THE UNITED METHODIST
HYMNAL

THE UNITED METHODIST
HYMNAL

Book of United Methodist Worship

THE UNITED METHODIST PUBLISHING HOUSE
NASHVILLE, TENNESSEE

THE UNITED METHODIST HYMNAL

Book of United Methodist Worship

Copyright © 1989 The United Methodist Publishing House

Sixth Printing, 1991

PEW EDITIONS

ISBN 0-687-43132-8 (Blue)
ISBN 0-687-43133-6 (Dark Red)
ISBN 0-687-43134-4 (Bright Red)
ISBN 0-687-43139-5 (Purple)
ISBN 0-687-43135-2 (Forest Green)
ISBN 0-687-43136-0 (Gray)
ISBN 0-687-43137-9 (Ivory)
ISBN 0-687-43138-7 (Maroon)
ISBN 0-687-43140-9 (Black Bonded Leather)
ISBN 0-687-43144-1 (Blue Bonded Leather)
ISBN 0-687-43145-X (Red Bonded Leather)
ISBN 0-687-43156-5 (Genuine Leather)
ISBN 0-687-43157-3 (General Conference)

MANUFACTURED IN THE UNITED STATES OF AMERICA

PREFACE

From the time of John and Charles Wesley, Methodist and Evangelical United Brethren hymnals have constituted the "worship book" of our corporate and private piety and praise. Hymn singing has been a vital and distinctive component of our worship of God. From our beginning we have been "a singing people."

Our hymnals serve as instruments by which the spiritual heritage received from the past is celebrated in the present and transmitted to future generations. Next to the Bible, our hymnals have been our most formative resource.

The United Methodist Hymnal, approved by the 1988 General Conference, is the latest entry in our long and distinguished line of hymnals and worship resources. It embodies our former Methodist and former Evangelical United Brethren traditions, yet it is the first substantial revision of content and format since the 1870s. It has more singable qualities and contains a broader base of musical styles than any of its predecessors. Its content reflects our Wesleyan heritage and witness: evangelical and ecumenical.

This Hymnal provides what the congregation needs for Sunday and other times of worship (including the sacraments): the rites of marriage and burial, and morning and evening prayer and praise. Additional worship materials are topically placed among the hymns; other prayers, litanies, and creeds follow the occasional services.

The core of this Hymnal is the abundance of well-known hymns from Greek, Latin, German, Scandinavian, Wesleyan, English, and North American traditions. Alongside these, the committee has placed representative evangelical hymns and songs from the recent popular repertory, as well as the proven hymns from the recent "hymnic explosion" of England and North America.

Much care has been taken to provide hymns and prayers from our rich ethnic diversity. More than 70 hymns are included to represent the Afro-American, Hispanic, Asian-American, and Native American heritages; prayers and other worship materials from these traditions are also included among the hymns.

Seventeen canticles from traditional and contemporary sources with sung or spoken responses are also included. Service music appropriate for the congregation is found within the services and among the hymns.

The psalms, with spoken or sung responses, occupy a more prominent position than in previous editions. One hundred psalms prescribed by the lectionary of the Consultation on Common Texts as well as psalms for special occasions are included.

The keyboard edition of The United Methodist Hymnal contains harmonic settings of the congregational responses for the psalms, the canticles and services of Holy Communion and Baptism.

The Hymnal Revision Committee has taken a commonsense approach to the preparation of a new hymnal and worship book: seeking the middle ground of evangelical hymnody held in common by the various traditions and constituencies, and identifying and retaining that "traditional core" of hymns that has the strongest potential value and usefulness to most local United Methodist congregations. It has set aside those that are little used by the denomination's mainstream and made room for new hymns which more fully reflect our continuing concerns for peace, justice, the care of the planet Earth, hunger, and the reconciling ministry of Christ's church to the world.

The committee began by recognizing a common problem: it is not possible to accede to all wishes in a single volume! Having shown a willingness to listen to the constituency, early in our work we made a firm commitment that this would be the people's hymnal, belonging to the whole United Methodist Church—a church uniquely inclusive in membership, episcopal and itinerate in government, and global and ecumenical in ministry.

We are confident that through this Hymnal the mutual bonds of our faith will unite us in a common celebration of what we have been and what, with God's help, we hope to become. It has been our challenge, delight, and satisfaction as a Hymnal Revision Committee to represent the church in this undertaking.

We commend this new Hymnal to you as the first official hymnal of The United Methodist Church.

THE HYMNAL REVISION COMMITTEE

RUEBEN P. JOB, *Chair*
RAQUEL GUTIÉRREZ-ACHON, *Vice-Chair*

GEORGE W. BASHORE
ROBERT C. BENNETT, *Chair—Tunes*
MARY BROOKE CASAD
HELEN GRAY CROTWELL
BONNIE JONES GEHWEILER, *Chair—Hymns*
  Subcommittee
W. T. HANDY, JR.
JACK HOLLAND HENTON
J. EDWARD HOY
BERYL INGRAM-WARD, *Chair—Ritual*
HAROLD DEAN JACOBS

EZRA EARL JONES, *General Secretary,*
  General Board of Discipleship

ROGER DESCHNER, *Secretary*
CARLTON R. YOUNG, *Editor*

HOPE OMACHI-KAWASHIMA
RONALD P. PATTERSON, *Chair—*
  Classification
CHARLES M. SMITH, *Chair—Psalter*
WILLIAM RANDOLPH SMITH
NANCY STARNES
LAURENCE HULL STOOKEY, *Chair—Worship*
  Resources Subcommittee
MARJORIE BEADLES TUELL, *Chair—Texts*
CHARLES H. WEBB, *Chair—Service Music*
J. LAVON WILSON

ROBERT K. FEASTER, *Publisher*

STAFF

GENERAL BOARD OF DISCIPLESHIP
  HOYT L. HICKMAN
  THOMAS A. LANGFORD III
  DIANA SANCHEZ

UNITED METHODIST PUBLISHING HOUSE
  NANCY REGEN BOZEMAN
  JAMES E. LEATH
  GARY ALAN SMITH

DIRECTIONS FOR SINGING

I. Learn these tunes before you learn any others; afterwards learn as many as you please.

II. Sing them exactly as they are printed here, without altering or mending them at all; and if you have learned to sing them otherwise, unlearn it as soon as you can.

III. Sing all. See that you join with the congregation as frequently as you can. Let not a slight degree of weakness or weariness hinder you. If it is a cross to you, take it up, and you will find it a blessing.

IV. Sing lustily and with a good courage. Beware of singing as if you were half dead, or half asleep; but lift up your voice with strength. Be no more afraid of your voice now, nor more ashamed of its being heard, than when you sung the songs of Satan.

V. Sing modestly. Do not bawl, so as to be heard above or distinct from the rest of the congregation, that you may not destroy the harmony; but strive to unite your voices together, so as to make one clear melodious sound.

VI. Sing in time. Whatever time is sung be sure to keep with it. Do not run before nor stay behind it; but attend close to the leading voices, and move therewith as exactly as you can; and take care not to sing too slow. This drawling way naturally steals on all who are lazy; and it is high time to drive it out from us, and sing all our tunes just as quick as we did at first.

VII. Above all sing spiritually. Have an eye to God in every word you sing. Aim at pleasing him more than yourself, or any other creature. In order to do this attend strictly to the sense of what you sing, and see that your heart is not carried away with the sound, but offered to God continually; so shall your singing be such as the Lord will approve here, and reward you when he cometh in the clouds of heaven.

From John Wesley's *Select Hymns*, 1761

CONTENTS

AFFIRMATIONS OF FAITH

PRAYERS OF CONFESSION, ASSURANCE, AND PARDON

THE LORD'S PRAYER

AMENS

INDEXES

GENERAL SERVICES

*This is the bond of perfectness
the anointing from above,
and all the law of life and peace
we find fulfilled in love.*

CHARLES WESLEY, ca. 1749

THE BASIC PATTERN OF WORSHIP

A recommended order of worship for United Methodists is presented on this and the following pages. This order for proclaiming God's Word and celebrating the Lord's Supper expresses the biblical, historical, and theological integrity of Christian worship. The several formats demonstrate its flexibility for different situations, but in its essentials it is one order.

The Basic Pattern of Worship described below makes plain the structure of all the General Services of the Church.

ENTRANCE

The people come together in the Lord's name. There may be greetings, music and song, prayer and praise.

PROCLAMATION AND RESPONSE

The Scriptures are opened to the people through the reading of lessons, preaching, witnessing, music, or other arts and media. Interspersed may be psalms, anthems, and hymns. Responses to God's Word include acts of commitment and faith with offerings of concerns, prayers, gifts, and service for the world and for one another.

THANKSGIVING AND COMMUNION

In services with Communion, the actions of Jesus in the Upper Room are reenacted:
taking the bread and cup,
giving thanks over the bread and cup,
breaking the bread, and
giving the bread and cup.

In services without Communion, thanks are given for God's mighty acts in Jesus Christ.

SENDING FORTH

The people are sent into ministry with the Lord's blessing.

AN ORDER OF SUNDAY WORSHIP USING THE BASIC PATTERN

This order shows the variety that is possible within the basic pattern of worship. It is a guide for those who plan worship, not an order to be followed by the congregation. The congregation may be guided through the service by a bulletin or by announcement, whether or not Holy Communion is celebrated. This order is the basis of the following forms of service provided for congregations that wish to use this book for all or part of the service of Holy Communion.

ENTRANCE

GATHERING

The people come together in the Lord's name. While they are gathering, one or more of the following may take place:
Informal greetings, conversation, and fellowship
Announcements and welcoming
Rehearsal of congregational music and other acts of worship
Informal prayer, singing, testimony
Quiet meditation and private prayer
Organ or other instrumental or vocal music

GREETING AND HYMN

Facing the people, the leader greets them in the Lord's name. Scripture sentences or responsive acts between leader and people declare that the Lord is present and empowers our worship. The hymn may precede or follow the greeting.

OPENING PRAYERS AND PRAISE

One or more of the following may be spoken or sung:
Prayer of the day, such as a collect
Prayer of confession and act of pardon
Litany, such as the "Lord, Have Mercy"

If an act of praise is desired, one or more of the following may be spoken or sung:
A "Glory to God in the Highest"
A psalm or other scripture song
The Gloria Patri
An anthem

PROCLAMATION AND RESPONSE

PRAYER FOR ILLUMINATION

The blessing of the Holy Spirit is invoked upon the reading, preaching, hearing, and doing of the Word. This may be included with the opening prayers, if there has not been an act of praise.

SCRIPTURE

Two or three Scripture readings should be used. If there are not Old Testament, Epistle, and Gospel readings at each service, care should be taken that over a period of time the people hear representative readings from each.

The Scripture readings may be interspersed with:

A psalm or psalm portions, sung or spoken, after the first reading
A hymn or song related to the Scriptures of the day, or a sung alleluia, before the final reading

SERMON

One or more of the Scripture readings is interpreted.

RESPONSE TO THE WORD

Responses may include one or more of the following:

Invitation to Christian discipleship, followed by a hymn of invitation or of response, or a baptism or confirmation hymn
Appropriate portions of the Baptismal Covenant:
    Holy Baptism
    Confirmation
    Reaffirmation of Faith
    Reception into The United Methodist Church
    Reception into the Local Congregation
A creed, except when already used in the Baptismal Covenant

CONCERNS AND PRAYERS

Joys and concerns to be included in the prayers may be expressed.
Prayer may take one or more of these forms:

Brief intercessions, petitions, and thanksgivings by the leader or members of the congregation. Each of these prayers may be followed by a common response, such as "Lord, hear our prayer," spoken or sung by all.
Litany of intercession and petition
Pastoral prayer

During this time persons may be invited to kneel at the communion rail.

CONFESSION, PARDON, AND PEACE

A prayer of confession and act of pardon are used here, if not used during the Entrance.

The people may offer one another signs of reconciliation and love, particularly when Holy Communion is celebrated.

OFFERING

An offering may include:

Monetary gifts
Other appropriate gifts, such as memorial gifts or other items to be dedicated
The bread and wine, if Holy Communion is to follow

As the gifts are received and presented, there may be:
A hymn
An anthem
A doxology or other musical response

THANKSGIVING

WITH HOLY COMMUNION

The pastor prepares the bread and cup.
The pastor and people join in the Great Thanksgiving.
All pray the Lord's Prayer.
The pastor breaks the bread and lifts the cup.
The bread and cup are given to the people.
The congregation may sing hymns.
The table is set in order.
There may be a brief prayer.

WITHOUT HOLY COMMUNION

A prayer of thanksgiving is offered.
All pray the Lord's Prayer.

SENDING FORTH

HYMN OR SONG AND DISMISSAL WITH BLESSING

Facing the people, the leader declares God's blessing.
The hymn may precede or follow the blessing.

GOING FORTH

One or more of the following may be included:
Organ or other instrumental voluntary
Silence before the congregation disperses
Informal greetings, conversation, and fellowship

A SERVICE OF WORD AND TABLE I

A congregation may use this text for the entire service.
Parts of the service marked in brackets [ ] are optional.

ENTRANCE

GATHERING

GREETING

The grace of the Lord Jesus Christ be with you.
And also with you.
The risen Christ is with us.
Praise the Lord!

HYMN OF PRAISE

OPENING PRAYER

The following or a prayer of the day is offered:

Almighty God,
to you all hearts are open, all desires known,
and from you no secrets are hidden.
Cleanse the thoughts of our hearts
by the inspiration of your Holy Spirit,
that we may perfectly love you,
and worthily magnify your holy name,
through Christ our Lord.
Amen.

[ACT OF PRAISE]

PROCLAMATION AND RESPONSE

PRAYER FOR ILLUMINATION

Lord, open our hearts and minds
by the power of your Holy Spirit,
that, as the Scriptures are read
and your Word proclaimed,
we may hear with joy what you say to us today.
Amen.

SCRIPTURE LESSON

[PSALM] *May be sung or spoken.*

[SCRIPTURE LESSON]

HYMN OR SONG

GOSPEL LESSON

SERMON

RESPONSE TO THE WORD

Responses may include one or more of the following acts:

Invitation to Christian discipleship, followed by a hymn of invitation or of response, or a baptism or confirmation hymn

Baptism, confirmation, reaffirmation of faith, or other reception of members

The following or another creed:

I believe in God, the Father Almighty,
   creator of heaven and earth.

I believe in Jesus Christ, his only Son, our Lord,
   who was conceived by the Holy Spirit,
   born of the Virgin Mary,
   suffered under Pontius Pilate,
   was crucified, died, and was buried;
   he descended to the dead.
   On the third day he rose again;
   he ascended into heaven,
   is seated at the right hand of the Father,
   and will come again to judge the living and the dead.

I believe in the Holy Spirit,
   the holy catholic* church,
   the communion of saints,
   the forgiveness of sins,
   the resurrection of the body,
   and the life everlasting. Amen.

CONCERNS AND PRAYERS

Brief intercessions, petitions, and thanksgivings may be prayed by the leader, or spontaneously by members of the congregation. To each of these, all may make a common response, such as: "Lord, hear our prayer."

Or, a litany of intercession and petition may be prayed.

Or, a pastoral prayer may be prayed.

INVITATION

Christ our Lord invites to his table all who love him,
   who earnestly repent of their sin
   and seek to live in peace with one another.
Therefore, let us confess our sin before God and one another.

*universal

CONFESSION AND PARDON

Merciful God,
we confess that we have not loved you with our whole heart.
We have failed to be an obedient church.
We have not done your will,
we have broken your law,
we have rebelled against your love,
we have not loved our neighbors,
and we have not heard the cry of the needy.
Forgive us, we pray.
Free us for joyful obedience,
through Jesus Christ our Lord.
Amen.

All pray in silence.

Leader to people:

Hear the good news:
  Christ died for us while we were yet sinners;
  that proves God's love toward us.
In the name of Jesus Christ, you are forgiven!

People to leader:

In the name of Jesus Christ, you are forgiven!

Leader and people:

Glory to God. Amen.

THE PEACE

Let us offer one another signs of reconciliation and love.

All exchange signs and words of God's peace.

OFFERING

As forgiven and reconciled people,
let us offer ourselves and our gifts to God.

A hymn, psalm, or anthem may be sung as the offering is received.

The bread and wine are brought by representatives of the people to the Lord's table with the other gifts, or uncovered if already in place.

A hymn, doxology, or other response may be sung as the gifts are presented.

If a Great Thanksgiving other than that which follows here is to be used, the service proceeds with "A Service of Word and Table III." Otherwise, the service continues as follows:

THANKSGIVING AND COMMUNION

TAKING THE BREAD AND CUP

The pastor takes the bread and cup, and the bread and wine are prepared for the meal.

THE GREAT THANKSGIVING

The musical settings on pages 17-25 may be used if desired.

The Lord be with you.

And also with you.

Lift up your hearts.

We lift them up to the Lord.

Let us give thanks to the Lord our God.

It is right to give our thanks and praise.

It is right, and a good and joyful thing,
　　always and everywhere to give thanks to you,
　　Father Almighty, creator of heaven and earth.
You formed us in your image
　　and breathed into us the breath of life.
When we turned away, and our love failed,
　　your love remained steadfast.
You delivered us from captivity,
　　made covenant to be our sovereign God,
　　and spoke to us through your prophets.
And so,
　　with your people on earth
　　and all the company of heaven
　　we praise your name and join their unending hymn:

Holy, holy, holy Lord, God of power and might,
heaven and earth are full of your glory.
　　Hosanna in the highest.
Blessed is he who comes in the name of the Lord.
　　Hosanna in the highest.

Holy are you, and blessed is your Son Jesus Christ.
Your Spirit anointed him
　　to preach good news to the poor,
　　to proclaim release to the captives
　　　　and recovering of sight to the blind,
　　to set at liberty those who are oppressed,
　　and to announce that the time had come
　　　　when you would save your people.
He healed the sick, fed the hungry, and ate with sinners.
By the baptism of his suffering, death, and resurrection
　　you gave birth to your church,
　　delivered us from slavery to sin and death,
　　and made with us a new covenant
　　　　by water and the Spirit.

When the Lord Jesus ascended,
he promised to be with us always,
in the power of your Word and Holy Spirit.

On the night in which he gave himself up for us,
he took bread, gave thanks to you, broke the bread,
gave it to his disciples, and said:
"Take, eat; this is my body which is given for you.
Do this in remembrance of me."

When the supper was over, he took the cup,
gave thanks to you, gave it to his disciples, and said:
"Drink from this, all of you;
this is my blood of the new covenant,
poured out for you and for many
for the forgiveness of sins.
Do this, as often as you drink it,
in remembrance of me."

And so,
in remembrance of these your mighty acts in Jesus Christ,
we offer ourselves in praise and thanksgiving
as a holy and living sacrifice,
in union with Christ's offering for us,
as we proclaim the mystery of faith.

Christ has died; Christ is risen; Christ will come again.

Pour out your Holy Spirit on us gathered here,
and on these gifts of bread and wine.
Make them be for us the body and blood of Christ,
that we may be for the world the body of Christ,
redeemed by his blood.

By your Spirit make us one with Christ,
one with each other,
and one in ministry to all the world,
until Christ comes in final victory
and we feast at his heavenly banquet.

Through your Son Jesus Christ,
with the Holy Spirit in your holy church,
all honor and glory is yours, almighty Father,
now and for ever.
Amen.

THE LORD'S PRAYER

And now, with the confidence of children of God, let us pray:

Our Father in heaven,
hallowed be your name,
your kingdom come,
your will be done,
on earth as in heaven.

Give us today our daily bread.
Forgive us our sins
   as we forgive those who sin against us.
Save us from the time of trial,
   and deliver us from evil.
For the kingdom, the power, and the glory are yours
   now and for ever. Amen.

BREAKING THE BREAD

The pastor breaks the bread in silence, or while saying:

Because there is one loaf,
we, who are many, are one body, for we all partake of the one loaf.
The bread which we break is a sharing in the body of Christ.

The pastor lifts the cup in silence, or while saying:

The cup over which we give thanks is a sharing in the blood of Christ.

GIVING THE BREAD AND CUP

The bread and wine are given to the people, with these or other words being exchanged:

The body of Christ, given for you. **Amen.**
The blood of Christ, given for you. **Amen.**

The congregation sings hymns while the bread and cup are given.

When all have received, the Lord's table is put in order.

The following prayer is then offered by the pastor or by all:

Eternal God, we give you thanks for this holy mystery
   in which you have given yourself to us.
Grant that we may go into the world
   in the strength of your Spirit,
     to give ourselves for others,
in the name of Jesus Christ our Lord.
Amen.

SENDING FORTH

HYMN OR SONG

DISMISSAL WITH BLESSING

Go forth in peace.
The grace of the Lord Jesus Christ,
and the love of God,
and the communion of the Holy Spirit
be with you all.

Amen.

GOING FORTH

A SERVICE OF WORD AND TABLE II

A congregation may use this text beginning with the invitation to the Lord's table. Preceding parts of the service are guided by a bulletin or by announcement.

The people gather in the Lord's name.
They offer prayer and praise.
The Scriptures are read and preached.
Responses of praise, faith, and prayer are offered.
The service continues with the invitation to the Lord's table.

INVITATION

Christ our Lord invites to his table all who love him,
    who earnestly repent of their sin
    and seek to live in peace with one another.
Therefore, let us confess our sin before God and one another.

CONFESSION AND PARDON

Merciful God,
we confess that we have not loved you with our whole heart.
We have failed to be an obedient church.
We have not done your will,
we have broken your law,
we have rebelled against your love,
we have not loved our neighbors,
and we have not heard the cry of the needy.
Forgive us, we pray.
Free us for joyful obedience,
through Jesus Christ our Lord. Amen.

All pray in silence.

Leader to people:

Hear the good news:
    Christ died for us while we were yet sinners;
    that proves God's love toward us.
In the name of Jesus Christ, you are forgiven!

People to leader:

In the name of Jesus Christ, you are forgiven!

Leader and people:

Glory to God. Amen.

THE PEACE

Let us offer one another signs of reconciliation and love.

All exchange signs and words of God's peace.

OFFERING

As forgiven and reconciled people,
let us offer ourselves and our gifts to God.

A hymn, psalm, or anthem may be sung as the offering is received.

The bread and wine are brought by representatives of the people to the Lord's table with the other gifts, or uncovered if already in place.

A hymn, doxology, or other response may be sung as the gifts are presented.

TAKING THE BREAD AND CUP

The pastor takes the bread and cup, and the bread and wine are prepared for the meal.

THE GREAT THANKSGIVING

One of the musical settings on pages 17-25 may be used if desired.

The Lord be with you.

And also with you.

Lift up your hearts.

We lift them up to the Lord.

Let us give thanks to the Lord our God.

It is right to give our thanks and praise.

It is right, and a good and joyful thing,
    always and everywhere to give thanks to you,
    Father Almighty, creator of heaven and earth.*

And so,
    with your people on earth
    and all the company of heaven
    we praise your name and join their unending hymn:

Holy, holy, holy Lord, God of power and might,
heaven and earth are full of your glory.
    Hosanna in the highest.
Blessed is he who comes in the name of the Lord.
    Hosanna in the highest.

Holy are you, and blessed is your Son Jesus Christ.*
By the baptism of his suffering, death, and resurrection
    you gave birth to your church,
    delivered us from slavery to sin and death,
    and made with us a new covenant
        by water and the Spirit.*

Words appropriate to the day, season, or occasion may be added at these points.

On the night in which he gave himself up for us
 he took bread, gave thanks to you, broke the bread,
 gave it to his disciples, and said:
"Take, eat; this is my body which is given for you.
Do this in remembrance of me."

When the supper was over, he took the cup,
 gave thanks to you, gave it to his disciples, and said:
"Drink from this, all of you;
 this is my blood of the new covenant,
 poured out for you and for many
  for the forgiveness of sins.
Do this, as often as you drink it,
 in remembrance of me."

And so,
in remembrance of these your mighty acts in Jesus Christ,
we offer ourselves in praise and thanksgiving
 as a holy and living sacrifice,
 in union with Christ's offering for us,
as we proclaim the mystery of faith.

Christ has died; Christ is risen; Christ will come again.

Pour out your Holy Spirit on us gathered here,
 and on these gifts of bread and wine.
Make them be for us the body and blood of Christ,
that we may be for the world the body of Christ,
 redeemed by his blood.*

By your Spirit make us one with Christ,
 one with each other,
 and one in ministry to all the world,
until Christ comes in final victory,
 and we feast at his heavenly banquet.

Through your Son Jesus Christ,
with the Holy Spirit in your holy church,
all honor and glory is yours, almighty Father,
 now and for ever.

Amen.

And now, with the confidence of children of God, let us pray:

THE LORD'S PRAYER

BREAKING THE BREAD

  The pastor breaks the bread and then lifts the cup, in silence or with appropriate words.

GIVING THE BREAD AND CUP

  The bread and wine are given to the people, with these or other words being exchanged:

The body of Christ, given for you. **Amen.**
The blood of Christ, given for you. **Amen.**

The congregation sings hymns while the bread and cup are given.

When all have received, the Lord's table is put in order.

The pastor or congregation may then give thanks after Communion.

HYMN OR SONG

DISMISSAL WITH BLESSING

Go forth in peace.
The grace of the Lord Jesus Christ,
and the love of God,
and the communion of the Holy Spirit
be with you all.

Amen.

GOING FORTH

A SERVICE OF WORD AND TABLE III

This text provides only congregational responses for Holy Communion.
The service through the Entrance and the Proclamation and Response is guided by a bulletin or by announcement.
This text may be used when a Service of Christian Marriage or a Service of Death and Resurrection includes Holy Communion.

THANKSGIVING AND COMMUNION

TAKING THE BREAD AND CUP

The pastor takes the bread and cup, and the bread and wine are prepared for the meal.

THE GREAT THANKSGIVING

One of the musical settings on pages 17-25 may be used if desired.

The Lord be with you.

And also with you.

Lift up your hearts.

We lift them up to the Lord.

Let us give thanks to the Lord our God.

It is right to give our thanks and praise.

The pastor gives thanks appropriate to the occasion, remembering God's acts of salvation, and concludes:

And so,
   with your people on earth
   and all the company of heaven
   we praise your name and join their unending hymn:

Holy, holy, holy Lord, God of power and might,
heaven and earth are full of your glory.
   Hosanna in the highest.
Blessed is he who comes in the name of the Lord.
   Hosanna in the highest.

The pastor continues the thanksgiving. The institution of the Lord's Supper is recalled. The pastor concludes:

And so,
in remembrance of these your mighty acts in Jesus Christ,
we offer ourselves in praise and thanksgiving
   as a holy and living sacrifice,
   in union with Christ's offering for us,
as we proclaim the mystery of faith.

Christ has died; Christ is risen; Christ will come again.

The pastor invokes the present work of the Holy Spirit and then praises the Trinity, concluding:

All honor and glory is yours, almighty Father (*God*), now and for ever.

Amen.

THE LORD'S PRAYER

BREAKING THE BREAD

The pastor breaks the bread and then lifts the cup, in silence or with appropriate words.

GIVING THE BREAD AND CUP

The bread and wine are given to the people, with appropriate words being exchanged.

The congregation sings hymns while the bread and cup are given.

When all have received, the Lord's table is put in order.

The pastor or congregation may give thanks after Communion.

SENDING FORTH

HYMN OR SONG

DISMISSAL WITH BLESSING

GOING FORTH

THE GREAT THANKSGIVING

The following musical settings may be used with
A Service of Word and Table I, II, and III

MUSICAL SETTING A

The Lord be with you.

And also with you.

Lift up your hearts.

We lift them up to the Lord.

Let us give thanks to the Lord our God.

It is right to give our thanks and praise.

The pastor gives thanks appropriate to the occasion, remembering God's acts of salvation, and concludes:

And so,
  with your people on earth
  and all the company of heaven
  we praise your name and join their unending hymn:

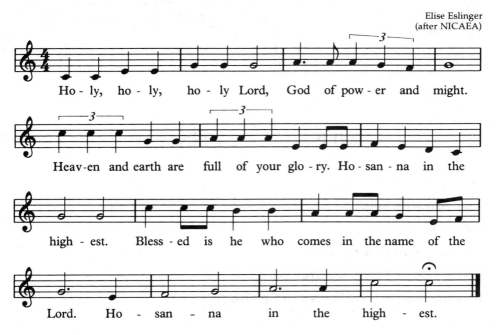

Elise Eslinger
(after NICAEA)

Ho-ly, ho-ly, ho-ly Lord, God of pow-er and might. Heav-en and earth are full of your glo-ry. Ho-san-na in the high-est. Bless-ed is he who comes in the name of the Lord. Ho-san-na in the high-est.

The pastor continues the thanksgiving. The institution of the Lord's Supper is recalled. The pastor concludes:

And so,
in remembrance of these your mighty acts in Jesus Christ,
we offer ourselves in praise and thanksgiving
    as a holy and living sacrifice,
    in union with Christ's offering for us,
as we proclaim the mystery of faith.

Elise Eslinger

Christ has died, Christ is ris - en, Christ will come a - gain!

Adapt. © 1989 The United Methodist Publishing House

The pastor invokes the present work of the Holy Spirit and then praises the Trinity, concluding:

All honor and glory is yours, almighty Father (*God*),
now and for ever.

Elise Eslinger

A - men, a - men a - men.

Adapt. © 1989 The United Methodist Publishing House

MUSICAL SETTING B

The Lord be with you.

And also with you.

Lift up your hearts.

We lift them up to the Lord.

Let us give thanks to the Lord our God.

It is right to give our thanks and praise.

The pastor gives thanks appropriate to the occasion, remembering God's acts of salvation, and concludes:

And so,
with your people on earth
and all the company of heaven
we praise your name and join their unending hymn:

James A. Kriewald

Ho - ly, ho - ly, ho - ly Lord, God of pow-er and might. Heaven and earth are full of your glo - ry, glo - ry. Ho - san - na in the high - est. Ho - high - est. Bless - ed is he who comes in the name of the Lord. Lord. Ho - san - na, ho - san - na, in the high - est, in the high - est.

Music © 1985 The United Methodist Publishing House

The pastor continues the thanksgiving. The institution of the Lord's Supper is recalled. The pastor concludes:

And so,
in remembrance of these your mighty acts in Jesus Christ,
we offer ourselves in praise and thanksgiving
    as a holy and living sacrifice,
    in union with Christ's offering for us,
as we proclaim the mystery of faith.

Music © 1985 The United Methodist Publishing House

The pastor invokes the present work of the Holy Spirit and then praises the Trinity,
concluding:

All honor and glory is yours, almighty Father (*God*),
now and for ever.

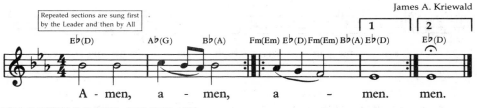

Music © 1985 The United Methodist Publishing House

MUSICAL SETTING C

The Lord be with you.

And also with you.

Lift up your hearts.

We lift them up to the Lord.

Let us give thanks to the Lord our God.

It is right to give our thanks and praise.

The pastor gives thanks appropriate to the occasion, remembering God's acts of salvation,
and concludes:

And so,
    with your people on earth
    and all the company of heaven
    we praise your name and join their unending hymn:

From *Deutsche Messe* by Franz Schubert; adapt. by Richard Proulx

Ho - ly, ho - ly, ho - ly Lord, God of

power and might. might.

Heav - en and earth are full,
Bless - ed is he who comes

full of your glo - ry. Ho -
in the name of the Lord.

san - na in the high - est, ho -

san - na in the high - est.

The pastor continues the thanksgiving. The institution of the Lord's Supper is recalled. The pastor concludes:

And so,
in remembrance of these your mighty acts in Jesus Christ,
we offer ourselves in praise and thanksgiving
   as a holy and living sacrifice,
   in union with Christ's offering for us,
as we proclaim the mystery of faith.

From *Deutsche Messe* by Franz Schubert; arr. by Charles H. Webb

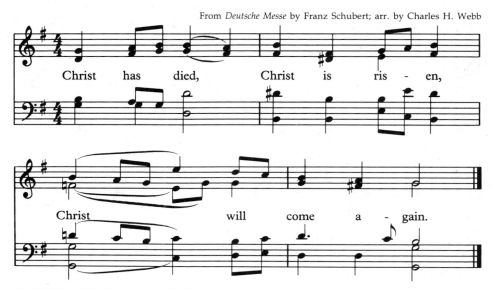

Arr. © 1989 The United Methodist Publishing House

The pastor invokes the present work of the Holy Spirit and then praises the Trinity, concluding:

All honor and glory is yours, almighty Father (*God*),
now and for ever.

From *Deutsche Messe* by Franz Schubert; arr. by Charles H. Webb

Arr. © 1989 The United Methodist Publishing House

MUSICAL SETTING D

The Lord be with you.

And also with you.

Lift up your hearts.

We lift them up to the Lord.

Let us give thanks to the Lord our God.

It is right to give our thanks and praise.

The pastor gives thanks appropriate to the occasion, remembering God's acts of salvation, and concludes:

And so,
  with your people on earth
  and all the company of heaven
  we praise your name and join their unending hymn:

Carlton R. Young

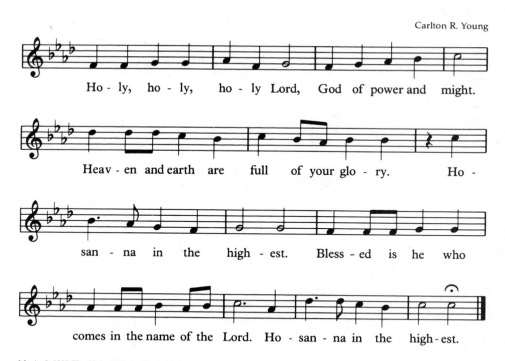

Ho - ly, ho - ly, ho - ly Lord, God of power and might. Heav - en and earth are full of your glo - ry. Ho - san - na in the high - est. Bless - ed is he who comes in the name of the Lord. Ho - san - na in the high - est.

Music © 1989 The United Methodist Publishing House

The pastor continues the thanksgiving. The institution of the Lord's Supper is recalled. The pastor concludes:

And so,
in remembrance of these your mighty acts in Jesus Christ,
we offer ourselves in praise and thanksgiving
    as a holy and living sacrifice,
    in union with Christ's offering for us,
as we proclaim the mystery of faith.

Carlton R. Young

Christ has died, Christ is ris - en, Christ will come a - gain!

Music © 1989 The United Methodist Publishing House

The pastor invokes the present work of the Holy Spirit and then praises the Trinity,
concluding:

All honor and glory is yours, almighty Father (*God*),
now and for ever.

Carlton R. Young

A - men, a - men, a - men.

Music © 1989 The United Methodist Publishing House

MUSICAL SETTING E

The Lord be with you.

And also with you.

Lift up your hearts.

We lift them up to the Lord.

Let us give thanks to the Lord our God.

It is right to give our thanks and praise.

The pastor gives thanks appropriate to the occasion, remembering God's acts of salvation,
and concludes:

And so,
    with your people on earth
    and all the company of heaven
    we praise your name and join their unending hymn:

William Mathias

Ho - ly, ho - ly,
ho - ly Lord, God of pow - er and might.
Heaven and earth are full of your glo-ry. Ho-san-na in the high-est.
Bless - ed is he who comes in the
name of the Lord. Ho-san - na in the high - est.

The pastor continues the thanksgiving. The institution of the Lord's Supper is recalled.
The pastor concludes:

And so,
in remembrance of these your mighty acts in Jesus Christ,
we offer ourselves in praise and thanksgiving
   as a holy and living sacrifice,
   in union with Christ's offering for us,
as we proclaim the mystery of faith.

William Mathias

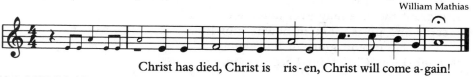

Christ has died, Christ is ris-en, Christ will come a-gain!

The pastor invokes the present work of the Holy Spirit and then praises the Trinity,
concluding:

All honor and glory is yours, almighty Father (*God*),
now and for ever.

William Mathias

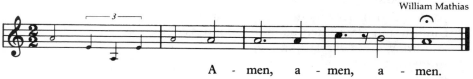

A - men, a - men, a - men.

A SERVICE OF WORD AND TABLE IV

This is a traditional text from the rituals of the former Methodist and former Evangelical United Brethren churches.

The people gather in the Lord's name.
They offer prayer and praise, which may include "Canticle of God's Glory" (No. 82)
The Scriptures are read and preached.
Responses of praise, faith, and prayer are offered.
The service continues as follows:

INVITATION

Ye that do truly and earnestly repent of your sins,
    and are in love and charity with your neighbors,
    and intend to lead a new life, following the commandments of God,
    and walking from henceforth in his holy ways:
Draw near with faith, and take this Holy Sacrament to your comfort,
    and make your humble confession to almighty God.

CONFESSION

Almighty God, Father of our Lord Jesus Christ,
    maker of all things, judge of all people:
We acknowledge and bewail our manifold sins and wickedness,
    which we from time to time most grievously have committed,
    by thought, word, and deed, against thy divine majesty.
We do earnestly repent,
    and are heartily sorry for these our misdoings;
    the remembrance of them is grievous unto us.
Have mercy upon us, have mercy upon us, most merciful Father.
For thy Son our Lord Jesus Christ's sake,
    forgive us all that is past;
and grant that we may ever hereafter
    serve and please thee in newness of life,
    to the honor and glory of thy name;
through Jesus Christ our Lord. Amen.

PRAYER FOR PARDON

Almighty God, our heavenly Father,
    who of thy great mercy hast promised forgiveness of sins
    to all them that with hearty repentance and true faith
    turn to thee:
Have mercy upon us;
    pardon and deliver us from all our sins;
    confirm and strengthen us in all goodness;
    and bring us to everlasting life;
    through Jesus Christ our Lord.

Amen.

WORDS OF ASSURANCE

Hear what comfortable words the Scriptures say
  to all that truly turn to the Lord:

The leader says one or more of the following sentences:

Come to me, all who labor and are heavy laden,
  and I will give you rest. (*Matthew 11:28*)

God so loved the world that he gave his only Son,
  that whoever believes in him
  should not perish but have eternal life. (*John 3:16*)

The saying is sure and worthy of full acceptance,
  that Christ Jesus came into the world to save sinners.
  (*1 Timothy 1:15*)

If we confess our sins,
  God is faithful and just,
  and will forgive our sins
  and cleanse us from all unrighteousness. (*1 John 1:9*)

If any one sins,
  we have an advocate with the Father,
  Jesus Christ the righteous;
and he is the expiation for our sins,
  and not for ours only
  but also for the sins of the whole world. (*From 1 John 2:1-2*)

Signs and words of God's peace may be exchanged at this point.

If an offering has not been received earlier in the service, it may be received at this time.

A hymn, psalm, or anthem may be sung as the offering is received.

A hymn, doxology, or other response may be sung as the gifts are brought to the Lord's table.

The bread and wine are brought by representatives of the people to the Lord's table, or uncovered if already in place.

TAKING THE BREAD AND CUP

The pastor takes the bread and cup, and the bread and wine are prepared for the meal.

THE GREAT THANKSGIVING

The Lord be with you.
And with thy spirit.
Lift up your hearts.
We lift them up unto the Lord.
Let us give thanks unto the Lord.
It is meet and right so to do.

It is very meet, right, and our bounden duty
  that we should at all times and in all places
  give thanks unto thee, O Lord,
  Holy Father, almighty, everlasting God.

Here the pastor may add a preface proper to the season. Then the pastor continues:

Therefore with angels and archangels,
  and with all the company of heaven,
  we laud and magnify thy glorious name,
  evermore praising thee and saying (singing):

Holy, holy, holy, Lord God of hosts:
Heaven and earth are full of thy glory!
  Glory be to thee, O Lord most high!
Blessed is he that cometh in the name of the Lord!
  Hosanna in the highest!

John Merbecke

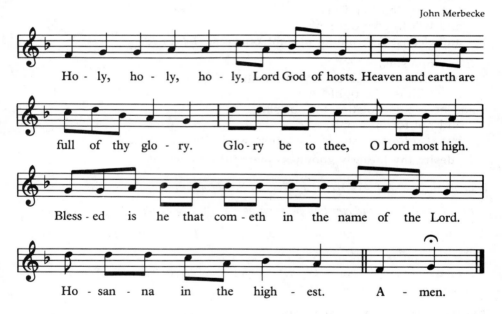

Ho - ly, ho - ly, ho - ly, Lord God of hosts. Heaven and earth are full of thy glo - ry. Glo - ry be to thee, O Lord most high. Bless - ed is he that com - eth in the name of the Lord. Ho - san - na in the high - est. A - men.

Almighty God, our heavenly Father,
who of thy tender mercy
  didst give thine only Son Jesus Christ
  to suffer death upon the cross for our redemption;
who made there, by the one offering of himself,
  a full, perfect, and sufficient sacrifice
  for the sins of the whole world;
and didst institute,
  and in his holy Gospel command us to continue,
  a perpetual memory of his precious death
  until his coming again:

Hear us, O merciful Father,
  we most humbly beseech thee;
and bless and sanctify with thy Word and Holy Spirit
  these thy gifts of bread and wine,
that we, receiving them
    according to thy Son our Savior Jesus Christ's holy institution,
    in remembrance of his passion, death, and resurrection,
    may be partakers of the divine nature through him:

Who, in the same night that he was betrayed, took bread;
  and when he had given thanks,
    he broke it, and gave it to his disciples, saying,
"Take, eat; this is my body which is given for you;
do this in remembrance of me."

Likewise after supper he took the cup;
  and when he had given thanks,
    he gave it to them, saying,
"Drink ye all of this;
    for this is my blood of the New Covenant,
    which is shed for you and for many,
    for the forgiveness of sins;
do this as oft as ye shall drink it,
  in remembrance of me."

O Lord, our heavenly Father,
  we, thy humble servants,
    desire thy fatherly goodness mercifully to accept
    this our sacrifice of praise and thanksgiving;
most humbly beseeching thee to grant that,
  by the merits and death of thy Son Jesus Christ,
  and through faith in his blood,
we and thy whole church may obtain
  forgiveness of our sins,
  and all other benefits of his passion.

And here we offer and present unto thee, O Lord,
  ourselves, our souls and bodies,
    to be a reasonable, holy, and lively sacrifice unto thee;
humbly beseeching thee
    that all we who are partakers of this Holy Communion
    may be filled with thy grace and heavenly benediction.

And although we be unworthy,
  through our manifold sins,
    to offer unto thee any sacrifice,
yet we beseech thee
    to accept this our bounden duty and service,
    not weighing our merits, but pardoning our offenses;

Through Jesus Christ our Lord,
   by whom, and with whom,
   in the unity of the Holy Spirit,
   all honor and glory be unto thee, O Father Almighty,
   world without end.
Amen.

If the Lord's Prayer has not been prayed earlier in the service it is prayed at this time.

BREAKING THE BREAD

The pastor breaks the bread and then lifts the cup, in silence or with appropriate words.

The following prayer may then be prayed:

PRAYER OF HUMBLE ACCESS

We do not presume to come to this thy table,
   O merciful Lord,
   trusting in our own righteousness,
   but in thy manifold and great mercies.
We are not worthy
   so much as to gather up the crumbs under thy table.
But thou art the same Lord,
   whose property is always to have mercy.
Grant us, therefore, gracious Lord,
   so to partake of this Sacrament of thy Son Jesus Christ,
   that we may walk in newness of life,
   may grow into his likeness,
   and may evermore dwell in him, and he in us. Amen.

Here may be sung or spoken:

O Lamb of God, that takest away the sins of the world, have mercy upon us.
O Lamb of God, that takest away the sins of the world, have mercy upon us.
O Lamb of God, that takest away the sins of the world, grant us thy peace.

John Merbecke

have mer - cy up - on us. O Lamb of God,
that tak - est a - way the sins of the world, grant us thy peace.

GIVING THE BREAD AND CUP

When the bread is given, one or both of the following sentences are said:

The body of our Lord Jesus Christ,
   which was given for thee,
     preserve thy soul and body unto everlasting life.

Take and eat this
   in remembrance that Christ died for thee,
   and feed on him in thy heart
   by faith with thanksgiving.

When the cup is given, one or both of the following sentences are said:

The blood of our Lord Jesus Christ,
   which was shed for thee,
     preserve thy soul and body unto everlasting life.

Drink this
   in remembrance that Christ's blood was shed for thee,
   and be thankful.

The congregation sings hymns while the bread and cup are given.

When all have received, the Lord's table is put in order, and a prayer may be offered.

HYMN OR SONG OF THANKSGIVING

DISMISSAL WITH BLESSING

The peace of God, which passeth all understanding,
   keep your hearts and minds
   in the knowledge and love of God,
   and of his Son Jesus Christ our Lord;
and the blessing of God Almighty,
   the Father, the Son, and the Holy Spirit,
   be among you, and remain with you always.

Amen.

GOING FORTH

CONCERNING THE SERVICES OF THE BAPTISMAL COVENANT

The Baptismal Covenant is God's word to us, proclaiming our adoption by grace, and our word to God promising our response of faith and love. Those within the covenant constitute the community we call the church; therefore, the services of the Baptismal Covenant are conducted during the public worship of the congregation where the person's membership is to be held, except in very unusual circumstances. These services are best placed in the order of worship as a response following the reading of Scripture and its exposition in the sermon.

Persons of any age are suitable candidates. Infants and others unable to take the vows for themselves are presented by parents and/or sponsors. There may also be sponsors when candidates can speak for themselves. Parents or sponsors should be members of Christ's holy church.

In cases of emergency the essential acts in baptism are the vows and the baptism with water in the name of the Father, and of the Son, and of the Holy Spirit. A candidate baptized outside of a congregational worship service should, if possible, be presented at a later time to the congregation.

Those baptized before they are old enough to take the vows for themselves make their personal profession of faith in the service called confirmation. Those who are able to take the vows for themselves at their baptism are not confirmed, for they have made their public profession of faith at the font.

After confirmation, or after baptism when candidates take the vows for themselves, Christians are encouraged to reaffirm the Baptismal Covenant from time to time. Such reaffirmation is not, however, to be understood as the Sacrament of Baptism. Baptism is not administered to any person more than once, for while our baptismal vows are less than reliable, God's promise to us in the sacrament is steadfast.

Reaffirmation of the Baptismal Covenant is particularly appropriate by an entire congregation at Easter, which recalls our death and resurrection with Christ. It is also especially appropriate for persons who are transferring into a congregation. When those being received into a congregation do not wish to reaffirm the Baptismal Covenant, only sections 14-16 of the service are used with those coming from another denomination and only sections 15-16 with those transferring from another United Methodist congregation.

The material marked by brackets [ ] is optional and may be omitted from the service.

Other approved services are found in *The Book of Ritual* of The Evangelical United Brethren Church (1959), pages 7-11 and 28-33, and *The Book of Worship for Church and Home* of The Methodist Church (1965), pages 7-14. Congregational responses for use with these services are found following The Baptismal Covenant II (page 44).

THE BAPTISMAL COVENANT I

HOLY BAPTISM
CONFIRMATION
REAFFIRMATION OF FAITH
RECEPTION INTO THE UNITED METHODIST CHURCH
RECEPTION INTO A LOCAL CONGREGATION

This service may be used for any of the above acts, or any combination of these that may be called for on a given occasion.

INTRODUCTION TO THE SERVICE

As persons are coming forward, an appropriate hymn of baptism or confirmation may be sung.

1   *The pastor makes the following statement to the congregation:*

Brothers and sisters in Christ:
Through the Sacrament of Baptism
  we are initiated into Christ's holy church.
We are incorporated into God's mighty acts of salvation
  and given new birth through water and the Spirit.
All this is God's gift, offered to us without price.

2   *If there are confirmations or reaffirmations, the pastor continues:*

Through confirmation,
  and through the reaffirmation of our faith,
  we renew the covenant declared at our baptism,
  acknowledge what God is doing for us,
  and affirm our commitment to Christ's holy church.

PRESENTATION OF CANDIDATES

3   *A representative of the congregation presents the candidates with the appropriate statements:*

I present *Name(s)* for baptism.
I present *Name(s)* for confirmation.
I present *Name(s)* to reaffirm *their* faith.
I present *Name(s)* who come(s) to this congregation from the
_____ Church.

RENUNCIATION OF SIN AND PROFESSION OF FAITH

4   *The pastor addresses parents or other sponsors and those candidates who can answer for themselves:*

On behalf of the whole church, I ask you:
Do you renounce the spiritual forces of wickedness,
    reject the evil powers of this world,
    and repent of your sin?

I do.

Do you accept the freedom and power God gives you
    to resist evil, injustice, and oppression
    in whatever forms they present themselves?

I do.

Do you confess Jesus Christ as your Savior,
put your whole trust in his grace,
and promise to serve him as your Lord,
in union with the church which Christ has opened
    to people of all ages, nations, and races?

I do.

5   *The pastor addresses parents or other sponsors of candidates not able to answer for themselves:*

Will you nurture *these children (persons)*
in Christ's holy church,
that by your teaching and example they may be guided
    to accept God's grace for themselves,
    to profess their faith openly,
    and to lead a Christian life?

I will.

6   *The pastor addresses candidates who can answer for themselves:*

According to the grace given to you,
will you remain *faithful members* of Christ's holy church
and serve as Christ's *representatives* in the world?

I will.

7   *If those who have answered for themselves have sponsors, the pastor addresses the sponsors:*

Will you who sponsor *these candidates*
support and encourage *them* in *their* Christian life?

I will.

8   *The pastor addresses the congregation:*

Do you, as Christ's body, the church,
reaffirm both your rejection of sin
    and your commitment to Christ?

We do.

Will you nurture one another in the Christian faith and life and include *these persons* now before you in your care?

With God's help we will proclaim the good news
    and live according to the example of Christ.
We will surround *these persons*
    with a community of love and forgiveness,
    that *they* may grow in *their* trust of God,
    and be found faithful in *their* service to others.
We will pray for *them*,
    that *they* may be true disciples
    who walk in the way that leads to life.

9   *The pastor addresses all:*

Let us join together in professing the Christian faith
    as contained in the Scriptures of the Old and New Testaments.

Do you believe in God the Father?

I believe in God, the Father Almighty,
    creator of heaven and earth.

Do you believe in Jesus Christ?

I believe in Jesus Christ, his only Son, our Lord,
    [who was conceived by the Holy Spirit,
    born of the Virgin Mary,
    suffered under Pontius Pilate,
    was crucified, died, and was buried;
    he descended to the dead.
    On the third day he rose again;
    he ascended into heaven,
    is seated at the right hand of the Father,
    and will come again to judge the living and the dead.]

Do you believe in the Holy Spirit?

I believe in the Holy Spirit,
    [the holy catholic* church,
    the communion of saints,
    the forgiveness of sins,
    the resurrection of the body,
    and the life everlasting.]

*universal

THANKSGIVING OVER THE WATER

10   *If there are baptisms, or if water is to be used for reaffirmation, the water may be poured into the font at this time, and the following prayer offered:*

The Lord be with you.

And also with you.

Let us pray.

Eternal Father:
When nothing existed but chaos,
   you swept across the dark waters
   and brought forth light.
In the days of Noah
   you saved those on the ark through water.
After the flood you set in the clouds a rainbow.
When you saw your people as slaves in Egypt,
   you led them to freedom through the sea.
Their children you brought through the Jordan
   to the land which you promised.

*Sing to the Lord, all the earth.
Tell of God's mercy each day.

In the fullness of time you sent Jesus,
   nurtured in the water of a womb.
He was baptized by John and anointed by your Spirit.
He called his disciples
   to share in the baptism of his death and resurrection
   and to make disciples of all nations.

*Declare his works to the nations,
his glory among all the people.

Pour out your Holy Spirit,
   to bless this gift of water and *those* who *receive* it,
   to wash away *their* sin
     and clothe *them* in righteousness
     throughout *their lives,*
   that, dying and being raised with Christ,
     they may share in his final victory.

*All praise to you, Eternal Father,
through your Son Jesus Christ,
who with you and the Holy Spirit
lives and reigns for ever.
Amen.

*One of the musical settings on pages 53-54 may be used if desired.

BAPTISM WITH LAYING ON OF HANDS

11 *As each candidate is baptized, the pastor says:*

Name, I baptize you in the name of the Father, and of the Son,
  and of the Holy Spirit.

The people respond:

Amen.

Immediately after the administration of the water, the pastor, and others if desired, place hands on the head of each candidate, as the pastor says to each:

The Holy Spirit work within you,
that being born through water and the Spirit,
you may be a faithful disciple of Jesus Christ.

The people respond:

Amen.

When all candidates have been baptized, the pastor invites the congregation to welcome them:

Now it is our joy to welcome our new *sisters and brothers* in Christ.
Through baptism
you are incorporated by the Holy Spirit
  into God's new creation
and made to share in Christ's royal priesthood.
We are all one in Christ Jesus.
With joy and thanksgiving we welcome you
  as *members* **of the family of Christ.**

CONFIRMATION OR REAFFIRMATION OF FAITH

12 *Here water may be used symbolically in ways that cannot be interpreted as baptism, as the pastor says:*

Remember your baptism and be thankful.

Amen.

As the pastor, and others if desired, place hands on the head of each person being confirmed or reaffirming faith, the pastor says to each:

Name, the Holy Spirit work within you,
that having been born through water and the Spirit,
you may live as a faithful disciple of Jesus Christ.

All respond:

Amen.

13 *When there is a congregational reaffirmation of the Baptismal Covenant, water may be used symbolically in ways that cannot be interpreted as baptism, as the pastor says:*

Remember your baptism and be thankful.

Amen.

RECEPTION INTO THE UNITED METHODIST CHURCH

14 *If there are persons coming into membership in The United Methodist Church from other denominations who have not yet been presented, they may be presented at this time.*

The pastor addresses all those transferring their membership into The United Methodist Church, together with those who, through baptism or in confirmation, have just professed their own faith:

As *members* of Christ's universal church,
will you be loyal to The United Methodist Church,
and do all in your power to strengthen its ministries?

I will.

RECEPTION INTO THE LOCAL CONGREGATION

15 *If there are persons joining this congregation from other United Methodist congregations who have not yet been presented, they may be presented at this time.*

The pastor addresses all those transferring membership into the congregation and those who have just professed their own faith, in baptism or in confirmation:

As *members* of this congregation,
will you faithfully participate in its ministries
   by your prayers, your presence,
   your gifts, and your service?

I will.

COMMENDATION AND WELCOME

16 *The pastor addresses the congregation:*

Members of the household of God,
I commend *these persons* to your love and care.
Do all in your power to increase *their* faith,
   confirm *their* hope, and perfect *them* in love.

The congregation responds:

We give thanks for all that God has already given you
   and we welcome you in Christian love.
As members together with you
   in the body of Christ
   and in this congregation
   of The United Methodist Church,
we renew our covenant
   faithfully to participate
   in the ministries of the church
   by our prayers, our presence,
   our gifts, and our service,
that in everything God may be glorified
   through Jesus Christ.

The pastor addresses those baptized, confirmed, or received:

The God of all grace,
 who has called us to eternal glory in Christ,
establish you and strengthen you
 by the power of the Holy Spirit,
that you may live in grace and peace.

One or more lay leaders may join with the pastor in acts of welcome and peace.

Appropriate thanksgivings and intercessions for those who have participated in these acts should be included in the concerns and prayers which follow.

It is most fitting that the service continue with Holy Communion, in which the union of the new members with the body of Christ is most fully expressed. The new members may receive first.

THE BAPTISMAL COVENANT II

HOLY BAPTISM
FOR CHILDREN AND OTHERS UNABLE TO
ANSWER FOR THEMSELVES

This service is to be used only when children or others unable to take the vows themselves are being baptized, and when there is not a youth or adult baptism, confirmation, or reaffirmation of faith.

When it is necessary to shorten the service, at least sections 4, 8, and 11 are used.

INTRODUCTION TO THE SERVICE

As persons are coming forward, an appropriate hymn of baptism or confirmation may be sung.

1 *The pastor makes the following statement to the congregation:*

Brothers and sisters in Christ:
Through the Sacrament of Baptism
 we are initiated into Christ's holy church.
We are incorporated into God's mighty acts of salvation
 and given new birth through water and the Spirit.
All this is God's gift, offered to us without price.

PRESENTATION OF CANDIDATES

3 *A representative of the congregation presents the candidates:*

I present *Name(s)* for baptism.

RENUNCIATION OF SIN AND PROFESSION OF FAITH

4   *The pastor addresses parents or other sponsors:*

On behalf of the whole church, I ask you:
Do you renounce the spiritual forces of wickedness,
   reject the evil powers of this world,
   and repent of your sin?

I do.

Do you accept the freedom and power God gives you
   to resist evil, injustice, and oppression
   in whatever forms they present themselves?

I do.

Do you confess Jesus Christ as your Savior,
put your whole trust in his grace,
and promise to serve him as your Lord,
in union with the church which Christ has opened
   to people of all ages, nations, and races?

I do.

Will you nurture *these children (persons)*
   in Christ's holy church,
that by your teaching and example they may be guided
   to accept God's grace for themselves,
   to profess their faith openly,
   and to lead a Christian life?

I will.

8   *The pastor addresses the congregation:*

Do you, as Christ's body, the church,
reaffirm both your rejection of sin
   and your commitment to Christ?

We do.

Will you nurture one another in the Christian faith and life and include *these persons* now before you in your care?

**With God's help we will proclaim the good news
   and live according to the example of Christ.
We will surround *these persons*
   with a community of love and forgiveness,
   that *they* may grow in *their* service to others.
We will pray for *them*,
   that *they* may be true *disciples*
   who *walk* in the way that leads to life.**

9   *The pastor addresses all:*

Let us join together in professing the Christian faith
   as contained in the Scriptures of the Old and New Testaments.

Do you believe in God the Father?

I believe in God, the Father Almighty,
creator of heaven and earth.

Do you believe in Jesus Christ?

I believe in Jesus Christ, his only Son, our Lord,
[who was conceived by the Holy Spirit,
born of the Virgin Mary,
suffered under Pontius Pilate,
was crucified, died, and was buried;
he descended to the dead.
On the third day he rose again;
he ascended into heaven,
is seated at the right hand of the Father,
and will come again to judge the living and the dead.]

Do you believe in the Holy Spirit?

I believe in the Holy Spirit,
[the holy catholic* church,
the communion of saints,
the forgiveness of sins,
the resurrection of the body,
and the life everlasting.]

THANKSGIVING OVER THE WATER

10 *The water may be poured into the font at this time, and the following prayer offered:*

The Lord be with you.

And also with you.

Let us pray.

Eternal Father:
When nothing existed but chaos,
   you swept across the dark waters
   and brought forth light.
In the days of Noah
   you saved those on the ark through water.
After the flood you set in the clouds a rainbow.
When you saw your people as slaves in Egypt,
   you led them to freedom through the sea.
Their children you brought through the Jordan
   to the land which you promised.

**Sing to the Lord, all the earth.
Tell of God's mercy each day.

---

*universal
**One of the musical responses on pages 53-54 may be used if desired.

In the fullness of time you sent Jesus,
nurtured in the water of a womb.
He was baptized by John and anointed by your Spirit.
He called his disciples
to share in the baptism of his death and resurrection
and to make disciples of all nations.

****Declare his works to the nations,
his glory among all the people.**

Pour out your Holy Spirit,
to bless this gift of water and *those* who *receive* it,
to wash away *their* sin
and clothe *them* in righteousness
throughout *their lives,*
that, dying and being raised with Christ,
they may share in his final victory.

****All praise to you, Eternal Father,
through your Son Jesus Christ,
who with you and the Holy Spirit
lives and reigns for ever.
Amen.**

BAPTISM WITH LAYING ON OF HANDS

11　*As each candidate is baptized, the pastor says:*

Name, I baptize you in the name of the Father,
and of the Son,
and of the Holy Spirit.

The people respond:

Amen.

Immediately after the administration of the water, the pastor, and others if desired place hands on the head of each candidate, as the pastor says to each:

The Holy Spirit work within you,
that being born through water and the Spirit
you may be a faithful disciple of Jesus Christ.

The people respond:

Amen.

When all candidates have been baptized, the pastor invites the congregation to welcome them:

Now it is our joy to welcome
our new *sisters and brothers* in Christ.

**Through baptism
you are incorporated by the Holy Spirit
    into God's new creation
and made to share in Christ's royal priesthood.
We are all one in Christ Jesus.
With joy and thanksgiving we welcome you
    as *members* of the family of Christ.**

COMMENDATION AND WELCOME

16   *The pastor addresses the congregation:*

Members of the household of God,
I commend *these persons* to your love and care.
Do all in your power to increase *their* faith,
    confirm *their* hope, and perfect *them* in love.

The congregation responds:

**We give thanks for all that God has already given you
    and we welcome you in Christian love.
As members together with you
    in the body of Christ
    and in this congregation
    of The United Methodist Church,
we renew our covenant
    faithfully to participate
    in the ministries of the church
    by our prayers, our presence,
    our gifts, and our service,
that in everything God may be glorified
    through Jesus Christ.**

The pastor addresses those baptized:

The God of all grace,
    who has called us to eternal glory in Christ,
establish you and strengthen you
    by the power of the Holy Spirit,
that you may live in grace and peace.

One or more lay leaders may join with the pastor in acts of welcome and peace.

Appropriate thanksgivings and intercessions for those who have participated in these acts should be included in the concerns and prayers which follow.

It is most fitting that the service continue with Holy Communion, in which the union of the new members with the body of Christ is most fully expressed. The new members may receive first.

THE CONGREGATIONAL PLEDGE 1

When using the service of the Baptism of Infants of the former Evangelical United Brethren Church, this congregational act is used, the people standing:

Pastor:

Do you as a congregation
accept the responsibility of assisting *these parents*
  in fulfillment of the baptismal vows,
and do you undertake to provide facilities and opportunities
  for Christian nurture and fellowship?

People:

We will, by the grace of God.

CONGREGATIONAL PLEDGE 2

When using the service of the Baptism of Children of the former Methodist Church, this congregational act is used, the people standing:

Pastor:

Members of the household of faith,
I commend to your love and care *this child,*
  whom we this day recognize as *a member* of the family of God.
Will you endeavor so to live
  that *this child* may grow in the knowledge and love of God,
  through our Savior Jesus Christ?

People:

With God's help
we will so order our lives after the example of Christ,
that *this child*, surrounded by steadfast love,
may be established in the faith,
and confirmed and strengthened
in the way that leads to life eternal.

Do you promise, according to the grace given you,
to keep God's holy will and commandments
and walk in the same all the days of your life
as *faithful members* of Christ's holy church?

I do.

BAPTISM

If there are no baptisms, the service continues with the Laying on of Hands.

Of the candidates for baptism, the pastor inquires:

Do you desire to be baptized in this faith?

I do.

As each candidate is baptized, the pastor says:

Name, I baptize you in the name of the Father,
　　and of the Son,
　　and of the Holy Spirit.

The people respond:

Amen.

LAYING ON OF HANDS, CONFIRMATION, OR REAFFIRMATION OF FAITH

As the pastor, and others if desired, place hands on the head of each person who has been baptized, or is being confirmed, or is reaffirming faith, the pastor says to each:

Name, the Lord defend you with his heavenly grace
and by his Spirit confirm you
　　in the faith and fellowship
　　of all true disciples of Jesus Christ.

The people respond:

Amen.

RECEPTION INTO THE UNITED METHODIST CHURCH

The pastor, addressing the people, may say:

Let those persons who are members of other communions
　　in Christ's holy church,
and who now desire to enter
　　into the fellowship of this congregation,
present themselves
　　to be received into the membership
　　of The United Methodist Church.

The pastor addresses all those transferring their membership into The United Methodist Church, together with those who, through baptism or confirmation, have just professed their faith:

Will you be loyal to The United Methodist Church,
and uphold it by your prayers, your presence,
   your gifts, and your service?

I will.

RECEPTION INTO THE LOCAL CONGREGATION

Then the pastor may say:

Let those who are members of other congregations
   of The United Methodist Church,
and who now desire to enter
   into the fellowship of this congregation,
   present themselves to be welcomed.

COMMENDATION AND WELCOME

Here a lay member, selected by the Administrative Board or Council, may join with the pastor in offering the hand of fellowship to all those received.

Then the pastor may have those received face the congregation and, causing the people to stand, address them, saying:

Brothers and sisters,
I commend to your love and care
   these persons whom we this day receive
   into the membership of this congregation.
Do all in your power
   to increase *their* faith,
   confirm *their* hope,
   and perfect *them* in love.

The congregation responds:

**We rejoice to recognize you
   as *members* of Christ's holy church,
and bid you welcome to this congregation
   of The United Methodist Church.
With you we renew our vows to uphold it
   by our prayers, our presence,
   our gifts, and our service.
With God's help we will so order our lives
   after the example of Christ**

**that, surrounded by steadfast love,
you may be established in the faith,
and confirmed and strengthened in the way
  that leads to life eternal.**

The pastor may give this or another blessing:

God the Father, God the Son, and God the Holy Spirit
bless, preserve, and keep you,
now and evermore.

The people respond:

Amen.

Appropriate thanksgivings and intercessions for those who have participated in these acts should be included in the concerns and prayers which follow.

It is most fitting that the service continue with Holy Communion, in which the union of the new members with the body of Christ is most fully expressed. The new members may receive first.

THE BAPTISMAL COVENANT IV

CONGREGATIONAL REAFFIRMATION OF THE BAPTISMAL COVENANT

This service is for use by a congregation when there are no candidates to be baptized, confirmed, or received into membership.

INTRODUCTION TO THE SERVICE

Brothers and sisters in Christ:

Through the Sacrament of Baptism
    we are initiated into Christ's holy church.
We are incorporated into God's mighty acts of salvation
    and given new birth through water and the Spirit.
All this is God's gift, offered to us without price.

Through the reaffirmation of our faith
we renew the covenant declared at our baptism,
    acknowledge what God is doing for us,
    and affirm our commitment to Christ's holy church.

RENUNCIATION OF SIN AND PROFESSION OF FAITH

On behalf of the whole church, I ask you:
Do you renounce the spiritual forces of wickedness,
    reject the evil powers of this world,
    and repent of your sin?

I do.

Do you accept the freedom and power God gives you
    to resist evil, injustice, and oppression
    in whatever forms they present themselves?

I do.

Do you confess Jesus Christ as your Savior,
put your whole trust in his grace,
and promise to serve him as your Lord,
in union with the church which Christ has opened
    to people of all ages, nations, and races?

I do.

According to the grace given to you,
will you remain faithful members of Christ's holy church
and serve as Christ's representatives in the world?

I will.

Let us join together in professing the Christian faith
    as contained in the Scriptures of the Old and New Testaments.

Do you believe in God the Father?

I believe in God, the Father Almighty,
creator of heaven and earth.

Do you believe in Jesus Christ?

I believe in Jesus Christ, his only Son, our Lord,
[who was conceived by the Holy Spirit,
born of the Virgin Mary,
suffered under Pontius Pilate,
was crucified, died, and was buried;
he descended to the dead.
On the third day he rose again;
he ascended into heaven,
is seated at the right hand of the Father,
and will come again to judge the living and the dead.]

Do you believe in the Holy Spirit?

I believe in the Holy Spirit,
[the holy catholic* church,
the communion of saints,
the forgiveness of sins,
the resurrection of the body,
and the life everlasting.]

THANKSGIVING OVER THE WATER

If water is to be used for reaffirmation, the water may be poured into the font at this time, and the following prayer offered:

The Lord be with you.

And also with you.

Let us pray.

Eternal Father:
When nothing existed but chaos,
   you swept across the dark waters
   and brought forth light.
In the days of Noah
   you saved those on the ark through water.
After the flood you set in the clouds a rainbow.
When you saw your people as slaves in Egypt,
   you led them to freedom through the sea.
Their children you brought through the Jordan
   to the land which you promised.

**Sing to the Lord, all the earth.
Tell of God's mercy each day.

*universal
***One of the musical settings on pages 53-54 may be used if desired.*

In the fullness of time you sent Jesus,
    nurtured in the water of a womb.
He was baptized by John and anointed by your Spirit.
He called his disciples
    to share in the baptism of his death and resurrection
    and to make disciples of all nations.

**Declare his works to the nations,
his glory among all people.

Pour out your Holy Spirit,
and by this gift of water call to our remembrance
    the grace declared to us in our baptism.
For you have washed away our sins,
    and you clothe us with righteousness throughout our lives,
    that dying and rising with Christ
    we may share in his final victory.

**All praise to you, Eternal Father,
through your Son Jesus Christ,
who with you and the Holy Spirit
lives and reigns for ever.
Amen.

REAFFIRMATION OF FAITH

Here water may be used symbolically in ways that cannot be interpreted as baptism, as the pastor says:

Remember your baptism and be thankful.

Amen.

The Holy Spirit work within you,
that having been born through water and the Spirit,
you may live as faithful disciples of Jesus Christ.

Amen.

THANKSGIVING

Let us rejoice in the faithfulness of our covenant God.

We give thanks for all that God has already given us.
As members of the body of Christ
    and in this congregation of The United Methodist Church,
we will faithfully participate in the ministries of the church
    by our prayers, our presence, our gifts, and our service,
    that in everything God may be glorified through Jesus Christ.

The pastor addresses those reaffirming the Baptismal Covenant:

The God of all grace,
    who has called us to eternal glory in Christ,
establish and strengthen you

by the power of the Holy Spirit,
that you may live in grace and peace.

Signs of peace may be exchanged.

It is most fitting that the service continue with Holy Communion.

BAPTISMAL COVENANT
MUSICAL RESPONSES

(1)

Charles H. Webb

Sing to the Lord, all the earth, tell of God's mer-cy each day.

Music © 1989 The United Methodist Publishing House

(2)

Charles H. Webb

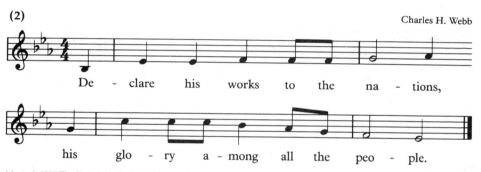

De - clare his works to the na - tions,

his glo - ry a - mong all the peo - ple.

Music © 1989 The United Methodist Publishing House

(3)

Charles H. Webb

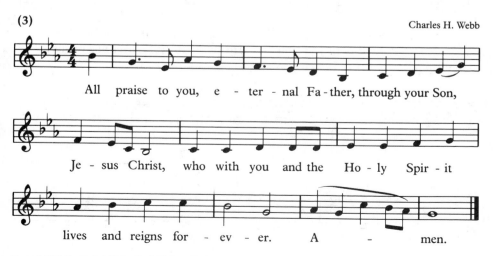

All praise to you, e - ter - nal Fa - ther, through your Son,

Je - sus Christ, who with you and the Ho - ly Spir - it

lives and reigns for - ev - er. A - men.

Music © 1989 The United Methodist Publishing House

Responses may be sung with repeats, leader or choir singing first, congregation repeating; OR the responses may be sung without repeats using only the second endings, except response 3, where all endings would be used.

Carlton R. Young

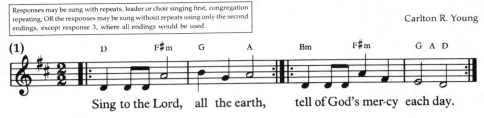

(1) Sing to the Lord, all the earth, tell of God's mer-cy each day.

Music © 1989 The United Methodist Publishing House

Carlton R. Young

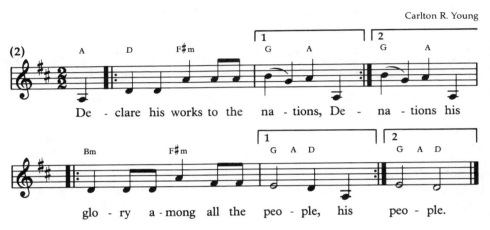

(2) De - clare his works to the na - tions, De - na - tions his

glo - ry a - mong all the peo - ple, his peo - ple.

Music © 1989 The United Methodist Publishing House

Carlton R. Young

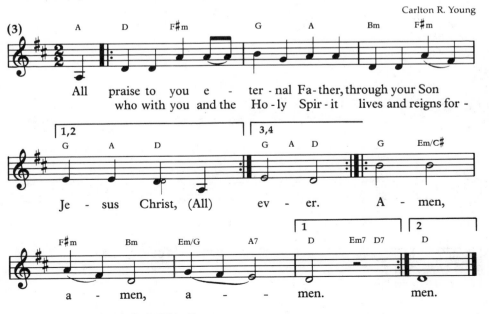

(3) All praise to you e - ter - nal Fa - ther, through your Son
who with you and the Ho - ly Spir - it lives and reigns for -

Je - sus Christ, (All) ev - er. A - men,

a - men, a - - men. men.

Music © 1989 The United Methodist Publishing House

HYMNS, CANTICLES & ACTS OF WORSHIP

Glory to God, and praise and love
* be ever, ever given;*
by saints below and saints above,
* the church in earth and heaven.*

CHARLES WESLEY, 1739

Beginning with stanza 7, "O For a Thousand Tongues to Sing" has traditionally been the opening hymn in Methodist hymnals throughout the world since the time of Wesley's *Collection of Hymns for the Use of the People Called Methodists* (1780). The number of stanzas tends to vary, but the complete eighteen, seventeen of which are included in No. 58, seem never to have been used as a hymn, and much of the poem's original content is little known. It was written in 1739 by Charles Wesley to commemorate his conversion on May 21, 1738, and was published in *Hymns and Sacred Poems* (1740) with the title "For the Anniversary Day of One's Conversion." The first six stanzas deal with Charles Wesley's own emotions upon his spiritual transformation. The climactic stanza, however, is apparently an echo of an expression used by Peter Böhler: "Had I a thousand tongues, I would praise him with them all!" This itself may have been a reminiscence of a hymn by Johann Mentzer (1658-1734) which was published in Freylinghausen's *Gesangbuch* (1704), beginning with the same words in German: "O dass ich tausend Zungen hätte."

O For a Thousand Tongues to Sing   57

1. O for a thou - sand tongues to sing my great Re - deem - er's praise, the glo - ries of my God and King, the tri - umphs of his grace!

2. My gra - cious Mas - ter and my God, as - sist me to pro - claim, to spread through all the earth a - broad the hon - ors of thy name.

3. Je - sus! the name that charms our fears, that bids our sor - rows cease; 'tis mu - sic in the sin - ner's ears, 'tis life, and health, and peace.

4. He breaks the power of can - celed sin, he sets the pris - oner free; his blood can make the foul - est clean; his blood a - vailed for me.

5. He speaks, and listen - ing to his voice, new life the dead re - ceive; the mourn - ful, bro - ken hearts re - joice, the hum - ble poor be - lieve.

*6. Hear him, ye deaf; his praise, ye dumb, your loos - ened tongues em - ploy; ye blind, be - hold your Sav - ior come, and leap, ye lame, for joy.

7. In Christ, your head, you then shall know, shall feel your sins for - given; an - tic - i - pate your heaven be - low, and own that love is heaven.

*May be omitted

WORDS: Charles Wesley, 1739   AZMON
MUSIC: Carl G. Gläser; arr. by Lowell Mason, 1839   CM

Alt. tune: RICHMOND

58 Glory to God, and Praise and Love

Glory to God, and praise and love
be ever, ever given,
by saints below and saints above,
the church in earth and heaven.

On this glad day the glorious Sun
of Righteousness arose;
on my benighted soul he shone
and filled it with repose.

Sudden expired the legal strife,
'twas then I ceased to grieve;
my second, real, living life
I then began to live.

Then with my heart I first believed,
believed with faith divine,
power with the Holy Ghost received
to call the Savior mine.

I felt my Lord's atoning blood
close to my soul applied;
me, me he loved, the Son of God,
for me, for me he died!

I found and owned his promise true,
ascertained of my part,
my pardon passed in heaven I knew
when written on my heart.

O for a thousand tongues to sing
my dear Redeemer's praise!
The glories of my God and King,
the triumphs of his grace.

My gracious Master and my God,
assist me to proclaim,
to spread through all the earth abroad
the honors of thy name.

Jesus! the name that charms our fears,
that bids our sorrows cease;
'tis music in the sinner's ears,
'tis life, and health, and peace!

He breaks the power of canceled sin,
he sets the prisoner free;
his blood can make the foulest clean;
his blood availed for me.

He speaks, and listening to his voice
new life the dead receive;
the mournful, broken hearts rejoice,
the humble poor believe.

Hear him, ye deaf, his praise, ye dumb,
your loosened tongues employ;
ye blind, behold your Savior come,
and leap, ye lame, for joy.

Look unto him, ye nations, own
your God, ye fallen race!
Look, and be saved through faith alone,
be justified by grace!

See all your sins on Jesus laid;
the Lamb of God was slain,
his soul was once an offering made
for every soul of man.

Harlots and publicans and thieves,
in holy triumph join!
Saved is the sinner that believes
from crimes as great as mine.

Murderers and all ye hellish crew,
ye sons of lust and pride,
believe the Savior died for you;
for me the Savior died.

With me, your chief, you then shall know,
shall feel your sins forgiven;
anticipate your heaven below
and own that love is heaven.

Charles Wesley, 1739

Mil Voces Para Celebrar

1. Mil vo - ces pa - ra ce - le - brar a
2. Mi buen Se - ñor, Maes - tro y Dios: que
3. El dul - ce nom - bre de Je - sús nos
4. Des - tru - ye el po - der del mal y
5. Él ha - bla y al o - ír su voz el
6. Es - cu - chen, sor - dos, al Se - ñor; a -
7. En Cris - to, pues, co - no - ce - rán la

mi Li - ber - ta - dor, las glo - rias de su
pue - da di - vul - gar tu gra - to nom - bre
li - bra del te - mor, en las tris - te - zas
brin - da li - ber - tad; al más im - pu - ro
muer - to vi - vi - rá; se a - le - gra el tris - te
la - be el mun - do a Dios, los co - jos sal - ten,
gra - cia del per - dón, y a - quí del cie - lo

ma - jes - tad, los triun - fos de su a - mor.
y su ho - nor, en cie - lo, tie - rra y mar.
tra - e luz, per - dón al pe - ca - dor.
pue - de dar pu - re - za y san - ti - dad.
co - ra - zón, los po - bres ha - llan paz.
ve - an hoy los cie - gos al Se - ñor.
go - za - rán, pues cie - lo es su a - mor.

WORDS: Charles Wesley, 1739; trans. by Federico J. Pagura, 1987
MUSIC: Carl G. Gläser; arr. by Lowell Mason, 1839

AZMON
CM

Alt. tune: RICHMOND

60   I'll Praise My Maker While I've Breath

Unison

1. I'll praise my Mak-er while I've breath; and when my voice
2. Hap-py are they whose hopes re-ly on Is-rael's God,
3. The Lord pours eye-sight on the blind; the Lord sup-ports
4. I'll praise my God who lends me breath; and when my voice

is lost in death, praise shall em-ploy my no-bler powers.
who made the sky and earth and seas, with all their train;
the faint-ing mind and sends the la-boring con-science peace.
is lost in death, praise shall em-ploy my no-bler powers.

My days of praise shall ne'er be past, while life, and thought,
whose truth for-ev-er stands se-cure, who saves th'op-pressed
God helps the stran-ger in dis-tress, the wid-ow and
My days of praise shall ne'er be past, while life, and thought,

and be-ing last, or im-mor-tal-i-ty en-dures.
and feeds the poor, for none shall find God's prom-ise vain.
the fa-ther-less, and grants the pris-oner sweet re-lease.
and be-ing last, or im-mor-tal-i-ty en-dures.

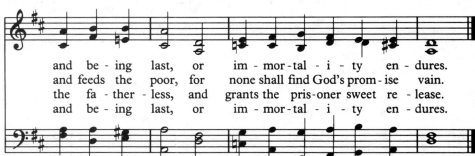

WORDS: Isaac Watts, 1719; alt. by John Wesley, 1737; alt. 1989 (Ps. 146)
MUSIC: Attr. to Matthäus Greiter, 1525; harm. by V. Earle Copes, 1963
Harm. © 1964 Abingdon Press

OLD 113th
888.888

Come, Thou Almighty King

1. Come, thou al-might-y King, help us thy name to sing, help us to praise! Fa-ther all glo-ri-ous, o'er all vic-to-ri-ous, come and reign o-ver us, An-cient of Days!

2. Come, thou in-car-nate Word, gird on thy might-y sword, our prayer at-tend! Come, and thy peo-ple bless, and give thy word suc-cess; Spir-it of ho-li-ness, on us de-scend!

3. Come, ho-ly Com-fort-er, thy sa-cred wit-ness bear in this glad hour. Thou who al-might-y art, now rule in ev-ery heart, and ne'er from us de-part, Spir-it of power!

4. To thee, great One in Three, e-ter-nal prais-es be, hence, ev-er-more. Thy sov-ereign maj-es-ty may we in glo-ry see, and to e-ter-ni-ty love and a-dore!

WORDS: Anon.
MUSIC: Felice de Giardini, 1769

ITALIAN HYMN
664.6664

Alt. tune: AMERICA

62 All Creatures of Our God and King

Unison

1. All crea-tures of our God and King, lift up your voice and with us
2. O broth-er wind, air, clouds, and rain, by which all crea-tures ye sus-
3. O sis-ter wa-ter, flow-ing clear, make mu-sic for thy Lord to
4. Dear moth-er earth, who day by day un-fold-est bless-ings on our
5. All ye who are of ten-der heart, for-giv-ing oth-ers, take your

Harmony   *Unison*

sing, O praise ye! Al-le-lu-ia! O broth-er sun with
tain, O praise ye! Al-le-lu-ia! Thou ris-ing morn, in
hear, Al-le-lu-ia! Al-le-lu-ia! O broth-er fire who
way, Al-le-lu-ia! Al-le-lu-ia! The flowers and fruits that
part, O praise ye! Al-le-lu-ia! Ye who long pain and

Refrain (Harmony)

gold-en beam, O sis-ter moon with sil-ver gleam!
praise re-joice, ye lights of eve-ning, find a voice!   O praise ye!
lights the night, pro-vid-ing warmth, en-hanc-ing sight,
in thee grow, let them God's glo-ry al-so show!
sor-row bear, praise God and on him cast your care!

WORDS: Francis of Assisi, ca. 1225; trans. by
  William H. Draper, 1925, adapt. 1987
MUSIC: *Geistliche Kirchengesänge*, 1623; harm. by Ralph Vaughan Williams, 1906

LASST UNS ERFREUEN
88.44.88 with Refrain

Unison

O praise ye! Al- le - lu - ia! Al- le- lu - ia! Al- le- lu - ia!

6. And thou, our sister, gentle death,
   waiting to hush our latest breath,
   Alleluia! Alleluia!
   Thou leadest home the child of God,
   and Christ our Lord the way has trod,
   Refrain

7. Let all things their Creator bless,
   and worship him in humbleness,
   O praise ye! Alleluia!
   Praise, praise the Father, praise the Son,
   and praise the Spirit, Three in One!
   Refrain

Blessed Be the Name
63

Bless-ed be the name! Bless-ed be the name! Bless-ed be the
name of the Lord! Bless - ed be the name!
Bless-ed be the name! Bless-ed be the name of the Lord!

WORDS: USA campmeeting chorus (Ps. 72:19)
MUSIC: USA campmeeting melody; arr. by Ralph E. Hudson, 1887

BLESSED BE THE NAME
Irr.

64 Holy, Holy, Holy! Lord God Almighty

1. Ho - ly, ho - ly, ho - ly! Lord God Al - might - y!
2. Ho - ly, ho - ly, ho - ly! All the saints a - dore thee,
3. Ho - ly, ho - ly, ho - ly! Though the dark-ness hide thee,
4. Ho - ly, ho - ly, ho - ly! Lord God Al - might - y!

Ear - ly in the morn - ing our song shall rise to thee.
cast - ing down their gold - en crowns a - round the glass - y sea;
though the eye of sin - ful man thy glo - ry may not see,
All thy works shall praise thy name, in earth and sky and sea.

Ho - ly, ho - ly, ho - ly! Mer - ci - ful and might - y,
cher - u - bim and ser - a - phim fall - ing down be - fore thee,
on - ly thou art ho - ly; there is none be - side thee,
Ho - ly, ho - ly, ho - ly! Mer - ci - ful and might - y,

God in three per - sons, bless - ed Trin - i - ty!
which wert, and art, and ev - er - more shalt be.
per - fect in power, in love and pur - i - ty.
God in three per - sons, bless - ed Trin - i - ty.

WORDS: Reginald Heber, 1826 (Rev. 4:8-11)
MUSIC: John B. Dykes, 1861

NICAEA
11 12.12 10

¡Santo! ¡Santo! ¡Santo!

65

1. ¡San-to! ¡San-to! ¡San - to! Se - ñor om - ni - po - ten - te,
2. ¡San-to! ¡San-to! ¡San - to! la in - men-sa mu-che - dum - bre
3. ¡San-to! ¡San-to! ¡San - to! por más que es-tés ve - la - do,
4. ¡San-to! ¡San-to! ¡San - to! la glo-ria de tu nom - bre

siem - pre el la - bio mí - o lo - o - res te da - rá.
de án - ge - les que cum - plen tu san - ta vo - lun - tad,
e im - po - si - ble se - a tu glo-ria con - tem - plar;
ve - mos en tus o - bras en cie - lo, tie-rra y mar;

¡San - to! ¡San - to! ¡San - to! te a - do - ro re - ve - ren - te,
an - te ti se pos - tra, ba - ña - da de tu lum - bre,
San - to tú e - res só - lo, y na - da hay a tu la - do
¡San - to! ¡San - to! ¡San - to! te a - do - ra - rá to - do hom - bre,

Dios en tres per - so - nas, ben - di - ta Tri - ni - dad.
an - te ti que has si - do, que e - res y se - rás.
en po - der per - fec - to, pu - re - za y ca - ri - dad.
Dios en tres per - so - nas, ben - di - ta Tri - ni - dad.

WORDS: Reginald Heber, 1826; trans. by Juan Bautista Cabrera (Rev. 4:8-11)
MUSIC: John B. Dykes, 1861

NICAEA
11 12.12 10

66 Praise, My Soul, the King of Heaven

1. Praise, my soul, the King of heav - en, to the throne thy
2. Praise the Lord for grace and fa - vor to all peo - ple
3. Fa - ther - like, God tends and spares us; well our fee - ble
4. An - gels in the heights, a - dor - ing, you be - hold God

trib - ute bring; ran-somed, healed, re - stored, for - giv - en,
in dis - tress; praise God, still the same as ev - er,
frame God knows; moth - er - like, God gent - ly bears us,
face to face; saints tri - um-phant, now a - dor - ing,

ev - er - more God's prais - es sing. Al - le - lu - ia!
slow to chide, and swift to bless. Al - le - lu - ia!
res - cues us from all our foes. Al - le - lu - ia!
gath - ered in from ev - ery race. Al - le - lu - ia!

Al - le - lu - ia! Praise the ev - er - last - ing King.
Al - le - lu - ia! Glo-rious now God's faith - ful - ness.
Al - le - lu - ia! Wide-ly yet God's mer - cy flows.
Al - le - lu - ia! Praise with us the God of grace.

WORDS: Henry F. Lyte, 1834 (Ps. 103)
MUSIC: John Goss, 1869

LAUDA ANIMA
87.87.87

Alt. tune: REGENT SQUARE

We, Thy People, Praise Thee

We, thy peo-ple, praise thee, praise thee, God of ev-ery na-tion!

We, thy peo-ple, praise thee, praise thee, Lord of Hosts e-ter-nal!

1. Days of won-der, days of beau-ty, days of rap-ture filled with light
2. For thy bless-ings, for thy boun-ty, joy-ful songs to thee we sing,

tell thy good-ness, tell thy mer-cies, tell thy glo-rious might.
songs of glo-ry, songs of tri-umph to our God and King.

We, thy peo-ple, praise thee, praise thee, praise thee ev-er-more!

WORDS: Kate Stearns Page, 1932
MUSIC: Franz Joseph Haydn, ca. 1780; arr. by Edith Lovell Thomas, 1935; alt.

ST. ANTHONY'S CHORALE
Irr.

Arr. © renewed 1963 Abingdon Press

68　When in Our Music God Is Glorified

Unison

1. When in our mu-sic God is glo-ri-fied,
2. How of-ten, mak-ing mu-sic, we have found
3. So has the church in lit-ur-gy and song,
4. And did not Je-sus sing a psalm that night
5. Let ev-ery in-stru-ment be tuned for praise!

and ad-o-ra-tion leaves no room for pride,
a new di-men-sion in the world of sound,
in faith and love, through cen-tu-ries of wrong,
when ut-most e-vil strove a-gainst the light?
Let all re-joice who have a voice to raise!

it is as though the whole cre-a-tion cried
as wor-ship moved us to a more pro-found
borne wit-ness to the truth in ev-ery tongue,
Then let us sing, for whom he won the fight:
And may God give us faith to sing al-ways

1, 2, 3, 4
Al-le-lu-ia!

5
Al-le-lu-ia!

WORDS: Fred Pratt Green, 1971 (Mk. 14:26)
MUSIC: Charles Villiers Stanford, 1904

Words © 1972 Hope Publishing Co.

ENGELBERG
10 10 10 with Alleluias

Alt. tune: SINE NOMINE

For True Singing

Glorious God, source of joy and righteousness,
enable us as redeemed and forgiven children
evermore to rejoice in singing your praises.
Grant that what we sing with our lips
we may believe in our hearts,
and what we believe in our hearts
we may practice in our lives;
so that being doers of the Word and not hearers only,
we may receive everlasting life;
through Jesus Christ our Lord. **Amen.**

Fred D. Gealy, USA, 20th cent.; alt. by Laurence Hull Stookey, 1987 (Ja. 1:22)

Alt. © 1989 The United Methodist Publishing House

Glory Be to the Father

70

WORDS: Lesser Doxology, 3rd-4th cent.
MUSIC: Charles Meineke, 1844

MEINEKE
Irr.

71 Glory Be to the Father

WORDS: Lesser Doxology, 3rd-4th cent.
MUSIC: Henry W. Greatorex, 1851

GREATOREX
Irr.

72 Gloria, Gloria

May be sung as a canon

WORDS: Luke 2:14;
MUSIC: Jacques Berthier and the Community of Taizé, 1979

GLORIA CANON
Irr.

O Worship the King

1. O worship the King, all - glo - rious a - bove,
2. O tell of God's might, O sing of God's grace,
3. The earth with its store of won - ders un - told,
4. Thy boun - ti - ful care, what tongue can re - cite?
5. Frail chil - dren of dust, and fee - ble as frail,

O grate - ful - ly sing God's power and God's love;
whose robe is the light, whose can - o - py space,
Al - might - y, thy power hath found - ed of old;
It breathes in the air, it shines in the light;
in thee do we trust, nor find thee to fail;

our Shield and De - fend - er, the An - cient of Days,
whose char - iots of wrath the deep thun - der - clouds form,
hath stab - lished it fast by a change - less de - cree,
it streams from the hills, it de - scends to the plain,
thy mer - cies how ten - der, how firm to the end,

pa - vil - ioned in splen - dor, and gird - ed with praise.
and dark is God's path on the wings of the storm.
and round it hath cast, like a man - tle, the sea.
and sweet - ly dis - tills in the dew and the rain.
our Mak - er, De - fend - er, Re - deem - er, and Friend.

WORDS: Robert Grant, 1833 (Ps. 104)
MUSIC: Attr. to Johann Michael Haydn; arr. by William Gardiner, 1815

LYONS
10 10.11 11

74   Canticle of Thanksgiving

(Jubilate)

RESPONSE 1 *(Thanksgiving & General)*

Make joy-ful noise, lift up your voice! Ye na-tions of the earth re-joice!

RESPONSE 2 *(General)*

Re - joice! Re - joice! Re - joice, give thanks, and sing.

R

Make a joyful noise unto the Lord, all ye lands.
Serve the Lord with gladness;
   come before his presence with singing.
Know ye that the Lord, he is God;
it is he that hath made us, and not we ourselves;
   we are his people, and the sheep of his pasture.
Enter into his gates with thanksgiving,
   and into his courts with praise;
be thankful unto him, and bless his name.
For the Lord is good;
his mercy is everlasting;
   and his truth endureth to all generations.   **R**

See No. 75 for a metrical version of this psalm and No. 821 for a modern language version.

WORDS: Psalm 100 (KJV); Response 1, Charles Wesley, adapt.; Response 2, Edward H. Plumptre
MUSIC: Response 1, Timothy E. Kimbrough; Response 2, Arthur H. Messiter

75   All People That on Earth Do Dwell

1. All   peo - ple that on   earth do   dwell, sing   to the Lord with
2. Know   that the Lord is   God in - deed; with - out our aid he
3. O   en - ter then his   gates with praise; ap - proach with joy his
4. For   why! the Lord our   God is   good; his   mer - cy is for -

WORDS: Attr. to William Kethe, 1561 (Ps. 100)   OLD 100th
MUSIC: Attr. to Louis Bourgeois, 1551   LM

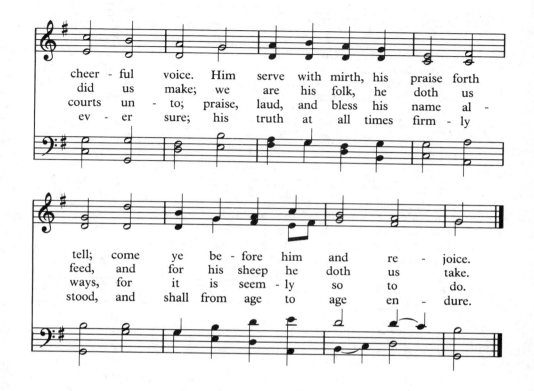

cheer - ful	voice.	Him	serve	with	mirth,	his	praise	forth
did	us	make;	we	are	his	folk,	he	doth	us
courts	un - to;	praise,	laud,	and	bless	his	name	al -
ev - er	sure;	his	truth	at	all	times	firm - ly

tell;	come	ye	be - fore	him	and	re -	joice.
feed,	and	for	his	sheep	he	doth	us	take.
ways,	for	it	is	seem - ly	so	to	do.
stood,	and	shall	from	age	to	age	en -	dure.

Trinity Sunday   76

Holy God,
you have given us grace,
    by the confession of the faith of your holy church,
    to acknowledge the mystery of the eternal Trinity
    and, in the power of your divine majesty, to worship the Unity.
Keep us steadfast in this faith and worship,
    and bring us at last to see in your eternal glory
        One God, now and forever. **Amen.**

After The Book of Common Prayer; alt.

77 How Great Thou Art

1. O Lord my God! when I in awe-some won - der
2. When through the woods and for - est glades I wan - der,
3. And when I think that God, his Son not spar - ing,
4. When Christ shall come with shout of ac - cla - ma - tion

con - sid - er all the *worlds thy hands have made,
and hear the birds sing sweet - ly in the trees;
sent him to die, I scarce can take it in;
and take me home, what joy shall fill my heart.

I see the stars, I hear the roll - ing thun - der,
when I look down from loft - y moun-tain gran - deur
that on the cross, my bur - den glad - ly bear - ing,
Then I shall bow in hum - ble ad - o - ra - tion,

thy power through - out the un - i - verse dis - played.
and hear the brook, and feel the gen - tle breeze;
he bled and died to take a - way my sin;
and there pro - claim, my God, how great thou art!

*Authors's original words are "works" and "mighty."

WORDS: Stuart K. Hine, 1953
MUSIC: Stuart K. Hine, 1953

© 1953, renewed 1981 Manna Music, Inc.

HOW GREAT THOU ART
Irr. with Refrain

Refrain

Then sings my soul, my Sav - ior God to thee;

how great thou art, how great thou art! Then sings my

soul, my Sav-ior God to thee; how great thou art, how great thou art!

Heleluyan

78

(Alleluia)

He - le - lu - yan, he - le - lu - yan; he - le, he - le - lu - yan;

he - le - lu - yan, he - le - lu - yan; he - le, he - le - lu - yan.

WORDS: Trad. Muscogee (Creek) Indian
MUSIC: Trad. Muscogee (Creek) Indian; transcription by Charles H. Webb

HELELUYAN
Irr.

79 Holy God, We Praise Thy Name

1. Holy God, we praise thy name; Lord of all, we
2. Hark, the glad celestial hymn angel choirs a-
3. Lo! the apostolic train joins thy sacred
4. Holy Father, Holy Son, Holy Spirit:
*5. Christ, thou art our glorious King, Son of God, en-

bow before thee; all on earth thy scepter claim;
bove are raising; cherubim and seraphim,
name to hallow; prophets swell the glad refrain,
three we name thee, though in essence only one;
throned in splendor; but deliverance to bring

all in heaven above adore thee. Infinite thy
in unceasing chorus praising, fill the heavens with
and the white-robed martyrs follow. And from morn to
undivided God we claim thee, and adoring
thou all honors didst surrender, and wast of a

vast domain; everlasting is thy reign.
sweet accord: Holy, holy, holy Lord.
set of sun, through the church the song goes on.
bend the knee while we own the mystery.
virgin born humbly on that blessed morn.

*May be omitted

WORDS: Sts. 1-4, Ignaz Franz, 18th cent.; trans. by Clarence Walworth, 1853;
sts. 5-7. F. Bland Tucker, 1982
MUSIC: *Katholisches Gesangbuch,* ca. 1774
Sts. 5-7 © 1985 The Church Pension Fund

GROSSER GOTT
78.78.77

*6. Thou didst take the sting from death,
Son of God, as Savior given;
on the cross thy dying breath
opened wide the realm of heaven.
In the glory of that land
thou art set at God's right hand.

*7. As our judge thou wilt appear,
Savior, who hast died to win us;
help thy servants, drawing near;
Lord, renew our hearts within us.
Grant that with thy saints we may
dwell in everlasting day.

Canticle of the Holy Trinity   80
(Te Deum Laudamus)

RESPONSE *(General)*

Sing praise to God, who reigns a-bove, the   God of all cre - a-tion.

R

We praise you, O God.
**We acclaim you as Lord;
all creation worships you,
Father everlasting.**
To you all angels, all the powers of heaven,
cherubim and seraphim, sing in endless praise:
**Holy, holy, holy Lord, God of power and might,
heaven and earth are full of your glory.**
The glorious company of the apostles praise you.
The noble fellowship of prophets praise you.
The white-robed army of martyrs praise you.
**Throughout the world the holy church acclaims you:
Father, of majesty unbounded,
your glorious, true and only Son,
and the Holy Spirit, advocate and guide.   R**

Continued on next page

WORDS: 4th-5th cent. hymn, ICET, rev. ELLC; Response, Johann J. Schütz; trans. by Frances E. Cox
MUSIC: Bohemian Brethren's *Kirchengesänge*

You, Christ, are the King of glory,
the eternal Son of the Father.
When you became incarnate to set us free
you humbly accepted the Virgin's womb.
You overcame the sting of death,
and opened the kingdom of heaven to all believers.
You are seated at God's right hand in glory.
We believe that you will come to be our judge.
Come then, Lord, and help your people,
bought with the price of your own blood,
and bring us with your saints
to glory everlasting. R

Versicles and Responses which may follow

Save your people, Lord, and bless your inheritance.
Govern and uphold them now and always.
Day by day we bless you.
We praise your name for ever.
Keep us today, Lord, from all sin.
Have mercy on us, Lord, have mercy.
Lord, show us your love and mercy;
for we put our trust in you.
In you, Lord, is our hope:
and we shall never hope in vain. R

See No. 79 for a metrical version of this ancient text.

81   ¡Canta, Débora, Canta!

WORDS: Luiza Cruz, 1973; English trans. by Gertrude C. Suppe, 1987;
   Spanish trans. by Raquel Gutiérrez-Achon, 1987 (Judges 5)
MUSIC: Luiza Cruz, 1973

DÉBORA
Irr.

1. Ma-dre de Is-ra-el, lí-der de_e-jér-ci-tos, can-ta un
2. To-dos los que can - tan, al-cen hoy sus vo - ces, can-ten un

1. Moth-er of Is-ra-el, lead-er of her ar - mies, sing a hymn of
2. We lift up our voic - es, ev-ery-one to-geth - er, sing-ing the

Estribillo (Refrain)

him-no_a tu Se - ñor. Por - que bue-no_es Dios, bue-no_es Dios, él es -
him-no de lo - or.

vic-tory to our God. For our God is good! God is good, and has
tri-umphs of our God.

co - ge a los hu-mil-des. Por - que bue - no_es Dios,

cho - sen those who are hum - ble. For our God is good!

bue - no_es Dios, él los for-ta-le-ce con su po - der.

God is good, and will strength-en the peo-ple with might!

82 Canticle of God's Glory

(Gloria in Excelsis)

Glory be to God on high, and on earth peace, good will to all.

We praise thee, we bless thee, we wor-ship thee, we glorify thee, we give

thanks to thee for thy great glo - ry: O Lord God, heaven-ly King,

God the Fa-ther Al-might - y. O Lord, the only begotten Son,

Je - sus Christ; O Lord God, Lamb of God, Son of the Fa - ther,

See No. 83 for a modern language version of this ancient text.

WORDS: Luke 2:14; John 1:29
MUSIC: Old Scottish Chant

83 Canticle of God's Glory
(Gloria in Excelsis)

RESPONSE *(General)*

Glo-ry to God in the high-est, and peace to God's peo-ple on earth.

R

> Glory to God in the highest,
> and peace to God's people on earth.
> Lord God, heavenly King,
> almighty God and Father,
> we worship you, we give you thanks,
> we praise you for your glory.   **R**

> Lord Jesus Christ, only Son of the Father,
> Lord God, Lamb of God,
> you take away the sin of the world:
> have mercy on us;
> you are seated at the right hand of the Father:
> receive our prayer.   **R**

> For you alone are the Holy One,
> you alone are the Lord,
> you alone are the Most High,
> Jesus Christ,
> with the Holy Spirit,
> in the glory of God the Father. Amen.   **R**

See No. 82 for a chanted version of this ancient text.

WORDS: Luke 2:14; John 1:29; ICET, rev. ELLC
MUSIC: Alexander Peloquin

Music © 1972 G.I.A. Publications, Inc.

84 Thank You, Lord

Thank you, Lord. Thank you, Lord.

WORDS: Trad.
MUSIC: Trad.; adapt. and arr. by William Farley Smith, 1986

THANK YOU, LORD
Irr.

Adapt. and arr. © 1989 The United Methodist Publishing House

Thank you, Lord. I just want to thank you, Lord.

We Believe in One True God 85

1. We be-lieve in one true God, Fa-ther, Son, and Ho-ly Ghost,
2. We be-lieve in Je - sus Christ, Son of God and Ma-ry's Son,
3. We con-fess the Ho - ly Ghost, who from both for - e'er pro-ceeds;

ev - er-pres-ent help in need, praised by all the heaven-ly host;
who de-scend-ed from his throne and for us sal - va-tion won;
who up-holds and com-forts us in all tri-als, fears, and needs.

by whose might-y power a - lone all is made and wrought and done.
by whose cross and death are we res-cued from sin's mis - er - y.
Blest and Ho-ly Trin-i - ty, praise for - ev - er be to thee!

WORDS: Tobias Clausnitzer, 1668; trans. by Catherine Winkworth, 1863
MUSIC: J. G. Werner's *Choralbuch*, 1815; arr. by William H. Havergal, 1861

RATISBON
77.77.77

86   Mountains Are All Aglow

1. Moun-tains are all a-glow with au-tumn col - ors so bright;
2. Ev - ery land so a - bun-dant-ly rich the har - vest bears;
3. Ear - ly spring is the time to sow all God's rich seeds of life.
4. Praise the Lord as we're plant - ing God's word deep in each heart.

riv - ers are filled with wa - ter, giv - ing life to our days.
ev - ery or - chard is filled with lus-cious, rip - ened new fruit.
Work-ing hard, till - ing God's earth; mak-ing prep - a - ra - tion.
God has sent sun-shine and the rain so the seed-lings may grow.

Gold - en fields wave their praise to God's boun - ti - ful har - vest;
Sun and rain by the Lord's de-sign shall come at pro-per time.
Look - ing for - ward to re-wards of har - vest so plen - ti - ful;
Des - ert lands which seem bar - ren, flow - ers still might bloom;

grate-ful - ly, sky - ward a - ris-ing, hear our joy-ous songs of praise!
Work-ing hard, God has giv - en us rea-sons for deep grat - i - tude.
prom-ised bless-ings will soon be ours in each rev - e - la - tion.
trust-ing in God's prom-is - es, our thanks to God we will show!

WORDS: Ok In Lim, 1967; trans. by Hae Jong Kim, 1988;   KAHM-SAH
    versification by Hope Omachi-Kawashima (Ps. 65:9-13; Acts 14:17)   13 13.13 15 with Refrain
MUSIC: Jae Hoon Park, 1967

87   What Gift Can We Bring

Unison

1. What gift can we bring, what pres - ent, what to - ken?
2. Give thanks for the past, for those who had vi - sion,
3. Give thanks for to - mor - row, full of sur - pris - es,
4. This gift we now bring, this pres - ent, this to - ken,

What words can con - vey it, the joy of this day?
who plant - ed and wa - tered so dreams could come true.
for know - ing what - ev - er to - mor - row may bring,
these words can con - vey it, the joy of this day!

When grate - ful we come, re - mem - ber - ing, re - joic - ing,
Give thanks for the now, for stud - y, for wor - ship,
the Word is our prom - ise al - ways, for - ev - er;
When grate - ful we come, re - mem - ber - ing, re - joic - ing,

what song can we of - fer in hon - or and praise?
for mis - sion that bids us turn prayer in - to deed.
we rest in God's keep - ing and live in God's love.
this song we now of - fer in hon - or and praise!

WORDS: Jane Marshall, 1980
MUSIC: Jane Marshall, 1980

ANNIVERSARY SONG
11 11.11 11

Maker, in Whom We Live

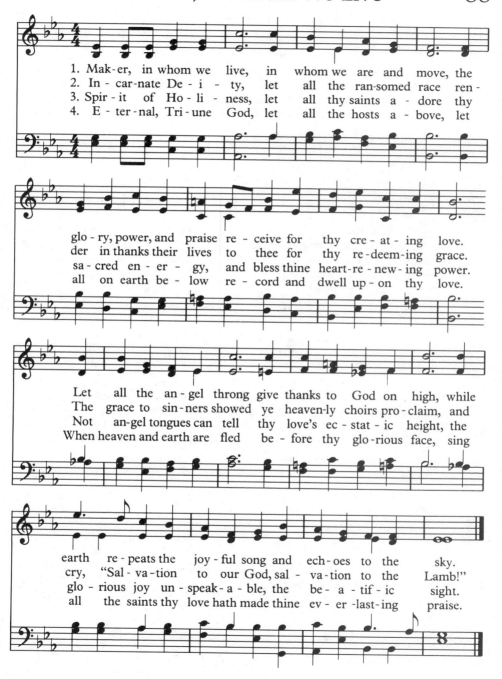

1. Mak-er, in whom we live, in whom we are and move, the
2. In - car-nate De - i - ty, let all the ran-somed race ren -
3. Spir - it of Ho - li - ness, let all thy saints a - dore thy
4. E - ter-nal, Tri - une God, let all the hosts a - bove, let

glo - ry, power, and praise re - ceive for thy cre - at - ing love.
der in thanks their lives to thee for thy re-deem-ing grace.
sa - cred en - er - gy, and bless thine heart-re - new-ing power.
all on earth be - low re - cord and dwell up - on thy love.

Let all the an - gel throng give thanks to God on high, while
The grace to sin-ners showed ye heaven-ly choirs pro - claim, and
Not an-gel tongues can tell thy love's ec - stat - ic height, the
When heaven and earth are fled be - fore thy glo-rious face, sing

earth re - peats the joy - ful song and ech-oes to the sky.
cry, "Sal - va -tion to our God, sal - va-tion to the Lamb!"
glo - rious joy un-speak-a - ble, the be - a - tif - ic sight.
all the saints thy love hath made thine ev - er-last-ing praise.

WORDS: Charles Wesley, 1747
MUSIC: George J. Elvey, 1868

DIADEMATA
SMD

89   Joyful, Joyful, We Adore Thee

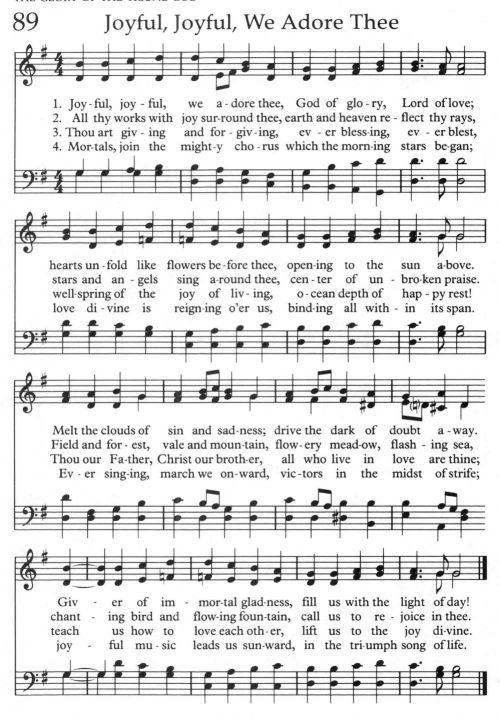

1. Joy-ful, joy-ful, we a-dore thee, God of glo-ry, Lord of love;
2. All thy works with joy sur-round thee, earth and heaven re-flect thy rays,
3. Thou art giv-ing and for-giv-ing, ev-er bless-ing, ev-er blest,
4. Mor-tals, join the might-y cho-rus which the morn-ing stars be-gan;

hearts un-fold like flowers be-fore thee, open-ing to the sun a-bove.
stars and an-gels sing a-round thee, cen-ter of un-bro-ken praise.
well-spring of the joy of liv-ing, o-cean depth of hap-py rest!
love di-vine is reign-ing o'er us, bind-ing all with-in its span.

Melt the clouds of sin and sad-ness; drive the dark of doubt a-way.
Field and for-est, vale and moun-tain, flow-ery mead-ow, flash-ing sea,
Thou our Fa-ther, Christ our broth-er, all who live in love are thine;
Ev-er sing-ing, march we on-ward, vic-tors in the midst of strife;

Giv-er of im-mor-tal glad-ness, fill us with the light of day!
chant-ing bird and flow-ing foun-tain, call us to re-joice in thee.
teach us how to love each oth-er, lift us to the joy di-vine.
joy-ful mu-sic leads us sun-ward, in the tri-umph song of life.

WORDS: Henry Van Dyke, 1907; st. 4 alt. 1989
MUSIC: Ludwig van Beethoven, 1824; arr. by Edward Hodges, 1864

HYMN TO JOY
87.87 D

Ye Watchers and Ye Holy Ones

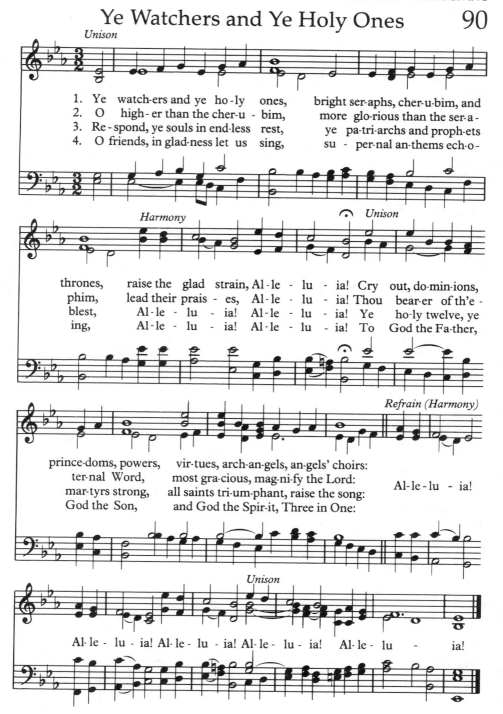

1. Ye watch-ers and ye ho-ly ones, bright ser-aphs, cher-u-bim, and
2. O high-er than the cher-u-bim, more glo-rious than the ser-a-
3. Re-spond, ye souls in end-less rest, ye pa-tri-archs and proph-ets
4. O friends, in glad-ness let us sing, su-per-nal an-thems ech-o-

thrones, raise the glad strain, Al-le-lu-ia! Cry out, do-min-ions,
phim, lead their prais-es, Al-le-lu-ia! Thou bear-er of th'e-
blest, Al-le-lu-ia! Al-le-lu-ia! Ye ho-ly twelve, ye
ing, Al-le-lu-ia! Al-le-lu-ia! To God the Fa-ther,

prince-doms, powers, vir-tues, arch-an-gels, an-gels' choirs:
ter-nal Word, most gra-cious, mag-ni-fy the Lord:
mar-tyrs strong, all saints tri-um-phant, raise the song: Al-le-lu-ia!
God the Son, and God the Spir-it, Three in One:

Al-le-lu-ia! Al-le-lu-ia! Al-le-lu-ia! Al-le-lu-ia!

WORDS: John Athelstan Laurie Riley, 1906
MUSIC: *Geistliche Kirchengesänge*, 1623; harm. by Ralph Vaughan Williams, 1906

LASST UNS ERFREUEN
88.44.88 with Refrain

91 Canticle of Praise to God
(Venite Exultemus)

WORDS: Psalm 95:1-7; 96:9, 13
MUSIC: William Boyce

For the Beauty of the Earth

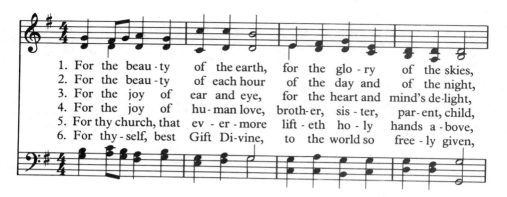

1. For the beau-ty of the earth, for the glo-ry of the skies,
2. For the beau-ty of each hour of the day and of the night,
3. For the joy of ear and eye, for the heart and mind's de-light,
4. For the joy of hu-man love, broth-er, sis-ter, par-ent, child,
5. For thy church, that ev-er-more lift-eth ho-ly hands a-bove,
6. For thy-self, best Gift Di-vine, to the world so free-ly given,

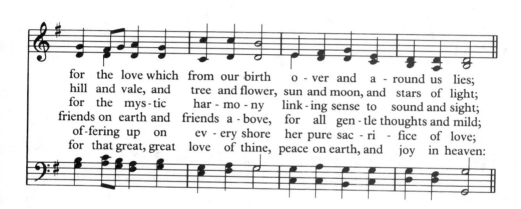

for the love which from our birth o-ver and a-round us lies;
hill and vale, and tree and flower, sun and moon, and stars of light;
for the mys-tic har-mo-ny link-ing sense to sound and sight;
friends on earth and friends a-bove, for all gen-tle thoughts and mild;
of-fering up on ev-ery shore her pure sac-ri-fice of love;
for that great, great love of thine, peace on earth, and joy in heaven:

Refrain

Lord of all, to thee we raise this our hymn of grate-ful praise.
* *Christ, our God, to thee we raise this our sac-ri-fice of praise.*

*For Holy Communion

WORDS: Folliot S. Pierpoint, 1864
MUSIC: Conrad Kocher, 1838; arr. by W. H. Monk, 1861

DIX
77.77.77

93 Let All the World in Every Corner Sing

Antiphon (Unison)

Let all the world in ev-ery cor-ner sing:

Harmony

my God and King! 1. The heavens are not too high,

God's praise may thith-er fly; the earth is not too low, God's prais-es

Antiphon (Unison)

there may grow. Let all the world in ev-ery cor-ner sing:

WORDS: George Herbert, 1633
MUSIC: Erik Routley, 1960

Music © 1976 Hinshaw Music, Inc.

AUGUSTINE
66.66 with Antiphon

my God and King! 2. The church with psalms must shout, no

door can keep them out. But, more than all, the heart must bear the

Antiphon (Unison)

long - est part. Let all the world in

ev - ery cor - ner sing: my God and King!

94 Praise God, from Whom All Blessings Flow

Praise God, from whom all bless-ings flow; praise
God, all crea-tures here be-low: Al - le - lu - ia! Al - le -

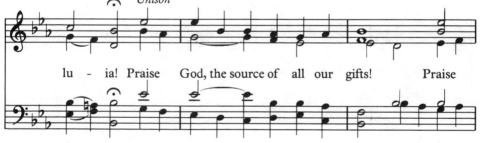

lu - ia! Praise God, the source of all our gifts! Praise

Je-sus Christ, whose power up-lifts! Praise the Spir - it, Ho-ly Spir - it!

WORDS: Thomas Ken, 1674; adapt. by Gilbert H. Vieira, 1978
MUSIC: *Geistliche Kirchengesänge*, 1623; harm. by Ralph Vaughan Williams, 1906

LASST UNS ERFREUEN
88.44.88 with Refrain

Adapt. © 1989 The United Methodist Publishing House,

Unison

Al- le - lu - ia! Al- le - lu - ia! Al - le - lu - ia!

Praise God, from Whom All Blessings Flow 95

Praise God, from whom all bless-ings flow; praise him, all crea-tures

here be - low; praise him a - bove, ye heaven - ly

host; praise Fa - ther, Son, and Ho - ly Ghost. A - men.

WORDS: Thomas Ken, 1674
MUSIC: Attr. to Louis Bourgeois, 1551

OLD 100th
LM

96 Praise the Lord Who Reigns Above

1. Praise the Lord who reigns a-bove and keeps his court be-low;
2. Cel - e - brate th'e - ter - nal God with harp and psal-ter - y,
3. God, in whom they move and live, let ev - ery crea-ture sing,

praise the ho - ly God of love and all his great-ness show;
tim- brels soft and cym - bals loud in this high praise a - gree;
glo - ry to their Mak- er give, and hom - age to their King.

praise him for his no - ble deeds, praise him for his match-less power;
praise with ev - ery tune - ful string; all the reach of heaven-ly art,
Hallow-ed be thy name be-neath, as in heaven on earth a-dored;

him from whom all good pro-ceeds let earth and heaven a - dore.
all the powers of mu - sic bring, the mu - sic of the heart.
praise the Lord in ev - ery breath, let all things praise the Lord.

WORDS: Charles Wesley, 1743 (Ps. 150)
MUSIC: *Foundery Collection*, 1742

AMSTERDAM
76.76.77.76

For the Fruits of This Creation

1. For the fruits of this cre-a-tion, thanks be to God;
2. In the just re-ward of la-bor, God's will is done;
3. For the har-vests of the Spir-it, thanks be to God;

for good gifts to ev-ery na-tion, thanks be to God;
in the help we give our neigh-bor, God's will is done;
for the good we all in-her-it, thanks be to God;

for the plow-ing, sow-ing, reap-ing, si-lent growth while we are sleep-ing,
in our world-wide task of car-ing for the hun-gry and de-spair-ing,
for the won-ders that as-tound us, for the truths that still con-found us,

fu-ture needs in earth's safe-keep-ing, thanks be to God.
in the har-vests we are shar-ing, God's will is done.
most of all, that love has found us, thanks be to God.

WORDS: Fred Pratt Green, 1970
MUSIC: Francis Jackson, 1957

EAST ACKLAM
84.84.888.4

Alt. tune: AR HYD Y NOS

98 To God Be the Glory

1. To God be the glo-ry, great things he hath done! So loved he the
2. O per-fect re-demp-tion, the pur-chase of blood, to ev-ery be-
3. Great things he hath taught us, great things he hath done, and great our re-

world that he gave us his Son, who yield-ed his life an a-
liev-er the prom-ise of God; the vil-est of-fend-er who
joic-ing thru Je-sus the Son; but pur-er, and high-er, and

tone-ment for sin, and o-pened the life-gate that all may go in.
tru-ly be-lieves, that mo-ment from Je-sus a par-don re-ceives.
great-er will be our won-der, our trans-port, when Je-sus we see.

Refrain

Praise the Lord, praise the Lord, let the earth hear his voice! Praise the

Lord, praise the Lord, let the peo-ple re-joice! O come to the Fa-ther thru

WORDS: Fanny J. Crosby, 1875
MUSIC: William H. Doane, 1875

TO GOD BE THE GLORY
11 11.11 11 with Refrain

Je-sus the Son, and give him the glo-ry, great things he hath done!

My Tribute

99

To God be the glo-ry, to God be the glo-ry,

to God be the glo-ry for the things he has done.

With his blood he has saved me; with his power he has raised me;

to God be the glo-ry for the things he has done.

WORDS: Andraé Crouch, 1971
MUSIC: Andraé Crouch, 1971

© 1971 Communiqué Music, Inc.

MY TRIBUTE
Irr.

100 God, Whose Love Is Reigning o'er Us

1. God, whose love is reign-ing o'er us, source of all, the
2. Word of God from na-ture bring - ing spring-time green and
3. Ho - ly God of an-cient glo - ry, choos-ing man and
4. Cove-nant, new a - gain in Je - sus, Star-child born to
5. Lift we then our hu-man voic - es in the songs that

end - ing true; hear the u - ni - ver - sal cho - rus
au - tumn gold; moun-tain streams like chil-dren sing - ing,
wom - an, too; A-br'am's faith and Sa - rah's sto - ry
set us free; sent to heal us, sent to teach us
faith would bring; live we then in hu - man choic - es

raised in joy - ful praise to you: Al - le - lu - ia,
o - cean waves like thun - der bold: Al - le - lu - ia,
formed a peo - ple bound to you. Al - le - lu - ia,
how love's chil - dren we might be. Al - le - lu - ia,
lives that, like our mu - sic, sing: Al - le - lu - ia,

Al - le - lu - ia, wor-ship an-cient, wor-ship new.
Al - le - lu - ia, as cre - a-tion's tale is told.
Al - le - lu - ia, to your cove-nant keep us true.
Al - le - lu - ia, ris - en Christ, our Sav - ior he!
Al - le - lu - ia, joined in love our prais - es ring!

WORDS: William Boyd Grove, 1980
MUSIC: John Goss, 1869
Words © 1980 William Boyd Grove

LAUDA ANIMA
87.87.87

From All That Dwell Below the Skies 101

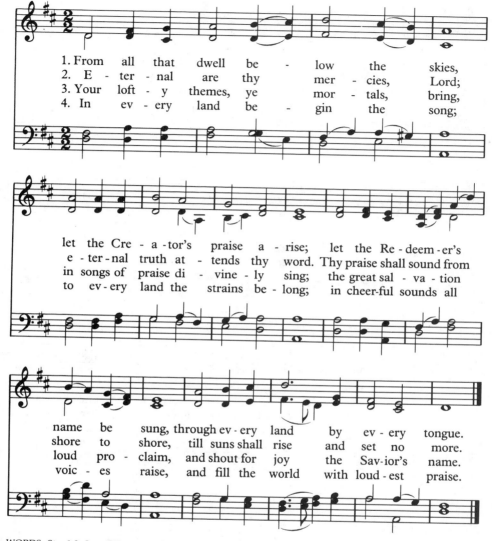

1. From all that dwell be - low the skies,
2. E - ter - nal are thy mer - cies, Lord;
3. Your loft - y themes, ye mor - tals, bring,
4. In ev - ery land be - gin the song;

let the Cre - a - tor's praise a - rise; let the Re - deem - er's
e - ter - nal truth at - tends thy word. Thy praise shall sound from
in songs of praise di - vine - ly sing; the great sal - va - tion
to ev - ery land the strains be - long; in cheer - ful sounds all

name be sung, through ev - ery land by ev - ery tongue.
shore to shore, till suns shall rise and set no more.
loud pro - claim, and shout for joy the Sav - ior's name.
voic - es raise, and fill the world with loud - est praise.

WORDS: Sts. 1-2, Isaac Watts; sts. 3-4, anon., ca. 1781 (Ps. 117)
MUSIC: John Hatton, 1793

DUKE STREET
LM

PRAISE AND THANKSGIVING, *see further:*

102 Now Thank We All Our God

1. Now thank we all our God, with heart and hands and voic - es,
2. O may this boun-teous God through all our life be near us,
3. All praise and thanks to God the Fa - ther now be giv - en;

who won-drous things has done, in whom this world re - joic - es;
with ev - er joy - ful hearts and bless-ed peace to cheer us;
the Son, and him who reigns with them in high - est heav - en;

who from our moth-ers' arms has blessed us on our way
and keep us still in grace, and guide us when per - plexed;
the one e - ter - nal God, whom earth and heaven a - dore;

with count-less gifts of love, and still is ours to - day.
and free us from all ills, in this world and the next.
for thus it was, is now, and shall be ev - er - more.

WORDS: Martin Rinkart, 1636; trans. by Catherine Winkworth, 1858
(Sir. 50:22-24)
MUSIC: Johann Crüger, 1647; harm. by Felix Mendelssohn, 1840

NUN DANKET
67.67.66.66

Immortal, Invisible, God Only Wise 103

1. Im - mor - tal, in - vis - i - ble, God on - ly wise,
2. Un - rest - ing, un - hast - ing, and si - lent as light,
3. To all, life thou giv - est, to both great and small;
4. Thou reign - est in glo - ry; thou dwell - est in light;

in light in - ac - ces - si - ble hid from our eyes,
nor want - ing, nor wast - ing, thou rul - est in might;
in all life thou liv - est, the true life of all;
thine an - gels a - dore thee, all veil - ing their sight;

most bless - ed, most glo - rious, the An - cient of Days,
thy jus - tice like moun - tains high soar - ing a - bove
we blos - som and flour - ish as leaves on the tree,
all laud we would ren - der: O help us to see

al - might - y, vic - to - rious, thy great name we praise.
thy clouds which are foun - tains of good - ness and love.
and with - er and per - ish, but naught chang - eth thee.
'tis on - ly the splen - dor of light hid - eth thee.

WORDS: Walter Chalmers Smith, 1867 (1 Tim. 1:17)
MUSIC: Welsh melody from *Canaidau y Cyssegr*, 1839; adapt. by John Roberts

ST. DENIO
11 11.11 11

104 Praising God of Many Names

O burning Mountain, O chosen Sun,
O perfect Moon, O fathomless Well,
O unattainable Height, O Clearness beyond measure,
O Wisdom without end, O Mercy without limit,
O Strength beyond resistance, O Crown beyond all majesty:
The humblest thing you created sings your praise. **Amen.**

Mechthild of Magdeburg, Germany, 13th cent.

105 God of Many Names

Unison

1. God of man - y names, gath - ered in - to One,
   God of hov - ering wings, womb and birth of time,

2. God of Jew - ish faith, ex - o - dus and law,
   God of Je - sus Christ, rab - bi of the poor,

3. God of wound - ed hands, web and loom of love,
   God of man - y names, gath - ered in - to One,

in your glo - ry come and meet us, mov - ing, end-less - ly be-com-ing;
joy - ful - ly we sing your prais-es, breath of life in ev - ery peo-ple,

in your glo - ry come and meet us, joy of Mir - i - am and Mo-ses;
joy - ful - ly we sing your prais-es, cru - ci - fied, a - live for - ev - er,

in your glo - ry come and meet us, car - pen - ter of new cre - a - tion;
joy - ful - ly we sing your prais-es, mov - ing, end-less - ly be-com-ing,

WORDS: Brian Wren, 1985
MUSIC: William P. Rowan, 1985
© 1986 Hope Publishing Co.

MANY NAMES
55.88 D

Hush, hush, hal-le-lu-jah, hal-le-lu-jah! Shout, shout, hal-le-lu-jah, hal-le-lu- jah!

Sing, sing, hal-le - lu-jah, hal-le-lu - jah! Sing God is love, God is love!

final only

God Is Able 106

Leader:

Is someone here moving toward the twilight of life and fearful of that which we call death?

People:

Why be afraid? God is able.

Leader:

Is someone here on the brink of despair because of the death of a loved one, the breaking of a marriage, or the waywardness of a child?

People:

Why despair? God is able to give us the power to endure that which cannot be changed.

Leader:

Is someone here anxious because of bad health?

People:

Why be anxious? Come what may, God is able.

All:

Surely God is able.

Martin Luther King, Jr., USA 20th cent.

107 La Palabra Del Señor Es Recta
(Righteous and Just Is the Word of Our Lord)

Estribillo, Unísono (Refrain, Unison)

La pa-la-bra del Se-ñor es rec-ta y sus o-bras son ma-
Righ-teous and just is the word of our Lord; faith-ful and mar-vel-ous

ra-vi-llo-sas. La jus-ti-cia y el de-re-cho
are the Lord's works. Jus-tice and right are what God loves,

tie-nen tro-nos a su dies-tra y de su mi-se-ri-cor-dia
they sit on thrones at God's right hand. And from the Lord's lov-ing-kind-ness

lle-na es-tá to-da la tie-rra. Y de su mi-se-ri-cor-dia
all the earth is filled with mer-cy, and from the Lord's lov-ing-kind-ness

a la Estrofa (to Verses) *Al Final (Final ending)*

lle-na es-tá to-da la tie-rra. tie-rra.
all the earth is filled with mer-cy! mer-cy!

WORDS: Juan Luis García; trans. by George Lockwood, 1987 (Ps. 33:4-11)
MUSIC: Juan Luis García

NELSON
LMD with Refrain

By permission of Juan Luis García; trans. © 1989 The United Methodist Publishing House

108 God Hath Spoken by the Prophets

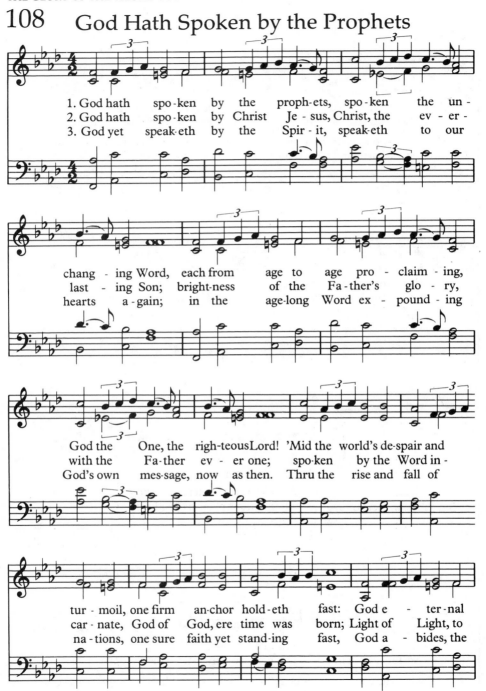

1. God hath spo-ken by the proph-ets, spo-ken the un-
2. God hath spo-ken by Christ Je - sus, Christ, the ev - er-
3. God yet speak-eth by the Spir - it, speak-eth to our

chang - ing Word, each from age to age pro - claim - ing,
last - ing Son; bright-ness of the Fa - ther's glo - ry,
hearts a - gain; in the age-long Word ex - pound - ing

God the One, the righ-teous Lord! 'Mid the world's de-spair and
with the Fa - ther ev - er one; spo-ken by the Word in -
God's own mes-sage, now as then. Thru the rise and fall of

tur - moil, one firm an-chor hold-eth fast: God e - ter-nal
car - nate, God of God, ere time was born; Light of Light, to
na - tions, one sure faith yet stand-ing fast, God a - bides, the

WORDS: George W. Briggs, 1952, alt.
MUSIC: Thomas J. Williams, 1890

EBENEZER
87.87 D

reigns for - ev - er, God the first, and God the last.
earth de - scend - ing, Christ, as God in hu - man form.
Word un - chang - ing, God the first, and God the last.

Creating God, Your Fingers Trace 109

Unison

1. Cre - at - ing God, your fin - gers trace the
2. Sus - tain - ing God, your hands up - hold earth's
3. Re - deem - ing God, your arms em - brace all
4. In - dwell - ing God, your gos - pel claims one

bold de - signs of far - thest space; let sun and moon and
mys - teries known or yet un - told; let wa - ter's fra - gile
now de - spised for creed or race; let peace, de - scend - ing
fam - ily with a bil - lion names; let ev - ery life be

stars and light and what lies hid - den praise your might.
blend with air, en - a - bling life, pro - claim your care.
like a dove, make known on earth your heal - ing love.
touched by grace un - til we praise you face to face.

WORDS: Jeffery Rowthorn, 1974
MUSIC: Attr. to Elkanah Kelsay Dare, 1799

KEDRON
LM

Words © 1979 The Hymn Society of America

110   A Mighty Fortress Is Our God

1. A might-y for-tress is our God, a bul-wark nev-er fail - ing;
2. Did we in our own strength con-fide, our striv-ing would be los - ing,
3. And though this world, with dev-ils filled, should threat-en to un - do us,
4. That word a -bove all earth-ly powers, no thanks to them, a -bid - eth;

our help-er he a - mid the flood of mor-tal ills pre - vail - ing.
were not the right man on our side, the man of God's own choos - ing.
we will not fear, for God hath willed his truth to tri-umph through us.
the Spir-it and the gifts are ours, thru him who with us sid - eth.

For still our an - cient foe doth seek to work us woe; his craft and
Dost ask who that may be? Christ Je-sus, it is he; Lord Sa - ba -
The Prince of Dark-ness grim, we trem-ble not for him; his rage we
Let goods and kin - dred go, this mor-tal life al - so; the bod -y

power are great, and armed with cru-el hate, on earth is not his e - qual.
oth, his name, from age to age the same, and he must win the bat - tle.
can en - dure, for lo, his doom is sure; one lit-tle word shall fell him.
they may kill; God's truth a - bid-eth still; his king-dom is for - ev - er.

WORDS: Martin Luther, ca. 1529; trans. by Frederick H. Hedge, 1853 (Ps. 46)   EIN' FESTE BURG
MUSIC: Martin Luther, ca. 1529; harm. from *The New Hymnal for American Youth*, 1930   87.87.66.667

How Can We Name a Love

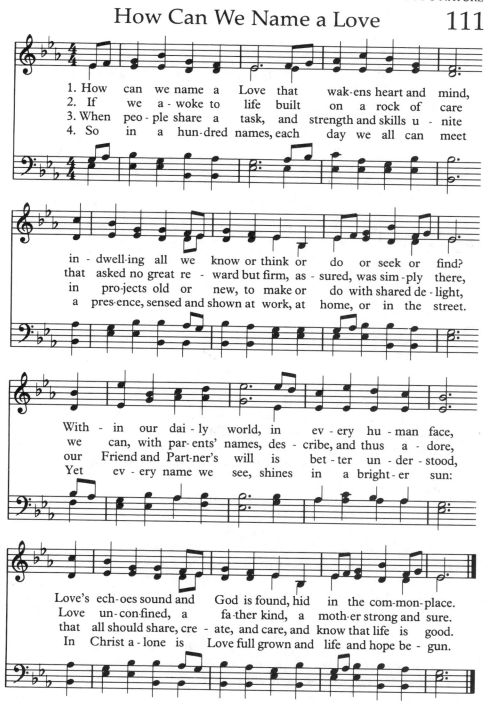

1. How can we name a Love that wak-ens heart and mind,
2. If we a-woke to life built on a rock of care
3. When peo-ple share a task, and strength and skills u - nite
4. So in a hun-dred names, each day we all can meet

in - dwell-ing all we know or think or do or seek or find?
that asked no great re - ward but firm, as-sured, was sim-ply there,
in pro-jects old or new, to make or do with shared de - light,
a pres-ence, sensed and shown at work, at home, or in the street.

With - in our dai - ly world, in ev-ery hu - man face,
we can, with par-ents' names, des - cribe, and thus a - dore,
our Friend and Part-ner's will is bet-ter un - der - stood,
Yet ev - ery name we see, shines in a bright-er sun:

Love's ech-oes sound and God is found, hid in the com-mon-place.
Love un-con-fined, a fa-ther kind, a moth-er strong and sure.
that all should share, cre - ate, and care, and know that life is good.
In Christ a - lone is Love full grown and life and hope be - gun.

WORDS: Brian Wren, 1973
MUSIC: Trad. English melody; adapt. by Franklin L. Sheppard, 1915
Words © 1975 Hope Publishing Co.

TERRA BEATA
SMD

112   Canticle of Wisdom

R

May God grant that I speak with judgment
    and have thoughts worthy of what I have received,
    for God is the God even of wisdom
    and the corrector of the wise.
Wisdom is more mobile than any motion;
    because of her purity, wisdom pervades and penetrates all things.
For she is a breath of the power of God,
    and a pure emanation of the glory of the Almighty;
    therefore nothing defiled gains entrance into wisdom.   **R**

For she is a reflection of eternal light,
    a spotless mirror of the working of God,
    an image of God's goodness.
Though wisdom is but one, she can do all things;
    while remaining in herself, wisdom renews all things;
in every generation wisdom passes into holy souls
    and makes them friends of God and prophets.
Truly God loves nothing so much as those who live with wisdom.   **R**

For she is more beautiful than the sun,
    and excels every constellation of the stars.
    Compared with the light, she is found to be superior.
For light is succeeded by the night,
    but against wisdom evil does not prevail.   **R**

WORDS: Wisdom of Solomon 7:15, 24-30, adapt.; Response 1, Harrell Beck; Response 2, Henry Sloane Coffin
MUSIC: Response 1, Carlton R. Young; Response 2, 15th cent. French

Adapt. and Response 1 © 1989 The United Methodist Publishing House

Source and Sovereign, Rock and Cloud   113

Unison

1. Source and Sov-ereign, Rock and Cloud, For-tress,
2. Word and Wis-dom, Root and Vine, Shep-herd,
3. Storm and Still-ness, Breath and Dove, Thun-der,

Foun-tain, Shel-ter, Light, Judge, De-fend-er,
Sav-ior, Ser-vant, Lamb, Well and Wa-ter,
Tem-pest, Whirl-wind, Fire, Com-fort, Coun-selor,

Mer-cy, Might, Life whose life all life en-dowed:
Bread and Wine, Way who leads us to I AM:
Pres-ence, Love, En-er-gies that nev-er tire:

Refrain

May the church at prayer re-call that no sin-gle ho-ly name

but the truth be-hind them all is the God whom we pro-claim.

WORDS: Thomas H. Troeger, 1987
MUSIC: Carol Doran, 1987

© 1987 Oxford University Press

GOD'S NAMES
77.77 with Refrain

114 Many Gifts, One Spirit

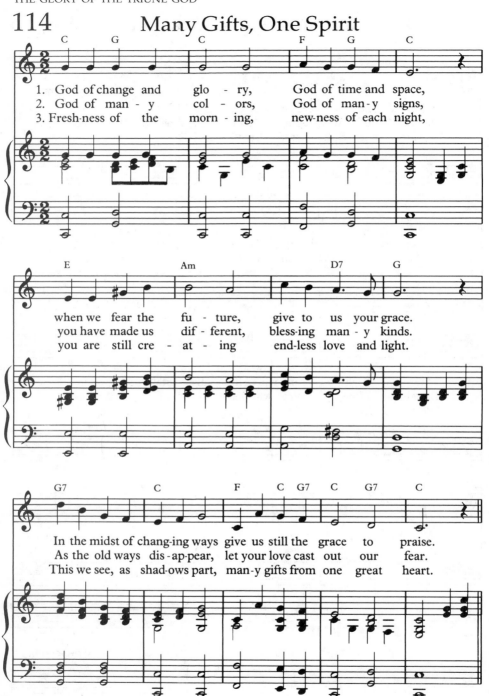

1. God of change and glo - ry, God of time and space,
2. God of man - y col - ors, God of man - y signs,
3. Fresh-ness of the morn - ing, new-ness of each night,

when we fear the fu - ture, give to us your grace.
you have made us dif - ferent, bless-ing man - y kinds.
you are still cre - at - ing end-less love and light.

In the midst of chang-ing ways give us still the grace to praise.
As the old ways dis - ap-pear, let your love cast out our fear.
This we see, as shad-ows part, man-y gifts from one great heart.

WORDS: Al Carmines, 1973
MUSIC: Al Carmines, 1973

KATHERINE
65.65.77

© 1974 Al Carmines

Refrain

Man-y gifts, one Spir-it, one love known in man-y ways.

In our dif-fer-ence is bless-ing, from di-ver-si - ty we praise one Giv-er,

one Lord, one Spir-it, one Word known in man-y ways,

hal-low-ing our days. For the Giv-er, for the gifts, praise, praise, praise!

115 How Like a Gentle Spirit

Unison

1. How like a gen - tle spir - it deep with - in
2. Let God be God wher - ev - er life may be;
3. God like a moth - er ea - gle hov - ers near
4. When in our vain pre - ten - sions we con - spire
5. Through all our fret - ful claims of sex and race

God reins our fer - vent pas - sions day by day,
let ev - ery tongue bear wit - ness to the call;
on might - y wings of pow - er man - i - fest;
to shape God's im - age as we see our own,
the un - i - ver - sal love of God shines through,

and gives us strength to chal - lenge and to win
all hu - man - kind is one by God's de - cree;
God like a gen - tle shep - herd stills our fear,
hark to the voice a - bove our base de - sire;
for God is love tran - scend - ing style and place

de - spite the per - ils of our cho - sen way.
let God be God, let God be God for all.
and com - forts us a - gainst a peace - ful breast.
God is the sculp - tor, we the bro - ken stone.
and all the i - dle op - tions we pur - sue.

WORDS: C. Eric Lincoln, 1987
MUSIC: Alfred Morton Smith, 1941

SURSUM CORDA
10 10.10 10

The God of Abraham Praise

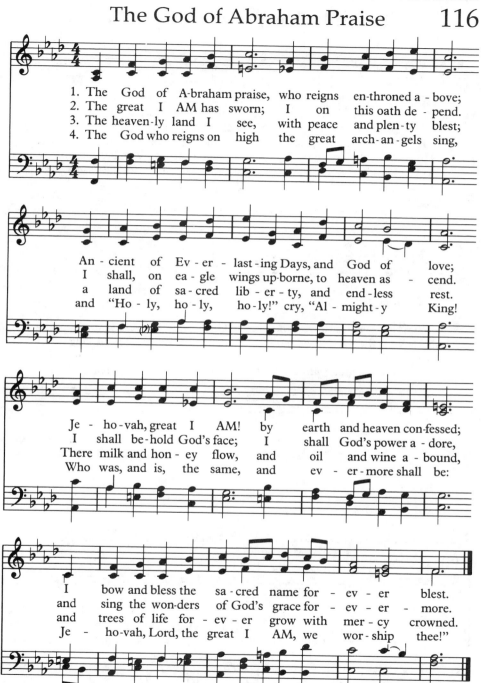

1. The God of A-braham praise, who reigns en-throned a - bove;
2. The great I AM has sworn; I on this oath de - pend.
3. The heaven-ly land I see, with peace and plen-ty blest;
4. The God who reigns on high the great arch-an-gels sing,

An - cient of Ev - er - last-ing Days, and God of love;
I shall, on ea - gle wings up-borne, to heaven as - cend.
a land of sa - cred lib - er - ty, and end - less rest.
and "Ho - ly, ho - ly, ho - ly!" cry, "Al - might - y King!

Je - ho-vah, great I AM! by earth and heaven con-fessed;
I shall be-hold God's face; I shall God's power a - dore,
There milk and hon - ey flow, and oil and wine a - bound,
Who was, and is, the same, and ev - er - more shall be:

I bow and bless the sa - cred name for - ev - er blest.
and sing the won-ders of God's grace for - ev - er - more.
and trees of life for - ev - er grow with mer - cy crowned.
Je - ho-vah, Lord, the great I AM, we wor - ship thee!"

WORDS: From *The Yigdal* of Daniel ben Judah, ca. 1400;
   para. by Thomas Olivers, 1760; alt.
MUSIC: Hebrew melody, *Sacred Harmony*, 1780; harm. from *Hymns Ancient and Modern*, 1875, alt.

LEONI
66.84 D

117   O God, Our Help in Ages Past

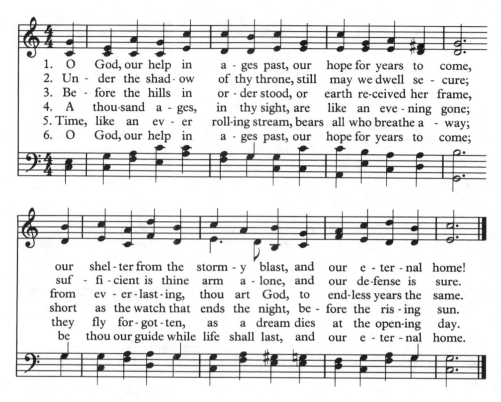

1. O God, our help in a - ges past, our hope for years to come,
2. Un - der the shad - ow of thy throne, still may we dwell se - cure;
3. Be - fore the hills in or - der stood, or earth re-ceived her frame,
4. A thou-sand a - ges, in thy sight, are like an eve - ning gone;
5. Time, like an ev - er roll-ing stream, bears all who breathe a - way;
6. O God, our help in a - ges past, our hope for years to come;

our shel - ter from the storm - y blast, and our e - ter - nal home!
suf - fi - cient is thine arm a - lone, and our de-fense is sure.
from ev - er-last-ing, thou art God, to end-less years the same.
short as the watch that ends the night, be - fore the ris - ing sun.
they fly for-got-ten, as a dream dies at the open-ing day.
be thou our guide while life shall last, and our e - ter - nal home.

WORDS: Isaac Watts, 1719 (Ps. 90)
MUSIC: Attr. to William Croft, 1708; harm. by W. H. Monk, 1861

ST. ANNE
CM

118   The Care the Eagle Gives Her Young

1. The care the ea - gle gives her young, safe in her loft - y nest,
2. As when the time to ven-ture comes, she stirs them out to flight,
3. And if we flut - ter help-less - ly, as fledg-ling ea-gles fall,

WORDS: R. Deane Postlethwaite (Dt. 32:11)
MUSIC: Jesse Seymour Irvine, 1872; harm. by TCL. Pritchard, 1929

CRIMOND
CM

Harm. by permission of Oxford University Press

is like the ten - der love of God for us made man-i - fest.
so we are pressed to bold - ly try, to strive for dar-ing height.
be - neath us lift God's might - y wings to bear us, one and all.

O God in Heaven 119

Unison

1. O God in heav- en, grant to thy chil-dren mer - cy and
2. Je - sus, Re - deem - er, may we re - mem-ber thy gra-cious
3. Spir-it de - scend-ing, whose is the bless-ing, strength for the

bless-ing, songs nev-er ceas-ing, love to u - nite us, grace to re -
pas -sion, thy res - ur - rec-tion. Wor-ship we bring thee, praise we shall
wea -ry, help for the need-y; sealed in our kin-ship, thine be our

deem us, O God in heav-en, dear Lord, our God.
sing thee, Je -sus, Re - deem-er, Je -sus, our Lord.
wor-ship, Spir-it de - scend-ing, Spir-it a - dored.

WORDS: Elena G. Maquiso, 1961; trans. by D. T. Niles, 1964   HALAD
MUSIC: Elena G. Maquiso, 1961; harm. by Charles H. Webb, 1987   5555.5554

120 Your Love, O God

Unison

1. Your love, O God, is broad like beach and mead-ow,
2. We long for free-dom where our tru-est be-ing
3. But there are walls that keep us all di-vid-ed;
4. O judge us, Lord, and in your judg-ment free us,

wide as the wind, and our e-ter-nal home.
is giv-en hope and cour-age to un-fold.
we fence each oth-er in with hate and war.
and set our feet in free-dom's o-pen space;

You leave us free to seek you or re-ject you,
We seek in free-dom space and scope for dream-ing,
Fear is the bricks and mor-tar of our pris-on,
take us as far as your com-pas-sion wan-ders

you give us room to an-swer "yes" or "no."
and look for ground where trees and plants can grow.
our pride of self, the pris-on coat we wear.
a-mong the chil-dren of the hu-man race.

WORDS: Anders Frostenson, 1968; trans. by Fred Kaan, 1972
MUSIC: Lars Åke Lundberg, 1968; harm. by Carlton R. Young, 1988

GUDS KÄRLEK
11 10.11 10 with Refrain

Alt. tune: FINLANDIA

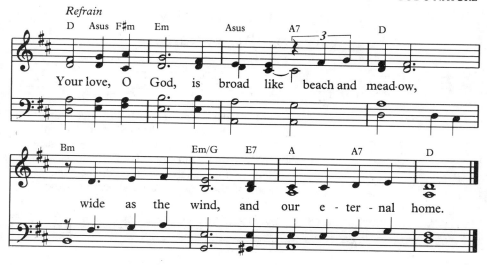

Refrain

Your love, O God, is broad like beach and mead-ow,
wide as the wind, and our e-ter-nal home.

There's a Wideness in God's Mercy 121

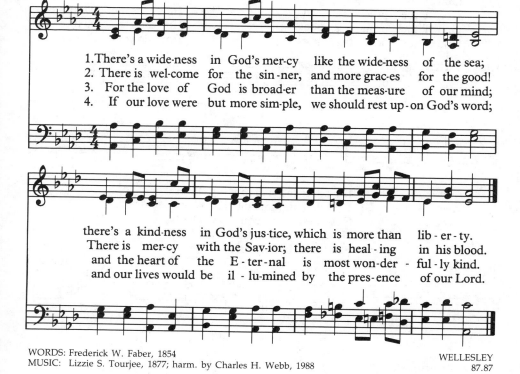

1. There's a wide-ness in God's mer-cy like the wide-ness of the sea;
2. There is wel-come for the sin-ner, and more grac-es for the good!
3. For the love of God is broad-er than the meas-ure of our mind;
4. If our love were but more sim-ple, we should rest up-on God's word;

there's a kind-ness in God's jus-tice, which is more than lib-er-ty.
There is mer-cy with the Sav-ior; there is heal-ing in his blood.
and the heart of the E-ter-nal is most won-der-ful-ly kind.
and our lives would be il-lu-mined by the pres-ence of our Lord.

WORDS: Frederick W. Faber, 1854
MUSIC: Lizzie S. Tourjee, 1877; harm. by Charles H. Webb, 1988

WELLESLEY
87.87

Harm. © 1989 The United Methodist Publishing House

Alt. tune: IN BABILONE

122
God of the Sparrow
God of the Whale

Unison

1. God of the spar - row God of the whale
2. God of the earth-quake God of the storm
3. God of the rain - bow God of the cross
4. God of the hun - gry God of the sick
5. God of the neigh-bor God of the foe
6. God of the a - ges God near at hand

God of the swirl - ing stars   How does the crea-ture say
God of the trum - pet blast   How does the crea-ture cry
God of the emp - ty grave   How does the crea-ture say
God of the prod - i – gal   How does the crea-ture say
God of the prun - ing hook   How does the crea-ture say
God of the lov - ing heart   How do your chil-dren say

1-5   **6**

Awe   How does the crea-ture say Praise
Woe   How does the crea-ture cry Save
Grace   How does the crea-ture say Thanks
Care   How does the crea-ture say Life
Love   How does the crea-ture say Peace
Joy   How do your chil-dren say   Home

*last time

WORDS: Jaroslav J. Vajda, 1983
MUSIC: Carl F. Schalk, 1983

ROEDER
546.77

El Shaddai

Translation of Hebrew:
El Shaddai: God Almighty
El Elyon: The Most High God
na Adonai: O Lord
Erkahmka: We will love you

WORDS: Michael Card and John Thompson, 1981
MUSIC: Michael Card and John Thompson, 1981

EL SHADDAI
Irr.

124   Seek the Lord

Unison

1. Seek the Lord who now is pres-ent, pray to One who
2. "Judge me not by hu-man stan-dards! As the vault of
3. "So my word re-turns not fruit-less; does not from its

is at hand. Let the wick-ed cease from sin-ning,
heav-en soars high a-bove the earth, so high-er
la-bors cease till it has a-chieved my pur-pose

e-vil-do-ers change their mind. On the sin-ful
are my thoughts and ways than yours." See how rain and
in a world of joy and peace." God is love! How

God has pit-y; those re-turn-ing God for-gives.
snow from heav-en make earth blos-som and bear fruit,
close the proph-et to that vi-tal gos-pel word!

WORDS: Fred Pratt Green, 1986 (Is. 55:6-11)
MUSIC: George Henry Day, 1940

GENEVA
87.87 D

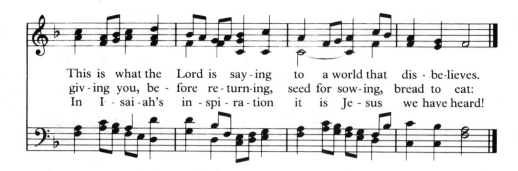

This is what the Lord is say-ing to a world that dis-be-lieves.
giv-ing you, be-fore re-turn-ing, seed for sow-ing, bread to eat:
In I - sai-ah's in-spi-ra-tion it is Je-sus we have heard!

Canticle of Covenant Faithfulness 125
(Quaerite Dominum)

RESPONSE *(General)*

Your face, Lord, do I seek. Hide not your face from me.

R

Seek the Lord who now is present,
　　call upon the Lord, who is near,
let the wicked forsake their way,
　　and the unrighteous their thoughts;
let them return, that the Lord may have mercy on them;
　　that our God may abundantly pardon.
For my thoughts are not your thoughts,
　　neither are your ways my ways, says the Lord.
　　For as the heavens are higher than the earth,
　　so are my ways higher than your ways
　　and my thoughts than your thoughts.

For as the rain and the snow come down from heaven,
　　and return not but water the earth,
　　making it bring forth and sprout,
　　giving seed to the sower and bread to the eater,
so shall my word be that goes forth from my mouth;
　　it shall not return to me empty,
　　but it shall accomplish that which I intend,
　　and prosper in the thing for which I sent it.

See No. 124 for a metrical version of this ancient text.

WORDS: Isaiah 55:6-11; adapt.; Response, Isaiah 55:6, adapt.
MUSIC: Thomas Hastings

Adapt. and words Response © 1989 The United Methodist Publishing House

GOD'S NATURE, *see further:*
386, 387 Come, O Thou Traveler Unknown

126 Sing Praise to God Who Reigns Above

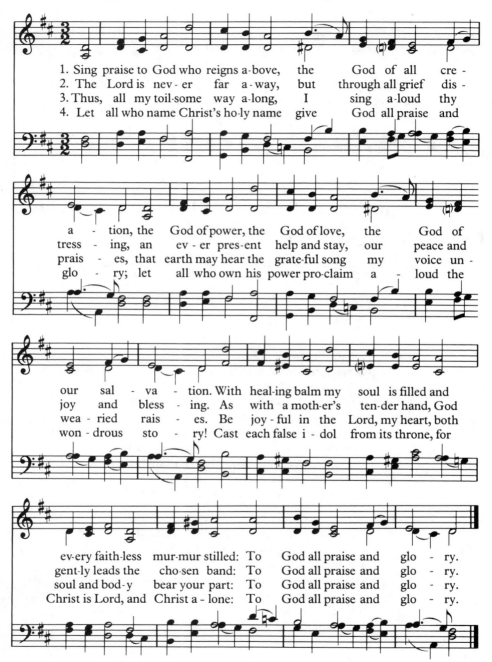

1. Sing praise to God who reigns a-bove, the God of all cre-
2. The Lord is nev-er far a-way, but through all grief dis-
3. Thus, all my toil-some way a-long, I sing a-loud thy
4. Let all who name Christ's ho-ly name give God all praise and

a - tion, the God of power, the God of love, the God of
tress - ing, an ev - er pres-ent help and stay, our peace and
prais - es, that earth may hear the grate-ful song my voice un -
glo - ry; let all who own his power pro-claim a - loud the

our sal - va - tion. With heal-ing balm my soul is filled and
joy and bless - ing. As with a moth-er's ten-der hand, God
wea - ried rais - es. Be joy - ful in the Lord, my heart, both
won - drous sto - ry! Cast each false i - dol from its throne, for

ev-ery faith-less mur-mur stilled: To God all praise and glo - ry.
gent-ly leads the cho-sen band: To God all praise and glo - ry.
soul and bod-y bear your part: To God all praise and glo - ry.
Christ is Lord, and Christ a - lone: To God all praise and glo - ry.

WORDS: Johann J. Schütz, 1675; trans. by Frances E. Cox, 1864 (Dt. 32:3)
MUSIC: Bohemian Brethren's *Kirchengesänge*, 1566; harm. by Maurice F. Bell, 1906

MIT FREUDEN ZART
87.87.887

Guide Me, O Thou Great Jehovah 127

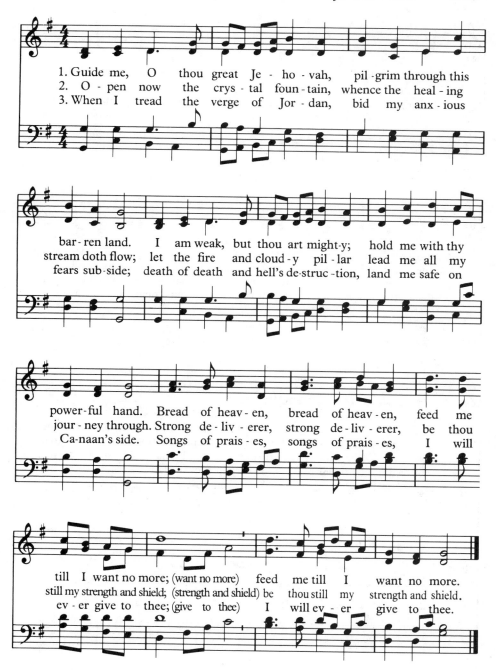

1. Guide me, O thou great Je - ho - vah, pil - grim through this
bar - ren land. I am weak, but thou art might - y; hold me with thy
power - ful hand. Bread of heav - en, bread of heav - en, feed me
till I want no more; (want no more) feed me till I want no more.

2. O - pen now the crys - tal foun - tain, whence the heal - ing
stream doth flow; let the fire and cloud - y pil - lar lead me all my
jour - ney through. Strong de - liv - erer, strong de - liv - erer, be thou
still my strength and shield; (strength and shield) be thou still my strength and shield.

3. When I tread the verge of Jor - dan, bid my anx - ious
fears sub - side; death of death and hell's de - struc - tion, land me safe on
Ca - naan's side. Songs of prais - es, songs of prais - es, I will
ev - er give to thee; (give to thee) I will ev - er give to thee.

WORDS: William Williams, 1745; trans. from the Welsh by Peter Williams and
the author, 1771
MUSIC: John Hughes, 1907

CWM RHONDDA
87.87.87

128 He Leadeth Me: O Blessed Thought

1. He lead - eth me: O bless - ed thought! O
2. Some - times mid scenes of deep - est gloom, some -
3. Lord, I would place my hand in thine, nor
4. And when my task on earth is done, when

words with heaven-ly com - fort fraught! What - e'er I do, wher -
times where E - den's bow - ers bloom, by wa - ters still, o'er
ev - er mur - mur nor re - pine; con - tent, what-ev - er
by thy grace the vic - tory's won, e'en death's cold wave I

e'er I be, still 'tis God's hand that lead - eth me.
trou - bled sea, still 'tis his hand that lead - eth me.
lot I see, since 'tis my God that lead - eth me.
will not flee, since God through Jor - dan lead - eth me.

Refrain

He lead - eth me, he lead - eth me, by

WORDS: Joseph H. Gilmore, 1862 (Ps. 23)
MUSIC: William B. Bradbury, 1864

HE LEADETH ME
LM with Refrain

his own hand he lead - eth me; his faith - ful fol - lower

I would be, for by his hand he lead - eth me.

Give to the Winds Thy Fears 129

1. Give to the winds thy fears; hope and be un - dis - mayed.
2. Through waves and clouds and storms, God gent - ly clears thy way;
3. Leave to God's sov-ereign sway to choose and to com - mand;
4. Let us in life, in death, thy stead-fast truth de - clare,

God hears thy sighs and counts thy tears, God shall lift up thy head.
wait thou God's time; so shall this night soon end in joy - ous day.
so shalt thou, won-dering, own that way, how wise, how strong this hand.
and pub-lish with our lat - est breath thy love and guard-ian care.

WORDS: Paul Gerhardt, 1653; trans. by John Wesley, 1739 (Ps. 37:5)
MUSIC: William H. Walter, 1894

FESTAL SONG
SM

130 God Will Take Care of You

1. Be not dis-mayed what-e'er be-tide, God will take care of you;
2. Through days of toil when heart doth fail, God will take care of you;
3. All you may need he will pro-vide, God will take care of you;
4. No mat-ter what may be the test, God will take care of you;

be-neath his wings of love a-bide, God will take care of you.
when dan-gers fierce your path as-sail, God will take care of you.
noth-ing you ask will be de-nied, God will take care of you.
lean, wea-ry one, up-on his breast, God will take care of you.

Refrain

God will take care of you, through ev-ery day, o'er all the way;

he will take care of you, God will take care of you.

WORDS: Civilla D. Martin, 1904
MUSIC: W. Stillman Martin, 1905

MARTIN
CM with Refrain

We Gather Together

1. We gath-er to-geth-er to ask the Lord's bless-ing;
2. Be-side us to guide us, our God with us join-ing,
3. We all do ex-tol thee, thou lead-er tri-um-phant,

he chas-tens and has-tens his will to make known.
or-dain-ing, main-tain-ing his king-dom di-vine;
and pray that thou still our de-fend-er wilt be.

The wick-ed op-press-ing now cease from dis-tress-ing.
so from the be-gin-ning the fight we were win-ning;
Let thy con-gre-ga-tion es-cape trib-u-la-tion;

Sing prais-es to his name; he for-gets not his own.
thou, Lord, wast at our side, all glo-ry be thine!
thy name be ev-er praised! O Lord, make us free!

WORDS: *Nederlandtsch Gedenckclanck*, 1626; trans. by Theodore Baker, 1894
MUSIC: 16th cent. Dutch melody; arr. by Edward Kremser, 1877

KREMSER
Irr.

132 All My Hope Is Firmly Grounded

1. All my hope is firm-ly ground-ed in the great and
2. Tell me, who can trust our na-ture, hu-man, weak, and
3. But in ev-ery time and sea-son, out of love's a-
4. Thank, O thank, our great Cre-a-tor, thru God's on-ly

liv-ing Lord; who, when-ev-er I most need him, nev-er
in-se-cure? Which of all the air-y cas-tles can the
bun-dant store, God sus-tains the whole cre-a-tion, fount of
Son this day; God a-lone, the heaven-ly pot-ter, made us

fails to keep his word. God I must whol-ly
hur-ri-cane en-dure? Built on sand, naught can
life for-ev-er-more. We who share earth and
out of earth and clay. Quick to heed, strong in

trust, God the ev-er good and just.
stand by our earth-ly wis-dom planned.
air count on God's un-fail-ing care.
deed, God shall all the peo-ple feed.

WORDS: Joachim Neander, 1680; trans. by Fred Pratt Green, 1986
MUSIC: Herbert Howells, 1930, 1977

MICHAEL
87.87.337

Trans. © 1989 Hope Publishing Co.; music © 1968 Novello and Co., Ltd.

Leaning on the Everlasting Arms 133

1. What a fel-low-ship, what a joy di-vine, lean-ing on the ev-er-
2. O how sweet to walk in this pil-grim way, lean-ing on the ev-er-
3. What have I to dread, what have I to fear, lean-ing on the ev-er-

last - ing arms; what a bless-ed-ness, what a peace is mine,
last - ing arms; O how bright the path grows from day to day,
last - ing arms? I have bless-ed peace with my Lord so near,

Refrain

lean - ing on the ev-er-last-ing arms. Lean - ing,
Lean-ing on Je - sus,

lean - ing, safe and se-cure from all a-larms; lean -
lean-ing on Je - sus, lean-ing on

ing, lean - ing,
Je - sus, lean-ing on Je - sus, lean-ing on the ev-er-last-ing arms.

WORDS: Elisha A. Hoffman, 1887 (Dt. 33:27)   SHOWALTER
MUSIC: Anthony J. Showalter, 1887   10 9.10 9 with Refrain

134 O Mary, Don't You Weep

Refrain

O Ma - ry, don't you weep, don't you mourn, O Ma - ry, don't you weep, don't you mourn; Pha-raoh's ar - my got drown - ded, O Ma - ry, don't you weep.

Fine

Leader

1. One of these morn - ings bright and fair, goin'- a take my wings and cleave the air;
2. When I get to heav-en goin'- a sing and shout, ain't no - bod-y there goin'- a turn me out;
3. When I get to heav-en goin'- a put on my shoes, goin'- a run a - bout and spread the news;

All

Pha-raoh's ar - my got drown - ded, O Ma - ry, don't you weep.

D.C.

WORDS: Afro-American spiritual (Jn. 20:11-18; Ex. 15:21)
MUSIC: Afro-American spiritual; adapt. and arr. by William Farley Smith, 1986

O MARY
Irr.

Adapt. and arr. © 1989 The United Methodist Publishing House

Canticle of Moses and Miriam

(Cantemus Domino)

RESPONSE *(General)*

Be ex - alt - ed, Lord, in your strength!

We will sing and praise your power.

R

Then Moses and the people of Israel sang this song to the Lord,
    saying,
"I will sing to the Lord, who has triumphed gloriously;
    the horse and its rider the Lord has thrown into the sea.
The Lord is my strength and my song,
    and has become my salvation;
this is my God whom I will praise.
    I will exalt my father's God
    who is a mighty warrior,
    whose name is the Lord.
Pharaoh's chariots and his host the Lord cast into the sea;
    and his chosen officers are sunk in the Red Sea.
The floods cover them;
    they went down into the depths like a stone.
Your right hand, O Lord, glorious in power,
    your right hand, O Lord, shatters the enemy.   R

"Who is like you, O Lord, among the gods?
    Who is like you, majestic in holiness,
    terrible in glorious deeds, doing wonders?
You stretched out your right hand,
    the earth swallowed them.
In your steadfast love,
    you have led the people whom you have redeemed;
you have guided them by your strength to your holy abode.   R

Continued on next page

WORDS: Exodus 15:1-6, 11-13, 17-18, 20-21, adapt; Response, Psalm 21:13, adapt.
MUSIC: Carlton R. Young

"You will bring them in,
　　and plant them on your own mountain,
　　the place, O Lord, which you have made for your abode,
　　the sanctuary, O Lord, which your hands have established.
The Lord will reign for ever and ever."　R

Then Miriam, the prophet, the sister of Aaron,
　　took a timbrel in her hand;
　　and all the women went out after her with timbrels and dancing,
　　and Miriam sang to them:
**"Sing to the Lord, who has triumphed gloriously;
　　the horse and its rider the Lord has thrown into the sea."　R**

136 The Lord's My Shepherd, I'll Not Want

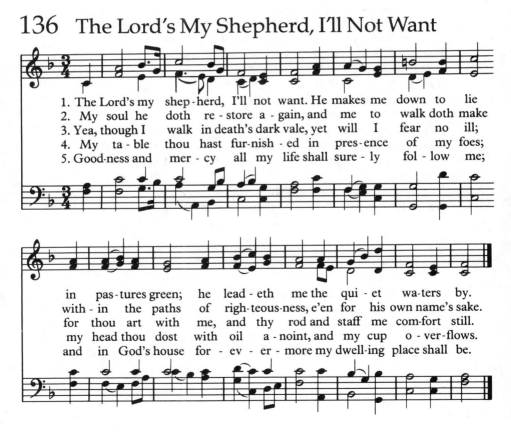

1. The Lord's my　shep-herd, I'll not want. He makes me　down to　lie
2. My soul he　doth re-store a-gain, and me to　walk doth make
3. Yea, though I　walk in death's dark vale, yet will I　fear no ill;
4. My ta-ble　thou hast fur-nish-ed in pres-ence　of my foes;
5. Good-ness and　mer-cy all my life shall sure-ly　fol-low me;

in pas-tures green; he lead-eth me the qui-et wa-ters by.
with-in the paths of righ-teous-ness, e'en for his own name's sake.
for thou art with me, and thy rod and staff me com-fort still.
my head thou dost with oil a-noint, and my cup o-ver-flows.
and in God's house for-ev-er-more my dwell-ing place shall be.

WORDS: *Scottish Psalter*, 1650 (Ps. 23)　　　　　　　　　　　　　　CRIMOND
MUSIC: Jesse Seymour Irvine, 1872; harm. by TCL. Pritchard, 1929　　CM

Harm. by permission of Oxford University Press.

Psalm 23 (King James Version)

RESPONSE 1 *(Lent, Christ the King & General)*

My shep-herd is the Lord, noth-ing in-deed shall I want.

RESPONSE 2 *(Easter & Funerals and Memorial Services)*

The Good Shep-herd comes that we may have life and have it a - bun - dant - ly.

R

1 The Lord is my shepherd; I shall not want.
2 **He maketh me to lie down in green pastures:**
   he leadeth me beside the still waters.
3 He restoreth my soul:
   he leadeth me in the paths of righteousness for his name's
      sake.
4 **Yea, though I walk through the valley of the shadow of death,**
   I will fear no evil: for thou art with me;
   thy rod and thy staff they comfort me.   R

5 Thou preparest a table before me
   in the presence of mine enemies:
   thou anointest my head with oil;
   my cup runneth over.
6 **Surely goodness and mercy shall follow me**
   all the days of my life:
   and I will dwell in the house of the Lord for ever.   R

WORDS: Psalm 23; Response 1, Psalm 23:1, Grail version; Response 2, John 10:10, adapt.
MUSIC: Response 1, Joseph Gelineau; Response 2, Richard Proulx
Response 1 © 1963 The Grail, by permission of G.I.A. Publications, Inc.; Response 2 © 1989 The United Methodist Publishing House

138   The King of Love My Shepherd Is

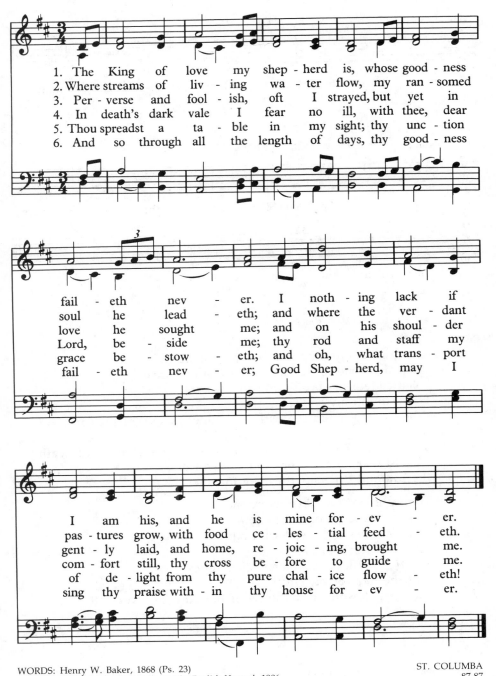

1. The King of love my shep-herd is, whose good-ness
2. Where streams of liv-ing wa-ter flow, my ran-somed
3. Per-verse and fool-ish, oft I strayed, but yet in
4. In death's dark vale I fear no ill, with thee, dear
5. Thou spreadst a ta-ble in my sight; thy unc-tion
6. And so through all the length of days, thy good-ness

fail-eth nev-er. I noth-ing lack if
soul he lead-eth; and where the ver-dant
love he sought me; and on his shoul-der
Lord, be-side me; thy rod and staff my
grace be-stow-eth; and oh, what trans-port
fail-eth nev-er; Good Shep-herd, may I

I am his, and he is mine for-ev-er.
pas-tures grow, with food ce-les-tial feed-eth.
gent-ly laid, and home, re-joic-ing, brought me.
com-fort still, thy cross be-fore to guide me.
of de-light from thy pure chal-ice flow-eth!
sing thy praise with-in thy house for-ev-er.

WORDS: Henry W. Baker, 1868 (Ps. 23)
MUSIC: Irish Melody; harm. from *The English Hymnal*, 1906

ST. COLUMBA
87.87

Praise to the Lord, the Almighty

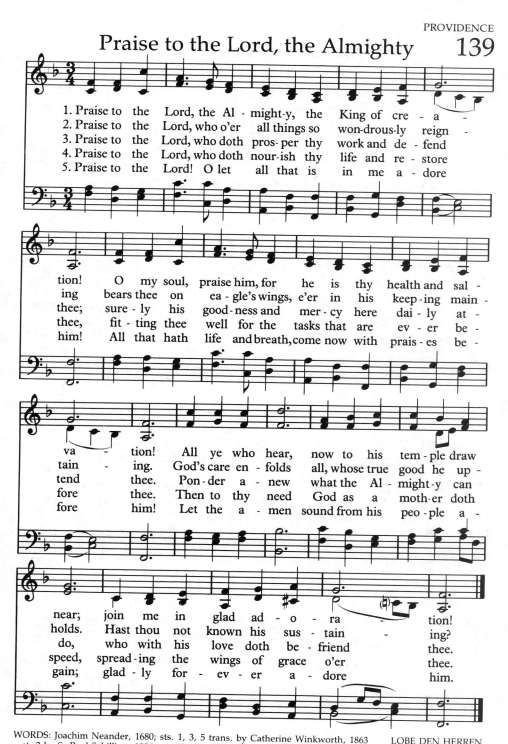

1. Praise to the Lord, the Al - might-y, the King of cre - a - tion! O my soul, praise him, for he is thy health and sal - va - tion! All ye who hear, now to his tem - ple draw near; join me in glad ad - o - ra - tion!

2. Praise to the Lord, who o'er all things so won-drous-ly reign - ing bears thee on ea - gle's wings, e'er in his keep-ing main - tain - ing. God's care en - folds all, whose true good he up - holds. Hast thou not known his sus - tain - ing?

3. Praise to the Lord, who doth pros- per thy work and de - fend thee; sure - ly his good - ness and mer - cy here dai - ly at - tend thee. Pon - der a - new what the Al - might-y can do, who with his love doth be - friend thee.

4. Praise to the Lord, who doth nour-ish thy life and re - store thee, fit - ting thee well for the tasks that are ev - er be - fore thee. Then to thy need God as a moth-er doth speed, spread-ing the wings of grace o'er thee.

5. Praise to the Lord! O let all that is in me a - dore him! All that hath life and breath, come now with prais - es be - fore him! Let the a - men sound from his peo - ple a - gain; glad - ly for - ev - er a - dore him.

WORDS: Joachim Neander, 1680; sts. 1, 3, 5 trans. by Catherine Winkworth, 1863
st. 2 by S. Paul Schilling, 1986; st. 4 by Rupert E. Davies, 1983 (Ps. 103:1-6; 150)
MUSIC: Erneuerten Gesangbuch, 1665; harm. by William Sterndale Bennett, 1864

LOBE DEN HERREN
14 14.478

Trans. sts. 2 and 4 © 1989 The United Methodist Publishing House

140 Great Is Thy Faithfulness

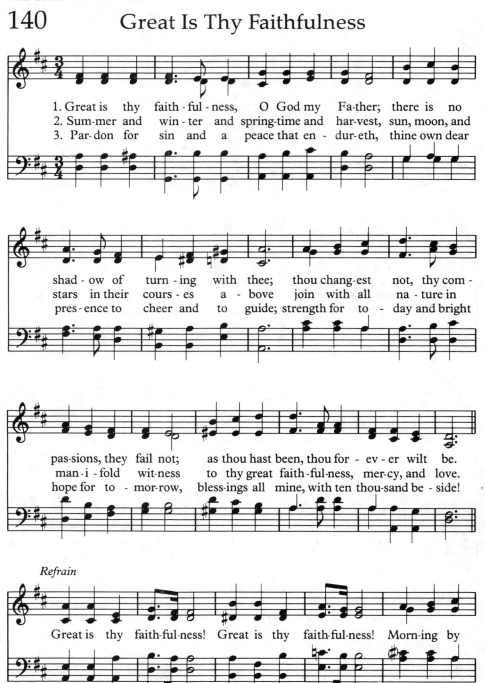

1. Great is thy faith-ful-ness, O God my Fa-ther; there is no
2. Sum-mer and win-ter and spring-time and har-vest, sun, moon, and
3. Par-don for sin and a peace that en - dur-eth, thine own dear

shad - ow of turn-ing with thee; thou chang-est not, thy com -
stars in their cours- es a - bove join with all na - ture in
pres - ence to cheer and to guide; strength for to - day and bright

pas-sions, they fail not; as thou hast been, thou for - ev - er wilt be.
man - i - fold wit-ness to thy great faith-ful-ness, mer-cy, and love.
hope for to - mor-row, bless-ings all mine, with ten thou-sand be - side!

Refrain

Great is thy faith-ful-ness! Great is thy faith-ful-ness! Morn-ing by

WORDS: Thomas O. Chisholm, 1923 (Lam. 3:22-23)
MUSIC: William M. Runyan, 1923

FAITHFULNESS
11 10.11 10 with Refrain

morn-ing new mer-cies I see; all I have need-ed thy
hand hath pro - vid-ed; great is thy faith-ful-ness, Lord, un-to me!

Children of the Heavenly Father 141

1. Chil-dren of the heaven-ly Fa-ther safe-ly in his bos-om gath-er;
2. God his own doth tend and nour-ish; in his ho-ly courts they flour-ish;
3. Nei-ther life nor death shall ev - er from the Lord his chil-dren sev - er;
4. Though he giv- eth or he tak-eth, God his chil-dren ne'er for-sak-eth;

nest-ling bird nor star in heav-en such a ref-uge e'er was giv-en.
from all e-vil things he spares them; in his might-y arms he bears them.
un - to them his grace he show-eth, and their sor-rows all he know-eth.
his the lov- ing pur-pose sole-ly to pre-serve them pure and ho - ly.

WORDS: Caroline V. Sandell-Berg, 1855; trans. by Ernst W. Olson, 1925   TRYGGARE KAN INGEN VARA
MUSIC: Swedish melody
88.88

Trans. © 1925, renewed 1953 Augsburg/Fortress

142 If Thou But Suffer God to Guide Thee

1. If thou but suf-fer God to guide thee, and hope in God through
2. On-ly be still, and wait God's lei-sure in cheer-ful hope, with
3. Sing, pray, and keep God's ways un-swerv-ing; so do thine own part

all thy ways, God will give strength, what-e'er be-tide thee,
heart con-tent to take what-e'er thy Mak-er's plea-sure
faith-ful-ly, and trust God's word; though un-de-serv-ing,

and bear thee through the e-vil days. Who trusts in God's un-
and all-dis-cern-ing love hath sent; we know our in-most
thou yet shalt find it true for thee. God nev-er yet for-

chang-ing love builds on the rock that naught can move.
wants are known, for we are called to be God's own.
sook at need the soul that trust-ed God in-deed.

WORDS: Georg Neumark, 1657; trans. by
    Catherine Winkworth, 1863 (Ps. 55:22)
MUSIC: Georg Neumark, 1657

WER NUR DEN LIEBEN GOTT
98.98.88

On Eagle's Wings

And God† will raise you* up on ea-gle's wings, bear you* on the breath of dawn, make you* to shine like the sun, and hold you* in the palm of God's‡ hand.

† or "you"
* or "us"
‡ or "your"

WORDS: Michael Joncas, 1979 (Ex. 19:4)
MUSIC: Michael Joncas, 1979; harm. by Carlton R. Young, 1988

ON EAGLE'S WINGS
Irr. with Refrain

© 1979, 1989 North American Liturgy Resources

PROVIDENCE, *see further:*

144 This Is My Father's World

1. This is my Father's world, and to my lis-tening ears all
2. This is my Father's world, the birds their car-ols raise, the
3. This is my Father's world. O let me ne'er for-get that

na - ture sings, and round me rings the mu - sic of the spheres.
morn-ing light, the lil - y white, de - clare their mak-er's praise.
though the wrong seems oft so strong, God is the rul - er yet.

This is my Father's world: I rest me in the thought of
This is my Father's world: he shines in all that's fair; in the
This is my Father's world: why should my heart be sad? The

rocks and trees, of skies and seas; his hand the won-ders wrought.
rust-ling grass I hear him pass; he speaks to me ev-ery-where.
Lord is King; let the heav-ens ring! God reigns; let the earth be glad!

WORDS: Maltbie D. Babcock, 1901
MUSIC: Trad. English melody; adapt. by Franklin L. Sheppard, 1915

TERRA BEATA
SMD

Morning Has Broken

1. Morn-ing has bro - ken like the first morn - ing;
2. Sweet the rain's new fall sun - lit from heav - en,
3. Mine is the sun - light! Mine is the morn - ing

black-bird has spo - ken like the first bird.
like the first dew - fall on the first grass.
born of the one light E - den saw play!

Praise for the sing - ing! Praise for the morn - ing!
Praise for the sweet - ness of the wet gar - den,
Praise with e - la - tion, praise ev - ery morn - ing,

Praise for them, spring - ing fresh from the Word!
sprung in com - plete - ness where his feet pass.
God's re - cre - a - tion of the new day!

WORDS: Eleanor Farjeon, 1931 (Lam. 3:22-23)
MUSIC: Trad. Gaelic melody; harm. by Carlton R. Young, 1988

BUNESSAN
55.54 D

146   At the Birth of a Child

Hail the day on which a child, _____(name)_____, was born. Rejoice! Let us all sing and praise her that gave birth to a *(son/daughter)* for whom she longed. Greet this day with joy. Our hearts are glad.

The Masai people
Kenya and Tanzania (1)

        Let us pray.
        O Creator, who dost all human beings create,
        thou hast a great worth on us conferred
        by bringing us this little child! **Amen.**

The Akamba people
Kenya (2)

(1) From *The Masai, Herders of East Africa* by Sonia Bleeker. © 1963 by Sonia Bleeker.
     Reprinted by permission of Morrow Junior Books
(2) © 1975 John S. Mbiti, by permission of SPCK

147   All Things Bright and Beautiful

Refrain (Unison)

All things bright and beau-ti-ful, all crea-tures great and small,

all things wise and won-der-ful: the Lord God made them all.

Fine

1. Each lit-tle flower that o-pens, each lit-tle bird that sings,
2. The pur-ple-head-ed moun-tains, the riv-er run-ning by,
3. The cold wind in the win-ter, the pleas-ant sum-mer sun,
4. God gave us eyes to see them, and lips that we might tell

WORDS: Cecil Frances Alexander, 1848 (Gen. 1:31)
MUSIC: 17th cent. English melody; arr. by Martin Shaw, 1915

ROYAL OAK
76.76 with Refrain

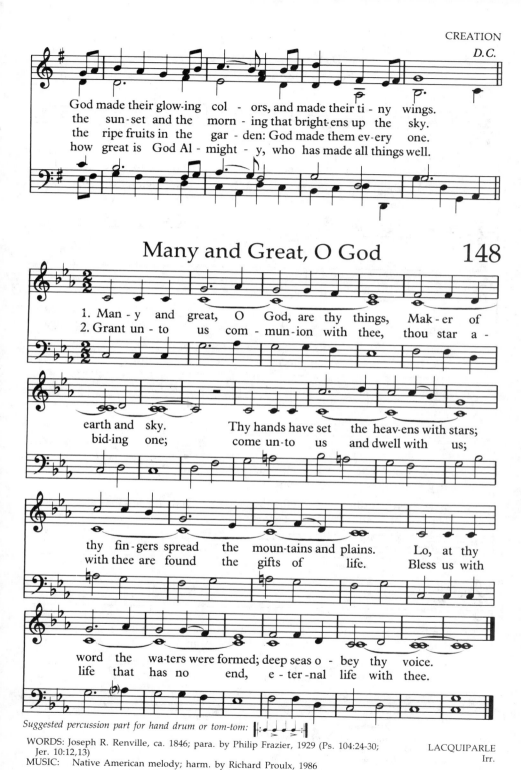

D.C.

God made their glow-ing col - ors, and made their ti - ny wings.
the sun-set and the morn - ing that bright-ens up the sky.
the ripe fruits in the gar - den: God made them ev-ery one.
how great is God Al - might - y, who has made all things well.

Many and Great, O God

148

1. Man - y and great, O God, are thy things, Mak - er of
2. Grant un - to us com - mun-ion with thee, thou star a -

earth and sky. Thy hands have set the heav-ens with stars;
bid-ing one; come un-to us and dwell with us;

thy fin - gers spread the moun-tains and plains. Lo, at thy
with thee are found the gifts of life. Bless us with

word the wa-ters were formed; deep seas o - bey thy voice.
life that has no end, e - ter-nal life with thee.

Suggested percussion part for hand drum or tom-tom:

WORDS: Joseph R. Renville, ca. 1846; para. by Philip Frazier, 1929 (Ps. 104:24-30;   LACQUIPARLE
    Jer. 10:12,13)   Irr.
MUSIC: Native American melody; harm. by Richard Proulx, 1986

Harm. © 1986 G.I.A. Publications, Inc.

149 Cantemos al Señor
(Let's Sing unto the Lord)

WORDS: Carlos Rosas; trans. by Roberto Escamilla, Elise S. Eslinger, and
George Lockwood, 1983, 1987 (Ps. 19)
MUSIC: Carlos Rosas; arr. by Raquel Mora Martinez

ROSAS
67.68 D with Refrain

150 God, Who Stretched the Spangled Heavens

1. God, who stretched the span-gled heav-ens, in-fi-nite in
2. Proud-ly rise our mod-ern cit-ies, state-ly build-ings,
3. We have ven-tured worlds un-dreamed of since the child-hood
4. As each far ho-ri-zon beck-ons, may it chal-lenge

time and place, flung the suns in burn-ing ra-diance
row on row; yet their win-dows, blank, un-feel-ing,
of our race; known the ec-sta-sy of wing-ing
us a-new, chil-dren of cre-a-tive pur-pose,

through the si-lent fields of space, we your chil-dren,
stare on can-yoned streets be-low, where the lone-ly
through un-trav-eled realms of space; probed the se-crets
serv-ing oth-ers, hon-oring you. May our dreams prove

in your like-ness, share in-ven-tive powers with you.
drift un-no-ticed in the cit-y's ebb and flow,
of the at-om, yield-ing un-i-mag-ined power,
rich with prom-ise, each en-deav-or well be-gun.

WORDS: Catherine Cameron, 1967
MUSIC: William Moore, 1825

Words © 1967 Hope Publishing Co.

HOLY MANNA
87.87 D

Alt. tune: AUSTRIA

Great Cre-a-tor, still cre-at-ing, show us what we yet may do.
lost to pur-pose and to mean-ing, scarce-ly car-ing where they go.
fac-ing us with life's de-struc-tion or our most tri-um-phant hour.
Great Cre-a-tor, give us guid-ance till our goals and yours are one.

God Created Heaven and Earth 151

Unison

1. God cre-at-ed heaven and earth, all things per-fect
2. Let us praise God's mer-cy great; all our needs that
3. God is one, will ev-er be; i-dols are mere
4. But God's grace be-yond com-pare saves us all from

brought to birth; God's great power made
love a-wait; God who fash-ions
van-i-ty; hand-made gods of
death's de-spair; so earth's crea-tures

dark and light, earth re-volv-ing day and night.
all that lives to each one a bless-ing gives.
wood and clay can-not help us when we pray.
small and great give thanks for that bless-ed state.

WORDS: Trad. Taiwanese hymn; trans. by Boris and Clare Anderson, 1983 (Gen. 1:1-5)   TOA-SIA
MUSIC: Trad. Taiwanese melody; harm. by I-to Loh, 1983   77.77

Trans. © 1983 Boris and Clare Anderson; harm. © 1983 The United Methodist Publishing House

152 I Sing the Almighty Power of God

1. I sing the al-might-y power of God, that made the moun-tains
2. I sing the good-ness of the Lord, who filled the earth with
3. There's not a plant or flower be-low, but makes thy glo-ries

rise, that spread the flow-ing seas a-broad, and built the loft - y skies.
food, who formed the crea-tures thru the Word, and then pro-nounced them good.
known, and clouds a - rise, and tem-pests blow, by or - der from thy throne;

I sing the wis-dom that or-dained the sun to rule the day;
Lord, how thy won-ders are dis-played, wher- e'er I turn my eye,
while all that bor-rows life from thee is ev - er in thy care;

the moon shines full at God's com-mand, and all the stars o - bey.
if I sur - vey the ground I tread, or gaze up - on the sky.
and ev-ery-where that we can be, thou, God, art pres - ent there.

WORDS: Isaac Watts, 1715
MUSIC: Trad. English melody; arr. by Ralph Vaughan Williams, 1906

FOREST GREEN
CMD

CREATION, *see further:*

62 All Creatures of Our God and King   588 All Things Come of Thee

Thou Hidden Source of Calm Repose 153

1. Thou hid – den source of calm re – pose, thou all – suf –
2. Thy might – y name sal – va – tion is, and keeps my
3. Je – sus, my all in all thou art, my rest in
4. In want my plen – ti – ful sup – ply, in weak – ness

fi - cient love di – vine, my help and ref - uge from my foes,
hap - py soul a – bove; com - fort it brings, and power and peace,
toil, my ease in pain, the heal - ing of my bro - ken heart,
my al - might - y power, in bonds my per - fect lib - er - ty,

se - cure I am if thou art mine; and lo! from sin and
and joy and ev - er - last - ing love; to me with thy dear
in war my peace, in loss my gain, my smile be - neath the
my light in Sa - tan's dark - est hour, in grief my joy un -

grief and shame I hide me, Je - sus, in thy name.
name are given par - don and ho - li - ness and heaven.
ty - rant's frown, in shame my glo - ry and my crown,
speak - a - ble, my life in death, my heaven in hell.

WORDS: Charles Wesley, 1749
MUSIC: Attr. to Dimitri S. Bortniansky, 1825

ST. PETERSBURG
88.88.88

154 All Hail the Power of Jesus' Name

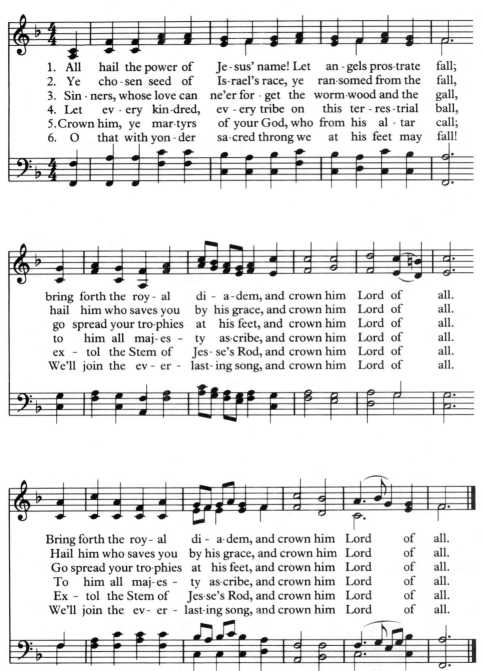

1. All hail the power of Je-sus' name! Let an-gels pros-trate fall;
2. Ye cho-sen seed of Is-rael's race, ye ran-somed from the fall,
3. Sin - ners, whose love can ne'er for - get the worm-wood and the gall,
4. Let ev - ery kin-dred, ev - ery tribe on this ter - res -trial ball,
5. Crown him, ye mar-tyrs of your God, who from his al - tar call;
6. O that with yon - der sa-cred throng we at his feet may fall!

bring forth the roy - al di - a-dem, and crown him Lord of all.
hail him who saves you by his grace, and crown him Lord of all.
go spread your tro-phies at his feet, and crown him Lord of all.
to him all maj-es - ty as-cribe, and crown him Lord of all.
ex - tol the Stem of Jes- se's Rod, and crown him Lord of all.
We'll join the ev - er - last-ing song, and crown him Lord of all.

Bring forth the roy- al di - a-dem, and crown him Lord of all.
Hail him who saves you by his grace, and crown him Lord of all.
Go spread your tro-phies at his feet, and crown him Lord of all.
To him all maj-es - ty as-cribe, and crown him Lord of all.
Ex - tol the Stem of Jes-se's Rod, and crown him Lord of all.
We'll join the ev - er - last-ing song, and crown him Lord of all.

WORDS: Edward Perronet, 1779; alt. by John Rippon, 1787
MUSIC: Oliver Holden, 1792

CORONATION
CM

All Hail the Power of Jesus' Name   155

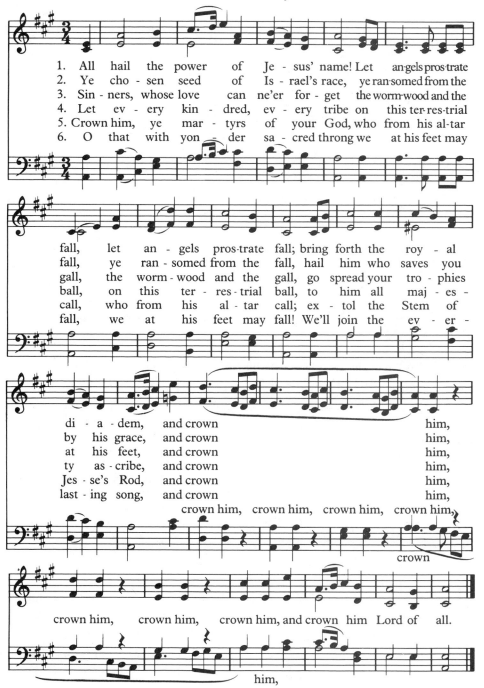

1. All hail the power of Je - sus' name! Let an-gels pros-trate
2. Ye cho - sen seed of Is - rael's race, ye ran-somed from the
3. Sin - ners, whose love can ne'er for - get the worm-wood and the
4. Let ev - ery kin - dred, ev - ery tribe on this ter-res-trial
5. Crown him, ye mar - tyrs of your God, who from his al-tar
6. O that with yon - der sa - cred throng we at his feet may

fall, let an - gels pros-trate fall; bring forth the roy - al
fall, ye ran - somed from the fall, hail him who saves you
gall, the worm - wood and the gall, go spread your tro - phies
ball, on this ter - res - trial ball, to him all maj - es -
call, who from his al - tar call; ex - tol the Stem of
fall, we at his feet may fall! We'll join the ev - er -

di - a - dem, and crown   him,
by his grace, and crown   him,
at his feet, and crown   him,
ty as - cribe, and crown   him,
Jes - se's Rod, and crown   him,
last - ing song, and crown   him,

crown him, crown him, crown him, crown him,
crown

crown him, crown him, crown him, and crown him Lord of all.

him,

WORDS: Edward Perronet, 1779; alt. by John Rippon, 1787
MUSIC: James Ellor, 1838

DIADEM
CM

156 I Love to Tell the Story

1. I love to tell the sto-ry of un-seen things a-
2. I love to tell the sto-ry; more won-der-ful it
3. I love to tell the sto-ry; 'tis pleas-ant to re-
4. I love to tell the sto-ry, for those who know it

bove, of Je-sus and his glo-ry, of Je-sus and his
seems than all the gold-en fan-cies of all our gold-en
peat what seems, each time I tell it, more won-der-ful-ly
best seem hun-ger-ing and thirst-ing to hear it like the

love. I love to tell the sto-ry, be-cause I know 'tis
dreams. I love to tell the sto-ry, it did so much for
sweet. I love to tell the sto-ry, for some have nev-er
rest. And when, in scenes of glo-ry, I sing the new, new

true; it sat-is-fies my long-ings as noth-ing else can do.
me; and that is just the rea-son I tell it now to thee.
heard the mes-sage of sal-va-tion from God's own ho-ly Word.
song, 'twill be the old, old sto-ry that I have loved so long.

Refrain

I love to tell the sto-ry, 'twill be my theme in glo-ry,

WORDS: Katherine Hankey, ca. 1868
MUSIC: William G. Fischer, 1869

HANKEY
76.76 D with Refrain

to tell the old, old sto-ry of Je-sus and his love.

Jesus Shall Reign 157

1. Je-sus shall reign wher - e'er the sun does its suc-
2. To Je-sus end-less prayer be made, and end-less
3. Peo-ple and realms of ev - ery tongue dwell on his
4. Bless-ings a-bound wher - e'er he reigns; all pris-oners
5. Let ev-ery crea-ture rise and bring hon-ors pe-

ces - sive jour - neys run; his king-dom spread from
prais - es crown his head; his name like sweet per-
love with sweet - est song; and in - fant voic - es
leap and loose their chains; the wea-ry find e -
cu - liar to our King; an - gels de - scend with

shore to shore, till moons shall wax and wane no more.
fume shall rise with ev-ery morn - ing sac-ri - fice.
shall pro - claim their ear-ly bless - ings on his name.
ter - nal rest, and all who suf - fer want are blest.
songs a - gain, and earth re - peat the loud a - men!

WORDS: Isaac Watts, 1719 (Ps. 72)   DUKE STREET
MUSIC: John Hatton, 1793   LM

158 Come, Christians, Join to Sing

1. Come, Chris-tians, join to sing: Al - le - lu - ia! A - men!
2. Come, lift your hearts on high: Al - le - lu - ia! A - men!
3. Praise yet the Lord a - gain: Al - le - lu - ia! A - men!

loud praise to Christ our King: Al - le - lu - ia! A - men!
Let prais-es fill the sky: Al - le - lu - ia! A - men!
Life shall not end the strain: Al - le - lu - ia! A - men!

Let all, with heart and voice, be - fore his throne re - joice;
He is our guide and friend; to us he'll con - de-scend;
On heav-en's bliss-ful shore his good-ness we'll a - dore,

praise is his gra-cious choice. Al - le - lu - ia! A - men!
his love shall nev - er end: Al - le - lu - ia! A - men!
sing - ing for - ev - er -more: Al - le - lu - ia! A - men!

WORDS: Christian Henry Bateman, 1843
MUSIC: Trad. melody; arr. by Benjamin Carr, 1824; harm. by Austin C. Lovelace, 1963

SPANISH HYMN
66.66 D

Harm. © 1964 Abingdon Press

Lift High the Cross

Refrain (Unison)

Lift high the cross, the love of Christ pro-claim

till all the world a-dore his sa-cred name.

Fine

Harmony

1. Come, Chris-tians, fol – low this tri-um-phant sign. The
2. Each new-born ser – vant of the Cru-ci – fied bears
3. O Lord, once lift – ed on the glo-rious tree, as
4. So shall our song of tri – umph ev – er be: Praise

D.C.

hosts of God in u-ni-ty com-bine.
on the brow the seal of him who died.
thou hast prom-ised, draw the world to thee.
to the Cru-ci – fied for vic-to – ry!

WORDS: George William Kitchin and Michael Robert Newbolt, 1916, alt.
MUSIC: Sydney Hugo Nicholson, 1916

CRUCIFER
10 10 with Refrain

160   Rejoice, Ye Pure in Heart

1. Re - joice, ye pure in heart; re - joice, give
2. Your clear ho - san - nas raise, and al - le -
3. Yes, on through life's long path, still chant - ing
4. At last the march shall end; the wea - ried
5. Praise God who reigns on high, the Lord whom

thanks, and sing; your glo - rious ban - ner
lu - ias loud; whilst an - swering ech - oes
as ye go; from youth to age, by
ones shall rest; the pil - grims find their
we a - dore, the Fa - ther, Son, and

wave on high, the cross of Christ your King.
up - ward float, like wreaths of in - cense cloud.
night and day, in glad - ness and in woe.
heaven - ly home, Je - ru - sa - lem the blest.
Ho - ly Ghost, one God for - ev - er - more.

Refrain

Re - joice, re - joice, re - joice, give thanks and sing.
Re - joice, re - joice,

WORDS: Edward H. Plumptre, 1865 (Ps. 20:4; 147:1; Phil. 4:4)
MUSIC: Arthur H. Messiter, 1889

MARION
SM with Refrain

Rejoice, Ye Pure in Heart

1. Re - joice, ye pure in heart; re - joice, give thanks, and sing; your glo - rious ban - ner wave on high, the cross of Christ your King.
2. Your clear ho - san - nas raise, and al - le - lu - ias loud; whilst an - swering ech - oes up - ward float, like wreaths of in - cense cloud.
3. Yes, on through life's long path, still chant-ing as ye go; from youth to age, by night and day, in glad - ness and in woe.
4. At last the march shall end; the wea-ried ones shall rest; the pil - grims find their heaven-ly home, Je - ru - sa - lem the blest.
5. Praise God who reigns on high, the Lord whom we a - dore, the Fa - ther, Son, and Ho - ly Ghost, one God for - ev - er - more.

Refrain

Ho - san - na! Ho - san - na! Re - joice, give thanks, and sing.

WORDS: Edward H. Plumptre, 1865 (Ps. 20:4; 147:1; Phil. 4:4)
MUSIC: Richard Wayne Dirksen, 1974

VINEYARD HAVEN
SM with Refrain

162 Alleluia, Alleluia

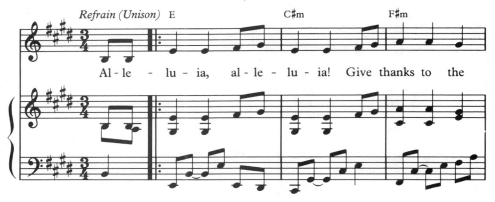

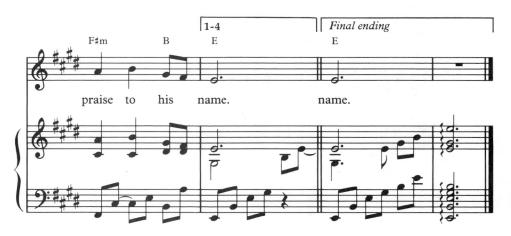

WORDS: Donald Fishel, 1973
MUSIC: Donald Fishel, 1973

ALLELUIA NO. 1
Irr.

© 1973 The Word of God

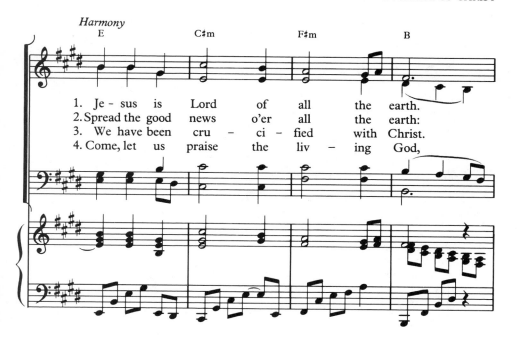

1. Je - sus is Lord of all the earth.
2. Spread the good news o'er all the earth:
3. We have been cru - ci - fied with Christ.
4. Come, let us praise the liv - ing God,

He is the King of cre - a - tion.
Je - sus has died and has ris - en.
Now we shall live for - ev - er.
joy - ful - ly sing to our Sav - ior.

Al - le -

163 Ask Ye What Great Thing I Know

1. Ask ye what great thing I know, that de-lights and
2. Who de-feats my fier-cest foes? Who con-soles my
3. Who is life in life to me? Who the death of
4. This is that great thing I know; this de-lights and

stirs me so? What the high re-ward I win? Whose the name I
sad-dest woes? Who re-vives my faint-ing heart, heal-ing all its
death will be? Who will place me on his right, with the count-less
stirs me so: faith in him who died to save, him who tri-umphed

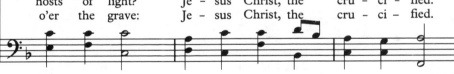

glo - ry in? Je - sus Christ, the cru - ci - fied.
hid - den smart? Je - sus Christ, the cru - ci - fied.
hosts of light? Je - sus Christ, the cru - ci - fied.
o'er the grave: Je - sus Christ, the cru - ci - fied.

WORDS: Johann C. Schwedler, 1741; trans. by Benjamin H. Kennedy, 1863   HENDON
(1 Cor. 2:2; Gal. 6:14)   77.77.7
MUSIC: H. A. César Malan, 1827; harm. by Lowell Mason, 1841

164 Come, My Way, My Truth, My Life

Unison

1. Come, my Way, my Truth, my Life: such a way as
2. Come, my Light, my Feast, my Strength: such a light as
3. Come, my Joy, my Love, my Heart: such a joy as

WORDS: George Herbert, 1633 (Jn. 14:6)   THE CALL
MUSIC: Ralph Vaughan Williams, 1911; adapt. by E. Harold Geer   77.77

gives us breath, such a truth as ends all strife,
shows a feast, such a feast as mends in length,
none can move, such a love as none can part,

such a life as kill - eth death.
such a strength as makes his guest.
such a heart as joys in love.

Hallelujah! What a Savior 165

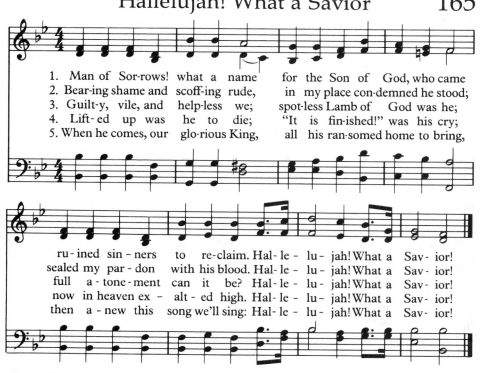

1. Man of Sor-rows! what a name for the Son of God, who came
2. Bear-ing shame and scoff-ing rude, in my place con-demned he stood;
3. Guilt-y, vile, and help-less we; spot-less Lamb of God was he;
4. Lift-ed up was he to die; "It is fin-ished!" was his cry;
5. When he comes, our glo-rious King, all his ran-somed home to bring,

ru-ined sin-ners to re-claim. Hal-le-lu-jah! What a Sav-ior!
sealed my par-don with his blood. Hal-le-lu-jah! What a Sav-ior!
full a-tone-ment can it be? Hal-le-lu-jah! What a Sav-ior!
now in heaven ex - alt-ed high. Hal-le-lu-jah! What a Sav-ior!
then a-new this song we'll sing: Hal-le-lu-jah! What a Sav-ior!

WORDS: Philip P. Bliss, 1875 (Is. 53)
MUSIC: Philip P. Bliss, 1875

HALLELUJAH! WHAT A SAVIOR
777.8

166 All Praise to Thee, for Thou, O King Divine

1. All praise to thee, for thou, O King di - vine, didst
2. Thou cam'st to us, in low - li - ness of thought; by
3. Let this mind be in us which was in thee,
4. Where-fore, by God's e - ter - nal pur-pose, thou
5. Let ev - ery tongue con - fess with one ac - cord in

yield the glo - ry that of right was thine,
thee the out - cast and the poor were sought,
who wast a ser - vant, that we might be free,
art high ex - alt - ed o'er all crea-tures now,
heaven and earth that Je - sus Christ is Lord;

that in our dark - ened hearts thy grace might shine:
and by thy death was God's sal - va - tion wrought:
hum - bling thy - self to death on Cal - va - ry:
and given the name to which all knees shall bow:
and God the Fa - ther be by all a - dored:

WORDS: F. Bland Tucker, 1938 (Phil. 2:5-11)
MUSIC: Ralph Vaughan Williams, 1906
Words © 1940, 1943, renewed 1971 The Church Pension Fund

SINE NOMINE
10 10 10 with Alleluias
Alt. tune: ENGELBERG

Canticle of Christ's Obedience 167

RESPONSE 1 *(General)*

Let this mind be in you which was al - so in Christ Je - sus.

RESPONSE 2 *(General)*

At the name of Je - sus ev - ery knee shall bow.

R

Christ Jesus, though he was in the form of God,
  did not count equality with God a thing to be grasped,
but emptied himself,
  taking the form of a servant,
  being born in our likeness.
And being found in human form
  he humbled himself and became obedient unto death,
  even death on a cross.
Therefore God has highly exalted him
  and bestowed on him the name which is above every name,
that at the name of Jesus every knee shall bow,
  in heaven and on earth and under the earth,
  and every tongue confess that Jesus Christ is Lord,
    to the glory of God the Father.   R

See Nos. 166 & 168 for metrical settings of this ancient text.

WORDS: Philippians 2:5-11, adapt.; Response 1, Philippians 2:5, adapt.; Response 2, Caroline M. Noel
MUSIC: Response 1, Gary Alan Smith; Response 2, Ralph Vaughan Williams

Adapt. and Response 1 © 1989 The United Methodist Publishing House; music Response 2 by permission of Oxford University Press

168   At the Name of Jesus

Unison

1. At the name of Je - sus ev -ery knee shall bow,
2. Hum-bled for a sea - son, to re-ceive a name
3. Bore it up tri - um - phant with its hu - man light,
4. In your hearts en - throne him; there let him sub - due

ev - ery tongue con - fess him King of glo - ry now;
from the lips of sin - ners un - to whom he came,
through all ranks of crea - tures to the cen - tral height,
all that is not ho - ly, all that is not true.

'tis the Fa - ther's plea - sure we should call him Lord,
faith-ful - ly he bore it, spot-less to the last,
to the throne of God - head, to the Fa - ther's breast;
Crown him as your cap - tain in temp-ta - tion's hour;

who from the be - gin - ning was the might - y Word.
brought it back vic - to - rious when from death he passed.
filled it with the glo - ry of that per - fect rest.
let his will en - fold you in its light and power.

WORDS: Caroline M. Noel, 1870 (Phil. 2:5-11)
MUSIC: Ralph Vaughan Williams, 1925

KING'S WESTON
65.65 D

In Thee Is Gladness

WORDS: Johann Lindemann, 1598; trans. by Catherine Winkworth, 1858
MUSIC: Giovanni Giacomo Gastoldi, 1593

IN DIR IST FREUDE
Irr.

170 O How I Love Jesus

1. There is a name I love to hear, I love to sing its worth;
2. It tells me of a Savior's love, who died to set me free;
3. It tells of one whose lov-ing heart can feel my deep-est woe;

it sounds like mu-sic in my ear, the sweet-est name on earth.
it tells me of his pre-cious blood, the sin-ner's per-fect plea.
who in each sor-row bears a part that none can bear be-low.

Refrain

O how I love Je - sus, O how I love Je - sus,

O how I love Je - sus, be - cause he first loved me!

WORDS: Frederick Whitfield, 1855
MUSIC: 19th cent. USA melody

O HOW I LOVE JESUS
CM with Refrain

There's Something About That Name 171

Je-sus, Je-sus, Je - sus! There's just some-thing a - bout that name! Mas-ter, Sav-ior, Je - sus! Like the fra-grance af - ter the rain. Je-sus, Je-sus, Je - sus! Let all heav-en and earth pro - claim: Kings and king-doms will all pass a - way, but there's some-thing a - bout that name!

WORDS: Gloria Gaither and William J. Gaither, 1970
MUSIC: William J. Gaither, 1970

THAT NAME
Irr.

172   My Jesus, I Love Thee

1. My Je-sus, I love thee, I know thou art mine; for
2. I love thee be-cause thou hast first lov-ed me, and
3. In man-sions of glo-ry and end-less de-light, I'll

thee all the fol-lies of sin I re-sign. My
pur-chased my par-don on Cal-va-ry's tree; I
ev-er a-dore thee in heav-en so bright; I'll

gra-cious Re-deem-er, my Sav-ior art thou; if
love thee for wear-ing the thorns on thy brow; if
sing with the glit-ter-ing crown on my brow; if

ev - er I loved thee, my Je - sus, 'tis now.
ev - er I loved thee, my Je - sus, 'tis now.
ev - er I loved thee, my Je - sus, 'tis now.

WORDS: William R. Featherstone, 1864
MUSIC: Adoniram J. Gordon, 1876

GORDON
11 11.11 11

Christ, Whose Glory Fills the Skies 173

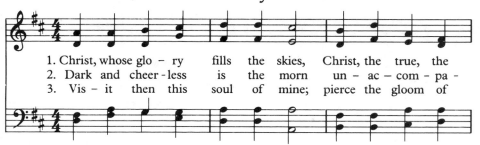

1. Christ, whose glo - ry fills the skies, Christ, the true, the
2. Dark and cheer - less is the morn un - ac - com - pa -
3. Vis - it then this soul of mine; pierce the gloom of

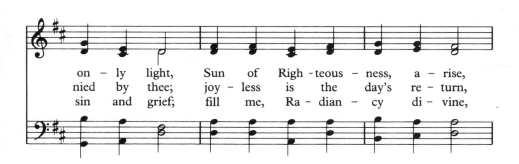

on - ly light, Sun of Righ - teous - ness, a - rise,
nied by thee; joy - less is the day's re - turn,
sin and grief; fill me, Ra - dian - cy di - vine,

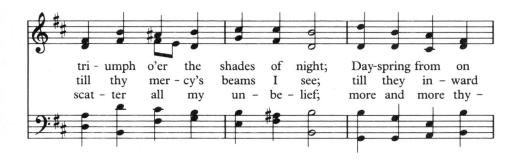

tri - umph o'er the shades of night; Day-spring from on
till thy mer - cy's beams I see; till they in - ward
scat - ter all my un - be - lief; more and more thy -

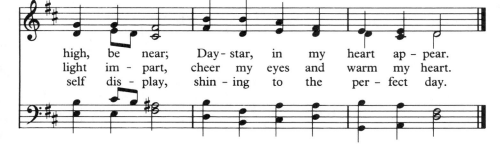

high, be near; Day - star, in my heart ap - pear.
light im - part, cheer my eyes and warm my heart.
self dis - play, shin - ing to the per - fect day.

WORDS: Charles Wesley, 1740
MUSIC: J. G. Werner's *Choralbuch*, 1815; harm. by William H. Havergal, 1861

RATISBON
77.77.77

174 His Name Is Wonderful

His name is won-der-ful, his name is won-der-ful, his name is won-der-ful, Je-sus, my Lord. He is the might-y King, Mas-ter of ev-ery-thing; his name is won-der-ful, Je-sus, my Lord. He's the great Shep-herd, the Rock of all a-ges, al-might-y God is he; bow down be-fore him, love and a-

WORDS: Audrey Mieir, 1959
MUSIC: Audrey Mieir, 1959

HIS NAME IS WONDERFUL
Irr.

dore him, his name is won-der-ful, Je - sus, my Lord.

Jesus, the Very Thought of Thee 175

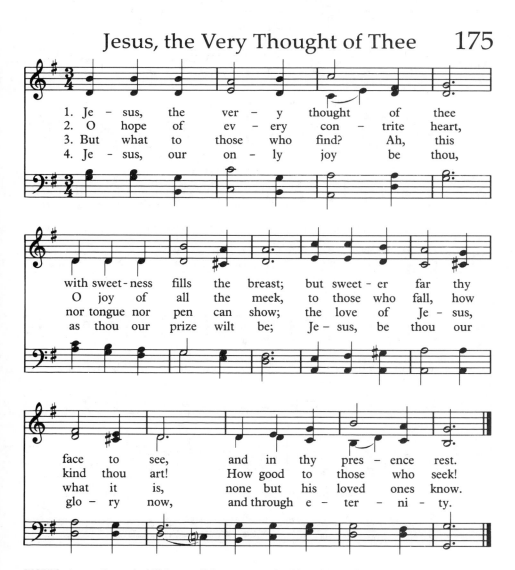

1. Je - sus, the ver - y thought of thee
2. O hope of ev - ery con - trite heart,
3. But what to those who find? Ah, this
4. Je - sus, our on - ly joy be thou,

with sweet-ness fills the breast; but sweet - er far thy
O joy of all the meek, to those who fall, how
nor tongue nor pen can show; the love of Je - sus,
as thou our prize wilt be; Je - sus, be thou our

face to see, and in thy pres - ence rest.
kind thou art! How good to those who seek!
what it is, none but his loved ones know.
glo - ry now, and through e - ter - ni - ty.

WORDS: Attr. to Bernard of Clairvaux, 12th cent.; trans. by Edward Caswall, 1849
MUSIC: John B. Dykes, 1866

ST. AGNES
CM

176 Majesty, Worship His Majesty

Maj - es - ty, worship his maj - es - ty; un - to

Je - sus be all glo - ry, hon - or, and praise. Maj - es - ty,

king-dom au - thor - i - ty, flow from his throne un - to his own;

his an-them raise. So ex - alt, lift up on high the name of

Je - sus. Mag-ni - fy, come glo-ri - fy Christ Je-sus, the King.

WORDS: Jack Hayford, 1981
MUSIC: Jack Hayford, 1981; arr. by Eugene Thomas, 1981

© 1981 Rocksmith Music c/o Trust Music Management

MAJESTY
Irr.

Maj – es – ty, wor-ship his maj – es – ty,

Je – sus who died, now glo – ri – fied, King of all kings.

He Is Lord 177

He is Lord, he is Lord! He is ris – en from the

dead and he is Lord! Ev – ery knee shall bow,

ev – ery tongue con – fess that Je – sus Christ is Lord.

WORDS: Philippians 2:9-11
MUSIC: Trad.; arr. by Tom Fettke, 1986

Arr. © 1986 Word, Inc.

HE IS LORD
Irr.

178 Hope of the World

Unison

1. Hope of the world, thou Christ of great com - pas - sion,
2. Hope of the world, God's gift from high-est heav - en,
3. Hope of the world, a - foot on dust - y high - ways,
4. Hope of the world, who by thy cross didst save us
5. Hope of the world, O Christ o'er death vic - tor - ious,

speak to our fear - ful hearts by con-flict rent.
bring-ing to hun - gry souls the bread of life,
show-ing to wan- dering souls the path of light,
from death and dark de - spair, from sin and guilt,
who by this sign didst con-quer grief and pain,

Save us, thy peo - ple, from con-sum-ing pas - sion,
still let thy spir - it un - to us be giv - en,
walk thou be - side us lest the tempt-ing by - ways
we ren - der back the love thy mer-cy gave us;
we would be faith - ful to thy gos - pel glo - rious;

who by our own false hopes and aims are spent.
to heal earth's wounds and end all bit - ter strife.
lure us a - way from thee to end - less night.
take thou our lives, and use them as thou wilt.
thou art our Lord! Thou dost for - ev - er reign.

WORDS: Georgia Harkness, 1954
MUSIC: V. Earle Copes, 1963

VICAR
11 10.11 10

O Sing a Song of Bethlehem

1. O sing a song of Beth-le-hem, of shep-herds watch-ing there,
2. O sing a song of Naz-a-reth, of sun-ny days of joy;
3. O sing a song of Gal-i-lee, of lake and woods and hill,
4. O sing a song of Cal-va-ry, its glo-ry and dis-may,

and of the news that came to them from an-gels in the air.
O sing of fra-grant flow-ers' breath, and of the sin-less Boy.
of him who walked up-on the sea and bade the waves be still.
of him who hung up-on the tree, and took our sins a-way.

The light that shone on Beth-le-hem fills all the world to-day;
For now the flowers of Naz-a-reth in ev-ery heart may grow;
For though like waves on Gal-i-lee, dark seas of trou-ble roll,
For he who died on Cal-va-ry is ris-en from the grave,

of Je-sus' birth and peace on earth the an-gels sing al-way.
now spreads the fame of his dear name on all the winds that blow.
when faith has heard the Mas-ter's word, falls peace up-on the soul.
and Christ, our Lord, by heaven a-dored, is might-y now to save.

WORDS: Louis F. Benson, 1889
MUSIC: English melody; arr. by Ralph Vaughan Williams, 1906

KINGSFOLD
CMD

180 Jesús Es Mi Rey Soberano
(O Jesus, My King and My Sovereign)

1. Je - sús es mi Rey so - be - ra - no, mi
2. Je - sús es mi_a - mi - go_an - he - la - do, y_en
3. Se - ñor, ¿qué pu - die - ra yo dar - te por

1. O Je - sus, my King and my Sov - ereign, my
2. O Je - sus, my friend and my yearn - ing, in
3. O Lord, tell me what could I give you for

go - zo_es can - tar su lo - or; es Rey, y me
som - bras o_en luz siem - pre va pa - cien - te_y hu -
tan - ta bon - dad pa - ra mí? ¿Me bas - ta ser -

joy is to sing him my praise. He's king, yet he
dark - ness and light al - ways near; he walks at my
all your great good - ness to me? Could this be e -

ve cual her - ma - no, es Rey y me_im -
mil - de_a mi la - do, a - yu - da_y con -
vir - te_y a - mar - te? ¿Es to - do_en - tre -

treats me like fam - ily, he's king, yet he
side, pa - tient, hum - ble, and gives me his
nough: serve and love you, com - mit - ting my

WORDS: Vicente Mendoza, 1920; trans. by Esther Frances, 1982, and
George Lockwood, 1988
MUSIC: Vicente Mendoza, 1920

MI REY Y MI AMIGO
Irr.

181 Ye Servants of God

1. Ye ser-vants of God, your Mas-ter pro-claim,
2. God rul-eth on high, al-might-y to save,
3. "Sal-va-tion to God, who sits on the throne!"
4. Then let us a-dore and give him his right,

and pub-lish a-broad his won-der-ful name;
and still he is nigh, his pres-ence we have;
Let all cry a-loud and hon-or the Son;
all glo-ry and power, all wis-dom and might;

the name all-vic-to-rious of Je-sus ex-tol,
the great con-gre-ga-tion his tri-umph shall sing,
the prais-es of Je-sus the an-gels pro-claim,
all hon-or and bless-ing with an-gels a-bove,

his king-dom is glo-rious and rules o-ver all.
as-crib-ing sal-va-tion to Je-sus, our King.
fall down on their fac-es and wor-ship the Lamb.
and thanks nev-er ceas-ing and in-fi-nite love.

WORDS: Charles Wesley, 1744 (Rev. 7:9-12)
MUSIC: Attr. to William Croft, 1708

HANOVER
10 10.11 11

Word of God, Come Down on Earth 182

1. Word of God, come down on earth, liv-ing rain from heaven de-scend-ing; touch our hearts and bring to birth faith and hope and love un-end-ing. Word al-might-y, we re-vere you; Word made flesh, we long to hear you.

2. Word e-ter-nal, throned on high, Word that brought to life cre-a-tion, Word that came from heaven to die, cru-ci-fied for our sal-va-tion, sav-ing Word, the world re-stor-ing, speak to us, your love out-pour-ing.

3. Word that caused blind eyes to see, speak and heal our mor-tal blind-ness; deaf we are: our heal-er be; loose our tongues to tell your kind-ness. Be our Word in pit-y spo-ken; heal the world, by our sin bro-ken.

4. Word that speaks your Fa-ther's love, one with God be-yond all tell-ing, Word that sends us from a-bove God the Spir-it, with us dwell-ing, Word of truth, to all truth lead us; Word of life, with one Bread feed us.

WORDS: James Quinn, 1969
MUSIC: Johann R. Ahle, 1664

Words © 1969 James Quinn

LIEBSTER JESU
78.78.88

183   Jesu, Thy Boundless Love to Me

Jesu, thy boundless love to me
no thought can reach, no tongue declare;
O knit my thankful heart to thee
and reign without a rival there.
Thine wholly, thine alone, I am;
be thou alone my constant flame.

O grant that nothing in my soul
may dwell, but thy pure love alone!
O may thy love possess me whole,
my joy, my treasure, and my crown.
Strange flames far from my soul remove,
my every act, word, thought, be love.

O Love, how cheering is thy ray!
All pain before thy presence flies!
Care, anguish, sorrow, melt away
where'er thy healing beams arise.
O Jesu, nothing may I see,
nothing hear, feel, or think, but thee!

In suffering be thy love my peace,
in weakness be thy love my power;
and when the storms of life shall cease,
Jesu, in that important hour,
in death as life be thou my guide,
and save me, who for me hast died.

Suggested Tune: ST. CATHERINE

This is an extract from one of John Wesley's translations from Paul Gerhardt, prepared in Savannah, Georgia, and published in 1739 in *Hymns and Sacred Poems*, under the title "Living by Christ." He later quoted stanza 2 at the end of his sermon "A Plain Account of Christian Perfection" as "the cry of my heart" upon leaving Georgia, rejected and disillusioned.

Of the Father's Love Begotten

184

WORDS: Aurelius Clemens Prudentius; trans. by John Mason Neale, 1851 and
  Henry W. Baker, 1859
MUSIC: 11th cent. *Sanctus* trope; arr. by C. Winfred Douglas, 1940

DIVINUM MYSTERIUM
87.87.887

Arr. © 1943, renewed 1981 The Church Pension Fund

185 When Morning Gilds the Skies

1. When morn-ing gilds the skies my heart a-wak-ing cries:
2. The night be-comes as day when from the heart we say:
3. Let all the earth a-round ring joy-ous with the sound:
4. Be this, while life is mine, my can-ti-cle di-vine:

May Je-sus Christ be praised! A-like at work and prayer,
May Je-sus Christ be praised! The powers of dark-ness fear
May Je-sus Christ be praised! In heaven's e-ter-nal bliss
May Je-sus Christ be praised! Be this th'e-ter-nal song

to Je-sus I re-pair: May Je-sus Christ be praised!
when this sweet chant they hear: May Je-sus Christ be praised!
the love-liest strain is this: May Je-sus Christ be praised!
through all the a-ges long: May Je-sus Christ be praised!

WORDS: *Katholisches Gesangbuch,* ca. 1744; sts. 1, 2, 4 trans. by Edward Caswall, 1854;   LAUDES DOMINI
   st. 3 by Robert S. Bridges, 1899   666.666
MUSIC: Joseph Barnby, 1868

186 Alleluia

1. Al-le-lu-ia, al-le-lu-ia, al-le-lu-ia, al-le-lu-ia,

WORDS: Jerry Sinclair, 1972   ALLELUIA
MUSIC: Jerry Sinclair, 1972   Irr.

al- le - lu - ia, al- le - lu - ia, al- le - lu - ia, al- le - lu - ia.

2. He's my Savior
3. I will praise Him

Rise, Shine, You People 187

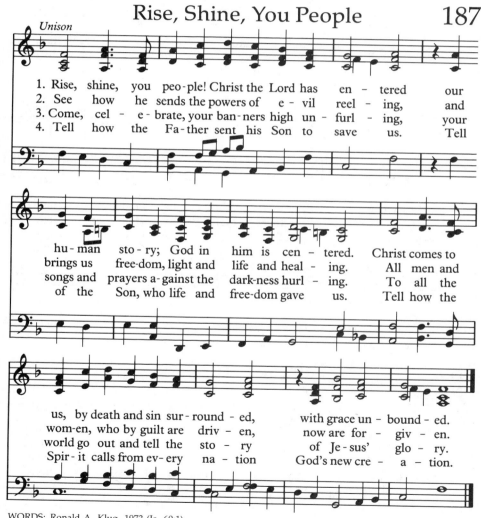

Unison

1. Rise, shine, you peo-ple! Christ the Lord has en - tered our
2. See how he sends the powers of e - vil reel - ing, and
3. Come, cel - e - brate, your ban-ners high un - furl - ing, your
4. Tell how the Fa-ther sent his Son to save us. Tell

hu - man sto - ry; God in him is cen - tered. Christ comes to
brings us free-dom, light and life and heal - ing. All men and
songs and prayers a-gainst the dark-ness hurl - ing. To all the
of the Son, who life and free-dom gave us. Tell how the

us, by death and sin sur - round - ed, with grace un - bound - ed.
wom-en, who by guilt are driv - en, now are for - giv - en.
world go out and tell the sto - ry of Je - sus' glo - ry.
Spir-it calls from ev-ery na - tion God's new cre - a - tion.

WORDS: Ronald A. Klug, 1973 (Is. 60:1)
MUSIC: Dale Wood, 1973

© 1974 Augsburg Publishing House

WOJTKIEWIECZ
11 11 11.5
Alt. tune: CHRISTE SANCTORUM

188 Christ Is the World's Light

1. Christ is the world's light, Christ and none oth - er; born in our
2. Christ is the world's peace, Christ and none oth - er; no one can
3. Christ is the world's life, Christ and none oth - er; sold once for
4. Give God the glo - ry, God and none oth - er; give God the

dark - ness, he be-came our broth - er. If we have seen him,
serve him and de-spise an - oth - er. Who else u - nites us,
sil - ver, mur-dered here, our broth - er; he, who re - deems us,
glo - ry, Spir - it, Son, and Fa - ther; give God the glo - ry,

we have seen the Fa - ther: Glo - ry to God on high!
one in God the Fa - ther? Glo - ry to God on high!
reigns with God the Fa - ther: Glo - ry to God on high!
God with us, my broth - er: Glo - ry to God on high!

WORDS: Fred Pratt Green, 1968
MUSIC: *Paris Antiphoner*, 1681; harm. by David Evans, 1927; alt.

CHRISTE SANCTORUM
10 11 11.6

Words © 1969 Hope Publishing Co.; harm. by permission of Oxford University Press

189 Fairest Lord Jesus

1. Fair - est Lord Je - sus, rul - er of all na - ture,
2. Fair are the mead - ows, fair - er still the wood - lands,
3. Fair is the sun - shine, fair - er still the moon - light,
4. Beau - ti - ful Sav - ior! Lord of all the na - tions!

WORDS: *Münster Gesangbuch*, 1677; trans. Joseph August Seiss, 1873
MUSIC: *Schlesische Volkslieder*, 1842; arr. by Richard Storrs Willis, 1850

ST. ELIZABETH
568.558

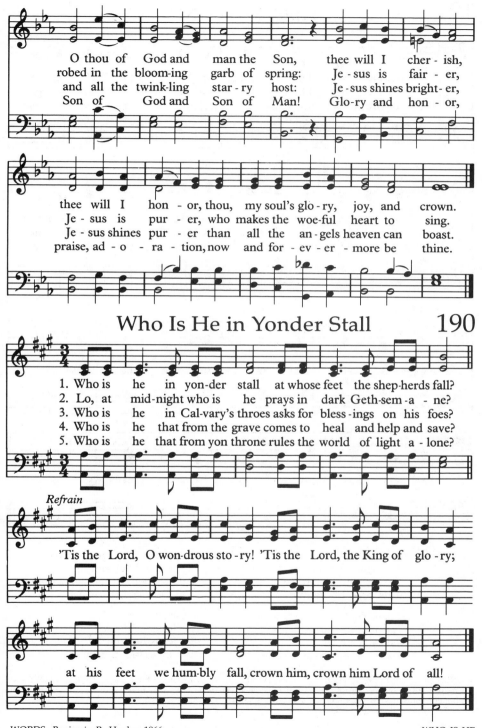

O thou of God and man the Son, thee will I cher-ish,
robed in the bloom-ing garb of spring: Je-sus is fair-er,
and all the twink-ling star-ry host: Je-sus shines bright-er,
Son of God and Son of Man! Glo-ry and hon-or,

thee will I hon-or, thou, my soul's glo-ry, joy, and crown.
Je-sus is pur-er, who makes the woe-ful heart to sing.
Je-sus shines pur-er than all the an-gels heaven can boast.
praise, ad-o-ra-tion, now and for-ev-er-more be thine.

Who Is He in Yonder Stall 190

1. Who is he in yon-der stall at whose feet the shep-herds fall?
2. Lo, at mid-night who is he prays in dark Geth-sem-a-ne?
3. Who is he in Cal-vary's throes asks for bless-ings on his foes?
4. Who is he that from the grave comes to heal and help and save?
5. Who is he that from yon throne rules the world of light a-lone?

Refrain

'Tis the Lord, O won-drous sto-ry! 'Tis the Lord, the King of glo-ry;

at his feet we hum-bly fall, crown him, crown him Lord of all!

WORDS: Benjamin R. Hanby, 1866
MUSIC: Benjamin R. Hanby, 1866

WHO IS HE
77 with Refrain

191 Jesus Loves Me

1. Je - sus loves me! This I know, for the Bi - ble tells me so.
2. Je - sus loves me! This I know, as he loved so long a - go,
3. Je - sus loves me still to - day, walk-ing with me on my way,

Lit - tle ones to him be-long; they are weak, but he is strong.
tak - ing chil-dren on his knee, say-ing, "Let them come to me."
want-ing as a friend to give light and love to all who live.

Refrain

Yes, Je - sus loves me! Yes, Je - sus loves me!

Yes, Je - sus loves me! The Bi - ble tells me so.

CHEROKEE
Tsisa a ki ke yu ha
Koh wel a khi no hih se
Tsu nah sti ka Tsu tse li
u hli ni ki tih ye hno

Tsis a ki ke yu
Tsis a ki ke yu
Tsis a ki ke yu
a khi no hih se ho.

GERMAN
Jesus liebt mich ganz gewiss,
Denn die Bibel sagt mir dies,
Alle Kinder schwach und klein,
Läd't Er herzlich zu sich ein.

Ja, Jesus liebt mich,
Ja, Jesus liebt mich,
Ja, Jesus liebt mich,
Die Bibel sagt mir dies.

WORDS: St. 1 Anna B. Warner, 1860; Sts. 2-3 David Rutherford McGuire; trans.:
Cherokee, Robert Bushyhead, 1962; German, *Psalter und Harfe*, 1876; Japanese
phonetic transcription, Mas Kawashima, 1988; Spanish, *Himnario Metodista*, 1968
MUSIC: William B. Bradbury, 1862

JESUS LOVES ME
77.77 with Refrain

Cherokee phonetic transcription © 1989 The United Methodist Publishing House; Japanese
phonetic transcription © 1989 The United Methodist Publishing House

JAPANESE
Shu ware o aisu,
Shu wa tsuyo kere ba,
Ware yowaku-tomo,
Osore wa araji.

Waga Shu Esu,
Waga Shu Esu,
Waga Shu Esu,
Ware o aisu.

SPANISH
Cris-to me a-ma, bien lo sé.
Su pa-la-bra me ha-ce ver.
Que los ni-ños son de A-quél,
Quien es nues-tro A-mi-go fiel.

Cris-to me a-ma,
Cris-to me a-ma,
La Bi-blia di-ce a-sí.

There's a Spirit in the Air 192

1,7. There's a Spir - it in the air, tell - ing Chris - tians ev - ery - where: Praise the love that Christ re - vealed, liv - ing, work - ing, in our world.

2. Lose your shy - ness, find your tongue; tell the world what God has done. God in Christ has come to stay. Live to - mor - row's life to - day!

3. When be - liev - ers break the bread, when a hun - gry child is fed, praise the love that Christ re - vealed, liv - ing, work - ing, in our world.

4. Still the Spir - it leads the fight, see - ing wrong and set - ting right: God in Christ has come to stay. Live to - mor - row's life to - day!

5. When a stran - ger's not a - lone, when the home - less find a home, praise the love that Christ re - vealed, liv - ing, work - ing, in our world.

6. May the Spir - it fill our praise, guide our thoughts and change our ways: God in Christ has come to stay. Live to - mor - row's life to - day!

WORDS: Brian Wren, 1969
MUSIC: Medieval French melody; harm. by Richard Redhead, 1853
Words © 1979 Hope Publishing Co.

ORIENTIS PARTIBUS
77.77

193 Jesus! the Name High over All

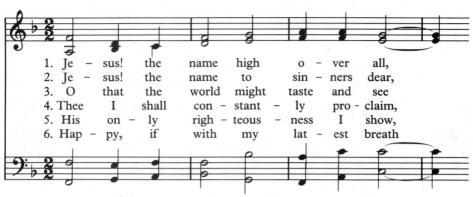

1. Je - sus! the name high o - ver all,
2. Je - sus! the name to sin - ners dear,
3. O that the world might taste and see
4. Thee I shall con - stant - ly pro - claim,
5. His on - ly righ - teous - ness I show,
6. Hap - py, if with my lat - est breath

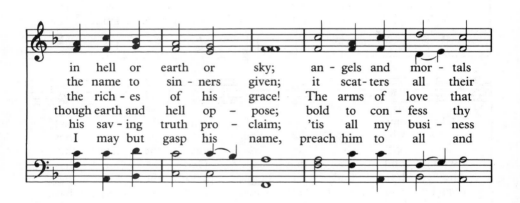

in hell or earth or sky; an - gels and mor - tals
the name to sin - ners given; it scat-ters all their
the rich - es of his grace! The arms of love that
though earth and hell op - pose; bold to con - fess thy
his sav - ing truth pro - claim; 'tis all my busi - ness
I may but gasp his name, preach him to all and

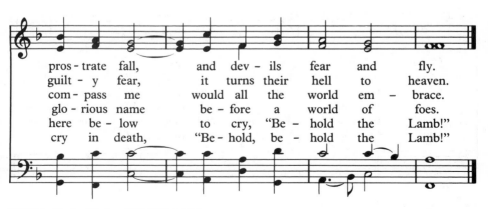

pros - trate fall, and dev - ils fear and fly.
guilt - y fear, it turns their hell to heaven.
com - pass me would all the world em - brace.
glo - rious name be - fore a world of foes.
here be - low to cry, "Be - hold the Lamb!"
cry in death, "Be - hold, be - hold the Lamb!"

WORDS: Charles Wesley, 1749 (Phil. 2:9-11)
MUSIC: Johann Crüger, 1647

GRÄFENBERG
CM

Morning Glory, Starlit Sky

1. Morn - ing glo - ry, star - lit sky, soar - ing
2. O - pen are the gifts of God, gifts of
3. Love that gives, gives ev - er - more, gives with
4. Drained is love in mak - ing full, bound in
5. There - fore he who shows us God help - less
6. Here is God: no mon - arch he, throned in

mu - sic, schol - ars' truth, flight of swal - lows,
love to mind and sense; hid - den is love's
zeal, with ea - ger hands; spares not, keeps not,
set - ting oth - ers free, poor in mak - ing
hangs up - on the tree, and the nails and
eas - y state to reign; here is God, whose

au - tumn leaves, mem - ory's trea - sure, grace of youth:
ag - o - ny, love's en - deav - or, love's ex - pense.
all out - pours, ven - tures all, its all ex - pends.
man - y rich, weak in giv - ing power to be.
crown of thorns tell of what God's love must be.
arms of love, ach - ing, spent, the world sus - tain.

WORDS: W. H. Vanstone, 1980 (1 Cor. 13:7)   MONKLAND
MUSIC: *Geistreiches Gesangbuch*, 1704; arr. by John Lees, 1824; harm. by John B. Wilkes, 1861   77.77

Words by permission of J.W. Shore Music

IN PRAISE OF CHRIST, *see further:*

195

Send Your Word

1. Send your Word, O Lord, like the rain, fall-ing down up-
2. Send your Word, O Lord, like the wind, blow-ing down up-
3. Send your Word, O Lord, like the dew, com-ing gent-ly up-

on the earth. Send your Word. We seek your end-less grace,
on the earth. Send your Word. We seek your won-drous power,
on the hills. Send your Word. We seek your end-less love.

with souls that hun-ger and thirst, sor-row and ag-o-nize.
pure-ness that re-jects all sins, though they per-sist and cling.
For life that suf-fers in strife with ad-ver-si-ties and hurts,

We would all be lost in dark with-out your guid-ing light.
Bring us to com-plete vic-tory; set us all free in-deed.
send your heal-ing power of love; we long for your new world.

WORDS: Yasushige Imakoma, 1965; trans. by Nobuaki Hanaoka, 1983
MUSIC: Shozo Koyama, 1965

MIKOTOBA
Irr.

© 1967 The Hymnal Committee of the United Church of Christ in Japan; trans. © 1983 The United Methodist Publishing House

Come, Thou Long-Expected Jesus 196

1. Come, thou long - ex - pect - ed Je - sus, born to set thy
2. Born thy peo - ple to de - liv - er, born a child and

peo - ple free; from our fears and sins re - lease us,
yet a King, born to reign in us for - ev - er,

let us find our rest in thee. Is-rael's strength and con - so -
now thy gra-cious king-dom bring. By thine own e - ter - nal

la - tion, hope of all the earth thou art; dear de - sire of
spir - it rule in all our hearts a - lone; by thine all suf -

ev - ery na - tion, joy of ev - ery long-ing heart.
fi - cient mer - it, raise us to thy glo-rious throne.

WORDS: Charles Wesley, 1744
MUSIC: Rowland H. Prichard, 1830; harm. from *The English Hymnal*, 1906

HYFRYDOL
87.87 D

197 Ye Who Claim the Faith of Jesus

WORDS: Sts. 1-3 Vincent Stucky Stratton Coles; st. 4 F. Bland Tucker, 1982 (Lk. 1:26-55)
MUSIC: David Hurd, 1983

JULION
87.87.87

Conclusion

My Soul Gives Glory to My God 198

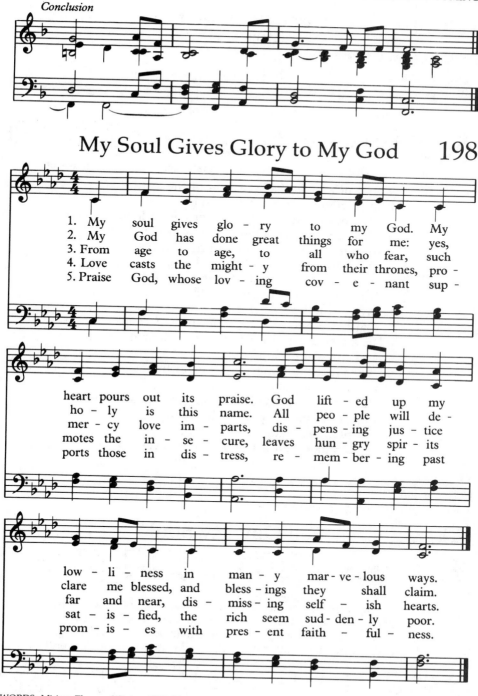

1. My soul gives glo - ry to my God. My
2. My God has done great things for me: yes,
3. From age to age, to all who fear, such
4. Love casts the might - y from their thrones, pro -
5. Praise God, whose lov - ing cov - e - nant sup -

heart pours out its praise. God lift - ed up my
ho - ly is this name. All peo - ple will de -
mer - cy love im - parts, dis - pens - ing jus - tice
motes the in - se - cure, leaves hun - gry spir - its
ports those in dis - tress, re - mem - ber - ing past

low - li - ness in man - y mar - ve - lous ways.
clare me blessed, and bless - ings they shall claim.
far and near, dis - miss - ing self - ish hearts.
sat - is - fied, the rich seem sud - den - ly poor.
prom - is - es with pres - ent faith - ful - ness.

WORDS: Miriam Therese Winter, 1987 (Lk. 1:46b-55)
MUSIC: Wyeth's *Repository of Sacred Music, Part Second*, 1813;
   harm. by Charles H. Webb, 1988

MORNING SONG
CM

199

Canticle of Mary
(Magnificat)

RESPONSE *(Advent & General)*

The glo - ry of the Lord shall be re-vealed; all flesh shall see it to - geth - er.

R My soul proclaims the greatness of the Lord,
my spirit rejoices in God my Savior,
who has looked with favor on me, a lowly servant.
From this day all generations shall call me blessed:
the Almighty has done great things for me
and holy is the name of the Lord,
whose mercy is on those who fear God
from generation to generation.
The arm of the Lord is strong,
and has scattered the proud in their conceit.
God has cast down the mighty from their thrones
and lifted up the lowly.
God has filled the hungry with good things
and sent the rich empty away.
God has come to the aid of Israel, the chosen servant,
remembering the promise of mercy,
the promise made to our forebears,
to Abraham and his children for ever.   R

See Nos. 198 and 200 for metrical versions of this biblical text.

WORDS: Luke 1:46b-55, ICET, rev. ELLC; Response, Isaiah 40:5, adapt.
MUSIC: Richard Proulx

200 *Unison*

Tell Out, My Soul

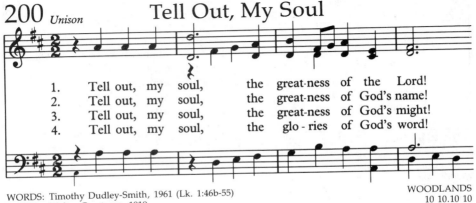

1. Tell out, my soul,   the great-ness of the   Lord!
2. Tell out, my soul,   the great-ness of God's name!
3. Tell out, my soul,   the great-ness of God's might!
4. Tell out, my soul,   the glo - ries of God's word!

WORDS: Timothy Dudley-Smith, 1961 (Lk. 1:46b-55)
MUSIC: Walter Greatorex, 1919

WOODLANDS
10 10.10 10

Un - num - bered bless - ings give my spir - it
Make known God's might, who won - drous deeds has
Powers and do - min - ions lay their glo - ry
Firm is the prom - ise and God's mer - cy

voice; ten - der to me the prom-ise of God's word;
done; God's mer-cy sure, from age to age the same;
by; proud hearts and stub - born wills are put to flight,
sure. Tell out, my soul, the great-ness of the Lord

in God my Sav - ior shall my heart re - joice.
God's ho - ly name, the Lord, the might - y One.
the hun - gry fed, the hum - ble lift - ed high.
to chil - dren's chil - dren and for - ev - er - more!

Advent

201

Merciful God,
you sent your messengers the prophets
to preach repentance and prepare the way for our salvation.
Give us grace to heed their warnings and forsake our sins,
that we may celebrate aright the commemoration of the nativity,
and may await with joy
the coming in glory of Jesus Christ our Redeemer;
who lives and reigns with you and the Holy Spirit,
One God, for ever and ever. **Amen.**

The Book of Common Prayer; alt. by Laurence Hull Stookey

Alt. © 1989 The United Methodist Publishing House

202 People, Look East

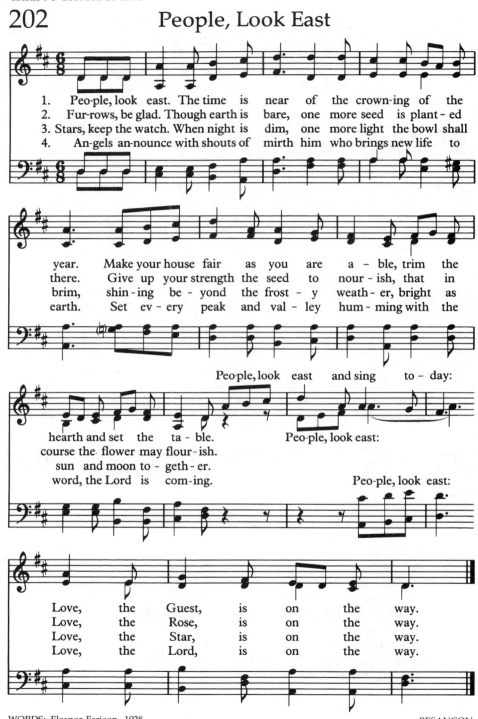

1. Peo-ple, look east. The time is near of the crown-ing of the
2. Fur-rows, be glad. Though earth is bare, one more seed is plant-ed
3. Stars, keep the watch. When night is dim, one more light the bowl shall
4. An-gels an-nounce with shouts of mirth him who brings new life to

year. Make your house fair as you are a – ble, trim the
there. Give up your strength the seed to nour – ish, that in
brim, shin – ing be – yond the frost – y weath – er, bright as
earth. Set ev – ery peak and val – ley hum – ming with the

People, look east and sing to – day:

hearth and set the ta – ble.   People, look east:
course the flower may flour – ish.
sun and moon to – geth – er.
word, the Lord is com – ing.   People, look east:

Love,	the	Guest,	is	on	the	way.
Love,	the	Rose,	is	on	the	way.
Love,	the	Star,	is	on	the	way.
Love,	the	Lord,	is	on	the	way.

WORDS: Eleanor Farjeon, 1928
MUSIC: Trad. French carol; harm. by Martin Shaw, 1928

BESANÇON
87.98.87

Words by permission of David Higham Assoc. Ltd.; harm. by permission of Oxford University Press

Hail to the Lord's Anointed

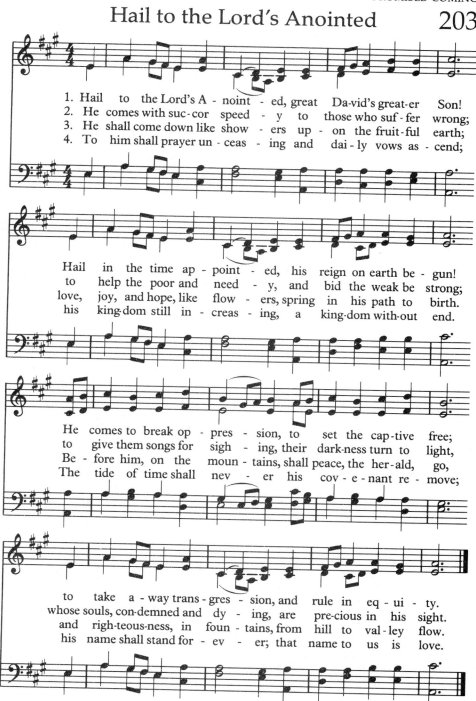

1. Hail to the Lord's A-noint-ed, great Da-vid's great-er Son!
2. He comes with suc-cor speed-y to those who suf-fer wrong;
3. He shall come down like show-ers up-on the fruit-ful earth;
4. To him shall prayer un-ceas-ing and dai-ly vows as-cend;

Hail in the time ap-point-ed, his reign on earth be-gun!
to help the poor and need-y, and bid the weak be strong;
love, joy, and hope, like flow-ers, spring in his path to birth.
his king-dom still in-creas-ing, a king-dom with-out end.

He comes to break op-pres-sion, to set the cap-tive free;
to give them songs for sigh-ing, their dark-ness turn to light,
Be-fore him, on the moun-tains, shall peace, the her-ald, go,
The tide of time shall nev-er his cov-e-nant re-move;

to take a-way trans-gres-sion, and rule in eq-ui-ty.
whose souls, con-demned and dy-ing, are pre-cious in his sight.
and right-teous-ness, in foun-tains, from hill to val-ley flow.
his name shall stand for-ev-er; that name to us is love.

WORDS: James Montgomery, 1821 (Ps. 72)
MUSIC: *Gesangbuch der H. W. k. Hofkapelle*, 1784, alt;
adapt. and harm. by W. H. Monk, 1868

ELLACOMBE
76.76 D

204 Emmanuel, Emmanuel

WORDS: Bob McGee, 1976 (Mt. 1:23)
MUSIC: Bob McGee, 1976

McGEE
Irr.

© 1976 C. A. Music (div. of Christian Artists Corp.)

Canticle of Light and Darkness

RESPONSE 1 *(Advent)*

The peo-ple who walked in dark-ness have seen a great light.

RESPONSE 2 *(Advent, Christmas & General)*

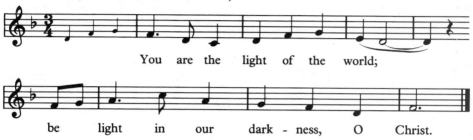

You are the light of the world;

be light in our dark - ness, O Christ.

RESPONSE 3 *(Christmas)*

O come, let us a - dore him, Christ, the Lord.

    R

       We look for light but find darkness,
          for brightness, but walk in gloom.
       We grope like those who have no eyes;
       we stumble at noon as in the twilight. **R**

       If I say, "Let only darkness cover me,
          and the light about me be night,"
       even the darkness is not dark to you,
       the night is bright as the day,
       for darkness is as light with you. **R**

       Blessed be your name, O God, for ever.
          You reveal deep and mysterious things;
       you are light and in you is no darkness.
       Our darkness is passing away
       and already the true light is shining. **R**

WORDS: Isaiah 9:2; 59:9-10; Psalm 139:11-12; Daniel 2:20, 22; 1 John 1:5, adapt. by Alan Luff;
   Response 1, Isaiah 9:2, adapt.; Response 2, Alan Luff; Response 3, trans. by Frederick Oakley and others
MUSIC: Response 1, Carlton R. Young; Response 2, Richard Proulx; Response 3, John F. Wade

Adapt., Responses 1 and 2 © 1989 The United Methodist Publishing House

206 I Want to Walk as a Child of the Light

1. I want to walk as a child of the light.
2. I want to see the bright-ness of God.
3. I'm look-ing for the com-ing of Christ.

I want to fol - low Je - sus.
I want to look at Je - sus.
I want to be with Je - sus.

God set the stars to give light to the world. The
Clear Sun of Righ-teous-ness, shine on my path, and
When we have run with pa-tience the race, we

star of my life is Je - sus.
show me the way to the Fa - ther.
shall know the joy of Je - sus.

WORDS: Kathleen Thomerson, 1966
MUSIC: Kathleen Thomerson, 1966

HOUSTON
10 7.10 8 with Refrain

In him there is no dark-ness at all. The
night and the day are both a – like. The
Lamb is the light of the cit-y of God.
Shine in my heart, Lord Je – sus.

Prepare the Way of the Lord 207

Pre - pare the way of the Lord. Pre - pare the way of the Lord,
and all peo-ple will see the sal - va-tion of our God. Pre -

WORDS: Isaiah 40:3; 52:10
MUSIC: Jacques Berthier and the Community of Taizé, 1984

PREPARE THE WAY
Irr.

Music © 1984 Les Presses de Taizé, by permission of G.I.A. Publications, Inc.

208 Canticle of Zechariah
(Benedictus)

RESPONSE *(Advent & General)*

Hail   to   the Lord's A – noint – ed,   great   Da-vid's great-er   Son.

R

Blessed be the Lord, the God of Israel,
    who has come to set the chosen people free.
The Lord has raised up for us
    a mighty Savior from the house of David.
Through the holy prophets, God promised of old
    to save us from our enemies,
    from the hands of all who hate us;
to show mercy to our forebears
    and to remember the holy covenant.
This was the oath God swore to our father Abraham:
to set us free from the hands of our enemies,
    free to worship without fear,
    holy and righteous in the Lord's sight,
    all the days of our life.   R

And you, child, shall be called the prophet of the Most High,
    for you will go before the Lord to prepare the way,
to give God's people knowledge of salvation
    by the forgiveness of their sins.
In the tender compassion of our God
    the dawn from on high shall break upon us,
to shine on those who dwell in darkness and the shadow of death,
    and to guide our feet into the way of peace.   R

WORDS: Luke 1:68-79; ICET, rev. ELLC; Response, James Montgomery
MUSIC: *Gesangbuch der H. W. k. Hofkapelle*

Blessed Be the God of Israel

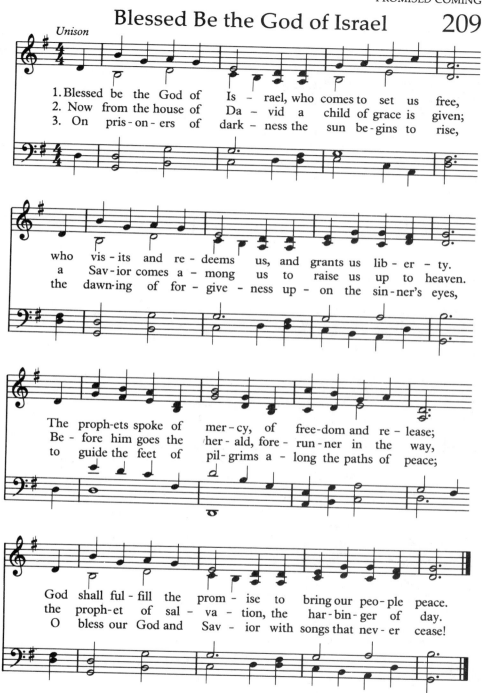

Unison

1. Blessed be the God of Is – rael, who comes to set us free,
2. Now from the house of Da – vid a child of grace is given;
3. On pris – on – ers of dark – ness the sun be – gins to rise,

who vis – its and re – deems us, and grants us lib – er – ty.
a Sav – ior comes a – mong us to raise us up to heaven.
the dawn – ing of for – give – ness up – on the sin – ner's eyes,

The proph – ets spoke of mer – cy, of free – dom and re – lease;
Be – fore him goes the her – ald, fore – run – ner in the way,
to guide the feet of pil – grims a – long the paths of peace;

God shall ful – fill the prom – ise to bring our peo – ple peace.
the proph – et of sal – va – tion, the har – bin – ger of day.
O bless our God and Sav – ior with songs that nev – er cease!

WORDS: Michael Perry, 1973 (Lk. 1:68-79)
MUSIC: Hal H. Hopson, 1983

MERLE'S TUNE
76.76 D

210

Toda la Tierra
(All Earth Is Waiting)

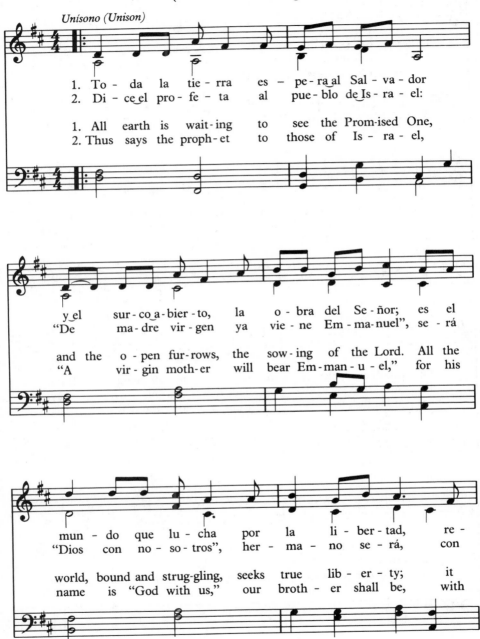

Unísono (Unison)

1. To - da la tie - rra es - pe - ra al Sal - va - dor
2. Di - ce el pro - fe - ta al pue - blo de Is - ra - el:

1. All earth is wait - ing to see the Prom - ised One,
2. Thus says the proph - et to those of Is - ra - el,

y el sur - co a - bier - to, la o - bra del Se - ñor; es el
"De ma - dre vir - gen ya vie - ne Em - ma - nuel", se - rá

and the o - pen fur - rows, the sow - ing of the Lord. All the
"A vir - gin moth - er will bear Em - man - u - el," for his

mun - do que lu - cha por la li - ber - tad, re -
"Dios con no - so - tros", her - ma - no se - rá, con

world, bound and strug - gling, seeks true lib - er - ty; it
name is "God with us," our broth - er shall be, with

WORDS: Catalonian text by Alberto Taulè, 1972; English trans. by
    Gertrude C. Suppe, 1987 (Is. 40:3-5)
MUSIC: Alberto Taulè, 1972; harm. by Skinner Chávez-Melo, 1988

TAULÈ
11 11.12 12

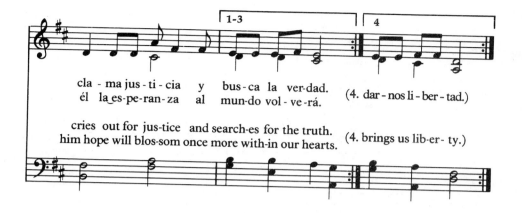

cla - ma jus - ti - cia   y   bus - ca la ver-dad.
él   la_es-pe-ran-za   al   mun-do vol - ve -rá.   (4. dar - nos li - ber - tad.)

cries out for jus-tice and search-es for the truth.
him hope will blos-som once more with-in our hearts.   (4. brings us lib-er- ty.)

3. Montes y valles habrá que preparar;
   nuevos caminos tenemos que trazar.
   Él está ya muy cerca, venidlo_a_encontrar,
   y todas las puertas abrid de par en par.

4. En una cueva Jesús apareció,
   pero_en el mundo está presente hoy.
   Vive_en nuestros hermanos, con ellos está;
   y vuelve de nuevo a darnos libertad.

———

3. Mountains and valleys will have to be made plain;
   open new highways, new highways for the Lord.
   He is now coming closer, so come all and see,
   and open the doorways as wide as wide can be.

4. In lowly stable the Promised One appeared,
   yet, feel his presence throughout the earth today,
   for he lives in all Christians and is with us now;
   again, with his coming he brings us liberty.

211 O Come, O Come, Emmanuel

1. O come, O come, Em - man - u - el, and ran-som cap-tive
2. O come, thou Wis-dom from on high, and or - der all things
3. O come, O come, great Lord of might, who to thy tribes on
4. O come, thou Root of Jes - se's tree, an en-sign of thy

Is - ra - el, that mourns in lone - ly ex - ile here
far and nigh; to us the path of knowl - edge show
Si - nai's height in an-cient times once gave the law
peo - ple be; be - fore thee ru - lers si - lent fall;

Refrain

un - til the Son of God ap - pear.
and cause us in her ways to go.
in cloud and maj-es - ty and awe. Re - joice! Re - joice! Em -
all peo-ples on thy mer - cy call.

man - u - el shall come to thee, O Is - ra - el.

WORDS: 9th cent. Latin; trans. st. 1, 3, 5ab, 6cd, 7ab *The Hymnal,* 1940; st. 2, Henry Sloane Coffin, 1916; st. 4, 5cd, 6ab, 7cd, Laurence Hull Stookey, 1986
MUSIC: 15th cent. French; arr. and harm. by Thomas Helmore, 1854

VENI EMMANUEL
LM with Refrain

Sts. 1, 3, 5ab, 6cd, 7ab © 1940, 1943, renewed 1981 The Church Pension Fund; trans. sts. 4, 5cd, 6ab, 7cd © 1989 The United Methodist Publishing House; antiphons © 1962 Sisters of St. Benedict

5. O come, thou Key of David, come,
and open wide our heavenly home.
The captives from their prison free,
and conquer death's deep misery.
Refrain

6. O come, thou Dayspring, come and cheer
our spirits by thy justice here;
disperse the gloomy clouds of night,
and death's dark shadows put to flight.
Refrain

7. O come, Desire of nations bind
all peoples in one heart and mind.
From dust thou brought us forth to life;
deliver us from earthly strife.
Refrain

Antiphons may be read before and between hymn stanzas.

Antiphon 1   O EMMANUEL, our King and Lawgiver, the Expected of the
nations and their Savior: **Come and save us, O Lord, our God.**

Antiphon 2   O WISDOM, who came forth from the mouth of the Most High,
reaching from end to end, and ordering all things mightily and
sweetly: **Come, and teach us the way of prudence.**

Antiphon 3   O ADONAI and Leader of the house of Israel, who appeared to
Moses in the flames of the bush and gave him the law on Sinai:
Come, and with your outstretched arm redeem us.

Antiphon 4   O ROOT OF JESSE, who stands for an ensign of the people,
before whom kings shall keep silence and to whom the Gentiles
shall make their supplication: **Come, and deliver us and tarry not.**

Antiphon 5   O KEY OF DAVID and Scepter of the house of Israel, who opens
and no one shuts, who shuts and no one opens: **Come, and bring
forth from prison the captive who sits in darkness and in the
shadow of death.**

Antiphon 6   O DAYSPRING, Brightness of the light eternal and Sun of
justice: **Come, and enlighten those who sit in darkness and in the
shadow of death.**

Antiphon 7   O KING OF THE GENTILES and their Desired One, Corner-
stone that makes both one: **Come, and deliver us whom you
formed out of the dust of the earth.**

212 Psalm 24 (King James Version)

RESPONSE 1 *(Advent, All Saints & General)*

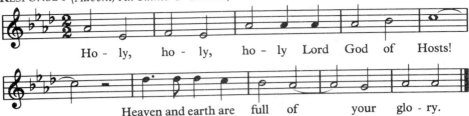

Ho - ly, ho - ly, ho - ly Lord God of Hosts!

Heaven and earth are full of your glo - ry.

RESPONSE 2 *(General)*

Who shall stand in God's ho - ly place?

Those with clean hands and with pure hearts.

R 1 The earth is the Lord's, and the fullness thereof;
the world, and they that dwell therein.

2 For he hath founded it upon the seas,
and established it upon the floods.

3 Who shall ascend into the hill of the Lord?
or who shall stand in his holy place?

4 He that hath clean hands, and a pure heart;
who hath not lifted up his soul unto vanity,
nor sworn deceitfully.

5 He shall receive the blessing from the Lord,
and righteousness from the God of his salvation.

6 This is the generation of them that seek him,
that seek thy face, O Jacob.   R

7 Lift up your heads, O ye gates;
and be ye lifted up, ye everlasting doors;
and the King of glory shall come in.

8 **Who is this King of glory?**
The Lord, strong and mighty,
the Lord, mighty in battle.

9 **Lift up your heads, O ye gates;**
even lift them up, ye everlasting doors;
and the King of glory shall come in.

10 Who is this King of glory?
The Lord of hosts,
he is the King of glory.   R

WORDS: Psalm 24; Response 1, Isaiah 6:3; Response 2, Psalm 24:3b,4a, adapt.
MUSIC: Response 1, Anon.; Response 2, Jane Marshall

Response 2 © 1989 The United Methodist Publishing House

Lift Up Your Heads, Ye Mighty Gates 213

1. Lift up your heads, ye might-y gates; be-hold, the King of glo-ry waits; the King of kings is draw-ing near; the Sav-ior of the world is here!

2. Fling wide the por-tals of your heart; make it a tem-ple, set a-part from earth-ly use for heaven's em-ploy, a-dorned with prayer and love and joy.

3. Re-deem-er, come, with us a-bide; our hearts to thee we o-pen wide; let us thy in-ner pres-ence feel; thy grace and love in us re-veal.

4. Thy Ho-ly Spir-it lead us on un-til our glo-rious goal is won; e-ter-nal praise, e-ter-nal fame be of-fered, Sav-ior, to thy name!

WORDS: Georg Weissel, 1642; trans. by Catherine Winkworth, 1855 (Ps. 24)
MUSIC: *Psalmodia Evangelica*, 1789

TRURO
LM

214 Savior of the Nations, Come

1. Sav - ior of the na - tions, come; Vir - gin's
2. Not by hu - man flesh and blood; by the
3. Won - drous birth! O won - drous Child of the
4. God the Fa - ther is his source, back to
5. Now thy man - ger's ha - lo bright hal - lows

Son, here make thy home! Mar - vel now, O
Spir - it of our God was the Word of
Vir - gin un - de - filed! Hu - man and di -
God he runs his course; down to death and
night with new - born light; let no night this

heaven and earth, that the Lord chose such a birth.
God made flesh, wom - an's off - spring, pure and fresh.
vine in one, ea - ger now his race to run!
hell de - scends, God's high throne he re - as - cends.
light sub - due, let our faith shine ev - er new.

WORDS: Sts. 1, 2 Martin Luther, 1523, trans. by
William Reynolds, 1851; st. 3-5 Martin L. Seltz, 1969
MUSIC: *Enchiridion Oder Handbüchlein*, 1524; harm. J. S. Bach; alt.

NUN KOMM, DER HEIDEN HEILAND
77.77

Sts. 3-5 © 1969 Concordia Publishing House

To a Maid Engaged to Joseph

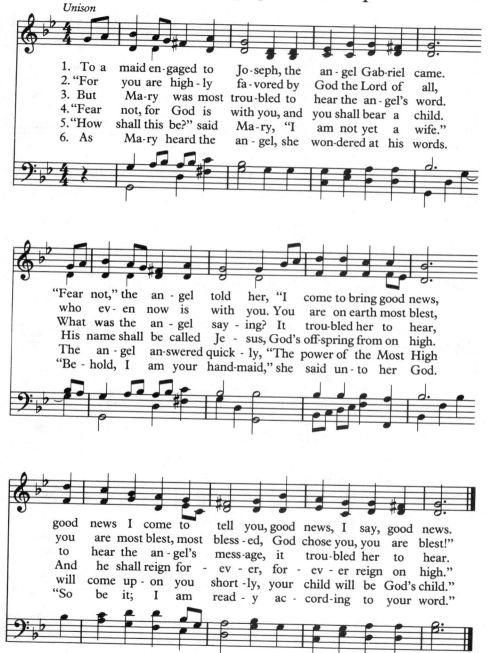

1. To a maid en-gaged to Jo-seph, the an-gel Gab-riel came.
2. "For you are high-ly fa-vored by God the Lord of all,
3. But Ma-ry was most trou-bled to hear the an-gel's word.
4. "Fear not, for God is with you, and you shall bear a child.
5. "How shall this be?" said Ma-ry, "I am not yet a wife."
6. As Ma-ry heard the an-gel, she won-dered at his words.

"Fear not," the an-gel told her, "I come to bring good news,
who ev-en now is with you. You are on earth most blest,
What was the an-gel say-ing? It trou-bled her to hear,
His name shall be called Je-sus, God's off-spring from on high.
The an-gel an-swered quick-ly, "The power of the Most High
"Be-hold, I am your hand-maid," she said un-to her God.

good news I come to tell you, good news, I say, good news.
you are most blest, most bless-ed, God chose you, you are blest!"
to hear the an-gel's mess-age, it trou-bled her to hear.
And he shall reign for-ev-er, for-ev-er reign on high."
will come up-on you short-ly, your child will be God's child."
"So be it; I am read-y ac-cord-ing to your word."

WORDS: Gracia Grindal, 1983 (Lk. 1:26-38)
MUSIC: Rusty Edwards, 1983

ANNUNCIATION
76.76.76

216   Lo, How a Rose E'er Blooming

1. Lo, how a Rose e'er bloom-ing from ten-der stem hath
2. I - sa - iah 'twas fore - told it, the Rose I have in
3. O Flower, whose fra-grance ten - der with sweet-ness fills the

sprung! Of Jes - se's lin - eage com-ing, as those of old have
mind; with Ma - ry we be - hold it, the Vir - gin Moth - er
air, dis - pel in glo-rious splen-dor the dark-ness ev - ery -

sung. It came, a flow-er - et bright, a - mid the
kind. To show God's love a - right, she bore to
where. True man yet ver - y God, from sin and

cold of win - ter, when half spent was the night.
us a Sav - ior, when half spent was the night.
death now save us, and share our ev - ery load.

WORDS: Sts. 1-2, 15th cent. German; trans. by Theodore Baker, 1894; st. 3 from
The Hymnal, 1940 (Is. 35:1-2)
MUSIC: *Alte Catholische Geistliche Kirchengesäng*, 1599; harm. by Michael Praetorius, 1609

ES IST EIN ROS
76.76.676

St. 3 © 1940, 1943, renewed 1971 The Church Pension Fund

PROMISED COMING, *see further:*

720   Wake, Awake, for Night Is Flying

Away in a Manger

1. A - way in a man - ger, no crib for a bed,
2. The cat - tle are low - ing, the ba - by a - wakes,
3. Be near me, Lord Je - sus, I ask thee to stay

the lit - tle Lord Je - sus laid down his sweet head.
but lit - tle Lord Je - sus, no cry - ing he makes;
close by me for - ev - er, and love me, I pray;

The stars in the sky looked down where he lay,
I love thee, Lord Je - sus, look down from the sky
bless all the dear chil - dren in thy ten - der care,

the lit - tle Lord Je - sus, a - sleep on the hay.
and stay by my cra - dle till morn - ing is nigh.
and fit us for heav - en to live with thee there.

WORDS: Anon. (Lk. 2:7)
MUSIC: James R. Murray, 1887

AWAY IN A MANGER
11 11.11 11

218 It Came upon the Midnight Clear

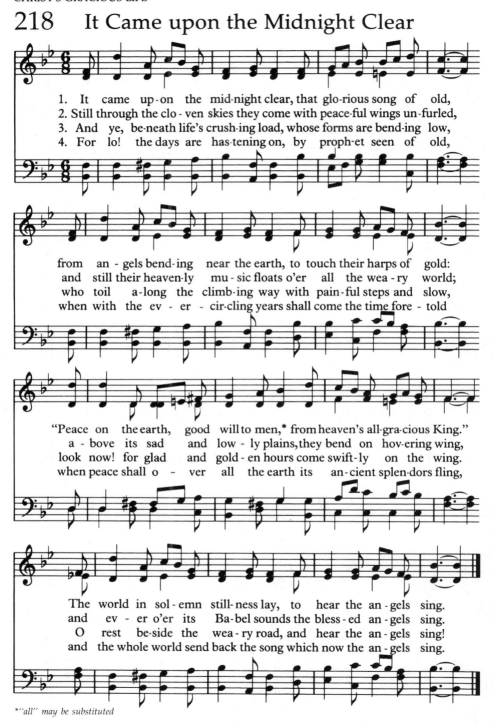

1. It came up-on the mid-night clear, that glo-rious song of old,
2. Still through the clo - ven skies they come with peace-ful wings un-furled,
3. And ye, be-neath life's crush-ing load, whose forms are bend-ing low,
4. For lo! the days are has-tening on, by proph-et seen of old,

from an - gels bend-ing near the earth, to touch their harps of gold:
and still their heaven-ly mu - sic floats o'er all the wea - ry world;
who toil a-long the climb-ing way with pain-ful steps and slow,
when with the ev - er - cir-cling years shall come the time fore - told

"Peace on the earth, good will to men,* from heaven's all-gra-cious King."
a - bove its sad and low - ly plains, they bend on hov-ering wing,
look now! for glad and gold - en hours come swift-ly on the wing.
when peace shall o - ver all the earth its an-cient splen-dors fling,

The world in sol - emn still-ness lay, to hear the an - gels sing.
and ev - er o'er its Ba-bel sounds the bless-ed an - gels sing.
O rest be-side the wea - ry road, and hear the an - gels sing!
and the whole world send back the song which now the an - gels sing.

*"all" may be substituted

WORDS: Edmund H. Sears, 1849 (Lk. 2:8-14)
MUSIC: Richard Storrs Willis, 1850

CAROL
CMD

What Child Is This

1. What child is this who, laid to rest, on Ma - ry's lap is sleep - ing? Whom an - gels greet with an - thems sweet, while shep - herds watch are keep - ing?

2. Why lies he in such mean es - tate where ox and ass are feed - ing? Good Chris - tians, fear, for sin - ners here the si - lent Word is plead - ing.

3. So bring him in - cense, gold, and myrrh, come, peas - ant, king, to own him; the King of kings sal - va - tion brings, let lov - ing hearts en - throne him.

Refrain

This, this is Christ the King, whom shep-herds guard and an - gels sing; haste, haste to bring him laud, the babe, the son of Ma - ry.

WORDS: William C. Dix, 1865 (Lk. 2:6-20; Mt. 2:1-12)
MUSIC: 16th cent. English melody

GREENSLEEVES
87.87 with Refrain

220 Angels from the Realms of Glory

1. An - gels from the realms of glo - ry, wing your flight o'er
2. Shep-herds, in the field a - bid - ing, watch-ing o'er your
3. Sa - ges, leave your con - tem- pla - tions, bright - er vi - sions
4. Saints, be - fore the al - tar bend-ing, watch-ing long in

all the earth; ye who sang cre - a - tion's sto - ry
flocks by night, God with us is now re - sid - ing;
beam a - far; seek the great De - sire of na - tions;
hope and fear; sud - den - ly the Lord, de-scend - ing,

Refrain

now pro - claim Mes - si - ah's birth:
yon - der shines the in - fant light: Come and wor - ship,
ye have seen his na - tal star:
in his tem - ple shall ap - pear:

come and wor - ship, wor - ship Christ, the new - born King.

WORDS: James Montgomery, 1816 (Lk. 2:8-20; Mt. 2:1-12; Mal. 3:1)
MUSIC: Henry T. Smart, 1867

REGENT SQUARE
87.87.87

In the Bleak Midwinter

1. In the bleak mid - win -ter, frost - y wind made moan,
2. Our God, heaven can-not hold him, nor earth sus - tain;
3. An - gels and arch - an - gels may have gath-ered there,
4. What can I give him, poor as I am?

earth stood hard as i - ron, wa - ter like a stone;
heaven and earth shall flee a - way when he comes to reign.
cher - u - bim and ser - a-phim throng - ed the air;
If I were a shep - herd, I would bring a lamb;

snow had fall - en, snow on snow, snow on snow,
In the bleak mid - win - ter a sta - ble place suf - ficed the
but his moth- er on - ly, in her maid-en bliss,
if I were a Wise Man, I would do my part; yet

in the bleak mid - win - ter, long a - go.
Lord God Al - might - y, Je - sus Christ.
wor-shiped the be - lov - ed with a kiss.
what I can I give him: give my heart.

WORDS: Christina G. Rossetti, 1872 (Lk. 2:8-14)
MUSIC: Gustav Holst, 1906

CRANHAM
Irr.

222

Niño Lindo
(Child So Lovely)

Estribillo, Unísono (Refrain, Unison)

Ni - ño lin - do, an - te ti me rin - do,
Child so love - ly, here I kneel be - fore you,

ni - ño lin - do, e - res tú mi Dios.
child so love - ly, you are Christ my God.

Ni - ño lin - do, an - te ti me rin - do;
Child so love - ly, here I kneel be - fore you,

1.

ni - ño lin - do, e - res tú mi Dios.
child so love - ly, you are Christ the Lord.

WORDS: Trad. Venezuelan; trans. by George Lockwood, 1987
MUSIC: Trad. Venezuelan melody

CARACAS
Irr. with Refrain

Trans. © 1989 The United Methodist Publishing House

Fine

2. (𝄐)

Dios.

Lord.

1. E - sa tu her-mo - su - ra; e - se tu can -
2. La vi - da, bien mí - o, y el al - ma tam -
3. A - diós, tier-no in - fan - te, a - diós, ni - ño, a -

1. You have heav-en's beau - ty, and God's pu - ri
2. All my life, my dar - ling, and my soul, as
3. Adi - os, ten - der ba - by, adi - os, child, adi -

dor, el al - ma me ro - ba, el al - ma me
bién; te o-frez - co, gus - to - so, te o-frez - co, gus -
diós. A - diós, dul-ce a - man - te, a - diós, dul-ce, a -

ty, steal-ing my de - vo - tion, steal-ing my af -
well; this is what I of - fer, of - fer joy-ous-
os; adi - os, sweet be - lov - ed, adi - os, sweet be -

D.C.

ro - ba, me ro ba el a - mor.
to - so, ren - di do a tus pies.
man - te, a - diós, ni - ño, a - diós.

fec - tion, steal - ing all my soul.
ly, fall - ing at your feet.
lov - ed; adi - os, child, adi - os.

223 Break Forth, O Beauteous Heavenly Light

1. Break forth, O beau-teous heaven-ly light, and ush-er in the
2. This night of won-der, night of joy, was born the Christ, our
3. Come, dear-est child, in - to our hearts, and leave your crib be -

morn - ing; O shep-herds, shrink not with af-fright, but
broth - er; he comes, not might-y to de-stroy, to
hind you! Let this be where the new life starts for

hear the an-gel's warn - ing. This child, now weak in
bid us love each oth - er. How could he quit his
all who seek and find you. To you the hon-or,

in - fan-cy, our con - fi-dence and joy shall be, the
king - ly state for such a world of greed and hate? What
thanks, and praise, for all your gifts this time of grace; come,

power of Sa-tan break - ing, our peace e - ter-nal mak - ing.
deep hu-mil - i - a - tion se-cured the world's sal-va - tion!
con-quer and de - liv - er this world, and us, for - ev - er.

WORDS: Johann Rist, 1641; st. 1 trans. by John Troutbeck, ca. 1885;
sts. 2, 3 by Fred Pratt Green, 1986 (Lk. 2:8-14)
MUSIC: Johann Schop, 1641; harm. by J. S. Bach, 1734

ERMUNTRE DICH
87.87.88.77

Trans. st. 2, 3 © 1989 Hope Publishing Co.

Good Christian Friends, Rejoice 224

1., 2., 3. Good Chris-tian friends, re - joice with heart and soul and

voice; give ye heed to what we say: News, news!
voice; now ye hear of end - less bliss: News, news!
voice; now ye need not fear the grave: News, news!

Je - sus Christ is born to - day! Ox and ass be -
Je - sus Christ was born for this! He hath o - pened
Jē - sus Christ was born to save! Calls you one and

fore him bow, and he is in the man - ger now.
heav - en's door, and ye are blest for - ev - er - more.
calls you all to gain his ev - er - last - ing hall.

Christ is born to - day, Christ is born to - day!
Christ was born for this, Christ was born for this!
Christ was born to save, Christ was born to save!

WORDS: 14th cent. Latin; trans. by John Mason Neale, 1855
MUSIC: German melody; harm. by Gary Alan Smith, 1988

IN DULCI JUBILO
66.727.78.55

225

Canticle of Simeon
(Nunc Dimittis)

RESPONSE *(Christmas & General)*

Lord, ev-ery na-tion on earth shall a - dore you.

R

Lord, now let your servant go in peace;
your word has been fulfilled:
my own eyes have seen the salvation
which you have prepared in the presence of all people,
a light to reveal you to the nations
and the glory of your people Israel. R

See No. 226 for a metrical setting of this ancient text.

WORDS: Luke 2:29-32, ICET, rev. ELLC; Response, Psalm 72:11, ICEL
MUSIC: Richard Proulx

Music © 1975 G.I.A. Publications, Inc.

226 My Master, See, the Time Has Come

1. My Mas-ter, see, the time has come to give your ser-vant leave
2. For I have seen sal - va-tion, Lord. Now may the whole world see

to go in peace, long wait-ed for, your prom-ise now ful - filled.
that light which is your Is-rael's boast en - light-ening ev-ery land.

WORDS: Luke 2:29-32   MORNING SONG
MUSIC: Wyeth's *Repository of Sacred Music, Part Second,* 1813;   CM
  harm. by Charles H. Webb, 1988

Words by permission of A P Watt Ltd.; harm. © 1989 The United Methodist Publishing House

The Friendly Beasts

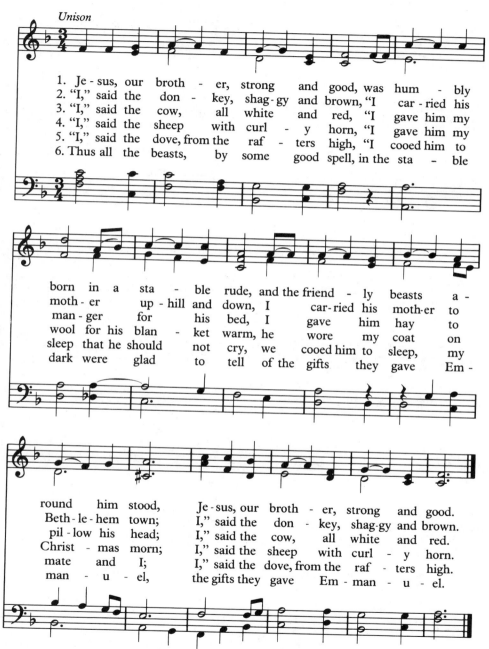

Unison

1. Je - sus, our broth - er, strong and good, was hum - bly
2. "I," said the don - key, shag - gy and brown, "I car - ried his
3. "I," said the cow, all white and red, "I gave him my
4. "I," said the sheep with curl - y horn, "I gave him my
5. "I," said the dove, from the raf - ters high, "I cooed him to
6. Thus all the beasts, by some good spell, in the sta - ble

born in a sta - ble rude, and the friend - ly beasts a -
moth - er up - hill and down, I car - ried his moth - er to
man - ger for his bed, I gave him hay to
wool for his blan - ket warm, he wore my coat on
sleep that he should not cry, we cooed him to sleep, my
dark were glad to tell of the gifts they gave Em -

round him stood, Je - sus, our broth - er, strong and good.
Beth - le - hem town; I," said the don - key, shag - gy and brown.
pil - low his head; I," said the cow, all white and red.
Christ - mas morn; I," said the sheep with curl - y horn.
mate and I; I," said the dove, from the raf - ters high.
man - u - el, the gifts they gave Em - man - u - el.

WORDS: 12th cent. French carol; trans. anon.; (Lk. 2:7)
MUSIC: Medieval French melody; harm. by Carlton R. Young, 1987

ORIENTIS PARTIBUS
Irr.

228

He Is Born
(Il Est Né)

Refrain (Unison)

He is born, the ho-ly Child, play the o-boe and
Il est né, le di-vin En-fant, jou-ez haut-bois rè-son-

bag-pipes mer-ri-ly! He is born, the ho-ly Child,
nez mu-set-tes! Il est né, le di-vin En-fant,

Fine   *Optional S.A.*

sing we all of the Sav-ior mild.
chan-tons tous son a-vè-ne-ment!

1. Thru long a-ges
2. O how love-ly,
3. Je-sus, Lord of

of the past, proph-ets have fore-told his com-ing;
O how pure is this per-fect child of heav-en;
all the world, com-ing as a child a-mong us,

WORDS: Trad. 19th cent. French carol; trans. anon.
MUSIC: 18th cent. French carol; harm. by Carlton R. Young, 1988

IL EST NÉ
78.77 with Refrain

D.C.

thru long a-ges of the past, now the time has come at last!
O how love-ly, O how pure, gra-cious gift to hu-man-kind!
Je-sus, Lord of all the world, grant to us thy heaven-ly peace.

Infant Holy, Infant Lowly 229

Unison

1. In-fant ho-ly, in-fant low-ly, for his bed a cat-tle
2. Flocks were sleep-ing, shep-herds keep-ing vig-il till the morn-ing

stall; ox-en low-ing, lit-tle know-ing, Christ the babe is Lord of
new saw the glo-ry, heard the sto-ry, tid-ings of a gos-pel

all. Swift are wing-ing an-gels sing-ing, no-els ring-ing, tid-ings
true. Thus re-joic-ing, free from sor-row, prais-es voic-ing, greet the

Interlude, Ending

bring-ing: Christ the babe is Lord of all.
mor-row: Christ the babe was born for you.

WORDS: Polish carol; trans. by Edith M. G. Reed, 1925 (Lk. 2:6-20)
MUSIC: Polish carol; arr. by Edith M. G. Reed, 1926; harm. by Austin C. Lovelace, 1964

W ZLOBIE LEZY
447.447.44447

Harm. © 1965 Abingdon Press

230 O Little Town of Bethlehem

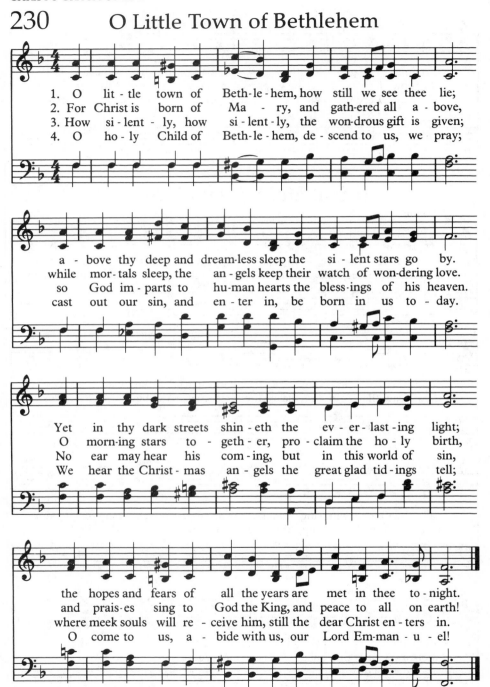

1. O lit-tle town of Beth-le-hem, how still we see thee lie;
2. For Christ is born of Ma - ry, and gath-ered all a - bove,
3. How si - lent - ly, how si - lent-ly, the won-drous gift is given;
4. O ho - ly Child of Beth-le-hem, de - scend to us, we pray;

a - bove thy deep and dream-less sleep the si - lent stars go by.
while mor-tals sleep, the an - gels keep their watch of won-dering love.
so God im - parts to hu-man hearts the bless-ings of his heaven.
cast out our sin, and en - ter in, be born in us to - day.

Yet in thy dark streets shin - eth the ev - er - last - ing light;
O morn-ing stars to - geth - er, pro - claim the ho - ly birth,
No ear may hear his com - ing, but in this world of sin,
We hear the Christ - mas an - gels the great glad tid - ings tell;

the hopes and fears of all the years are met in thee to - night.
and prais-es sing to God the King, and peace to all on earth!
where meek souls will re - ceive him, still the dear Christ en - ters in.
O come to us, a - bide with us, our Lord Em-man - u - el!

WORDS: Phillips Brooks, ca. 1868
MUSIC: Lewis H. Redner, 1868

ST. LOUIS
86.86.76.86

Alt. tune: FOREST GREEN

Christmas

Eternal God,
by the birth of Jesus Christ you gave yourself to the world.
Grant that, being born in our hearts,
    he may save us from all our sins,
        and restore within us the image and likeness of our Creator,
to whom be everlasting praise and glory,
    world without end. **Amen.**

The Book of Hymns, 1966; alt. by Laurence Hull Stookey
Alt. © 1989 The United Methodist Publishing House

When Christmas Morn Is Dawning   232

1. When Christ-mas morn is dawn-ing, I wish that I could be
2. How kind of you, our Sav-ior, for us to come to earth.
3. We need you, O Lord Je-sus, to be our dear-est friend.

there by the man-ger - cra - dle, God's Son, new-born, to see.
O may we not by sin - ning, de - spise your low -ly birth.
Your love will guard and guide us and keep us to life's end.

There by the man-ger - cra - dle, God's Son, new-born, to see.
O may we not by sin - ning, de - spise your low - ly birth.
Your love will guard and guide us and keep us to life's end.

WORDS: Attr. to Elisabeth Ehrenborg-Posse, 1856; trans. by
Joel W. Lundeen, 1978 (Lk. 2:7)
MUSIC: German folk tune

WIR HATTEN GEBAUET
76.76.76

Trans. © 1978 Lutheran Book of Worship

233

En el Frío Invernal
(Cold December Flies Away)

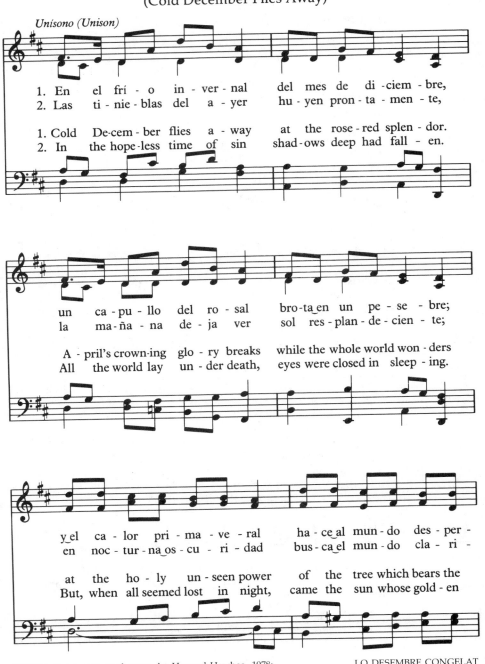

Unísono (Unison)

1. En el frí - o in - ver - nal del mes de di - ciem - bre,
2. Las ti - nie - blas del a - yer hu - yen pron - ta - men - te,

1. Cold De-cem-ber flies a - way at the rose-red splen - dor.
2. In the hope-less time of sin shad-ows deep had fall - en.

un ca - pu - llo del ro - sal bro-ta en un pe - se - bre;
la ma - ña - na de - ja ver sol res - plan - de - cien - te;

A - pril's crown-ing glo - ry breaks while the whole world won - ders
All the world lay un - der death, eyes were closed in sleep - ing.

y el ca - lor pri - ma - ve - ral ha - ce al mun - do des - per -
en noc - tur - na os - cu - ri - dad bus - ca el mun - do cla - ri -

at the ho - ly un - seen power of the tree which bears the
But, when all seemed lost in night, came the sun whose gold - en

WORDS: Catalonian carol; trans. by Howard Hawhee, 1978;
   Spanish by Skinner Chávez-Melo, 1987 (Is. 35:1-2)
MUSIC: Catalonian carol; harm. by Skinner Chávez-Melo, 1987

LO DESEMBRE CONGELAT
Irr.

tar, ¡qué fra - gan - te_o - lor de tan be - lla flor! yo_e-sa ro-, yo_e-sa
dad, ¡qué fe - li - ci - dad es - ta Na -vi - dad! ya la lu-, ya la

flower. On the bless-ed tree blooms the red-dest flower, on the tree blooms the
light brings un-end-ing joy, brings the end-less joy of our hope, high-est

ro-, yo_e-sa ro - sa_an-he - lo del jar - dín del cie - lo.
lu-, ya la luz di - vi - na al mun - do_i- lu - mi - na.

rose here in love's own gar - den, full and strong in glo - ry.
hope, of our hope's bright dawn-ing, Son be -loved of heav - en.

3. Va_el capullo_a florecer rosa blanca_y pura,
   su fragancia va_a_ofrecer a toda criatura;
   ese_aroma sin igual nueva vida da_al mortal,
   es de Dios el don, sumo galardón
   que al mun-, que al mun-,
   que al mundo_ha dado, es su Hijo_amado.

   ———

3. Now the bud has come to bloom, and the world awakens.
   In the lily's purest flower dwells a wondrous fragrance.
   And it spreads to all the earth from the moment of its birth;
   and its beauty lives. In the flower it lives,
   in the flower, and it spreads
   in its heavenly brightness, sweet perfume delightful.

234 O Come, All Ye Faithful

1. O come, all ye faith-ful, joy-ful and tri - um-phant, O
1. A - des - te, fi - de - les, lae - ti tri - um - phan - tes; ve -
2. True God of true God, Light from Light E - ter - nal,
3. Sing, choirs of an - gels, sing in ex - ul - ta - tion; O
* 4. See how the shep-herds, sum-moned to his cra - dle,

come ye, O come ye, to Beth - le - hem.
ni - te, ve - ni - te in Beth - le - hem.
lo, he shuns not the Vir - gin's womb;
sing, all ye cit - i - zens of heaven a - bove!
leav - ing their flocks, draw nigh to gaze;

Come and be - hold him, born the King of an - gels;
Na - tum vi - de - te Re - gem an - ge - lor - um.
Son of the Fa - ther, be - got - ten, not cre - at - ed;
Glo - ry to God, all glo - ry in the high - est;
we too will thith - er bend our joy - ful foot - steps;

Refrain

O come, let us a - dore him, O come, let us a - dore him,
Ve - ni - te a - do - re - mus, ve - ni - te a - do - re - mus,

O come, let us a - dore him, Christ the Lord.
ve - ni - te a - do - re - mus, Do - mi - num.

*5. Child, for us sinners
poor and in the manger,
we would embrace thee
with love and awe.
Who would not love thee,
loving us so dearly?
Refrain

** 6. Yea, Lord, we greet thee,
born this happy morning,
Jesus, to thee be
all glory given.
Word of the Father,
now in flesh appearing:
Refrain

*May be omitted.
**For Christmas Eve/Day

WORDS: John F. Wade, ca. 1743; trans. by Frederick Oakeley, 1841, and others
MUSIC: John F. Wade, ca. 1743; harm. from *Collections of Motetts or Antiphons*, 1792

ADESTE FIDELES
Irr.

Rock-a-Bye, My Dear Little Boy   235

1. Rock - a - bye, my dear lit - tle boy, dear lit - tle boy,
2. Lit - tle Je - sus, In - fant Di - vine, In - fant Di - vine,

won - der of won - ders, my bless - ing and joy; slum - ber as I
one with the Fa - ther, yet born to be mine; as I rock you

gen - tly hold you, let my ten - der love en - fold you; gift of God to
calm - ly sleep - ing, an - gel guards their watch are keep - ing; pre - cious child, one

me and the world, here in my arms lies so peace - ful - ly curled.
day we shall see what love has des - tined for you and for me.

WORDS: Czech carol; trans. by Jaroslav J. Vajda, 1987
MUSIC: Czech carol; melody collected by Martin Shaw, 1928

ROCKING
Irr.

Trans. © 1987 Jaroslav J. Vajda; music by permission of Oxford University Press

236 While Shepherds Watched Their Flocks

1.. While shep-herds watched their flocks by night, all seat - ed
2. "Fear not!" said he, for might - y dread had seized their
3. "To you, in Da - vid's town, this day is born of
4. "The heaven-ly babe you there shall find to hu - man
5. Thus spake the ser - aph and forth - with ap - peared a
6. "All glo - ry be to God on high, and to the

on the ground, the an - gel of the Lord came down,
trou - bled mind. "Glad tid - ings of great joy I bring
Da - vid's line a Sav - ior, who is Christ the Lord,
view dis - played, all mean - ly wrapped in swath-ing bands,
shin - ing throng of an - gels prais - ing God on high,
earth be peace; good will hence-forth from heaven to earth

and glo - ry shone a - round, and glo - ry shone a - round.
to all of hu - man - kind, to all of hu - man - kind.
and this shall be the sign, and this shall be the sign:
and in a man - ger laid, and in a man - ger laid."
who thus ad - dressed their song, who thus ad - dressed their song:
be - gin and nev - er cease, be - gin and nev - er cease!"

WORDS: Nahum Tate, 1700 (Lk. 2:8-14)
MUSIC: *Harmonia Sacra*, 1812; arr. from G. F. Handel, 1728

CHRISTMAS
CM
Alt. tune: WINCHESTER OLD

Sing We Now of Christmas

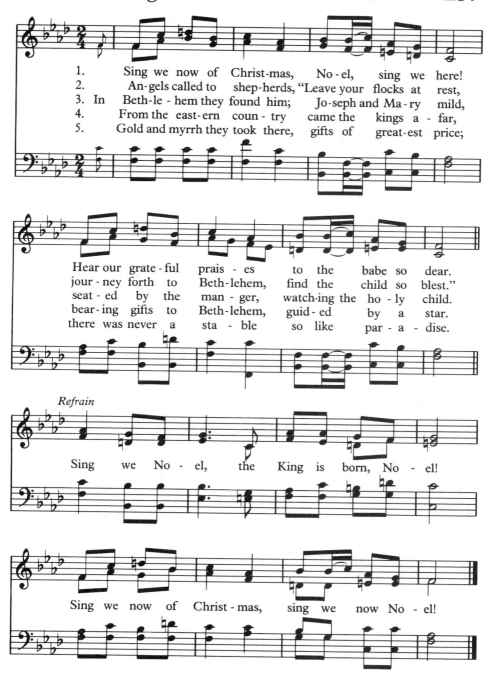

1. Sing we now of Christ-mas, No - el, sing we here!
2. An - gels called to shep-herds, "Leave your flocks at rest,
3. In Beth-le - hem they found him; Jo-seph and Ma - ry mild,
4. From the east-ern coun - try came the kings a - far,
5. Gold and myrrh they took there, gifts of great-est price;

Hear our grate - ful prais - es to the babe so dear.
jour - ney forth to Beth-lehem, find the child so blest."
seat - ed by the man - ger, watch-ing the ho - ly child.
bear - ing gifts to Beth-lehem, guid - ed by a star.
there was never a sta - ble so like par - a - dise.

Refrain

Sing we No - el, the King is born, No - el!

Sing we now of Christ - mas, sing we now No - el!

WORDS: Trad. French carol (Lk. 2:8-20; Mt. 2:1-12)
MUSIC: Trad. French carol; harm. by Martin Shaw, 1928

FRENCH CAROL
11 10.10 11

Harm. by permission of Oxford University Press

238 Angels We Have Heard on High

1. An-gels we have heard on high sweet-ly sing-ing o'er the plains,
2. Shep-herds, why this ju - bi - lee? Why your joy - ous strains pro-long?
3. Come to Beth-le - hem and see Christ whose birth the an - gels sing;
4. See him in a man - ger laid, whom the choirs of an - gels praise;

and the moun-tains in re - ply ech - o - ing their joy - ous strains.
What the glad-some tid - ings be which in - spire your heaven- ly song?
come, a - dore on bend - ed knee, Christ the Lord, the new - born King.
Ma - ry, Jo - seph, lend your aid, while our hearts in love we raise.

Refrain

Glo - - - - - - ri - a,

in ex - cel - sis De - o! Glo - - -

WORDS: Trad. French carol; trans. *Crown of Jesus*, 1862, alt. (Lk. 2:6-20)
MUSIC: French carol melody; arr. by Edward Shippen Barnes, 1937;
   harm. by Austin C. Lovelace, 1964

GLORIA
77.77 with Refrain

Harm. © 1964 Abingdon Press

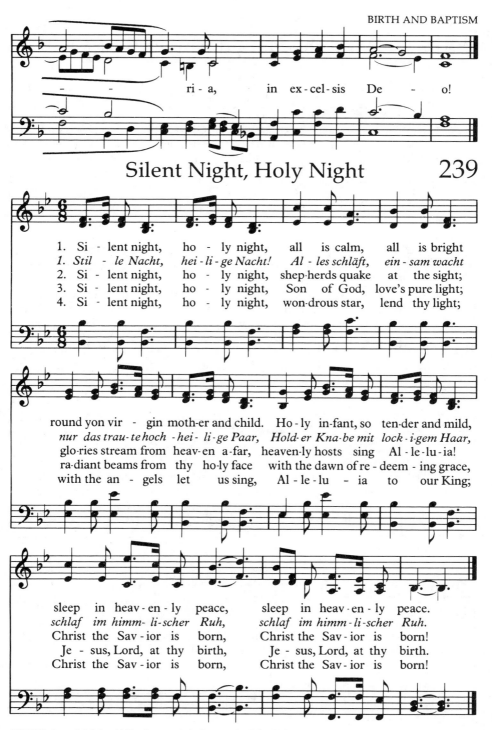

Silent Night, Holy Night 239

1. Si - lent night, ho - ly night, all is calm, all is bright
1. *Stil - le Nacht, hei - li - ge Nacht! Al - les schläft, ein - sam wacht*
2. Si - lent night, ho - ly night, shep·herds quake at the sight;
3. Si - lent night, ho - ly night, Son of God, love's pure light;
4. Si - lent night, ho - ly night, won·drous star, lend thy light;

round yon vir - gin moth·er and child. Ho - ly in·fant, so ten·der and mild,
nur das trau·te hoch ·hei· li -ge Paar, Hold· er Kna·be mit lock·i·gem Haar,
glo·ries stream from heav·en a·far, heaven·ly hosts sing Al - le·lu·ia!
ra·diant beams from thy ho·ly face with the dawn of re - deem - ing grace,
with the an - gels let us sing, Al - le·lu - ia to our King;

sleep in heav - en·ly peace, sleep in heav·en·ly peace.
schlaf im himm- li-scher Ruh, schlaf im himm - li-scher Ruh.
Christ the Sav - ior is born, Christ the Sav - ior is born!
Je - sus, Lord, at thy birth, Je - sus, Lord, at thy birth.
Christ the Sav - ior is born, Christ the Sav - ior is born!

WORDS: Joseph Mohr, 1818, alt.; sts. 1, 2, 3 trans. by John F. Young; st. 4 trans. anon. (Lk. 2:6-20)
MUSIC: Franz Gruber, 1818

STILLE NACHT
Irr.

240 Hark! the Herald Angels Sing

1. Hark! the her - ald an - gels sing, "Glo - ry to the new-born King;
2. Christ, by high - est heaven a - dored; Christ, the ev - er - last - ing Lord;
3. Hail the heaven-born Prince of Peace! Hail the Sun of Righ-teous-ness!

peace on earth, and mer - cy mild, God and sin - ners rec - on-ciled!"
late in time be - hold him come, off-spring of a vir-gin's womb.
Light and life to all he brings, risen with heal - ing in his wings.

Joy - ful, all ye na - tions rise, join the tri - umph of the skies;
Veiled in flesh the God-head see; hail th'in - car - nate De - i - ty,
Mild he lays his glo - ry by, born that we no more may die,

with th'an-gel - ic host pro-claim, "Christ is born in Beth-le-hem!"
pleased with us in flesh to dwell, Je - sus, our Em - man - u - el.
born to raise us from the earth, born to give us sec-ond birth.

WORDS: Charles Wesley, 1739; alt. by George Whitefield, 1753, and others (Lk. 2:8-14)   MENDELSSOHN
MUSIC: Felix Mendelssohn, 1840; arr. by William H. Cummings, 1856   77.77 D with Refrain

Refrain

Hark! the her-ald an-gels sing, "Glo-ry to the new-born King!"

That Boy-Child of Mary 241

Refrain (Unison)

That boy-child of Ma-ry was born in a sta-ble, a man-ger his

Fine

cra-dle in Beth-le-hem.

1. What shall we call him,
2. His name is Je-sus,
3. How can he save us,
4. Gift of the Fa-ther,
5. One with the Fa-ther,
6. Glad-ly we praise him,

D.C.

child of the man-ger? What name is giv-en in Beth-le-hem?
God ev-er with us, God giv-en for us in Beth-le-hem.
how can he help us, born here a-mong us in Beth-le-hem?
to hu-man moth-er, makes him our broth-er of Beth-le-hem.
he is our Sav-ior, heav-en-sent help-er of Beth-le-hem.
love and a-dore him, give our-selves to him of Beth-le-hem.

WORDS: Tom Colvin, 1969 (Lk. 2:7) BLANTYRE
MUSIC: Trad. Malawi melody; adapt. by Tom Colvin, 1969 Irr.
© 1969 Hope Publishing Co.

242 Love Came Down at Christmas

1. Love came down at Christ-mas, Love all love-ly, Love di-vine;
2. Wor-ship we the God-head, Love in-car-nate, Love di-vine;
3. Love shall be our to-ken; love be yours and love be mine;

Love was born at Christ-mas; star and an-gels gave the sign.
wor-ship we our Je-sus, but where-with for sa-cred sign?
love to God and all men,* love for plea and gift and sign.

*"neighbor" may be substituted for "all men"

WORDS: Christina G. Rossetti, 1885
MUSIC: Trad. Irish melody; harm. by David Evans, 1927; alt.

GARTAN
67.67

Harm. by permission of Oxford University Press

243 De Tierra Lejana Venimos
(From a Distant Home)

Unisono (Unison)

1. De tie-rra le-ja-na ve-ni-mos a ver-te,
2. Al re-cién na-ci-do que es Rey de los re-yes,

1. From a dist-tant home the Sav-ior we come seek-ing,
2. Glow-ing gold I bring the new-born babe so ho-ly,

nos sir-ve de guí-a la es-tre-lla de O-rien-te.
o-ro le re-ga-lo pa-ra or-nar sus sie-nes.

us-ing as our guide the star so bright-ly beam-ing.
to-ken of his power to reign a-bove in glo-ry.

WORDS: Trad. Puerto Rican carol; trans. by George K. Evans (Mt. 2:1-12)
MUSIC: Trad. Puerto Rican carol

ISLA DEL ENCANTO
12 12 with Refrain

Trans. © 1963, 1980 Walter Ehret and George K. Evans, by permission of Walton Music Corp.

Estribillo (Refrain)

Oh bri - llan - te_es - tre - lla que_a-nun-cias la_au - ro - ra
Glo-ria_en las al - tu - ras al Hi - jo de Dios,

Love-ly east - ern star that tells us of God's morn - ing,
Glo-ry in the high - est to the Son of Heav - en,

no nos fal - te nun - ca tu luz bien-he - cho - ra.
Glo-ria_en las al - tu - ras

heav-en's won-drous light, O nev - er cease thy shin - ing!
and up - on the earth be

y_en la tie - rra_a - mor.

peace and love to all.

3. Como_es Dios el Niño le regalo_incienso,
   perfume con alma que sube_hasta_el cielo.
   Estribillo

4. Al Niño del cielo que bajó_a la tierra,
   le regalo mirra que_inspira tristeza.
   Estribillo

3. Frankincense I bring the child of God's own choosing,
   token of our prayers to heaven ever rising.
   Refrain

4. Bitter myrrh have I to give the infant Jesus,
   token of the pain that he will bear to save us.
   Refrain

244 'Twas in the Moon of Wintertime

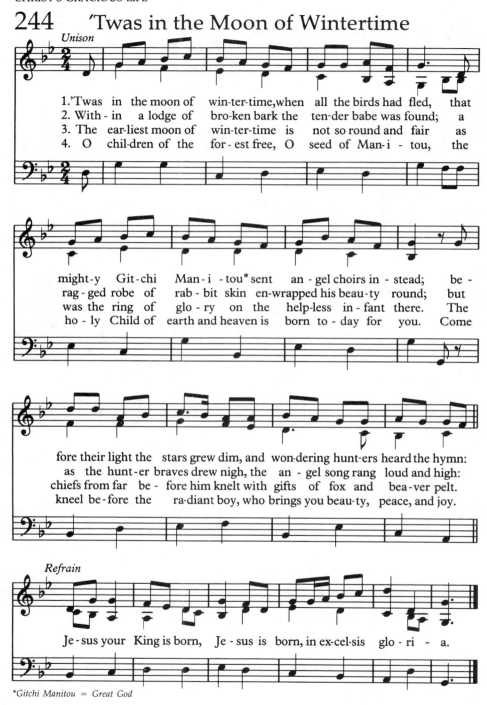

Unison

1. 'Twas in the moon of win-ter-time, when all the birds had fled, that
2. With-in a lodge of bro-ken bark the ten-der babe was found; a
3. The ear-liest moon of win-ter-time is not so round and fair as
4. O chil-dren of the for-est free, O seed of Man-i - tou,* the

might-y Git-chi Man-i -tou* sent an - gel choirs in - stead; be -
rag - ged robe of rab - bit skin en-wrapped his beau-ty round; but
was the ring of glo - ry on the help-less in - fant there. The
ho - ly Child of earth and heaven is born to - day for you. Come

fore their light the stars grew dim, and won-dering hunt-ers heard the hymn:
as the hunt-er braves drew nigh, the an - gel song rang loud and high:
chiefs from far be - fore him knelt with gifts of fox and bea-ver pelt.
kneel be-fore the ra-diant boy, who brings you beau-ty, peace, and joy.

Refrain

Je - sus your King is born, Je - sus is born, in ex-cel-sis glo - ri - a.

*Gitchi Manitou = Great God

WORDS: Jean de Brebeuf, ca. 1643; trans. by Jesse Edgar Middleton, 1926
MUSIC: French Canadian melody

JESOUS AHATONHIA
86.86.86 with Refrain

Trans. by permission of Frederick Harris Music Co. Ltd.

The First Noel

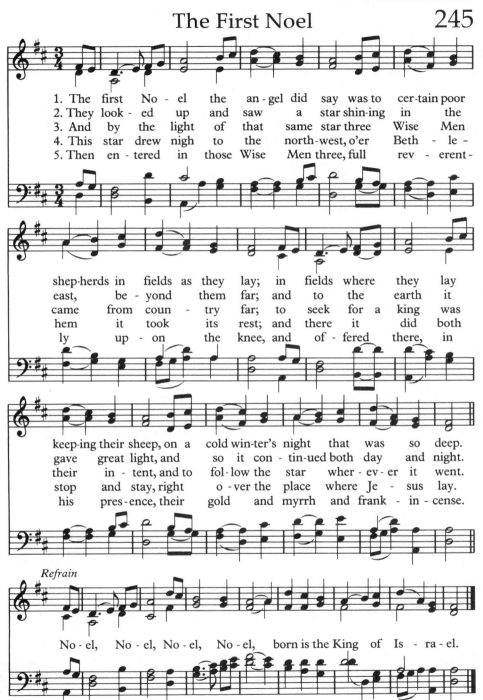

1. The first No - el the an - gel did say was to cer-tain poor
2. They look - ed up and saw a star shin-ing in the
3. And by the light of that same star three Wise Men
4. This star drew nigh to the north-west, o'er Beth - le -
5. Then en - tered in those Wise Men three, full rev - erent -

shep-herds in fields as they lay; in fields where they lay
east, be - yond them far; and to the earth it
came from coun - try far; to seek for a king was
hem it took its rest; and there it did both
ly up - on the knee, and of - fered there, in

keep-ing their sheep, on a cold win-ter's night that was so deep.
gave great light, and so it con - tin-ued both day and night.
their in - tent, and to fol-low the star wher - ev - er it went.
stop and stay, right o - ver the place where Je - sus lay.
his pres - ence, their gold and myrrh and frank - in - cense.

Refrain

No - el, No - el, No - el, No - el, born is the King of Is - ra - el.

WORDS: Trad. English carol (Lk. 2:8-14; Mt. 2:1-12)
MUSIC: Trad. English carol; harm. from *Christmas Carols New and Old*, 1871

THE FIRST NOEL
Irr. with Refrain

246 Joy to the World

1. Joy to the world, the Lord is come!
2. Joy to the world, the Sav - ior reigns!
3. No more let sins and sor - rows grow,
4. He rules the world with truth and grace,

Let earth re - ceive her King; let
Let all their songs em - ploy; while
nor thorns in - fest the ground; he
and makes the na - tions prove the

ev - ery heart pre - pare him room,
fields and floods, rocks, hills, and plains
comes to make his bless - ings flow
glo - ries of his righ - teous - ness,

WORDS: Issac Watts, 1719 (Ps. 98:4-9)
MUSIC: Arr. from G. F. Handel, 1741, by Lowell Mason, 1848

ANTIOCH
CM with Repeat

247 O Morning Star, How Fair and Bright

1. O Morn - ing Star, how fair and bright thou
2. Thou heaven - ly Bright - ness! Light di - vine! O
3. What joy to know, when life is past, the

beam - est forth in truth and light, O
deep with - in my heart now shine, and
Lord we love is first and last, the

Sov - ereign meek and low - ly! Thou
make thee there an al - tar! Fill
end and the be - gin - ning! He

Root of Jes - se, Da - vid's Son, my
me with joy and strength to be thy
will one day, O glo - rious grace, trans -

WORDS: Philipp Nicolai, 1599; trans. by
  Catherine Winkworth, 1863; trans. st. 3
  Lutheran Book of Worship, 1978
MUSIC: Philipp Nicolai, 1599; harm. by J. S. Bach, ca. 1731

WIE SCHÖN LEUCHTET DER MORGENSTERN
887.887.4.84.8

Trans. st. 3 © 1978 Lutheran Book of Worship

Lord and Mas - ter, thou hast won my
mem - ber, ev - er joined to thee in
port us to that hap - py place be -

heart to serve thee sole - ly! Thou art ho - ly,
love that can - not fal - ter; toward thee long - ing
yond all tears and sin - ning! A - men! A - men!

fair and glo - rious, all - vic - to - rious, rich in bless -
doth pos - sess me; turn and bless me; here in sad -
Come, Lord Je - sus! Crown of glad - ness, we are yearn -

ing, rule and might o'er all pos - sess - ing.
ness eye and heart long for thy glad - ness!
ing for the day of your re - turn - ing.

248 On This Day Earth Shall Ring

1. On this day
2. His the doom,
3. God's bright star,
4. On this day

earth shall ring
ours the mirth;
o'er his head,
an - gels sing;

with the song
when he came
Wise Men three
with their song

chil - dren sing
down to earth,
to him led;
earth shall ring,

to the Lord,
Beth - le - hem
kneel they low
prais - ing Christ,

Christ our King,
saw his birth;
by his bed,
heav - en's King,

born on earth to
ox and ass be -
lay their gifts be -
born on earth to

WORDS: *Piae Cantiones*, 1582; trans. by Jane M. Joseph (Lk. 2:6-14; Mt. 2:1-12)
MUSIC: Melody from *Piae Cantiones*, 1582; arr. by Gustav Holst, 1925

PERSONENT HODIE
666.66 with Refrain

save   us;   him the   Fa - ther gave us.
side   him,   from the   cold would hide him.
fore   him,   praise him and   a - dore him.
save   us;   peace and love he   gave us.

Refrain

* Id - e - o - o - o,   id - e - o - o - o,

id - e - o   glo - ri - a   in ex - cel - sis De - o!

*therefore

249

There's a Song in the Air

1. There's a song in the air! There's a star in the sky!
2. There's a tu-mult of joy o'er the won-der-ful birth,
3. In the light of that star lie the a-ges im-pearled;
4. We re-joice in the light, and we ech-o the song

There's a moth-er's deep prayer and a ba-by's low cry!
for the vir-gin's sweet boy is the Lord of the earth.
and that song from a-far has swept o-ver the world.
that comes down through the night from the heav-en-ly throng.

And the star rains its fire while the beau-ti-ful sing,
Ay! the star rains its fire while the beau-ti-ful sing,
Ev-ery hearth is a-flame, and the beau-ti-ful sing
Ay! we shout to the love-ly e-van-gel they bring,

for the man-ger of Beth-le-hem cra-dles a King!
for the man-ger of Beth-le-hem cra-dles a King!
in the homes of the na-tions that Je-sus is King!
and we greet in his cra-dle our Sav-ior and King!

WORDS: Josiah G. Holland, 1874
MUSIC: Karl P. Harrington, 1904

CHRISTMAS SONG
66.66.12 12

Once in Royal David's City

250

1. Once in roy - al Da-vid's cit - y stood a low - ly cat - tle
2. He came down to earth from heav - en who is God and Lord of
3. Je - sus is our child-hood's pat - tern; day by day, like us he
4. And our eyes at last shall see him, through his own re-deem-ing

shed, where a moth - er laid her ba - by in a
all, and his shel - ter was a sta - ble, and his
grew; he was lit - tle, weak, and help - less, tears and
love; for that child so dear and gen - tle is our

man - ger for his bed; Ma - ry, lov - ing moth - er
cra - dle was a stall. With the poor, the scorned, the
smiles like us he knew; and he feel - eth for our
Lord in heaven a - bove; and he leads his chil - dren

mild, Je - sus Christ, her lit - tle child.
low - ly lived on earth our Sav - ior ho - ly.
sad - ness, and he shar - eth in our glad - ness.
on to the place where he is gone.

WORDS: Cecil Frances Alexander, 1848 (Lk. 2:7)
MUSIC: Henry J. Gauntlett, 1849

IRBY
87.87.77

251 Go, Tell It on the Mountain

Refrain

Go, tell it on the moun-tain, o-ver the hills and ev-ery-where;

go, tell it on the moun-tain, that Je - sus Christ is born. *Fine*

1. While shep-herds kept their watch-ing o'er si - lent flocks by night,
2. The shep-herds feared and trem-bled, when lo! a - bove the earth,
3. Down in a low - ly man-ger the hum - ble Christ was born,

D.C.

be - hold through-out the heav-ens there shone a ho - ly light.
rang out the an - gel cho-rus that hailed the Sav-ior's birth.
and God sent us sal - va-tion that bless - ed Christ-mas morn.

WORDS: Afro-American spiritual; adapt. by
  John W. Work, Jr., 1907 (Lk. 2:8-20)
MUSIC: Afro-American spiritual; adapt. and arr. by
  William Farley Smith, 1986

GO TELL IT ON THE MOUNTAIN
Irr. with Refrain

When Jesus Came to Jordan

252

WORDS: Fred Pratt Green, 1973 (Mt. 3:13-17; Mk. 1:9-11; Lk. 3:21-22)
MUSIC: Attr. to William Walker, 1835; harm. by Carlton R. Young, 1988

COMPLAINER
76.76 D

253 Baptism of the Lord

Father in heaven,
at the baptism of Jesus in the River Jordan
    you proclaimed him your beloved Son
    and anointed him with the Holy Spirit.
Grant that all who are baptized into his name
    may keep the covenant they have made,
    and boldly confess him as Lord and Savior,
who with you and the Holy Spirit lives and reigns,
One God, in glory everlasting. **Amen.**

After *The Book of Common Prayer* (Mt. 3:13-17; Mk. 1:9-11; Lk. 3:21-22)

254 We Three Kings

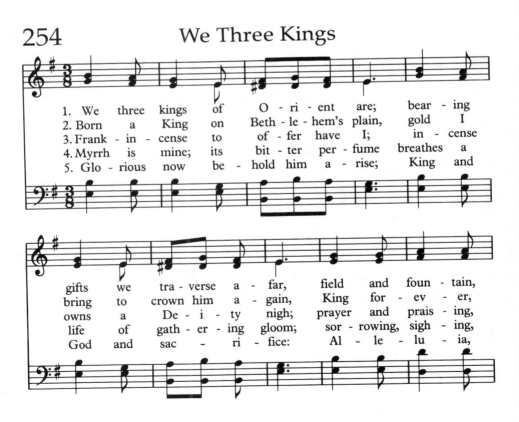

1. We three kings of O - ri - ent are; bear - ing
2. Born a King on Beth - le - hem's plain, gold I
3. Frank - in - cense to of - fer have I; in - cense
4. Myrrh is mine; its bit - ter per - fume breathes a
5. Glo - rious now be - hold him a - rise; King and

gifts we tra - verse a - far, field and foun - tain,
bring to crown him a - gain, King for - ev - er,
owns a De - i - ty nigh; prayer and prais - ing,
life of gath - er - ing gloom; sor - rowing, sigh - ing,
God and sac - ri - fice: Al - le - lu - ia,

WORDS: John H. Hopkins, Jr., 1857 (Mt. 2:1-12)
MUSIC: John H. Hopkins, Jr., 1857

KINGS OF ORIENT
88.446 with Refrain

moor and moun - tain, fol - low - ing yon - der star.
ceas - ing nev - er, o - ver us all to reign.
voic - es rais - ing, wor-ship - ing God on high.
bleed - ing, dy - ing, sealed in the stone - cold tomb.
Al - le - lu - ia, sounds through the earth and skies.

Refrain

O star of won - der, star of light, star with roy - al beau-ty bright,

west-ward lead-ing, still pro - ceed-ing, guide us to thy per-fect light.

Epiphany   255

O God,
  you made of one blood all nations,
    and, by a star in the East,
      revealed to all peoples him whose name is Emmanuel.
Enable us who know your presence with us
  so to proclaim his unsearchable riches
    that all may come to his light
      and bow before the brightness of his rising,
who lives and reigns with you and the Holy Spirit,
  now and for ever. **Amen.**

Laurence Hull Stookey, USA, 20th Cent. (Mt. 2:1-12)

© 1989 The United Methodist Publishing House

BIRTH AND BAPTISM, *see further:*

190 Who Is He in Yonder Stall

256 We Would See Jesus

1. We would see Je - sus; lo! his star is shin - ing
2. We would see Je - sus, Ma - ry's son most ho - ly,
3. We would see Je - sus, on the moun-tain teach - ing,
4. We would see Je - sus, in his work of heal - ing,
5. We would see Je - sus, in the ear - ly morn - ing,

a - bove the sta - ble while the an - gels sing;
light of the vil - lage life from day to day;
with all the lis - tening peo - ple gath - ered round;
at ev - en - tide be - fore the sun was set;
still as of old he call - eth, "Fol - low me!"

there in a man - ger on the hay re - clin - ing;
shin - ing re - vealed through ev - ery task most low - ly,
while birds and flowers and sky a - bove are preach - ing
di - vine and hu - man, in his deep re - veal - ing
Let us a - rise, all mean - er ser - vice scorn - ing;

haste, let us lay our gifts be - fore the King.
the Christ of God, the life, the truth, the way.
the bless - ed - ness which sim - ple trust has found.
of God made flesh, in lov - ing ser - vice met.
Lord, we are thine, we give our - selves to thee.

WORDS: J. Edgar Park, 1913
MUSIC: Herbert B. Turner, 1907

CUSHMAN
11 10.11 10

We Meet You, O Christ

Unison

1. We meet you, O Christ, in man-y a guise;
2. In mil-lions a-live, a-way and a-broad;
3. We hear you, O man, in ag-o-ny cry;
4. You choose to be made at one with the earth;

your im-age we see in sim-ple and wise.
in-volved in our life, you live down the road.
for free-dom you march, in ri-ots you die.
the dark of the grave pre-pares for your birth.

You live in a pal-ace, ex-ist in a shack;
Im-pris-oned in sys-tems, you long to be free;
Your face in the pa-pers we read and we see.
Your death is your ris-ing, cre-a-tive your word;

we see you, the gar-dener, a tree on your back.
we see you, Lord Je-sus, still bear-ing your tree.
The tree must be plant-ed by hu-man de-cree.
the tree springs to life and our hope is re-stored.

WORDS: Fred Kaan, 1966
MUSIC: Carl F. Schalk, 1987

STANLEY BEACH
10 10.11 11

Words © 1968 Hope Publishing Co.; music © 1989 The United Methodist Publishing House

258 O Wondrous Sight! O Vision Fair

1. O won - drous sight! O vi - sion fair
2. From age to age the tale de - clares
3. The law and proph - ets there have place,
4. With shin - ing face and bright ar - ray,
5. And faith - ful hearts are raised on high

of glo - ry that the church shall share,
how with the three dis - ci - ples there
two cho - sen wit - ness - es of grace;
Christ deigns to man - i - fest that day
by this great vi - sion's mys - ter - y;

which Christ up - on the moun - tain shows,
where Mo - ses and E - li - jah meet,
the Fa - ther's voice from out the cloud
what glo - ry shall be theirs a - bove
for which in joy - ful strains we raise

where bright - er than the sun he glows!
the Lord holds con - verse high and sweet.
pro - claims his on - ly Son a - loud.
who joy in God with per - fect love.
the voice of prayer, the hymn of praise.

WORDS: *Sarum Breviary*, 1495; trans. by John Mason Neale, 1851
    (Mt. 17:1-8; Mk. 9:2-8; Lk. 9:28-36)
MUSIC: William Knapp, 1738; harm. from *Hymns Ancient and Modern*, 1875

WAREHAM
LM

Transfiguration

Holy God,
  upon the mountain you revealed our Messiah,
    who by his death and resurrection
      would fulfill both the law and the prophets.
By his transfiguration enlighten our path
    that we may dare to suffer with him in the service of humanity
    and so share in the everlasting glory of him
    who lives and reigns with you and the Holy Spirit,
    One God, for ever. **Amen.**

Laurence Hull Stookey, USA, 20th Cent. (Mt. 17:1-8; Mk. 9:2-8; Lk. 9:28-36)
© 1989 The United Methodist Publishing House

Christ, upon the Mountain Peak   260

Unison

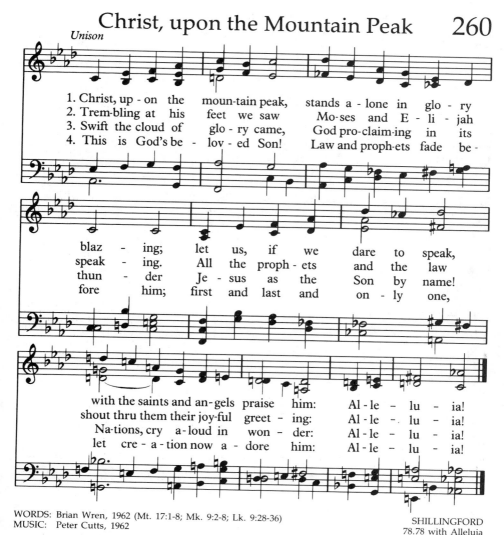

1. Christ, up-on the moun-tain peak, stands a-lone in glo-ry
2. Trem-bling at his feet we saw Mo-ses and E-li-jah
3. Swift the cloud of glo-ry came, God pro-claim-ing in its
4. This is God's be-lov-ed Son! Law and proph-ets fade be-

blaz - ing; let us, if we dare to speak,
speak - ing. All the proph-ets and the law
thun - der, Je - sus as the Son by name!
fore him; first and last and on - ly one,

with the saints and an-gels praise him: Al - le - lu - ia!
shout thru them their joy-ful greet - ing: Al - le - lu - ia!
Na-tions, cry a-loud in won - der: Al - le - lu - ia!
let cre - a-tion now a - dore him: Al - le - lu - ia!

WORDS: Brian Wren, 1962 (Mt. 17:1-8; Mk. 9:2-8; Lk. 9:28-36)
MUSIC: Peter Cutts, 1962

© 1977 Hope Publishing Co.

SHILLINGFORD
78.78 with Alleluia

Alt. tune: LIEBSTER JESU

261 Lord of the Dance

WORDS: Sydney Carter, 1963
MUSIC: 19th cent. Shaker tune; adapt. by Sydney Carter, 1963;
harm. by Gary Alan Smith, 1988

LORD OF THE DANCE
Irr. with Refrain

Heal Me, Hands of Jesus

262

1. Heal me, hands of Je - sus, and search out all my pain; restore my hope, re-move my fear, and bring me peace a - gain.
2. Cleanse me, blood of Je - sus, take bit - ter-ness a - way; let
me for-give as one for-given and bring me peace to - day.
3. Know me, mind of Je - sus, and show me all my sin; dis-
pel the mem-o - ries of guilt and bring me peace with-in.
4. Fill me, joy of Je - sus; anx - i - e - ty shall cease, and
heaven's se-ren- i - ty be mine, for Je-sus brings me peace!

WORDS: Michael Perry, 1982
MUSIC: Norman L. Warren, 1982

SUTTON COMMON
SM

© 1982 Hope Publishing Co.

263 When Jesus the Healer Passed Through Galilee

1. When Jesus the heal-er passed through Gal-i-lee,
2. A par-a-lyzed man was let down through a roof.
3. The death of his daugh-ter caused Jai-rus to weep. Heal
4. When blind Bar-ti-mae-us cried out to the Lord,
5. The lep-ers were healed and the de-mons cast out.

       the deaf came to hear and the
       His sins were for-giv-en, his
us, heal us to-day! The Lord took her hand, and he
       His faith made him whole and his
       A bent wom-an straight-ened to

blind came to see.
walk-ing the proof.
raised her from sleep. Heal us, Lord Je-sus!
sight was re-stored.
laugh and to shout.

6. The twelve were commissioned and sent out in twos
   Heal us, heal us today!
   to make the sick whole and to spread the good news.
   Heal us, Lord Jesus!

7. There's still so much sickness and suffering today.
   Heal us, heal us today!
   We gather together for healing and pray:
   Heal us, Lord Jesus!

WORDS: Peter D. Smith, 1979
MUSIC: Peter D. Smith, 1979

HEALER
11 6.11 5

Silence, Frenzied, Unclean Spirit 264

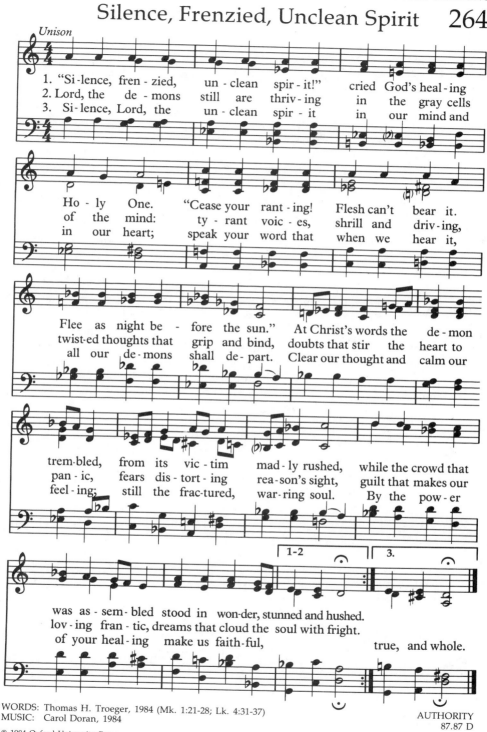

Unison

1. "Si-lence, fren-zied, un-clean spir-it!" cried God's heal-ing
2. Lord, the de-mons still are thriv-ing in the gray cells
3. Si-lence, Lord, the un-clean spir-it in our mind and

Ho-ly One. "Cease your rant-ing! Flesh can't bear it.
of the mind: ty-rant voic-es, shrill and driv-ing,
in our heart; speak your word that when we hear it,

Flee as night be-fore the sun." At Christ's words the de-mon
twist-ed thoughts that grip and bind, doubts that stir the heart to
all our de-mons shall de-part. Clear our thought and calm our

trem-bled, from its vic-tim mad-ly rushed, while the crowd that
pan-ic, fears dis-tort-ing rea-son's sight, guilt that makes our
feel-ing; still the frac-tured, war-ring soul. By the pow-er

1-2

was as-sem-bled stood in won-der, stunned and hushed.
lov-ing fran-tic, dreams that cloud the soul with fright.

3.

of your heal-ing make us faith-ful, true, and whole.

WORDS: Thomas H. Troeger, 1984 (Mk. 1:21-28; Lk. 4:31-37)
MUSIC: Carol Doran, 1984

AUTHORITY
87.87 D

Alt. tune: EBENEZER

265   O Christ, the Healer

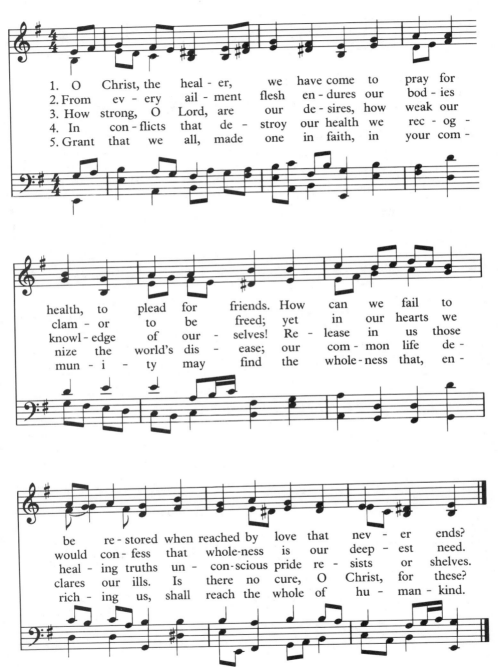

1. O Christ, the heal - er, we have come to pray for
2. From ev - ery ail - ment flesh en - dures our bod - ies
3. How strong, O Lord, are our de - sires, how weak our
4. In con - flicts that de - stroy our health we rec - og -
5. Grant that we all, made one in faith, in your com -

health, to plead for friends. How can we fail to
clam - or to be freed; yet in our hearts we
knowl - edge of our - selves! Re - lease in us those
nize the world's dis - ease; our com - mon life de -
mun - i - ty may find the whole - ness that, en -

be re - stored when reached by love that nev - er ends?
would con - fess that whole - ness is our deep - est need.
heal - ing truths un - con - scious pride re - sists or shelves.
clares our ills. Is there no cure, O Christ, for these?
rich - ing us, shall reach the whole of hu - man - kind.

WORDS: Fred Pratt Green, 1967
MUSIC: *Geistliche Lieder* (Klug), 1543; harm. by J. S. Bach, 1725

ERHALT UNS HERR
LM

Heal Us, Emmanuel, Hear Our Prayer 266

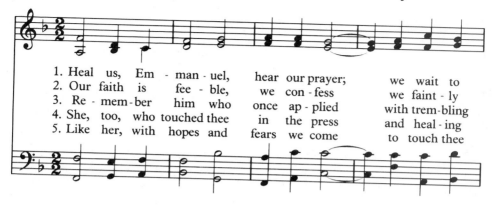

1. Heal us, Em - man - uel, hear our prayer; we wait to
2. Our faith is fee - ble, we con - fess we faint - ly
3. Re - mem - ber him who once ap - plied with trem - bling
4. She, too, who touched thee in the press and heal - ing
5. Like her, with hopes and fears we come to touch thee

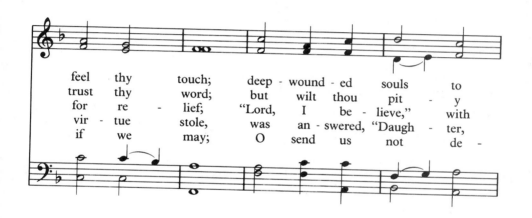

feel thy touch; deep - wound - ed souls to
trust thy word; but wilt thou pit - y
for re - lief; "Lord, I be - lieve," with
vir - tue stole, was an - swered, "Daugh - ter,
if we may; O send us not de -

thee re - pair, and Sav - ior, we are such.
us the less? Be that far from thee, Lord!
tears he cried; "O help my un - be - lief!"
go in peace: thy faith hath made thee whole."
spair - ing home; send none un - healed a - way.

WORDS: William Cowper, 1779 (Mk. 9:14-27; Mt. 9:20-22; Mk. 5:25-34; Lk. 8:43-48)
MUSIC: Johann Crüger, 1647

GRÄFENBERG
CM

267 O Love, How Deep

1. O love, how deep, how broad, how high,
   it fills the heart with ec - sta - sy,
   that God, the Son of God, should take
   our mor - tal form for mor - tals' sake!

2. For us bap - tized, for us he bore
   his ho - ly fast and hun - gered sore,
   for us temp - ta - tion sharp he knew;
   for us the tempt - er o - ver - threw.

3. For us he prayed; for us he taught;
   for us his dai - ly works he wrought;
   by words and signs and ac - tions thus
   still seek - ing not him - self, but us.

4. For us to e - vil power be - trayed,
   scourged, mocked, in pur - ple robe ar - rayed,
   he bore the shame - ful cross and death,
   for us gave up his dy - ing breath.

5. For us he rose from death a - gain;
   for us he went on high to reign;
   for us he sent his Spir - it here,
   to guide, to strength - en, and to cheer.

6. All glo - ry to our Lord and God
   for love so deep, so high, so broad:
   the Trin - i - ty whom we a - dore,
   for - ev - er and for - ev - er - more.

WORDS: 15th cent. Latin; trans. by Benjamin Webb, 1854; alt.
MUSIC: English melody; harm. from *Hymns Ancient and Modern, Revised*, 1950

DEO GRACIAS
LM

Lent

O God our deliverer, you led your people of old through the wilderness and brought them to the promised land. Guide now the people of your church, that, following our Savior, we may walk through the wilderness of this world toward the glory of the world to come; through Jesus Christ our Lord, who lives and reigns with you and the Holy Spirit, One God, now and forever. **Amen.**

The Lutheran Book of Worship, 1978
© 1978, 1989 Augsburg Publishing House

Lord, Who Throughout These Forty Days 269

1. Lord, who through-out these for-ty days for us didst fast and pray, teach us with thee to mourn our sins and close by thee to stay.
2. As thou with Sa-tan didst con-tend, and didst the vic-tory win, O give us strength in thee to fight, in thee to con-quer sin.
3. As thou didst hun-ger bear, and thirst, so teach us, gra-cious Lord, to die to self, and chief-ly live by thy most ho-ly word.
4. And through these days of pen-i-tence, and through thy pas-sion-tide, yea, ev-er-more in life and death, Je-sus, with us a-bide.
5. A-bide with us, that so, this life of suf-fering o-ver past, an Eas-ter of un-end-ing joy we may at-tain at last.

WORDS: Claudia F. Hernaman, 1873 (Mt. 4:1-11; Mk. 1:12-13; Lk. 4:1-13)
MUSIC: USA folk melody; arr. by Annabel Morris Buchanan, 1938; harm. by Charles H. Webb, 1988

LAND OF REST
CM

Harm. © 1989 The United Methodist Publishing House

270 The Lord's Prayer

Our Father who art in heaven, hal - low - ed be thy name,

thy kingdom come,
thy will be done on earth as it is in heaven. Give us this day our

dai - ly bread; and forgive us our trespasses
as we forgive those who

tres - pass a - gainst us. And lead us not into
temptation, but de - liv - er

us from e - vil, for thine is the king -
dom, and the power
and the glory for - ev - er. A - men.

WORDS: Matthew 6:9-13
MUSIC: Lowell Mason, 1824

GREGORIAN
Irr.

The Lord's Prayer

1. Our Fa-ther, which art in heav-en,
2. Done on earth as it is in heav-en,
3. And for - give all our debts,
4. Lead us not in - to temp-ta-tion, hal-low-ed - a be thy
5. Thine is the king-dom, pow-er, and glo-ry,
6. A - men, a - men, a - men,

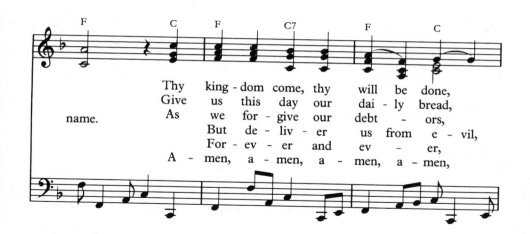

name.

Thy king - dom come, thy will be done,
Give us this day our dai - ly bread,
As we for - give our debt - ors,
But de - liv - er us from e - vil,
For - ev - er and ev - er,
A - men, a - men, a - men, a - men,

hal – low – ed – a be thy name.

Fine

WORDS: Matthew 6:9-13; adapt. by J. Jefferson Cleveland and Verolga Nix, 1981
MUSIC: West Indian folk tune; arr. by Carlton R. Young, 1988

WEST INDIAN
Irr.

Adapt. © 1981 Abingdon Press; arr. © 1989 The United Methodist Publishing House

272 Sing of Mary, Pure and Lowly

1. Sing of Ma-ry, pure and lowly, maid-en moth-er, wise and mild. Sing of God's own Son most ho-ly, who be-came her lit-tle child. Fair-est child of fair-est moth-er, God the Lord who came to earth, Word made flesh, our ver-y

2. Sing of Je-sus, son of Ma-ry, in the home at Naz-a-reth. Toil and la-bor can-not wea-ry love en-dur-ing un-to death. Con-stant was the love he gave her, though it drove him from her side, forth to preach, and

3. Joy-ful moth-er, full of glad-ness, in thine arms thy Lord was borne. Mourn-ful moth-er, full of sad-ness, all thy heart with pain was torn. Glo-rious moth-er, now re-ward-ed with a crown at Je-sus' hand, age to age thy name re-

WORDS: Roland Ford Palmer, 1938
MUSIC: Skinner Chávez-Melo, 1985

RAQUEL
87.87 D

broth - er, takes our na - ture by his birth.
suf - fer, till on Cal - va - ry he died.
cord - ed shall be blest in ev - ery land.

Jesus' Hands Were Kind Hands 273

Unison

1. Je - sus' hands were kind hands, do - ing good to all,
2. Take my hands, Lord Je - sus, let them work for you;

heal - ing pain and sick - ness, bless - ing chil - dren small,
make them strong and gen - tle, kind in all I do.

wash - ing tir - ed feet, and sav - ing those who fall;
Let me watch you, Je - sus, till I'm gen - tle too,

Je - sus' hands were kind hands, do - ing good to all.
till my hands are kind hands, quick to work for you.

WORDS: Margaret Cropper, 1975
MUSIC: Old French melody; harm. by Carlton R. Young, 1988

AU CLAIR DE LA LUNE
65.65 D

274 Woman in the Night

Unison

1. Wom-an in the night, spent from giv-ing birth,
2. Wom-an in the crowd, creep-ing up be-hind,
3. Wom-an at the well, ques-tion the Mes-siah;
4. Wom-an at the feast, let the righ-teous stare;
5. Wom-an in the house, nur-tured to be meek,
6. Wom-en on the road, wel-comed and re-stored,

guard our pre-cious light; peace is on the earth!
touch-ing is al-lowed; seek and you will find!
find your friends and tell; drink your heart's de-sire!
come and go in peace; love him with your hair!
leave your sec-ond place; lis-ten, think, and speak!
trav-el far and wide; wit-ness to the Lord!

Refrain

Come and join the song, wom-en, chil-dren, men;

Je-sus makes us free to live a-gain!

WORDS: Brian Wren, 1982
MUSIC: Charles H. Webb, 1987

HAIZ
55.55 with Refrain

7. Women on the hill,
   stand when men have fled!
   Christ needs loving still,
   though your hope is dead.
   Refrain

8. Women in the dawn,
   care and spices bring;
   earliest to mourn;
   earliest to sing!
   Refrain

The Kingdom of God 275

Unison

1. The king-dom of God is like a grain of mus-tard seed.
2. For when it is sown, it grows in - to the larg - est plant,
3. It grows so birds can rest in - side its crown of leaves,
4. And so we can lik - en it to seeds which make a tree

When it is sown in the earth, it is the small - est seed.
great - er than all of the herbs, and grows in - to a tree.
deep in its shad - ows, a - way from an - y e - vil prey.
larg - er than all of the trees from just the small - est seed.

Refrain

It is like the king-dom of God and a mys - ter - y.

WORDS: Gracia Grindal, 1985 (Mt. 13:31-32; Mk. 4:30-32)
MUSIC: Austin C. Lovelace, 1985

MUSTARD SEED
76.76.85

© 1987 Hope Publishing Co.

276 The First One Ever

1. The first one ev - er, oh, ev - er to know of the birth of Je - sus was the Maid Ma - ry, was Ma - ry the Maid of Gal - i - lee, and bless - ed is she, is she who be - lieves. Oh,

2. The first one ev - er, oh, ev - er to know of Mes - si - ah, Je - sus, when he said, "I am he," was the Sa - mar - i - tan wom - an who drew from the well, and bless - ed is she, is she who per - ceives. Oh,

3. The first ones ev - er, oh, ev - er to know of the ris - ing of Je - sus, his glo - ry to be, were Ma - ry, Jo - an - na, and Mag - da - lene, and bless - ed are they, are they who see. Oh,

WORDS: Linda Wilberger Egan, 1980, alt. (Lk. 1:26-38, 45; Jn. 4:7-26; Lk. 24:1-11)
MUSIC: Linda Wilberger Egan, 1980

BALLAD
Irr.

© 1980, 1983 Linda Wilberger Egan

277   Tell Me the Stories of Jesus

Unison (Optional S.A.)

1. Tell me the sto - ries of Je - sus I love to hear;
2. First let me hear how the chil - dren stood round his knee,
3. In - to the cit - y I'd fol - low the chil - dren's band,

things I would ask him to tell me if he were here:
and I shall fan - cy his bless - ing rest - ing on me;
wav - ing a branch of the palm tree high in my hand;

scenes by the way - side, tales of the sea,
words full of kind - ness, deeds full of grace,
one of his her - alds, yes, I would sing

sto - ries of Je - sus, tell them to me.
all in the love - light of Je - sus' face.
loud - est ho - san - nas, "Je - sus is King!"

WORDS: William H. Parker, 1885 (Mt. 19:13-15; 21:8-9;
  Mk. 10:13-16; 11:8-10; Jn. 12:13)
MUSIC: Frederick A. Challinor, 1903

STORIES OF JESUS
84.84.54.54

LIFE AND TEACHING, *see further:*

432   Jesu, Jesu   398   Jesus Calls Us O'er the Tumult

Hosanna, Loud Hosanna

1. Ho - san - na, loud ho - san - na, the lit - tle chil-dren sang;
2. From Ol - i - vet they fol - lowed mid an ex - ult-ant crowd,
3. "Ho - san - na in the high - est!" that an-cient song we sing,

through pil-lared court and tem - ple the love-ly an-them rang.
the vic - tor palm branch wav - ing, and chant-ing clear and loud.
for Christ is our Re - deem - er, the Lord of heaven our King.

To Je - sus, who had blessed them close fold-ed to his breast,
The Lord of earth and heav - en rode on in low-ly state,
O may we ev - er praise him with heart and life and voice,

the chil-dren sang their prais - es, the sim-plest and the best.
nor scorned that lit - tle chil - dren should on his bid-ding wait.
and in his bliss-ful pres - ence e - ter-nal-ly re - joice!

WORDS: Jeanette Threlfall, 1873 (Mt. 21:8-9; Mk. 11:8-10; Jn. 12:12-13)
MUSIC: *Gesangbuch der H. W. k. Hofkapelle*, 1784; adapt. and harm. by W. H. Monk, 1868

ELLACOMBE
76.76 D

279

Mantos y Palmas
(Filled with Excitement)

Unísono (Unison)

1. Man - tos y pal - mas es - par - cien - do, va
2. Co - mo en la en - tra - da de Je - ru - sa - lén,

1. Filled with ex - cite - ment, all the hap - py throng
2. As in that en - trance to Je - ru - sa - lem,

el pue-blo a - le - gre de Je - ru - sa-lén. A - llá a lo
to - dos can - ta - mos a Je - sús el Rey, al Cris-to

spread cloaks and branch-es on the cit - y streets. There in the
we sing ho - san - nas to the Christ, our King, to the liv-ing

le - jos se em-pie - za a mi-rar en un po - lli - no al Hi-
vi - vo que nos lla - ma hoy pa - ra se-guir-le con a -

dis-tance they be - gin to see, rid - ing on a don-key, comes the
Sav-ior who still calls to-day, ask-ing us to fol-low him with

Estribillo (Refrain)

jo de Dios.
mor y fe.

Mien-tras mil vo - ces re - sue-nan por do-quier; ho -

Son of God.
love and faith.

From ev-ery cor - ner a thou-sand voic-es sing

WORDS: Rubén Ruiz Avila, 1972; trans. by Gertrude C. Suppe, 1979, 1987
(Mt. 21:8-9; Mk. 11:8-10; Lk. 19:36-38; Jn.12:12-13)
MUSIC: Rubén Ruiz Avila, 1972; arr. by Alvin Schutmaat

HOSANNA
10 10.10 11 with Refrain

© 1972, 1979, 1989 The United Methodist Publishing House

280 All Glory, Laud, and Honor

WORDS: Theodulph of Orleans, 8-9th cent.; trans. by John Mason Neale, 1851
  (Mt. 21:8-9; Mk. 11:8-10; Lk. 19:36-38; Jn. 12:12-13)
MUSIC: Melchior Teschner, 1615; harm. by W. H. Monk, 1861

ST. THEODULPH
76.76 D

Passion/Palm Sunday

Almighty God,
you sent your Son, our Savior Jesus Christ,
　　to suffer death on the cross.
Grant that we may share in his obedience to your will
　　and in the glorious victory of his resurrection;
through Jesus Christ our Lord,
　　who lives and reigns with you and the Holy Spirit,
　　One God, now and ever. **Amen.**

The Lutheran Book of Worship, 1978; alt. by Laurence Hull Stookey, 1987

© 1978, 1989 Augsburg Publishing House

'Tis Finished! The Messiah Dies　282

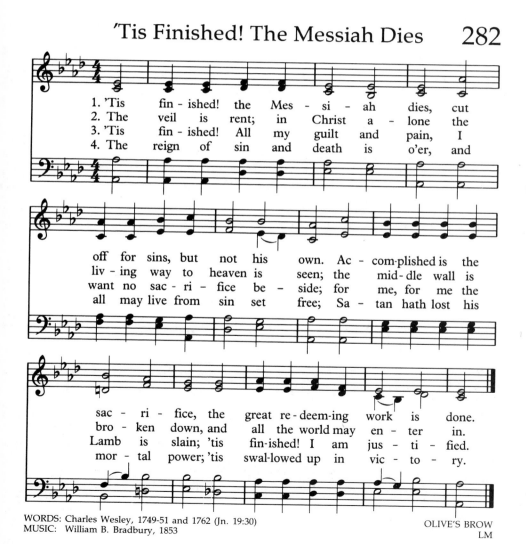

1. 'Tis fin-ished! the Mes-si-ah dies, cut off for sins, but not his own. Ac-com-plished is the sac-ri-fice, the great re-deem-ing work is done.
2. The veil is rent; in Christ a-lone the liv-ing way to heaven is seen; the mid-dle wall is bro-ken down, and all the world may en-ter in.
3. 'Tis fin-ished! All my guilt and pain, I want no sac-ri-fice be-side; for me, for me the Lamb is slain; 'tis fin-ished! I am jus-ti-fied.
4. The reign of sin and death is o'er, and all may live from sin set free; Sa-tan hath lost his mor-tal power; 'tis swal-lowed up in vic-to-ry.

WORDS: Charles Wesley, 1749-51 and 1762 (Jn. 19:30)
MUSIC: William B. Bradbury, 1853

OLIVE'S BROW
LM

283 Holy Thursday

Gracious God,
   your Anointed One, on the night before he suffered,
     instituted the sacrament of his body and blood.
Mercifully grant that we may receive it thankfully
   in remembrance of Jesus Christ our Lord,
   who in these holy mysteries
   gives us a pledge of eternal life. **Amen.**

After *The Book of Common Prayer* (Mt. 26:26-29; Mk. 14:22-25;
  Lk. 22:17-20; 1 Cor. 11:23-26)

284 Good Friday

Almighty God,
   graciously behold this your family,
for whom our Lord Jesus Christ was willing
   to be betrayed into the hands of sinners,
   and to suffer death upon the cross;
who now lives and reigns with you and the Holy Spirit,
   One God, for ever and ever. **Amen.**

After *The Book of Common Prayer*

285 To Mock Your Reign, O Dearest Lord

1. To mock your reign, O dear - est Lord, they
2. In mock ac - claim, O gra - cious Lord, they
3. A scep - tered reed, O pa - tient Lord, they

WORDS: Fred Pratt Green, 1972 (Mt. 27:27-31; Mk. 15:16-20; Jn. 19:1-5)   KINGSFOLD
MUSIC: English melody; arr. by Ralph Vaughan Williams, 1906   CMD
Words © 1973 Hope Publishing Co.

made a crown of thorns; set you with taunts a -
snatched a pur - ple cloak; your pas - sion turned, for
thrust in - to your hand, and act - ed out their

long that road from which no one re - turns.
all they cared, in - to a sol - dier's joke.
grim cha - rade to its ap - point - ed end.

They could not know, as we do now, how
They could not know, as we do now, that
They could not know, as we do now, though

glo - rious is that crown; that thorns would flower up -
though we mer - it blame, you will your robe of
em - pires rise and fall, your king - dom shall not

on your brow, your sor - rows heal our own.
mer - cy throw a - round our na - ked shame.
cease to grow till love em - brac - es all.

286 O Sacred Head, Now Wounded

1. O sa-cred Head, now wound - ed, with grief and shame weighed down,
2. What thou, my Lord, hast suf - fered was all for sin - ners' gain;
3. What lan-guage shall I bor - row to thank thee, dear-est friend,

now scorn-ful-ly sur - round - ed with thorns, thine on - ly crown:
mine, mine was the trans - gres - sion, but thine the dead - ly pain.
for this thy dy - ing sor - row, thy pit - y with-out end?

how pale thou art with an - guish, with sore a - buse and scorn!
Lo, here I fall, my Sav - ior! 'Tis I de-serve thy place;
O make me thine for - ev - er; and should I faint-ing be,

How does that vis - age lan - guish which once was bright as morn!
look on me with thy fa - vor, vouch-safe to me thy grace.
Lord, let me nev - er, nev - er out - live my love to thee.

WORDS: Anon. Latin; trans. by Paul Gerhardt, 1656,
and James W. Alexander, 1830 (Mt. 27:27-31; Mk. 15:16-20; Jn. 19:1-5)
MUSIC: Hans L. Hassler, 1601; harm. by J. S. Bach, 1729, alt.

PASSION CHORALE
76.76 D

O Love Divine, What Hast Thou Done 287

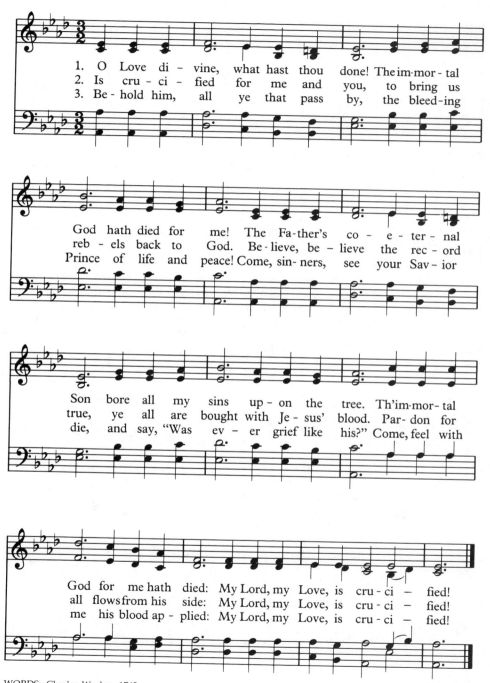

1. O Love di - vine, what hast thou done! The im-mor - tal
2. Is cru - ci - fied for me and you, to bring us
3. Be - hold him, all ye that pass by, the bleed-ing

God hath died for me! The Fa-ther's co - e - ter - nal
reb - els back to God. Be - lieve, be - lieve the rec - ord
Prince of life and peace! Come, sin - ners, see your Sav - ior

Son bore all my sins up - on the tree. Th'im-mor - tal
true, ye all are bought with Je - sus' blood. Par - don for
die, and say, "Was ev - er grief like his?" Come, feel with

God for me hath died: My Lord, my Love, is cru - ci - fied!
all flows from his side: My Lord, my Love, is cru - ci - fied!
me his blood ap - plied: My Lord, my Love, is cru - ci - fied!

WORDS: Charles Wesley, 1742
MUSIC: Isaac B. Woodbury, 1850

SELENA
88.88.88

288   Were You There

1. Were you there when they cru-ci-fied my Lord? (were you
2. Were you there when they nailed him to the tree? (were you
3. Were you there when they pierced him in the side? (were you
4. Were you there when the sun re-fused to shine? (were you
5. Were you there when they laid him in the tomb? (were you

there) Were you there when they cru-ci-fied my Lord? (were you
there) Were you there when they nailed him to the tree? (were you
there) Were you there when they pierced him in the side? (were you
there) Were you there when the sun re-fused to shine? (were you
there) Were you there when they laid him in the tomb? (were you

Refrain

there)   Oh!   some-times it caus-es

me to trem-ble, trem-ble, trem-ble.   Were you

WORDS: Afro-American spiritual
MUSIC: Afro-American spiritual; adapt. and arr. by William Farley Smith, 1986

WERE YOU THERE
Irr.

Adapt. and arr. © 1989 The United Methodist Publishing House

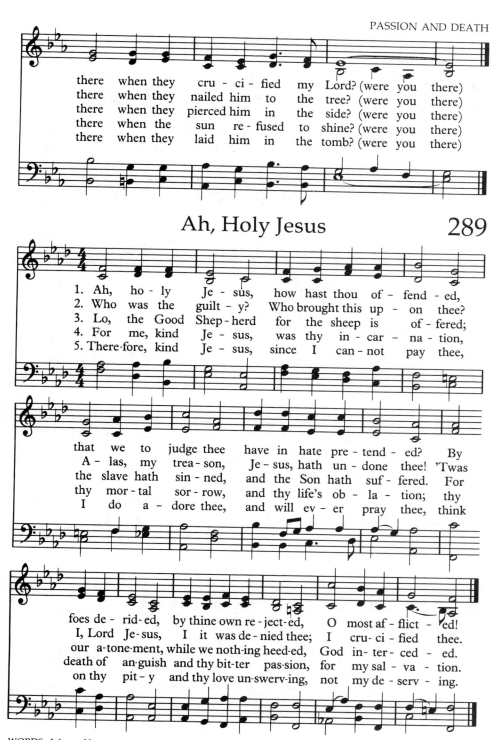

there when they cru - ci - fied my Lord? (were you there)
there when they nailed him to the tree? (were you there)
there when they pierced him in the side? (were you there)
there when the sun re - fused to shine? (were you there)
there when they laid him in the tomb? (were you there)

Ah, Holy Jesus

289

1. Ah, ho - ly Je - sus, how hast thou of - fend - ed,
2. Who was the guilt - y? Who brought this up - on thee?
3. Lo, the Good Shep - herd for the sheep is of - fered;
4. For me, kind Je - sus, was thy in - car - na - tion,
5. There-fore, kind Je - sus, since I can - not pay thee,

that we to judge thee have in hate pre - tend - ed? By
A - las, my trea - son, Je - sus, hath un - done thee! 'Twas
the slave hath sin - ned, and the Son hath suf - fered. For
thy mor - tal sor - row, and thy life's ob - la - tion; thy
I do a - dore thee, and will ev - er pray thee, think

foes de - rid - ed, by thine own re - ject - ed, O most af - flict - ed!
I, Lord Je - sus, I it was de - nied thee; I cru - ci - fied thee.
our a-tone-ment, while we noth-ing heed-ed, God in - ter - ced - ed.
death of an-guish and thy bit-ter pas-sion, for my sal - va - tion.
on thy pit - y and thy love un-swerv-ing, not my de - serv - ing.

WORDS: Johann Heermann, 1630; trans. by Robert S. Bridges, 1899
MUSIC: Johann Crüger, 1640

HERZLIEBSTER JESU
11 11 11.5

290 Go to Dark Gethsemane

1. Go to dark Geth-sem-a-ne, ye that feel the temp-ter's power; your Re-deem-er's con-flict see, watch with him one bit-ter hour. Turn not from his griefs a-way; learn of Je-sus Christ to pray.

2. See him at the judg-ment hall, beat-en, bound, re-viled, ar-raigned; O the worm-wood and the gall! O the pangs his soul sus-tained! Shun not suf-fering, shame, or loss; learn of Christ to bear the cross.

3. Cal-vary's mourn-ful moun-tain climb; there, a-dor-ing at his feet, mark that mir-a-cle of time, God's own sac-ri-fice com-plete. "It is fin-ished!" hear him cry; learn of Je-sus Christ to die.

4. Ear-ly has-ten to the tomb where they laid his breath-less clay; all is sol-i-tude and gloom. Who has tak-en him a-way? Christ is risen! He meets our eyes; Sav-ior, teach us so to rise.

WORDS: James Montgomery, 1820, 1825, alt.
MUSIC: Richard Redhead, 1853

REDHEAD 76
77.77.77

He Never Said a Mumbalin' Word 291

1. They cru-ci-fied my Lord,
2. They nailed him to the tree,
3. They pierced him in the side,
4. His blood came trick-ling down,
5. He hung his head and died,

and he nev-er said a mum-ba-lin' word;

they cru-ci-fied my Lord,
they nailed him to the tree,
they pierced him in the side,
his blood came trick-ling down,
he hung his head and died,

and he nev-er said a mum-ba-lin' word, not a

word, not a word, not a word.
(not a word)   (not a word)   (not a mum-balin' word)

WORDS: Afro-American spiritual
MUSIC: Afro-American spiritual; adapt. and arr. by William Farley Smith, 1986

SUFFERER
Irr.

Adapt. and arr. © 1989 The United Methodist Publishing House

292 What Wondrous Love Is This

1. What won-drous love is this, O my soul, O my soul,
2. What won-drous love is this, O my soul, O my soul,
3. To God and to the Lamb I will sing, I will sing,
4. And when from death I'm free, I'll sing on, I'll sing on,

what won-drous love is this, O my soul! What
what won-drous love is this, O my soul! What
to God and to the Lamb, I will sing; to
and when from death I'm free, I'll sing on; and

won-drous love is this that caused the Lord of bliss to
won-drous love is this, that caused the Lord of life to
God and to the Lamb who is the great I AM, while
when from death I'm free, I'll sing and joy-ful be, and

bear the dread-ful curse for my soul, for my soul, to
lay a-side his crown for my soul, for my soul, to
mil-lions join the theme I will sing, I will sing; while
through e-ter-ni-ty I'll sing on, I'll sing on, and

WORDS: USA folk hymn
MUSIC: USA folk hymn; harm. by Paul J. Christiansen, 1955

WONDROUS LOVE
12 9.12 9

bear	the	dread	- ful	curse	for	my	soul.
lay	a	- side	his	crown	for	my	soul.
mil	- lions	join	the	theme	I	will	sing.
through	e	- ter	- ni	- ty	I'll	sing	on.

Behold the Savior of Mankind 293

Behold the Savior of mankind
nailed to the shameful tree;
how vast the love that him inclined
to bleed and die for thee!

Hark how he groans! while nature shakes,
and earth's strong pillars bend!
The temple's veil in sunder breaks,
the solid marbles rend.

'Tis done! the precious ransom's paid!
"Receive my soul!" he cries;
see where he bows his sacred head!
He bows his head and dies!

But soon he'll break death's envious chain
and in full glory shine.
O Lamb of God, was ever pain,
was ever love like thine?

Written by Samuel Wesley (1662-1735), this is one of the few relics of his papers found after the fire which destroyed the Epworth rectory during the night of February 9, 1709, when his son, young John Wesley, was rescued as a "brand plucked out of the burning." It was first printed in John Wesley's hymnbook *A Collection of Psalms and Hymns* (Charleston, 1737), under the title "On the Crucifixion."

294 Alas! and Did My Savior Bleed

1. A - las! and did my Sav - ior bleed, and
2. Was it for crimes that I have done, he
3. Well might the sun in dark - ness hide, and
4. Thus might I hide my blush - ing face while
5. But drops of tears can ne'er re - pay the

did my Sov-ereign die? Would he de - vote that
groaned up - on the tree? A - maz - ing pit - y!
shut its glo - ries in, when God, the might - y
his dear cross ap - pears; dis - solve my heart in
debt of love I owe. Here, Lord, I give my -

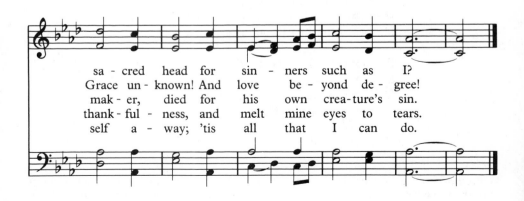

sa - cred head for sin - ners such as I?
Grace un - known! And love be - yond de - gree!
mak - er, died for his own crea - ture's sin.
thank - ful - ness, and melt mine eyes to tears.
self a - way; 'tis all that I can do.

WORDS: Isaac Watts, 1707
MUSIC: Attr. to Hugh Wilson, 1827

MARTYRDOM
CM

In the Cross of Christ I Glory

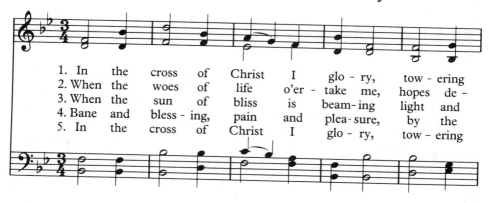

1. In the cross of Christ I glo - ry, tow - ering
2. When the woes of life o'er - take me, hopes de -
3. When the sun of bliss is beam- ing light and
4. Bane and bless - ing, pain and plea- sure, by the
5. In the cross of Christ I glo - ry, tow - ering

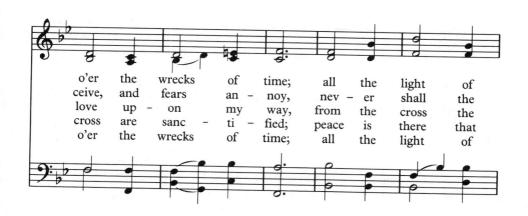

o'er the wrecks of time; all the light of
ceive, and fears an - noy, nev - er shall the
love up - on my way, from the cross the
cross are sanc - ti - fied; peace is there that
o'er the wrecks of time; all the light of

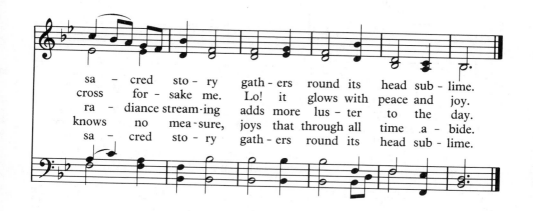

sa - cred sto - ry gath - ers round its head sub - lime.
cross for - sake me. Lo! it glows with peace and joy.
ra - diance stream- ing adds more lus - ter to the day.
knows no mea - sure, joys that through all time a - bide.
sa - cred sto - ry gath - ers round its head sub - lime.

WORDS: John Bowring, 1825
MUSIC: Ithamar Conkey, 1849

RATHBUN
87.87

296 Sing, My Tongue, the Glorious Battle

Unison

1. Sing, my tongue, the glorious battle, sing the ending of the fray; now above the cross, the trophy, sound the loud triumphant lay: tell how Christ, the world's Redeemer, as a victim won the day.

2. Tell how, when at length the fullness of th'appointed time was come, Christ, the Word, was born of woman, left for us his heavenly home; showed us human life made perfect, shone as light amid the gloom.

3. Thus, with thirty years accomplished, went he forth from Nazareth, destined, dedicated, willing, wrought his work, and met his death. Like a lamb he humbly yielded on the cross his dying breath.

4. Faithful cross, thou sign of triumph, now for us the noblest tree, none in foliage, none in blossom, none in fruit thy peer may be; symbol of the world's redemption, for the weight that hung on thee!

5. Unto God be praise and glory: to the Father and the Son, to th'eternal Spirit honor now and evermore be done; praise and glory in the highest, while unending ages run.

WORDS: Venantius Honorius Fortunatus, 6th cent.; trans. by Percy Dearmer, 1931
MUSIC: French carol melody; harm. from *The English Hymnal*, 1906, alt.

PICARDY
87.87.87

Beneath the Cross of Jesus

1. Be - neath the cross of Je - sus I fain would take my stand,
2. Up - on that cross of Je - sus mine eye at times can see
3. I take, O cross, thy shad - ow for my a - bid-ing place;

the shad-ow of a might-y rock with- in a wea-ry land;
the ver - y dy-ing form of One who suf-fered there for me;
I ask no oth - er sun-shine than the sun-shine of his face;

a home with-in the wil-der-ness, a rest up-on the way,
and from my strick-en heart with tears two won-ders I con - fess:
con - tent to let the world go by, to know no gain nor loss,

from the burn-ing of the noon-tide heat, and the bur-den of the day.
the won-ders of re - deem-ing love and my un-wor-thi - ness.
my sin-ful self my on-ly shame, my glo - ry all the cross.

WORDS: Elizabeth C. Clephane, 1872
MUSIC: Frederick C. Maker, 1881

ST. CHRISTOPHER
76.86.86.86

298 When I Survey the Wondrous Cross

1. When I sur-vey the won-drous cross on which the Prince of Glo-ry died, my rich-est gain I count but loss, and pour con-tempt on all my pride.
2. For-bid it, Lord, that I should boast, save in the death of Christ, my God; all the vain things that charm me most, I sac-ri-fice them to his blood.
3. See, from his head, his hands, his feet, sor-row and love flow min-gled down. Did e'er such love and sor-row meet, or thorns com-pose so rich a crown?
4. Were the whole realm of na-ture mine, that were an of-fering far too small; love so a-maz-ing, so di-vine, de-mands my soul, my life, my all.

WORDS: Isaac Watts, 1707 (Gal. 6:14)
MUSIC: Lowell Mason, 1824

HAMBURG
LM

299 When I Survey the Wondrous Cross

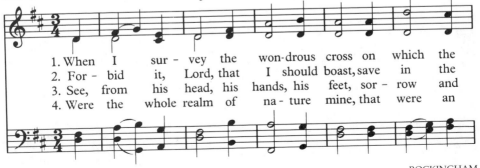

1. When I sur-vey the won-drous cross on which the
2. For-bid it, Lord, that I should boast, save in the
3. See, from his head, his hands, his feet, sor-row and
4. Were the whole realm of na-ture mine, that were an

WORDS: Isaac Watts, 1707 (Gal. 6:14)
MUSIC: Anon.; arr. by Edward Miller, 1790

ROCKINGHAM
LM

Prince of Glo - ry died, my rich - est gain I
death of Christ, my God; all the vain things that
love flow min - gled down. Did e'er such love and
of - fering far too small; love so a - maz - ing,

count but loss, and pour con - tempt on all my pride.
charm me most, I sac - ri - fice them to his blood.
sor - row meet, or thorns com - pose so rich a crown?
so di - vine, de - mands my soul, my life, my all.

O the Lamb

300

O the Lamb, the lov - ing Lamb, the lamb of

Cal - va - ry! The Lamb that was slain, yet

lives a - gain to in - ter - cede for me!

WORDS: 19th cent. campmeeting song; adapt. by Ellen Jane Lorenz, 1980
MUSIC: 19th cent. USA campmeeting melody; arr. by Ellen Jane Lorenz, 1980

THE LAMB
Irr.

301 Jesus, Keep Me Near the Cross

1. Je - sus, keep me near the cross; there a pre - cious foun - tain,
2. Near the cross, a trem-bling soul, love and mer - cy found me;
3. Near the cross! O Lamb of God, bring its scenes be - fore me;
4. Near the cross I'll watch and wait, hop - ing, trust - ing ev - er,

free to all, a heal - ing stream, flows from Cal-vary's moun - tain.
there the bright and morn-ing star sheds its beams a - round me.
help me walk from day to day with its shad - ow o'er me.
till I reach the gold - en strand just be-yond the riv - er.

Refrain

In the cross, in the cross, be my glo - ry ev - er,

till my rap-tured soul shall find rest be-yond the riv - er.

WORDS: Fanny J. Crosby, 1869
MUSIC: William H. Doane, 1869

NEAR THE CROSS
76.76 with Refrain

PASSION AND DEATH, *see further:*

425 O Crucified Redeemer

Christ the Lord Is Risen Today 302

1. Christ the Lord is risen to-day, Al - le - lu - ia!
2. Love's re-deem-ing work is done, Al - le - lu - ia!
3. Lives a-gain our glo-rious King, Al - le - lu - ia!
4. Soar we now where Christ has led, Al - le - lu - ia!
* 5. Hail the Lord of earth and heaven, Al - le - lu - ia!
* 6. King of glo-ry, soul of bliss, Al - le - lu - ia!

Earth and heaven in cho-rus say, Al - le - lu - ia!
Fought the fight, the bat-tle won, Al - le - lu - ia!
Where, O death, is now thy sting? Al - le - lu - ia!
Fol-lowing our ex - alt-ed Head, Al - le - lu - ia!
Praise to thee by both be given, Al - le - lu - ia!
Ev - er - last-ing life is this, Al - le - lu - ia!

Raise your joys and tri - umphs high, Al - le - lu - ia!
Death in vain for - bids him rise, Al - le - lu - ia!
Once he died our souls to save, Al - le - lu - ia!
Made like him, like him we rise, Al - le - lu - ia!
Thee we greet tri - um - phant now, Al - le - lu - ia!
Thee to know, thy power to prove, Al - le - lu - ia!

Sing, ye heavens, and earth re - ply, Al - le - lu - ia!
Christ has o - pened par - a - dise, Al - le - lu - ia!
Where's thy vic - tory, boast-ing grave? Al - le - lu - ia!
Ours the cross, the grave, the skies, Al - le - lu - ia!
Hail the Res - ur - rec-tion, thou, Al - le - lu - ia!
Thus to sing, and thus to love, Al - le - lu - ia!

WORDS: Charles Wesley, 1739
MUSIC: *Lyra Davidica*, 1708

EASTER HYMN
77.77 D

303 The Day of Resurrection

1. The day of res-ur-rec-tion! Earth, tell it out a-broad;
2. Our hearts be pure from e-vil, that we may see a-right
3. Now let the heavens be joy-ful! Let earth the song be-gin!

the pass-o-ver of glad-ness, the pass-o-ver of God.
the Lord in rays e-ter-nal of res-ur-rec-tion light;
Let the round world keep tri-umph, and all that is there-in!

From death to life e-ter-nal, from earth un-to the sky,
and lis-tening to his ac-cents, may hear, so calm and plain,
Let all things seen and un-seen their notes in glad-ness blend,

our Christ hath brought us o-ver, with hymns of vic-to-ry.
his own "All hail!" and, hear-ing, may raise the vic-tor strain.
for Christ the Lord hath ris-en, our joy that hath no end.

WORDS: John of Damascus; trans. by John Mason Neale, 1862
MUSIC: Henry T. Smart, 1835

LANCASHIRE
76.76 D

Easter People, Raise Your Voices 304

1. Eas - ter peo - ple, raise your voic - es, sounds of heaven in
2. Fear of death can no more stop us from our press - ing
3. Ev - ery day to us is Eas - ter, with its res - ur -

earth should ring. Christ has brought us heav - en's choic - es;
here be - low. For our Lord em - pow - ered us to
rec - tion song. When in trou - ble move the fast - er

heaven - ly mu - sic, let it ring. Al - le - lu - ia!
tri - umph o - ver ev - ery foe. Al - le - lu - ia!
to our God who rights the wrong. Al - le - lu - ia!

Al - le - lu - ia! Eas - ter peo - ple, let us sing.
Al - le - lu - ia! On to vic - tory now we go.
Al - le - lu - ia! See the power of heaven - ly throngs.

WORDS: William M. James, 1979
MUSIC: Henry T. Smart, 1867

REGENT SQUARE
87.87.87

Words © 1979 The United Methodist Publishing House

305 Camina, Pueblo de Dios
(Walk On, O People of God)

Estribillo, Unísono (Refrain, Unison)

Ca - mi - na, pue-blo de Dios, ca - mi - na, pue-blo de Dios.

Walk on, O peo-ple of God; walk on, O peo-ple of God!

Nue-va ley, nue-va a - lian-za, en la nue-va cre-a - ción.

A new law, God's new al - li-ance, all cre - a-tion is re - born.

Fine

Ca - mi - na, pue-blo de Dios, ca - mi - na, pue-blo de Dios.

Walk on, O peo-ple of God; walk on, O peo-ple of God!

1. Mi-ra a-llá en el Cal - va-rio en la ro - ca hay u -na cruz;
2. Cris - to to-ma en su cuer-po el pe - ca - do, la es-cla-vi - tud.

1. Look on Cal-va-ry's sum-mit; on the rock there tow-ers a cross;
2. Christ takes in-to his bod - y all our sin, en-slave-ment, and pain;

WORDS: Cesareo Gabaraín; trans. by George Lockwood, 1987
MUSIC: Cesareo Gabaraín; harm. by Juan Luis García, 1987

NUEVA CREACIÓN
78.78 D with Refrain

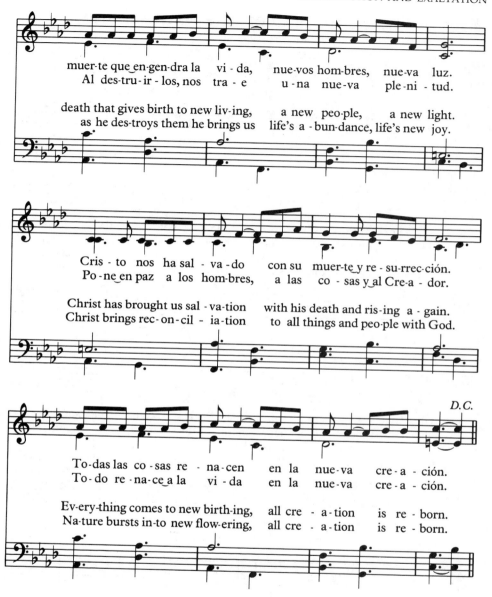

muer-te que_en-gen-dra la vi - da, nue-vos hom-bres, nue-va luz.
Al des-tru-ir - los, nos tra - e u -na nue-va ple -ni - tud.

death that gives birth to new liv-ing, a new peo-ple, a new light.
as he des-troys them he brings us life's a -bun-dance, life's new joy.

Cris - to nos ha sal - va-do con su muer-te_y re - su-rrec-ción.
Po -ne en paz a los hom-bres, a las co - sas y_al Cre-a - dor.

Christ has brought us sal -va-tion with his death and ris-ing a - gain.
Christ brings rec-on-cil - ia-tion to all things and peo-ple with God.

D.C.

To-das las co -sas re - na-cen en la nue-va cre-a - ción.
To- do re -na-ce_a la vi - da en la nue-va cre-a - ción.

Ev-ery-thing comes to new birth-ing, all cre - a-tion is re - born.
Na-ture bursts in-to new flow-ering, all cre - a-tion is re - born.

3. Cielo y tierra se_abrazan,
   nuestra alma halla_el perdón.
   Vuelven a_abrirse los cielos
   para_el hombre pecador.
   Israel peregrino,
   vive_y canta tu redención.
   Hay nuevos mundos abiertos
   en la nueva creación.
   Estribillo

3. Heaven and earth are embracing,
   and our souls find pardon at last.
   Now heaven's gates are reopened
   to the sinner, to us all.
   Israel walks a journey;
   now we live, salvation's our song;
   Christ's resurrection has freed us.
   There are new worlds to explore.
   Refrain

306 The Strife Is O'er, the Battle Done

Antiphon (at the beginning and after stanza 4)

Al - le - lu - ia! Al - le - lu - ia! Al - le - lu - ia!

1. The strife is o'er, the bat - tle done;
2. The powers of death have done their worst,
3. The three sad days are quick - ly sped;
4. Lord, by the stripes which wound - ed thee,

the vic - to - ry of life is won; the song of
but Christ their le - gions hath dis - persed; let shouts of
he ris - es glo - rious from the dead; all glo - ry
from death's dread sting thy ser - vants free, that we may

tri - umph has be - gun: Al - le - lu - ia!
ho - ly joy out - burst: Al - le - lu - ia!
to our ris - en Head! Al - le - lu - ia!
live, and sing to thee: Al - le - lu - ia!

WORDS: Anon. Latin, 1695; trans. by Francis Pott, 1861
MUSIC: Giovanni P. da Palestrina, 1591; arr. by W. H. Monk, 1861

VICTORY
888 with Alleluias

Christ Is Risen

Unison

1. Christ is ris - en! Shout Ho - san - na! Cel - e -
   brate this day of days. Christ is ris - en! Hush in won - der;
   all cre - a - tion is a - mazed. In the de - sert all - sur -
   round - ing, see, a spread - ing tree has grown. Heal - ing leaves of
   grace a - bound - ing bring a taste of love un - known.

2. Christ is ris - en! Raise your spir - its from the
   cav - erns of des - pair. Walk with glad - ness in the morn - ing.
   See what love can do and dare. Drink the wine of res - ur -
   rec - tion, not a ser - vant, but a friend; Je - sus is our
   strong com - pan - ion. Joy and peace shall nev - er end.

3. Christ is ris - en! Earth and heav - en nev - er -
   more shall be the same. Break the bread of new cre - a - tion
   where the world is still in pain. Tell its grim, de - mon - ic
   cho - rus: "Christ is ris - en! Get you gone!" God the First and
   Last is with us. Sing Ho - san - na ev - ery - one!

WORDS: Brian Wren, 1984
MUSIC: Polish carol; arr. by Edith M. G. Reed, 1926; harm. by Austin C. Lovelace, 1964

W ZLOBIE LEZY
447.447 D

308

Thine Be the Glory

1. Thine be the glo - ry, ris - en, con - quering Son;
2. Lo! Je - sus meets thee, ris - en from the tomb;
3. No more we doubt thee, glo - rious Prince of life!

end - less is the vic - tory thou o'er death hast won.
lov - ing - ly he greets thee, scat - ters fear and gloom.
Life is naught with - out thee; aid us in our strife.

An - gels in bright rai - ment rolled the stone a - way,
Let the church with glad - ness hymns of tri - umph sing,
Make us more than con - querors, through thy death - less love;

kept the fold - ed grave-clothes where thy bod - y lay.
for our Lord now liv - eth; death hath lost its sting.
bring us safe through Jor - dan to thy home a - bove.

Refrain

Thine be the glo - ry, ris - en, con - quering Son;

WORDS: Edmond L. Budry, 1904; trans. by R. Birch Hoyle, 1923
MUSIC: *Harmonia Sacra*, ca. 1753; arr. from G. F. Handel, 1747

JUDAS MACCABEUS
55.65.65.65

Trans. by permission of The World Student Christian Federation

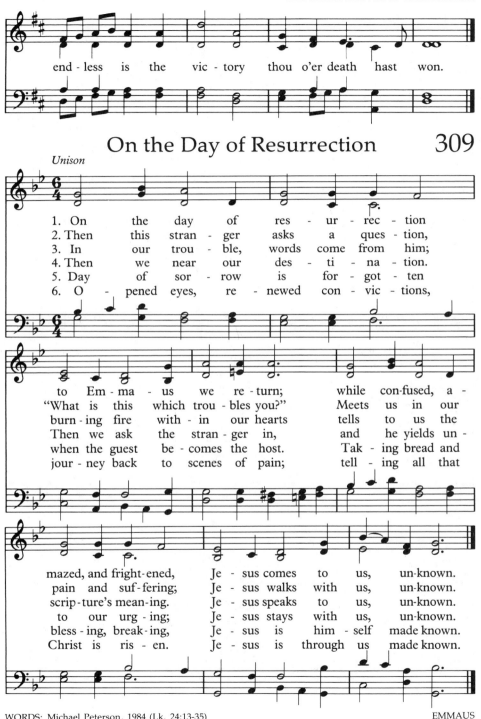

On the Day of Resurrection 309

Unison

1. On the day of res-ur-rec-tion
2. Then this stran-ger asks a ques-tion,
3. In our trou-ble, words come from him;
4. Then we near our des-ti-na-tion.
5. Day of sor-row is for-got-ten
6. O-pened eyes, re-newed con-vic-tions,

to Em-ma-us we re-turn; while con-fused, a-
"What is this which trou-bles you?" Meets us in our
burn-ing fire with-in our hearts tells to us the
Then we ask the stran-ger in, and he yields un-
when the guest be-comes the host. Tak-ing bread and
jour-ney back to scenes of pain; tell-ing all that

mazed, and fright-ened, Je-sus comes to us, un-known.
pain and suf-fering; Je-sus walks with us, un-known.
scrip-ture's mean-ing. Je-sus speaks to us, un-known.
to our urg-ing; Je-sus stays with us, un-known.
bless-ing, break-ing, Je-sus is him-self made known.
Christ is ris-en. Je-sus is through us made known.

WORDS: Michael Peterson, 1984 (Lk. 24:13-35)
MUSIC: Mark Sedio, 1984; harm. by Charles H. Webb, 1987

EMMAUS
87.87

310

He Lives

1. I serve a ris - en Sav - ior, he's in the world to - day;
2. In all the world a - round me I see his lov - ing care,
3. Re - joice, re-joice, O Chris-tian, lift up your voice and sing

I know that he is liv - ing, what - ev - er foes may say.
and though my heart grows wea - ry, I nev - er will de - spair.
e - ter - nal hal - le - lu - jahs to Je - sus Christ the King!

I see his hand of mer - cy, I hear his voice of cheer,
I know that he is lead - ing through all the storm - y blast;
The hope of all who seek him, the help of all who find;

and just the time I need him, he's al - ways near.
the day of his ap - pear-ing will come at last.
none oth - er is so lov-ing, so good and kind.

WORDS: Alfred H. Ackley, 1933
MUSIC: Alfred H. Ackley, 1933

ACKLEY
76.76.76.74 with Refrain

311 Now the Green Blade Riseth

1. Now the green blade ris - eth, from the bur - ied grain,
2. In the grave they laid him, Love who had been slain,
3. Forth he came at Eas - ter, like the ris - en grain,
4. When our hearts are win - try, griev - ing, or in pain,

wheat that in the dark earth man - y days has lain;
think - ing that he nev - er would a - wake a - gain,
Je - sus who for three days in the grave had lain;
Je - sus' touch can call us back to life a - gain,

Love lives a - gain, that with the dead has been:
laid in the earth like grain that sleeps un - seen:
quick from the dead my ris - en Lord is seen:
fields of our hearts that dead and bare have been:

Refrain

Love is come a - gain, like wheat that spring-eth green.

WORDS: J. M. C. Crum, 1928, alt.
MUSIC: Trad. French carol; harm. by Martin Shaw, 1928

FRENCH CAROL
11 10.10 11

Harm. by permission of Oxford University Press

Hail the Day That Sees Him Rise 312

1. Hail the day that sees him rise, Al - le - lu - ia!
2. There the glo-rious tri-umph waits, Al - le - lu - ia!
3. See! the heaven its Lord re-ceives, Al - le - lu - ia!
4. See! he lifts his hands a-bove, Al - le - lu - ia!

To his throne a - bove the skies, Al - le - lu - ia!
Lift your heads, e - ter - nal gates, Al - le - lu - ia!
Yet he loves the earth he leaves, Al - le - lu - ia!
See! he shows the prints of love, Al - le - lu - ia!

Christ, a - while to mor - tals given, Al - le - lu - ia!
Christ hath con-quered death and sin, Al - le - lu - ia!
Though re - turn - ing to his throne, Al - le - lu - ia!
Hark! his gra - cious lips be - stow, Al - le - lu - ia!

Re - as - cends his na - tive heaven, Al - le - lu - ia!
Take the King of glo - ry in, Al - le - lu - ia!
Still he calls the world his own, Al - le - lu - ia!
Bless-ings on his church be - low, Al - le - lu - ia!

WORDS: Charles Wesley, 1739
MUSIC: Robert Williams, 1817; harm. by David Evans, 1927

LLANFAIR
77.77 with Alleluias

Harm. by permission of Oxford University Press

313

Cristo Vive
(Christ Is Risen)

1. ¡Cris - to vi - ve, fue - ra_el llan - to, los la -
2. Que si Cris - to no vi - vie - ra va - na

1. Christ is ris - en, Christ is liv - ing, dry your
2. If the Lord had nev - er ris - en, we'd have

men - tos y_el pe - sar! Ni la muer - te ni_el se -
fue - ra nues - tra fe; mas se cum - ple su pro -

tears, be un - a - fraid! Death and dark - ness could not
noth - ing to be - lieve; but his prom - ise can be

pul - cro lo_han po - di - do su - je - tar.
me - sa: 'Por - que vi - vo, vi - vi - réis.'

hold him, nor the tomb in which he lay.
trust - ed: "You will live, be - cause I live."

No bus - quéis en - tre los muer - tos al que
Si_en A - dán en - tró la muer - te, por Je -

Do not look a - mong the dead for one who
As we share the death of A - dam, so in

WORDS: Nicolás Martínez, 1960; trans. by Fred Kaan, 1972 (1 Cor. 15)
MUSIC: Pablo D. Sosa, 1960

CENTRAL
87.87 D

siem - pre_ha de vi - vir, ¡Cris - to vi - ve! es - tas
sús la vi - da_en - tró; no te - máis, el triun-fo_es

lives for - ev - er - more; tell the world that Christ is
Christ we live a - gain; death has lost its sting and

nue - vas por do - quier de - jad o - ír.
vues - tro: ¡El Se - ñor re - su - ci - tó!

ris - en, make it known he goes be - fore.
ter - ror, Christ the Lord has come to reign.

3. Si_es verdad que de la muerte
   el pecado es aguijón,
   no temáis pues Jesucristo
   nos da vida_y salvación.
   Gracias demos al Dios Padre
   que nos da seguridad,
   que quien cree en Jesucristo
   vive por la_eternidad.

---

3. Death has lost its old dominion,
   let the world rejoice and shout!
   Christ, the firstborn of the living,
   gives us life and leads us out.
   Let us thank our God, who causes
   hope to spring up from the ground.
   Christ is risen, Christ is giving
   life eternal, life profound.

314

In the Garden
(I Come to the Garden Alone)

1. I come to the gar-den a-lone while the dew is
2. He speaks, and the sound of his voice is so sweet the
3. I'd stay in the gar-den with him though the night a-

still on the ros-es, and the voice I hear fall-ing on my ear,
birds hush their sing-ing, and the mel-o-dy that he gave to me
round me be fall-ing, but he bids me go; thru the voice of woe

Refrain

the Son of God dis-clos-es.
with-in my heart is ring-ing. And he walks with me, and he
his voice to me is call-ing.

talks with me, and he tells me I am his own; and the

joy we share as we tar-ry there, none oth-er has ev-er known.

WORDS: C. Austin Miles, 1913 (Jn. 20:11-18)
MUSIC: C. Austin Miles, 1913; adapt. by Charles H. Webb, 1987

GARDEN
89.557 with Refrain

Adapt. © 1989 The United Methodist Publishing House

Come, Ye Faithful, Raise the Strain 315

1. Come, ye faith-ful, raise the strain of tri-um-phant glad-ness;
2. 'Tis the spring of souls to-day; Christ hath burst his pris-on,
3. Now the queen of sea-sons, bright with the day of splen-dor,
4. Neith-er might the gates of death, nor the tomb's dark por-tal,
5. "Al-le-lu-ia!" now we cry to our King im-mor-tal,

God hath brought forth Is-ra-el in-to joy from sad-ness;
and from three days' sleep in death as a sun hath ris-en;
with the roy-al feast of feasts, comes its joy to ren-der;
nor the watch-ers, nor the seal hold thee as a mor-tal;
who, tri-um-phant, burst the bars of the tomb's dark por-tal;

loosed from Phar-aoh's bit-ter yoke Ja-cob's sons and daugh-ters,
all the win-ter of our sins, long and dark, is fly-ing
comes to glad Je-ru-sa-lem, who with true af-fec-tion
but to-day a-midst the twelve thou didst stand, be-stow-ing
"Al-le-lu-ia!" with the Son, God the Fa-ther prais-ing,

led them with un-moist-ened foot through the Red Sea wa-ters.
from his light, to whom we give laud and praise un-dy-ing.
wel-comes in un-wea-ried strains Je-sus' res-ur-rec-tion.
that thy peace which ev-er-more pass-eth hu-man know-ing.
"Al-le-lu-ia!" yet a-gain to the Spir-it rais-ing.

WORDS: John of Damascus; trans. by John Mason Neale, 1859 (Ex. 15)
MUSIC: Arthur S. Sullivan, 1872

ST. KEVIN
76.76 D

Alt. tune: AVE VIRGO VIRGINUM

316

He Rose

1. They cru - ci - fied my Sav - ior and
2. Then Jo - seph begged his bod - y and
3. Sis - ter Ma - ry she came run - ning, a -
4. An an - gel came from heav - en and

nailed him to the tree, they cru - ci - fied my
laid it in the tomb, then Jo - seph begged his
look - ing for my Lord, Sis - ter Ma - ry she came
rolled the stone a - way, an an - gel came from

Sav - ior and nailed him to the tree, they
bod - y and laid it in the tomb, then
run - ning, a - look - ing for my Lord, Sis - ter
heav - en and rolled the stone a - way, an

cru - ci - fied my Sav - ior and nailed him to the tree,
Jo - seph begged his bod - y and laid it in the tomb,
Ma - ry she came run - ning, a - look - ing for my Lord,
an - gel came from heav - en and rolled the stone a - way,

WORDS: Afro-American spiritual
MUSIC: Afro-American spiritual; adapt. and arr. by William Farley Smith, 1986
ASCENSIUS
76.76.76.9 with Refrain

Adapt. and arr. © 1989 The United Methodist Publishing House

317 O Sons and Daughters, Let Us Sing

1. O sons and daugh - ters, let us sing!
2. That Eas - ter morn at break of day,
3. An an - gel clad in white they see,
4. That night the a - pos - tles met in fear;
5. On this most ho - ly day of days

The King of heaven, the glo - rious King,
the faith - ful wom - en went their way
who sat and spake un - to the three,
a - midst them came their Lord most dear,
our hearts and voic - es, Lord, we raise

o'er death and hell rose tri - umph - ing.
to seek the tomb where Je - sus lay.
"Your Lord doth go to Gal - i - lee."
and said, "My peace be on all here."
to thee, in ju - bi - lee and praise.

Refrain

Al - le - lu - ia! Al - le - lu - ia!

WORDS: Jean Tisserand, 15th cent.; trans. by John Mason Neale, 1851, alt.   O FILII ET FILIAE
MUSIC: 15th cent. French carol; harm. by Charles H. Webb, 1987   888 with Alleluias
Harm. © 1989 The United Methodist Publishing House

6. When Thomas first the tidings heard,
how they had seen the risen Lord,
he doubted the disciples' word.
Refrain

7. "My pierced side, O Thomas, see;
my hands, my feet, I show to thee;
not faithless but believing be."
Refrain

8. No longer Thomas then denied;
he saw the feet, the hands, the side;
"Thou art my Lord and God," he cried.
Refrain

9. How blest are they who have not seen,
and yet whose faith hath constant been,
for they eternal life shall win.
Refrain

Stanzas 1-5 for Easter Sunday; stanzas 1 and 6-9 for the second Sunday of Easter.

Christ Is Alive 318

1. Christ is a-live! Let Chris-tians sing. His cross stands emp-ty to the sky. Let streets and homes with prais-es ring. His love in death shall nev-er die.
2. Christ is a-live! No long-er bound to dis-tant years in Pal-es-tine, he comes to claim the here and now and dwell in ev-ery place and time.
3. Not throned a-far, re-mote-ly high, un-touched, un-moved by hu-man pains, but dai-ly, in the midst of life, our Sav-ior in the God-head reigns.
4. In ev-ery in-sult, rift, and war, where col-or, scorn, or wealth di-vide, he suf-fers still, yet loves the more, and lives, though ev-er cru-ci-fied.
5. Christ is a-live, and comes to bring good news to this and ev-ery age, till earth and all cre-a-tion ring with joy, with jus-tice, love, and praise.

WORDS: Brian Wren, 1968, alt.
MUSIC: *Psalmodia Evangelica*, 1789

TRURO
LM

Words © 1975 Hope Publishing Co.

319 Christ Jesus Lay in Death's Strong Bands

1. Christ Jesus lay in death's strong bands, for our offenses given; but now at God's right hand he stands, and brings us life from heaven; wherefore let us joyful be, and sing to

2. It was a strange and dreadful strife when life and death contended; the victory remained with life; the reign of death was ended. Stripped of power, no more it reigns, an empty

3. So let us keep the festival whereto the Lord invites us; Christ is himself the joy of all, the Sun that warms and lights us. By his grace he doth impart eternal

4. Then let us feast this Easter day on the true bread of heaven; the Word of grace hath purged away the old and wicked leaven. Christ alone our souls will feed; he is our

WORDS: Martin Luther, 1524; trans. by Richard Massie, 1854
MUSIC: *Geistliche Gesangbüchlein,* 1524;
arr. and harm. by J. S. Bach, 1724

CHRIST LAG IN TODESBANDEN
87.87.78.74

God right thank - ful - ly loud songs of Al - le -
form a - lone re - mains; death's sting is lost for -
sun - shine to the heart; the night of sin is
meat and drink in - deed; faith lives up - on no

lu - ia!
ev - er! Al - le - lu - ia!
end - ed!
oth - er!

Easter Vigil or Day 320

Almighty God,
through Jesus Christ you overcame death
and opened to us the gate of everlasting life.
Grant that we,
who celebrate the day of our Lord's resurrection,
may, by the renewing of your Spirit
arise from the death of sin to the life of righteousness;
through Jesus Christ our Lord. **Amen.**

The Book of Hymns, 1966

Sundays of Easter 321

Almighty God,
you give us the joy of celebrating our Lord's resurrection.
Give us also the joys of life in your service,
and bring us at last to the full joy of life eternal;
through Jesus Christ our Lord. **Amen.**

The Lutheran Book of Worship, 1978

322 Up from the Grave He Arose

1. Low in the grave he lay, Je - sus my Sav - ior,
2. Vain - ly they watch his bed, Je - sus my Sav - ior;
3. Death can - not keep its prey, Je - sus my Sav - ior;

wait - ing the com - ing day, Je - sus my Lord!
vain - ly they seal the dead, Je - sus my Lord!
he tore the bars a - way, Je - sus my Lord!

Refrain

Up from the grave he a - rose, with a
(he a - rose)

might - y tri - umph o'er his foes; he a -
(o'er his foes)

WORDS: Robert Lowry, 1874
MUSIC: Robert Lowry, 1874

CHRIST AROSE
65.64 with Refrain

rose a vic - tor from the dark do - main, and he
lives for - ev - er, with his saints to reign. He a -
rose! He a - rose! Hal- le - lu -jah! Christ a - rose!
(he a-rose) (he a-rose)

The Ascension 323

Everliving God,
your eternal Christ once dwelt on earth,
    confined by time and space.
Give us faith to discern in every time and place
    the presence among us
    of him who is head over all things and fills all,
even Jesus Christ our ascended Lord. **Amen.**

Laurence Hull Stookey, USA, 20th cent. (Lk. 24:51; Acts 1:9-11; Eph. 1:16-23)
© 1989 The United Methodist Publishing House

324 Hail Thee, Festival Day

Refrain (Unison)

Hail thee, fes-ti-val day! blest day to be hal-lowed for-ev-er;

Fine

(Easter) day when our Lord was raised, break-ing the king-dom of death.
(Ascension) day when our ris-en Lord rose in the heav-ens to reign.
(Pentecost) day when the Ho-ly Ghost shone in the world full of grace.

1. (Easter) All the fair beau-ty of earth, from the
1. (Ascension) He who was nailed to the cross is
1. (Pentecost) Bright and in like-ness of fire, on

3. (All seasons) God the Al-might-y, the Lord, the
5. (All seasons) Spir-it of life and of power, now

death of the win-ter a-ris-ing! Ev-ery good
Rul-er and Lord of all peo-ple. All things cre-
those who a-wait your ap-pear-ing, you whom the

Rul-er of earth and the heav-ens, guard us from
flow in us, fount of our be-ing, light that en-

WORDS: Venantius Honorius Fortunatus; trans. from *The English Hymnal*, 1906, alt.
MUSIC: Ralph Vaughan Williams, 1906

SALVE FESTA DIES
79.77 with Refrain

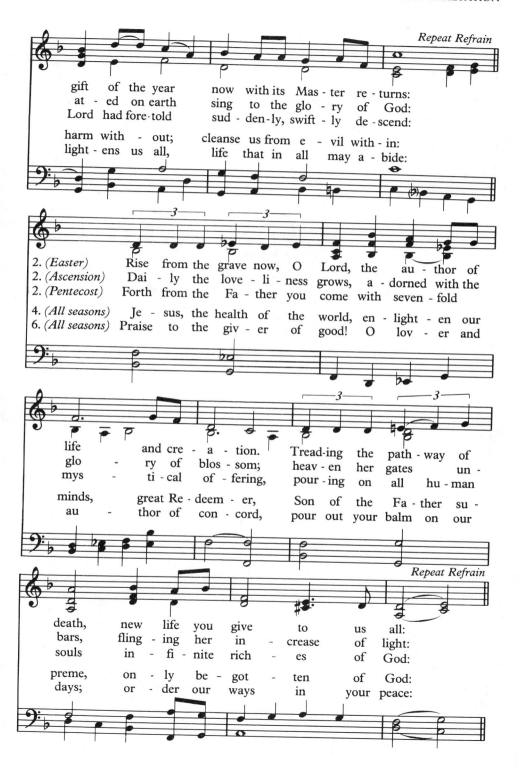

Repeat Refrain

gift of the year   now with its Mas-ter re-turns:
at - ed on earth   sing to the glo-ry of God:
Lord had fore-told   sud-den-ly, swift-ly de-scend:

harm with - out;   cleanse us from e - vil with-in:
light - ens us all,   life that in all may a - bide:

2. (Easter)   Rise from the grave now, O Lord, the au - thor of
2. (Ascension)   Dai - ly the love - li - ness grows, a - dorned with the
2. (Pentecost)   Forth from the Fa - ther you come with seven - fold
4. (All seasons)   Je - sus, the health of the world, en - light - en our
6. (All seasons)   Praise to the giv - er of good! O lov - er and

life   and cre - a - tion.   Tread-ing the path - way of
glo - ry of blos - som;   heav - en her gates un -
mys - ti - cal of - fering,   pour-ing on all hu - man
minds,   great Re - deem - er, Son of the Fa - ther su -
au - thor of con - cord,   pour out your balm on our

Repeat Refrain

death,   new life you give to us all:
bars,   fling - ing her in - crease of light:
souls   in - fi - nite rich - es of God:
preme,   on - ly be - got - ten of God:
days;   or - der our ways in your peace:

325 Hail, Thou Once Despised Jesus

1. Hail, thou once de - spis - ed Je - sus! Hail, thou Gal - i -
2. Pas - chal Lamb, by God ap - point - ed, all our sins on
3. Je - sus, hail! en - throned in glo - ry, there for - ev - er
4. Wor - ship, hon - or, power, and bless - ing Christ is wor - thy

le - an King! Thou didst suf - fer to re - lease us; thou didst
thee were laid; by al - might - y love a - noint - ed, thou hast
to a - bide; all the heaven - ly hosts a - dore thee, seat - ed
to re - ceive; loud - est prais - es, with - out ceas - ing, right it

free sal - va - tion bring. Hail, thou u - ni - ver - sal
full a - tone - ment made. Ev - ery sin may be for -
at thy Fa - ther's side. There for sin - ners thou art
is for us to give. Help, ye bright an - gel - ic

Sav - ior, who hast borne our sin and shame! By thy mer - its
giv - en through the vir - tue of thy blood; o - pened is the
plead - ing; there thou dost our place pre - pare; thou for saints art
spir - its, bring your sweet - est, no - blest lays; help to sing of

WORDS: Attr. to John Bakewell, 1757, and Martin Madan, 1760, alt. (Rev. 4:2-11)
MUSIC: Trad. Dutch melody; arr. by Julius Roentgen, 1906

IN BABILONE
87.87 D

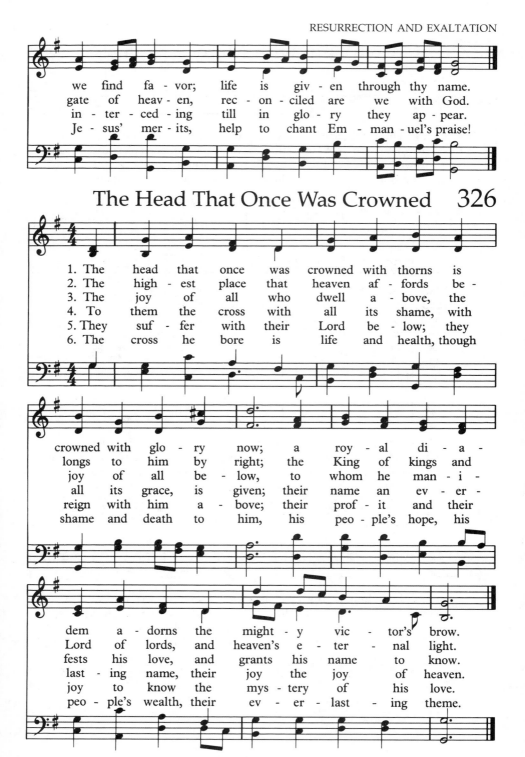

we find fa - vor; life is giv - en through thy name.
gate of heav - en, rec - on - ciled are we with God.
in - ter - ced - ing till in glo - ry they ap - pear.
Je - sus' mer - its, help to chant Em - man - uel's praise!

The Head That Once Was Crowned 326

1. The head that once was crowned with thorns is
2. The high - est place that heaven af - fords be -
3. The joy of all who dwell a - bove, the
4. To them the cross with all its shame, with
5. They suf - fer with their Lord be - low; they
6. The cross he bore is life and health, though

crowned with glo - ry now; a roy - al di - a -
longs to him by right; the King of kings and
joy of all be - low, to whom he man - i -
all its grace, is given; their name an ev - er -
reign with him a - bove; their prof - it and their
shame and death to him, his peo - ple's hope, his

dem a - dorns the might - y vic - tor's brow.
Lord of lords, and heaven's e - ter - nal light.
fests his love, and grants his name to know.
last - ing name, their joy the joy of heaven.
joy to know the mys - tery of his love.
peo - ple's wealth, their ev - er - last - ing theme.

WORDS: Thomas Kelly, 1820 (Heb. 2:9-10)
MUSIC: Attr. to Jeremiah Clark, 1707; harm. by W. H. Monk, 1868

ST. MAGNUS
CM

327 Crown Him with Many Crowns

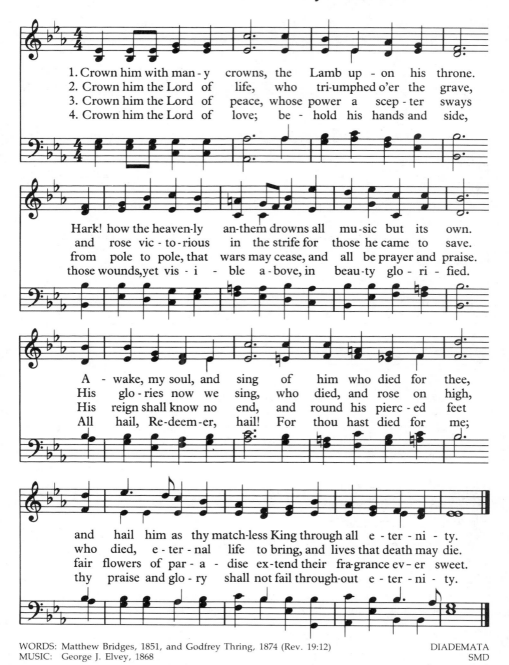

1. Crown him with man-y crowns, the Lamb up-on his throne.
2. Crown him the Lord of life, who tri-umphed o'er the grave,
3. Crown him the Lord of peace, whose power a scep-ter sways
4. Crown him the Lord of love; be-hold his hands and side,

Hark! how the heaven-ly an-them drowns all mu-sic but its own.
and rose vic-to-rious in the strife for those he came to save.
from pole to pole, that wars may cease, and all be prayer and praise.
those wounds, yet vis-i-ble a-bove, in beau-ty glo-ri-fied.

A-wake, my soul, and sing of him who died for thee,
His glo-ries now we sing, who died, and rose on high,
His reign shall know no end, and round his pierc-ed feet
All hail, Re-deem-er, hail! For thou hast died for me;

and hail him as thy match-less King through all e-ter-ni-ty.
who died, e-ter-nal life to bring, and lives that death may die.
fair flowers of par-a-dise ex-tend their fra-grance ev-er sweet.
thy praise and glo-ry shall not fail through-out e-ter-ni-ty.

WORDS: Matthew Bridges, 1851, and Godfrey Thring, 1874 (Rev. 19:12)   DIADEMATA
MUSIC: George J. Elvey, 1868   SMD

RESURRECTION AND EXALTATION, *see further:*

636 Christian People, Raise Your Song   715, 716 Rejoice, the Lord Is King
177 He Is Lord

Surely the Presence of the Lord · · · 328

Sure-ly the pres-ence of the Lord is in this place;
I can feel his might-y pow-er and his grace.
I can hear the brush of an-gels' wings,
I see glo-ry on each face; sure-ly the
pres-ence of the Lord is in this place.

WORDS: Lanny Wolfe, 1977
MUSIC: Lanny Wolfe, 1977

WOLFE
11 11.9 7 12

329 Prayer to the Holy Spirit

O Great Spirit,
    whose breath gives life to the world,
    and whose voice is heard in the soft breeze:
We need your strength and wisdom.
Cause us to walk in beauty. Give us eyes
    ever to behold the red and purple sunset.
Make us wise so that we may understand
    what you have taught us.
Help us learn the lessons you have hidden
    in every leaf and rock.
Make us always ready to come to you
    with clean hands and steady eyes,
so when life fades, like the fading sunset,
    our spirits may come to you without shame. **Amen.**

Trad. Native American prayer

330 Daw-Kee, Aim Daw-Tsi-Taw
(Great Spirit, Now I Pray)

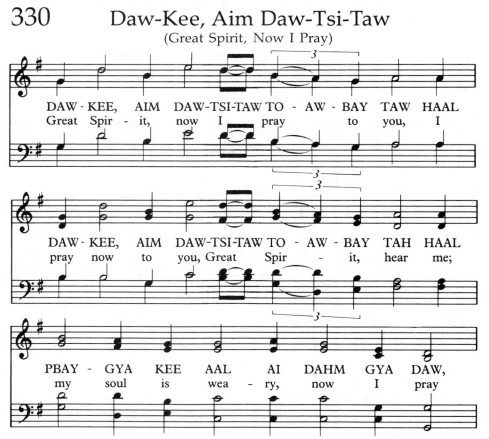

DAW - KEE,   AIM   DAW-TSI-TAW TO - AW - BAY   TAW   HAAL
Great Spir - it,   now   I   pray   to   you,   I

DAW - KEE,   AIM   DAW-TSI-TAW TO - AW - BAY   TAH   HAAL
pray   now   to   you, Great   Spir - it,   hear   me;

PBAY - GYA   KEE   AAL   AI   DAHM   GYA   DAW,
my   soul   is   wea - ry,   now   I   pray

WORDS: Kiowa prayer; para. by Libby Littlechief, 1981
MUSIC: Native American melody; arr. by Charles Boynton, 1981

KIOWA
Irr.

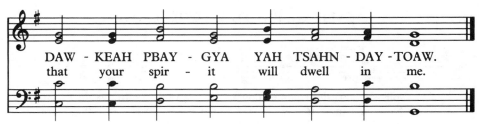

DAW - KEAH PBAY - GYA   YAH TSAHN - DAY -TOAW.
that   your   spir - it   will   dwell   in   me.

Holy Spirit, Come, Confirm Us   331

1. Ho - ly   Spir - it,   come, con - firm   us   in   the
2. Ho - ly   Spir - it,   come, con - sole   us,   come as
3. Ho - ly   Spir - it,   come, re - new   us,   come your -
4. Ho - ly   Spir - it,   come, pos - sess   us,   you   the

truth that Christ makes   known;   we have faith   and   un - der -
ad - vo - cate   to   plead;   lov - ing   Spir - it from the
self   to make us   live;   ho - ly through your lov - ing
love of Three in   One,   Ho - ly   Spir - it   of   the

stand - ing through your   help - ing   gifts   a - lone.
Fa - ther,   grant in   Christ the   help   we   need.
pres - ence,   ho - ly   through the   gifts   you   give.
Fa - ther,   Ho - ly   Spir - it   of   the   Son.

WORDS: Brian Foley   FOR THE BREAD
MUSIC: V. Earle Copes, 1960   87.87

332 Spirit of Faith, Come Down

1. Spir-it of faith, come down, re-veal the things of God,
2. No one can tru-ly say that Je-sus is the Lord,
3. O that the world might know the all-a-ton-ing Lamb!
4. In-spire the liv-ing faith (which who-so-e'er re-ceive,

and make to us the God-head known, and wit-ness
un-less thou take the veil a-way and breathe the
Spir-it of faith, de-scend and show the vir-tue
the wit-ness in them-selves they have and con-scious-

with the blood. 'Tis thine the blood to ap-ply
liv-ing Word. Then, on-ly then, we feel
of his name; the grace which all may find,
ly be-lieve), the faith that con-quers all,

and give us eyes to see, who did for ev-ery
our in-terest in his blood, and cry with joy un-
the sav-ing power, im-part, and tes-ti-fy to
and doth the moun-tain move, and saves who-e'er on

WORDS: Charles Wesley, 1746
MUSIC: *Sacred Harp* (Mason), 1840

BEALOTH
SMD

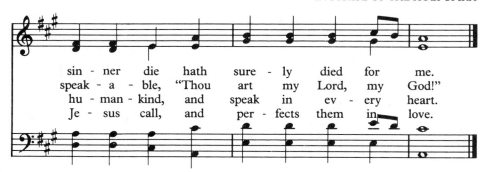

sin - ner die hath sure - ly died for me.
speak - a - ble, "Thou art my Lord, my God!"
hu - man - kind, and speak in ev - ery heart.
Je - sus call, and per - fects them in love.

I'm Goin' a Sing When the Spirit Says Sing 333

1. I'm goin' - a sing* when the Spir - it says sing,

I'm goin' - a sing when the Spir - it says sing,

I'm goin' - a sing when the Spir - it says sing, and o -

bey the Spir - it of the Lord.

*2. pray 3. moan 4. shout

WORDS: Afro-American spiritual
MUSIC: Afro-American spiritual; adapt. by William Farley Smith, 1986

I'M GOIN'A SING
Irr.

334 Sweet, Sweet Spirit

There's a sweet, sweet Spir-it in this place, and I know that it's the Spir-it of the Lord; there are sweet ex-pres-sions on each face, and I know they feel the pres-ence of the Lord.

Refrain

Sweet Ho-ly Spir-it, sweet heav-en-ly Dove, stay right here

WORDS: Doris Akers, 1962
MUSIC: Doris Akers, 1962

SWEET, SWEET SPIRIT
Irr. with Refrain

with us, fill-ing us with your love; and for these bless-ings

we lift our hearts in praise; with-out a doubt we'll know

that we have been re-vived when we shall leave this place.

An Invitation to the Holy Spirit 335

O God, the Holy Spirit,
    come to us, and among us;
    come as the wind, and cleanse us;
    come as the fire, and burn;
    come as the dew, and refresh;
convict, convert, and consecrate
    many hearts and lives
        to our great good
        and to thy greater glory;
and this we ask for Jesus Christ's sake. **Amen.**

Eric Milner-White, England, 20th cent.

By permission of SPCK

336   Of All the Spirit's Gifts to Me

1. Of all the Spir-it's gifts to me, I
2. The Spir-it shows me love's the root of
3. The Spir-it shows if I pos-sess a
4. Though what's a-head is mys-ter-y, and
5. We go in peace, but made a-ware that,

pray that I may nev-er cease to take and
ev-ery gift sent from a-bove, of ev-ery
love no e-vil can de-stroy; how-ev-er
life it-self is ours on lease, each day the
in a need-y world like this, our clear-est

trea-sure most these three: love, joy, and peace.
flower, of ev-ery fruit, that God is love.
great is my dis-tress, then this is joy.
Spir-it says to me, "Go forth in peace!"
pur-pose is to share love, joy, and peace.

WORDS: Fred Pratt Green, 1979   MEYER
MUSIC: *Seelenfreud* (J. Meyer, 1692)   88.84

IN PRAISE OF THE HOLY SPIRIT, *see further:*

Only Trust Him

1. Come, ev - ery soul by sin op-pressed, there's
2. For Je - sus shed his pre - cious blood rich
3. Yes, Je - sus is the truth, the way that
4. Come then and join this ho - ly band, and

mer - cy with the Lord; and he will sure - ly
bless - ings to be - stow; plunge now in - to the
leads you in - to rest; be - lieve in him with -
on to glo - ry go, to dwell in that ce -

give you rest, by trust - ing in his Word.
crim - son flood that wash - es bright as snow.
out de - lay, and you are ful - ly blest.
les - tial land where joys im - mor - tal flow.

Refrain

On - ly trust him, on - ly trust him, on - ly trust him now.

He will save you, he will save you, he will save you now.

WORDS: John H. Stockton, 1874
MUSIC: John H. Stockton, 1869

STOCKTON
CM with Refrain

338
Where He Leads Me

1. I can hear my Sav - ior call - ing,
2. I'll go with him through the gar - den,
3. I'll go with him through the judg - ment,
4. He will give me grace and glo - ry,

I can hear my Sav - ior call - ing,
I'll go with him through the gar - den,
I'll go with him through the judg - ment,
he will give me grace and

I can hear my Sav - ior
I'll go with him through the
I'll go with him through the
he will give me grace and

call - ing, "Take thy cross and fol-low, fol - low me."
gar - den, I'll go with him, with him all the way.
judg - ment, I'll go with him, with him all the way.
glo - ry, and go with me, with me all the way.

Refrain

Where he leads me I will fol - low, where he leads me

I will fol - low, where he leads me I will

WORDS: E. W. Blandy, 1890 (Mk. 8:34; Mt. 8:19)
MUSIC: John S. Norris, 1890

NORRIS
888.9 with Refrain

fol - low; I'll go with him, with him all the way.

Come, Sinners, to the Gospel Feast 339

1. Come, sin - ners, to the gos - pel feast; let ev - ery
2. Sent by my Lord, on you I call; the in - vi -
3. Come, all ye souls by sin op - pressed, ye rest - less
4. My mes - sage as from God re - ceive; ye all may
5. This is the time, no more de - lay! This is the

soul be Je - sus' guest. Ye need not one be
ta - tion is to all. Come, all the world! Come,
wan - derers af - ter rest; ye poor, and maimed, and
come to Christ and live. O let his love your
Lord's ac - cept - ed day. Come thou, this mo - ment,

left be - hind, for God hath bid all hu - man - kind.
sin - ner, thou! All things in Christ are read - y now.
halt, and blind, in Christ a heart - y wel - come find.
hearts con - strain, nor suf - fer him to die in vain.
at his call, and live for him who died for all.

WORDS: Charles Wesley, 1747 (Lk. 14:16-24)
MUSIC: *Katholisches Gesangbuch*, ca. 1774; adapt. from *Metrical Psalter*, 1855

HURSLEY
LM

340 Come, Ye Sinners, Poor and Needy

1. Come, ye sin - ners, poor and need - y, weak and
2. Come, ye thirst - y, come, and wel - come, God's free
3. Come ye wea - ry, hea - vy lad - en, lost and
4. Let not con - science make you lin - ger, nor of

wound - ed, sick and sore; Je - sus read - y
boun - ty glo - ri - fy; true be - lief and
ruin - ed by the fall; if you tar - ry
fit - ness fond - ly dream; all the fit - ness

stands to save you, full of pit - y, love, and power.
true re - pen - tance, ev - ery grace that brings you nigh.
till you're bet - ter, you will nev - er come at all.
he re - quir - eth is to feel your need of him.

Refrain

I will a - rise and go to Je - sus;

WORDS: Joseph Hart, 1759
MUSIC: *The Southern Harmony*, 1835; harm. by Charles H. Webb, 1987

Harm. © 1989 The United Methodist Publishing House

RESTORATION
87.87 with Refrain

Alt. tune: BEACH SPRING

he will em-brace me with his arms; in the arms of
my dear Sav-ior, O there are ten thou-sand charms.

I Sought the Lord 341

1. I sought the Lord, and af-ter-ward I knew he moved my
2. Thou didst reach forth thy hand and mine en-fold; I walked and
3. I find, I walk, I love, but oh, the whole of love is

soul to seek him, seek-ing me. It was not I that
sank not on the storm-vexed sea. 'Twas not so much that
but my an-swer, Lord, to thee! For thou wert long be-

found, O Sav-ior true; no, I was found of thee.
I on thee took hold, as thou, dear Lord, on me.
fore-hand with my soul; al-ways thou lov-edst me.

WORDS: Anon., ca. 1890
MUSIC: George W. Chadwick, 1890

PEACE
10 10.10 6

342 Where Shall My Wondering Soul Begin

Where shall my wondering soul begin?
How shall I all to heaven aspire?
A slave redeemed from death and sin,
a brand plucked from eternal fire,
how shall I equal triumphs raise,
and sing my great deliverer's praise?

O how shall I the goodness tell,
Father, which thou to me hast showed?
That I, a child of wrath and hell,
I should be called a child of God!
Should know, should feel my sins forgiven,
blest with this antepast of heaven!

And shall I slight my Father's love,
or basely fear his gifts to own?
Unmindful of his favors prove,
shall I, the hallowed cross to shun,
refuse his righteousness to impart,
by hiding it within my heart?

Outcasts of men, to you I call,
harlots and publicans and thieves;
he spreads his arms to embrace you all,
sinners alone his grace receive.
No need of him the righteous have;
he came the lost to seek and save.

Come, O my guilty brethren, come,
groaning beneath your load of sin;
his bleeding heart shall make you room,
his open side shall take you in.
He calls you now, invites you home:
come, O my guilty brethren, come.

For you the purple current flowed
in pardon from his wounded side,
languished for you the eternal God,
for you the Prince of Glory died.
Believe, and all your guilt's forgiven,
only believe—and yours is heaven.

This is generally thought to be part of the 8-verse hymn which Charles Wesley wrote shortly after his conversion, perhaps the one intended in the comment on the conversion of his brother on May 24, 1738: "Towards ten, my brother was brought in triumph by a troop of our friends, and declared, 'I believe.' We sang the hymn with great joy, and parted with prayer."

Come Back Quickly to the Lord

343

1.-3. Come back quick-ly to the Lord, just come back to the Lord.

Though how grave your sins may be, or how bur-den-some they
Our Lord waits ev-ery day with his doors kept o-pen
Though you think that you have sinned and aren't fit to be his

seem, there is no sin he can-not bear, nor
wide. He is anx-ious-ly wait-ing for you ev-ery
child, God will cel-e-brate with a big feast, when re-

sin-ner not ac-cept, for the bo-som of our
day and ev-ery night. The Lord is wait-ing
pen-tance brings you home. So, come back to his

lov-ing Lord is much great-er than all the skies.
through the night for a child who has gone a-stray.
o-pen arms, come back quick-ly un-to the Lord.

WORDS: Young Taik Chun, 1943; trans. by Sang E. Chun and Ivy G. Chun, 1988 (Lk. 15:11-32) KOREA
MUSIC: Jae Hoon Park   Irr.

© 1989 The United Methodist Publishing House

344 Tú Has Venido a la Orilla
(Lord, You Have Come to the Lakeshore)

Unísono (Unison)

1. Tú has ve - ni - do a la o - ri - lla,
2. Tú sa - bes bien lo que ten - go:

1. Lord, you have come to the lake - shore
2. You know so well my pos - ses - sions;

no has bus - ca - do ni a sa - bios ni a ri - cos,
en mi bar - ca no hay o - ro ni es - pa - das,

look - ing nei - ther for wealth-y nor wise ones;
my boat car - ries no gold and no weap - ons;

tan só - lo quie - res que yo te si - ga.
tan só - lo re - des y mi tra - ba - jo.

you on - ly asked me to fol - low hum - bly.
you will find there my nets and la - bor.

Estribillo (Refrain)

Se - ñor, me has mi - ra - do a los o - jos

O Lord, with your eyes you have searched me,

WORDS: Cesareo Gabaraín; trans. by Gertrude C. Suppe, George
Lockwood, and Raquel Gutiérrez-Achon, 1987 (Mt. 4:18-22;
Mk. 1:16-20; Lk. 5:1-11)
MUSIC: Cesareo Gabaraín; harm. by Skinner Chávez-Melo, 1987

PESCADOR DE HOMBRES
Irr. with Refrain

y son-rien - do   has di-cho mi nom - bre;
and while smil - ing   have spo-ken my name;

en la a - re - na   he de-ja-do mi bar - ca;
now my boat's left   on the shore-line be-hind me;

jun -to a ti   bus-ca-ré o-tro mar.
by your side   I will seek oth-er seas.

3. Tú necesitas mis manos,
   mi cansancio que a otros descanse,
   amor que quiera seguir amando.
   Estribillo

4. Tú, pescador de otros mares,
   ansia eterna de almas que esperan,
   amigo bueno, que así me llamas.
   Estribillo

3. You need my hands, full of caring
   through my labors to give others rest,
   and constant love that keeps on loving.
   Refrain

4. You, who have fished other oceans,
   ever longed for by souls who are waiting,
   my loving friend, as thus you call me.
   Refrain

345 'Tis the Old Ship of Zion

2. Ain't no danger in the water,
3. It was good for my dear mother,
4. It was good for my dear father,
5. It will take us all to heaven,

Other traditional words for the refrain: Give me that old time religion, . . . it is good enough for me.

WORDS: Afro-American spiritual   YARMOUTH
MUSIC: Afro-American spiritual; adapt. and arr. by William Farley Smith, 1986   Irr.

Adapt. and arr. © 1989 The United Methodist Publishing House

Sinners, Turn: Why Will You Die   346

Sinners, turn: why will you die?
God, your Maker, asks you why.
God, who did your being give,
made you himself, that you might live;
he the fatal cause demands,
asks the work of his own hands.
Why, you thankless creatures, why
will you cross his love, and die?

Sinners, turn: why will you die?
God, your Savior, asks you why.
God, who did your souls retrieve,
died himself, that you might live.
Will you let him die in vain?
Crucify your Lord again?
Why, you ransomed sinners, why
will you slight his grace, and die?

Sinners, turn: why will you die?
God, the Spirit, asks you why;
he, who all your lives hath strove,
wooed you to embrace his love.
Will you not his grace receive?
Will you still refuse to live?
Why, you long-sought sinners, why
will you grieve your God, and die?

You, on whom he favors showers,
you, possessed of nobler powers,
you, of reason's powers possessed,
you, with will and memory blest,
you, with finer sense endued,
creatures capable of God;
noblest of his creatures, why,
why will you forever die?

You, whom he ordained to be
transcripts of the Trinity,
you, whom he in life doth hold,
you, for whom himself was sold,
you, on whom he still doth wait,
whom he would again create;
made by him, and purchased, why,
why will you forever die?

You, who own his record true,
you, his chosen people, you,
you, who call the Savior Lord,
you, who read his written Word,
you, who see the gospel light,
claim a crown in Jesu's right;
why will you, ye Christians, why
will the house of Israel die?

Turn, he cries, ye sinners, turn;
by his life your God hath sworn;
he would have you turn and live,
he would all the world receive;
he hath brought to all the race
full salvation by his grace;
he hath no one soul passed by;
why will you resolve to die?

Can ye doubt, if God is love,
if to all his mercies move?
Will ye not his word receive?
Will ye not his oath believe?
See, the suffering God appears!
Jesus weeps! Believe his tears!
Mingled with his blood they cry,
why will you resolve to die?

Suggested tune: MESSIAH

Charles Wesley, 1742 (Ezek. 18:31-32)

347

Spirit Song

1. O let the Son of God en-fold you with his
(2. O come and) sing this song with glad-ness as your

Spir - it and his love. Let him fill your heart and
hearts are filled with joy. Lift your hands in sweet sur -

sat - is - fy your soul. O let him have the things that
ren - der to his name. O give him all your tears and

hold you, and his Spir - it like a dove will de -
sad - ness; give him all your years of pain, and you'll

WORDS: John Wimber, 1979
MUSIC: John Wimber, 1979

© 1979 Mercy Publishing

SPIRIT SONG
9 7 11 D

348 Softly and Tenderly Jesus Is Calling

1. Soft - ly and ten - der - ly Je - sus is call - ing,
2. Why should we tar - ry when Je - sus is plead - ing,
3. Time is now fleet - ing, the mo - ments are pass - ing,
4. O for the won - der - ful love he has prom - ised,

call - ing for you and for me; see, on the por - tals he's
plead-ing for you and for me? Why should we lin - ger and
pass - ing from you and from me; shad - ows are gath - er - ing,
prom-ised for you and for me! Though we have sinned, he has

wait - ing and watch - ing, watch - ing for you and for me.
heed not his mer-cies, mer-cies for you and for me?
death-beds are com - ing, com - ing for you and for me.
mer - cy and par - don, par - don for you and for me.

Refrain

Come home, come home; you who are
Come home, come home;

WORDS: Will L. Thompson, 1880
MUSIC: Will L. Thompson, 1880

THOMPSON
11 7.11 7 with Refrain

wea-ry, come home; ear-nest-ly, ten-der-ly,

Je - sus is call-ing, call-ing, O sin-ner, come home!

Turn Your Eyes upon Jesus 349

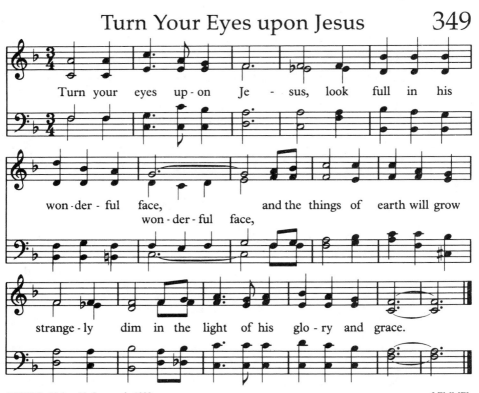

Turn your eyes up-on Je - sus, look full in his

won-der-ful face,
won-der-ful face, and the things of earth will grow

strange-ly dim in the light of his glo-ry and grace.

WORDS: Helen H. Lemmel, 1922
MUSIC: Helen H. Lemmel, 1922

LEMMEL
Irr.

350 Come, All of You

1. Come, all of you, come, men and wom-en, come for-ward,
2. Come, all of you, come, bear-ers of bur-den, come for-ward,
3. Come, all of you, come, trou-ble – mind-ed, come for-ward,
4. Come, all of you, come, hun-gry and poor, come for-ward,

drink of the wa-ter pro-vid-ed for you;
I will give you rest; don't wait for long;
I will give you peace, the peace-ful mind;
buy your milk and wine with-out mon-ey;

all of you who are thirst-y, come to me to drink
all of you who are wea-ry, come to me, the Christ
all of you who are hun-gry, come to me, re-ceive
come for free, bring no pen-ny; come to me, re-ceive the

from the wa-ter of life, pro-vid-ed by Je-sus your Lord.
Je-sus the Lord of all, the Sav-ior, King of hu-man-kind.
bread and the wa-ter of life, pro-vid-ed by Je-sus your Lord.
bread and the wa-ter of life, pro-vid-ed by Je-sus your Lord.

WORDS: Laotian hymn; trans. by Cher Lue Vang, 1987 (Rev. 22:17; Mt. 11:28;
    Jn. 14:27; Is. 55:1-2)
MUSIC: Thai folksong

SOI SON TUD
Irr.

Trans. © 1989 The United Methodist Publishing House

INVITATION, *see further:*

379 Blow Ye the Trumpet, Blow

398 Jesus Calls Us o'er the Tumult

Pass Me Not, O Gentle Savior

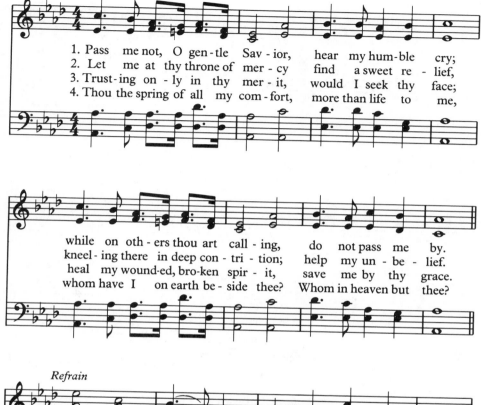

1. Pass me not, O gen-tle Sav-ior, hear my hum-ble cry;
2. Let me at thy throne of mer-cy find a sweet re-lief,
3. Trust-ing on-ly in thy mer-it, would I seek thy face;
4. Thou the spring of all my com-fort, more than life to me,

while on oth-ers thou art call-ing, do not pass me by.
kneel-ing there in deep con-tri-tion; help my un-be-lief.
heal my wound-ed, bro-ken spir-it, save me by thy grace.
whom have I on earth be-side thee? Whom in heaven but thee?

Refrain

Sav - ior, Sav - ior, hear my hum - ble cry;

while on oth - ers thou art call - ing, do not pass me by.

WORDS: Fanny J. Crosby, 1868
MUSIC: William H. Doane, 1870

PASS ME NOT
85.85 with Refrain

352

It's Me, It's Me, O Lord
(Standing in the Need of Prayer)

WORDS: Afro-American spiritual
MUSIC: Afro-American spiritual; arr. by William Farley Smith, 1986

Arr. © 1989 The United Methodist Publishing House

PENITENT
Irr.

Not my broth - er, not my sis - ter, but it's

me, O Lord, stand-ing in the need of prayer.

2. Not the preacher, not the deacon,
3. Not my father, not my mother,

Ash Wednesday 353

O God,
maker of every thing and judge of all that you have made,
from the dust of the earth you have formed us
and from the dust of death you would raise us up.
By the redemptive power of the cross,
create in us clean hearts
and put within us a new spirit,
that we may repent of our sins
and lead lives worthy of your calling;
through Jesus Christ our Lord. **Amen.**

Laurence Hull Stookey, USA, 20th cent. (Gen. 3:19; Ps. 51:10; 1 Th. 2:12)
© 1989 The United Methodist Publishing House

I Surrender All

1. All to Je-sus I sur-ren-der; all to him I freely give; I will ev-er love and trust him, in his pres-ence dai-ly live.
2. All to Je-sus I sur-ren-der; hum-bly at his feet I bow, world-ly plea-sures all for-sak-en; take me, Je-sus, take me now.
3. All to Je-sus I sur-ren-der; make me, Sav-ior, whol-ly thine; let me feel the Ho-ly Spir-it, tru-ly know that thou art mine.
4. All to Je-sus I sur-ren-der; Lord, I give my-self to thee; fill me with thy love and pow-er; let thy bless-ing fall on me.
5. All to Je-sus I sur-ren-der; now I feel the sa-cred flame. O the joy of full sal-va-tion! Glo-ry, glo-ry to his name!

Refrain (Harmony)

I sur-ren-der all, I sur-ren-der all, I sur-ren-der all,

WORDS: J. W. Van Deventer, 1896
MUSIC: W. S. Weeden, 1896

SURRENDER
87.87 with Refrain

all to thee, my bless-ed Sav-ior, I sur-ren-der all.

Depth of Mercy

355

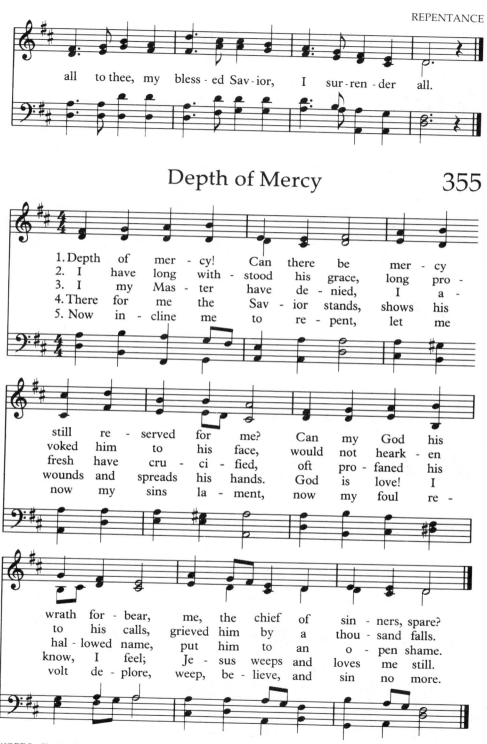

1. Depth of mer - cy! Can there be mer - cy
2. I have long with - stood his grace, long pro -
3. I my Mas - ter have de - nied, I a -
4. There for me the Sav - ior stands, shows his
5. Now in - cline me to re - pent, let me

still re - served for me? Can my God his
voked him to his face, would not heark - en
fresh have cru - ci - fied, oft pro - faned his
wounds and spreads his hands. God is love! I
now my sins la - ment, now my foul re -

wrath for - bear, me, the chief of sin - ners, spare?
to his calls, grieved him by a thou - sand falls.
hal - lowed name, put him to an o - pen shame.
know, I feel; Je - sus weeps and loves me still.
volt de - plore, weep, be - lieve, and sin no more.

WORDS: Charles Wesley, 1740
MUSIC: Adapt. from Orlando Gibbons, 1623

CANTERBURY
77.77

356

Pues Si Vivimos
(When We Are Living)

Unísono (Unison)

1. Pues si vi - vi - mos, pa-ra Él vi - vi - mos
2. En es - ta vi - da, fru-tos he - mos de dar.

1. When we are liv - ing, it is in Christ Je - sus,
2. Through all our liv - ing, we our fruits must give.

y si mo - ri - mos pa-ra Él mo - ri - mos.
Las o - bras bue - nas son pa-ra o - fren-dar.

and when we're dy - ing, it is in the Lord.
Good works of ser - vice are for of - fer - ing.

Sea que vi - va - mos o que mu - ra - mos,
Ya sea que de - mos o que re - ci - ba - mos,

Both in our liv - ing and in our dy - ing,
When we are giv - ing, or when re - ceiv - ing,

WORDS: St. 1 anon., trans. by Elise S. Eslinger, 1983; sts. 2,3,4
Roberto Escamilla, 1983, trans. by George Lockwood, 1987 (Rom. 14:8)
MUSIC: Trad. Spanish melody; harm. from *Celebremos*, 1983

SOMOS DEL SEÑOR
Irr.

Trans. © 1989 The United Methodist Publishing House

3. En la tristeza y en el dolor,
   en la belleza y en el amor,
   sea que suframos o que gocemos,
   Estribillo

4. En este mundo, hemos de encontrar
   gente que llora y sin consolar.
   Sea que ayudemos o que alimentemos,
   Estribillo

---

3. 'Mid times of sorrow and in times of pain,
   when sensing beauty or in love's embrace,
   whether we suffer, or sing rejoicing,
   Refrain

4. Across this wide world, we shall always find
   those who are crying with no peace of mind,
   but when we help them, or when we feed them,
   Refrain

357 Just as I Am, Without One Plea

1. Just as I am, with - out one plea,
but that thy blood was shed for me,
and that thou bidst me come to thee,

2. Just as I am, and wait - ing not
to rid my soul of one dark blot,
to thee whose blood can cleanse each spot,

3. Just as I am, though tossed a - bout
with many a con - flict, many a doubt,
fight - ings and fears with - in, with - out,

4. Just as I am, poor, wretch - ed, blind;
sight, rich - es, heal - ing of the mind,
yea, all I need in thee to find,

5. Just as I am, thou wilt re - ceive,
wilt wel - come, par - don, cleanse, re - lieve;
be - cause thy prom - ise I be - lieve,

6. Just as I am, thy love un - known
hath bro - ken ev - ery bar - rier down;
now, to be thine, yea, thine a - lone,

Refrain

O Lamb of God, I come, I come.

WORDS: Charlotte Elliott, 1835
MUSIC: William B. Bradbury, 1849

WOODWORTH
LM

Dear Lord and Father of Mankind 358

1. Dear Lord and Father of mankind, for-
2. In simple trust like theirs who heard, be-
3. O sabbath rest by Galilee, O
4. Drop thy still dews of quietness, till
5. Breathe through the heats of our desire thy

give our foolish ways; re-clothe us in our
side the Syrian sea, the gracious calling
calm of hills above, where Jesus knelt to
all our strivings cease; take from our souls the
coolness and thy balm; let sense be dumb, let

rightful mind, in purer lives thy
of the Lord, let us, like them, with-
share with thee the silence of e-
strain and stress, and let our ordered
flesh retire; speak through the earthquake,

service find, in deeper reverence, praise.
out a word, rise up and follow thee.
ternity, interpreted by love!
lives confess the beauty of thy peace.
wind, and fire, O still, small voice of calm.

WORDS: John Greenleaf Whittier, 1872
MUSIC: Frederick C. Maker, 1887

REST
86.886

359 Alas! and Did My Savior Bleed

1. A - las! and did my Sav - ior bleed, and
2. Was it for crimes that I have done, he
3. Well might the sun in dark - ness hide, and
4. Thus might I hide my blush - ing face while
5. But drops of tears can ne'er re - pay the

did my Sov - ereign die? Would he de - vote that
groaned up - on the tree? A - maz - ing pit - y!
shut its glo - ries in, when God, the might - y
his dear cross ap - pears; dis - solve my heart in
debt of love I owe. Here, Lord, I give my -

sa - cred head for sin - ners such as I?
Grace un - known! And love be - yond de - gree!
mak - er, died for his own crea - ture's sin.
thank - ful - ness, and melt mine eyes to tears.
self a - way; 'tis all that I can do.

Refrain

At the cross, at the cross, where I first saw the

WORDS: Isaac Watts, 1707; refrain by Ralph E. Hudson, 1885
MUSIC: Anon.; arr. by Ralph E. Hudson, ca. 1885

HUDSON
CM with Refrain

light, and the bur-den of my heart rolled a-way;

it was there by faith I re-ceived my sight,

and now I am hap-py all the day.

Freedom in Christ 360

Gracious God,
  make me sensitive to all the evidences of your goodness;
  and may I, trusting in you,
  free myself of the terror of death,
  and feel free to live intensely and happily
  the life you have given me. **Amen.**

Rubem Alves, Brazil, 20th cent.

From *I Believe in the Resurrection of the Body*, trans. © 1986 Fortress Press

REPENTANCE, *see further:*

361 Rock of Ages, Cleft for Me

1. Rock of A - ges, cleft for me, let me
2. Not the la - bors of my hands can ful -
3. Noth - ing in my hand I bring, sim - ply
4. While I draw this fleet - ing breath, when mine

hide my - self in thee; let the wa - ter and the blood,
fill thy law's de - mands; could my zeal no res - pite know,
to the cross I cling; na - ked, come to thee for dress;
eyes shall close in death, when I soar to worlds un - known,

from thy wound - ed side which flowed, be of sin the
could my tears for - ev - er flow, all for sin could
help - less, look to thee for grace; foul, I to the
see thee on thy judg - ment throne, Rock of A - ges,

dou - ble cure; save from wrath and make me pure.
not a - tone; thou must save, and thou a - lone.
foun - tain fly; wash me, Sav - ior, or I die.
cleft for me, let me hide my - self in thee.

WORDS: Augustus M. Toplady, 1776
MUSIC: Thomas Hastings, 1830

TOPLADY
77.77.77

Nothing but the Blood

1. What can wash a - way my sin? Noth-ing but the blood of
2. For my par - don this I see: noth-ing but the blood of
3. Noth-ing can for sin a - tone: noth-ing but the blood of
4. This is all my hope and peace: noth-ing but the blood of

Je - sus. What can make me whole a - gain?
Je - sus. For my cleans - ing this my plea:
Je - sus. Naught of good that I have done:
Je - sus. This is all my righ - teous - ness:

Refrain

Noth-ing but the blood of Je - sus.
noth-ing but the blood of Je - sus. O pre - cious
noth-ing but the blood of Je - sus.
noth-ing but the blood of Je - sus.

is the flow that makes me bright as snow; no oth - er

fount I know; noth-ing but the blood of Je - sus.

WORDS: Robert Lowry, 1876
MUSIC: Robert Lowry, 1876

PLAINFIELD
78.78 with Refrain

363 And Can It Be that I Should Gain

1. And can it be that I should gain an
2. 'Tis mys-tery all: th'Im-mor-tal dies! Who
3. He left his Fa - ther's throne a - bove (so
4. Long my im-pris - oned spir - it lay, fast
5. No con-dem-na - tion now I dread; Je -

in - terest in the Sav-ior's blood! Died he for
can ex - plore his strange de - sign? In vain the
free, so in - fi - nite his grace!), emp - tied him -
bound in sin and na-ture's night; thine eye dif -
sus, and all in him, is mine; a - live in

me? who caused his pain! For me? who him to
first - born ser - aph tries to sound the depths of
self of all but love, and bled for Ad - am's
fused a quick-ening ray; I woke, the dun - geon
him, my liv - ing Head, and clothed in righ - teous -

death pur - sued? A - maz - ing love! How can it
love di - vine. 'Tis mer - cy all! Let earth a -
help - less race. 'Tis mer - cy all, im - mense and
flamed with light; my chains fell off, my heart was
ness di - vine, bold I ap-proach th'e - ter - nal

WORDS: Charles Wesley, 1739 (Acts 16:26)
MUSIC: Thomas Campbell, 1835

SAGINA
88.88.88 with Repeat

364

Because He Lives

1. God sent his Son, they called him Je - sus;
2. How sweet to hold a new-born ba - by,
3. And then one day I'll cross the riv - er;

he came to love, heal, and for - give;
and feel the pride and joy he* gives;
I'll fight life's fi - nal war with pain;

he lived and died to buy my par - don,
but great - er still the calm as - sur - ance,
and then as death gives way to vic - tory,

an emp - ty grave is there to prove my Sav - ior lives.
this child can face un-cer-tain days be-cause he lives.
I'll see the lights of glo - ry and I'll know he reigns.

*Jesus

WORDS: Gloria and William J. Gaither, 1971
MUSIC: William J. Gaither, 1971

RESURRECTION
98.9 11 with Refrain

© 1971 William. J. Gaither

Refrain

Be-cause he lives, I can face to-mor-row;

be-cause he lives, all fear is gone;

be-cause I know he holds the fu-ture,

and life is worth the liv-ing just be-cause he lives.

365 Grace Greater than Our Sin

WORDS: Julia H. Johnston, 1911 (Rom. 5:20)
MUSIC: Daniel B. Towner, 1910

MOODY
99.99 with Refrain

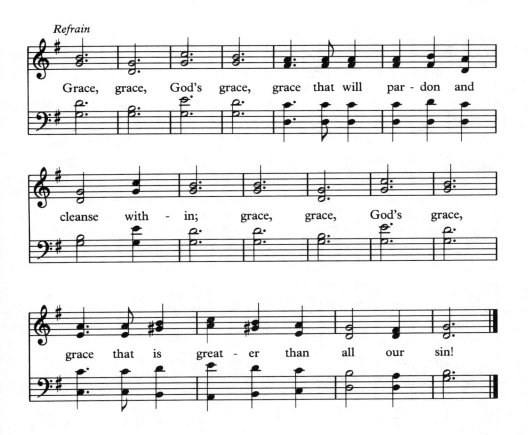

Refrain

Grace, grace, God's grace, grace that will par-don and cleanse with-in; grace, grace, God's grace, grace that is great-er than all our sin!

For Guidance

366

O God,
    just as we look into a mirror to see any soiled spots on our face,
so let us look to you
    in order to understand the things that we have done amiss.
We are like a reed shaken in the wind;
we are inexpressibly weak.
Leave us not to ourselves,
    but dwell in our hearts and guide our thoughts and actions. **Amen.**

Korea, 20th cent.

367 He Touched Me

1. Shack-led by a heav-y bur-den, neath a load of
2. Since I met this bless-ed Sav-ior, since he cleansed and

guilt and shame, then the hand of Je - sus touched me,
made me whole, I will nev-er cease to praise him;

Refrain

and now I am no long-er the same. He touched me, O he
I'll shout it while e - ter-ni-ty rolls.

touched me, and O the joy that floods my soul! Some-thing

hap-pened, and now I know, he touched me and made me whole.

WORDS: William J. Gaither, 1963 (Mt. 8:3; Mk. 1:41; Lk. 5:13)
MUSIC: William J. Gaither, 1963

HE TOUCHED ME
Irr. with Refrain

© 1963 William J. Gaither

PARDON, *see further:*

389 Freely, Freely
99 My Tribute

282 'Tis Finished! the Messiah Dies
98 To God Be the Glory

My Hope Is Built

1. My hope is built on noth-ing less than Je - sus' blood and righ-teous-ness. I dare not trust the sweet-est frame, but whol-ly lean on Je - sus' name.
2. When dark-ness veils his love-ly face, I rest on his un - chang-ing grace. In ev - ery high and storm-y gale, my an - chor holds with - in the veil.
3. His oath, his cov - e - nant, his blood sup - port me in the whelm-ing flood. When all a - round my soul gives way, he then is all my hope and stay.
4. When he shall come with trum - pet sound, O may I then in him be found! Dressed in his righ - teous - ness a - lone, fault - less to stand be - fore the throne!

Refrain

On Christ the sol - id rock I stand, all oth - er ground is sink - ing sand; all oth - er ground is sink - ing sand.

WORDS: Edward Mote, 1834
MUSIC: William B. Bradbury, 1863

THE SOLID ROCK
LM with Refrain

369 Blessed Assurance

1. Bless - ed as - sur - ance, Je - sus is mine!
2. Per - fect sub - mis - sion, per - fect de - light,
3. Per - fect sub - mis - sion, all is at rest;

O what a fore - taste of glo - ry di - vine!
vi - sions of rap - ture now burst on my sight;
I in my Sav - ior am hap - py and blest,

Heir of sal - va - tion, pur - chase of God,
an - gels de - scend - ing bring from a - bove
watch - ing and wait - ing, look - ing a - bove,

born of his Spir - it, washed in his blood.
ech - oes of mer - cy, whis - pers of love.
filled with his good - ness, lost in his love.

WORDS: Fanny J. Crosby, 1873
MUSIC: Phoebe P. Knapp, 1873

ASSURANCE
9 10.9 9 with Refrain

370 Victory in Jesus

1. I heard an old, old story, how a Sav-ior came
2. I heard a-bout his heal-ing, of his cleans-ing power
3. I heard a-bout a man-sion he has built for me

from glo-ry, how he gave his life on Cal-va-ry
re-veal-ing, how he made the lame to walk a-gain
in glo-ry, and I heard a-bout the streets of gold

to save a wretch like me; I heard a-bout his
and caused the blind to see; and then I cried, "Dear
be-yond the crys-tal sea; a-bout the an-gels

groan-ing, of his pre-cious blood's a-ton-ing,
Je-sus, come and heal my bro-ken spir-it,"
sing-ing and the old re-demp-tion sto-ry,

then I re-pent-ed of my sins and won the
and some-how Je-sus came and brought to me the
and some sweet day I'll sing up there the song of

WORDS: Eugene M. Bartlett, 1939
MUSIC: Eugene M. Bartlett, 1939

HARTFORD
Irr. with Refrain

371   I Stand Amazed in the Presence

1. I stand a - mazed in the pres - ence of
2. For me it was in the gar - den he
3. In pit - y an - gels be - held him, and
4. He took my sins and my sor - rows, he
5. When with the ran - somed in glo - ry his

Je - sus the Naz - a - rene, and won - der
prayed: "Not my will, but thine." He had no
came from the world of light to com - fort
made them his ver - y own; he bore the
face I at last shall see, 'twill be my

how he could love me, a sin - ner, con-demned, un - clean.
tears for his own griefs, but sweat-drops of blood for mine.
him in the sor - rows he bore for my soul that night.
bur - den to Cal - vary, and suf - fered and died a - lone.
joy through the a - ges to sing of his love for me.

Refrain

How mar - vel-ous! How won-der-ful! And my song shall ev - er be:
O how mar-vel-ous!   O how won-der-ful!

WORDS: Charles H. Gabriel, 1905 (Lk. 22:41-44)
MUSIC: Charles H. Gabriel, 1905

MY SAVIOR'S LOVE
87.87 with Refrain

How mar-vel-ous! How won-der-ful is my Sav-ior's love for me!
O how mar-vel-ous! O how won-der-ful

How Can We Sinners Know 372

1. How can we sin - ners know our sins on
2. What we have felt and seen, with con - fi -
3. We who in Christ be - lieve that he for
4. We by his Spir - it prove and know the
5. The meek and low - ly heart that in our
6. Our na - ture's turned, our mind trans - formed in

earth for - given? How can my gra - cious
dence we tell, and can pub - lish to the
us hath died, we all his un - known
things of God, the things which free - ly
Sav - ior was, to us that Spir - it
all its powers, and both the wit - ness -

Sav - ior show my name in - scribed in heaven?
ends of earth the signs in - fal - li - ble.
peace re - ceive and feel his blood ap - plied.
of his love he hath on us be - stowed.
doth im - part and signs us with his cross.
es are joined, the Spirit of God with ours.

WORDS: Charles Wesley, 1749
MUSIC: *Genevan Psalter*, 1551; adapt. by William Crotch, 1836

ST. MICHAEL
SM

373 Nothing Between

WORDS: Charles Albert Tindley, ca. 1906
MUSIC: Charles Albert Tindley, ca. 1906; arr. by F. A. Clark

NOTHING BETWEEN
10 9.11 9 with Refrain

374 Standing on the Promises

1. Stand-ing on the prom - is - es of Christ my King,
2. Stand-ing on the prom - is - es that can - not fail,
3. Stand-ing on the prom - is - es of Christ the Lord,
4. Stand-ing on the prom - is - es I can - not fall,

through e - ter - nal a - ges let his prais - es ring;
when the howl - ing storms of doubt and fear as - sail,
bound to him e - ter - nal - ly by love's strong cord,
lis - tening ev - ery mo - ment to the Spir - it's call,

glo - ry in the high - est, I will shout and sing,
by the liv - ing Word of God I shall pre - vail,
o - ver - com - ing dai - ly with the Spir - it's sword,
rest - ing in my Sav - ior as my all in all,

stand - ing on the prom - is - es of God.
stand - ing on the prom - is - es of God.
stand - ing on the prom - is - es of God.
stand - ing on the prom - is - es of God.

WORDS: R. Kelso Carter, 1886 (Eph. 6:14-17)
MUSIC: R. Kelso Carter, 1886

PROMISES
11 11.11 9 with Refrain

375 There Is a Balm in Gilead

There is a balm in Gil-e-ad to make the wound-ed whole; there is a balm in Gil-e-ad to heal the sin-sick soul.

1. Some - times I feel dis - cour - aged, and think my work's in vain. But then the Ho - ly
2. Don't ev - er feel dis - cour - aged, for Je - sus is your friend, and if you look for
3. If you can't preach like Pe - ter, if you can't pray like Paul, just tell the love of

WORDS: Afro-American spiritual (Jer. 8:22)
MUSIC: Afro-American spiritual; adapt. and arr. by William Farley Smith, 1986

BALM IN GILEAD
Irr.

D.S.

Spir - it   re - vives   my soul   a - gain.
knowl - edge   he'll   ne'er   re - fuse   to   lend.
Je - sus,   and   say   he died   for   all.

Dona Nobis Pacem

376

Do - na   no - bis   pa - cem, pa - cem.   Do - na

no - bis   pa - cem.   Do - na   no - bis   pa - cem.

Do - na   no - bis   pa - cem.   Do - na

no - bis   pa - cem.   Do - na   no - bis   pa - cem.

*May be sung as a canon

WORDS: Trad. Latin
MUSIC: Trad.

DONA NOBIS PACEM
Irr.

377   It Is Well with My Soul

1. When peace, like a riv - er, at - tend - eth my way,
2. Though Sa - tan should buf - fet, though tri - als should come,
3. My sin, oh, the bliss of this glo - ri - ous thought!
4. And, Lord, haste the day when my faith shall be sight,

when sor - rows like sea bil - lows roll; what - ev - er my
let this blest as - sur - ance con - trol, that Christ has re -
My sin, not in part but the whole, is nailed to the
the clouds be rolled back as a scroll; the trump shall re -

lot, thou hast taught me to say, It is well, it is
gard - ed my help - less es - tate, and hath shed his own
cross, and I bear it no more, praise the Lord, praise the
sound, and the Lord shall de - scend, e - ven so, it is

Refrain

well with my soul.
blood for my soul.   It is well   with my soul,
Lord, O my soul!
well with my soul.   It is well   with my soul,

it is well, it is well with my soul.

WORDS: Horatio G. Spafford, 1873
MUSIC: Philip P. Bliss, 1876

VILLE DU HAVRE
11 8.11 9 with Refrain

Amazing Grace

1. A - maz - ing grace! How sweet the sound that
2. 'Twas grace that taught my heart to fear, and
3. Through man - y dan - gers, toils, and snares, I
4. The Lord has prom - ised good to me, his
5. Yea, when this flesh and heart shall fail, and
6. When we've been there ten thou - sand years, bright

saved a wretch like me! I once was lost, but
grace my fears re - lieved; how pre - cious did that
have al - read - y come; 'tis grace hath brought me
word my hope se - cures; he will my shield and
mor - tal life shall cease, I shall pos - sess, with -
shin - ing as the sun, we've no less days to

now am found; was blind, but now I see.
grace ap - pear the hour I first be - lieved.
safe thus far, and grace will lead me home.
por - tion be, as long as life en - dures.
in the veil, a life of joy and peace.
sing God's praise than when we'd first be - gun.

Cherokee
OOH NAY THLA NAH, HEE OO WAY GEE.'
E GAH GWOO YAH HAY EE.
NAW GWOO JOE SAH, WE YOU LOW SAY,
E GAH GWOO YAH HO NAH.

Navajo
NIZHÓNÍGO JOOBA' DITTS' A'
YISDÁSHÍÍTÍNÍGÍÍ,
LAH YÓÓÍÍYÁ, K'AD SHÉNÁHOOSDZIN,
DOO EESH'ÍÍ DA ŃT'ÉÉ.

Kiowa
DAW K'EE DA HA DAWTSAHY HE TSOW'HAW
DAW K'EE DA HA DAWTSAHY HEE.
BAY DAWTSAHY TAW, GAW AYM OW THAH T'AW,
DAW K'EE DA HA DAWTSAHY H'EE.

Creek
PO YA FEK CHA HE THLAT AH TET
AH NON AH CHA PA KAS
CHA FEE KEE O FUNNAN LA KUS
UM E HA TA LA YUS.

Choctaw
SHILOMBISH HOLITOPA MA!
ISHMMINTI PULLA CHA
HATAK ILBUSHA PIA HA
IS PI YUKPALASHKE.

WORDS: John Newton, 1779; st. 6 anon.; phonetic transcription Cherokee, Kiowa,   AMAZING GRACE
   Creek, Choctaw as sung in Oklahoma Indian Missionary Conference; Navajo phonetic   CM
   transcription by Albert Tsosi (1 Chr. 17:16-17)
MUSIC: 19th cent. USA melody; harm. by Edwin O. Excell, 1900

379 Blow Ye the Trumpet, Blow

1. Blow ye the trum-pet, blow! The glad-ly sol-emn sound
2. Je - sus, our great high priest, hath full a - tone-ment made;
3. Ex - tol the Lamb of God, the all - a - ton - ing Lamb;
4. Ye slaves of sin and hell, your lib-er-ty re - ceive,

let all the na-tions know, to earth's re - mot-est bound:
ye wea-ry spir-its, rest; ye mourn-ful souls, be glad:
re - demp-tion in his blood through-out the world pro - claim:
and safe in Je - sus dwell, and blest in Je-sus' live:

The year of ju-bi - lee is come! The year of ju - bi -

lee is come! Re - turn, ye ran-somed sin - ners, home.

5. Ye who have sold for nought
your heritage above
shall have it back unbought,
the gift of Jesus' love:
The year of jubilee is come!
The year of jubilee is come!
Return, ye ransomed sinners, home.

6. The gospel trumpet hear,
the news of heavenly grace;
and saved from earth, appear
before your Savior's face:
The year of jubilee is come!
The year of jubilee is come!
Return to your eternal home.

WORDS: Charles Wesley, 1750 (Lev. 25:8-17)
MUSIC: Lewis Edson, ca. 1782

LENOX
66.66.88

There's Within My Heart a Melody 380

1. There's with-in my heart a mel-o-dy
2. All my life was wrecked by sin and strife,
3. Though some-times he leads through wa-ters deep,
4. Feast-ing on the rich-es of his grace,
5. Soon he's com-ing back to wel-come me

Je-sus whis-pers sweet and low: Fear not, I am with thee,
dis-cord filled my heart with pain; Je-sus swept a-cross the
tri-als fall a-cross the way, though some-times the path seems
rest-ing neath his shel-tering wing, al-ways look-ing on his
far be-yond the star-ry sky; I shall wing my flight to

peace, be still, in all of life's ebb and flow.
bro-ken strings, stirred the slum-bering chords a-gain.
rough and steep, see his foot-prints all the way.
smil-ing face, that is why I shout and sing.
worlds un-known; I shall reign with him on high.

Refrain

Je-sus, Je-sus, Je-sus, sweet-est name I know,

fills my ev-ery long-ing, keeps me sing-ing as I go.

WORDS: Luther B. Bridgers, 1910
MUSIC: Luther B. Bridgers, 1910

SWEETEST NAME
97.97 with Refrain

381 Savior, Like a Shepherd Lead Us

1. Sav - ior, like a shep-herd lead us, much we
2. We are thine, thou dost be - friend us, be the
3. Thou hast prom-ised to re - ceive us, poor and
4. Ear - ly let us seek thy fa - vor, ear - ly

need thy ten-der care; in thy pleas-ant pas-tures
guard-ian of our way; keep thy flock, from sin de-
sin - ful though we be; thou hast mer - cy to re-
let us do thy will; bless - ed Lord and on - ly

feed us, for our use thy folds pre - pare.
fend us, seek us when we go a - stray.
lieve us, grace to cleanse and power to free.
Sav - ior, with thy love our bos - oms fill.

Bless - ed Je - sus, bless - ed Je - sus! Thou hast
Bless - ed Je - sus, bless - ed Je - sus! Hear, O
Bless - ed Je - sus, bless - ed Je - sus! We will
Bless - ed Je - sus, bless - ed Je - sus! Thou hast

WORDS: Attr. to Dorothy A. Thrupp, 1836 (Jn. 10:1-29)
MUSIC: William B. Bradbury, 1859

BRADBURY
87.87 D

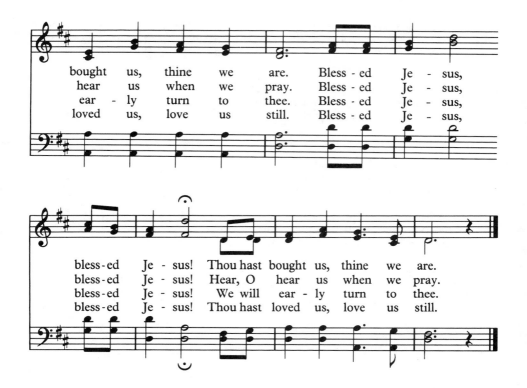

bought us, thine we are. Bless - ed Je - sus,
hear us when we pray. Bless - ed Je - sus,
ear - ly turn to thee. Bless - ed Je - sus,
loved us, love us still. Bless - ed Je - sus,

bless - ed Je - sus! Thou hast bought us, thine we are.
bless - ed Je - sus! Hear, O hear us when we pray.
bless - ed Je - sus! We will ear - ly turn to thee.
bless - ed Je - sus! Thou hast loved us, love us still.

ASSURANCE, *see further:*

382 Have Thine Own Way, Lord

1. - 4. Have thine own way, Lord! Have thine own way!

Thou art the pot - ter; I am the clay.
Search me and try me, Sav - ior to - day!
Wound - ed and wea - ry, help me I pray!
Hold o'er my be - ing ab - so - lute sway.

Mold me and make me af - ter thy will,
Wash me just now, Lord, wash me just now,
Pow - er, all pow - er, sure - ly is thine!
Fill with thy Spir - it till all shall see

while I am wait - ing, yield - ed and still.
as in thy pres - ence hum - bly I bow.
Touch me and heal me, Sav - ior di - vine!
Christ on - ly, al - ways, liv - ing in me!

WORDS: Adelaide A. Pollard, 1902 (Jer. 18:6)　　　　　　　　　　　　　ADELAIDE
MUSIC: George C. Stebbins, 1907　　　　　　　　　　　　　　　　　　　54.54 D

This Is a Day of New Beginnings 383

Unison

1. This is a day of new be - gin - nings,
2. For by the life and death of Je - sus,
3. Then let us, with the Spir - it's dar - ing,
4. Christ is a - live, and goes be - fore us
*5. In faith we'll gath - er round the ta - ble

time to re - mem - ber and move on,
God's might - y Spir - it, now as then,
step from the past and leave be - hind
to show and share what love can do.
to taste and share what love can do.

time to be - lieve what love is bring - ing,
can make for us a world of dif - ference,
our dis - ap - point - ment, guilt, and griev - ing,
This is a day of new be - gin - nings;
This is a day of new be - gin - nings;

[1-3]

lay - ing to rest the pain that's gone.
as faith and hope are born a - gain.
seek - ing new paths, and sure to find.
our God is mak - ing all things
our God is mak - ing all things

[4 or 5]

new.
new.

*Alternate text for Holy Communion

WORDS: Brian Wren, 1978; alt. 1987 (Rev. 21:5)
MUSIC: Carlton R. Young, 1984
Words © 1983, 1987 Hope Publishing Co.; music © 1987 Hope Publishing Co.

BEGINNINGS
98.98

384 Love Divine, All Loves Excelling

1. Love di - vine, all loves ex - cell - ing, joy of heaven, to
2. Breathe, O breathe thy lov - ing Spir - it in - to ev - ery
3. Come, Al - might - y to de - liv - er, let us all thy
4. Fin - ish, then, thy new cre - a - tion; pure and spot - less

earth come down; fix in us thy hum - ble dwell - ing;
trou - bled breast! Let us all in thee in - her - it;
life re - ceive; sud - den - ly re - turn and nev - er,
let us be. Let us see thy great sal - va - tion

all thy faith - ful mer - cies crown! Je - sus, thou art
let us find that sec - ond rest. Take a - way our
nev - er - more thy tem - ples leave. Thee we would be
per - fect - ly re - stored in thee; changed from glo - ry

all com - pas - sion, pure, un - bound - ed love thou art; vis - it
bent to sin - ning; Al - pha and O - me - ga be; end of
al - ways bless - ing, serve thee as thy hosts a - bove, pray and
in - to glo - ry, till in heaven we take our place, till we

WORDS: Charles Wesley, 1747
MUSIC: John Zundel, 1870

BEECHER
87.87 D

Alt. tune: HYFRYDOL

us with thy sal - va - tion; en - ter ev - ery trem-bling heart.
faith, as its be - gin - ning, set our hearts at lib - er - ty.
praise thee with-out ceas-ing, glo - ry in thy per - fect love.
cast our crowns be - fore thee, lost in won-der, love, and praise.

Let Us Plead for Faith Alone 385

1. Let us plead for faith a - lone, faith which
2. Ac - tive faith that lives with - in, con - quers
3. Let us for this faith con - tend, sure sal -
4. On - ly let us per - se - vere till we

by our works is shown; God it is who
hell and death and sin, hal - lows whom it
va - tion is the end; heaven al - read - y
see our Lord ap - pear, nev - er from the

jus - ti - fies, on - ly faith the grace ap - plies,
first made whole, forms the Sav - ior in the soul.
is be - gun, ev - er - last - ing life is won.
Rock re - move, saved by faith which works by love.

WORDS: Charles Wesley, 1740 (Eph. 2:8-10)   SAVANNAH
MUSIC: *Foundery Collection*, 1742   77.77

386 Come, O Thou Traveler Unknown

Unison

1. Come, O thou Trav - el - er un - known,
2. I need not tell thee who I am,
3. Yield to me now, for I am weak,
4. 'Tis Love! 'tis Love! Thou diedst for me,

whom still I hold, but can - not see!
my mis - er - y and sin de - clare;
but con - fi - dent in self - de - spair!
I hear thy whis - per in my heart.

My com - pa - ny be - fore is gone,
thy - self hast called me by my name,
Speak to my heart, in bless - ing speak,
The morn - ing breaks, the shad - ows flee,

and I am left a - lone with thee.
look on thy hands and read it there.
be con - quered by my in - stant prayer.
pure, U - ni - ver - sal Love thou art.

WORDS: Charles Wesley, 1742 (Gen. 32:24-32)
MUSIC: Trad. Scottish melody; harm. by Carlton R. Young, 1963

CANDLER
LMD

Harm. © 1964 Abingdon Press

With thee all night I mean to stay,
But who, I ask thee, who art thou?
Speak, or thou nev - er hence shalt move,
To me, to all, thy mer - cies move;

and wres - tle till the break of day;
Tell me thy name, and tell me now.
and tell me if thy name is Love.
thy na - ture and thy name is Love.

with thee all night I mean to stay,
But who, I ask thee, who art thou?
Speak, or thou nev - er hence shalt move,
To me, to all, thy mer - cies move;

and wres - tle till the break of day.
Tell me thy name, and tell me now.
and tell me if thy name is Love.
thy na - ture and thy name is Love.

387 Come, O Thou Traveler Unknown

Come, O thou Traveler unknown,
whom still I hold, but cannot see!
My company before is gone,
and I am left alone with thee;
with thee all night I mean to stay
and wrestle till the break of day.

I need not tell thee who I am,
my misery and sin declare;
thyself hast called me by my name,
look on thy hands and read it there.
But who, I ask thee, who art thou?
Tell me thy name, and tell me now.

In vain thou strugglest to get free,
I never will unloose my hold;
art thou the man that died for me?
The secret of thy love unfold;
wrestling, I will not let thee go
till I thy name, thy nature know.

Wilt thou not yet to me reveal
thy new, unutterable name?
Tell me, I still beseech thee, tell,
to know it now resolved I am;
wrestling, I will not let thee go,
till I thy name, thy nature know.

'Tis all in vain to hold thy tongue
or touch the hollow of my thigh;
though every sinew be unstrung,
out of my arms thou shalt not fly;
wrestling I will not let thee go
till I thy name, thy nature know.

What though my shrinking flesh complain
and murmur to contend so long?
I rise superior to my pain:
when I am weak then I am strong,
and when my all of strength shall fail
I shall with the God-man prevail.

My strength is gone, my nature dies,
I sink beneath thy weighty hand,
faint to revive, and fall to rise;
I fall, and yet by faith I stand;
I stand and will not let thee go
till I thy name, thy nature know.

Yield to me now—for I am weak
but confident in self-despair!
Speak to my heart, in blessing speak,
be conquered by my instant prayer:
speak, or thou never hence shalt move,
and tell me if thy name is Love.

'Tis Love! 'tis Love! thou diedst for me,
I hear thy whisper in my heart.
The morning breaks, the shadows flee,
pure Universal Love thou art:
to me, to all, thy mercies move—
thy nature, and thy name is Love.

My prayer hath power with God; the grace
unspeakable I now receive;
through faith I see thee face to face,
I see thee face to face, and live!
In vain I have not wept and strove—
thy nature, and thy name is Love.

I know thee, Savior, who thou art,
Jesus, the feeble sinner's friend;
nor wilt thou with the night depart,
but stay and love me to the end:
thy mercies never shall remove,
thy nature, and thy name is Love.

The Sun of Righteousness on me
hath risen with healing in his wings:
withered my nature's strength; from thee
my soul its life and succor brings;
my help is all laid up above;
thy nature, and thy name is Love.

Contented now upon my thigh
I halt, till life's short journey end;
all helplessness, all weakness I
on thee alone for strength depend;
nor have I power from thee to move:
thy nature, and thy name is Love.

Lame as I am, I take the prey,
hell, earth, and sin with ease overcome;
I leap for joy, pursue my way,
and as a bounding hart fly home,
through all eternity to prove
thy nature, and thy name is Love.

John Wesley ended his obituary tribute to his brother Charles at the Methodist Conference in 1788: "His least praise was, his talent for poetry: although Dr. [Isaac] Watts did not scruple to say that 'that single poem, Wrestling Jacob, was worth all the verses he himself had written.'" A little over two weeks after his brother's death, John Wesley tried to teach the hymn at Bolton, but broke down when he came to the lines "my company before is gone, and I am left alone with thee." The poem was first published in the brothers' *Hymns and Sacred Poems* of 1742, expounding Genesis 32:24-32, influenced by Matthew Henry's exposition.

O Come and Dwell in Me 388

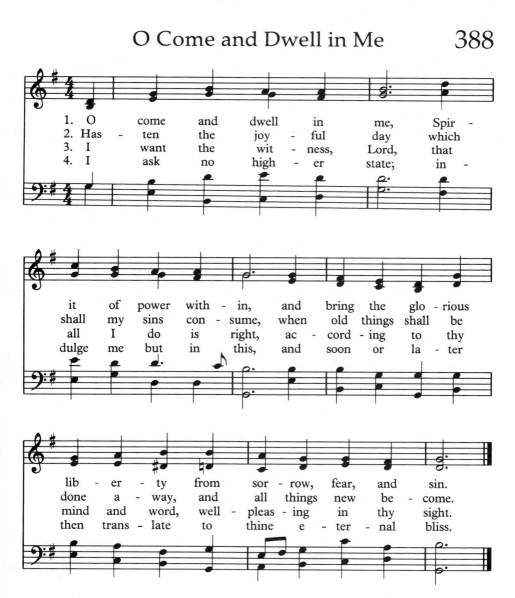

1. O come and dwell in me, Spir-it of power with-in, and bring the glo-rious lib-er-ty from sor-row, fear, and sin.
2. Has-ten the joy-ful day which shall my sins con-sume, when old things shall be done a-way, and all things new be-come.
3. I want the wit-ness, Lord, that all I do is right, ac-cord-ing to thy mind and word, well-pleas-ing in thy sight.
4. I ask no high-er state; in-dulge me but in this, and soon or la-ter then trans-late to thine e-ter-nal bliss.

WORDS: Charles Wesley, 1762 (2 Cor. 3:17; 5:17; Heb. 11:5)
MUSIC: *Genevan Psalter*, 1551; adapt. by William Crotch, 1836

ST. MICHAEL
SM

389

Freely, Freely

1. God for-gave my sin in Je - sus' name, I've been
2. All power is given in Je - sus' name, in

born a - gain in Je - sus' name, and in Je - sus' name I
earth and heaven in Je - sus' name, and in Je - sus' name I

come to you, to share his love as he told me to.
come to you, to share his power as he told me to.

Refrain

He said, "Free - ly, free - ly you have re - ceived,

free - ly, free - ly give. Go in my name, and be -

WORDS: Carol Owens, 1972 (Mt. 10:8; 28:18-20)   FREELY, FREELY
MUSIC: Carol Owens, 1972   99.99 with Refrain

Forgive Our Sins as We Forgive 390

1. "For - give our sins as we for - give," you
2. How can your par - don reach and bless the
3. In blaz - ing light your cross re - veals the
4. Lord, cleanse the depths with - in our souls, and

taught us, Lord, to pray; but you a - lone can
un - for - giv - ing heart that broods on wrongs and
truth we dim - ly knew: what triv - ial debts are
bid re - sent - ment cease; then, bound to all in

grant us grace to live the words we say.
will not let old bit - ter - ness de - part?
owed to us, how great our debt to you!
bonds of love, our lives will spread your peace.

WORDS: Rosamond E. Herklots, 1966 (Mt. 6:12)
MUSIC: *Supplement to Kentucky Harmony*, 1820

DETROIT
CM

391 O Happy Day, That Fixed My Choice

1. O hap - py day, that fixed my choice on thee, my
2. O hap - py bond, that seals my vows to him who
3. It's done: the great trans - ac - tion's done! I am the
4. Now rest, my long - di - vid - ed heart, fixed on this
5. High heaven, that heard the sol - emn vow, that vow re -

Sav - ior and my God! Well may this glow - ing
mer - its all my love! Let cheer - ful an - thems
Lord's and he is mine; he drew me and I
bliss - ful cen - ter, rest. Here have I found a
newed shall dai - ly hear, till in life's lat - est

heart re - joice, and tell its rap - tures all a - broad.
fill his house, while to that sa - cred shrine I move.
fol - lowed on, charmed to con - fess the voice di - vine.
no - bler part; here heaven-ly plea - sures fill my breast.
hour I bow and bless in death a bond so dear.

Refrain

Hap - py day, hap - py day, when Je - sus washed my

WORDS: Philip Doddridge, 1755; refrain from *Wesleyan Sacred Harp*, 1854 (2 Chr. 15:15)   HAPPY DAY
MUSIC: Anon.; refrain attr. to Edward F. Rimbault, 1854   LM with Refrain

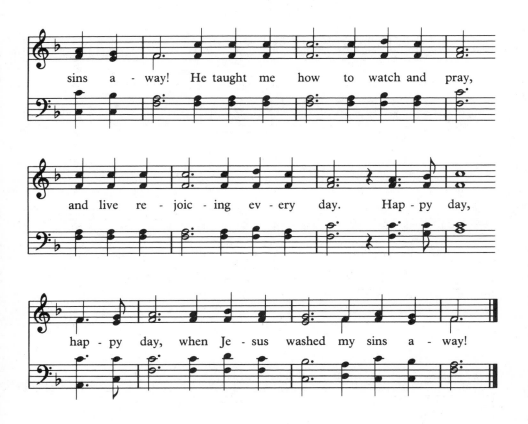

sins a - way! He taught me how to watch and pray,

and live re - joic - ing ev - ery day. Hap - py day,

hap - py day, when Je - sus washed my sins a - way!

Prayer for a New Heart   392

Thou who art over us,
Thou who art one of us,
Thou who *art:*
   Give me a pure heart, that I may see thee;
   a humble heart, that I may hear thee;
   a heart of love, that I may serve thee;
   a heart of faith, that I may abide in thee. **Amen.**

Dag Hammerskjöld, Sweden, 20th cent. (Mt. 5:8)

From *Markings* © 1964 Alfred A. Knopf, Inc. and Faber & Faber, Ltd.

393   Spirit of the Living God

Spir - it of the liv-ing God, fall a-fresh on me.

Spir - it of the liv - ing God, fall a-fresh on me.

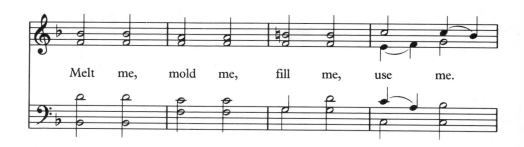

Melt me, mold me, fill me, use me.

Spir - it of the liv - ing God, fall a-fresh on me.

WORDS: Daniel Iverson, 1926; adapt. (Acts 11:15)
MUSIC: Daniel Iverson, 1926

LIVING GOD
75.75.875

Something Beautiful

394

Some-thing beau-ti-ful, some-thing good;

all my con-fu-sion he un-der-stood;

all I had to of-fer him was bro-ken-ness and

strife, but he made some-thing beau-ti-ful of my life.

WORDS: Gloria Gaither, 1971
MUSIC: William J. Gaither, 1971

SOMETHING BEAUTIFUL
Irr.

REBIRTH AND THE NEW CREATURE, *see further:*

311 Now the Green Blade Riseth

395   Take Time to Be Holy

1. Take time to be ho - ly, speak oft with thy Lord;
2. Take time to be ho - ly, the world rush - es on;
3. Take time to be ho - ly, let him be thy guide,
4. Take time to be ho - ly, be calm in thy soul,

a - bide in him al - ways, and feed on his word.
spend much time in se - cret with Je - sus a - lone.
and run not be - fore him, what - ev - er be - tide.
each thought and each mo - tive be - neath his con - trol.

Make friends of God's chil - dren, help those who are weak,
By look - ing to Je - sus, like him thou shalt be;
In joy or in sor - row, still fol - low the Lord,
Thus led by his spir - it to foun-tains of love,

for - get - ting in noth - ing his bless-ing to seek.
thy friends in thy con - duct his like - ness shall see.
and, look - ing to Je - sus, still trust in his word.
thou soon shalt be fit - ted for ser - vice a - bove.

WORDS: William D. Longstaff, ca. 1882 (1 Pet. 1:16)
MUSIC: George C. Stebbins, 1890

HOLINESS
65.65 D

O Jesus, I Have Promised

396

1. O Je - sus, I have prom-ised to serve thee to the end;
2. O let me feel thee near me! The world is ev - er near;
3. O let me hear thee speak-ing in ac - cents clear and still,
4. O Je - sus, thou hast prom-ised to all who fol - low thee

be thou for-ev - er near me, my Mas - ter and my friend.
I see the sights that daz - zle, the tempt-ing sounds I hear;
a - bove the storms of pas - sion, the mur-murs of self - will.
that where thou art in glo - ry there shall thy ser-vant be.

I shall not fear the bat - tle if thou art by my side,
my foes are ev - er near me, a - round me and with - in;
O speak to re - as - sure me, to has - ten or con - trol;
And Je - sus, I have prom-ised to serve thee to the end;

nor wan - der from the path - way if thou wilt be my guide.
but Je - sus, draw thou near - er, and shield my soul from sin.
O speak, and make me lis - ten, thou guard-ian of my soul.
O give me grace to fol - low, my Mas-ter and my Friend.

WORDS: John E. Bode, ca. 1866 (Lk. 9:57)
MUSIC: Arthur H. Mann, 1881

ANGEL'S STORY
76.76 D

397 I Need Thee Every Hour

1. I need thee ev-ery hour, most gra-cious Lord;
2. I need thee ev-ery hour; stay thou near - by;
3. I need thee ev-ery hour, in joy or pain;
4. I need thee ev-ery hour; teach me thy will;
5. I need thee ev-ery hour, most Ho - ly One;

no ten - der voice like thine can peace af - ford.
temp - ta - tions lose their power when thou art nigh.
come quick - ly and a - bide, or life is vain.
and thy rich prom-is - es in me ful - fill.
O make me thine in - deed, thou bless - ed Son.

Refrain

I need thee, O I need thee; ev - ery hour I need thee;

O bless me now, my Sav - ior, I come to thee.

WORDS: Annie S. Hawks, 1872 (Jn. 15:5)
MUSIC: Robert Lowry, 1873

NEED
64.64 with Refrain

Jesus Calls Us

398

1. Je - sus calls us o'er the tu - mult of our
2. As of old the a - pos - tles heard it by the
3. Je - sus calls us from the wor - ship of the
4. In our joys and in our sor - rows, days of
5. Je - sus calls us! By thy mer - cies, Sav - ior,

life's wild, rest - less sea; day by day his
Gal - i - le - an lake, turned from home and
vain world's gold - en store, from each i - dol
toil and hours of ease, still he calls, in
may we hear thy call, give our hearts to

sweet voice sound - eth, say - ing, "Chris - tian, fol - low me!"
toil and kin - dred, leav - ing all for Je - sus' sake.
that would keep us, say - ing, "Chris - tian, love me more!"
cares and plea - sures, "Chris - tian, love me more than these!"
thine o - be - dience, serve and love thee best of all.

WORDS: Cecil Frances Alexander, 1852 (Mt. 4:18-22)
MUSIC: William H. Jude, 1874

GALILEE
87.87

399 Take My Life, and Let It Be

WORDS: Frances R. Havergal, 1873 (Rom. 12:1)
MUSIC: Louis J. F. Hérold, 1839; arr. by George Kingsley, 1839

MESSIAH
77.77 D

Come, Thou Fount of Every Blessing 400

1. Come, thou Fount of ev-ery bless-ing, tune my heart to
2. Here I raise mine Eb-e-ne-zer; hith-er by thy
3. O to grace how great a debt-or dai-ly I'm con-

sing thy grace; streams of mer-cy, nev-er ceas-ing,
help I'm come; and I hope, by thy good plea-sure,
strained to be! Let thy good-ness, like a fet-ter,

call for songs of loud-est praise. Teach me some me-lo-dious
safe-ly to ar-rive at home. Je-sus sought me when a
bind my wan-der-ing heart to thee. Prone to wan-der, Lord, I

son-net, sung by flam-ing tongues a-bove. Praise the mount! I'm
stran-ger, wan-der-ing from the fold of God; he, to res-cue
feel it, prone to leave the God I love; here's my heart, O

fixed up-on it, mount of thy re-deem-ing love.
me from dan-ger, in-ter-posed his pre-cious blood.
take and seal it, seal it for thy courts a-bove.

WORDS: Robert Robinson, 1758 (1 Sam. 7:12)
MUSIC: Wyeth's *Repository of Sacred Music, Part Second*, 1813

NETTLETON
87.87 D

401   For Holiness of Heart

Lord, I want to be more holy in my heart.
  Here is the citadel of all my desiring,
    where my hopes are born
    and all the deep resolutions of my spirit take wings.
In this center, my fears are nourished,
    and all my hates are nurtured.
Here my loves are cherished,
    and all the deep hungers of my spirit are honored
    without quivering and without shock.
In my heart, above all else,
    let love and integrity envelop me
    until my love is perfected and the last vestige
    of my desiring is no longer in conflict with thy Spirit.
Lord, I want to be more holy in my heart. **Amen.**

Howard Thurman, USA, 20th cent.
By permission of The Howard Thurman Educational Trust

402   Lord, I Want to Be a Christian

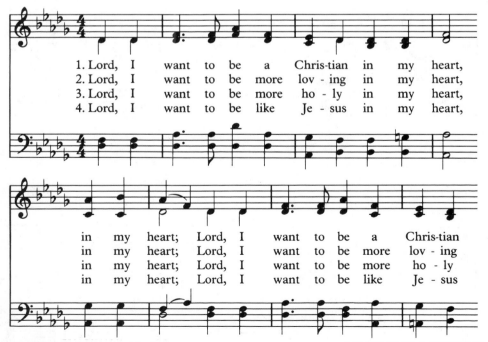

1. Lord, I want to be a Christian in my heart,
in my heart; Lord, I want to be a Christian

2. Lord, I want to be more loving in my heart,
in my heart; Lord, I want to be more loving

3. Lord, I want to be more holy in my heart,
in my heart; Lord, I want to be more holy

4. Lord, I want to be like Jesus in my heart,
in my heart; Lord, I want to be like Jesus

WORDS: Afro-American spiritual
MUSIC: Afro-American spiritual; adapt. and arr. by
  William Farley Smith, 1986

I WANT TO BE A CHRISTIAN
Irr.

Adapt. and arr. © 1989 The United Methodist Publishing House.

in my heart. In my heart,
(in my heart) (in my heart)
in my heart, Lord, I want to
(in my heart)
be a Chris-tian in my heart. (in my heart)
be more lov - ing in my heart. (in my heart)
be more ho - ly in my heart. (in my heart)
be like Je - sus in my heart. (in my heart)

For True Life 403

Govern all by thy wisdom, O Lord,
  so that my soul may always be serving thee
    as thou dost will,
    and not as I may choose.
Do not punish me, I beseech thee,
  by granting that which I wish or ask,
    if it offend thy love, which would always live in me.
Let me die to myself, that I may serve thee;
  let me live to thee, who in thyself art the true life. **Amen.**

Teresa of Avila, Spain, 16th cent.

404 Every Time I Feel the Spirit

Refrain

Ev-ery time I feel the Spir-it mov-ing in my heart, I will pray. Yes, ev-ery time I feel the Spir-it mov-ing in my heart, I will pray.

Fine

1. Up-on the moun-tain, my Lord spoke, out his mouth came fire and smoke. All a-round me looks so
2. Jor-dan riv-er runs right cold, chills the bod-y, not the soul. Ain't but one train on this

WORDS: Afro-American spiritual (Rom. 8:15-17)
MUSIC: Afro-American spiritual; adapt. and arr. by William Farley Smith, 1986

PENTECOST
Irr.

Adapt. and arr. © 1989 The United Methodist Publishing House

Seek Ye First 405

WORDS: Karen Lafferty, 1972 (Mt. 6:33; 7:7)
MUSIC: Karen Lafferty, 1972

SEEK YE
Irr.

406 Canticle of Prayer

WORDS: Romans 8:26; Luke 11:9-10; adapt. by Alan Luff, 1962, alt.
MUSIC: Erik Routley, 1969

PRAYER CANTICLE
Irr.

Close to Thee

1. Thou my ev - er - last - ing por - tion, more than friend or life to me, all a - long my pil - grim jour - ney, Sav-ior, let me walk with thee.

2. Not for ease or world - ly plea - sure, nor for fame my prayer shall be; glad - ly will I toil and suf - fer, on - ly let me walk with thee.

3. Lead me through the vale of shad - ows, bear me o'er life's fit - ful sea; then the gate of life e - ter - nal may I en - ter, Lord, with thee.

Refrain

Close to thee, close to thee, close to thee, close to thee,

all a - long my pil - grim jour - ney, Sav - ior, let me walk with thee.

glad - ly will I toil and suf - fer, on - ly let me walk with thee.

then the gate of life e - ter - nal may I en - ter, Lord, with thee.

WORDS: Fanny J. Crosby, 1874
MUSIC: Silas J. Vail, 1874

CLOSE TO THEE
87.87 with Refrain

408 The Gift of Love

1. Though I may speak with brav-est fire,
2. Though I may give all I pos-sess,
3. Come, Spir-it, come, our hearts con-trol,

and have the gift to all in - spire,
and striv-ing so my love pro-fess,
our spir-its long to be made whole.

and have not love, my words are vain,
but not be given by love with - in,
Let in - ward love guide ev - ery deed;

as sound-ing brass, and hope-less gain.
the prof-it soon turns strange-ly thin.
by this we wor - ship, and are freed.

WORDS: Hal Hopson, 1972 (1 Cor. 13:1-3) GIFT OF LOVE
MUSIC: Trad. English melody; adapt. by Hal Hopson, 1972 LM

409 For Grace to Labor

The things, good Lord, that we pray for, give us the grace to labor for.
Amen.

Thomas More, England, 16th cent.

I Want a Principle Within

410

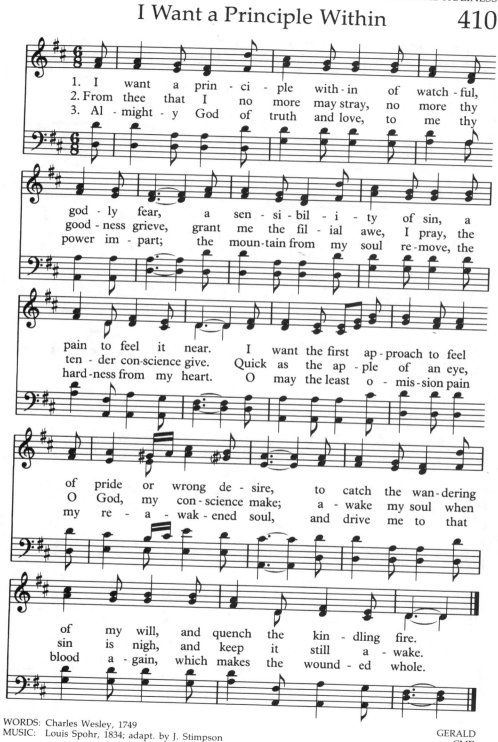

1. I want a principle within of watchful godly fear, a sensibility of sin, a pain to feel it near. I want the first approach to feel of pride or wrong desire, to catch the wandering of my will, and quench the kindling fire.

2. From thee that I no more may stray, no more thy goodness grieve, grant me the filial awe, I pray, the tender conscience give. Quick as the apple of an eye, O God, my conscience make; awake my soul when sin is nigh, and keep it still awake.

3. Almighty God of truth and love, to me thy power impart; the mountain from my soul remove, the hardness from my heart. O may the least omission pain my reawakened soul, and drive me to that blood again, which makes the wounded whole.

WORDS: Charles Wesley, 1749
MUSIC: Louis Spohr, 1834; adapt. by J. Stimpson

GERALD
CMD

411 Dear Lord, Lead Me Day by Day

1. Dear Lord, lead me day by day; make me stead-fast,
2. Dear Lord, lead me day by day; make me fol-low
3. Now with con-fi-dence I sing joy-ous prais-es

wise, and strong; hap-py most of all to know that my
and o-bey faith-ful-ly your words of life, that your
to our God, and with up-right heart I give ten-der

dear Lord loves me so.
love ev-er a-bide.
care and sym-pa-thy.

Refrain

Praise to God, fount of love,

praise from morn till the set of sun; praise at home,

praise in church; praise to God ev-ery-where on earth.

WORDS: Francisca Asuncion, 1983
MUSIC: Philippine folk melody; arr. by Francisca Asuncion, 1983

COTTAGE GROVE
77.77 with Refrain

© 1983 The United Methodist Publishing House

Prayer of John Chrysostom 412

Almighty God,
you have given us grace at this time
  with one accord to make our common supplication to you;
and you have promised through your well-beloved Son
  that when two or three are gathered together in his name,
    you will be in the midst of them.
Fulfill now, O Lord, our desires and petitions
  as may be best for us;
  granting us in this world knowledge of your truth,
    and in the age to come life everlasting. **Amen.**

After *The Book of Common Prayer*, Greek, 5th cent. (Mt. 18:19-20)

A Charge to Keep I Have 413

1. A charge to keep I have, a God to glo - ri - fy,
2. To serve the pres - ent age, my call-ing to ful - fill;
3. Arm me with jeal - ous care, as in thy sight to live,
4. Help me to watch and pray, and on thy - self re - ly,

a nev - er - dy - ing soul to save, and fit it for the sky.
O may it all my powers en-gage to do my Mas-ter's will!
and oh, thy ser - vant, Lord, pre-pare a strict ac-count to give!
as - sured, if I my trust be-tray, I shall for - ev - er die.

WORDS: Charles Wesley, 1762 (Lev. 8:35)
MUSIC: Lowell Mason, 1832

BOYLSTON
SM

414 Thou Hidden Love of God

1. Thou hid-den love of God, whose height, whose depth un-fath-omed no one knows, I see from far thy beau-teous light, and in-ly sigh for thy re-pose; my heart is pained, nor can it be

2. 'Tis mer-cy all that thou hast brought my mind to seek its peace in thee; yet while I seek, but find thee not, no peace my wan-dering soul shall see. O when shall all my wan-derings end,

3. Is there a thing be-neath the sun that strives with thee my heart to share? Ah, tear it thence and reign a-lone, the Lord of ev-ery mo-tion there; then shall my heart from earth be free,

4. O Love, thy sov-ereign aid im-part to save me from low-thought-ed care; chase this self-will from all my heart, from all its hid-den maz-es there; make me thy du-teous child that I

5. Each mo-ment draw from earth a-way my heart that low-ly waits thy call; speak to my in-most soul and say, "I am thy love, thy God, thy all!" To feel thy power, to hear thy voice,

WORDS: Gerhard Tersteegen, 1729; trans. by John Wesley, 1736 (Gal. 2:20)
MUSIC: *Geistliche Lieder*, 1539; harm. from J. S. Bach, 1726

VATER UNSER
88.88.88

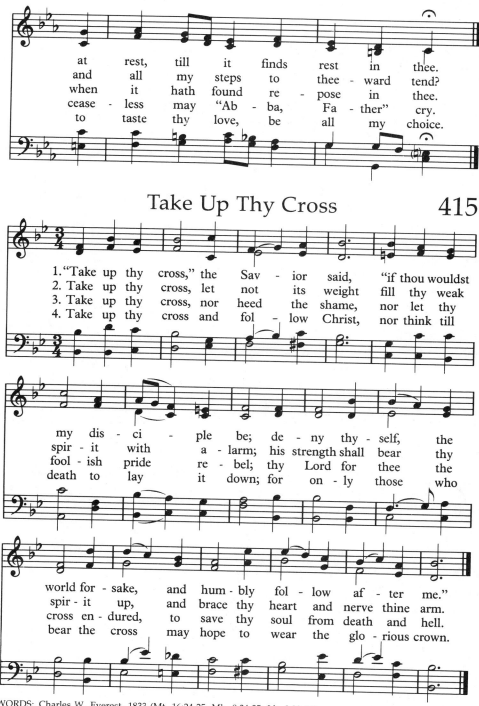

at rest, till it finds rest in thee.
and all my steps to thee - ward tend?
when it hath found re - pose in thee.
cease - less may "Ab - ba, Fa - ther" cry.
to taste thy love, be all my choice.

Take Up Thy Cross 415

1. "Take up thy cross," the Sav - ior said, "if thou wouldst
2. Take up thy cross, let not its weight fill thy weak
3. Take up thy cross, nor heed the shame, nor let thy
4. Take up thy cross and fol - low Christ, nor think till

my dis - ci - ple be; de - ny thy - self, the
spir - it with a - larm; his strength shall bear thy
fool - ish pride re - bel; thy Lord for thee the
death to lay it down; for on - ly those who

world for - sake, and hum - bly fol - low af - ter me."
spir - it up, and brace thy heart and nerve thine arm.
cross en - dured, to save thy soul from death and hell.
bear the cross may hope to wear the glo - rious crown.

WORDS: Charles W. Everest, 1833 (Mt. 16:24-25; Mk. 8:34-35; Lk. 9:23-24)
MUSIC: William Gardiner's *Sacred Melodies*, 1815

GERMANY
LM

416 Come Out the Wilderness

WORDS: Afro-American spiritual
MUSIC: Afro-American spiritual, adapt. and arr. by William Farley Smith, 1986

TURNER
Irr.

417 O For a Heart to Praise My God

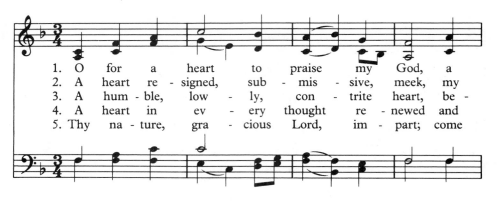

1. O for a heart to praise my God, a
2. A heart re - signed, sub - mis - sive, meek, my
3. A hum - ble, low - ly, con - trite heart, be -
4. A heart in ev - ery thought re - newed and
5. Thy na - ture, gra - cious Lord, im - part; come

heart from sin set free, a heart that al - ways
great Re - deem - er's throne, where on - ly Christ is
liev - ing, true, and clean, which nei - ther life nor
full of love di - vine, per - fect and right and
quick - ly from a - bove; write thy new name up -

feels thy blood so free - ly shed for me.
heard to speak, where Je - sus reigns a - lone.
death can part from Christ who dwells with - in.
pure and good, a cop - y, Lord, of thine.
on my heart, thy new, best name of Love.

WORDS: Charles Wesley, 1742 (Ps. 51:10)
MUSIC: Thomas Haweis, 1792

RICHMOND
CM

We Are Climbing Jacob's Ladder 418

1. We are climb - ing Ja - cob's lad - der; we are
2. Ev - ery round goes high - er, high - er; ev - ery
3. Sin - ner, do you love my Je - sus? Sin - ner,
4. If you love him, why not serve him? If you
5. We are climb - ing high - er, high - er; we are

(yes, Lord)

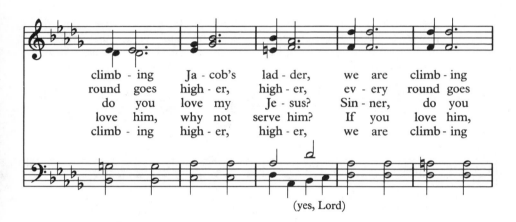

climb - ing Ja - cob's lad - der, we are climb - ing
round goes high - er, high - er, ev - ery round goes
do you love my Je - sus? Sin - ner, do you
love him, why not serve him? If you love him,
climb - ing high - er, high - er, we are climb - ing

(yes, Lord)

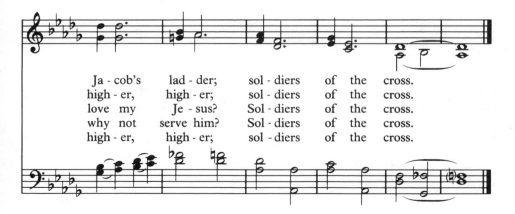

Ja - cob's lad - der; sol - diers of the cross.
high - er, high - er; sol - diers of the cross.
love my Je - sus? Sol - diers of the cross.
why not serve him? Sol - diers of the cross.
high - er, high - er; sol - diers of the cross.

WORDS: Afro-American spiritual (Gen. 28:10-17)
MUSIC: Afro-American spiritual; adapt. and arr. by William Farley Smith, 1986

JACOB'S LADDER
Irr.

419 I Am Thine, O Lord

1. I am thine, O Lord, I have heard thy voice, and it
2. Con-se-crate me now to thy ser-vice, Lord, by the
3. O the pure de-light of a sin-gle hour that be-
4. There are depths of love that I can-not know till I

told thy love to me; but I long to rise in the
power of grace di-vine; let my soul look up with a
fore thy throne I spend, when I kneel in prayer, and with
cross the nar-row sea; there are heights of joy that I

arms of faith and be clos-er drawn to thee.
stead-fast hope, and my will be lost in thine.
thee, my God, I com-mune as friend with friend!
may not reach till I rest in peace with thee.

Refrain

Draw me near - er, near-er, bless-ed Lord, to the
near - er, near - er,

WORDS: Fanny J. Crosby, 1875 (Heb. 10:22)
MUSIC: William H. Doane, 1875

I AM THINE
10 7.10 7 with Refrain

cross where thou hast died. Draw me near-er, near-er,

near-er, bless-ed Lord, to thy pre-cious, bleed-ing side.

Breathe on Me, Breath of God 420

1. Breathe on me, Breath of God, fill me with life a-new,
2. Breathe on me, Breath of God, un-til my heart is pure,
3. Breathe on me, Breath of God, till I am whol-ly thine,
4. Breathe on me, Breath of God, so shall I nev-er die,

that I may love what thou dost love, and do what thou wouldst do.
un-til with thee I will one will, to do and to en-dure.
till all this earth-ly part of me glows with thy fire di-vine.
but live with thee the per-fect life of thine e-ter-ni-ty.

WORDS: Edwin Hatch, 1878 (Jn. 20:22)
MUSIC: Robert Jackson, 1888

TRENTHAM
SM

421 Make Me a Captive, Lord

1. Make me a cap-tive, Lord, and then I shall be free.
2. My heart is weak and poor un-til it mas-ter find;
3. My power is faint and low till I have learned to serve;
4. My will is not my own till thou hast made it thine;

Force me to ren-der up my sword, and I shall
it has no spring of ac-tion sure, it va-ries
it lacks the need-ed fire to glow, it lacks the
if it would reach a mon-arch's throne, it must its

con-queror be. I sink in life's a-larms when
with the wind. It can-not free-ly move till
breeze to nerve. It can-not drive the world un-
crown re-sign. It on-ly stands un-bent a-

by my-self I stand; im-pris-on me with-
thou hast wrought its chain; en-slave it with thy
til it-self be driven; its flag can on-ly
mid the clash-ing strife, when on thy bos-om

WORDS: George Matheson, 1890 (Eph. 3:1)
MUSIC: George J. Elvey, 1868

DIADEMATA
SMD

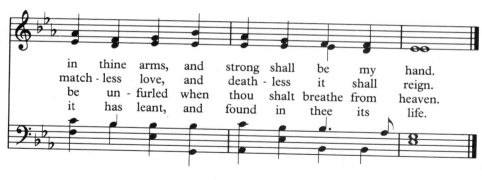

in thine arms, and strong shall be my hand.
match-less love, and death-less it shall reign.
be un-furled when thou shalt breathe from heaven.
it has leant, and found in thee its life.

Jesus, Thine All-Victorious Love 422

1. Je - sus, thine all - vic - to - rious love shed
2. O that in me the sa - cred fire might
3. O that it now from heaven might fall and
4. Re - fin - ing fire, go through my heart, il -

in my heart a - broad; then shall my feet no
now be - gin to glow; burn up the dross of
all my sins con - sume! Come, Ho - ly Ghost, for
lu - mi - nate my soul; scat - ter thy life through

long - er rove, root - ed and fixed in God.
base de - sire and make the moun - tains flow!
thee I call, Spir - it of burn - ing, come!
ev - ery part and sanc - ti - fy the whole.

WORDS: Charles Wesley, 1740
MUSIC: Carl G. Gläser; arr. by Lowell Mason, 1839

AZMON
CM

423 Finding Rest in God

Thou hast made us for thyself, O Lord, and our hearts are restless until they find rest in thee.

Augustine of Hippo, North Africa, 4th cent. (Mt. 11:28)

In comparison with this big world, the human heart is only a small thing. Though the world is so large, it is utterly unable to satisfy this tiny heart. The ever-growing soul and its capacity can be satisfied only in the infinite God. As water is restless until it reaches its level, so the soul has not peace until it rests in God.

Sundar Singh, India, 20th cent.

424 Must Jesus Bear the Cross Alone

1. Must Je - sus bear the cross a - lone, and all the world go free? No, there's a cross for ev - ery - one, and there's a cross for me.
2. How hap - py are the saints a - bove, who once went sor - rowing here! But now they taste un - min - gled love, and joy with - out a tear.
3. The con - se - crat - ed cross I'll bear till death shall set me free; and then go home my crown to wear, for there's a crown for me.

WORDS: Thomas Shepherd and others, 1855
MUSIC: George N. Allen, 1844

MAITLAND
CM

PERSONAL HOLINESS, *see further:*

290 Go to Dark Gethsemane
373 Nothing Between My Soul and My Savior
585 This Little Light of Mine
298, 299 When I Survey the Wondrous Cross

O Crucified Redeemer

1. O cru - ci - fied Re - deem - er, whose life-blood we have spilt,
2. We hear your cry of an - guish, we see your life out - poured
3. The groan-ing of cre - a - tion wrung out by pain and care,

to you we raise our guilt - y hands, and hum-bly own our guilt.
where bat - tle-fields run red with blood, our neigh-bors' blood, O Lord;
the an-guish of a mil - lion hearts that break in dumb de - spair;

To - day we see your pas-sion spread o - pen to our gaze;
and in that oth - er bat - tle, the fight for dai - ly bread,
O cru - ci - fied Re - deem - er, these are your cries of pain;

the crowd-ed street, the coun-try road, its Cal - va - ry dis - plays.
where might is right and self is king, we see your thorn-crowned head.
O may they break our self - ish hearts, and love come in to reign.

WORDS: Timothy Rees, 1946
MUSIC: Welsh hymn melody; harm. by David Evans, 1927

LLANGLOFFAN
76.76 D

Words by permission of Community of Resurrection, Mirfield, UK; harm. by permission of
Oxford University Press

426 Behold a Broken World

1. Be - hold a bro - ken world, we pray, where
2. A dream of swords to sick - les bent, of
3. Where ev - ery bat - tle flag is furled and
4. No force of arms shall there pre - vail nor
5. O Prince of Peace, who died to save, a
6. Bring, Lord, your bet - ter world to birth, your

want and war in - crease, and grant us, Lord, in
spears to scythe and spade, the weap - ons of our
ev - ery trum - pet stilled, where wars shall cease in
jus - tice cease its sway; nor shall their loft - iest
lost world to re - deem, and rose in tri - umph
king - dom, love's do - main, where peace with God, and

this our day, the an - cient dream of peace:
war - fare spent, a world of peace re - made;
all the world, a wak - ing dream ful - filled.
vi - sions fail the dream - ers of the day.
from the grave, be - hold our wak - ing dream.
peace on earth, and peace e - ter - nal reign.

WORDS: Timothy Dudley-Smith, 1985 (Is. 2:1-4; Mic. 4:1-4)
MUSIC: Max Miller, 1984

MARSH CHAPEL
CM

Where Cross the Crowded Ways of Life 427

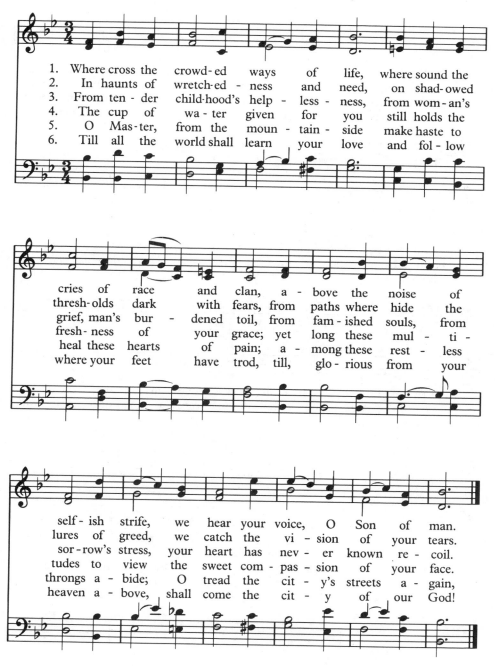

1. Where cross the crowd-ed ways of life, where sound the
2. In haunts of wretch-ed - ness and need, on shad-owed
3. From ten - der child-hood's help - less - ness, from wom-an's
4. The cup of wa - ter given for you still holds the
5. O Mas-ter, from the moun - tain-side make haste to
6. Till all the world shall learn your love and fol - low

cries of race and clan, a - bove the noise of
thresh-olds dark with fears, from paths where hide the
grief, man's bur - dened toil, from fam - ished souls, from
fresh-ness of your grace; yet long these mul - ti -
heal these hearts of pain; a - mong these rest - less
where your feet have trod, till, glo - rious from your

self - ish strife, we hear your voice, O Son of man.
lures of greed, we catch the vi - sion of your tears.
sor-row's stress, your heart has nev - er known re - coil.
tudes to view the sweet com - pas - sion of your face.
throngs a - bide; O tread the cit - y's streets a - gain,
heaven a - bove, shall come the cit - y of our God!

WORDS: Frank Mason North, 1903 (Mt. 22:9)
MUSIC: William Gardiner's *Sacred Melodies*, 1815

GERMANY
LM

428 For the Healing of the Nations

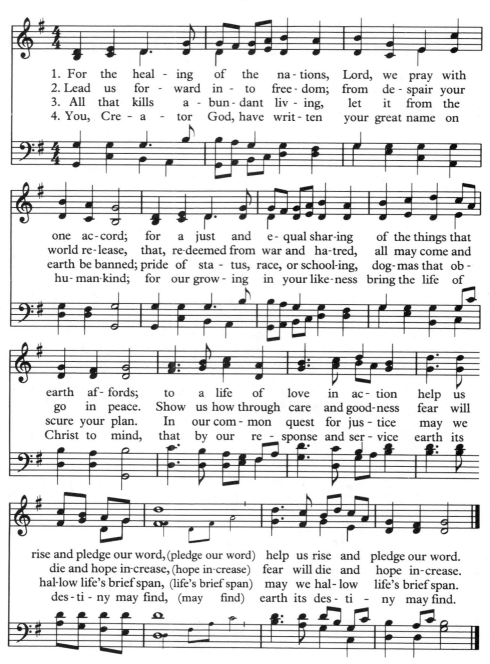

1. For the heal-ing of the na-tions, Lord, we pray with
2. Lead us for-ward in-to free-dom; from de-spair your
3. All that kills a-bun-dant liv-ing, let it from the
4. You, Cre-a-tor God, have writ-ten your great name on

one ac-cord; for a just and e-qual shar-ing of the things that
world re-lease, that, re-deemed from war and ha-tred, all may come and
earth be banned; pride of sta-tus, race, or school-ing, dog-mas that ob-
hu-man-kind; for our grow-ing in your like-ness bring the life of

earth af-fords; to a life of love in ac-tion help us
go in peace. Show us how through care and good-ness fear will
scure your plan. In our com-mon quest for jus-tice may we
Christ to mind, that by our re-sponse and ser-vice earth its

rise and pledge our word, (pledge our word) help us rise and pledge our word.
die and hope in-crease, (hope in-crease) fear will die and hope in-crease.
hal-low life's brief span, (life's brief span) may we hal-low life's brief span.
des-ti-ny may find, (may find) earth its des-ti-ny may find.

WORDS: Fred Kaan, 1965 (Rev. 21:1-22:5)
MUSIC: John Hughes, 1907
Words © 1968 Hope Publishing Co.

CWM RHONDDA
87.87.87

For Our Country

O God, keep our whole country under your protection. Wipe out sin from this land; lift it up from the depth of sorrow, O Lord, our shining light. Save us from deep grief and misfortune, Lord of all nations. Bless us with your wisdom, so that the poor may not be oppressed and the rich may not be oppressors. Make this a nation having no ruler except God, a nation having no authority but that of Love. **Amen.**

Toyohiko Kagawa, Japan, 20th cent.

© 1950 by Harper & Brothers

O Master, Let Me Walk with Thee   430

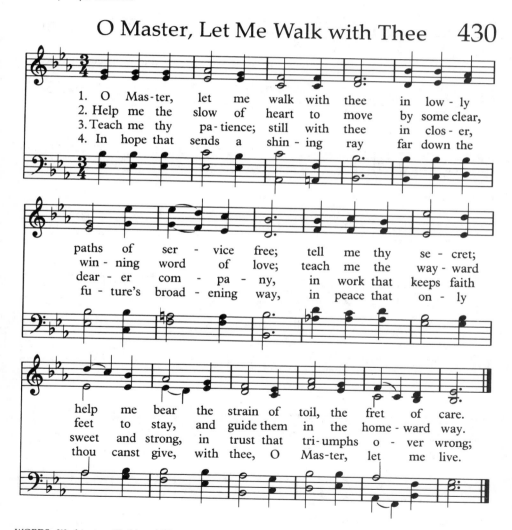

1. O Mas-ter, let me walk with thee in low-ly
2. Help me the slow of heart to move by some clear,
3. Teach me thy pa-tience; still with thee in clos-er,
4. In hope that sends a shin-ing ray far down the

paths of ser - vice free; tell me thy se - cret;
win - ning word of love; teach me the way - ward
dear - er com - pa - ny, in work that keeps faith
fu - ture's broad - ening way, in peace that on - ly

help me bear the strain of toil, the fret of care.
feet to stay, and guide them in the home - ward way.
sweet and strong, in trust that tri - umphs o - ver wrong;
thou canst give, with thee, O Mas - ter, let me live.

WORDS: Washington Gladden, 1879
MUSIC: H. Percy Smith, 1874

MARYTON
LM

431 Let There Be Peace on Earth

Let there be peace on earth, and let it be-gin with me; let there be peace on earth, the peace that was meant to be. *With God our cre-a-tor, chil-dren all are we. Let us walk with each oth-er in per-fect har-mo-ny.

*Original words: With God as our Father, brothers all are we. Let me walk with my brother in perfect harmony.

WORDS: Sy Miller and Jill Jackson
MUSIC: Sy Miller and Jill Jackson; harm. by Charles H. Webb, 1987

WORLD PEACE
Irr.

432

Jesu, Jesu

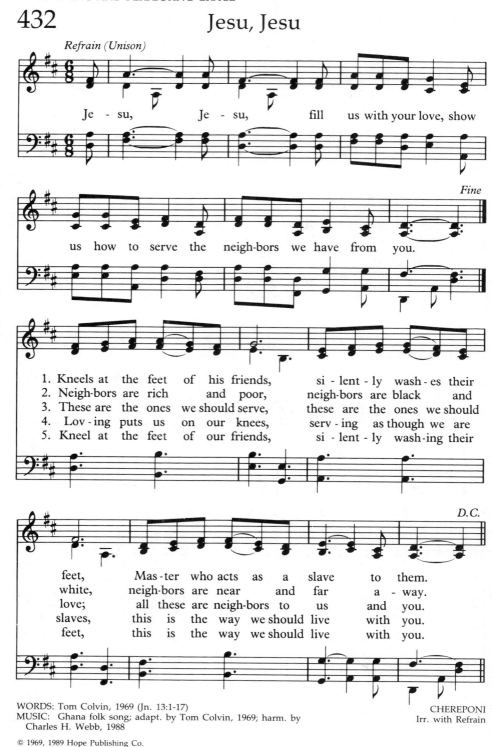

Refrain (Unison)

Je - su, Je - su, fill us with your love, show

Fine

us how to serve the neigh-bors we have from you.

1. Kneels at the feet of his friends, si - lent - ly wash - es their
2. Neigh-bors are rich and poor, neigh-bors are black and
3. These are the ones we should serve, these are the ones we should
4. Lov - ing puts us on our knees, serv - ing as though we are
5. Kneel at the feet of our friends, si - lent - ly wash-ing their

D.C.

feet, Mas - ter who acts as a slave to them.
white, neigh-bors are near and far a - way.
love; all these are neigh-bors to us and you.
slaves, this is the way we should live with you.
feet, this is the way we should live with you.

WORDS: Tom Colvin, 1969 (Jn. 13:1-17)
MUSIC: Ghana folk song; adapt. by Tom Colvin, 1969; harm. by
    Charles H. Webb, 1988

CHEREPONI
Irr. with Refrain

All Who Love and Serve Your City 433

Unison

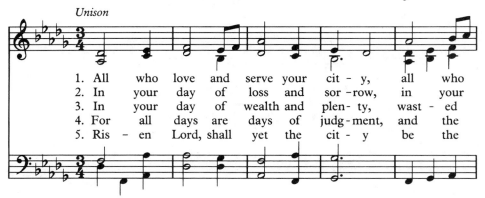

1. All who love and serve your cit - y, all who
2. In your day of loss and sor -row, in your
3. In your day of wealth and plen- ty, wast - ed
4. For all days are days of judg-ment, and the
5. Ris - en Lord, shall yet the cit - y be the

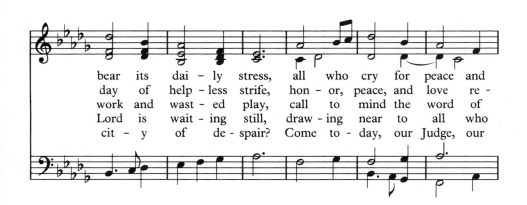

bear its dai — ly stress, all who cry for peace and
day of help - less strife, hon - or, peace, and love re -
work and wast - ed play, call to mind the word of
Lord is wait - ing still, draw - ing near to all who
cit - y of de - spair? Come to - day, our Judge, our

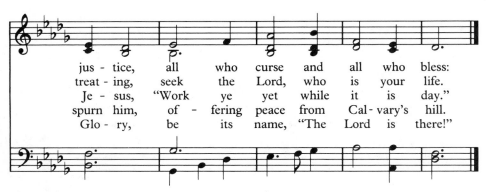

jus - tice, all who curse and all who bless:
treat - ing, seek the Lord, who is your life.
Je - sus, "Work ye yet while it is day."
spurn him, of - fering peace from Cal - vary's hill.
Glo - ry, be its name, "The Lord is there!"

WORDS: Erik Routley, 1966 (Lk. 19:41; Ezk. 48:35)   CHARLESTOWN
MUSIC: USA melody; harm. and arr. by Carlton R. Young, 1964   87.87

434

Cuando El Pobre
(When the Poor Ones)

Unísono (Unison)

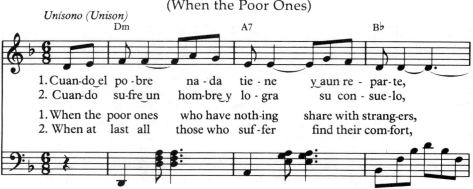

1. Cuan-do el po-bre na-da tie-ne y aun re - par-te,
2. Cuan-do su-fre un hom-bre y lo - gra su con - sue-lo,

1. When the poor ones who have noth-ing share with strang-ers,
2. When at last all those who suf-fer find their com-fort,

cuan-do el hom-bre pa-sa sed y a-gua nos da,
cuan-do es-pe-ra y no se can - sa de es-pe-rar,

when the thirst-y wa-ter give un -to us all,
when they hope though e -ven hope seems hope-less-ness,

cuan-do el dé-bil a su her-ma-no for-ta - le-ce,
cuan-do a - ma-mos, aun-que el o-dio nos ro - de-e,

when the crip-pled in their weak-ness strength-en oth-ers,
when we love though hate at times seems all a-round us,

WORDS: J. A. Olivar and Miguel Manzano; trans. by
George Lockwood (Mt. 25:31-46)
MUSIC: J. A. Olivar and Miguel Manzano; arr. by Alvin Schutmaat

EL CAMINO
12 11 12 with Refrain

Estribillo (Refrain)

va Dios mis-mo en nues-tro mis - mo ca - mi - nar,

then we know that God still goes that road with us,

va Dios mis-mo en nues-tro mis - mo ca-mi -nar.

then we know that God still goes that road with us.

3. Cuando crece la alegría y nos inunda,
   cuando dicen nuestros labios la verdad,
   cuando amamos el sentir de los sencillos,
   Estribillo

4. Cuando abunda el bien y llena los hogares,
   cuando un hombre donde hay guerra pone paz,
   cuando "hermano" le llamamos al extraño,
   Estribillo

———

3. When our joy fills up our cup to overflowing,
   when our lips can speak no words other than true,
   when we know that love for simple things is better,
   Refrain

4. When our homes are filled with goodness in abundance,
   when we learn how to make peace instead of war,
   when each stranger that we meet is called a neighbor,
   Refrain

435   O God of Every Nation

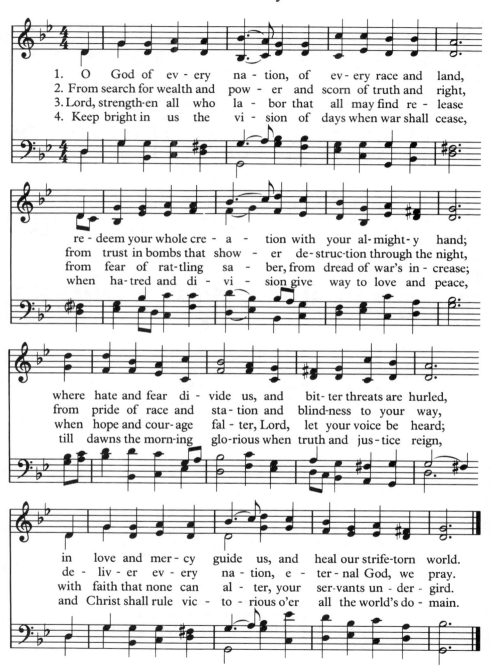

1. O God of ev-ery na-tion, of ev-ery race and land,
2. From search for wealth and pow-er and scorn of truth and right,
3. Lord, strength-en all who la-bor that all may find re-lease
4. Keep bright in us the vi-sion of days when war shall cease,

re-deem your whole cre-a-tion with your al-might-y hand;
from trust in bombs that show-er de-struc-tion through the night,
from fear of rat-tling sa-ber, from dread of war's in-crease;
when ha-tred and di-vi-sion give way to love and peace,

where hate and fear di-vide us, and bit-ter threats are hurled,
from pride of race and sta-tion and blind-ness to your way,
when hope and cour-age fal-ter, Lord, let your voice be heard;
till dawns the morn-ing glo-rious when truth and jus-tice reign,

in love and mer-cy guide us, and heal our strife-torn world.
de-liv-er ev-ery na-tion, e-ter-nal God, we pray.
with faith that none can al-ter, your ser-vants un-der-gird.
and Christ shall rule vic-to-rious o'er all the world's do-main.

WORDS: William W. Reid, Jr., 1958
MUSIC: Welsh hymn melody; harm. by David Evans, 1927

LLANGLOFFAN
76.76 D

Words © 1958, renewed 1986 The Hymn Society of America; harm. by permission of Oxford University Press

The Voice of God Is Calling

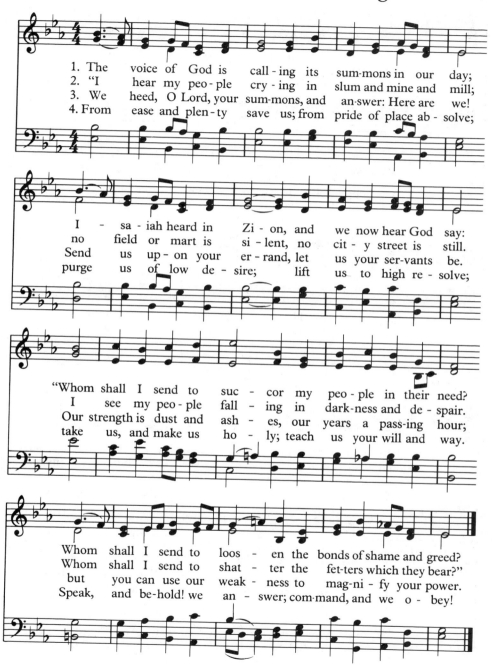

1. The voice of God is call-ing its sum-mons in our day;
2. "I hear my peo-ple cry-ing in slum and mine and mill;
3. We heed, O Lord, your sum-mons, and an-swer: Here are we!
4. From ease and plen-ty save us; from pride of place ab - solve;

I - sa - iah heard in Zi - on, and we now hear God say:
no field or mart is si - lent, no cit - y street is still.
Send us up - on your er - rand, let us your ser-vants be.
purge us of low de - sire; lift us to high re - solve;

"Whom shall I send to suc - cor my peo - ple in their need?
I see my peo - ple fall - ing in dark-ness and de - spair.
Our strength is dust and ash - es, our years a pass-ing hour;
take us, and make us ho - ly; teach us your will and way.

Whom shall I send to loos - en the bonds of shame and greed?
Whom shall I send to shat - ter the fet-ters which they bear?"
but you can use our weak - ness to mag-ni - fy your power.
Speak, and be-hold! we an - swer; com-mand, and we o - bey!

WORDS: John Haynes Holmes, 1913 (Is. 6:8)
MUSIC: William Lloyd, 1840

MEIRIONYDD
76.76 D

437 This Is My Song

1. This is my song, O God of all the na-tions,
2. My coun-try's skies are blu-er than the o-cean,
3. This is my prayer, O Lord of all earth's king-doms:

a song of peace for lands a-far and mine.
and sun-light beams on clo-ver-leaf and pine;
Thy king-dom come; on earth thy will be done.

This is my home, the coun-try where my heart is;
but oth-er lands have sun-light too, and clo-ver,
Let Christ be lift-ed up till all shall serve him,

here are my hopes, my dreams, my ho-ly shrine;
and skies are ev-ery-where as blue as mine.
and hearts u-nit-ed learn to live as one.

but oth-er hearts in oth-er lands are beat-ing
O hear my song, thou God of all the na-tions,
O hear my prayer, thou God of all the na-tions;

WORDS: Sts. 1,2 Lloyd Stone, 1934; st. 3, Georgia Harkness, ca. 1939
MUSIC: Jean Sibelius, 1899; arr. from *The Hymnal*, 1933

FINLANDIA
11 10.11 10.11 10

with hopes and dreams as true and high as mine.
a song of peace for their land and for mine.
my-self I give thee; let thy will be done.

Forth in Thy Name, O Lord 438

1. Forth in thy name, O Lord, I go, my dai-ly
2. The task thy wis-dom hath as-signed, O let me
3. Thee may I set at my right hand, whose eyes mine
4. For thee de-light-ful-ly em-ploy what-e'er thy

la-bor to pur-sue; thee, on-ly thee, re-
cheer-ful-ly ful-fill; in all my works thy
in-most sub-stance see, and la-bor on at
boun-teous grace hath given; and run my course with

solved to know in all I think or speak or do.
pres-ence find, and prove thy good and per-fect will.
thy com-mand, and of-fer all my works to thee.
e-ven joy, and close-ly walk with thee to heaven.

WORDS: Charles Wesley, 1749
MUSIC: John Hatton, 1793

DUKE STREET
LM

439   We Utter Our Cry

1. We ut - ter our cry: that peace may pre - vail,
2. We cry from the fright of our dai - ly scene
3. We lift up our hearts for chil - dren un - born;
*4. Cre - a - tor of life, come, share out, we pray,
*5. Come with us, Lord; love, in pro - test and march,
6. What - ev - er the ill or pres - sure we face,

that earth will sur - vive, and faith must not fail.
for strength to say "No" to all that is mean:
give wis - dom, O God, that we may hand on,
your Spir - it on earth, re - veal - ing the Way
and help us to fire with pas - sion your church,
Lord, heart - en and heal, give in - sight and grace

We pray with our life for the world in our care,
de - signs bear - ing cha - os, ex - tinc - tion of life,
re - plen - ished and tend - ed, this good plan - et Earth,
to lead - ers con - fer - ring round ta - bles for peace,
to match all our state - ments and loft - y re - solve
to think and make peace with each heart - beat and breath,

*May be omitted

WORDS: Fred Kaan, 1983
MUSIC: *Paderborn Gesangbuch*, 1765; harm. by Sydney H. Nicholson, 1916
Words © 1984 Hope Publishing Co.

PADERBORN
10 10.11 11

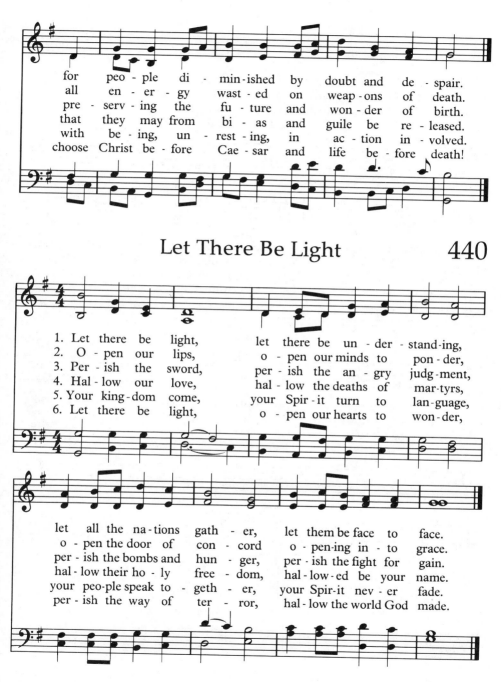

for   peo - ple   di - min-ished   by   doubt and   de - spair.
all   en - er - gy   wast - ed   on   weap-ons   of   death.
pre - serv - ing   the   fu - ture   and   won - der   of   birth.
that   they   may from   bi - as   and   guile   be   re - leased.
with   be - ing,   un - rest - ing,   in   ac - tion   in - volved.
choose Christ be - fore   Cae - sar   and   life   be - fore   death!

Let There Be Light   440

1. Let there   be   light,   let there be un - der - stand-ing,
2. O - pen our   lips,   o - pen our minds to   pon - der,
3. Per - ish   the   sword,   per - ish the an - gry   judg-ment,
4. Hal - low   our   love,   hal - low the deaths of   mar-tyrs,
5. Your king-dom   come,   your Spir - it turn to   lan-guage,
6. Let there   be   light,   o - pen our hearts to   won - der,

let   all the na - tions   gath - er,   let them be face   to   face.
o - pen the door of   con - cord   o - pen-ing in - to   grace.
per - ish the bombs and   hun - ger,   per - ish the fight for   gain.
hal - low their ho - ly   free - dom,   hal - low - ed be your   name.
your peo-ple speak to - geth - er,   your Spir - it nev - er   fade.
per - ish the way of   ter - ror,   hal - low the world God   made.

WORDS: Frances W. Davis
MUSIC: Robert J. B. Fleming, 1967

Music by permission of Mrs. Robert J. B. Fleming

CONCORD
47.76

441 What Does the Lord Require

1. What does the Lord re - quire for praise and
2. Rul - ers of earth, give ear! Should you not
3. All who gain wealth by trade, for whom the
4. How shall our life ful - fill God's law so

of - fer - ing? What sac - ri - fice, de - sire, or trib - ute
jus - tice know? Will God your plead-ing hear, while crime and
work - er toils, think not to win God's aid, if greed your
hard and high? Let Christ en-due our will with grace to

bid you bring? Do just - ly; love mer - cy; walk
cruel - ty grow? Do just - ly; love mer - cy; walk
com - merce soils. Do just - ly; love mer - cy; walk
for - ti - fy. Then just - ly, in mer - cy, we'll

hum - bly with your God.
hum - bly with your God.
hum - bly with your God.

hum - bly walk with God.

WORDS: Albert F. Bayly, 1949; alt. (Mic. 6:6-8)
MUSIC: Erik Routley, 1968

SHARPTHORNE
66.66.336

Words © 1949 Albert F. Bayly; music © 1969 Hope Publishing Co.

Weary of All Trumpeting

442

Unison

1. Wea - ry of all trum - pet-ing, wea - ry of all kill - ing,
2. Cap - tain Christ, O low - ly Lord, ser - vant King, your dy - ing
3. To the tri - umph of your cross sum - mon all the liv - ing;

wea - ry of all songs that sing prom - ise, non - ful - fill - ing,
bade us sheathe the fool - ish sword, bade us cease de - ny - ing.
sum - mon us to live by loss, gain - ing all by giv - ing;

we would raise, O Christ, one song; we would join in sing - ing
Trum-pet with your Spir-it's breath through each height and hol - low,
suf-fering all, that we may see tri - umph in sur - ren - der;

that great mu-sic pure and strong where-with heaven is ring-ing.
in - to your self-giv-ing death, call us all to fol - low.
leav - ing all, that we may be part-ners in your splen-dor.

WORDS: Martin Franzmann, 1971
MUSIC: Hugo Distler, 1938; harm. by Richard Proulx, 1975

TRUMPETS
76.76 D

443 O God Who Shaped Creation

1. O God who shaped cre - a - tion at earth's cha - o - tic dawn,
2. O God, with pain and an - guish a moth-er sees her child
3. Al-though your heart is bro - ken when peo-ple scorn your ways,
4. O God, when trin-kets tar - nish and plea-sures lose their charm,
5. In mer-cy and com - pas - sion your good-ness is re - vealed;

your word of power was spo - ken, and lo! the dark was gone!
em - bark on dead-end path - ways, al - lur -ing, but de - filed;
you nev - er cease your search - ing through e - vil's dark-some maze;
when, wea-ried by our wan - dering, we seek your o - pened arm,
with ten - der-ness you touch us, and bro-ken hearts are healed.

You framed us in your im - age, you brought us in - to birth,
so too your heart is bro - ken when hate and lust in - crease,
and when we cease our run - ning, your joys, O God, a - bound
with moth - er - like com - pas - sion you share your warm em - brace;
You claim us as your chil - dren, you strip our pride-ful shame;

you blessed our in - fant foot - steps and shared your splen-dored earth.
when worlds you birthed and nur - tured spurn ways that lead to peace.
like joy of search-ing wom - an when trea-sured coin is found.
you set for us a ban - quet and heal us through your grace.
with free-dom born of mer - cy we bless your ho - ly name!

WORDS: William W. Reid, Jr., 1987 (Gen. 1:1-3, 26-27) TUOLUMNE
MUSIC: Dale Wood, 1968, 1988 76.76 D

O Young and Fearless Prophet

444

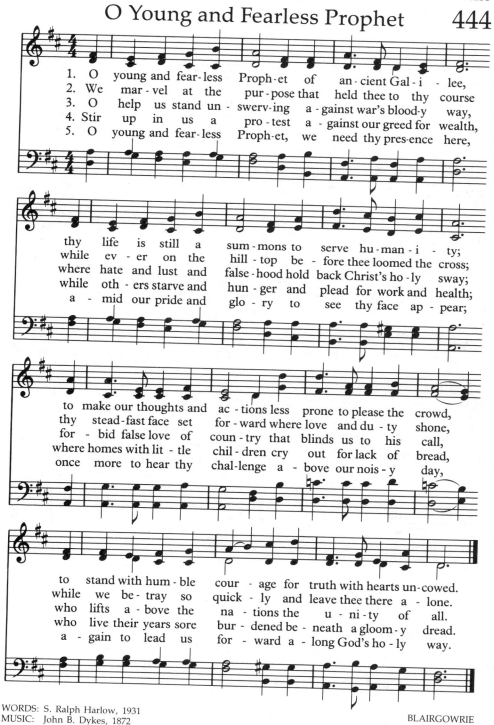

1. O young and fear-less Proph-et of an-cient Gal-i-lee,
2. We mar-vel at the pur-pose that held thee to thy course
3. O help us stand un-swerv-ing a-gainst war's blood-y way,
4. Stir up in us a pro-test a-gainst our greed for wealth,
5. O young and fear-less Proph-et, we need thy pres-ence here,

thy life is still a sum-mons to serve hu-man-i-ty;
while ev-er on the hill-top be-fore thee loomed the cross;
where hate and lust and false-hood hold back Christ's ho-ly sway;
while oth-ers starve and hun-ger and plead for work and health;
a-mid our pride and glo-ry to see thy face ap-pear;

to make our thoughts and ac-tions less prone to please the crowd,
thy stead-fast face set for-ward where love and du-ty shone,
for-bid false love of coun-try that blinds us to his call,
where homes with lit-tle chil-dren cry out for lack of bread,
once more to hear thy chal-lenge a-bove our nois-y day,

to stand with hum-ble cour-age for truth with hearts un-cowed.
while we be-tray so quick-ly and leave thee there a-lone.
who lifts a-bove the na-tions the u-ni-ty of all.
who live their years sore bur-dened be-neath a gloom-y dread.
a-gain to lead us for-ward a-long God's ho-ly way.

WORDS: S. Ralph Harlow, 1931
MUSIC: John B. Dykes, 1872

BLAIRGOWRIE
13 13.13 13

445 Happy the Home When God Is There

1. Hap - py the home when God is there,
2. Hap - py the home where Je - sus' name
3. Hap - py the home where prayer is heard,
4. Lord, let us in our homes a - gree

and love fills ev - ery breast; when one their wish, and
is sweet to ev - ery ear; where chil - dren ear - ly
and praise is wont to rise; where par - ents love the
this bless - ed peace to gain; u - nite our hearts in

one their prayer, and one their heaven - ly rest.
speak his fame, and par - ents hold him dear.
sa - cred Word and all its wis - dom prize.
love to thee, and love to all will reign.

WORDS: Henry Ware, Jr., 1846
MUSIC: John B. Dykes, 1866

ST. AGNES
CM

446 Serving the Poor

Make us worthy, Lord,
  to serve those throughout the world who live and die in poverty or hunger.
Give then, through our hands, this day their daily bread;
  and by our understanding love, give peace and joy. **Amen.**

Mother Teresa of Calcutta, Yugoslavia, 20th cent.

Our Parent, by Whose Name

447

1. Our Parent, by whose name all parent-hood is known,
2. O Jesus, who, a child with-in an earth-ly home,
3. Blest Spir-it, who can bind our hearts in u-ni-ty,

who in your love pro-claim each fam-i-ly your own:
with heart still un-de-filed did to a-dult-hood come:
and teach us so to find the love from self set free:

di-rect all par-ents, guard-ing well, with con-stant love
our chil-dren bless in ev-ery place, that they may all
in all our hearts such love in-crease that ev-ery home,

as sen-ti-nel, the homes in which your peo-ple dwell.
be-hold your face, and know-ing you may grow in grace.
by this re-lease, may be the dwell-ing place of peace.

WORDS: F. Bland Tucker, 1939; alt.
MUSIC: John David Edwards, ca. 1838

RHOSYMEDRE
66.66.888

448 Go Down, Moses

1. When Is-rael was in E-gypt's land, let my peo-ple
2. "Thus saith the Lord," bold Mo-ses said, let my peo-ple
3. No more shall they in bond-age toil, let my peo-ple
4. We need not al-ways weep and mourn, let my peo-ple
5. Come, Mo-ses, you will not get lost, let my peo-ple

go; op-pressed so hard they could not stand,
go; "if not, I'll smite your first-born dead,"
go; let them come out with E-gypt's spoil,
go; and wear those slav-ery chains for-lorn,
go; stretch out your rod and come a-cross,

let my peo-ple go.

Refrain

Go down, (go down) Mo-ses, (Mo-ses) way down in E-gypt's land; tell old Pha-raoh to let my peo-ple go!

WORDS: Afro-American spiritual (Ex. 3:7-12)
MUSIC: Afro-American spiritual; adapt. and arr. by William Farley Smith, 1986

TUBMAN
85.85 with Refrain

Adapt. and arr. © 1989 The United Methodist Publishing House

6. As Israel stood by the water's side,
   at God's command it did divide,
   Refrain

7. When they had reached the other shore,
   they sang a song of triumph o'er,
   Refrain

8. O Moses, the cloud shall cleave the way,
   a fire by night, a shade by day,
   Refrain

9. Your foes shall not before you stand,
   and you'll possess fair Canaan's land,
   Refrain

10. This world's a wilderness of woe,
    O let us on to Canaan go,
    Refrain

11. O let us all from bondage flee,
    and let us all in Christ be free,
    Refrain

Our Earth We Now Lament to See   449

Our earth we now lament to see
with floods of wickedness overflowed,
with violence, wrong, and cruelty,
one wide-extended field of blood,
where men like fiends each other tear
in all the hellish rage of war.

As listed on Abaddon's side,
they mangle their own flesh, and slay;
Tophet is moved, and opens wide
its mouth for its enormous prey;
and myriads sink beneath the grave,
and plunge into the flaming wave.

O might the universal Friend
this havoc of his creatures see!
Bid our unnatural discord end,
declare us reconciled in thee!
Write kindness on our inward parts
and chase the murderer from our hearts!

Who now against each other rise,
the nations of the earth constrain
to follow after peace, and prize
the blessings of thy righteous reign,
the joys of unity to prove,
the paradise of perfect love!

Charles Wesley, 1758

450 Creator of the Earth and Skies

Unison

1. Cre - a - tor of the earth and skies, to whom all
2. We have not known you: to the skies our mon - u -
3. We have not loved you: far and wide the wreck - age
4. We long to end this world - wide strife: How shall we

truth and power be - long, grant us your truth to
ments of fol - ly soar; and all our self - wrought
of our ha - tred spreads; and e - vils wrought by
fol - low in your way? Speak to us all your

make us wise; grant us your power to make us strong.
mis - er - ies have made us trust our - selves the more.
hu - man pride re - coil on un - re - pen - tant heads.
words of life, un - til our dark - ness turn to day.

WORDS: Donald Hughes, 1964, 1969 alt.   UFFINGHAM
MUSIC: Jeremiah Clark, 1707   LM

Words by permission of The Methodist Publishing House, England

SOCIAL HOLINESS, *see further:*

Be Thou My Vision

451

1. Be thou my vi - sion, O Lord of my heart;
2. Be thou my wis - dom, and thou my true word;
3. Great God of heav - en, my vic - to - ry won,

naught be all else to me, save that thou art.
I ev - er with thee and thou with me, Lord;
may I reach heav - en's joys, O bright heaven's Sun!

Thou my best thought, by day or by night,
thou and thou on - ly, first in my heart,
Heart of my own heart, what - ev - er be - fall,

wak - ing or sleep - ing, thy pres - ence my light.
great God of heav - en, my trea - sure thou art.
still be my vi - sion, O Rul - er of all.

WORDS: Ancient Irish; trans. by Mary E. Byrne, 1905; versed by Eleanor H. Hull, 1912, alt. SLANE
MUSIC: Trad. Irish melody; harm. by Carlton R. Young, 1963 10 10.9 10

Alt. © 1989 The United Methodist Publishing House; harm. © 1964 Abingdon Press

452 My Faith Looks Up to Thee

1. My faith looks up to thee, thou Lamb of
2. May thy rich grace im - part strength to my
3. While life's dark maze I tread, and griefs a -
4. When ends life's tran - sient dream, when death's cold,

Cal - va - ry, Sav - ior di - vine! Now hear me
faint - ing heart, my zeal in - spire! As thou hast
round me spread, be thou my guide; bid dark - ness
sul - len stream shall o'er me roll; blest Sav - ior,

while I pray, take all my guilt a - way,
died for me, O may my love to thee
turn to day, wipe sor - row's tears a - way,
then in love, fear and dis - trust re - move;

O let me from this day be whol - ly thine!
pure, warm, and change - less be, a liv - ing fire!
nor let me ev - er stray from thee a - side.
O bear me safe a - bove, a ran - somed soul!

WORDS: Ray Palmer, 1875
MUSIC: Lowell Mason, 1831

OLIVET
664.6664

More Love to Thee, O Christ 453

1. More love to thee, O Christ, more love to thee!
2. Once earth-ly joy I craved, sought peace and rest;
3. Let sor-row do its work, come grief and pain;
4. Then shall my lat-est breath whis-per thy praise;

Hear thou the prayer I make on bend-ed knee.
now thee a-lone I seek, give what is best.
sweet are thy mes-sen-gers, sweet their re-frain,
this be the part-ing cry my heart shall raise;

This is my ear-nest plea: More love, O Christ, to thee;
This all my prayer shall be: More love, O Christ, to thee;
when they can sing with me: More love, O Christ, to thee;
this still its prayer shall be: More love, O Christ, to thee;

more love to thee, more love to thee!
more love to thee, more love to thee!
more love to thee, more love to thee!
more love to thee, more love to thee!

WORDS: Elizabeth P. Prentiss, 1869
MUSIC: William H. Doane, 1870

MORE LOVE TO THEE
64.64.66.44

454 Open My Eyes, That I May See

1. O-pen my eyes, that I may see glimps-es of truth thou
2. O-pen my ears, that I may hear voic-es of truth thou
3. O-pen my mouth, and let me bear glad-ly the warm truth

hast for me; place in my hands the won-der-ful key
send-est clear; and while the wave-notes fall on my ear,
ev-ery-where; o-pen my heart and let me pre-pare

Refrain

that shall un-clasp and set me free.
ev-ery-thing false will dis-ap-pear. Si-lent-ly now I
love with thy chil-dren thus to share.

wait for thee, read-y, my God, thy will to see.

O-pen my eyes,
O-pen my ears, il-lu-mine me, Spir-it di-vine!
O-pen my heart,

WORDS: Clara H. Scott, 1895
MUSIC: Clara H. Scott, 1895

OPEN MY EYES
88.98 with Refrain

Not So in Haste, My Heart 455

1. Not so in haste, my heart! Have faith in God, and wait;
2. He nev-er com-eth late; he know-eth what is best;
3. Un-til he com-eth, rest, nor grudge the hours that roll;
4. Are soon-est at the goal that is not gained with speed;

al-though he lin-ger long, he nev-er comes too late.
vex not thy-self in vain; un-til he com-eth, rest.
the feet that wait for God are soon-est at the goal.
then hold thee still, my heart, for I shall wait his lead.

WORDS: Bradford Torrey, ca. 1875
MUSIC: Austrian melody; harm. by Joseph T. Cooper, 1879

DOLOMITE CHANT
66.66

For Courage to Do Justice 456

O Lord,
    open my eyes that I may see the needs of others;
    open my ears that I may hear their cries;
    open my heart so that they need not be without succor;
let me not be afraid to defend the weak because of the anger of the strong,
    nor afraid to defend the poor because of the anger of the rich.
Show me where love and hope and faith are needed,
    and use me to bring them to those places.
And so open my eyes and my ears
    that I may this coming day be able to do some work of peace for thee. **Amen.**

Alan Paton, South Africa, 20th cent.

457 For the Sick

God of compassion, source of life and health:
strengthen and relieve your servant(s), *Name(s)*,
and give your power of healing
   to those who minister to *their* needs,
that those for whom our prayers are offered
   may find help in weakness
   and have confidence in your loving care;
through him who healed the sick
   and is the physician of our souls,
   even Jesus Christ our Lord. **Amen.**

The Book of Common Prayer; alt. by Laurence Hull Stookey

Alt. © 1989 The United Methodist Publishing House

458 Dear Lord, for All in Pain

Unison

1. Dear Lord, for all in pain we pray to thee;
   O come and smite again thine en-e-my.
2. Give to thy ser-vants skill to soothe and bless,
   and to the tired and ill give qui-et-ness.
3. And, Lord, to those who know pain may not cease,
   come near, that e-ven so they may have peace.

WORDS: Amy W. Carmichael, 1931
MUSIC: Kenneth D. Smith, 1928; alt.

RAPHAEL
64.64

Words © 1933 Dohnavur Fellowship; music reprinted by permission of Kenneth D. Smith

The Serenity Prayer 459

God, grant me
    the serenity to accept the things I cannot change,
    the courage to change the things I can,
    and the wisdom to distinguish the one from the other. **Amen.**

Anonymous

In Time of Illness 460

O God, who dost forgive our iniquities and heal our diseases, we cry unto thee.
    Our strength has been brought low, and we know not what the future holds.
      In our bodies, there is pain; in our souls, anxiety and unrest.
If it may be, restore us to health.
We ask no miracle of deliverance,
    and if in the order of nature our suffering must continue,
      help us to accept it without rebellion.
If it must lead us toward the valley of the shadow,
    help us to fear no evil,
      but to go bravely into thy nearer presence.
In thy good keeping, all is well.
    Into thy hands we commend our bodies and our spirits.
    Do with us as thou wilt. **Amen.**

Georgia Harkness, USA, 20th cent.

© 1943 Whitmore & Stone, renewed 1970 Georgia Harkness

For Those Who Mourn 461

Gracious God,
    as your Son wept with Mary and Martha at the tomb of Lazarus,
look with compassion on those who grieve,
    [especially *Name(s)*].
Grant them the assurance of your presence now
    and faith in your eternal goodness,
that in them may be fulfilled the promise
    that those who mourn shall be comforted;
through Jesus Christ our Lord. **Amen.**

Laurence Hull Stookey, USA, 20th cent. (Jn. 11:35; Mt. 5:4)

© 1989 The United Methodist Publishing House

462 'Tis So Sweet to Trust in Jesus

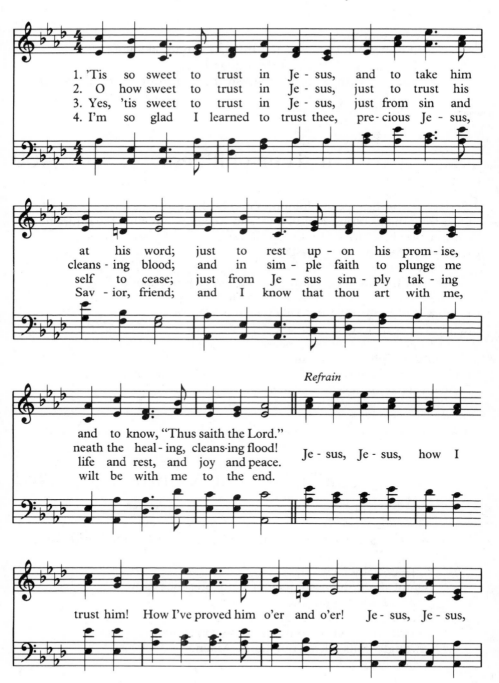

1. 'Tis so sweet to trust in Je - sus, and to take him at his word; just to rest up - on his prom - ise, and to know, "Thus saith the Lord."
2. O how sweet to trust in Je - sus, just to trust his cleans - ing blood; and in sim - ple faith to plunge me neath the heal - ing, cleans-ing flood!
3. Yes, 'tis sweet to trust in Je - sus, just from sin and self to cease; just from Je - sus sim - ply tak - ing life and rest, and joy and peace.
4. I'm so glad I learned to trust thee, pre - cious Je - sus, Sav - ior, friend; and I know that thou art with me, wilt be with me to the end.

Refrain

Je - sus, Je - sus, how I trust him! How I've proved him o'er and o'er! Je - sus, Je - sus,

WORDS: Louisa M. R. Stead, 1882
MUSIC: William J. Kirkpatrick, 1882

TRUST IN JESUS
87.87 with Refrain

pre - cious Je - sus! O for grace to trust him more!

Lord, Speak to Me 463

1. Lord, speak to me, that I may speak in
2. O strength - en me, that while I stand firm
3. O teach me, Lord, that I may teach the
4. O fill me with thy full - ness, Lord, un -
5. O use me, Lord, use ev - en me, just

liv - ing ech - oes of thy tone; as thou hast sought, so
on the rock, and strong in thee, I may stretch out a
pre - cious things thou dost im - part; and wing my words, that
til my ver - y heart o'er - flow in kin - dling thought and
as thou wilt, and when, and where, un - til thy bless - ed

let me seek thine err - ing chil - dren lost and lone.
lov - ing hand to wres - tlers with the trou - bled sea.
they may reach the hid - den depths of many a heart.
glow - ing word, thy love to tell, thy praise to show.
face I see, thy rest, thy joy, thy glo - ry share.

WORDS: Frances R. Havergal, 1872 (Rom. 14:7)
MUSIC: Adapt. from Robert Schumann, 1839

CANONBURY
LM

464 I Will Trust in the Lord

1. I will trust in the Lord, I will trust in the Lord,

I will trust in the Lord, till I die;

I will trust in the Lord, I will trust in the Lord,

I will trust in the Lord, till I die.

2. Sister, will you trust ... till you die
3. Brother, will you trust ... till you die
4. Preacher, will you trust ... till you die

WORDS: Afro-American spiritual (Ps. 37:3)
MUSIC: Afro-American spiritual; adapt. and arr. by William Farley Smith, 1987

I WILL TRUST
Irr.

Holy Spirit, Truth Divine 465

1. Ho - ly Spir - it, Truth di - vine, dawn up -
2. Ho - ly Spir - it, Love di - vine, glow with -
3. Ho - ly Spir - it, Power di - vine, fill and
4. Ho - ly Spir - it, Right di - vine, King with -

on this soul of mine; Word of God and
in this heart of mine; kin - dle ev - ery
nerve this will of mine; grant that I may
in my con - science reign; be my Lord, and

in - ward light, wake my spir - it, clear my sight.
high de - sire; per - ish self in thy pure fire.
strong - ly live, brave - ly bear, and no - bly strive.
I shall be firm - ly bound, for - ev - er free.

WORDS: Samuel Longfellow, 1864
MUSIC: Adapt. from Orlando Gibbons, 1623

CANTERBURY
77.77

An Invitation to Christ 466

Come, my Light, and illumine my darkness.
Come, my Life, and revive me from death.
Come, my Physician, and heal my wounds.
Come, Flame of divine love, and burn up the thorns of my sins,
  kindling my heart with the flame of thy love.
Come, my King, sit upon the throne of my heart and reign there.
For thou alone art my King and my Lord. **Amen.**

Dimitri of Rostov, Russia, 17th cent.

By permission of A. R. Mowbray & Co., Ltd.

467

Trust and Obey

1. When we walk with the Lord in the light of his word,
2. Not a bur - den we bear, not a sor - row we share,
3. But we nev - er can prove the de - lights of his love
4. Then in fel - low - ship sweet we will sit at his feet,

what a glo - ry he sheds on our way!
but our toil he doth rich - ly re - pay;
un - til all on the al - tar we lay;
or we'll walk by his side in the way;

While we do his good will, he a - bides with us still,
not a grief or a loss, not a frown or a cross,
for the fa - vor he shows, for the joy he be - stows,
what he says we will do, where he sends we will go;

and with all who will trust and o - bey.
but is blest if we trust and o - bey.
are for them who will trust and o - bey.
nev - er fear, on - ly trust and o - bey.

WORDS: John H. Sammis, 1887 (1 Jn 1:7)
MUSIC: Daniel B. Towner, 1887

TRUST AND OBEY
669 D with Refrain

Refrain

Trust and o - bey, for there's no oth - er way to be

hap - py in Je - sus, but to trust and o - bey.

Dear Jesus, in Whose Life I See 468

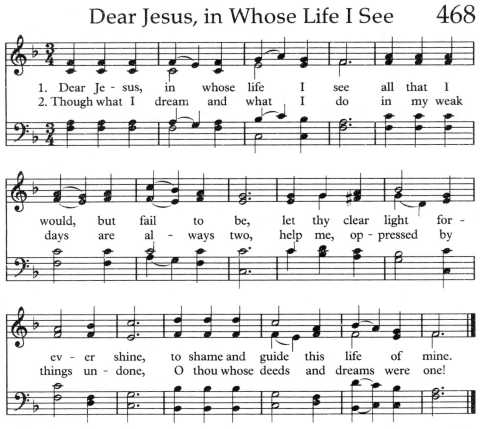

1. Dear Je - sus, in whose life I see all that I
2. Though what I dream and what I do in my weak

would, but fail to be, let thy clear light for-
days are al - ways two, help me, op - pressed by

ev - er shine, to shame and guide this life of mine.
things un - done, O thou whose deeds and dreams were one!

WORDS: John Hunter, 1889
MUSIC: *Katholisches Gesangbuch*, 1774; adapt. from *Metrical Psalter*, 1855

HURSLEY
LM

469 Jesus Is All the World to Me

1. Je-sus is all the world to me, my life, my joy, my all;
2. Je-sus is all the world to me, my friend in tri-als sore;
3. Je-sus is all the world to me, and true to him I'll be;
4. Je-sus is all the world to me, I want no bet-ter friend;

he   is   my strength from   day   to   day,   with-
I   go   to   him   for   bless - ings, and   he
O   how could I   this   friend   de - ny,   when
I   trust him   now, I'll   trust   him   when   life's

out   him   I   would fall.   When I   am   sad,   to
gives them o'er   and   o'er.   He sends the sun - shine
he's   so   true   to   me?   Fol - low - ing him   I
fleet - ing days shall   end.   Beau - ti - ful life   with

him   I   go,   no oth - er   one   can   cheer me so;
and   the rain,   he sends the har - vest's gold - en grain;
know I'm right,   he watch - es o'er   me   day and night;
such   a friend, beau - ti - ful life that has   no end;

WORDS: Will L. Thompson, 1904
MUSIC: Will L. Thompson, 1904

ELIZABETH
86.86.844.3

when I am sad, he makes me glad, he's my friend.
sun-shine and rain, har-vest of grain, he's my friend.
fol-low-ing him by day and night, he's my friend.
e-ter-nal life, e-ter-nal joy, he's my friend.

My God, I Love Thee 470

1. My God, I love thee, not be-cause I
2. Thou, O my Je-sus, thou didst me up-
3. Then why, O bless-ed Je-sus Christ, should
4. Not with the hope of gain-ing aught, not
5. So would I love thee, dear-est Lord, and

hope for heaven there-by, nor yet be-cause, if
on the cross em-brace; for me didst bear the
I not love thee well? Not for the sake of
seek-ing a re-ward, but as thy-self hast
in thy praise will sing; be-cause thou art my

I love not, I must for-ev-er die.
nails and spear and man-i-fold dis-grace.
win-ning heaven, nor of es-cap-ing hell.
lov-ed me, O ev-er-last-ing Lord.
lov-ing God and my e-ter-nal King.

WORDS: Latin, 17th cent.; trans. by Edward Caswall, 1849
MUSIC: Est's *Whole Booke of Psalmes*, 1592;
   harm. from *Hymns Ancient and Modern*, 1861

WINCHESTER OLD
CM

Alt. tune: ST. COLUMBA

471 Move Me

Move me, move me; move me to do thy will.

Move me, move me; move me to do thy will.

WORDS: Richard Alan Henderson, 1978
MUSIC: Richard Alan Henderson, 1978

© 1978 Richard Alan Henderson

MOVE ME
Irr.

472 Near to the Heart of God

1. There is a place of qui - et rest, near to the heart of God;
2. There is a place of com-fort sweet, near to the heart of God;
3. There is a place of full re-lease, near to the heart of God;

a place where sin can - not mo-lest, near to the heart of God.
a place where we our Sav - ior meet, near to the heart of God.
a place where all is joy and peace, near to the heart of God.

WORDS: Cleland B. McAfee, 1903
MUSIC: Cleland B. McAfee, 1903

McAFEE
CM with Refrain

Refrain

O Je - sus, blest Re - deem - er, sent from the heart of God,

hold us who wait be - fore thee near to the heart of God.

Lead Me, Lord 473

Lead me, Lord, lead me in thy right-teous-ness;

make thy way plain be - fore my face. For it is thou, Lord,

thou, Lord on - ly, that mak-est me dwell in safe - ty.

*Optional ending

WORDS: Psalms 5:8, 4:8
MUSIC: Samuel Sebastian Wesley, 1861

LEAD ME, LORD
Irr.

474   Precious Lord, Take My Hand

1. Pre-cious Lord, take my hand, lead me on, let me stand,
2. When my way grows drear, pre-cious Lord, lin-ger near,
3. When the dark-ness ap-pears and the night draws near,

I am tired, I am weak, I am worn;
when my life is al-most gone,
and the day is past and gone,

through the storm, through the night, lead me on to the light:
hear my cry, hear my call, hold my hand lest I fall:
at the riv-er I stand, guide my feet, hold my hand:

Refrain

Take my hand, pre-cious Lord, lead me home.

WORDS: Thomas A. Dorsey, 1932
MUSIC: Thomas A. Dorsey, 1932

PRECIOUS LORD
Irr.

Come Down, O Love Divine

1. Come down, O Love di – vine, seek thou this soul of mine,
2. O let it free – ly burn, till earth-ly pas - sions turn
3. And so the yearn - ing strong, with which the soul will long,

and vis - it it with thine own ar – dor glow – ing;
to dust and ash – es in its heat con - sum – ing;
shall far out - pass the power of hu - man tell – ing;

O Com-fort - er, draw near, with - in my heart ap – pear,
and let thy glo - rious light shine ev - er on my sight,
for none can guess its grace, till Love cre - ate a place

and kin - dle it, thy ho - ly flame be - stow – ing.
and clothe me round, the while my path il - lum – ing.
where - in the Ho - ly Spir - it makes a dwell – ing.

WORDS: Bianco of Siena, 15th cent.; trans. by Richard F. Littledale, 1867, alt.
MUSIC: Ralph Vaughan Williams, 1906

DOWN AMPNEY
6 6 11 D

476   Lonely the Boat

1. Lone-ly the boat, sail-ing at sea, tossed on a
2. Strong winds a-rose in all their rage, toss-ing the
3. Trem-bling with fear, deep in de-spair, look-ing for
4. "Plead-ing for your mer-cy, O Lord, e-ven a
5. "Storms in our lives, cru-el and cold, sure-ly will

cold, storm-y night; cru-el the sea which seemed so wide,
ti-ny lone boat; waves bil-low-ing high, toss-ing the boat,
help all a-round, the sail-or saw light from a-bove,
sin-ner like me; com-mand, O Lord, calm to the sea,
a-rise a-gain, threat-en-ing lives, threat-en-ing us

with waves so high. This sin-gle ship
lost and a-float. The sail-or stood
"Help can be found; my God is here
as in Gal-i-lee! Please save my life
on life's wild sea. Power-ful and great,

WORDS: Helen Kim; trans. by Hae Jong Kim; para. by Linda and Doug Sugano;   BAI
  versed by Hope Omachi-Kawashima, 1987 (Mt. 8:23-27; Mk. 4:35-41; Lk. 8:22-25)   Irr.
MUSIC: Dong Hoon Lee, 1967

sailed the deep sea, straight in - to the gale; O Lord,
all a-lone, won-dering what to do; O Lord,
in my small boat, stand-ing by my side; O I
from all dan-ger, grant a peace-ful life; O please
God's hand is there, firm-ly in con - trol. O Lord,

great is the per - il, dan-gers to all as - sail.
so help-less was he, won-der-ing what to do.
trust in the Sav-ior, now in my life a - bide.
be mer - ci - ful, Lord, in times of calm and strife.
calm peace comes from you, peace comes to my lone soul."

For Illumination 477

Open wide the window of our spirits, O Lord, and fill us full of light; open wide
the door of our hearts, that we may receive and entertain thee with all our
powers of adoration and love. **Amen.**

Christina G. Rossetti, England, 19th cent.

478

Jaya Ho
(Victory Hymn)

Refrain

Ja-ya   ho   a-ho

*Ja-ya ho ja-ya ho ja-ya ho ja-ya ho ja-ya ho ja-ya ho

ja-ya   ho   a-ho ja-ya ho   a-ho ja-ya   ho   a-ho

ja-ya   ho   ja-ya ho ja-ya   ho   ja-ya ho ja-ya   ho ja-ya ho ho

Fine

ja-ya ja-ya ja-ya ja-ya   ho   ja-ya ja-ya ja-ya ja-ya   ho.

Leader

1. We come be-fore thee,   O Great and Ho-ly,
1. *Te - re sa - na mukh ham hain   a - te.*
2. Lord, let us see thee, grant us a vi-sion!

All

1.   O Great and Ho-ly.
1.   *Ham hain   a - te.*
2. Grant us a vi-sion!

*pronounced Jáhee-yah

WORDS: Anon. Hindi; trans. by Katherine R. Rohrbough, 1958;
  phonetic transcription from the Hindi by I-to Loh, 1988
MUSIC: Trad. Hindi melody; arr. by Victor Sherring, 1955

VICTORY HYMN
10 5.10 5.11 11 with Refrain

Phonetic transcription © 1989 The United Methodist Publishing House

479 Jesus, Lover of My Soul

1. Je - sus, lov - er of my soul, let me to thy
2. Oth - er ref - uge have I none, hangs my help - less
3. Thou, O Christ, art all I want, more than all in
4. Plen - teous grace with thee is found, grace to cov - er

bos - om fly, while the near - er wa - ters roll,
soul on thee; leave, ah! leave me not a - lone,
thee I find; raise the fall - en, cheer the faint,
all my sin; let the heal - ing streams a - bound,

while the tem - pest still is high. Hide me, O my
still sup - port and com - fort me. All my trust on
heal the sick, and lead the blind. Just and ho - ly
make and keep me pure with - in. Thou of life the

Sav - ior, hide, till the storm of life is past;
thee is stayed, all my help from thee I bring;
is thy name, I am all un - righ - teous - ness;
foun - tain art, free - ly let me take of thee;

WORDS: Charles Wesley, 1740 (Wis. 11:26)
MUSIC: Joseph Parry, 1879

ABERYSTWYTH
77.77 D

safe in - to the ha - ven guide; O re - ceive my soul at last.
cov - er my de - fense-less head with the shad-ow of thy wing.
false and full of sin I am; thou art full of truth and grace.
spring thou up with - in my heart; rise to all e - ter - ni - ty.

O Love That Wilt Not Let Me Go   480

1. O Love that wilt not let me go,   I rest my
2. O Light that fol-lowest all my way,   I yield my
3. O Joy that seek - est me through pain,   I can - not
4. O Cross that lift - est up my head,   I dare not

wea-ry soul in thee;   I give thee back the life I owe,   that
flick-ering torch to thee;   my heart re-stores its bor-rowed ray,   that
close my heart to thee;   I trace the rain-bow thru the rain,   and
ask to fly from thee;   I lay in dust life's glo-ry dead,   and

in thine o-cean depths its flow may rich - er, full - er be.
in thy sun-shine's blaze its day may bright-er, fair - er be.
feel the prom-ise is not vain, that morn shall tear - less be.
from the ground there blos-soms red life that shall end - less be.

WORDS: George Matheson, 1882
MUSIC: Albert L. Peace, 1884

ST. MARGARET
88.886

481 The Prayer of Saint Francis

Lord, make me an instrument of thy peace;
where there is hatred, let me sow love;
where there is injury, pardon;
where there is doubt, faith;
where there is despair, hope;
where there is darkness, light;
and where there is sadness, joy.

O Divine Master,
grant that I may not so much seek
to be consoled as to console;
to be understood, as to understand;
to be loved, as to love;
for it is in giving that we receive,
it is in pardoning that we are pardoned,
and it is in dying that we are born to eternal life.

Francis of Assisi, Italy, 13th cent.

482 Lord, Have Mercy

Repeated sections are sung first by the Leader and then by All.

Lord, have mer - cy. Christ, have
Ky - ri - e e - le - i - son. Chris - te e -

mer - cy. Lord, have mer - cy. mer - cy.
le - i - son. Ky - ri - e e - le - i - son. le - i - son.

WORDS: Ancient Greek
MUSIC: James A. Kriewald, 1985

KRIEWALD KYRIE
Irr.

Music © 1985 The United Methodist Publishing House

Kyrie Eleison

Ky - ri - e e - lei - son. Ky - ri - e e - lei - son.

Ky - ri - e e e - le - i - son.

WORDS: Ancient Greek
MUSIC: Russian Orthodox Liturgy

ORTHODOX KYRIE
Irr.

Kyrie Eleison

Ky - ri - e, Ky - ri - e, e - le - i - son.

WORDS: Ancient Greek
MUSIC: Jacques Berthier and the Community of Taizé, 1979

TAIZÉ KYRIE
Irr.

Music © 1979 Les Presses de Taizé, by permission of G.I.A. Publications, Inc.

Let Us Pray to the Lord

Leader *All*

Let us pray to the Lord. Lord, have mer - cy.
Christ, have mer - cy.
Lord, have mer - cy.

MUSIC: Byzantine Chant; harm. by Robert Batistini, 1984

PETITIONS LITANY
Irr.

Harm. © 1984 G.I.A. Publications, Inc.

486 Alleluia

Al - le - lu - ia. Al - le - lu - ia. Al - le - lu - ia.

MUSIC: John Schiavone, 1978

Chant Mode VI

Music © 1978 G.I.A. Publications, Inc.

487 This Is Our Prayer

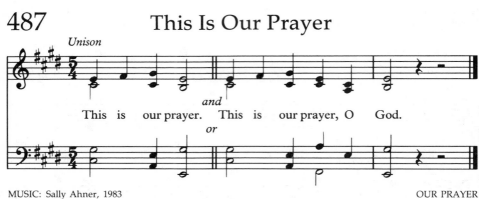

This is our prayer. This is our prayer, O God.

MUSIC: Sally Ahner, 1983

OUR PRAYER
Irr.

© 1989 The United Methodist Publishing House

488 Jesus, Remember Me

Je - sus, re - mem-ber me when you come in-to your king-dom.

Je - sus, re - mem-ber me when you come in-to your king-dom.

WORDS: Luke 23:42

REMEMBER ME

MUSIC: Jacques Berthier and the Community of Taizé, 1981

Irr.

Music © 1981 Les Presses de Taizé, by permission of G.I.A. Publications, Inc.

For God's Gifts

489

O Holy God,
 open unto me
  light for my darkness,
  courage for my fear,
  hope for my despair.
O loving God,
 open unto me
  wisdom for my confusion,
  forgiveness for my sins,
  love for my hate.

O God of peace,
 open unto me
  peace for my turmoil,
  joy for my sorrow,
  strength for my weakness.
O generous God,
 open my heart
  to receive all your gifts.
   Amen.

Howard Thurman, USA, 20th cent.
By permission of The Howard Thurman Educational Trust

Hear Us, O God

490

Unison

Hear us, O God.
or
Lord, hear our prayer.

MUSIC: Sally Ahner, 1983
© 1989 The United Methodist Publishing House

HEAR US
Irr.

Remember Me

491

Re - mem - ber me, re - mem - ber me,

O Lord, re - mem - ber me.

WORDS: Trad. (Lk. 23:42)
MUSIC: Trad.; harm. by J. Jefferson Cleveland, 1981

Harm. © 1981 Abingdon Press

CLEVELAND
Irr.

492 Prayer Is the Soul's Sincere Desire

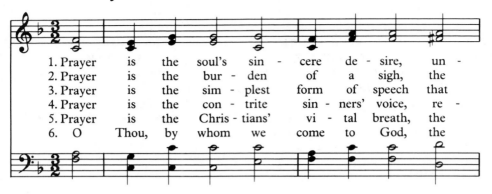

1. Prayer is the soul's sin - cere de - sire, un -
2. Prayer is the bur - den of a sigh, the
3. Prayer is the sim - plest form of speech that
4. Prayer is the con - trite sin - ners' voice, re -
5. Prayer is the Chris - tians' vi - tal breath, the
6. O Thou, by whom we come to God, the

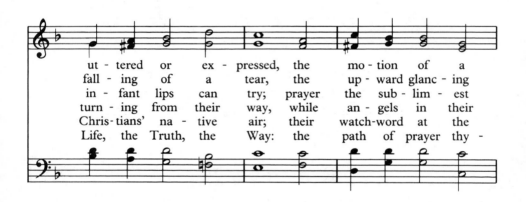

ut - tered or ex - pressed, the mo - tion of a
fall - ing of a tear, the up - ward glanc - ing
in - fant lips can try; prayer the sub - lim - est
turn - ing from their way, while an - gels in their
Chris - tians' na - tive air; their watch-word at the
Life, the Truth, the Way: the path of prayer thy -

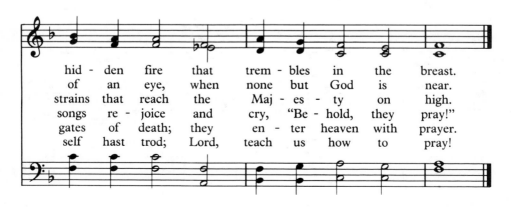

hid - den fire that trem - bles in the breast.
of an eye, when none but God is near.
strains that reach the Maj - es - ty on high.
songs re - joice and cry, "Be - hold, they pray!"
gates of death; they en - ter heaven with prayer.
self hast trod; Lord, teach us how to pray!

WORDS: James Montgomery, 1818
MUSIC: USA campmeeting melody; harm. by Robert G. McCutchan, 1935

CAMPMEETING
CM

Three Things We Pray 493

Thanks be to thee, O Lord Jesus Christ, for all the benefits which thou hast given us; for all the pains and insults which thou hast borne for us. O most merciful Redeemer, friend, and brother, may we know thee more clearly, love thee more dearly, and follow thee more nearly, for thine own sake. **Amen.**

Richard of Chichester, England, 13th cent.

Kum Ba Yah 494
(Come By Here)

2. Someone's praying, Lord.
3. Someone's crying, Lord.
4. Someone needs you, Lord.
5. Someone's singing, Lord.
6. Let us praise the Lord.

WORDS: Afro-American spiritual
MUSIC: Afro-American spiritual; harm. by Carlton R. Young, 1988

DESMOND
Irr.

Harm. © 1989 The United Methodist Publishing House

The Sufficiency of God 495

God, of your goodness give me yourself; for you are sufficient for me. I cannot properly ask anything less, to be worthy of you. If I were to ask less, I should always be in want. In you alone do I have all. **Amen.**

Juliana of Norwich, England, 15th cent.

496 Sweet Hour of Prayer

1. Sweet hour of prayer! sweet hour of prayer! that calls me
2. Sweet hour of prayer! sweet hour of prayer! the joys I
3. Sweet hour of prayer! sweet hour of prayer! thy wings shall

from a world of care, and bids me at my
feel, the bliss I share of those whose anx - ious
my pe - ti - tion bear to him whose truth and

Fa - ther's throne make all my wants and wish - es known.
spir - its burn with strong de - sires for thy re - turn!
faith - ful - ness en - gage the wait - ing soul to bless.

In sea - sons of dis - tress and grief, my soul has
With such I has - ten to the place where God my
And since he bids me seek his face, be - lieve his

of - ten found re - lief, and oft es - caped the
Sav - ior shows his face, and glad - ly take my
word, and trust his grace, I'll cast on him my

WORDS: William Walford, 1845
MUSIC: William B. Bradbury, 1861

SWEET HOUR
LMD

tempt- er's snare by thy re - turn, sweet hour of prayer!
sta - tion there, and wait for thee, sweet hour of prayer!
ev - ery care, and wait for thee, sweet hour of prayer!

Send Me, Lord

497

Leader

Send me, Lord.

All

1. Send me, Je -sus, send me, Je - sus, send me,
   Je -sus, lead me, Je - sus, lead me,
   Je -sus, fill me, Je - sus, fill me,

1, 2

2. Lead me, Lord.
3. Fill me, Lord.

3

Je - sus, send me, Lord.
Je - sus, lead me, Lord.
Je - sus, fill me,

2. Lead me,
3. Fill me,

Lord.

WORDS: Trad. South African (Is. 6:8)
MUSIC: Trad. South African

THUMA MINA
Irr.

© 1984 Utryck

498 My Prayer Rises to Heaven

Refrain (Unison)

My prayer ris-es to heaven, to the mys-ter-y of God's power, as the smoke as-cends when the pre-cious in-cense burns.

Have mer-cy on us, Lord, and grant us your grace.

My voice glo-ri-fies the Lord God of maj-es-ty,

as the night bird sings at the dawn-ing of the day.

WORDS: Dao Kim (Ps. 141:2)
MUSIC: Dao Kim

VIETNAM
Irr.

By permission of Vietnamese Ministries

This my of-fer-ing to God, the Lord of all.

1. As the thirst-y earth looks to heaven for life - giv-ing
2. O Lord God, how I wish that I could live with
3. O Lord God, you are love and jus - tice and

rain to save flow - er and tree,
you for the rest of my life;
truth; all your judg - ments are just.

so I raise my hands high in prayer: de - fend me from all
dwell-ing in your house I would feel as - sured that my
O Lord God, you are truth be - yond com -

peo - ple who try to harm me.
prayers would be al - ways in your sight.
pare. Lord, in you do I trust.

499

Serenity

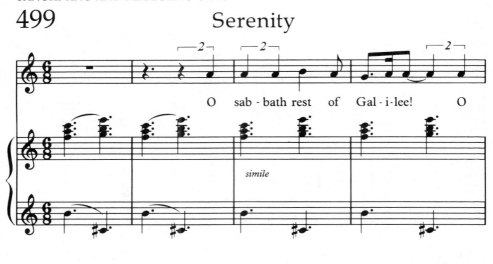

O sab-bath rest of Gal-i-lee! O

simile

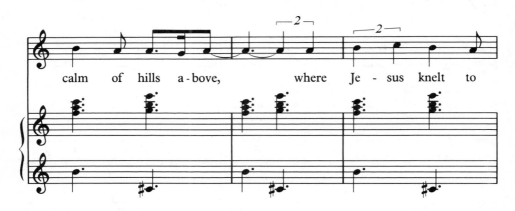

calm of hills a-bove, where Je - sus knelt to

share with thee the si - lence of e-ter-ni-ty in-

WORDS: John Greenleaf Whittier, 1872
MUSIC: Charles E. Ives, ca. 1909

SERENITY
86.886

500 Spirit of God, Descend upon My Heart

1. Spir - it of God, de - scend up - on my heart;
2. I ask no dream, no proph - et ec - sta - sies,
3. Hast thou not bid me love thee, God and King?
4. Teach me to feel that thou art al - ways nigh;
5. Teach me to love thee as thine an - gels love,

wean it from earth; through all its puls - es move;
no sud - den rend - ing of the veil of clay,
All, all thine own, soul, heart and strength and mind.
teach me the strug - gles of the soul to bear.
one ho - ly pas - sion fill - ing all my frame;

stoop to my weak - ness, might - y as thou art,
no an - gel vis - i - tant, no o - pening skies;
I see thy cross; there teach my heart to cling.
To check the ris - ing doubt, the reb - el sigh,
the kin - dling of the heaven - de - scend - ed Dove,

and make me love thee as I ought to love.
but take the dim - ness of my soul a - way.
O let me seek thee, and O let me find!
teach me the pa - tience of un - an - swered prayer.
my heart an al - tar, and thy love the flame.

WORDS: George Croly, 1867 (Gal. 5:25)
MUSIC: Frederick C. Atkinson, 1870

MORECAMBE
10 10.10 10

O Thou Who Camest from Above   501

1. O Thou who cam - est from a - bove,
2. There let it for thy glo - ry burn
3. Je - sus, con - firm my heart's de - sire
4. Read - y for all thy per - fect will,

the pure ce - les - tial fire to im - part,
with in - ex - tin - guish - a - ble blaze,
to work and speak and think for thee;
my acts of faith and love re - peat,

kin - dle a flame of sa - cred love
and trem - bling to its source re - turn,
still let me guard the ho - ly fire,
till death thy end - less mer - cies seal,

up - on the mean al - tar of my heart.
in hum - ble prayer and fer - vent praise.
and still stir up thy gift in me.
and make my sac - ri - fice com - plete.

WORDS: Charles Wesley, 1762 (Lev. 6:13)   HEREFORD
MUSIC: Samuel Sebastian Wesley, 1872   LM

502 Thy Holy Wings, O Savior

1. Thy ho-ly wings, O Sav-ior, spread gent-ly o-ver me,
2. O wash me in the wa-ters of No-ah's cleans-ing flood;

and let me rest se-cure-ly through good and ill in thee.
give me a will-ing spir-it, a heart both clean and good.

Harmony

O be my strength and por-tion, my rock and hid-ing place,
And take in-to thy keep-ing thy chil-dren great and small,

Unison

and let my ev-ery mo-ment be lived with-in thy grace.
and while we sweet-ly slum-ber, en-fold us one and all.

WORDS: Caroline V. Sandell-Berg, 1865; trans. by Gracia Grindal, 1983
   (Ps. 91:4; 73:26; 119:114; 51:10; 1 Pet. 3:18-22)
MUSIC: Swedish folk tune; harm. by LaRhae Knatterud, 1983

BRED DINA VIDA VINGAR
76.76 D

Let It Breathe on Me

Let it breathe on me; let it breathe on me;

let the breath of the Lord now breathe on me.

Let it breathe on me; let it breathe on me;

let the breath of the Lord now breathe on me.

WORDS: Magnolia Lewis-Butts, 1942 (Jn. 20:22)
MUSIC: Magnolia Lewis-Butts, 1942

LET IT BREATHE
Irr.

504   The Old Rugged Cross

1. On a hill far a-way stood an old rug-ged cross,
2. O that old rug-ged cross, so de-spised by the world,
3. In that old rug-ged cross, stained with blood so di-vine,
4. To the old rug-ged cross I will ev-er be true,

the em-blem of suf-fering and shame;
has a won-drous at-trac-tion for me;
a won-drous beau-ty I see,
its shame and re-proach glad-ly bear;

and I love that old cross where the dear-est and best
for the dear Lamb of God left his glo-ry a-bove
for 'twas on that old cross Je-sus suf-fered and died,
then he'll call me some day to my home far a-way,

for a world of lost sin-ners was slain.
to bear it to dark Cal-va-ry.
to par-don and sanc-ti-fy me.
where his glo-ry for-ev-er I'll share.

WORDS: George Bennard, 1913 (1 Cor. 1:22-25)
MUSIC: George Bennard, 1913

THE OLD RUGGED CROSS
Irr. with Refrain

Refrain

So I'll cher-ish the old rug-ged cross,
cross, the old rug-ged cross,

till my tro-phies at last I lay down;

I will cling to the old rug-ged cross,
cross, the old rug-ged cross,

and ex-change it some day for a crown.

505 When Our Confidence Is Shaken

1. When our con-fi-dence is shak-en in be-liefs we
2. So-lar sys-tems, void of mean-ing, freeze the spir-it
3. In the dis-ci-pline of pray-ing, when it's hard-est
4. God is love, and thus re-deems us in the Christ we

thought se-cure, when the spir-it in its sick-ness
in-to stone; al-ways our re-search-es lead us
to be-lieve; in the drudg-er-y of car-ing,
cru-ci-fy; this is God's e-ter-nal an-swer

seeks but can-not find a cure, God is ac-tive
to the ul-ti-mate un-known. Faith must die, or
when it's not e-nough to grieve; faith, ma-tur-ing,
to the world's e-ter-nal why. May we in this

in the ten-sions of a faith not yet ma-ture.
come full cir-cle to its source in God a-lone.
learns ac-cep-tance of the in-sights we re-ceive.
faith ma-tur-ing be con-tent to live and die!

WORDS: Fred Pratt Green, 1971
MUSIC: From *Chants Ordinaires de l'office divin*, 1881; harm. from *The English Hymnal*, 1906

GRAFTON
87.87.87

Words © 1971 Hope Publishing Co.

Wellspring of Wisdom

1. Well-spring of Wis-dom, hear our cry. The way a-head is parched and dry. We seek a source to sat-is-fy our thirst for sanc-ti-fy-ing wa-ters, wis-dom for your faith-filled sons and daugh-ters.

2. Dawn of a New Day, put to flight the ter-rors of a nu-clear night. As bear-ers of your lov-ing light, we hud-dle clos-er to your fire, lift the lamp of hope a lit-tle high-er.

3. Gar-den of Grace, your gifts a-bound, the sa-cred signs are all a-round, the whole of earth is ho-ly ground. We learn, from all of life ex-press-ing, how to grow in sow-ing seeds of bless-ing.

4. Call to Com-pas-sion, help us bring our burn-ing need for nur-tur-ing, the emp-ti-ness of ev-ery-thing to your em-brace, as we en-deav-or to pro-claim your ho-ly name for-ev-er.

WORDS: Miriam Therese Winter, 1987
MUSIC: Miriam Therese Winter, 1987; harm. by Don McKeever, 1987

WELLSPRING
888.9 10

© 1989 Medical Mission Sisters

507

Through It All

Through it all, through it all,

I've learned to trust in Je-sus, I've learned to trust in God;

through it all, through it all,

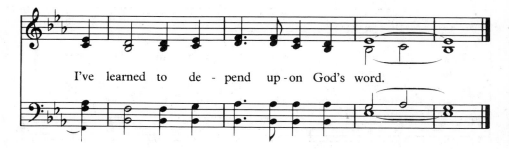

I've learned to de-pend up-on God's word.

WORDS: Andraé Crouch, 1971
MUSIC: Andraé Crouch, 1971

© 1971 Manna Music, Inc.

THROUGH IT ALL
Irr.

Faith, While Trees Are Still in Blossom 508

1. Faith, while trees are still in blos - som, plans the
2. Long be - fore the dawn is break - ing, faith an -
3. Long be - fore the rains were com - ing, No - ah
4. Faith, up - lift - ed, tamed the wa - ter of the
5. Faith be - lieves that God is faith - ful: God will

pick - ing of the fruit; faith can feel the thrill of
tic - i - pates the sun. Faith is ea - ger for the
went and built an ark. A - bra - ham, the lone - ly
un - di - vid - ed sea, and the peo - ple of the
be what God will be! Faith ac - cepts the call, re -

har - vest when the buds be - gin to sprout.
day - light, for the work that must be done.
mi - grant, saw the light be - yond the dark.
He - brews found the path that made them free.
spond - ing, "I am will - ing, Lord, send me."

WORDS: Anders Frostenson, 1960; trans. by Fred Kaan, 1972 (Heb.11)
MUSIC: V. Earle Copes, 1960

FOR THE BREAD
87.87

PRAYER, TRUST, HOPE, *see further:*

509

Jesus, Savior, Pilot Me

1. Je - sus, Sav - ior, pi - lot me o - ver
2. As a moth - er stills her child, thou canst
3. When at last I near the shore, and the

life's tem - pes - tuous sea; un- known waves be - fore me
hush the o - cean wild; bois-terous waves o - bey thy
fear - ful break - ers roar 'twixt me and the peace - ful

roll, hid - ing rock and treach-erous shoal. Chart and
will, when thou sayest to them, "Be still!" Won-drous
rest, then, while lean - ing on thy breast, may I

com - pass came from thee; Je - sus, Sav - ior, pi - lot me.
sov - ereign of the sea, Je - sus, Sav - ior, pi - lot me.
hear thee say to me, "Fear not, I will pi - lot thee."

WORDS: Edward Hopper, 1871 (Mt. 8:23-27; Mk. 4:35-41; Lk. 8:22-25)
MUSIC: John E. Gould, 1871

PILOT
77.77.77

Come, Ye Disconsolate

1. Come, ye dis-con-so-late, wher-e'er ye lan-guish,
2. Joy of the des-o-late, light of the stray-ing,
3. Here see the bread of life; see wa-ters flow-ing

come to the mer-cy seat, fer-vent-ly kneel.
hope of the pen-i-tent, fade-less and pure!
forth from the throne of God, pure from a-bove.

Here bring your wound-ed hearts, here tell your an-guish;
Here speaks the Com-fort-er, ten-der-ly say-ing,
Come to the feast of love; come, ev-er know-ing

earth has no sor-row that heaven can-not heal.
"Earth has no sor-row that heaven can-not cure."
earth has no sor-row but heaven can re-move.

WORDS: Thomas Moore, 1816; alt. by Thomas Hastings, 1831
MUSIC: Samuel Webbe, Sr., 1792

CONSOLATOR
11 10.11 10

511   Am I a Soldier of the Cross

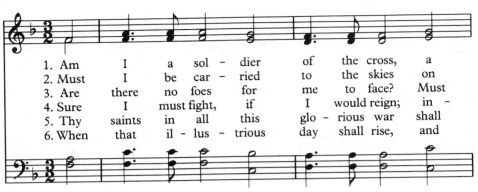

1. Am   I   a   sol – dier   of   the   cross,   a
2. Must   I   be   car – ried   to   the   skies   on
3. Are   there   no   foes   for   me   to   face?   Must
4. Sure   I   must fight,   if   I   would reign;   in –
5. Thy   saints   in   all   this   glo – rious war   shall
6. When   that   il – lus – trious   day   shall rise,   and

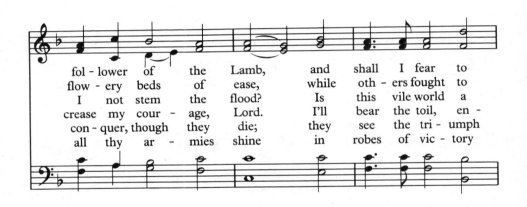

    fol – lower   of   the   Lamb,   and   shall   I   fear   to
    flow – ery   beds   of   ease,   while   oth – ers fought   to
    I   not   stem   the   flood?   Is   this   vile world   a
    crease my   cour – age,   Lord.   I'll   bear   the toil,   en –
    con – quer, though   they   die;   they   see   the tri – umph
    all   thy   ar – mies   shine   in   robes   of vic – tory

    own   his cause,   or   blush   to   speak   his   name?
    win   the prize,   and   sailed through blood – y   seas?
    friend   to grace,   to   help   me   on   to   God?
    dure   the pain,   sup – port – ed   by   thy   word.
    from   a – far,   by   faith   they   bring   it   nigh.
    through   the skies,   the   glo – ry   shall   be   thine.

WORDS: Isaac Watts, *Sermons*, 1721-24 (1 Cor. 16:13)
MUSIC: Thomas A. Arne, 1762; arr. by Ralph Harrison, 1784

ARLINGTON
CM

Stand By Me

1. When the storms of life are rag-ing,
2. In the midst of trib - u - la-tion,
3. In the midst of faults and fail-ures, stand by me; (stand by me)
4. In the midst of per - se - cu-tion,
5. When I'm grow - ing old and fee - ble,

when the storms of life are rag-ing,
in the midst of trib - u - la-tion,
in the midst of faults and fail-ures, stand by me. (stand by me)
in the midst of per - se - cu-tion,
when I'm grow-ing old and fee - ble,

When the world is toss - ing me, like a ship up-on the sea,
When the host of hell as - sail, and my strength be-gins to fail,
When I've done the best I can, and my friends mis-un-der-stand,
When my foes in war ar - ray un - der-take to stop my way,
When my life be-comes a bur-den, and I'm near-ing chil - ly Jor-dan,

thou who rul - est wind and wa-ter,
thou who nev - er lost a bat-tle,
thou who know-est all a-bout me, stand by me. (stand by me)
thou who sav - ed Paul and Si-las,
O thou Lil - y of the Val-ley,

WORDS: Charles Albert Tindley, ca. 1906 (Mt. 8:23-27; Mk. 4:35-41; Lk. 8:22-25)
MUSIC: Charles Albert Tindley, ca. 1906; arr. by William Farley Smith, 1989
Arr. © 1989 The United Methodist Publishing House

STAND BY ME
83.83.77.83

513   Soldiers of Christ, Arise

1. Sol - diers of Christ, a - rise, and put your ar - mor on,
2. Stand then in his great might, with all his strength en - dued,
3. Pray with-out ceas - ing, pray, (your Cap - tain gives the word)
4. From strength to strength go on, wres - tle and fight and pray,

strong in the strength which God sup-plies thru his e - ter - nal Son;
but take to arm you for the fight the pan - o - ply of God;
his sum-mons cheer-ful - ly o - bey and call up - on the Lord;
tread all the powers of dark-ness down and win the well-fought day.

strong in the Lord of Hosts, and in his might - y power,
that hav - ing all things done, and all your con - flicts passed,
to God your ev - ery want in in - stant prayer dis - play,
Still let the Spir - it cry in all his sol - diers, "Come!"

who in the strength of Je - sus trusts is more than con-quer - or.
ye may o'er-come thru Christ a-lone and stand en-tire at last.
pray al - ways, pray and nev - er faint, pray, with-out ceas-ing pray.
till Christ the Lord de-scends from high and takes the con-querors home.

WORDS: Charles Wesley, 1749 (Eph. 6:13-18)
MUSIC: George J. Elvey, 1868

DIADEMATA
SMD

Stand Up, Stand Up for Jesus

514

1. Stand up, stand up for Je - sus, ye sol - diers of the cross;
2. Stand up, stand up for Je - sus, the trum-pet call o - bey;
3. Stand up, stand up for Je - sus, stand in his strength a - lone;
4. Stand up, stand up for Je - sus, the strife will not be long;

lift high his roy - al ban - ner, it must not suf - fer loss.
forth to the might-y con - flict, in this his glo-rious day.
the arm of flesh will fail you, ye dare not trust your own.
this day the noise of bat - tle, the next the vic-tor's song.

From vic - tory un - to vic - tory his ar - my shall he lead,
Ye that are brave now serve him a - gainst un-num-bered foes;
Put on the gos - pel ar - mor, each piece put on with prayer;
To those who van-quish e - vil a crown of life shall be;

till ev - ery foe is van-quished, and Christ is Lord in - deed.
let cour - age rise with dan - ger, and strength to strength op - pose.
where du - ty calls or dan - ger, be nev - er want-ing there.
they with the King of Glo - ry shall reign e - ter - nal - ly.

WORDS: George Duffield, Jr., 1858 (Eph. 6:10-17)
MUSIC: George J. Webb, 1830

WEBB
76.76 D

515 Out of the Depths I Cry to You

1. Out of the depths I cry to you; O Lord, now
2. All things you send are full of grace; you crown our
3. It is in God that we shall hope, and not in
4. My soul is wait-ing for the Lord as one who

hear me call - ing. In-cline your ear to my dis - tress
lives with fa - vor. All our good works are done in vain
our own mer - it; we rest our fears in God's good Word
longs for morn - ing; no watch-er waits with great-er hope

in spite of my re – bel - ling. Do not re - gard my
with-out our Lord and Sav - ior. We praise the God who
and trust the Ho - ly Spir - it, whose prom-ise keeps us
than I for Christ's re - turn - ing. I hope as Is - rael

sin - ful deeds. Send me the grace my
gives us faith and saves us from the
strong and sure; we trust the ho - ly
in the Lord, who sends re - demp - tion

WORDS: Martin Luther, 1524; trans. by Gracia Grindal (Ps. 130; 120:1-2)   AUS TIEFER NOT
MUSIC: Attr. to Martin Luther, 1524; harm. by Austin C. Lovelace, 1963   87.87.887

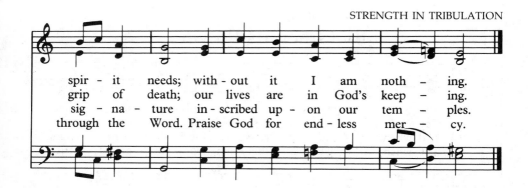

spir - it needs; with - out it I am noth – ing.
grip of death; our lives are in God's keep – ing.
sig - na - ture in - scribed up - on our tem – ples.
through the Word. Praise God for end - less mer – cy.

Canticle of Redemption 516
(De Profundis)

RESPONSE *(General)*

In my dis - tress I cry to the Lord:

de - liv - er me, O Lord.

R
Out of the deep have I called unto thee, O Lord;
  Lord, hear my voice.
O let thine ears consider well the voice of my complaint.
If thou, Lord, wilt be extreme to mark what is done amiss,
  O Lord, who may abide it?
For there is mercy with thee;
  therefore shalt thou be feared.
I look for the Lord; my soul doth wait for him;
  in his word is my trust.
My soul fleeth unto the Lord before the morning watch;
  I say before the morning watch.
O Israel, trust in the Lord,
  for with the Lord there is mercy,
  and with him is plenteous redemption.
And he shall redeem Israel
  from all their sins.   R

See No. 515 for a metrical setting of this biblical text.

WORDS: Psalm 130; Response, Psalm 120:1-2, adapt.
MUSIC: Jane Marshall, 1987

Response © 1989 The United Methodist Publishing House

517 By Gracious Powers

1. By gra-cious powers so won-der-ful-ly shel - tered,
2. Yet is this heart by its old foe tor - ment - ed,
3. And when this cup you give is filled to brim - ming
4. Yet when a - gain in this same world you give us

and con - fi - dent - ly wait-ing, come what may,
still e - vil days bring bur - dens hard to bear;
with bit - ter sor - row, hard to un - der - stand,
the joy we had, the bright-ness of your sun,

we know that God is with us night and morn - ing,
O give our fright-ened souls the sure sal - va - tion
we take it thank-ful - ly and with-out trem - bling,
we shall re - mem - ber all the days we lived through,

and nev - er fails to greet us each new day.
for which, O Lord, you taught us to pre - pare.
out of so good and so be - loved a hand.
and our whole life shall then be yours a - lone.

(♮ last time)

WORDS: Dietrich Bonhoeffer, 1944; trans. by Fred Pratt Green, 1972
MUSIC: Charles Hubert Hastings Parry, 1904

INTERCESSOR
11 10.11 10

O Thou, in Whose Presence

1. O Thou, in whose pres - ence my soul takes de -
2. Where dost thou, dear Shep - herd, re - sort with thy
3. O why should I wan - der, an a - lien from
4. Re - store, my dear Sav - ior, the light of thy
5. He looks! and ten thou - sands of an - gels re -

light, on whom in af - flic - tion I call,
sheep, to feed them in pas - tures of love?
thee, or cry in the des - ert for bread?
face, thy soul - cheer - ing com - fort im - part;
joice, and myr - i - ads wait for his word.

my com - fort by day and my song in the
Say, why in the val - ley of death should I
Thy foes will re - joice when my sor - rows they
and let the sweet to - kens of par - don - ing
He speaks! and e - ter - ni - ty, filled with his

night, my hope, my sal - va - tion, my all!
weep, or a - lone in this wil - der - ness rove?
see, and smile at the tears I have shed.
grace bring joy to my des - o - late heart.
voice, re - ech - oes the praise of the Lord.

WORDS: Joseph Swain, 1791 (Ps. 23)
MUSIC: Wyeth's *Repository of Sacred Music, Part Second,* 1813;
  harm. by Austin C. Lovelace, 1963

DAVIS
11 8.11 8

519   Lift Every Voice and Sing

1. Lift ev - ery voice and sing, till earth and heav - en ring,
2. Ston - y the road we trod, bit - ter the chas - tening rod,
3. God of our wea - ry years, God of our si - lent tears,

ring with the har - mo - nies of lib - er - ty;
felt in the days when hope un - born had died;
thou who hast brought us thus far on the way;

let our re - joic - ing rise high as the lis - tening skies,
yet with a stead - y beat, have not our wea - ry feet
thou who hast by thy might led us in - to the light,

let it re - sound loud as the roll - ing sea.
come to the place for which our fa - thers sighed?
keep us for - ev - er in the path, we pray.

WORDS: James Weldon Johnson, 1921
MUSIC: J. Rosamond Johnson, 1921

LIFT EVERY VOICE
Irr.

Sing a song full of the faith that the dark past has taught us;
We have come o-ver a way that with tears has been wa-tered;
Lest our feet stray from the plac-es, our God, where we met thee;

sing a song full of the hope that the pres-ent has brought us;
we have come, tread-ing our path thru the blood of the slaugh - tered,
lest our hearts drunk with the wine of the world, we for - get thee;

fac-ing the ris - ing sun of our new day be - gun,
out from the gloom - y past, till now we stand at last
shad-owed be - neath thy hand, may we for - ev - er stand,

let us march on till vic - to - ry is won.
where the white gleam of our bright star is cast.
true to our God, true to our na - tive land.

520 Nobody Knows the Trouble I See

Refrain

No-bod-y knows the trou-ble I see, no-bod-y
knows but Je - sus; oh, no - bod - y knows the
trou - ble I see, glo - ry hal - le - lu - jah!

1. Some-times I'm up, some-times I'm down,
2. Al-though you see me going long so, Oh, yes, Lord!
3. What makes old Sa-tan hate me so?

Some - times I'm al-most to the ground,
I have my trou-bles here be-low, Oh, yes, Lord! Oh,
Cause he got me once and let me go,

WORDS: Afro-American spiritual
MUSIC: Afro-American spiritual; adapt. and arr. by William Farley Smith, 1986

DUBOIS
Irr. with Refrain

Adapt. and arr. © 1989 The United Methodist Publishing House

I Want Jesus to Walk with Me

521

1. I want Je - sus to walk with me. (walk with me)
2. In my tri - als, Lord, walk with me. (walk with me)
3. When I'm trou - bled, Lord, walk with me. (walk with me)

I want Je - sus to walk with me. (walk with me)
In my tri - als, Lord, walk with me. (walk with me)
When I'm trou - bled, Lord, walk with me. (walk with me)

All a - long my pil - grim jour - ney,
When my heart is al - most break - ing,
When my head is bowed in sor - row,

Lord, I want Je - sus to walk with me. (walk with me)

WORDS: Afro-American spiritual
MUSIC: Afro-American spiritual; adapt. by William Farley Smith, 1986

SOJOURNER
888.9

Adapt. © 1989 The United Methodist Publishing House

522 Leave It There

1. If the world from you with-hold of its sil-ver and its gold,
2. If your bod-y suf-fers pain, and your health you can't re-gain,
3. When your en-e-mies as-sail, and your heart be-gins to fail,
4. When your youth-ful days are done, and old age is steal-ing on,

and you have to get a-long with mea-ger fare,
and your soul is al-most sink-ing in de-spair,
don't for-get that God in heav-en an-swers prayer;
and your bod-y bends be-neath the weight of care,

just re-mem-ber in his Word how he feeds the lit-tle bird,
Je-sus knows the pain you feel, he can save and he can heal,
he will make a way for you, and will lead you safe-ly through,
he will nev-er leave you then, he'll go with you to the end,

take your bur-den to the Lord and leave it there.

WORDS: Charles Albert Tindley, ca. 1906
MUSIC: Charles Albert Tindley, ca. 1906; arr. by Charles A. Tindley, Jr., 1916

LEAVE IT THERE
7 7 11 D with Refrain

Refrain

Leave it there, (leave it there) leave it there, (leave it there)

take your bur-den to the Lord and leave it there.

(leave it there)

If you trust and nev-er doubt, he will sure-ly bring you out;

take your bur-den to the Lord and leave it there. (leave it there)

523

Saranam, Saranam
(Refuge)

Je - sus, Sav - ior, Lord, lo, to thee I fly:

Sar - a - nam, Sar - a - nam, Sar - a - nam;

thou the Rock, my ref - uge that's higher than I:

Sar - a - nam, Sar - a - nam, Sar - a - nam.

WORDS: Trad. Pakistani; trans. by D. T. Niles, 1963 (Ps. 61: Heb. 13:8)
MUSIC: Trad. Punjabi melody; arr. by Shanti Rasanayagam, 1962

Trans. and arr. by permission of Christian Conference of Asia

PUNJABI
Irr. with Refrain

1. In the midst of foes I cry to thee,
2. In thy tent give me a dwell – ing place,
3. O that I my vows to thee may pay,
4. Yes – ter – day, to – day, for – e'er the same,

from the ends of earth wher – ev – er I may be;
and be – neath thy wings may I find shel - tering grace;
and that by thy faith - ful - ness to me each day
lo, the her – i - tage of all who bear thy name;

my strength in help - less - ness, O an - swer me:
O lift on me the sun - shine of thy face:
may live, and on thy love my bur - dens lay:
to ran - som them from sin the Sav - ior came:

Sar – a – nam, Sar – a – nam, Sar – a – nam.

524   Beams of Heaven as I Go

1. Beams of heaven as I go, through this
2. Of-ten-times my sky is clear, joy a-
3. Hard-er yet may be the fight; right may
4. Bur-dens now may crush me down, dis-ap-

wil-der-ness be-low, guide my feet in peace-ful ways,
bounds with-out a tear; though a day so bright be-gun,
of-ten yield to might; wick-ed-ness a while may reign;
point-ments all a-round; trou-bles speak in mourn-ful sigh,

turn my mid-nights in-to days. When in the
clouds may hide to-mor-row's sun. There'll be a
Sa-tan's cause may seem to gain. There is a
sor-row through a tear-stained eye. There is a

dark-ness I would grope, faith al-ways sees a star of hope,
day that's al-ways bright, a day that nev-er yields to night,
God that rules a-bove, with hand of power and heart of love;
world where plea-sure reigns, no mourn-ing soul shall roam its plains,

WORDS: Charles Albert Tindley, ca. 1906
MUSIC: Charles Albert Tindley, ca. 1906; arr. by J. Edward Hoy, 1984

SOMEDAY
77.77.88.96 with Refrain

and soon from all life's grief and dan-ger I shall be free some-day.
and in its light the streets of glo-ry I shall be-hold some-day.
if I am right, he'll fight my bat-tle, I shall have peace some-day.
and to that land of peace and glo-ry I want to go some-day.

Refrain

I do not know how long 'twill be, nor what the fu-ture holds for me, but this I know: if Je-sus leads me, I shall get home some-day.

525 We'll Understand It Better By and By

1. We are tossed and driv-en on the rest-less sea of time;
2. We are of-ten des-ti-tute of the things that life de-mands,
3. Tri-als dark on ev-ery hand, and we can-not un-der-stand
4. Temp - ta-tions, hid-den snares of - ten take us un-a-wares,

som - ber skies and howl-ing tem-pests oft suc – ceed a bright sun-shine;
want of food and want of shel-ter, thirst- y hills and bar-ren lands;
all the ways that God would lead us to that bless - ed prom-ised land;
and our hearts are made to bleed for a thought-less word or deed;

in that land of per -fect day, when the mists have rolled a --way,
we are trust - ing in the Lord, and ac - cord - ing to God's word,
but he guides us with his eye, and we'll fol - low till we die,
and we won - der why the test when we try to do our best,

we will un – der-stand it bet - ter by and by.
we will un – der-stand it bet - ter by and by.
for we'll un – der-stand it bet - ter by and by.
but we'll un – der-stand it bet - ter by and by.

WORDS: Charles Albert Tindley, ca. 1906 (1 Cor. 13:12)
MUSIC: Charles Albert Tindley, ca. 1906; arr. by F. A. Clark, 1906

BY AND BY
Irr. with Refrain

Refrain

By and by, when the morn - ing comes,

when the saints of God are gath - ered home,

we'll tell the sto - ry how we've o - ver-come,

for we'll un - der-stand it bet - ter by and by. (by and by)

526   What a Friend We Have in Jesus

1. What a friend we have in Je - sus,
   all our
   sins and griefs to bear!
   What a priv - i - lege to car - ry
   ev - ery-thing to God in prayer!
   O what peace we of - ten for - feit,
   O what need-less pain we bear,
   all be - cause we do not car - ry
   ev - ery-thing to God in prayer.

2. Have we tri - als and temp - ta - tions?
   Is there trou-ble an - y - where?
   We should nev-er be dis - cour - aged;
   take it to the Lord in prayer.
   Can we find a friend so faith - ful
   who will all our sor-rows share?
   Je - sus knows our ev - ery weak-ness;
   take it to the Lord in prayer.

3. Are we weak and heav - y la - den,
   cum - bered with a load of care?
   Pre - cious Sav-ior, still our ref - uge;
   take it to the Lord in prayer.
   Do thy friends de-spise, for - sake thee?
   Take it to the Lord in prayer!
   In his arms he'll take and shield thee;
   thou wilt find a sol - ace there.

WORDS: Joseph M. Scriven, ca. 1855
MUSIC: Charles C. Converse, 1868

CONVERSE
87.87 D

Do, Lord, Remember Me

527

1. Do, Lord, do, Lord, do, Lord, re-mem-ber me;
(have mer-cy)
do, Lord, do, Lord, do, Lord, re-mem-ber me;
(sing the song, chil-dren)
do, Lord, do, Lord, do, Lord, re-mem-ber me; sing-ing

D.C.

[1-4] do, Lord, re-mem-ber me.
[5] do, Lord, re-mem-ber me.
(oh glo-ry)

2. I took Jesus as my Savior, do, Lord, remember me.
3. When I'm in trouble, do, Lord, remember me.
4. When I am dying, do, Lord, remember me.
5. I got a home in gloryland that outshines the sun.

WORDS: Afro-American spiritual (Lk. 23:42)
MUSIC: Afro-American spiritual; adapt. and arr. by William Farley Smith, 1986

DITMUS
Irr.

Adapt. and arr. © 1989 The United Methodist Publishing House

528   Nearer, My God, to Thee

1. Near - er, my God, to thee, near - er to thee!
2. Though like the wan - der - er, the sun gone down,
3. There let the way ap - pear, steps un - to heaven;
4. Then, with my wak - ing thoughts bright with thy praise,
5. Or if, on joy - ful wing cleav - ing the sky,

E'en though it be a cross that rais - eth me,
dark - ness be o - ver me, my rest a stone;
all that thou send - est me, in mer - cy given;
out of my ston - y griefs Beth - el I'll raise;
sun, moon, and stars for - got, up - ward I fly,

still all my song shall be, near - er, my God, to thee;
yet in my dreams I'd be near - er, my God, to thee;
an - gels to beck - on me near - er, my God, to thee;
so by my woes to be near - er, my God, to thee;
still all my song shall be, near - er, my God, to thee;

near - er, my God, to thee, near - er to thee!

WORDS: Sarah F. Adams, 1841 (Gen. 28:10-22)
MUSIC: Lowell Mason, 1856

BETHANY
64.64.6664

How Firm a Foundation

529

1. How firm a foun - da - tion, ye saints of the Lord,
2. "Fear not, I am with thee, O be not dis - mayed,
3. "When through the deep wa - ters I call thee to go,
4. "When through fi - ery tri - als thy path - ways shall lie,
5. "The soul that on Je - sus still leans for re - pose,

is laid for your faith in his ex - cel - lent word!
for I am thy God and will still give thee aid;
the riv - ers of woe shall not thee o - ver - flow;
my grace, all - suf - fi - cient, shall be thy sup - ply;
I will not, I will not de - sert to its foes;

What more can he say than to you he hath said,
I'll strength- en and help thee, and cause thee to stand
for I will be with thee, thy trou - bles to bless,
the flame shall not hurt thee; I on - ly de - sign
that soul, though all hell should en - deav - or to shake,

to you who for ref - uge to Je - sus have fled?
up - held by my righ - teous, om - ni - po - tent hand.
and sanc - ti - fy to thee thy deep - est dis - tress.
thy dross to con - sume, and thy gold to re - fine.
I'll nev - er, no, nev - er, no, nev - er for - sake."

WORDS: "K" in Rippon's *Selection of Hymns*, 1787 (2 Tim. 2:19; Heb. 13:5; Is. 43:1-2)
MUSIC: Early USA melody; harm. from *Tabor*, 1866

FOUNDATION
11 11.11 11

530   Are Ye Able

1. "Are ye a - ble," said the Mas - ter, "to be
2. Are ye a - ble to re - mem - ber, when a
3. Are ye a - ble when the shad - ows close a -
4. Are ye a - ble? Still the Mas - ter whis - pers

cru - ci - fied with me?" "Yea," the sturd - y dream - ers
thief lifts up his eyes, that his par - doned soul is
round you with the sod, to be - lieve that spir - it
down e - ter - ni - ty, and he - ro - ic spir - its

an - swered, "to the death we fol - low thee."
wor - thy of a place in par - a - dise?
tri - umphs, to com - mend your soul to God?
an - swer, now as then in Gal - i - lee.

Refrain

Lord, we are a - ble. Our spir - its are thine.

WORDS: Earl Marlatt, 1926 (Mk. 10:35-40)
MUSIC: Harry S. Mason, 1924

BEACON HILL
Irr.

Re - mold them, make us, like thee, di - vine.

Thy guid - ing ra - diance a - bove us shall be

a bea - con to God, to love, and loy - al - ty.

For Overcoming Adversity 531

Lord, we pray not for tranquillity,
  nor that our tribulations may cease;
we pray for thy spirit and thy love,
  that thou grant us strength and grace to overcome adversity;
    through Jesus Christ. **Amen.**

Girolamo Savonarola, Italy, 15th cent.

532

Jesus, Priceless Treasure

1. Je - sus, price - less trea - sure, source of pur - est plea - sure,
2. In thine arms I rest me; foes who would mo - lest me
3. Hence, all thoughts of sad - ness! For the Lord of glad - ness,

tru - est friend to me, long my heart hath pant - ed,
can - not reach me here. Though the earth be shak - ing,
Je - sus, en - ters in. Those who love the Fa - ther,

till it well - nigh faint - ed, thirst - ing af - ter thee.
ev - ery heart be quak - ing, Je - sus calms our fear;
though the storms may gath - er, still have peace with - in;

Thine I am, O spot - less Lamb, I will suf - fer
sin and hell in con - flict fell with their heav - iest
yea, what - e'er we here must bear, still in thee lies

WORDS: Johann Franck, 1653; trans. by Catherine Winkworth, 1863
MUSIC: *Praxis Pietatis Melica*, 1656; harm. by J. S. Bach, 1723

JESU, MEINE FREUDE
665.665.786

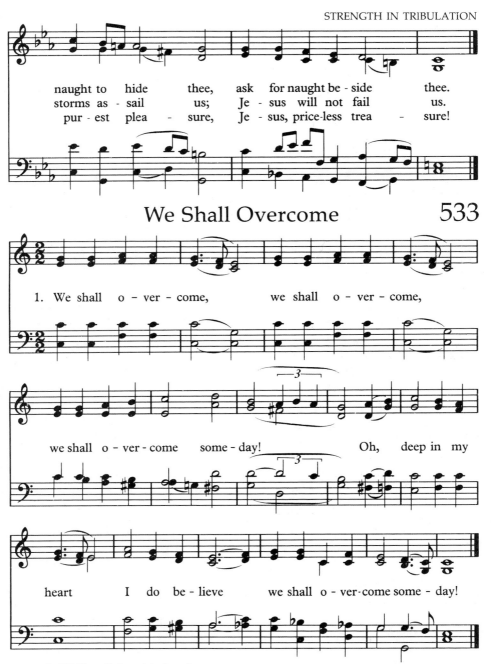

naught to hide thee, ask for naught be-side thee.
storms as - sail us; Je - sus will not fail us.
pur - est plea - sure, Je - sus, price-less trea - sure!

We Shall Overcome 533

1. We shall o - ver - come, we shall o - ver - come,

we shall o - ver - come some - day! Oh, deep in my

heart I do be - lieve we shall o - ver-come some - day!

2. We'll walk hand in hand.
3. We shall all be free.
4. We shall live in peace.
5. The Lord will see us through.

WORDS: Afro-American spiritual
MUSIC: Afro-American spiritual; adapt. by William Farley Smith, 1986

MARTIN
Irr.

Adapt. © 1989 The United Methodist Publishing House

534

Be Still, My Soul

1. Be still, my soul: the Lord is on your side.
2. Be still, my soul: your God will un-der-take
3. Be still, my soul: the hour is has-tening on

Bear pa-tient-ly the cross of grief or pain;
to guide the fu-ture, as in a-ges past.
when we shall be for-ev-er with the Lord,

leave to your God to or-der and pro-vide;
Your hope, your con-fi-dence let noth-ing shake;
when dis-ap-point-ment, grief, and fear are gone,

in ev-ery change God faith-ful will re-main.
all now mys-te-rious shall be bright at last.
sor-row for-got, love's pur-est joys re-stored.

WORDS: Katharina von Schlegel, 1752; trans. by Jane Borthwick, 1855 (Ps. 46:10)
MUSIC: Jean Sibelius, 1899; arr. from *The Hymnal*, 1933

FINLANDIA
11 10.11 10.11 10

Arr. © 1933, renewed 1961 Presbyterian Board of Christian Education

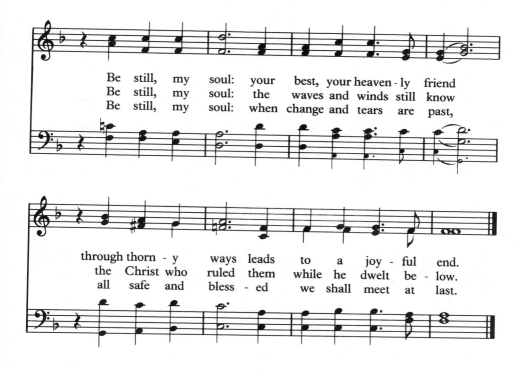

Be still, my soul: your best, your heaven - ly friend
Be still, my soul: the waves and winds still know
Be still, my soul: when change and tears are past,

through thorn - y ways leads to a joy - ful end.
the Christ who ruled them while he dwelt be - low.
all safe and bless - ed we shall meet at last.

A Refuge amid Distraction 535

Like an ant on a stick both ends of which are burning,
   I go to and fro without knowing what to do,
     and in great despair.
Like the inescapable shadow that follows me,
   the dead weight of sin haunts me.
Graciously look upon me.
Thy love is my refuge. **Amen.**

Trad., India

536

Precious Name

1. Take the name of Je - sus with you,
2. Take the name of Je - sus ev - er,
3. O the pre - cious name of Je - sus!
4. At the name of Je - sus bow - ing,

child of sor - row and of woe;
as a shield from ev - ery snare;
How it thrills our souls with joy,
fall - ing pros - trate at his feet,

it will joy and com - fort give you;
if temp - ta - tions round you gath - er,
when his lov - ing arms re - ceive us,
King of kings in heaven we'll crown him,

WORDS: Lydia Baxter, 1870 (Phil. 2:9-11)
MUSIC: William H. Doane, 1871

PRECIOUS NAME
87.87 with Refrain

Refrain

take it then, wher-e'er you go.
breathe that ho - ly name in prayer.
and his songs our tongues em - ploy!
when our jour - ney is com - plete.

Pre-cious name, O how sweet!
Pre-cious name, O how sweet!

Hope of earth and joy of heaven. Pre-cious name,
Pre-cious name,

O how sweet! Hope of earth and joy of heaven.
O how sweet, how sweet!

537   Filled with the Spirit's Power

1. Filled with the Spir-it's power, with one ac-cord
2. Now with the mind of Christ set us on fire,
3. Wid-en our love, good Spir-it, to em-brace

the in-fant church con-fessed its ris-en Lord.
that u-ni-ty may be our great de-sire.
in your strong care all those of ev-ery race.

O Ho-ly Spir-it, in the church to-day
Give joy and peace; give faith to hear your call,
Like wind and fire with life a-mong us move,

no less your power of fel-low-ship dis-play.
and read-i-ness in each to work for all.
till we are known as Christ's, and Chris-tians prove.

WORDS: John R. Peacey, 1969 (Acts 2)   SHELDONIAN
MUSIC: Cyril V. Taylor, 1943   10 10.10 10

Wind Who Makes All Winds That Blow 538

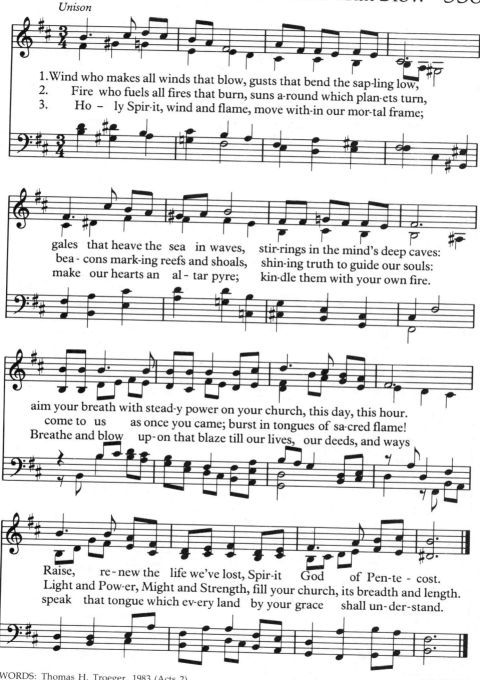

Unison

1. Wind who makes all winds that blow, gusts that bend the sap-ling low,
2. Fire who fuels all fires that burn, suns a-round which plan-ets turn,
3. Ho - ly Spir-it, wind and flame, move with-in our mor-tal frame;

gales that heave the sea in waves, stir-rings in the mind's deep caves:
bea - cons mark-ing reefs and shoals, shin-ing truth to guide our souls:
make our hearts an al - tar pyre; kin-dle them with your own fire.

aim your breath with stead-y power on your church, this day, this hour.
come to us as once you came; burst in tongues of sa-cred flame!
Breathe and blow up-on that blaze till our lives, our deeds, and ways

Raise, re - new the life we've lost, Spir-it God of Pen-te - cost.
Light and Pow-er, Might and Strength, fill your church, its breadth and length.
speak that tongue which ev-ery land by your grace shall un-der-stand.

WORDS: Thomas H. Troeger, 1983 (Acts 2)
MUSIC: Carol Doran, 1985

FALCONE
77.77 D

539   O Spirit of the Living God

1. O Spir - it of the liv - ing God, thou
2. Blow, wind of God! With wis - dom blow un -
3. Teach us to ut - ter liv - ing words of
4. So shall we know the power of Christ who

light and fire di - vine, de - scend up - on thy
til our minds are free from mists of er - ror,
truth which all may hear, the lan - guage all may
came this world to save; so shall we rise with

church once more, and make it tru - ly thine.
clouds of doubt, which blind our eyes to thee.
un - der - stand when love speaks loud and clear;
him to life which soars be - yond the grave;

Fill it with love and joy and power, with
Burn, wing - ed fire! In - spire our lips with
till ev - ery age and race and clime shall
and earth shall win true ho - li - ness, which

WORDS: Henry H. Tweedy, 1935 (Acts 2)
MUSIC: Trad. English melody; arr. by Ralph Vaughan Williams, 1906

FOREST GREEN
CMD

righ - teous - ness and peace; till Christ shall dwell in
flam - ing love and zeal, to preach to all thy
blend their creeds in one, and earth shall form one
makes thy chil - dren whole; till, per - fect - ed by

hu - man hearts, and sin and sor - row cease.
great good news, God's glo - rious com - mon - weal.
fam - i - ly by whom thy will is done.
thee, we reach cre - a - tion's glo - rious goal!

I Love Thy Kingdom, Lord 540

1. I love thy king-dom, Lord, the house of thine a - bode, the
2. I love thy church, O God! Her walls be - fore thee stand dear
3. For her my tears shall fall, for her my prayers as - cend, to
4. Be - yond my high - est joy I prize her heaven-ly ways, her
5. Sure as thy truth shall last, to Zi - on shall be given the

church our blest Re - deem - er saved with his own pre - cious blood.
as the ap - ple of thine eye, and grav - en on thy hand.
her my cares and toils be given, till toils and cares shall end.
sweet com - mu - nion, sol - emn vows, her hymns of love and praise.
bright- est glo - ries earth can yield, and bright - er bliss of heaven.

WORDS: Timothy Dwight, 1801
MUSIC: Aaron Williams, *The New Universal Psalmodist*, 1770

ST. THOMAS
SM

541 See How Great a Flame Aspires

1. See how great a flame as – pires, kin – dled
2. When he first the work be – gun, small and
3. Saints of God, your Sav – ior praise, who the
4. Saw ye not the cloud a – rise, lit – tle

by a spark of grace. Je – sus' love the
fee – ble was his day; now the Word doth
door hath o – pened wide; he hath given the
as a hu – man hand? Now it spreads a –

na – tions fires, sets the king – doms on a blaze.
swift – ly run, now it wins its wid – ening way;
word of grace, Je – sus' word is glo – ri – fied;
long the skies, hangs o'er all the thirst – y land.

To bring fire on earth he came, kin – dled
more and more it spreads and grows, ev – er
Je – sus might – y to re – deem, who a –
Lo! the prom – ise of a shower drops al –

WORDS: Charles Wesley, 1749 (Lk. 12:49; 1 Kg. 18:44-45)
MUSIC: Welsh hymn melody; harm. by Carlton R. Young, 1963, alt.

ARFON (MAJOR)
77.77 D

Harm. © 1964 Abingdon Press

in   some   hearts   it   is;   O   that   all   might
might - y   to   pre - vail;   sin's   strong - holds   it
lone   the   work   hath wrought;   wor - thy   is   the
read - y   from   a - bove;   but   the   Lord   will

catch   the   flame,   all   par - take   the   glo - rious   bliss!
now   o'er - throws,   shakes   the   trem - bling   gates   of   hell.
work   of   him,   him   who   spake   a   world from naught.
short - ly   pour   all   the   spir - it   of   his   love.

Day of Pentecost   542

God of grace,
  you sent the promised gift of the Holy Spirit
    upon the apostles and the women,
    upon Mary the mother of Jesus and upon his brothers.
Fill your church with power,
    kindle flaming hearts within us,
    and cause us to proclaim your mighty works in every tongue,
    that all may call on you and be saved;
  through Jesus Christ our Lord. **Amen.**

WORDS: Laurence Hull Stookey, USA, 20th cent. (Acts 1:4, 13-14; 2:3, 11, 21)

543   O Breath of Life

1. O Breath of Life, come sweep-ing through us,
2. O Wind of God, come, bend us, break us,
3. O Breath of Love, come, breathe with-in us,

re - vive your church with life and power.
till hum - bly we con - fess our need.
re - new - ing thought and will and heart.

O Breath of Life, come, cleanse, re - new us,
Then in your ten - der - ness re - make us;
Come, love of Christ, a - fresh to win us;

and fit your church to meet this hour.
re - vive, re - store, for this we plead.
re - vive your church in ev - ery part.

WORDS: Bessie Porter Head, 1920 (Acts 2; Jn. 20:22)
MUSIC: David Ashley White, 1987

BISHOP POWELL
98.98

Music © 1989 The United Methodist Publishing House

Like the Murmur of the Dove's Song 544

Unison

1. Like the mur-mur of the dove's song, like the chal-lenge of her
2. To the mem-bers of Christ's bod-y, to the branch-es of the
3. With the heal-ing of di-vi-sion, with the cease-less voice of

flight, like the vig-or of the wind's rush, like the
Vine, to the church in faith as-sem-bled, to her
prayer, with the power to love and wit-ness, with the

new flame's ea-ger might: Come, Ho-ly Spir - it, come.
midst as gift and sign: Come, Ho-ly Spir - it, come.
peace be-yond com-pare: Come, Ho-ly Spir - it, come.

WORDS: Carl P. Daw, Jr., 1981 (Acts 2)
MUSIC: Peter Cutts, 1968

BRIDEGROOM
87.87.6

Words © 1982 Hope Publishing Co.; music © 1969 Hope Publishing Co.

BORN OF THE SPIRIT, *see further:*

324 Hail Thee, Festival Day

332 Spirit of Faith, Come Down

545 The Church's One Foundation

1. The church's one foun - da - tion is Je - sus Christ her Lord;
2. E - lect from ev - ery na - tion, yet one o'er all the earth;
3. Though with a scorn-ful won-der we see her sore op-pressed,
4. Mid toil and trib-u - la - tion, and tu-mult of her war,
5. Yet she on earth hath un-ion with God the Three in One,

she is his new cre - a - tion by wa-ter and the Word.
her char-ter of sal - va - tion, one Lord, one faith, one birth;
by schis-ms rent a - sun - der, by her e-sies dis-tressed,
she waits the con-sum - ma - tion of peace for - ev - er - more;
and mys-tic sweet com - mu - nion with those whose rest is won.

From heaven he came and sought her to be his ho-ly bride;
one ho-ly name she bless-es, par-takes one ho-ly food,
yet saints their watch are keep-ing; their cry goes up, "How long?"
till, with the vi-sion glo-rious, her long-ing eyes are blest,
O hap-py ones and ho-ly! Lord, give us grace that we

with his own blood he bought her, and for her life he died.
and to one hope she press-es, with ev-ery grace en - dued.
And soon the night of weep-ing shall be the morn of song.
and the great church vic - to - rious shall be the church at rest.
like them, the meek and low - ly, on high may dwell with thee.

WORDS: Samuel J. Stone, 1866
MUSIC: Samuel Sebastian Wesley, 1864

AURELIA
76.76 D

The Church's One Foundation   546

The church's one foundation
is Jesus Christ our Lord;
we are his new creation
by water and the Word;
from heaven he came and sought us
that we might ever be
his living servant people,
by his own death set free.

Called forth from every nation,
yet one o'er all the earth;
our charter of salvation:
one Lord, one faith, one birth.
One holy name professing
and at one table fed,
to one hope always pressing,
by Christ's own Spirit led.

Though with a scornful wonder
the world sees us oppressed,
by schisms rent asunder,
by heresies distressed,
yet saints their watch are keeping;
their cry goes up, "How long?"
But soon the night of weeping
shall be the morn of song.

Mid toil and tribulation,
and tumult of our war,
we wait the consummation
of peace forevermore;
till with the vision glorious
our longing eyes are blest,
and the great church victorious
shall be the church at rest.

We now on earth have union
with God the Three in One,
and share through faith communion
with those whose rest is won.
Oh, happy ones, and holy!
Lord, give us grace that we
like them, the meek and lowly,
on high may dwell with thee.

Samuel J. Stone, 1866; adapt. by Laurence Hull Stookey, 1983

547 O Church of God, United

1. O church of God, u - nit - ed to serve one
   com - mon Lord, pro - claim to all one mes - sage, with
   hearts in glad ac - cord. Christ ev - er goes be -
   fore us; we fol - low day by day with

2. From ev - ery land and na - tion the or - dered
   ranks ap - pear; to serve one val - iant lead - er they
   come from far and near. They chant their one con -
   fes - sion, they praise one liv - ing Lord, and

3. Though creeds and tongues may dif - fer, they speak, O
   Christ, of thee; and in thy lov - ing spir - it we
   shall one peo - ple be. Lord, may our faith - ful
   ser - vice and sin - gle - ness of aim pro -

4. May thy great prayer be an - swered that we may
   all be one, close bound, by love u - nit - ed in
   thee, God's bless - ed Son: to bring a sin - gle
   wit - ness, to make the path - way bright, that

WORDS: Frederick B. Morley, 1953 (Acts 2:5-11)
MUSIC: *Gesangbuch der H. W. k. Hofkappelle*, 1784, alt.

ELLACOMBE
76.76 D

Alt. tune: AURELIA

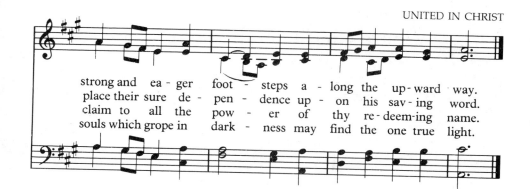

strong and ea - ger foot - steps a - long the up - ward way.
place their sure de - pen - dence up - on his sav - ing word.
claim to all the pow - er of thy re - deem - ing name.
souls which grope in dark - ness may find the one true light.

In Christ There Is No East or West 548

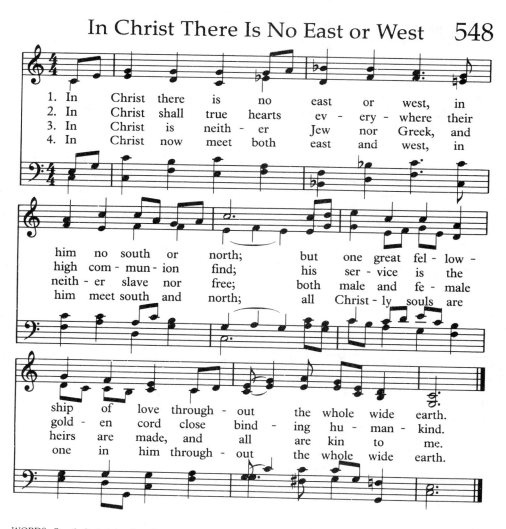

1. In Christ there is no east or west, in
2. In Christ shall true hearts ev - ery - where their
3. In Christ is neith - er Jew nor Greek, and
4. In Christ now meet both east and west, in

him no south or north; but one great fel - low -
high com - mun - ion find; his ser - vice is the
neith - er slave nor free; both male and fe - male
him meet south and north; all Christ - ly souls are

ship of love through - out the whole wide earth.
gold - en cord close bind - ing hu - man - kind.
heirs are made, and all are kin to me.
one in him through - out the whole wide earth.

WORDS: Sts. 1, 2, 4, John Oxenham, 1913; st. 3, Laurence Hull Stookey, 1987 (Gal. 3:28)
MUSIC: Afro-American spiritual; adapt. and harm. by Harry T. Burleigh, 1939

McKEE
CM

St. 3 © 1989 The United Methodist Publishing House

Alt. tune: ST. PETER

549 Where Charity and Love Prevail

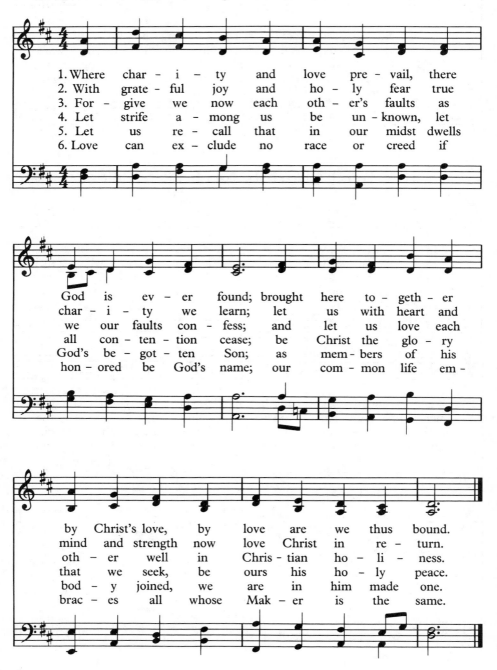

1. Where char-i-ty and love pre-vail, there
2. With grate-ful joy and ho-ly fear true
3. For-give we now each oth-er's faults as
4. Let strife a-mong us be un-known, let
5. Let us re-call that in our midst dwells
6. Love can ex-clude no race or creed if

God is ev-er found; brought here to-geth-er
char-i-ty we learn; let us with heart and
we our faults con-fess; and let us love each
all con-ten-tion cease; be Christ the glo-ry
God's be-got-ten Son; as mem-bers of his
hon-ored be God's name; our com-mon life em-

by Christ's love, by love are we thus bound.
mind and strength now love Christ in re-turn.
oth-er well in Chris-tian ho-li-ness.
that we seek, be ours his ho-ly peace.
bod-y joined, we are in him made one.
brac-es all whose Mak-er is the same.

WORDS: 9th cent. Latin; trans. by Omer Westendorf, 1961 (1 Jn. 4:16) ST. PETER
MUSIC: Alexander R. Reinagle, 1836; harm. from *Hymns Ancient and Modern*, 1861 CM

Trans. © 1961 World Library Publications, Inc.

Christ, from Whom All Blessings Flow 550

1. Christ, from whom all bless - ings flow, per - fect - ing the saints be - low, hear us, who thy na - ture share, who thy mys - tic bod - y are.
2. Join us, in one spir - it join, let us still re - ceive of thine; still for more on thee we call, thou who fill - est all in all.
3. Move and ac - tu - ate and guide, di - verse gifts to each di - vide; placed ac - cord - ing to thy will, let us all our work ful - fill;
4. Nev - er from thy ser - vice move, need - ful to each oth - er prove; use the grace on each be - stowed, tem - pered by the art of God.
5. Man - y are we now, and one, we who Je - sus have put on; there is neith - er bond nor free, male nor fe - male, Lord, in thee.
6. Love, like death, hath all de - stroyed, ren - dered all dis - tinc - tions void; names and sects and par - ties fall; thou, O Christ, art all in all!

WORDS: Charles Wesley, 1740 (1 Cor. 12:4-31; Gal. 3:27-28)
MUSIC: Adapt. from Orlando Gibbons, 1623

CANTERBURY
77.77

551 Awake, O Sleeper

Unison

1. A - wake, O sleep - er, rise from death, and Christ shall
2. To us on earth he came to bring from sin and
3. There is one bod - y and one hope, one Spir - it
4. Then walk in love as Christ has loved, who died that
5. For us Christ lived, for us he died, and con-quered

give you light; so learn his love, its
fear re - lease, to give the Spir - it's
and one call, one Lord, one faith, and
he might save; with kind and gen - tle
in the strife. A - wake, a - rise, go

length and breadth, its full - ness, depth, and height.
u - ni - ty, the ver - y bond of peace.
one bap - tism, one Fa - ther of us all.
hearts for - give as God in Christ for - gave.
forth in faith, and Christ shall give you life.

WORDS: F. Bland Tucker, 1980 (Rom. 13:11-14; Eph. 4:4-6)
MUSIC: Max Miller, 1984

MARSH CHAPEL
CM

Here, O Lord, Your Servants Gather 552

Unison

1. Here, O Lord, your ser-vants gath-er, hand we link with hand;
1. *Se - ka - i no to - mo to te o tsu - na - gi,*
2. Man-y are the tongues we speak, scat-tered are the lands,
3. Na-ture's se-crets o - pen wide, chang-es nev - er cease.
4. Grant, O God, an age re-newed, filled with death-less love;

look-ing toward our Sav-ior's cross, joined in love we stand.
Jyu - ji - ka no mo - to ni ta - tsu wa - re - ra,
yet our hearts are one in God, one in love's de - mands.
Where, oh where, can wea - ry souls find the source of peace?
help us as we work and pray, send us from a - bove

As we seek the realm of God, we u - nite to pray:
Ka - mi no mi - ku - ni o me a te to shi,
E'en in dark-ness hope ap-pears, call - ing age and youth:
Un - to all those sore dis-tressed, torn by end-less strife:
truth and cour-age, faith and power, need-ed in our strife:

Je - sus, Sav - ior, guide our steps, for you are the Way.
Shu Ye - su no mi - chi o su - su - mi yu - kan.
Je - sus, teach-er, dwell with us, for you are the Truth.
Je - sus, heal-er, bring your balm, for you are the Life.
Je - sus, Mas-ter, be our Way, be our Truth, our Life.

WORDS: Tokuo Yamaguchi, 1958; trans. by Everett M. Stowe, 1958;
phonetic transcription from the Japanese by I-to Loh, 1988
MUSIC: Isao Koizumi, 1958

TOKYO
77.77

553 And Are We Yet Alive

1. And are we yet a - live, and see each
2. Pre - served by power di - vine to full sal -
3. What trou - bles have we seen, what might - y
4. Yet out of all the Lord hath brought us
5. Then let us make our boast of his re -
6. Let us take up the cross till we the

oth - er's face? Glo - ry and thanks to
va - tion here, a - gain in Je - sus'
con - flicts past, fight - ings with - out, and
by his love; and still he doth his
deem - ing power, which saves us to the
crown ob - tain, and glad - ly reck - on

Je - sus give for his al - might - y grace!
praise we join, and in his sight ap - pear.
fears with - in, since we as - sem - bled last!
help af - ford, and hides our life a - bove.
ut - ter - most, till we can sin no more.
all things loss so we may Je - sus gain.

WORDS: Charles Wesley, 1749
MUSIC: Johann G. Nägeli; arr. by Lowell Mason, 1845

DENNIS
SM

All Praise to Our Redeeming Lord 554

1. All praise to our re - deem - ing Lord, who
2. He bids us build each oth - er up; and,
3. The gift which he on one be - stows, we
4. E'en now we think and speak the same, and
5. We all par - take the joy of one; the
6. And if our fel - low - ship be - low in

joins us by his grace, and bids us, each to
gath - ered in - to one, to our high call - ing's
all de - light to prove, the grace through ev - ery
cor - dial - ly a - gree, con - cen - tered all, through
com - mon peace we feel, a peace to sen - sual
Je - sus be so sweet, what height of rap - ture

each re - stored, to - geth - er seek his face.
glo - rious hope we hand in hand go on.
ves - sel flows in pur - est streams of love.
Je - sus' name, in per - fect har - mo - ny.
minds un - known, a joy un - speak - a - ble.
shall we know when round his throne we meet!

WORDS: Charles Wesley, 1747
MUSIC: Sylvanus B. Pond, 1836; harm. by Austin C. Lovelace, 1963

ARMENIA
CM

555 Forward Through the Ages

1. For-ward through the a – ges, in un – bro – ken line,
2. Wid – er grows the king – dom, reign of love and light;
3. Not a – lone we con – quer, not a – lone we fall;

move the faith – ful spir – its at the call di – vine;
for it we must la – bor, till our faith is sight.
in each loss or tri – umph lose or tri – umph all.

gifts in dif – fering mea – sure, hearts of one ac – cord,
Proph – ets have pro – claimed it, mar – tyrs tes – ti – fied,
Bound by God's far pur – pose in one liv – ing whole,

man – i – fold the ser – vice, one the sure re – ward.
po – ets sung its glo – ry, he – roes for it died.
move we on to – geth – er to the shin – ing goal.

WORDS: Frederick Lucian Hosmer, 1908
MUSIC: Arthur S. Sullivan, 1871

ST. GERTRUDE
65.65 D with Refrain

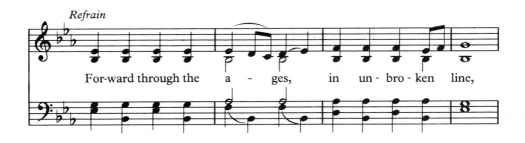

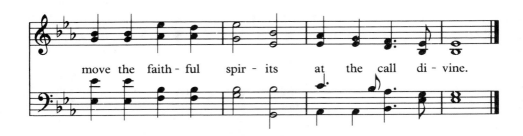

Refrain

For-ward through the a - ges, in un - bro - ken line,

move the faith - ful spir - its at the call di - vine.

Litany for Christian Unity 556

Let us ask the Lord to strengthen in all Christians faith in Christ, the Savior of the world.
Listen to us, O Lord.
Let us ask the Lord to sustain and guide Christians with his gifts along the way to full unity.
Listen to us, O Lord.
Let us ask the Lord for the gift of unity and peace for the world.
Listen to us, O Lord.
Let us pray. We ask you, O Lord, for the gifts of your Spirit.
 Enable us to penetrate the depth of the whole truth,
  and grant that we may share with others
   the goods you have put at our disposal.
 Teach us to overcome divisions. Send us your Spirit
  to lead to full unity your sons and daughters in full charity,
   in obedience to your will; through Christ our Lord. **Amen.**

Karol Wojtyla (Pope John Paul II), Poland, 20th cent.

By permission of The Crossroad Publishing Co.

557 Blest Be the Tie That Binds

1. Blest be the tie that binds our hearts in
2. Be - fore our Fa - ther's throne we pour our
3. We share each oth - er's woes, our mu - tual
4. When we a - sun - der part, it gives us

Chris - tian love; the fel - low - ship of
ar - dent prayers; our fears, our hopes, our
bur - dens bear; and of - ten for each
in - ward pain; but we shall still be

kin - dred minds is like to that a - bove.
aims are one, our com - forts and our cares.
oth - er flows the sym - pa - thiz - ing tear.
joined in heart, and hope to meet a - gain.

WORDS: John Fawcett, 1782
MUSIC: Johann G. Nägeli; arr. by Lowell Mason, 1845

DENNIS
SM

558 We Are the Church

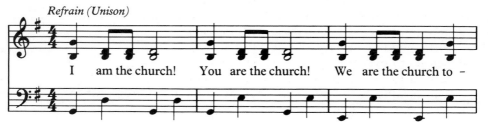

Refrain (Unison)

I am the church! You are the church! We are the church to -

WORDS: Richard K. Avery and Donald S. Marsh, 1972
MUSIC: Richard K. Avery and Donald S. Marsh, 1972

PORT JERVIS
77.87 with Refrain

geth – er! All who fol - low Je - sus,

Fine

all a - round the world! Yes, we're the church to – geth - er!

1. The church is not a build-ing, the church is not a stee - ple,
2. We're man - y kinds of peo - ple, with man - y kinds of fac - es,
3. Some-times the church is march-ing, some-times it's brave-ly burn-ing,
4. And when the peo - ple gath-er, there's sing – ing and there's pray-ing,
5. At Pen - te - cost some peo - ple re - ceived the Ho - ly Spir - it

D.C.

the church is not a rest-ing place, the church is a peo - ple.
all col - ors and all a - ges, too, from all times and plac - es.
some - times it's rid-ing, some-times hid-ing, al - ways it's learn-ing.
there's laugh - ing and there's cry-ing some-times, all of it say-ing:
and told the Good News through the world to all who would hear it.

559 Christ Is Made the Sure Foundation

1. Christ is made the sure foun - da - tion, Christ the head and cor - ner - stone; cho - sen of the Lord and pre - cious, bind - ing all the church in one; ho - ly Zi - on's help for - ev - er, and her con - fi - dence a - lone.

2. To this tem - ple, where we call thee, come, O Lord of Hosts, to - day! With thy faith - ful lov - ing - kind - ness hear thy peo - ple as they pray, and thy full - est ben - e - dic - tion shed with - in its walls al - way.

3. Here vouch - safe to all thy ser - vants what they ask of thee to gain; what they gain from thee for - ev - er with the bless - ed to re - tain, and here - af - ter in thy glo - ry ev - er - more with thee to reign.

4. Laud and hon - or to the Fa - ther, laud and hon - or to the Son, laud and hon - or to the Spir - it, ev - er three and ev - er one; one in might and one in glo - ry, while un - end - ing a - ges run.

WORDS: 7th cent. Latin; trans. by John Mason Neale, 1851
(Eph. 2:20-22; 1 Pet. 2:4-7)
MUSIC: Henry Purcell, ca. 1680; adapt. by Ernest Hawkins, 1842

WESTMINSTER ABBEY
87.87.87

Help Us Accept Each Other

1. Help us ac-cept each oth-er as Christ ac-cept-ed us;
2. Teach us, O Lord, your les-sons, as in our dai-ly life
3. Let your ac-cep-tance change us, so that we may be moved
4. Lord, for to-day's en-coun-ters with all who are in need,

teach us as sis-ter, broth-er, each per-son to em-brace.
we strug-gle to be hu-man and search for hope and faith.
in liv-ing sit-u-a-tions to do the truth in love;
who hun-ger for ac-cep-tance, for right-teous-ness and bread,

Be pres-ent, Lord, a-mong us, and bring us to be-lieve
Teach us to care for peo-ple, for all, not just for some,
to prac-tice your ac-cep-tance, un-til we know by heart
we need new eyes for see-ing, new hands for hold-ing on;

we are our-selves ac-cept-ed and meant to love and live.
to love them as we find them, or as they may be-come.
the ta-ble of for-give-ness and laugh-ter's heal-ing art.
re-new us with your Spir-it; Lord, free us, make us one!

WORDS: Fred Kaan, 1974 (Jn. 15:12)
MUSIC: John Ness Beck, 1977

ACCEPTANCE
76.76 D

561   Jesus, United by Thy Grace

1. Je - sus, u - nit - ed by thy grace
2. Help us to help each oth - er, Lord,
3. Up un - to thee, our liv - ing Head,
4. Touched by the lode - stone of thy love,
5. To thee, in - sep - a - ra - bly joined,
6. This is the bond of per - fect - ness,

and each to each en - deared, with con - fi - dence we
each oth - er's cross to bear; let all their friend - ly
let us in all things grow; till thou hast made us
let all our hearts a - gree, and ev - er toward each
let all our spir - its cleave; O may we all the
thy spot - less char - i - ty; O let us, still we

seek thy face and know our prayer is heard.
aid af - ford, and feel each oth - er's care.
free in - deed and spot - less here be - low.
oth - er move, and ev - er move toward thee.
lov - ing mind that was in thee re - ceive.
pray, pos - sess the mind that was in thee.

WORDS: Charles Wesley, 1742
MUSIC: John B. Dykes, 1866

ST. AGNES
CM

Jesus, Lord, We Look to Thee 562

1. Je - sus, Lord, we look to thee; let us in thy name a - gree; show thy - self the Prince of Peace, bid our strife for - ev - er cease.
2. By thy rec - on - cil - ing love ev - ery stum - bling block re - move; each to each u - nite, en - dear; come, and spread thy ban - ner here.
3. Make us of one heart and mind, gen - tle, cour - te - ous, and kind, low - ly, meek, in thought and word, al - to - geth - er like our Lord.
4. Let us for each oth - er care, each the oth - er's bur - dens bear; to thy church the pat - tern give, show how true be - liev - ers live.
5. Free from an - ger and from pride, let us thus in God a - bide; all the depths of love ex - press, all the heights of ho - li - ness.
6. Let us then with joy re - move to the fam - i - ly a - bove; on the wings of an - gels fly, show how true be - liev - ers die.

WORDS: Charles Wesley, 1749
MUSIC: *Foundery Collection*, 1742

SAVANNAH
77.77

563

Father, We Thank You

Unison

1. Fa-ther, we thank you,
2. Lord, you have made all
3. Watch o'er your church, O Lord,
4. As grain, once scat-tered

(Piano or *Organ)

(Organ pedal)

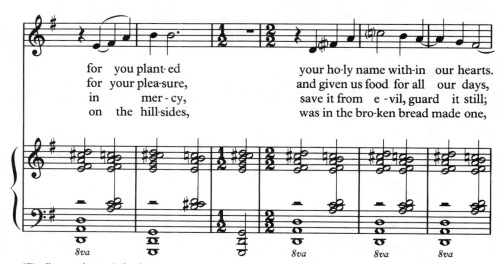

for you plant-ed
for your plea-sure,
in mer-cy,
on the hill-sides,

your ho-ly name with-in our hearts.
and given us food for all our days,
save it from e-vil, guard it still;
was in the bro-ken bread made one,

*Tie all repeated notes in hands

WORDS: Greek, 2nd cent.; trans. by F. Bland Tucker and others, 1939, 1982; alt.
MUSIC: William Albright, 1973

ALBRIGHT
98.98

Knowl-edge and faith and life im-mor - tal
giv-ing in Christ the bread e-ter - nal;
per-fect it in your love, u-nite it,
so from all lands your church be gath - ered

Ending

Je-sus your Son to us im - parts.
yours is the power, be yours the praise.
cleansed and con-formed un-to your will.
in-to your king-dom by your Son.

For the Unity of Christ's Body 564

Help each of us, gracious God,
   to live in such magnanimity and restraint
that the Head of the church may never have cause to say to any one of us,
   "This is my body, broken by you." **Amen.**

Chinese Prayer

565   Father, We Thank You

1. Fa-ther, we thank you, for you plant-ed your ho-ly
2. Watch o'er your church, O Lord, in mer-cy, save it from

name with-in our hearts. Knowl-edge and faith and life im-mor-tal
e-vil, guard it still; per-fect it in your love, u-nite it,

Je-sus your Son to us im-parts. Lord, you have made all for your
cleansed and con-formed un-to your will. As grain, once scat-tered on the

plea-sure, and given us food for all our days, giv-ing in
hill-sides, was in the bro-ken bread made one, so from all

Christ the bread e-ter-nal; yours is the power, be yours the praise.
lands your church be gath-ered in-to your king-dom by your Son.

WORDS: Greek, 2nd cent.; trans. by F. Bland Tucker and others, 1939, 1982
MUSIC: Attr. to Louis Bourgeois, 1551; harm. by John Wilson, 1979

RENDEZ À DIEU
98.98 D

Blest Be the Dear Uniting Love

566

1. Blest be the dear u - nit - ing love that will not let us part; our bod - ies may far off re - move, we still are one in heart.
2. Joined in one spir - it to our Head, where he ap - points we go, and still in Je - sus' foot - steps tread, and do his work be - low.
3. O may we ev - er walk in him, and noth - ing know be - side, noth - ing de - sire, noth - ing es - teem, but Je - sus cru - ci - fied!
4. We all are one who him re - ceive, and each with each a - gree, in him the One, the Truth, we live; blest point of u - ni - ty!
5. Par - tak - ers of the Sav - ior's grace, the same in mind and heart, nor joy, nor grief, nor time, nor place, nor life, nor death can part.

WORDS: Charles Wesley, 1742 (1 Cor. 2:2)
MUSIC: William Havergal, 1847; arr. by Lowell Mason, 1850

EVAN
CM

UNITED IN CHRIST, *see further:*

646 Canticle of Love   114 Many Gifts, One Spirit

567 Heralds of Christ

*Trumpets, before
each stanza*

1. Her-alds of Christ, who bear the King's com-
2. Through des-ert ways, dark fen, and deep mo-
3. Lord, give us faith and strength the road to

mands, im-mor-tal tid-ings in your mor-tal hands,
rass, through jun-gles, slug-gish seas, and moun-tain pass,
build, to see the prom-ise of the day ful-filled,

pass on and car-ry swift the news you bring;
build now the road, and fal-ter not, nor stay;
when war shall be no more, and strife shall cease

make straight, make straight the high-way of the King.
pre-pare a-cross the earth the King's high-way.
up-on the high-way of the Prince of Peace.

WORDS: Laura S. Copenhaver, 1915
MUSIC: George W. Warren, 1894

NATIONAL HYMN
10 10.10 10

Christ for the World We Sing

568

1. Christ for the world we sing, the world to
2. Christ for the world we sing, the world to
3. Christ for the world we sing, the world to
4. Christ for the world we sing, the world to

Christ we bring, with lov - ing zeal; the poor, and
Christ we bring, with fer - vent prayer; the way - ward
Christ we bring, with one ac - cord; with us the
Christ we bring, with joy - ful song; the new - born

them that mourn, the faint and o - ver - borne,
and the lost, by rest - less pas - sions tossed,
work to share, with us re - proach to dare,
souls, whose days, re - claimed from er - ror's ways,

sin - sick and sor - row - worn, whom Christ doth heal.
re - deemed at count - less cost, from dark de - spair.
with us the cross to bear, for Christ our Lord.
in - spired with hope and praise, to Christ be - long.

WORDS: Samuel Wolcott, 1869
MUSIC: Felice de Giardini, 1769

ITALIAN HYMN
664.6664

569 We've a Story to Tell to the Nations

1. We've a sto - ry to tell to the na - tions,
2. We've a song to be sung to the na - tions,
3. We've a mes - sage to give to the na - tions,
4. We've a Sav - ior to show to the na - tions,

that shall turn their hearts to the right, a
that shall lift their hearts to the Lord, a
that the Lord who reign - eth a - bove hath
who the path of sor - row hath trod, that

sto - ry of truth and mer - cy, a sto - ry of
song that shall con - quer e - vil and shat - ter the
sent us his Son to save us, and show us that
all of the world's great peo - ples might come to the

peace and light, a sto - ry of peace and light.
spear and sword, and shat - ter the spear and sword.
God is love, and show us that God is love.
truth of God, might come to the truth of God.

WORDS: H. Ernest Nichol, 1896
MUSIC: H. Ernest Nichol, 1896

MESSAGE
10 8.87 with Refrain

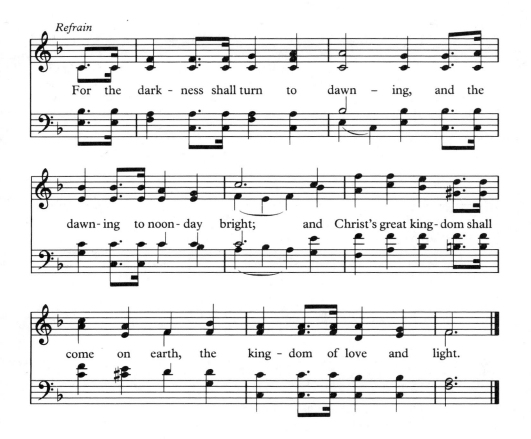

Refrain

For the dark-ness shall turn to dawn – ing, and the
dawn-ing to noon-day bright; and Christ's great king-dom shall
come on earth, the king – dom of love and light.

Prayer of Ignatius of Loyola   570

Teach us, good Lord,
    to serve you as you deserve;
    to give and not to count the cost;
    to fight and not to heed the wounds;
    to toil and not to seek for rest;
    to labor and not to ask for any reward,
      except that of knowing that we do your will;
through Jesus Christ our Lord. **Amen.**

Ignatius of Loyola, Spain, 16th cent.

571   Go, Make of All Disciples

1. "Go, make of all dis - ci - ples." We hear the call, O Lord,
2. "Go, make of all dis - ci - ples," bap - tiz - ing in the name
3. "Go, make of all dis - ci - ples." We at thy feet would stay
4. "Go, make of all dis - ci - ples." We wel-come thy com - mand.

that comes from thee, our Fa - ther, in thy e - ter - nal Word.
of Fa - ther, Son, and Spir - it, from age to age the same.
un - til each life's vo - ca - tion ac - cents thy ho - ly way.
"Lo, I am with you al - ways." We take thy guid - ing hand.

In - spire our ways of learn - ing through ear - nest, fer - vent prayer,
We call each new dis - ci - ple to fol - low thee, O Lord,
We cul - ti - vate the na - ture God plants in ev - ery heart,
The task looms large be - fore us; we fol - low with - out fear;

and let our dai - ly liv - ing re - veal thee ev - ery - where.
re - deem-ing soul and bod - y by wa - ter and the Word.
re - veal-ing in our wit - ness the mas - ter teach-er's art.
in heaven and earth thy pow - er shall bring God's king-dom here.

WORDS: Leon M. Adkins, 1955, alt. (Mt. 28:19-20)   LANCASHIRE
MUSIC: Henry T. Smart, 1835   76.76 D

Pass It On

Unison

1. It on - ly takes a spark to get a fire
2. What a won - drous time is spring, when all the trees are
3. I wish for you, my friend, this hap - pi-ness that

go - ing, and soon all those a - round can
bud - ding; the birds be-gin to sing, the
I've found; you can de-pend on him, it

warm up in its glow-ing. That's how it is with
flow - ers start their bloom-ing. That's how it is with
mat - ters not where you're bound. I'll shout it from the

God's love once you've ex - pe-ri-enced it; you spread his love to
God's love once you've ex - pe-ri-enced it; you want to sing, it's
moun-tain-top; I want my world to know; the Lord of love has

ev - ery-one; you want to pass it on.
fresh like spring, you want to pass it on.
come to me, I want to pass it on.

WORDS: Kurt Kaiser, 1969
MUSIC: Kurt Kaiser, 1969

© 1969 Communiqué Music, Inc.

PASS IT ON
Irr.

573 O Zion, Haste

1. O Zi - on, haste, thy mis- sion high ful - fill - ing,
2. Be - hold how man - y thou-sands still are ly - ing
3. Pro - claim to ev - ery peo - ple, tongue, and na - tion
4. Give of thine own to bear the mes-sage glo - rious;

to tell to all the world that God is light,
bound in the dark - some pris - on -house of sin,
that God, in whom they live and move, is love;
give of thy wealth to speed them on their way;

that he who made all na - tions is not will - ing
with none to tell them of the Sav- ior's dy - ing,
tell how he stooped to save his lost cre - a - tion,
pour out thy soul for them in prayer vic - to - rious;

one soul should per - ish, lost in shades of night.
or of the life he died for them to win.
and died on earth that we might live a - bove.
O Zi - on, haste to bring the bright - er day.

WORDS: Mary A. Thomson, 1894
MUSIC: James Walch, 1875

TIDINGS
11 10.11 10 with Refrain

Refrain

Pub - lish glad tid - ings, tid - ings of peace;

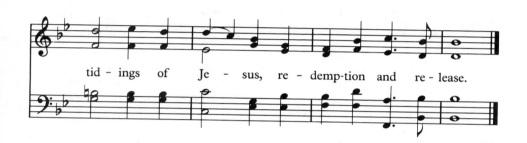

tid - ings of Je - sus, re - demp-tion and re - lease.

For Renewal of the Church 574

Renew your church, Lord,
your people in this land.
Save us from cheap words
and self-deception in your service.

In the power of your Spirit
transform us,
and shape us
by your cross. **Amen.**

South Africa, 20th cent.

© 1986 John de Gruchy

575 Onward, Christian Soldiers

1. On-ward, Chris-tian sol - diers, march-ing as to war,
2. At the sign of tri - umph Sa-tan's host doth flee;
3. Like a might-y ar - my moves the church of God;
4. Crowns and thrones may per - ish, king-doms rise and wane,
5. On-ward then, ye peo - ple, join our hap-py throng,

with the cross of Je - sus go - ing on be - fore.
on then, Chris-tian sol - diers, on to vic-to - ry!
broth-ers, we are tread - ing where the saints have trod.
but the church of Je - sus con-stant will re - main.
blend with ours your voic - es in the tri - umph song.

Christ, the roy - al Mas - ter, leads a-gainst the foe;
Hell's foun - da - tions quiv - er at the shout of praise;
We are not di - vid - ed, all one bod - y we,
Gates of hell can nev - er gainst that church pre - vail;
Glo - ry, laud, and hon - or un - to Christ the King,

for - ward in - to bat - tle see his ban-ners go!
broth-ers, lift your voic - es, loud your an-thems raise.
one in hope and doc - trine, one in char - i - ty.
we have Christ's own prom - ise, and that can-not fail.
this through count-less a - ges men and an - gels sing.

WORDS: Sabine Baring-Gould, 1864
MUSIC: Arthur S. Sullivan, 1871

ST. GERTRUDE
65.65 D with Refrain

Refrain

On-ward, Chris-tian sol – diers, march-ing as to war,

with the cross of Je – sus go – ing on be - fore.

Rise Up, O Men of God 576

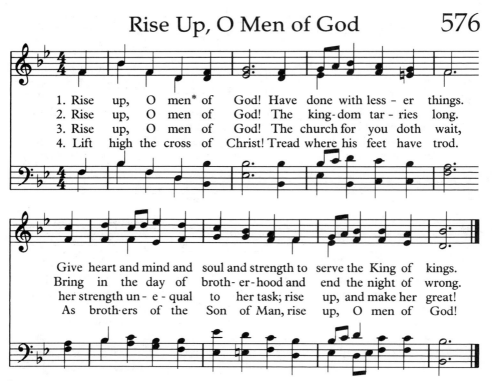

1. Rise up, O men* of God! Have done with less – er things.
2. Rise up, O men of God! The king-dom tar - ries long.
3. Rise up, O men of God! The church for you doth wait,
4. Lift high the cross of Christ! Tread where his feet have trod.

Give heart and mind and soul and strength to serve the King of kings.
Bring in the day of broth- er-hood and end the night of wrong.
her strength un - e - qual to her task; rise up, and make her great!
As broth-ers of the Son of Man, rise up, O men of God!

"Ye saints" may be substituted for "O men."

WORDS: William P. Merrill, 1911
MUSIC: William H. Walter, 1894

FESTAL SONG
SM

577 God of Grace and God of Glory

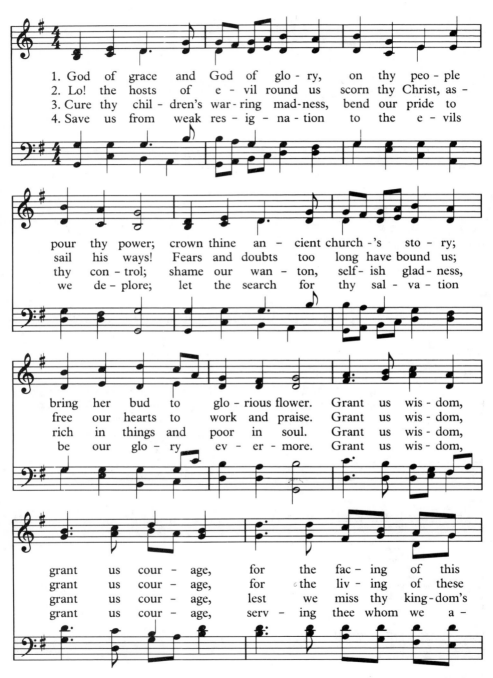

1. God of grace and God of glo - ry, on thy peo - ple
2. Lo! the hosts of e - vil round us scorn thy Christ, as -
3. Cure thy chil - dren's war - ring mad-ness, bend our pride to
4. Save us from weak res - ig - na - tion to the e - vils

pour thy power; crown thine an - cient church -'s sto - ry;
sail his ways! Fears and doubts too long have bound us;
thy con - trol; shame our wan - ton, self- ish glad - ness,
we de - plore; let the search for thy sal - va - tion

bring her bud to glo - rious flower. Grant us wis - dom,
free our hearts to work and praise. Grant us wis - dom,
rich in things and poor in soul. Grant us wis - dom,
be our glo - ry ev - er - more. Grant us wis - dom,

grant us cour - age, for the fac - ing of this
grant us cour - age, for the liv - ing of these
grant us cour - age, lest we miss thy king-dom's
grant us cour - age, serv - ing thee whom we a -

WORDS: Harry Emerson Fosdick, 1930
MUSIC: John Hughes, 1907
Words by permission of Elinor Fosdick Downs

CWM RHONDDA
87.87.87

hour, (of this hour) for the fac – ing of this hour.
days, (of these days) for the liv – ing of these days.
goal, (king-dom's goal) lest we miss thy king – dom's goal.
dore, (we a – dore) serv – ing thee whom we a – dore.

God of Love and God of Power   578

1. God of love and God of power, grant us in this burn-ing hour
2. We are not the first to be ban-ished by our fears from thee;
3. All our lives be – long to thee, thou our fi – nal loy – al – ty;
4. God of love and God of power, make us wor-thy of this hour;

grace to ask these gifts of thee, dar – ing hearts and spir – its free.
give us cour-age, let us hear heav-en's trum-pets ring-ing clear.
slaves are we when – e'er we share that de – vo – tion an – y – where.
of-fering lives if it's thy will, keep-ing free our spir – its still.

God of love and God of power, thou hast called us for this hour.

WORDS: Gerald H. Kennedy, ca. 1939
MUSIC: Joachim Neander, 1680

UNSER HERRSCHER
77.77.77

579 Lord God, Your Love Has Called Us Here

1. Lord God, your love has called us here, as we, by love, for
2. We come with self-in-flict-ed pains of bro-ken trust and
3. Lord God, in Christ you call our name, and then re-ceive us
4. Then take the towel, and break the bread, and hum-ble us, and
5. Lord God, in Christ you set us free your life to live, your

love were made; your liv-ing like-ness still we bear, though
cho-sen wrong, half-free, half-bound by in-ner chains, by
as your own; not through some mer-it, right, or claim, but
call us friends; suf-fer and serve till all are fed, and
joy to share; give us your Spir-it's lib-er-ty to

marred, dis-hon-ored, dis-o-beyed; we come, with all our
so-cial forc-es swept a-long, by powers and sys-tems
by your gra-cious love a-lone; we strain to glimpse your
show how grand-ly love in-tends to work till all cre-
turn from guilt and dull de-spair, and of-fer all that

heart and mind, your call to hear, your love to find.
close con-fined, yet seek-ing hope for hu-man-kind.
mer-cy seat, and find you kneel-ing at our feet.
a-tion sings, to fill all worlds, to crown all things.
faith can do, while love is mak-ing all things new.

WORDS: Brian Wren, 1973
MUSIC: Henry Carey, ca. 1723; harm. from *The English Hymnal*, 1906

CAREY'S (SURREY)
88.88.88

Lead On, O King Eternal

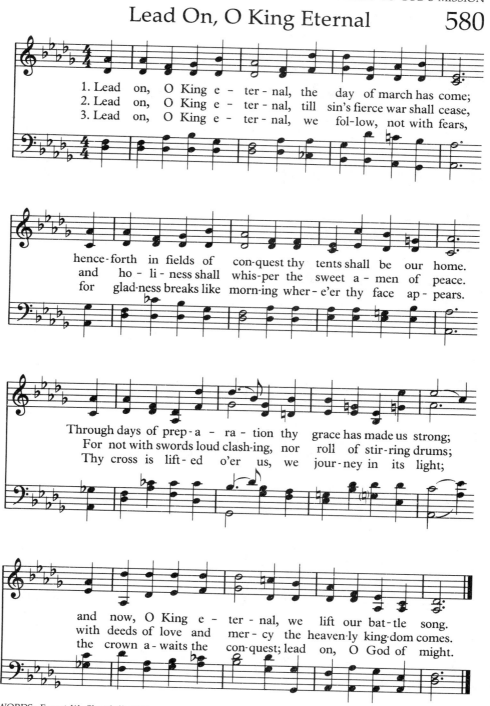

1. Lead on, O King e-ter-nal, the day of march has come;
2. Lead on, O King e-ter-nal, till sin's fierce war shall cease,
3. Lead on, O King e-ter-nal, we fol-low, not with fears,

hence-forth in fields of con-quest thy tents shall be our home.
and ho-li-ness shall whis-per the sweet a-men of peace.
for glad-ness breaks like morn-ing wher-e'er thy face ap-pears.

Through days of prep-a-ra-tion thy grace has made us strong;
For not with swords loud clash-ing, nor roll of stir-ring drums;
Thy cross is lift-ed o'er us, we jour-ney in its light;

and now, O King e-ter-nal, we lift our bat-tle song.
with deeds of love and mer-cy the heaven-ly king-dom comes.
the crown a-waits the con-quest; lead on, O God of might.

WORDS: Ernest W. Shurtleff, 1887
MUSIC: Henry T. Smart, 1835

LANCASHIRE
76.76 D

581 Lord, Whose Love Through Humble Service

1. Lord, whose love through hum-ble ser-vice bore the weight of hu-man need, who up-on the cross, for-sak-en, of-fered mer-cy's per-fect deed: we, your ser-vants, bring the wor-ship not of voice a-lone, but heart, con-se-crat-ing

2. Still your chil-dren wan-der home-less; still the hun-gry cry for bread; still the cap-tives long for free-dom; still in grief we mourn our dead. As, O Lord, your deep com-pas-sion healed the sick and freed the soul, use the love your

3. As we wor-ship, grant us vi-sion, till your love's re-veal-ing light in its height and depth and great-ness dawns up-on our quick-ened sight, mak-ing known the needs and bur-dens your com-pas-sion bids us bear, stir-ring us to

4. Called by wor-ship to your ser-vice, forth in your dear name we go to the child, the youth, the a-ged, love in liv-ing deeds to show; hope and health, good will and com-fort, coun-sel, aid, and peace we give, that your ser-vants,

WORDS: Albert F. Bayly, 1961, alt.
MUSIC: Attr. to B. F. White, 1844; harm. by Ronald A. Nelson, 1978

BEACH SPRING
87.87 D

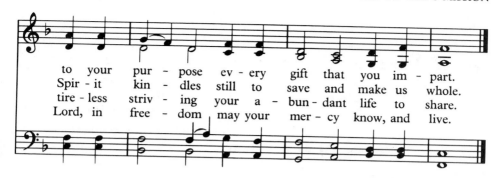

to your pur - pose ev - ery gift that you im - part.
Spir - it kin - dles still to save and make us whole.
tire - less striv - ing your a - bun - dant life to share.
Lord, in free - dom may your mer - cy know, and live.

Whom Shall I Send? 582

Unison

1. Whom shall I send? our Mak - er cries; and man - y,
2. For who can serve a God so pure, or claim to
3. And yet, be - liev - ing God who calls knows what we
4. Those who are called God pu - ri - fies, and dai - ly

when they hear God's voice, are sure where their vo -
speak in such a name, while doubt makes ev - ery
are and still may be, our past de - feats, our
gives us strength to bend our thoughts, our skills, our

ca - tion lies; but man - y shrink from such a choice.
step un - sure, and self con - fus - es ev - ery aim?
fu - ture falls, we dare to an - swer: Lord, send me!
en - er - gies, and life it - self to this one end.

WORDS: Fred Pratt Green, 1970 (Is. 6:8)
MUSIC: *Grenoble Antiphoner*, 1753; adapt. by Ralph Vaughan Williams, 1906; harm. by Basil Harwood, 1908
Words © 1971 Hope Publishing Co.

DEUS TUORUM MILITUM
LM

583 Sois la Semilla
(You Are the Seed)

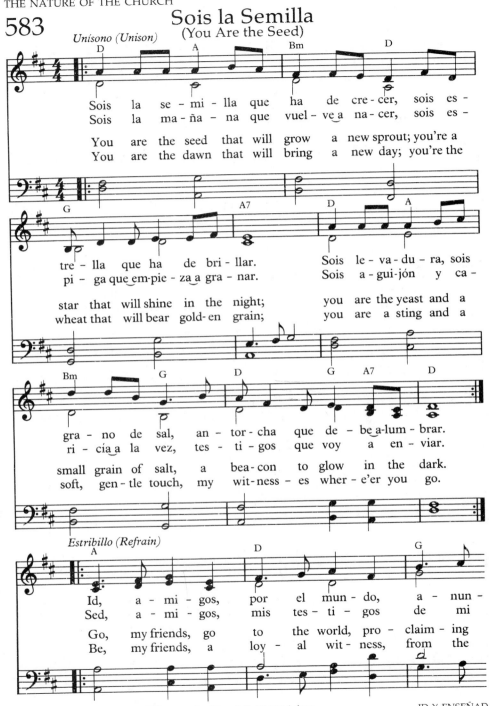

Unísono (Unison)

Sois la se-mi-lla que ha de cre-cer, sois es-
Sois la ma-ña-na que vuel-ve a na-cer, sois es-

You are the seed that will grow a new sprout; you're a
You are the dawn that will bring a new day; you're the

tre-lla que ha de bri-llar. Sois le-va-du-ra, sois
pi-ga que em-pie-za a gra-nar. Sois a-gui-jón y ca-

star that will shine in the night; you are the yeast and a
wheat that will bear gold-en grain; you are a sting and a

gra-no de sal, an-tor-cha que de-be a-lum-brar.
ri-cía a la vez, tes-ti-gos que voy a en-viar.

small grain of salt, a bea-con to glow in the dark.
soft, gen-tle touch, my wit-ness-es wher-e'er you go.

Estribillo (Refrain)

Id, a-mi-gos, por el mun-do, a-nun-
Sed, a-mi-gos, mis tes-ti-gos de mi

Go, my friends, go to the world, pro-claim-ing
Be, my friends, a loy-al wit-ness, from the

WORDS: Cesareo Gabaraín, 1979; trans. by Raquel Gutiérrez-Achon
and Skinner Chávez-Melo (Mt. 28:19-20)
MUSIC: Cesareo Gabaraín, 1979; harm. by Skinner Chávez-Melo, 1987

ID Y ENSEÑAD
10 9.10 8 with Refrain

cian - do el a - mor,   men - sa - je - ros de la vi - da,
re - su - rrec - ción.   Id lle - van - do mi pre - sen - cia;
love to all,   mes - sen - gers of my for - giv - ing peace,
dead I a - rose;   "Lo, I'll be with you for - ev - er,

de la paz y el per - dón.   con vo - so - tros es - toy.
e - ter - nal love.   till the end of the world."

2.
Sois una llama que ha de encender
resplandores de fe y caridad.
Sois los pastores que han de llevar
al mundo por sendas de paz.
Sois los amigos que quise escoger,
sois palabra que intento esparcir.
Sois reino nuevo que empieza a engendrar
justicia, amor y verdad.
Estribillo

3.
Sois fuego y sabia que vine a traer,
sois la ola que agita la mar.
La levadura pequeña de ayer
fermenta la masa del pan.
Una ciudad no se puede esconder,
ni los montes se han de ocultar,
en vuestras obras que buscan el bien
el mundo al Padre verá.
Estribillo

2.
You are the flame that will lighten the dark,
sending sparkles of hope, faith, and love;
you are the shepherds to lead the whole world
through valleys and pastures of peace.
You are the friends that I chose for myself,
the word that I want to proclaim.
You are the new kingdom built on a rock
where justice and truth always reign.
Refrain

3.
You are the life that will nurture the plant;
you're the waves in a turbulent sea;
yesterday's yeast is beginning to rise,
a new loaf of bread it will yield.
There is no place for a city to hide,
nor a mountain can cover its might;
may your good deeds show a world in despair
a path that will lead all to God.
Refrain

584 Lord, You Give the Great Commission

1. Lord, you give the great com-mis-sion: "Heal the sick and
2. Lord, you call us to your ser-vice: "In my name bap-
3. Lord, you make the com-mon ho-ly: "This my bod-y,
4. Lord, you show us love's true mea-sure: "Fa-ther, what they
5. Lord, you bless with words as-sur-ing: "I am with you

preach the word." Lest the church ne-glect its mis-sion,
tize and teach." That the world may trust your prom-ise,
this my blood." Let us all, for earth's true glo-ry,
do, for-give." Yet we hoard as pri-vate trea-sure
to the end." Faith and hope and love re-stor-ing,

and the gos-pel go un-heard, help us wit-ness
life a-bun-dant meant for each, give us all new
dai-ly lift life heav-en-ward, ask-ing that the
all that you so free-ly give. May your care and
may we serve as you in-tend and, a-mid the

to your pur-pose with re-newed in-teg-ri-ty.
fer-vor, draw us clos-er in com-mun-i-ty.
world a-round us share your chil-dren's lib-er-ty.
mer-cy lead us to a just so-ci-e-ty.
cares that claim us, hold in mind e-ter-ni-ty.

WORDS: Jeffery Rowthorn, 1978 (Lk. 9:2; Mt. 28:19-20; Lk. 23:34)
MUSIC: Cyril V. Taylor, 1941

ABBOT'S LEIGH
87.87 D

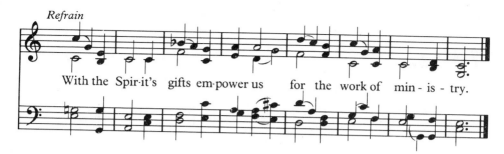

Refrain

With the Spir·it's gifts em·power us for the work of min - is - try.

This Little Light of Mine 585

1. This lit - tle light of mine, I'm goin'- a let it shine,

this lit - tle light of mine, I'm goin'- a let it shine;

this lit - tle light of mine, I'm goin'- a let it shine,

let it shine, let it shine, let it shine. (let it shine)

2. Everywhere I go
3. All through the night

WORDS: Afro-American spiritual (Mt. 5:14-16)
MUSIC: Afro-American spiritual; adapt. by William Farley Smith, 1987

LATTIMER
Irr.

Adapt. © 1989 The United Methodist Publishing House

586 Let My People Seek Their Freedom

1. "Let my peo-ple seek their free-dom in the
2. "Let my peo-ple seek their free-dom in the
3. When we mur-mur on the moun-tains for the
4. In the mael-strom of the na-tions, in the

wil - der - ness a - while, from the slave pens of the
wil - der - ness a - while, from the ag-ing shrines and
old E - gyp - tian plains, when we miss our an - cient
jour-neying in - to space, in the clash of gen - er -

Del - ta, from the ghet - tos on the Nile":
struc - tures, from the clois - ter and the aisle":
bond - age, and the hope, the prom - ise, wanes;
a - tions, in the hun - ger - ing for grace,

so God spoke from out of Si - nai, so God spoke and
so the Son of God has spo - ken, and the storm clouds
then the rock shall yield its wa - ter and the man-na
in our ag - o - ny and glo - ry, we are called to

WORDS: T. Herbert O'Driscoll, 1971 (Dt. 8:14-18)   EBENEZER
MUSIC: Thomas J. Williams, 1890   87.87 D

it was done, and a peo-ple crossed the
are un-furled, for God's peo-ple must be
fall by night, and with vi-sions of a
new-er ways by the Lord of our to -

wa-ters toward the ris - ing of the sun.
scat-tered to be ser - vants in the world.
fu-ture shall we march to - ward the light.
mor-rows and the God of earth's to - days.

Bless Thou the Gifts 587

Unison

Bless thou the gifts our hands have brought; bless

thou the work our hearts have planned. Ours is the faith, the

will, the thought; the rest, O God, is in thy hand.

WORDS: Samuel Longfellow, ca. 1886
MUSIC: *Grenoble Antiphoner*, 1753; adapt. by Ralph Vaughan Williams, 1906;
harm. by Basil Harwood, 1908

DEUS TUORUM MILITUM
LM

Alt. tune: CANONBURY

588 All Things Come of Thee

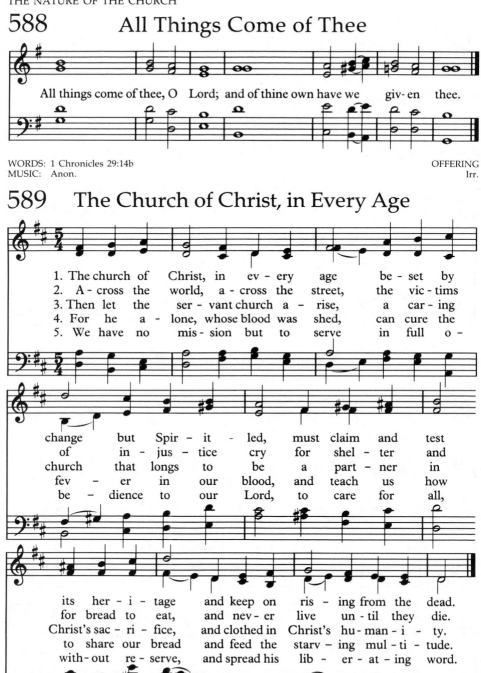

All things come of thee, O Lord; and of thine own have we giv-en thee.

WORDS: 1 Chronicles 29:14b
MUSIC: Anon.

OFFERING
Irr.

589 The Church of Christ, in Every Age

1. The church of Christ, in ev-ery age be-set by
2. A-cross the world, a-cross the street, the vic-tims
3. Then let the ser-vant church a-rise, a car-ing
4. For he a-lone, whose blood was shed, can cure the
5. We have no mis-sion but to serve in full o-

change but Spir-it-led, must claim and test
of in-jus-tice cry for shel-ter and
church that longs to be a part-ner in
fev-er in our blood, and teach us how
be-dience to our Lord, to care for all,

its her-i-tage and keep on ris-ing from the dead.
for bread to eat, and nev-er live un-til they die.
Christ's sac-ri-fice, and clothed in Christ's hu-man-i-ty.
to share our bread and feed the starv-ing mul-ti-tude.
with-out re-serve, and spread his lib-er-at-ing word.

WORDS: Fred Pratt Green, 1969
MUSIC: Lee Hastings Bristol, Jr., 1962

DICKINSON COLLEGE
LM

Words © 1971 Hope Publishing Co.; music © 1962 Theodore Presser Co.

Christ Loves the Church

590

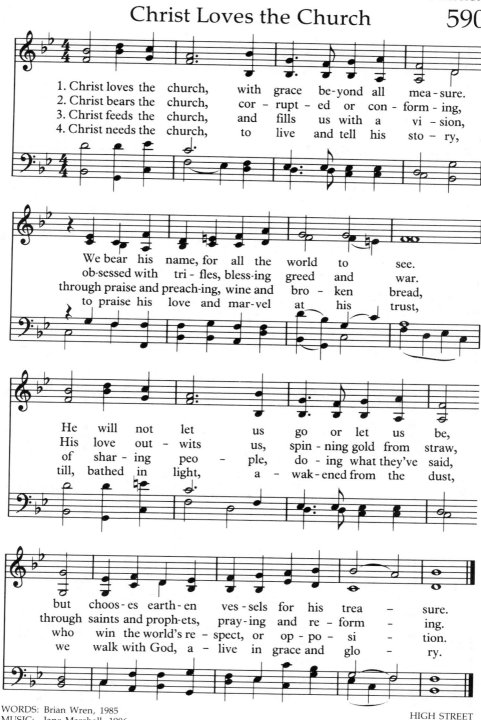

1. Christ loves the church, with grace be-yond all mea-sure.
2. Christ bears the church, cor - rupt - ed or con - form - ing,
3. Christ feeds the church, and fills us with a vi - sion,
4. Christ needs the church, to live and tell his sto - ry,

We bear his name, for all the world to see.
ob-sessed with tri - fles, bless-ing greed and war.
through praise and preach-ing, wine and bro - ken bread,
to praise his love and mar-vel at his trust,

He will not let us go or let us be,
His love out - wits us, spin - ning gold from straw,
of shar - ing peo - ple, do - ing what they've said,
till, bathed in light, a - wak-ened from the dust,

but choos-es earth-en ves-sels for his trea - sure.
through saints and proph-ets, pray-ing and re - form - ing.
who win the world's re - spect, or op - po - si - tion.
we walk with God, a - live in grace and glo - ry.

WORDS: Brian Wren, 1985
MUSIC: Jane Marshall, 1986

© 1986 Hope Publishing Co.

HIGH STREET
11 10.10 11

591   Rescue the Perishing

1. Rescue the perishing, care for the dying,
2. Though they are slighting him, still he is waiting,
3. Down in the human heart, crushed by the tempter,
4. Rescue the perishing, duty demands it;

snatch them in pity from sin and the grave;
waiting the penitent child to receive;
feelings lie buried that grace can restore;
strength for thy labor the Lord will provide;

weep o'er the erring one, lift up the fallen,
plead with them earnestly, plead with them gently;
touched by a loving heart, wakened by kindness,
back to the narrow way patiently win them;

tell them of Jesus, the mighty to save.
he will forgive if they only believe.
chords that were broken will vibrate once more.
tell the poor wanderer a Savior has died.

Refrain

Rescue the perishing, care for the dying;

WORDS: Fanny J. Crosby, 1869
MUSIC: William H. Doane, 1870

RESCUE
6 5 10 D

Je – sus is mer – ci – ful, Je – sus will save.

When the Church of Jesus 592

Unison

1. When the church of Je – sus shuts its out – er door,
2. If our hearts are lift – ed where de – vo – tion soars
3. Lest the gifts we of – fer, mon-ey, tal – ents, time,

lest the roar of traf – fic drown the voice of prayer,
high a – bove this hun – gry, suf-fering world of ours,
serve to salve our con – science, to our se – cret shame,

may our prayers, Lord, make us ten times more a – ware
lest our hymns should drug us to for – get its needs,
Lord, re-prove, in – spire us by the way you give;

that the world we ban – ish is our Chris – tian care.
forge our Chris-tian wor – ship in – to Chris – tian deeds.
teach us, dy – ing Sav – ior, how true Chris – tians live.

WORDS: Fred Pratt Green, 1968 (Jas. 2:14-17)
MUSIC: Ralph Vaughan Williams, 1925

KING'S WESTON
65.65 D

593 Here I Am, Lord

Unison

1. I, the Lord of sea and sky,   I have heard my peo-ple cry.
   I who made the stars of night,   I will make their dark-ness bright.

2. I, the Lord of snow and rain,   I have borne my peo-ple's pain.
   I will break their hearts of stone,   give them hearts for love a-lone.

3. I, the Lord of wind and flame,   I will tend the poor and lame,
   Fin-est bread I will pro-vide   till their hearts be sat-is-fied.

All who dwell in dark and sin   my hand will save.
Who will bear my light to them?

I have wept for love of them.   They turn a-way.
I will speak my word to them.

I will set a feast for them.   My hand will save.
I will give my life to them.

2.

Whom shall I send?
Whom shall I send?
Whom shall I send?

Refrain (Harmony)

Here I am, Lord.

WORDS: Dan Schutte, 1981 (Is. 6:8)
MUSIC: Dan Schutte, 1981; adapt. by Carlton R. Young, 1988

HERE I AM, LORD
77.74 D with Refrain

Is it I, Lord? I have heard you call-ing in the night. I will go, Lord, if you lead me. I will hold your peo - ple in my heart.

CALLED TO GOD'S MISSION, *see further:*

97 For the Fruits of This Creation   650 Give Me the Faith Which Can Remove

594   Come, Divine Interpreter

Come, divine Interpreter,
bring me eyes thy book to read,
ears the mystic words to hear,
words which did from thee proceed,
words that endless bliss impart,
kept in an obedient heart.

All who read, or hear, are blessed,
if thy plain commands we do;
of thy kingdom here possessed,
thee we shall in glory view
when thou comest on earth to abide,
reign triumphant at thy side.

Charles Wesley, 1762

595   Whether the Word Be Preached or Read

Whether the Word be preached or read,
no saving benefit I gain
from empty sounds or letters dead;
unprofitable all and vain,
unless by faith thy word I hear
and see its heavenly character.

Unmixed with faith, the Scripture gives
no comfort, life, or light to see,
but me in darker darkness leaves,
implunged in deeper misery,
overwhelmed with nature's sorest ills.
The Spirit saves, the letter kills.

If God enlighten through his Word,
I shall my kind Enlightener bless;
but void and naked of my Lord,
what are all verbal promises?
Nothing to me, till faith divine
inspire, inspeak, and make them mine.

Jesus, the appropriating grace
'tis thine on sinners to bestow.
Open mine eyes to see thy face,
open my heart thyself to know.
And then I through thy Word obtain
sure present, and eternal gain.

Charles Wesley, 1783 (2 Cor. 3:5-6)

Blessed Jesus, at Thy Word

596

1. Bless-ed Je-sus, at thy word we are gath-ered
2. All our knowl-edge, sense, and sight lie in deep-est
3. Glo-rious Lord, thy-self im-part! Light of light, from

all to hear thee; let our hearts and souls be stirred
dark-ness shroud-ed, till thy spir-it breaks our night
God pro-ceed-ing, o-pen thou our ears and heart;

now to seek and love and fear thee, by thy teach-ings
with the beams of truth un-cloud-ed. Thou a-lone to
help us by thy spir-it's plead-ing; hear the cry thy

sweet and ho-ly, drawn from earth to love thee sole-ly.
God canst win us; thou must work all good with-in us.
peo-ple rais-es; hear, and bless our prayers and prais-es.

WORDS: Tobias Clausnitzer, 1663; trans. by Catherine Winkworth, 1858
MUSIC: Johann R. Ahle, 1664

LIEBSTER JESU
78.78.88

597 For the Spirit of Truth

From the cowardice that dares not face new truth,
from the laziness that is contented with half-truth,
from the arrogance that thinks it knows all truth,
Good Lord, deliver me. **Amen.**

Prayer from Kenya

598 O Word of God Incarnate

1. O Word of God in - car - nate, O Wis - dom
2. The church from you, our Sav - ior, re - ceived the
3. The Scrip - ture is a ban - ner be - fore God's
4. O make your church, dear Sav - ior, a lamp of

from on high, O Truth un-changed, un - chang - ing, O
gift di - vine, and still that light is lift - ed o'er
host un - furled; it is a shin - ing bea - con a -
pur - est gold, to bear be - fore the na - tions your

Light of our dark sky: we praise you for the
all the earth to shine. It is the sa - cred
bove the dark - ling world. It is the chart and
true light as of old. O teach your wan - dering

ra - diance that from the hal -lowed page, a lan - tern
ves - sel where gems of truth are stored; it is the
com - pass that o'er life's surg - ing tide, mid mists and
pil - grims by this their path to trace, till, clouds and

WORDS: William W. How, 1867
MUSIC: *Gesangbuch*, Meiningen, 1693; harm. by Felix Mendelssohn, 1847

MUNICH
76.76 D

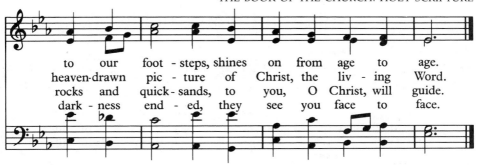

to our foot - steps, shines on from age to age.
heaven-drawn pic - ture of Christ, the liv - ing Word.
rocks and quick-sands, to you, O Christ, will guide.
dark - ness end - ed, they see you face to face.

Break Thou the Bread of Life 599

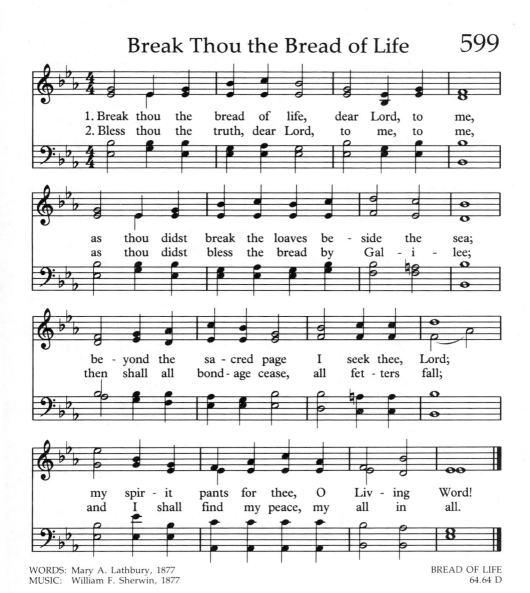

1. Break thou the bread of life, dear Lord, to me,
2. Bless thou the truth, dear Lord, to me, to me,

as thou didst break the loaves be - side the sea;
as thou didst bless the bread by Gal - i - lee;

be - yond the sa - cred page I seek thee, Lord;
then shall all bond - age cease, all fet - ters fall;

my spir - it pants for thee, O Liv - ing Word!
and I shall find my peace, my all in all.

WORDS: Mary A. Lathbury, 1877
MUSIC: William F. Sherwin, 1877

BREAD OF LIFE
64.64 D

600 Wonderful Words of Life

1. Sing them o - ver a - gain to me, won-der-ful words of life;
2. Christ, the bless-ed one, gives to all won-der-ful words of life;
3. Sweet-ly ech - o the gos - pel call, won-der-ful words of life;

let me more of their beau - ty see, won-der-ful words of life;
sin - ner, list to the lov - ing call, won-der-ful words of life;
of - fer par-don and peace to all, won-der-ful words of life;

words of life and beau - ty teach me faith and du - ty.
all so free - ly giv - en, woo - ing us to heav - en.
Je - sus, on - ly Sav - ior, sanc - ti - fy for - ev - er.

Refrain

Beau-ti - ful words, won-der-ful words, won-der-ful words of life.

Beau-ti - ful words, won-der-ful words, won-der-ful words of life.

WORDS: Philip P. Bliss, 1874
MUSIC: Philip P. Bliss, 1874

WORDS OF LIFE
86.86.66

Thy Word Is a Lamp

601

WORDS: Amy Grant, 1984 (Ps. 119:105)
MUSIC: Michael W. Smith 1984; arr. by Keith Phillips

THY WORD
Irr. with Refrain

602 Concerning the Scriptures

Blessed Lord, you have caused all holy Scriptures to be written for our learning. Grant us so to hear them, read, mark, learn, and inwardly digest them, that we may embrace and ever hold fast the blessed hope of everlasting life, which you have given us in our Savior Jesus Christ, who lives and reigns with you and the Holy Spirit, One God, forever and ever. **Amen.**

After *The Book of Common Prayer*

603 Come, Holy Ghost, Our Hearts Inspire

1. Come, Ho - ly Ghost, our hearts in - spire, let us thine in - fluence prove; source of the old pro - phet - ic fire, foun - tain of life and love.
2. Come, Ho - ly Ghost (for moved by thee the proph - ets wrote and spoke), un - lock the truth, thy - self the key, un - seal the sa - cred book.
3. Ex - pand thy wings, ce - les - tial Dove, brood o'er our na - ture's night; on our dis - or - dered spir - its move, and let there now be light.
4. God, through the Spir - it we shall know if thou with - in us shine, and sound, with all thy saints be - low, the depths of love di - vine.

WORDS: Charles Wesley, 1740
MUSIC: Est's *Whole Booke of Psalmes,* 1592; harm. from *Hymns Ancient and Modern,* 1861

WINCHESTER OLD
CM

THE BOOK OF THE CHURCH: HOLY SCRIPTURE, *see further:*

Praise and Thanksgiving Be to God 604

1. Praise and thanks - giv - ing be to God our mak - er,
2. Not our own ho - li - ness nor that we have striv - en
3. Come, Ho - ly Spir - it, come in vis - i - ta - tion;
4. Praise to the Fa - ther, Son, and Ho - ly Spir - it;

source of all bless - ing, prod - i - gal cre - a - tor.
brings us the peace which you, O Christ, have giv - en.
you are the truth, our hope, and our sal - va - tion.
one Lord, one faith, one source of ev - ery mer - it.

Bap - tized and made your own, now we come be -
Bap - tized and set a - part, strength - en us, O
Bap - tize with joy and power, give, O Dove de -
Here now re - new your church through this wa - ter

fore you, while we a - dore you.
Sav - ior, with grace and fa - vor.
scend - ing, life nev - er end - ing.
giv - en; grant peace from heav - en.

WORDS: H. Francis Yardley, 1982 (Lk. 3:21-22)
MUSIC: *Paris Antiphoner*, 1681; harm. by David Evans, 1927; alt.

CHRISTE SANCTORUM
11 11 11.5

Words © 1982 H. Francis Yardley; harm. by permission of Oxford University Press

605 Wash, O God, Our Sons and Daughters

1. Wash, O God, our sons and daugh-ters, where your cleans-ing
2. We who bring them long for nur-ture; by your milk may
3. O how deep your ho-ly wis-dom! Un-im-ag-ined,

wa-ters flow. Num-ber them a-mong your peo-ple;
we be fed. Let us join your feast, par-tak-ing
all your ways! To your name be glo-ry, hon-or!

bless as Christ blessed long a-go. Weave them gar-ments bright and
cup of bless-ing, liv-ing bread. God, re-new us, guide our
With our lives we wor-ship, praise! We your peo-ple stand be-

spark-ling; com-pass them with love and light. Fill, a-noint them;
foot-steps; free from sin and all its snares, one with Christ in
fore you, wa-ter-washed and Spir-it-born. By your grace, our

send your Spir-it, ho-ly dove and heart's de-light.
liv-ing, dy-ing, by your Spir-it, chil-dren, heirs.
lives we of-fer. Re-cre-ate us; God, trans-form!

WORDS: Ruth Duck, 1987 (Jn. 3:3-8)
MUSIC: Attr. to B. F. White, 1844; harm. by Ronald A. Nelson, 1978

BEACH SPRING
87.87 D

Come, Let Us Use the Grace Divine 606

1. Come, let us use the grace di-vine, and all with
2. The cov-enant we this mo-ment make be ev-er
3. Thee, Fa-ther, Son, and Ho-ly Ghost, let all our

one ac-cord, in a per-pet-ual cove-nant join
kept in mind; we will no more our God for-sake,
hearts re-ceive, pres-ent with thy ce-les-tial host

our-selves to Christ the Lord; give up our-selves, thru
or cast these words be-hind. We nev-er will throw
the peace-ful an-swer give; to each cov-e-nant the

Je-sus' power, his name to glo-ri-fy; and prom-ise,
off the fear of God who hears our vow; and if thou
blood ap-ply which takes our sins a-way, and reg-is-

in this sa-cred hour, for God to live and die.
art well pleased to hear, come down and meet us now.
ter our names on high and keep us to that day!

WORDS: Charles Wesley, 1762 (Jer. 50:5)
MUSIC: English melody; arr. by Ralph Vaughan Williams, 1906

KINGSFOLD
CMD

607 A Covenant Prayer in the Wesleyan Tradition

I am no longer my own, but thine.
Put me to what thou wilt, rank me with whom thou wilt.
Put me to doing, put me to suffering.
Let me be employed by thee or laid aside for thee,
exalted for thee or brought low for thee.
Let me be full, let me be empty.
Let me have all things, let me have nothing.
I freely and heartily yield all things
to thy pleasure and disposal.
And now, O glorious and blessed God,
Father, Son, and Holy Spirit,
thou art mine, and I am thine. So be it.
And the covenant which I have made on earth,
let it be ratified in heaven. **Amen.**

608 This Is the Spirit's Entry Now

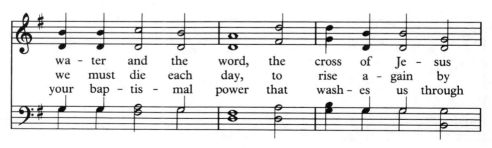

WORDS: Thomas E. Herbranson, 1972 (Rom. 6:3-4)
MUSIC: Carl G. Gläzer; arr. by Lowell Mason, 1839

AZMON
CM

Words © 1972 Thomas E. Herbranson

on your brow, the seal both felt and heard.
his de - sign as fol - lowers of his way.
all our days. Lord, cleanse a - gain this hour.

You Have Put On Christ 609

You have put on Christ, in

*Ped.

Christ you have been bap - tized. Al - le - lu -

ia! Al - le - lu - ia!

*Notes with stems down in bass clef are to be played on organ pedals.

WORDS: From the Rite of Baptism for Children, ICEL (Gal. 3:27)
MUSIC: Howard Hughes, S.M., 1977

BAPTIZED IN CHRIST
Irr.

610 We Know That Christ Is Raised

1. We know that Christ is raised and dies no more.
2. We share by wa-ter in his sav-ing death.
3. A new cre-a-tion comes to life and grows

Em-braced by death, he broke its fear-ful hold,
Re-born, we share with him an Eas-ter life
as Christ's new bod-y takes on flesh and blood.

and our de-spair he turned to blaz-ing joy.
as liv-ing mem-bers of a liv-ing Christ.
The un-i-verse re-stored and whole will sing:

Al - le - lu - ia! Al - le - lu - ia!

WORDS: John Brownlow Geyer, 1969 (Rom. 6:3-11)
MUSIC: Charles Villiers Stanford, 1904

ENGELBERG
10 10 10 with Alleluias

Words by permission of John Brownlow Geyer

Child of Blessing, Child of Promise 611

1. Child of bless - ing, child of prom - ise, bap - tized with the Spir - it's sign; with this wa - ter God has sealed you un - to love and grace di - vine.
2. Child of love, our love's ex - pres - sion, love's cre - a - tion, loved in - deed! Fresh from God, re - fresh our spir - its, in - to joy and laugh - ter lead.
3. Child of joy, our dear - est trea - sure, God's you are, from God you came. Back to God we hum - bly give you; live as one who bears Christ's name.
4. Child of God your lov - ing Par - ent, learn to know whose child you are. Grow to laugh and sing and wor - ship, trust and love God more than all.

WORDS: Ronald S. Cole-Turner, 1981
MUSIC: Attr. to C. F. Witt, 1715; adapt. by Henry J. Gauntlett, 1861

STUTTGART
87.87

Words © 1981 Ronald S. Cole-Turner

BAPTISM, CONFIRMATION, REAFFIRMATION, *see further:*

502 Thy Holy Wings, O Savior

612 Deck Thyself, My Soul, with Gladness

WORDS: Johann Franck, 1649; trans. by Catherine Winkworth, 1863 (Jn. 6:35-58) SCHMÜCKE DICH
MUSIC: Johann Crüger, 1653 LMD

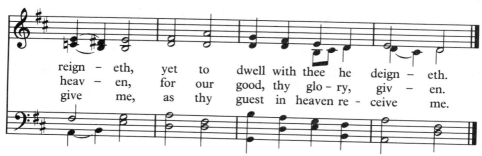

reign – eth, yet to dwell with thee he deign – eth.
heav – en, for our good, thy glo – ry, giv – en.
give me, as thy guest in heaven re – ceive me.

O Thou Who This Mysterious Bread 613

1. O Thou who this mys – ter – ious bread didst
2. Un – seal the vol – ume of thy grace, ap –
3. Of thee com – mun – ing still, we mourn till
4. En – kin – dle now the heaven – ly zeal, and

in Em – ma – us break, re – turn, here – with our
ply the gos – pel word; o – pen our eyes to
thou the veil re – move; talk with us, and our
make thy mer – cy known, and give our par – doned

souls to feed, and to thy fol – lowers speak.
see thy face, our hearts to know the Lord.
hearts shall burn with flames of fer – vent love.
souls to feel that God and love are one.

WORDS: Charles Wesley, 1745 (Lk. 24:13-35)
MUSIC: USA folk melody; arr. by Annabel Morris Buchanan, 1938;
  harm. by Charles H. Webb, 1988

LAND OF REST
CM

614 For the Bread Which You Have Broken

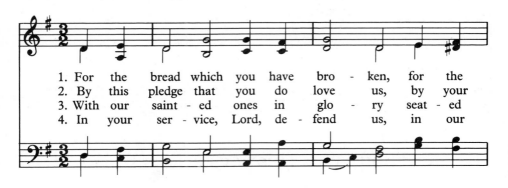

1. For the bread which you have bro - ken, for the
2. By this pledge that you do love us, by your
3. With our saint - ed ones in glo - ry seat - ed
4. In your ser - vice, Lord, de - fend us, in our

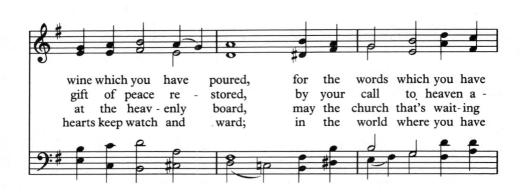

wine which you have poured, for the words which you have
gift of peace re - stored, by your call to heaven a -
at the heav - enly board, may the church that's wait - ing
hearts keep watch and ward; in the world where you have

spo - ken, now we give you thanks, O Lord.
bove us, hal - low all our lives, O Lord.
for you keep love's tie un - bro - ken, Lord.
sent us, let your king - dom come, O Lord.

WORDS: Louis F. Benson, 1924 (Mt. 26:26-29; Mk. 14:22-25; Lk. 22:15-20;
1 Cor. 11:23-26)
MUSIC: V. Earle Copes, 1960

FOR THE BREAD
87.87

For the Bread Which You Have Broken   615

Unison

1. For the bread which you have bro-ken, for the
1. *Mí - pau Chú Lí ūi goán lâi peh, Phû - tô -*
2. By this pledge that you do love us, by your
3. With our saint-ed ones in glo-ry seat-ed
4. In your ser-vice, Lord, de-fend us, in our

wine which you have poured, for the words which
chiú ūi goán lâi thîn; Ūi Lí só kóng
gift of peace re-stored, by your call to
at the heav-enly board, may the church that's
hearts keep watch and ward; in the world where

you have spo-ken, now we give you thanks, O Lord.
oáh - miā ê oē, Chú goán kám - siā, sim lâi gîm.
heaven a-bove us, hal-low all our lives, O Lord.
wait-ing for you keep love's tie un - bro-ken, Lord.
you have sent us, let your king-dom come, O Lord.

WORDS: Louis F. Benson, 1924; phonetic transcription from the Taiwanese
 by I-to Loh, 1988 (Mt. 26:26-29; Mk. 14:22-25; Lk. 22:15-20; 1 Cor. 11:23-26)
MUSIC: I-to Loh, 1970

BENG-LI
87.87

616   Come, Sinners, to the Gospel Feast

1. Come, sin - ners, to the gos - pel feast, let ev - ery
2. Do not be - gin to make ex - cuse; ah! do not
3. Come and par - take the gos - pel feast, be saved from
4. See him set forth be - fore your eyes; be - hold the
5. Ye who be - lieve his rec - ord true shall sup with

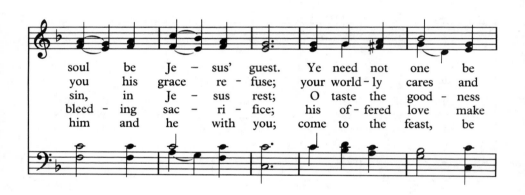

soul be Je - sus' guest. Ye need not one be
you his grace re - fuse; your world - ly cares and
sin, in Je - sus rest; O taste the good - ness
bleed - ing sac - ri - fice; his of - fered love make
him and he with you; come to the feast, be

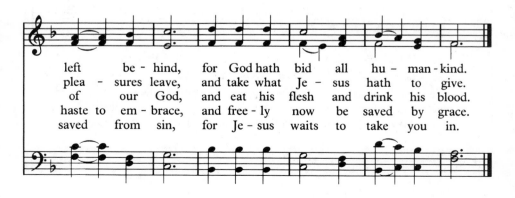

left be - hind, for God hath bid all hu - man - kind.
plea - sures leave, and take what Je - sus hath to give.
of our God, and eat his flesh and drink his blood.
haste to em - brace, and free - ly now be saved by grace.
saved from sin, for Je - sus waits to take you in.

WORDS: Charles Wesley, 1747 (Lk. 14:16-24)   HURSLEY
MUSIC: *Katholisches Gesangbuch*, ca. 1774; adapt. from *Metrical Psalter*, 1855   LM

I Come with Joy

Unison

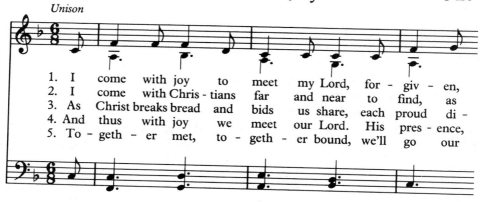

1. I come with joy to meet my Lord, for - giv - en,
2. I come with Chris - tians far and near to find, as
3. As Christ breaks bread and bids us share, each proud di -
4. And thus with joy we meet our Lord. His pres - ence,
5. To - geth - er met, to - geth - er bound, we'll go our

loved and free, in awe and won - der to re - call his
all are fed, the new com-mun - i - ty of love in
vi - sion ends. The love that made us makes us one, and
al - ways near, is in such friend - ship bet - ter known; we
dif - ferent ways, and as his peo - ple in the world, we'll

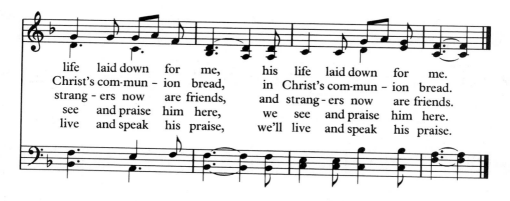

life laid down for me, his life laid down for me.
Christ's com-mun - ion bread, in Christ's com-mun - ion bread.
strang - ers now are friends, and strang-ers now are friends.
see and praise him here, we see and praise him here.
live and speak his praise, we'll live and speak his praise.

WORDS: Brian Wren, 1968 (1 Cor. 10:16-17)
MUSIC: *The Southern Harmony*, 1835; harm. by Charles H. Webb, 1987

DOVE OF PEACE
CM

Words © 1971 Hope Publishing Co.; harm. © 1989 The United Methodist Publishing House

618 Let Us Break Bread Together

1. Let us break bread to-geth-er on our knees, (on our knees)
(2. Let us) drink wine to-geth-er on our knees, (on our knees)
(3. Let us) praise God to-geth-er on our knees, (on our knees)

let us break bread to-geth-er on our knees. (on our knees)
let us drink wine to-geth-er on our knees. (on our knees)
let us praise God to-geth-er on our knees. (on our knees)

When I fall on my knees with my face to the ris-ing sun,

O Lord, have mer-cy on me. (on me) 2. Let us
3. Let us

*May end after stanza 3

WORDS: Afro-American spiritual (Acts 2:42)
MUSIC: Afro-American spiritual; adapt. and arr. by William Farley Smith, 1986

LET US BREAK BREAD
10 10 with Refrain

Adapt. and arr. © 1989 The United Methodist Publishing House

me) 4. Let us praise God to - geth-er on our knees, (on our knees)

let us praise God to - geth-er on our knees. (on our knees)

When I fall on my knees with my face to the ris - ing sun,

Fine

O Lord, have mer-cy if you please. (if you please)

619 Now the Silence

Now the si - lence Now the peace Now the emp - ty hands up-

lift - ed Now the kneel - ing Now the plea Now the Fa - ther's

arms in wel - come Now the hear - ing Now the power

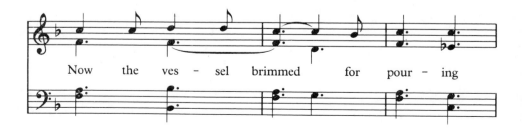

Now the ves - sel brimmed for pour - ing

WORDS: Jaroslav J. Vajda, 1968
MUSIC: Carl F. Schalk, 1969

© 1969 Hope Publishing Co.

NOW
Irr.

620 One Bread, One Body

WORDS: John B. Foley, 1978 (1 Cor. 10:16-17; Gal. 3:28; 1 Cor. 12)
MUSIC: John B. Foley, 1978; harm. by Gary Alan Smith, 1988

ONE BREAD, ONE BODY
44.6 with Refrain

1. Gen-tile or Jew, ser-vant or free,
2. Man-y the gifts, man-y the works,
3. Grain for the fields, scat-tered and grown,

wom- an or man, no more.
one in the Lord of all. One
gath-ered to one, for all.

Be Present at Our Table, Lord 621

Be pres- ent at our ta - ble, Lord; be here and
ev - ery - where a - dored; thy crea - tures bless, and
grant that we may feast in par - a - dise with thee.

WORDS: John Cennick, 1741, alt.
MUSIC: Attr. to Louis Bourgeois, 1551

OLD 100th
LM

622 There Is a Fountain Filled with Blood

1. There is a foun - tain filled with blood drawn
2. The dy - ing thief re - joiced to see that
3. Dear dy - ing Lamb, thy pre - cious blood shall
4. E'er since, by faith, I saw the stream thy
5. Then in a no - bler, sweet - er song, I'll

from Em - man - uel's veins; and sin - ners plunged be -
foun - tain in his day; and there may I, though
nev - er lose its power till all the ran - somed
flow - ing wounds sup - ply, re - deem - ing love has
sing thy power to save, when this poor lisp - ing,

neath that flood lose all their guilt - y stains.
vile as he, wash all my sins a - way.
church of God be saved, to sin no more.
been my theme, and shall be till I die.
stam - mering tongue lies si - lent in the grave.

WORDS: William Cowper, ca. 1771 (Zech. 13:1)
MUSIC: 19th cent., USA campmeeting melody

CLEANSING FOUNTAIN
CMD

Lose all their guilt - y stains, lose all their
Wash all my sins a - way, wash all my
Be saved, to sin no more, be saved, to
And shall be till I die, and shall be
Lies si - lent in the grave, lies si - lent

guilt - y stains; and sin - ners plunged be -
sins a - way; and there may I, though
sin no more; till all the ran - somed
till I die; re - deem - ing love has
in the grave; when this poor lisp - ing,

neath that flood lose all their guilt - y stains.
vile as he, wash all my sins a - way.
church of God be saved, to sin no more.
been my theme, and shall be till I die.
stam - mering tongue lies si - lent in the grave.

623 Here, O My Lord, I See Thee

1. Here, O my Lord, I see thee face to face;
2. This is the hour of ban – quet and of song;
3. Here would I feed up – on the bread of God,
4. Too soon we rise; the sym – bols dis – ap – pear;
5. Feast af – ter feast thus comes and pass – es by;

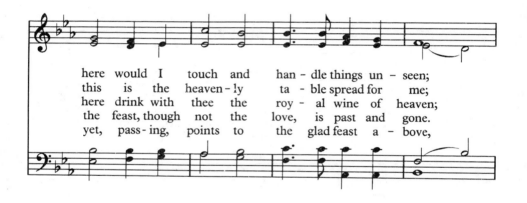

here would I touch and han – dle things un – seen;
this is the heaven – ly ta – ble spread for me;
here drink with thee the roy – al wine of heaven;
the feast, though not the love, is past and gone.
yet, pass – ing, points to the glad feast a – bove,

here grasp with firm – er hand e – ter – nal grace,
here let me feast, and feast – ing, still pro – long
here would I lay a – side each earth – ly load,
The bread and wine re – move; but thou art here,
giv – ing sweet fore – taste of the fes – tal joy,

WORDS: Horatius Bonar, 1857 (Rev. 19:6-9)
MUSIC: Edward Dearle, 1874

PENITENTIA
10 10.10 10

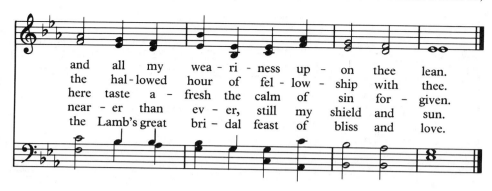

and all my wea - ri - ness up - on thee lean.
the hal - lowed hour of fel - low - ship with thee.
here taste a - fresh the calm of sin for - given.
near - er than ev - er, still my shield and sun.
the Lamb's great bri - dal feast of bliss and love.

Bread of the World 624

1. Bread of the world in mer - cy bro - ken, wine of the
2. Look on the heart by sor - row bro - ken, look on the

soul in mer - cy shed, by whom the words of life were
tears by sin - ners shed; and be thy feast to us the

spo - ken, and in whose death our sins are dead:
to - ken that by thy grace our souls are fed.

WORDS: Reginald Heber, 1827 (Jn. 6:35-58)
MUSIC: John S. B. Hodges, 1868

EUCHARISTIC HYMN
98.98

Alt. tune: RENDEZ À DIEU

625

Come, Let Us Eat

1. Come, let us eat, for now the feast is spread.
2. Come, let us drink, for now the wine is poured.
3. In his pres-ence now we meet and rest,
4. Rise, then, to spread a-broad God's might-y Word.

Come, let us eat, for now the feast is spread.
Come, let us drink, for now the wine is poured.
In his pres-ence now we meet and rest.
Rise, then, to spread a-broad God's might-y Word.

Our Lord's bod-y let us take to-geth-er.
Je-sus' blood poured let us drink to-geth-er.
In the pres-ence of our Lord we gath-er.
Je-sus ris-en will bring in the king-dom.

Our Lord's bod-y let us take to-geth-er.
Je-sus' blood poured let us drink to-geth-er.
In the pres-ence of our Lord we gath-er.
Je-sus ris-en will bring in the king-dom.

WORDS: Sts. 1-3, Billema Kwillia, 1970; trans. by Margaret D. Miller;
st. 4, Gilbert E. Doan, 1972; alt. (1 Cor. 5:7-8)
MUSIC: Billema Kwillia, 1970; harm. by Leland Sateren, 1972

A VA DE
10 10

Let All Mortal Flesh Keep Silence 626

Unison

1. Let all mor-tal flesh keep si-lence, and with fear and
2. King of kings, yet born of Ma-ry, as of old on
3. Rank on rank the host of heav-en spreads its van-guard
4. At his feet the six-winged ser-aph, cher-u-bim, with

trem-bling stand; pon-der noth-ing earth-ly-mind-ed,
earth he stood, Lord of lords, in hu-man ves-ture,
on the way, as the Light of light de-scend-eth
sleep-less eye, veil their fac-es to the pres-ence,

for with bless-ing in his hand, Christ our God to
in the bod-y and the blood; he will give to
from the realms of end-less day, that the powers of
as with cease-less voice they cry: Al-le-lu-ia,

earth de-scend — eth, our full hom-age to de — mand.
all the faith — ful his own self for heaven-ly food.
hell may van — ish as the dark-ness clears a — way.
Al-le-lu — ia, Al-le-lu-ia, Lord Most High!

WORDS: Liturgy of St. James, 4th cent.; trans. by Gerard Moultrie, 1864 (Jn. 6:35-58; Rev. 4)
MUSIC: French carol melody; harm. from *The English Hymnal*, 1906, alt.

PICARDY
87.87.87

627 O the Depth of Love Divine

Unison

1. O the depth of love di - vine, the un -
2. Let the wis - est mor - tals show how
3. How can spir - its heaven - ward rise, by
4. Sure and re - al is the grace, the

fath - o - ma - ble grace! Who shall say how
we the grace re - ceive; fee - ble el - e -
earth - ly mat - ter fed, drink here - with di -
man - ner be un - known; on - ly meet us

bread and wine God in - to us con - veys!
ments be - stow a power not theirs to give.
vine sup - plies and eat im - mor - tal bread?
in thy ways and per - fect us in one.

How the bread his flesh im - parts, how the
Who ex - plains the won - drous way, how through
Ask the Fa - ther's wis - dom how: Christ who
Let us taste the heaven - ly powers, Lord, we

WORDS: Charles Wesley, 1745 (Jn. 6:35-58)
MUSIC: Carlton R. Young, 1986

STOOKEY
76.76.77.76

Alt. tune: AMSTERDAM

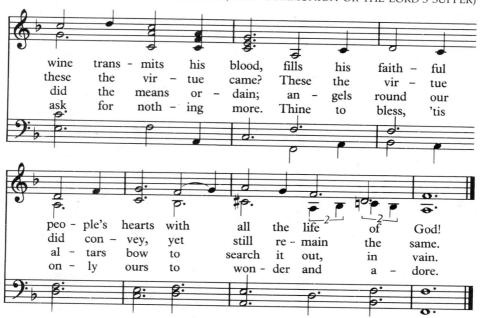

wine trans - mits his blood, fills his faith - ful
these the vir - tue came? These the vir - tue
did the means or - dain; an - gels round our
ask for noth - ing more. Thine to bless, 'tis

peo - ple's hearts with all the life of God!
did con - vey, yet still re - main the same.
al - tars bow to search it out, in vain.
on - ly ours to won - der and a - dore.

Eat This Bread

628

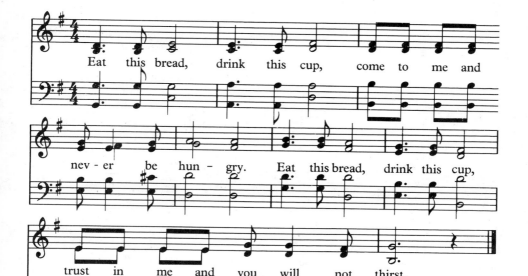

Eat this bread, drink this cup, come to me and
nev - er be hun - gry. Eat this bread, drink this cup,
trust in me and you will not thirst.

WORDS: Robert Batastini and the Taizé Community, 1982 (Jn. 6:35)
MUSIC: Jacques Berthier, 1982

BERTHIER
Irr.

629 You Satisfy the Hungry Heart

Refrain (Unison)

You sat-is-fy the hun-gry heart with gift of fin-est wheat. Come, give to us, O sav-ing Lord, the bread of life to eat.

1. As when the shep-herd calls his sheep, they know and heed his voice, so
2. With joy-ful lips we sing to you our praise and grat-i-tude, that
3. Is not the cup we bless and share the blood of Christ out-poured? Do
4. The mys-ter-y of your pres-ence, Lord, no mor-tal tongue can tell; whom
5. You give your-self to us, O Lord; then self-less let us be, to

WORDS: Omer Westendorf, 1977 (Jn. 6:34; 10:1-5; 1 Cor. 10:16-17)
MUSIC: Robert E. Kreutz, 1977

GIFT OF FINEST WHEAT
CM with Refrain

D.C.

when you call your fam-ily, Lord, we fol - low and re - joice.
you should count us wor-thy, Lord, to share this heaven-ly food.
not one cup, one loaf, de-clare our one - ness in the Lord?
all the world can - not con-tain comes in our hearts to dwell.
serve each oth - er in your name in truth and char-i - ty.

Become to Us the Living Bread 630

1. Be-come to us the liv - ing bread by which the Chris-tian
2. Be-come the nev - er - fail - ing wine, the spring of joy that
3. May Chris-tians all with one ac - cord u - nite a - round the

life is fed, re-newed, and great - ly com-fort - ed:
shall in - cline our hearts to bear the cov-enant sign:
sa - cred board to praise your ho - ly name, O Lord:

Refrain

Al - le - lu - ia! Al - le - lu - ia! Al - le - lu - ia!

WORDS: Miriam Drury, 1970 (Jn. 6:35-58)
MUSIC: *Schönes Geistliches Gesangbuch*, 1609;
harm. from *The Pilgrim Hymnal*, 1958

GELOBT SEI GOTT
888 with Alleluias

631 O Food to Pilgrims Given

1. O food to pil-grims giv - en, O bread of life from
2. O stream of love past tell - ing, O pur-est foun-tain,
3. O Je - sus, by thee bid - den, we here a - dore thee,

heav - en, O man - na from on high! We hun - ger;
well - ing from out the Sav-ior's side! We faint with
hid - den in forms of bread and wine. Grant when the

Lord, sup - ply us, nor thy de - lights de -
thirst; re - vive us, of thine a - bun - dance
veil is ris - en, we may be - hold, in

ny us, whose hearts to thee draw nigh.
give us, and all we need pro - vide.
heav - en, thy coun - te - nance di - vine.

WORDS: *Maintzich Gesangbuch*, 1661; trans. by John Athelstan Laurie Riley, 1906 (Jn. 6:35-58)
MUSIC: German melody, 15th cent.; adapt. by Heinrich Isaac, 1539; harm. by J. S. Bach, 1729

O WELT, ICH MUSS DICH LASSEN
776 D

Draw Us in the Spirit's Tether

632

1. Draw us in the Spir-it's te - ther, for when hum - bly
2. As dis - ci - ples used to gath - er in the name of
3. All our meals and all our liv - ing make as sac - ra -

in thy name, two or three are met to - geth - er,
Christ to sup, then with thanks to God the Fa - ther
ments of thee, that by car - ing, help-ing, giv - ing,

thou art in the midst of them. Al-le - lu - ia!
break the bread and bless the cup: Al-le - lu - ia!
we may true dis - ci - ples be. Al-le - lu - ia!

Al - le - lu - ia! Touch we now thy gar - ment's hem.
Al - le - lu - ia! So now bind our friend - ship up.
Al - le - lu - ia! We will serve thee faith - ful - ly.

WORDS: Percy Dearmer, 1931 (Mt. 18:20)
MUSIC: Harold Friedell, 1957

UNION SEMINARY
87.87.44.7

633 The Bread of Life for All Is Broken

Unison

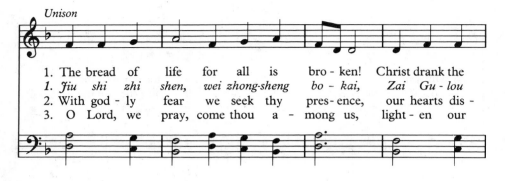

1. The bread of life for all is bro - ken! Christ drank the
1. *Jiu shi zhi shen, wei zhong-sheng bo - kai, Zai Gu - lou*
2. With god - ly fear we seek thy pres - ence, our hearts dis -
3. O Lord, we pray, come thou a - mong us, light - en our

cup on Gol - go - tha. God's grace we trust, and spread with
di, tong in ku - bei; Meng en xin - zhong, feng ming chang
tressed by peo - ple's grief. Thy ho - ly face is stained with
eyes, bright - ly ap - pear! Em - man - u - el, heaven's joy un -

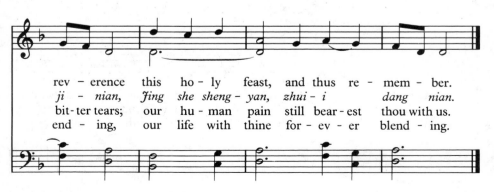

rev - erence this ho - ly feast, and thus re - mem - ber.
ji - nian, Jing she sheng - yan, zhui - i dang nian.
bit - ter tears; our hu - man pain still bear - est thou with us.
end - ing, our life with thine for - ev - er blend - ing.

WORDS: Timothy Tingfang Lew, 1936; trans. by Walter Reginald Oxenham Taylor, 1943; SHENG EN
  phonetic transcription from the Chinese by I-to Loh, 1988 98.98
MUSIC: Su Yin-Lan, 1934; harm. by Robert C. Bennett, 1988

Now Let Us from This Table Rise 634

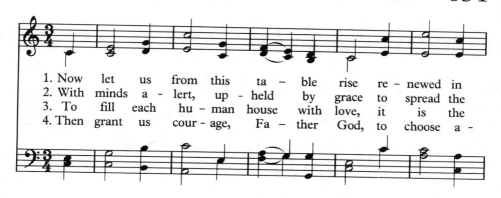

1. Now let us from this ta – ble rise re – newed in
2. With minds a – lert, up – held by grace to spread the
3. To fill each hu – man house with love, it is the
4. Then grant us cour – age, Fa – ther God, to choose a –

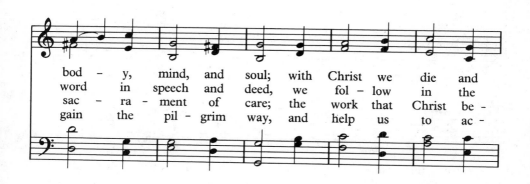

bod – y, mind, and soul; with Christ we die and
word in speech and deed, we fol – low in the
sac – ra – ment of care; the work that Christ be –
gain the pil – grim way, and help us to ac –

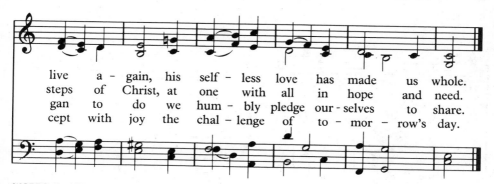

live a – gain, his self – less love has made us whole.
steps of Christ, at one with all in hope and need.
gan to do we hum – bly pledge our – selves to share.
cept with joy the chal – lenge of to – mor – row's day.

WORDS: Fred Kaan, 1964
MUSIC: *Grenoble Antiphoner*, 1753, harm. by Ralph Vaughan Williams, 1906;
   adapt. by Basil Harwood, 1908

DEUS TUORUM MILITUM
LM

635 Because Thou Hast Said

1. Be - cause thou hast said: "Do this for my sake,"
2. 'Tis here we look up and grasp at thy mind,

the mys - ti - cal bread we glad - ly par - take;
'tis here that we hope thine im - age to find;

we thirst for the Spir - it that flows from a - bove,
the means of be - stow - ing thy gifts we em - brace;

and long to in - her - it thy full - ness of love.
but all things are ow - ing to Je - sus' grace.

WORDS: Charles Wesley, 1748
MUSIC: *Paderborn Gesangbuch*, 1765; harm. by Sydney Hugo Nicholson, 1916

PADERBORN
10 10.11 11

Christian People, Raise Your Song 636

1. Chris-tian peo-ple, raise your song, chase a-way all griev-ing.
2. Come to wel-come Christ to-day, God's great rev-e-la-tion,

Sing your joy and be made strong, our Lord's life re-ceiv-ing.
who has pi-o-neered the way of the new cre-a-tion.

Na-ture's gifts of wheat and vine now are set be-fore us;
Greet the Christ, our ris-en King, glad-ly re-cog-niz-ing,

as we of-fer bread and wine, Christ comes to re-store us.
as with joy we greet the spring out of win-ter ris-ing.

WORDS: Colin P. Thompson, 1975 (1 Cor. 15:22)
MUSIC: J. Horn's *Gesangbuch*, 1544; harm. from *The English Hymnal,* 1906

AVE VIRGO VIRGINUM
76.76 D

Words by permission of Saint Andrew Press

637

Una Espiga

(Sheaves of Summer)

Unísono (Unison)

1. U - na es - pi - ga do - ra - da por el sol,
2. Com - par - ti - mos la mis - ma co - mu - nión,

1. Sheaves of sum - mer turned gold - en by the sun,
2. We are shar - ing the same com - mun-ion meal,

el ra - ci - mo que cor - ta el vi - ña - dor,
so - mos tri - go del mis - mo sem-bra - dor,

grapes in bunch - es cut down when ripe and red,
we are wheat by the same great Sow-er sown;

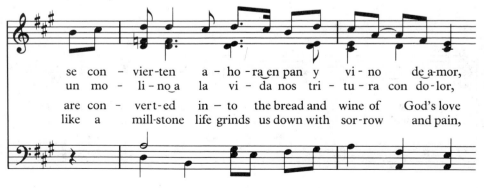

se con - vier-ten a - ho - ra en pan y vi - no de a-mor,
un mo - li - no a la vi - da nos tri - tu - ra con do-lor,

are con - vert-ed in — to the bread and wine of God's love
like a mill-stone life grinds us down with sor-row and pain,

WORDS: Cesareo Gabaraín, 1973; trans. by George Lockwood
MUSIC: Cesareo Gabaraín, 1973; harm. by Skinner Chávez-Melo, 1973

UNA ESPIGA
Irr.

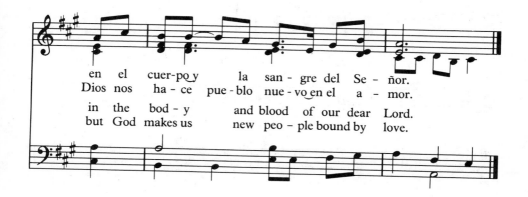

en el   cuer-po y   la   san - gre del   Se - ñor.
Dios nos   ha - ce   pue - blo   nue - vo en el   a - mor.

in   the   bod - y   and blood of our dear   Lord.
but God makes us   new peo - ple bound by   love.

3. Como granos que han hecho el mismo pan,
   como notas que tejen un cantar,
   como gotas de agua que se funden en el mar,
   los cristianos un cuerpo formarán.

4. En la mesa de Dios se sentarán,
   como hijos su pan compartirán,
   una misma esperanza caminando cantarán,
   en la vida como hermanos se amarán.

___

3. Like the grains which become one same whole loaf,
   like the notes that are woven into song,
   like the droplets of water that are blended in the sea,
   we, as Christians, one body shall become.

4. At God's table together we shall sit.
   As God's children, Christ's body we will share.
   One same hope we will sing together as we walk along.
   Brothers, sisters, in life, in love, we'll be.

638 This Is the Feast of Victory

WORDS: Revelation 5:12-13; trans. by John W. Arthur, 1970
MUSIC: Richard Hillert, 1975, alt.

FESTIVAL CANTICLE
Irr. with Refrain

Final Antiphon

This is the feast of vic-to-ry for our God.

Al-le - lu - ia! Al-le - lu - ia! Al-le - lu - ia!

Bread and Justice 639

O God, just as the disciples heard Christ's words of promise and began to eat the bread and drink the wine in the suffering of a long remembrance and in the joy of a hope, grant that we may hear your words, spoken in each thing of everyday affairs:

> Coffee, on our table in the morning;
> the simple gesture of opening a door to go out, free;
> the shouts of children in the parks;
> a familiar song, sung by an unfamiliar face;
> a friendly tree that has not yet been cut down.

May simple things speak to us of your mercy, and tell us that life can be good.

And may these sacramental gifts make us remember those who do not receive them:

> who have their lives cut every day, in the bread absent from the table;
> in the door of the hospital, the prison, the welfare home that does not open;
> in sad children, feet without shoes, eyes without hope;
> in war hymns that glorify death;
> in deserts where once there was life.

Christ was also sacrificed; and may we learn that we participate in the saving sacrifice of Christ when we participate in the suffering of his little ones. **Amen.**

Rubem Alves, Brazil, 20th cent.

I Believe in the Resurrection of the Body, trans. © 1986 Fortress Press

640 Take Our Bread

Refrain (Unison)

Take our bread, we ask you; take our hearts, we love you.

Take our lives, O Fa-ther, we are yours, we are yours.

1. Yours as we stand at the ta-ble you set;
2. Your ho-ly peo-ple stand-ing washed in your blood,

yours as we eat the bread our hearts can't for-get.
Spir-it-filled yet hun-gry we a-wait your food. We are

We are the sign of your life with us yet,
poor, but we've brought our-selves the best we could;

WORDS: Joe Wise, 1966
MUSIC: Joe Wise, 1966

TAKE OUR BREAD
Irr. with Refrain

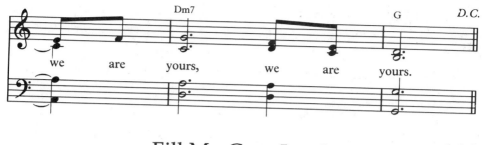

Fill My Cup, Lord 641

WORDS: Richard Blanchard, 1959 (Jn. 4:5-15; 6:35)
MUSIC: Richard Blanchard, 1959; arr. by Eugene Clark, 1971
© 1959 Sacred Songs

FILL MY CUP
Irr.

EUCHARIST (HOLY COMMUNION OR THE LORD'S SUPPER), *see further:*

642 As Man and Woman We Were Made

Unison

1. As man and wom-an we were made that love be found and
2. Now Je-sus lived and gave his love to make our life and
3. And Je-sus died to live a-gain, so praise the love that,
4. Then spread the ta-ble, clear the hall, and cel-e-brate till

life be-gun, so praise the Lord who made us two, and
lov-ing new; so cel-e-brate with him to-day and
come what may, can bring the dawn and clear the skies, and
day is done; let peace go deep be-tween us all and

praise the Lord when two are one: praise for the love that
drink the joy he of-fers you, that makes the sim-ple
waits to wipe all tears a-way; and let us hope for
joy be shared by ev-ery-one; laugh and make mer-ry

comes to life through child or par-ent, hus-band, wife.
mo-ment shine and chang-es wa-ter in-to wine.
what shall be, be-liev-ing where we can-not see.
with your friends, and praise the love that nev-er ends!

WORDS: Brian Wren, 1973 (Gen. 1:27; Jn. 2:1-11)
MUSIC: Trad. English melody; arr. and harm. by Ralph Vaughan Williams, 1919
Words © 1983 Hope Publishing Co.

SUSSEX CAROL
88.88.88

When Love Is Found

1. When love is found and hope comes home,
2. When love has flowered in trust and care,
3. When love is tried as loved ones change,
4. When love is torn and trust be - trayed,
5. Praise God for love, praise God for life,

sing and be glad that two are one.
build both each day, that love may dare
hold still to hope though all seems strange,
pray strength to love till tor - ments fade,
in age or youth, in hus - band, wife.

When love ex - plodes and fills the sky,
to reach be - yond home's warmth and light,
till ease re - turns, and love grows wise
till lov - ers keep no score of wrong,
Lift up your hearts, let love be fed

praise God and share our Mak - er's joy.
to serve and strive for truth and right.
through lis - tening ears and o - pened eyes.
but hear through pain love's Eas - ter song.
through death and life in bro - ken bread.

WORDS: Brian Wren, 1978
MUSIC: Trad. English melody; adapt. by Hal Hopson, 1972

GIFT OF LOVE
LM

Words © 1983 Hope Publishing Co.; music © 1972 Hope Publishing Co.

644

Jesus, Joy of Our Desiring

1. Je-sus, joy of our de-sir-ing, ho-ly wis-dom,
love most bright; drawn by thee, our souls as-pir-ing soar to
un-cre-at-ed light. Word of God, our flesh that fash-ioned,
with the fire of life im-pas-sioned, striv-ing still to
truth un-known, soar-ing, dy-ing round thy throne.

2. Through the way where hope is guid-ing, hark, what peace-ful
mu-sic rings; where the flock, in thee con-fid-ing, drink of
joy from death-less springs. Theirs is beau-ty's fair-est plea-sure;
theirs is wis-dom's ho-liest trea-sure. Thou dost ev-er
lead thine own in the love of joys un-known.

WORDS: Martin Janus, 1661; trans. anon.
MUSIC: Johann Schop, arr. by J. S. Bach, 1723

JESU, JOY OF MAN'S DESIRING
87.87.88.77

O Perfect Love

1. O per - fect Love, all hu - man thought tran - scend - ing,
2. O per - fect Life, be thou their full as - sur - ance
3. Grant them the joy which bright - ens earth - ly sor - row;

low - ly we kneel in prayer be - fore thy throne,
of ten - der char - i - ty and stead - fast faith,
grant them the peace which calms all earth - ly strife,

that theirs may be the love which knows no end - ing,
of pa - tient hope and qui - et, brave en - dur - ance,
and to life's day the glo - rious un - known mor - row

whom thou for - ev - er - more dost join in one.
with child - like trust that fears nor pain nor death.
that dawns up - on e - ter - nal love and life.

WORDS: Dorothy B. Gurney, 1883
MUSIC: Joseph Barnby, 1890

PERFECT LOVE
11 10.11 10

646 Canticle of Love

RESPONSE 1 *(General)*

This is my com-mand-ment, that you love one an-oth-er as I have loved you.

RESPONSE 2 *(Marriage)*

And two shall be-come one in love, for we are mem-bers of Christ's bod-y.

R

Let love be genuine and live in harmony;
    hate what is evil, hold fast to what is good.
    Outdo one another in showing honor;
    be humble and never conceited.
Love is stronger than death
    and jealousy is cruel as the grave.
    Floods cannot drown love
    and wealth cannot buy it.   R

Put love above all else;
    let Christ's peace rule your hearts.
    Always be forgiving,
    as Christ has forgiven you.
Love is not jealous or boastful,
    arrogant, rude, or stubborn,
    irritable, resentful, or possessive.
    Love is patient and kind.   R

Do not love in word or speech only;
    love also in deed and truth.
    Receive each other in sincerity,
    find mercy and grow old together.

Love rejoices in the right;
it bears, believes, hopes,
and endures all things,
for love is faithful and endless. R

When the Lord builds the house,
the labor is never in vain.
Happy are those who take refuge in God;
those who serve the Lord are redeemed. R

Your Love, O God, Has Called Us Here 647

Unison

1. Your love, O God, has called us here, for all love
2. O gra-cious God, you con - se - crate all that is
3. O God of love, in - spire our life, re - veal your

finds its source in you, the per - fect love that
love - ly, good, and true. Bless those who in your
will in all we do; join ev - ery hus - band,

casts out fear, the love that Christ makes ev - er new.
pres - ence wait and ev - ery day their love re - new.
ev - ery wife in mu - tual love and love for you.

WORDS: Russell Schulz-Widmar, 1982
MUSIC: M. Lee Suitor, 1984

CORNISH
LM

Words © 1982 Russell Schulz-Widmar; music © 1984 M. Lee Suitor

MARRIAGE, *see further:*

164 Come, My Way, My Truth, My Life   549 Where Charity and Love Prevail

648 God the Spirit, Guide and Guardian

1. God the Spir - it, guide and guard - ian, wind - sped flame and
2. Christ our Sav - ior, sov - ereign, shep - herd, word made flesh, love
3. Great Cre - a - tor, life - be - stow - er, truth be - yond all
4. Tri - une God, mys - te - rious be - ing, un - di - vid - ed

hov - ering dove, **breath of life** and voice of proph - ets, sign of
cru - ci - fied, teach - er, heal - er, suf - fering ser - vant, friend of
thought's re - call, **fount of** wis - dom, womb of mer - cy, giv - ing
and di - verse, deep - er than our minds can fath - om, great - er

bless - ing, power of love: give to those who lead your
sin - ners, foe of pride: in your tend - ing may all
and for - giv - ing all: as you know our strength and
than our creeds re - hearse: help us in our var - ied

peo - ple fresh a - noint - ing of your grace; send them forth as
pas - tors* learn and live a shep - herd's care; grant them cour - age
weak - ness, so may those the church ex - alts o - ver - see her
call - ings your full im - age to pro - claim, that our min - is -

*When appropriate, "ministers" may be substituted for "pastors."

WORDS: Carl P. Daw, Jr., 1987
MUSIC: Rowland H. Prichard, 1844; harm. from *The English Hymnal*, 1906
Words © 1989 Hope Publishing Co.

HYFRYDOL
87.87 D

How Shall They Hear the Word of God 649

bold a - pos - tles to your church in ev - ery place.
and com - pas - sion shown through word and deed and prayer.
life stead - fast - ly yet not o - ver - look her faults.
tries u - nit - ing may give glo - ry to your name.

1. How shall they hear the word of God un - less the
2. How shall they call to God for help un - less they
3. How shall the gos - pel be pro-claimed that sin - ners

truth is told? How shall the sin - ful be set free,
have be - lieved? How shall the poor be giv - en hope,
may re - pent? How shall the world find peace at last

the sor - row - ful con - soled? To all who speak the
the pris - on - er re - prieved? To those who help the
if her - alds are not sent? So send us, Lord, for

truth to - day, im - part your Spir - it, Lord, we pray.
blind to see, give light and love and clar - i - ty.
we re - joice to speak of Christ with life and voice.

WORDS: Michael Perry, 1982 (Rom. 10:14-15)
MUSIC: *Choralbuch* (Koch), 1816

AUCH JETZT MACHT GOTT
86.86.88

Words © 1982 Hope Publishing Co.

650 Give Me the Faith Which Can Remove

1. Give me the faith which can re-move and sink the
2. I would the pre-cious time re-deem, and long-er
3. My tal-ents, gifts, and grac-es, Lord, in-to thy
4. En-large, in-flame, and fill my heart with bound-less

moun-tain to a plain; give me the child-like pray-ing love,
live for this a-lone, to spend and to be spent for them
bless-ed hands re-ceive; and let me live to preach thy word,
char-i-ty di-vine, so shall I all my strength ex-ert,

which longs to build thy house a-gain; thy love, let it my
who have not yet my Sav-ior known; ful-ly on these my
and let me to thy glo-ry live; my ev-ery sa-cred
and love them with a zeal like thine, and lead them to thy

heart o'er-power, and all my sim-ple soul de-vour.
mis-sion prove, and on-ly breathe, to breathe thy love.
mo-ment spend in pub-lish-ing the sin-ner's Friend.
o-pen side, the sheep for whom the Shep-herd died.

WORDS: Charles Wesley, 1749 (Mk. 11:20-25)　　　　CAREY'S (SURREY)
MUSIC: Henry Carey, ca. 1732; harm. from *The English Hymnal*, 1906　　88.88.88

Come, Holy Ghost, Our Souls Inspire 651

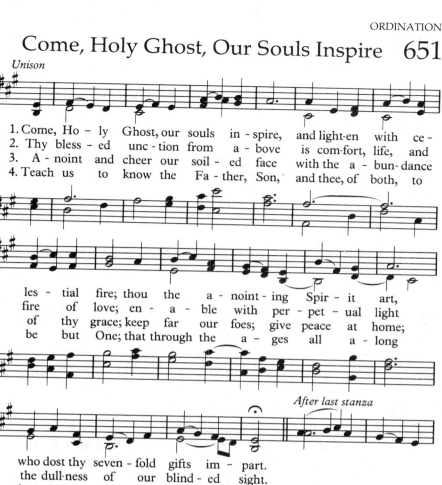

Unison

1. Come, Ho - ly Ghost, our souls in - spire, and light-en with ce -
2. Thy bless - ed unc - tion from a - bove is com-fort, life, and
3. A - noint and cheer our soil - ed face with the a - bun-dance
4. Teach us to know the Fa - ther, Son, and thee, of both, to

les - tial fire; thou the a - noint - ing Spir - it art,
fire of love; en - a - ble with per - pet - ual light
of thy grace; keep far our foes; give peace at home;
be but One; that through the a - ges all a - long

After last stanza

who dost thy sev - en - fold gifts im - part.
the dull-ness of our blind - ed sight.
where thou art guide, no ill can come.
this, this may be our end - less song; Praise to thy e -

ter - nal mer-it, Fa - ther, Son, and Ho - ly Spir-it. A - men.

WORDS: Attr. to Rhabanus Maurus, 8th-9th cent.; trans. by John Cosin, 1627
MUSIC: *Vesperale Romanum*, Mechlin, 1848; adapt. from *Hymns for Church and School*, 1964

VENI CREATOR
LM

ORDINATION, *see further:*

501 O Thou Who Camest from Above   582 Whom Shall I Send
408 The Gift of Love

652   Canticle of Remembrance

RESPONSE 1 *(General)*

The righ-teous live for-ev-er;

their re-ward is with the Lord.

RESPONSE 2 *(General)*

With my song I give thanks and praise,

for the Lord is my strength and shield.

R
The souls of the righteous are in the hand of God
    and no torment will ever touch them.
In the eyes of the foolish they seem to have died,
    and their departure was thought to be an affliction,
and their going from us to be their destruction;
    but they are at peace.
For though in our sight they were punished,
    their hope is full of immortality.   R

Having been disciplined a little, they will receive great good,
    because God tested them and found them worthy;
like gold in the furnace God tried them,
    and like a sacrificial burnt offering God accepted them.
In the time of their visitation they will shine forth,
    and will run like sparks through the stubble.
They will govern nations and rule over peoples,
    and the Lord will reign over them for ever.
Those who trust in God will understand truth,
    and the faithful will abide in love,
because grace and mercy are upon the elect,
    and God watches over the holy ones.   R

WORDS: Wisdom of Solomon 3:1-9, adapt.; Response 1, Wisdom of Solomon 3:1-9, adapt;
  Response 2, Psalm 28:7, adapt.
MUSIC: Response 1, *Gesangbuch*, Meiningen, adapt. by Timothy E. Kimbrough; Response 2, Jane Marshall

Christ the Victorious

653

1. Christ the Vic - to - ri - ous, give to your ser - vants
2. On - ly Im - mor - tal One, might - y Cre - a - tor!
3. God - spo - ken proph - e - cy, word at cre - a - tion:
4. Christ the Vic - to - ri - ous, give to your ser - vants

rest with your saints in the re - gions of light.
We are your crea - tures and chil - dren of earth.
"You came from dust and to dust shall re - turn."
rest with your saints in the re - gions of light.

Grief and pain end - ed, and sigh - ing no long - er,
From earth you formed us, both glo - rious and mor - tal,
Yet at the grave shall we raise up our glad song,
Grief and pain end - ed, and sigh - ing no long - er,

there may they find ev - er - last - ing life.
and to the earth shall we all re - turn.
"Al - le - lu - ia, al - le - lu - ia!"
there may they find ev - er - last - ing life.

WORDS: Carl P. Daw, Jr., 1982
MUSIC: Alexis Lvov, 1833

RUSSIAN HYMN
11 10.11 9

654 How Blest Are They Who Trust in Christ

1. How blest are they who trust in Christ when we and
   those we love must part; we yield them up, for
   go they must, but do not lose them from our heart.

2. In rip-ened age, their har-vest reaped, or gone from
   us in youth or prime, in Christ they have e-
   ter-nal life, re-leased from all the bonds of time.

3. In Christ, who tast-ed death for us, we rise a-
   bove our na-tural grief, and wit-ness to a
   strick-en world the strength and splen-dor of be-lief.

WORDS: Fred Pratt Green, 1972
MUSIC: H. Percy Smith, 1874
Words © 1972 The Hymn Society of America

MARYTON
LM
Alt. tune: ROCKINGHAM

655 Fix Me, Jesus

Refrain

Oh, fix me, oh, fix me,
(Je - sus) (Je - sus)

WORDS: Afro-American spiritual (Rev. 6:11; 7:9-14)
MUSIC: Afro-American spiritual; adapt. and arr. by William Farley Smith
adapt. and arr. © 1989 The United Methodist Publishing House

FIX ME, JESUS
Irr.

Fine

oh, fix me; fix me, Je-sus, fix me.

Leader   *All*

1. Fix me for my long white robe, fix me, Je-sus, fix me.
2. Fix me for my jour-ney home, fix me, Je-sus, fix me.

Leader   *All*   *D.C.*

Fix me for my star-ry crown, fix me, Je-sus, fix me.
Fix me for my dy-ing bed, fix me, Je-sus, fix me.

If Death My Friend and Me Divide   656

If death my friend and me divide,
thou dost not, Lord, my sorrow chide,
or frown my tears to see;
restrained from passionate excess,
thou bidst me mourn in calm distress
for them that rest in thee.

I feel a strong immortal hope,
which bears my mournful spirit up
beneath its mountain load;
redeemed from death, and grief, and pain,
I soon shall find my friend again
within the arms of God.

Pass a few fleeting moments more
and death the blessing shall restore
which death has snatched away;
for me thou wilt the summons send,
and give me back my parted friend
in that eternal day.

Charles Wesley, 1762

657

This Is the Day

WORDS: Psalm 118:24; adapt. by Les Garrett, 1967
MUSIC: Les Garrett, 1967

© 1967, 1980 Scripture in Song

THIS IS THE DAY
Irr.

This Is the Day the Lord Hath Made 658

This is the day the Lord hath made; he
calls the hours his own. Let heaven re - joice, let
earth be glad, and praise sur - round the throne.

WORDS: Isaac Watts, 1719 (Ps. 118:24)
MUSIC: Attr. to Lucius Chapin, ca. 1813

TWENTY-FOURTH
CM

Jesus Our Friend and Brother 659

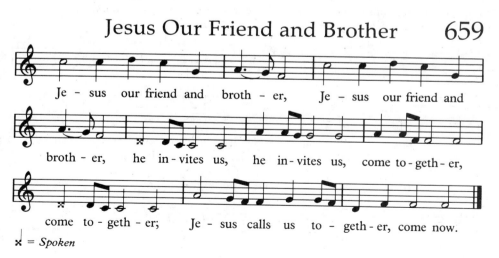

Je - sus our friend and broth - er, Je - sus our friend and
broth - er, he in - vites us, he in - vites us, come to - geth - er,
come to - geth - er; Je - sus calls us to - geth - er, come now.

× = Spoken

WORDS: Attr. to Ova'hehe; trans. by David Graber and others, 1982 (Jn. 15:14-15)
MUSIC: Attr. to Ova'hehe; transcribed by David Graber, 1982

ESENEHANE JESUS
Irr.

Trans. and music transcription © 1982 by Mennonite Leaders' Council

660

God Is Here

1. God is here! As we your peo-ple meet to of-fer
2. Here are sym-bols to re-mind us of our life-long
3. Here our chil-dren find a wel-come in the Shep-herd's
4. Lord of all, of church and king-dom, in an age of

praise and prayer, may we find in full-er mea-sure
need of grace; here are ta-ble, font, and pul-pit;
flock and fold; here as bread and wine are tak-en,
change and doubt keep us faith-ful to the gos-pel;

what it is in Christ we share. Here, as in the world a-
here the cross has cen-tral place. Here in hon-es-ty of
Christ sus-tains us, as of old. Here the ser-vants of the
help us work your pur-pose out. Here, in this day's ded-i-

round us, all our var-ied skills and arts wait the
preach-ing, here in si-lence, as in speech, here, in
Ser-vant seek in wor-ship to ex-plore what it
ca-tion, all we have to give, re-ceive; we, who

WORDS: Fred Pratt Green, 1978
MUSIC: Cyril V. Taylor, 1941

ABBOT'S LEIGH
87.87 D

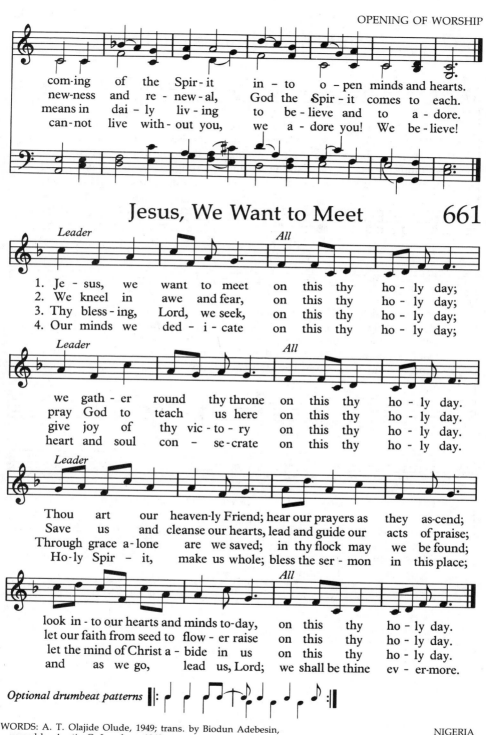

com-ing of the Spir-it in-to o-pen minds and hearts.
new-ness and re-new-al, God the Spir-it comes to each.
means in dai-ly liv-ing to be-lieve and to a-dore.
can-not live with-out you, we a-dore you! We be-lieve!

Jesus, We Want to Meet 661

Leader *All*

1. Je - sus, we want to meet on this thy ho - ly day;
2. We kneel in awe and fear, on this thy ho - ly day;
3. Thy bless - ing, Lord, we seek, on this thy ho - ly day;
4. Our minds we ded - i - cate on this thy ho - ly day;

Leader *All*

we gath - er round thy throne on this thy ho - ly day.
pray God to teach us here on this thy ho - ly day.
give joy of thy vic - to - ry on this thy ho - ly day.
heart and soul con - se -crate on this thy ho - ly day.

Leader

Thou art our heaven-ly Friend; hear our prayers as they as-cend;
Save us and cleanse our hearts, lead and guide our acts of praise;
Through grace a-lone are we saved; in thy flock may we be found;
Ho-ly Spir - it, make us whole; bless the ser - mon in this place;

All

look in - to our hearts and minds to-day, on this thy ho - ly day.
let our faith from seed to flow - er raise on this thy ho - ly day.
let the mind of Christ a - bide in us on this thy ho - ly day.
and as we go, lead us, Lord; we shall be thine ev - er-more.

Optional drumbeat patterns

WORDS: A. T. Olajide Olude, 1949; trans. by Biodun Adebesin,
    versed by Austin C. Lovelace, 1962
MUSIC: A. T. Olajide Olude, 1949

NIGERIA
Irr.

Trans. and versification © 1964 Abingdon Press

662   Stand Up and Bless the Lord

1. Stand up and bless the Lord, ye peo - ple of his choice; stand up and bless the Lord your God with heart and soul and voice.
2. Though high a - bove all praise, a - bove all bless - ing high, who would not fear his ho - ly name, and laud and mag - ni - fy?
3. O for the liv - ing flame from his own al - tar brought, to touch our lips, our minds in - spire, and wing to heaven our thought!
4. God is our strength and song, and his sal - va - tion ours; then be his love in Christ pro - claimed with all our ran - somed powers.
5. Stand up and bless the Lord; the Lord your God a - dore; stand up and bless his glo - rious name, hence - forth for - ev - er - more.

WORDS: James Montgomery (Neh. 9:5)
MUSIC: *Genevan Psalter*, 1551; adapt. by William Crotch, 1836

ST. MICHAEL
SM

OPENING OF WORSHIP, *see further:*

91   Canticle of Praise to God   579   Lord God, Your Love Has Called Us Here
478   Jaya Ho Jaya Ho

Savior, Again to Thy Dear Name 663

1. Savior, again to thy dear name we raise
   with one accord our parting hymn of praise;
   guard thou the lips from sin, the hearts from shame,
   that in this house have called upon thy name.

2. Grant us thy peace upon our homeward way;
   with thee began, with thee shall end the day.
   From harm and danger keep thy children free,
   for dark and light are both alike to thee.

3. Grant us thy peace throughout our earthly life;
   peace to thy church from error and from strife;
   peace to our land, the fruit of truth and love;
   peace in each heart, thy Spirit from above;

4. Thy peace in life, the balm of every pain;
   thy peace in death, the hope to rise again;
   then, when thy voice shall bid our conflict cease,
   call us, O Lord, to thine eternal peace.

WORDS: John Ellerton, 1866; alt.
MUSIC: Edward J. Hopkins, 1869

ELLERS
10 10.10 10

664 Sent Forth by God's Blessing

Unison

1. Sent forth by God's bless-ing, our true faith con-fess-ing,
2. With praise and thanks-giv-ing to God ev-er liv-ing,

the peo-ple of God from this dwell-ing take leave.
the tasks of our ev-ery-day life we will face.

The ser-vice is end-ed, O now be ex-tend-ed
Our faith ev-er shar-ing, in love ev-er car-ing,

the fruits of our wor-ship in all who be-lieve.
em-brac-ing God's chil-dren of each tribe and race.

The seed of the teach-ing, re-cep-tive souls reach-ing,
With your grace you feed us, with your light now lead us;

WORDS: Omer Westendorf, 1964
MUSIC: Welsh folk tune; harm. by Leland Sateren, 1972

THE ASH GROVE
6 6 11.6 6 11 D

Words © 1964 World Library Publications, Inc.; harm. © 1972
Contemporary Worship 4: Hymns for Baptism and Holy Communion

shall blos - som in ac - tion for God and for all.
u - nite us as one in this life that we share.

God's grace did in - vite us, and love shall u - nite us
Then may all the liv - ing with praise and thanks - giv - ing

to work for God's king - dom and an - swer the call.
give hon - or to Christ and that name which we bear.

Go Now in Peace

665

Keyboard, handbells, and/or Orff instruments

Go now in peace, go now in peace, may the love of

God sur-round you ev-ery-where, ev-ery-where you may go.

Fine

May be sung as a canon

WORDS: Natalie Sleeth, 1976 (Lk. 2:29)
MUSIC: Natalie Sleeth, 1976

GO IN PEACE
Irr.

666

Shalom to You

Unison

Sha - lom to you now, sha - lom, my friends.

May God's full mer - cies bless you, my friends.

In all your liv – ing and through your lov - ing,

Christ be your sha - lom, Christ be your sha - lom.

WORDS: Elise S. Eslinger, 1980
MUSIC: Trad. Spanish melody; harm. by Carlton R. Young, 1989
Words © 1983 The United Methodist Publishing House; harm. © 1989 The United Methodist Publishing House

SOMOS DEL SEÑOR
Irr.

667

Shalom

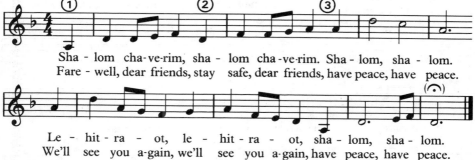

Sha - lom cha - ve-rim, sha - lom cha -ve-rim. Sha - lom, sha - lom.
Fare - well, dear friends, stay safe, dear friends, have peace, have peace.

Le - hit - ra - ot, le - hit - ra - ot, sha - lom, sha - lom.
We'll see you a-gain, we'll see you a-gain, have peace, have peace.

May be sung as a round
Pronounced: Shah - lohm Kah - vey - reem, Leh - heet - rah - oht

WORDS: Trad. Hebrew blessing; trans. by Roger N. Deschner, 1982
MUSIC: Israeli melody
Trans. © 1982 The United Methodist Publishing House

SHALOM
Irr.

Let Us Now Depart in Thy Peace 668

Unison

Let us now de-part in thy peace, bless-ed Je-sus.

Send us to our homes with God's love in our hearts.

Let not the bus-y world claim all our loy-al-ties.

(Optional)

Keep us ev-er mind-ful, dear Lord, of thee. A-men.

*See 903 for extended Amen.

WORDS: New Mexican folk song; adapt. by Lee Hastings Bristol, Jr. 1961 (Lk. 2:29)
MUSIC: New Mexican folk song; adapt. by Lee Hastings Bristol, Jr. 1961

A LA PUERTA
12 11.12 10

Adapt. © 1961 Concordia Publishing House

The Apostolic Blessing 669

The grace of the Lord Jesus Christ,
and the love of God,
and the communion of the Holy Spirit
be with you all. **Amen.**

2 Corinthians 13:14

670 Go Forth for God

1. Go forth for God, go to the world in peace;
2. Go forth for God, go to the world in love;
3. Go forth for God, go to the world in strength;
4. Go forth for God, go to the world in joy,

be of good cour - age, armed with heaven - ly grace,
strength - en the faint, give cour - age to the weak;
hold fast the good, be ur - gent for the right;
to serve God's peo - ple ev - ery day and hour,

in God's good Spir - it dai - ly to in - crease,
help the af - flict - ed; rich - ly from a - bove
ren - der to no one e - vil; Christ at length
and serv - ing Christ, our ev - ery gift em - ploy,

till in the king - dom we see face to face.
God's love sup - plies the grace and power we seek.
shall o - ver - come all dark - ness with his light.
re - joic - ing in the Ho - ly Spir - it's power.

WORDS: John R. Peacey, 1975
MUSIC: *Genevan Psalter*, 1551; harm. by C. Winfred Douglas, 1940, alt.

GENEVA 124
10 10.10 10.10

Words by permission of Mildred E. Peacey

Go forth for God, go to the world in peace.
Go forth for God, go to the world in love.
Go forth for God, go to the world in strength.
Go forth for God, go to the world in joy.

Lord, Dismiss Us with Thy Blessing 671

1. Lord, dis - miss us with thy bless-ing; fill our hearts with
2. Thanks we give and ad - o - ra - tion for thy gos - pel's

joy and peace; let us each, thy love pos - sess - ing,
joy - ful sound. May the fruits of thy sal - va - tion

tri - umph in re - deem - ing grace. O re - fresh us,
in our hearts and lives a - bound; ev - er faith - ful,

O re - fresh us, trav - eling through this wil - der - ness.
ev - er faith - ful to the truth may we be found.

WORDS: Attr. to John Fawcett, 1773
MUSIC: *The European Magazine and Review*, 1792; harm. from
The Methodist Hymn and Tune Book, 1889, alt.

SICILIAN MARINERS
87.87.87

672 God Be with You till We Meet Again

1. God be with you till we meet again; by his
2. God be with you till we meet again; neath his
3. God be with you till we meet again; when life's
4. God be with you till we meet again; keep love's

coun-sels guide, up-hold you, with his sheep se-cure-ly
wings se-cure-ly hide you, dai-ly man-na still pro-
per-ils thick con-found you, put his arms un-fail-ing
ban-ner float-ing o'er you, smite death's threat-ening wave be-

fold you;
vide you; God be with you till we meet a-gain.
round you;
fore you;

Refrain

Till we meet, till we meet, till we
(till we meet, till we meet a-gain)

meet at Je-sus' feet; till we meet,
(till we meet) (till we meet,

WORDS: Jeremiah E. Rankin, 1880
MUSIC: William G. Tomer, 1880

GOD BE WITH YOU
98.89 with Refrain

till we meet,
till we meet a - gain) God be with you till we meet a - gain.

God Be with You till We Meet Again 673

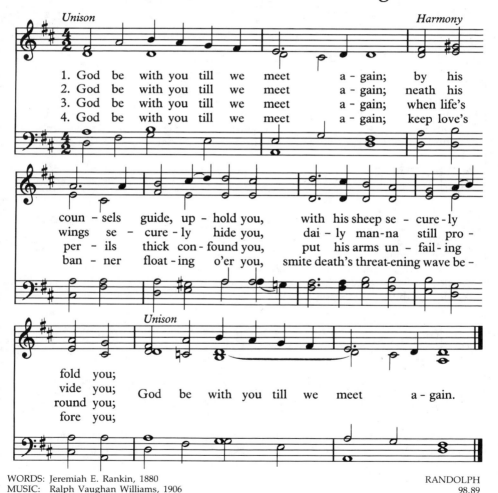

Unison   *Harmony*

1. God be with you till we meet a - gain; by his
2. God be with you till we meet a - gain; neath his
3. God be with you till we meet a - gain; when life's
4. God be with you till we meet a - gain; keep love's

coun - sels guide, up - hold you, with his sheep se - cure - ly
wings se - cure - ly hide you, dai - ly man - na still pro -
per - ils thick con - found you, put his arms un - fail - ing
ban - ner float - ing o'er you, smite death's threat-ening wave be -

Unison

fold you;
vide you;   God be with you till we meet a - gain.
round you;
fore you;

WORDS: Jeremiah E. Rankin, 1880
MUSIC: Ralph Vaughan Williams, 1906

RANDOLPH
98.89

CLOSING OF WORSHIP, *see further:*

674   See the Morning Sun Ascending

1. See the morn-ing sun as-cend-ing, ra-diant in the
2. So may we, in low-ly sta-tion, join the cho-ris-
3. For thy lov-ing-kind-ness ev-er shed up-on our
4. "Wis-dom, hon-or, power, and bless-ing!" with the an-gel-ic

east-ern sky; hear the an-gel voic-es blend-ing
ters a-bove; sing-ing with the whole cre-a-tion,
earth-ly way; for thy mer-cy, ceas-ing nev-er,
host we cry; round thy throne, thy name con-fess-ing,

in their praise to God on high! Al-le-lu-ia!
prais-ing thee for thy great love. Al-le-lu-ia!
for thy bless-ing day by day: Al-le-lu-ia!
Lord, we would to thee draw nigh. Al-le-lu-ia!

Al-le-lu-ia! Glo-ry be to God on high!
Al-le-lu-ia! Glo-ry be to God a-bove!
Al-le-lu-ia! Glo-ry be to God al-way!
Al-le-lu-ia! Glo-ry be to God on high!

WORDS: Charles Parkin, 1953 (Rev. 5:11-14; 7:11-12)
MUSIC: Joachim Neander, 1680

UNSER HERRSCHER
77.77.77

As the Sun Doth Daily Rise

1. As the sun doth dai - ly rise, bright - ening all the morn - ing skies, so to thee with one ac - cord lift we up our hearts, O Lord.
2. Day by day pro - vide us food, for from thee come all things good; strength un - to our souls af - ford from thy liv - ing bread, O Lord.
3. Be our guard in sin and strife; be the lead - er of our life; lest from thee we stray a - broad, stay our way - ward feet, O Lord.
4. Quick - ened by the Spir - it's grace all thy ho - ly will to trace while we dai - ly search thy Word, wis - dom true im - part, O Lord.
5. Praise we, with the heaven - ly host, Fa - ther, Son, and Ho - ly Ghost; thee would we with one ac - cord praise and mag - ni - fy, O Lord.

WORDS: Latin hymn; trans. by J. Masters; adapt. by Horatio Nelson, 1864
MUSIC: *The Parish Choir*, 1850; harm. by W. H. Monk, 1861

INNOCENTS
77.77

For a New Day

676

We give you hearty thanks for the rest of the past night
and for the gift of a new day, with its opportunities of pleasing you.
Grant that we may so pass its hours in the perfect freedom of your service,
that at eventide we may again give thanks unto you. **Amen.**

Eastern Orthodox Prayer

677 Listen, Lord (A Prayer)

O Lord, we come this morning knee-bowed and body-bent before thy throne of grace. O Lord—this morning—bow our hearts beneath our knees, and our knees in some lonesome valley. We come this morning like empty pitchers to a full fountain, with no merits of our own. O Lord, open up a window of heaven, and lean out far over the battlements of glory, and listen this morning, **Amen.**

James Weldon Johnson, USA, 20th cent.

© 1927 The Viking Press, Inc., renewed 1955 Grace Nail Johnson.

678 Rise to Greet the Sun

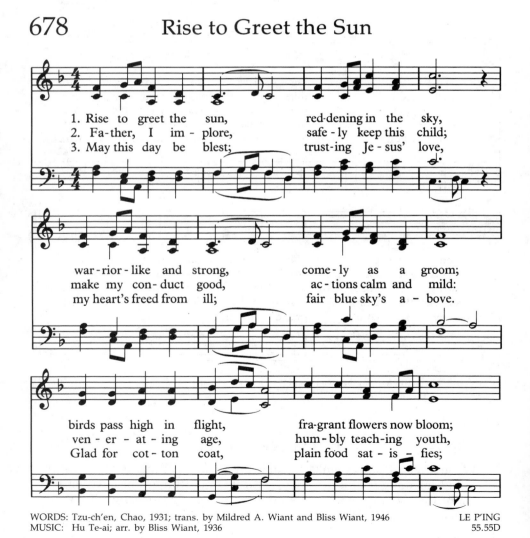

1. Rise to greet the sun, red-dening in the sky,
2. Fa-ther, I im-plore, safe-ly keep this child;
3. May this day be blest; trust-ing Je-sus' love,

war-rior-like and strong, come-ly as a groom;
make my con-duct good, ac-tions calm and mild:
my heart's freed from ill; fair blue sky's a-bove.

birds pass high in flight, fra-grant flowers now bloom;
ven-er-at-ing age, hum-bly teach-ing youth,
Glad for cot-ton coat, plain food sat-is-fies;

WORDS: Tzu-ch'en, Chao, 1931; trans. by Mildred A. Wiant and Bliss Wiant, 1946
MUSIC: Hu Te-ai; arr. by Bliss Wiant, 1936

LE P'ING
55.55D

Trans. 1965 © Bliss Wiant

with the gra-cious light   I my toil re - sume.
al - ways serv-ing thee,   shar-ing thy rich truth.
all my count-less needs   thy kind hand sup - plies.

O Splendor of God's Glory Bright   679

1. O splen - dor of God's glo - ry bright, O thou that
2. O thou true Sun, on us thy glance let fall in
3. The Fa - ther, too, our prayers im - plore, Fa - ther of
4. To guide what - e'er we no - bly do, with love all

bring - est light from light; O Light of light, light's
roy - al ra - di - ance; the Spir - it's sanc - ti -
glo - ry ev - er - more; the Fa - ther of all
en - vy to sub - due; to make ill for - tune

liv - ing spring, O day, all days il - lu - min - ing.
fy - ing beam up - on our earth - ly sens - es stream.
grace and might, to ban - ish sin from our de - light.
turn to fair, and give us grace our wrongs to bear.

WORDS: Ambrose of Milan, 4th cent.; trans. by Robert S. Bridges, 1899
MUSIC: William Knapp, 1738

WAREHAM
LM

680   Father, We Praise Thee

1. Fa-ther, we praise thee, now the night is o-ver; ac-tive and
2. Mon-arch of all things, fit us for thy man-sions; ban-ish our
3. All-ho-ly Fa-ther, Son, and e-qual Spir-it, Trin-i-ty

watch-ful, stand we all be-fore thee; sing-ing, we of-fer
weak-ness, health and whole-ness send-ing; bring us to heav-en,
bless-ed, send us thy sal-va-tion; thine is the glo-ry,

prayer and med-i-ta-tion; thus we a-dore thee.
with thy saints u-nit-ed; joy with-out end-ing.
gleam-ing and re-sound-ing through all cre-a-tion.

WORDS: Attr. to Gregory the Great, 6th cent.; trans. by Percy Dearmer, 1906   CHRISTE SANCTORUM
MUSIC: *Paris Antiphoner*, 1681; harm. by David Evans, 1927; alt.   11 11 11.5

Harm. by permission of Oxford University Press

MORNING, *see further:*

For Help for the Forthcoming Day 681

Almighty and everlasting God, you have safely brought us to the beginning of this day. Defend us with your mighty power, and grant that this day we fall into no sin, neither run into any kind of danger, but that all our doings, ordered by your governance, may be always righteous in your sight; through Jesus Christ our Lord. **Amen.**

After *The Book of Common Prayer*; alt. Laurence Hull Stookey, 1987
Alt. © 1989 The United Methodist Publishing House

All Praise to Thee, My God, This Night 682

1. All praise to thee, my God, this night, for all the bless-ings of the light! Keep me, O keep me, King of kings, be-neath thine own al-might-y wings.
2. For-give me, Lord, for thy dear Son, the ill that I this day have done, that with the world, my-self, and thee, I, ere I sleep, at peace may be.
3. Teach me to live, that I may dread the grave as lit-tle as my bed. Teach me to die, that so I may rise glo-rious at the judg-ment day.
4. O may my soul on thee re-pose, and with sweet sleep mine eye-lids close, sleep that may me more vig-orous make to serve my God when I a-wake.
5. Praise God, from whom all bless-ings flow; praise him, all crea-tures here be-low; praise him a-bove, ye heav-enly host; praise Fa-ther, Son, and Ho-ly Ghost.

May be sung as a unison canon

WORDS: Thomas Ken, ca. 1674
MUSIC: Thomas Tallis, ca. 1567

TALLIS' CANON
LM

683 The Day Is Past and Over

1. The day is past and o - ver; all thanks, O Lord, to
2. The joys of day are o - ver; we lift our hearts to
3. The toils of day are o - ver; we raise our hymn to
4. Be thou our souls' pre - serv - er, O God, for thou dost

thee! We pray thee that of - fense - less the hours of
thee, and call on thee that sin - less the hours of
thee, and ask that free from per - il the hours of
know how man - y are the per - ils through which we

dark may be. O Je - sus, keep us in thy sight,
dark may be. O Je - sus, make their dark - ness light,
dark may be. O Je - sus, keep us in thy sight,
have to go. Lord Je - sus Christ, O hear our call,

and guard us through the com - ing night.
and guard us through the com - ing night.
and guard us through the com - ing night.
and guard and save us from them all.

WORDS: Anon. Greek, prob. 6th cent.;
    trans. by John Mason Neale, 1853
MUSIC: Bartholomäus Gesius, 1601; harm. by J. S. Bach, 1724

DU FRIEDENSFÜRST, HERR JESU CHRIST
76.76.88

Christ, Mighty Savior

Unison

1. Christ, might- y Sav - ior, Light of all cre – a - tion,
2. Now comes the day's end as the sun is set - ting,
3. There-fore we come now eve – ning rites to of - fer,
4. Give heed, we pray you, to our sup - pli - ca - tion,
5. Though bod- ies slum - ber, hearts shall keep their vig - il,

you make the day - time ra – diant with the sun - light
mir - ror of day - break, pledge of res - ur - rec - tion;
joy - ful - ly chant - ing ho – ly hymns to praise you,
that you may grant us par - don for of - fens - es,
for - ev - er rest - ing in the peace of Je - sus,

and to the night give glit – ter-ing a - dorn - ment,
while in the heav – ens choirs of stars ap - pear - ing
with all cre - a - tion join – ing hearts and voic - es
strength for our weak hearts, rest for ach-ing bod - ies,
in light or dark - ness wor – ship-ing our Sav - ior

stars in the heav – ens.
hal – low the night – fall.
sing – ing your glo – ry.
sooth – ing the wea – ry.
now and for – ev – er.

WORDS: Mozarabic hymn, 10th cent.; trans. by Alan G. McDougall;
rev. Anne LeCroy, 1982
MUSIC: David Hurd, 1984

MIGHTY SAVIOR
11 11 11.5

685 Now, on Land and Sea Descending

1. Now, on land and sea de-scend-ing, brings the night its
2. Soon as dies the sun-set glo-ry, stars of heaven shine
3. Now, our wants and bur-dens leav-ing to God's care who
4. As the dark-ness deep-ens o'er us, lo! e-ter-nal

peace pro-found; let our ves-per hymn be blend-ing
out a-bove, tell-ing still the an-cient sto-ry,
cares for all, cease we fear-ing, cease we griev-ing;
stars a-rise; hope and faith and love rise glo-rious,

with the ho-ly calm a-round. Ju-bi-la-te! Ju-bi-la-te!
their Cre-a-tor's change-less love. Ju-bi-la-te! Ju-bi-la-te!
touched by God our bur-dens fall. Ju-bi-la-te! Ju-bi-la-te!
shin-ing in the Spir-it's skies. Ju-bi-la-te! Ju-bi-la-te!

Ju-bi-la-te! A-men! Let our ves-per
Ju-bi-la-te! A-men! Tell-ing still the
Ju-bi-la-te! A-men! Cease we fear-ing,
Ju-bi-la-te! A-men! Hope and faith and

WORDS: Samuel Longfellow, 1859
MUSIC: *A Selection of Popular National Airs*, 1818

VESPER HYMN
87.87.86.87

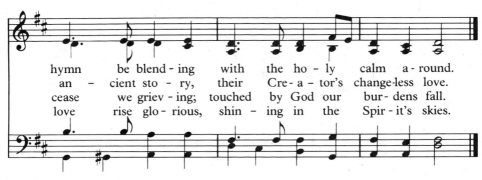

hymn be blend - ing with the ho - ly calm a - round.
an - cient sto - ry, their Cre - a - tor's change-less love.
cease we griev - ing; touched by God our bur - dens fall.
love rise glo - rious, shin - ing in the Spir - it's skies.

O Gladsome Light 686

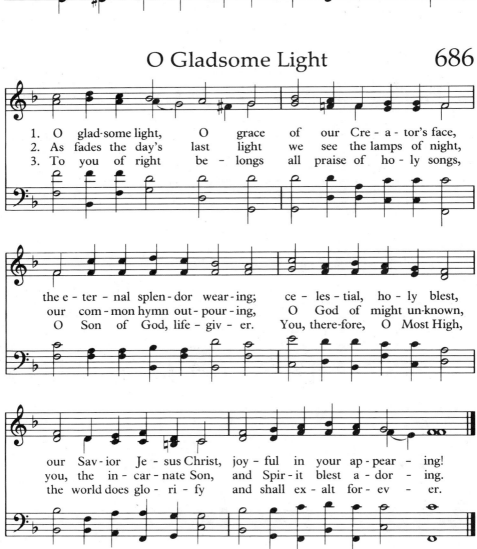

1. O glad-some light, O grace of our Cre - a - tor's face,
2. As fades the day's last light we see the lamps of night,
3. To you of right be - longs all praise of ho - ly songs,

the e - ter - nal splen - dor wear - ing; ce - les - tial, ho - ly blest,
our com - mon hymn out - pour - ing; O God of might un-known,
O Son of God, life - giv - er. You, there-fore, O Most High,

our Sav - ior Je - sus Christ, joy - ful in your ap - pear - ing!
you, the in - car - nate Son, and Spir - it blest a - dor - ing.
the world does glo - ri - fy and shall ex - alt for - ev - er.

WORDS: Ancient Greek hymn; trans. by Robert S. Bridges, 1899
MUSIC: Louis Bourgeois, 1547; harm. by Claude Goudimel, 1551

LE CANTIQUE DE SIMÉON
667.667

687 Day Is Dying in the West

1. Day is dy - ing in the west; heaven is touch - ing
2. Lord of life, be - neath the dome of the u - ni -
3. While the deep - ening shad - ows fall, heart of love en -
4. When for - ev - er from our sight pass the stars, the

earth with rest; wait and wor - ship while the night
verse, thy home, gath - er us who seek thy face
fold - ing all, through the glo - ry and the grace
day, the night, Lord of an - gels, on our eyes

sets the eve - ning lamps a - light through all the sky.
to the fold of thy em - brace, for thou art nigh.
of the stars that veil thy face, our hearts as - cend.
let e - ter - nal morn - ing rise and shad - ows end.

Refrain

Ho - ly, ho - ly, ho - ly, Lord God of Hosts! Heaven and earth are

WORDS: Mary A. Lathbury, 1878 (Is. 6:3)
MUSIC: William F. Sherwin, 1877

CHAUTAUQUA
77.774 with Refrain

God, That Madest Earth and Heaven 688

1. God, that mad-est earth and heav-en, dark-ness and light,
2. When the con-stant sun re-turn-ing un-seals our eyes,

who the day for toil hast giv-en, for rest the night: may thine
may we, born a-new like morn-ing, to la-bor rise. Gird us

an-gel guards de-fend us, slum-ber sweet thy mer-cy send us;
for the task that calls us, let not ease and self en-thrall us,

ho-ly dreams and hopes at-tend us, this live-long night.
strong through thee what-e'er be-fall us, O God most wise!

WORDS: St. 1, Reginald Heber, 1827; st. 2, Frederick Lucian Hosmer, 1912 (Gen. 1:1-15) AR HYD Y NOS
MUSIC: Trad. Welsh melody; harm. by Luther Orlando Emerson, 1906 84.84.888.4

689   At the Close of Day

O Lord my God, I thank thee that thou hast brought this day to its close. I thank thee that thou dost give rest to body and soul. Thy hand has been over me, guarding me and preserving me.

Forgive my feeble faith and all the wrong I have done this day, and help me to forgive all who have wronged me.

Grant that I may sleep in peace beneath thy care, and defend me from the temptations of darkness. Into thy hands I commend my loved ones, I commend this household, I commend my body and soul. O God, thy holy name be praised. **Amen.**

Dietrich Bonhoeffer, Germany, 20th cent.

690   The Day Thou Gavest, Lord, Is Ended

1. The day thou gav - est, Lord, is end - ed; the
2. We thank thee that thy church, un - sleep-ing while
3. As o'er each con - ti - nent and is - land the
4. So be it, Lord; thy throne shall nev - er, like

dark - ness falls at thy be - hest; to thee our morn - ing
earth rolls on - ward in - to light, through all the world her
dawn leads on an - oth - er day, the voice of prayer is
earth's proud em - pires, pass a - way. Thy king - dom stands, and

hymns as - cend-ed; thy praise shall hal - low now our rest.
watch is keep-ing, and rests not now by day or night.
nev - er si - lent, nor die the strains of praise a - way.
grows for - ev - er, till all thy crea - tures own thy sway.

WORDS: John Ellerton, 1870 (Ps. 113:2-3)
MUSIC: Clement Cottevill Scholefield, 1874

ST. CLEMENT
98.98

For Protection at Night 691

Dear Jesus, as a hen covers her chicks with her wings to keep them safe,
do thou this night protect us under your golden wings. **Amen.**

Trad., India (Mt. 23:37; Lk. 13:34)

Creator of the Stars of Night 692

Unison

1. Cre - a - tor of the stars of night, thy peo - ple's ev - er -
2. At the great name of Je - sus now all knees must bend, all

last - ing light, O Christ, thou Sav - ior of us all,
hearts must bow; and things ce - les - tial thee shall own,

D.C.

we pray thee, hear us when we call.
and things ter - res - trial, Lord a - lone. A - men.

WORDS: Anon. Latin, 9th cent.; trans. from *The Hymnal*, 1940 (Phil. 2:10-11) CONDITOR ALME
MUSIC: Plainsong, Mode IV; harm. by C. Winfred Douglas, 1943, alt. LM

Trans. © 1940, 1943, renewed 1971 The Church Pension Fund; harm. © 1943, renewed 1971 The Church Pension Fund

For a Peaceful Night 693

O God, you have let me pass the day in peace;
let me pass the night in peace, O Lord who has no lord.
There is no strength but in you. You alone have no obligation.
Under your hand I pass the night. You are my Mother and my Father. **Amen.**

Trad. prayer of the Boran people

EVENING, *see further:*

694 Come, Ye Thankful People, Come

1. Come, ye thank - ful peo - ple, come, raise the song of
2. All the world is God's own field, fruit as praise to
3. For the Lord our God shall come, and shall take the
4. E - ven so, Lord, quick - ly come, bring thy fi - nal

har - vest home; all is safe - ly gath - ered in, ere the
God we yield; wheat and tares to - geth - er sown are to
har - vest home; from the field shall in that day all of -
har - vest home; gath - er thou thy peo - ple in, free from

win - ter storms be - gin. God our Mak - er doth pro - vide
joy or sor - row grown; first the blade and then the ear,
fens - es purge a - way, giv - ing an - gels charge at last
sor - row, free from sin, there, for - ev - er pu - ri - fied,

for our wants to be sup - plied; come to God's own
then the full corn shall ap - pear; Lord of har - vest,
in the fire the tares to cast; but the fruit - ful
in thy pres - ence to a - bide; come, with all thine

WORDS: Henry Alford, 1844, alt. (Mk. 4:26-29; Mt. 13:36-43)
MUSIC: George J. Elvey, 1858

ST. GEORGE'S WINDSOR
77.77 D

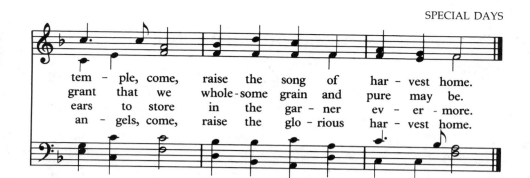

tem - ple, come,   raise the   song   of   har - vest home.
grant   that   we   whole-some grain   and   pure   may   be.
ears   to   store   in   the   gar - ner   ev - er - more.
an - gels,   come,   raise the   glo - rious   har - vest home.

O Lord, May Church and Home Combine 695

1. O   Lord,   may church   and   home com - bine   to
2. Let   all   un - wor - thy   aims   de - part,   im -
3. Shine, Light   di - vine;   re - veal   thy   face   where
4. May   stead - fast   faith   and   ear - nest prayer   keep

teach   thy   per - fect   way,   with   gen - tle - ness   and
bue   us   with   thy   grace;   with - in   the home   let
dark - ness else   might   be.   Grant, Love   di - vine,   in
sa - cred vows   se - cure;   build thou   a   hal - lowed

love   like   thine,   that   none   shall ev - er   stray.
ev - ery heart   be - come   thy dwell - ing   place.
ev - ery place   glad   fel - low-ship   with   thee.
dwell - ing where   true   joy   and peace   en - dure.

WORDS: Carlton C. Buck, 1961
MUSIC: USA folk melody; arr. by Annabel Morris Buchanan, 1938;
  harm. by Charles H. Webb, 1988

LAND OF REST
CM

696 America the Beautiful

1. O beau-ti-ful for spa-cious skies, for am-ber waves of grain; for pur-ple moun-tain maj-es-ties a-bove the fruit-ed plain! A-mer-i-ca! A-mer-i-ca! God shed his grace on thee, and crown thy good with broth-er-hood from sea to shin-ing sea.

2. O beau-ti-ful for he-roes proved in lib-er-at-ing strife, who more than self their coun-try loved, and mer-cy more than life! A-mer-i-ca! A-mer-i-ca! May God thy gold re-fine, till all suc-cess be no-ble-ness, and ev-ery gain di-vine.

3. O beau-ti-ful for pa-triot dream that sees be-yond the years thine al-a-bas-ter cit-ies gleam, un-dimmed by hu-man tears! A-mer-i-ca! A-mer-i-ca! God mend thine ev-ery flaw, con-firm thy soul in self-con-trol, thy lib-er-ty in law.

WORDS: Katharine Lee Bates, 1904
MUSIC: Samuel A. Ward, 1888

MATERNA
CMD

America
(My Country, 'Tis of Thee)

1. My coun - try, 'tis of thee, sweet land of
2. My na - tive coun - try, thee, land of the
3. Let mu - sic swell the breeze, and ring from
4. Our fa - thers' God, to thee, au - thor of

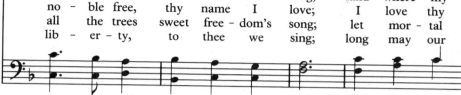

lib - er - ty, of thee I sing; land where my
no - ble free, thy name I love; I love thy
all the trees sweet free - dom's song; let mor - tal
lib - er - ty, to thee we sing; long may our

fa - thers died, land of the pil - grims' pride,
rocks and rills, thy woods and tem - pled hills;
tongues a - wake; let all that breathe par - take;
land be bright with free - dom's ho - ly light;

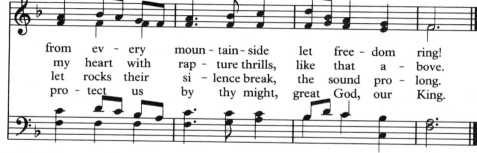

from ev - ery moun - tain - side let free - dom ring!
my heart with rap - ture thrills, like that a - bove.
let rocks their si - lence break, the sound pro - long.
pro - tect us by thy might, great God, our King.

WORDS: Samuel F. Smith, 1832
MUSIC: *Thesaurus Musicus*, 1744

AMERICA
664.6664

698 God of the Ages

Trumpets, before each stanza

1. God of the a - ges, whose al-might-y hand
2. Thy love di - vine hath led us in the past;
3. From war's a-larms, from dead-ly pes - ti - lence,
4. Re-fresh thy peo - ple on their toil-some way;

leads forth in beau - ty all the star - ry band
in this free land with thee our lot is cast;
be thy strong arm our ev - er sure de - fense;
lead us from night to nev - er - end - ing day;

of shin - ing worlds in splen - dor through the skies,
be thou our rul - er, guard-ian, guide, and stay,
thy true re - li - gion in our hearts in - crease;
fill all our lives with love and grace di - vine,

our grate - ful songs be - fore thy throne a - rise.
thy Word our law, thy paths our cho - sen way.
thy boun - teous good - ness nour - ish us in peace.
and glo - ry, laud, and praise be ev - er thine.

WORDS: Daniel C. Roberts, 1876
MUSIC: George W. Warren, 1894

NATIONAL HYMN
10 10.10 10

Come, and Let Us Sweetly Join

1. Come, and let us sweet - ly join, Christ to praise in hymns di - vine; give we all with one ac - cord glo - ry to our com - mon Lord.

2. Hands and hearts and voic - es raise, sing as in the an - cient days; an - te - date the joys a - bove, cel - e - brate the feast of love.

3. Je - sus, dear ex - pect - ed Guest, thou art bid - den to the feast; for thy - self our hearts pre - pare; come, and sit, and ban - quet there.

4. Sanc - ti - fy us, Lord, and bless, breathe thy Spir - it, give thy peace; thou thy - self with - in us move, make our feast a feast of love.

WORDS: Charles Wesley, 1740
MUSIC: Adapt. from Orlando Gibbons, 1623

CANTERBURY
77.77

700 Abide with Me

1. A - bide with me; fast falls the e - ven - tide;
2. Swift to its close ebbs out life's lit - tle day;
3. I need thy pres - ence ev - ery pass - ing hour.
4. I fear no foe, with thee at hand to bless;
5. Hold thou thy cross be - fore my clos - ing eyes;

the dark - ness deep - ens; Lord, with me a - bide.
earth's joys grow dim; its glo - ries pass a - way;
What but thy grace can foil the tempt - er's power?
ills have no weight, and tears no bit - ter - ness.
shine through the gloom and point me to the skies.

When oth - er help - ers fail and com - forts flee,
change and de - cay in all a - round I see;
Who, like thy - self, my guide and stay can be?
Where is death's sting? Where, grave, thy vic - to - ry?
Heaven's morn - ing breaks, and earth's vain shad - ows flee;

Help of the help - less, O a - bide with me.
O Thou who chang - est not, a - bide with me.
Through cloud and sun - shine, Lord, a - bide with me.
I tri - umph still, if thou a - bide with me.
in life, in death, O Lord, a - bide with me.

WORDS: Henry F. Lyte, 1847 (Lk. 24:29)
MUSIC: W. H. Monk, 1861

EVENTIDE
10 10.10 10

When We All Get to Heaven

1. Sing the won-drous love of Je - sus; sing his mer - cy
2. While we walk the pil - grim path-way, clouds will o - ver -
3. Let us then be true and faith-ful, trust - ing, serv - ing
4. On - ward to the prize be - fore us! Soon his beau - ty

and his grace. In the man-sions bright and bless - ed
spread the sky; but when trav - eling days are o - ver,
ev - ery day; just one glimpse of him in glo - ry
we'll be-hold; soon the pearl - y gates will o - pen;

he'll pre - pare for us a place.
not a shad - ow, not a sigh.
will the toils of life re - pay.
we shall tread the streets of gold.

Refrain

When we all get to

heav - en, what a day of re - joic - ing that will be!

When we all see Je - sus, we'll sing and shout the vic - to - ry!

WORDS: Eliza E. Hewitt, 1898
MUSIC: Emily D. Wilson, 1898

HEAVEN
87.87 with Refrain

702 Sing with All the Saints in Glory

1. Sing with all the saints in glo-ry, sing the res-ur-
2. O what glo-ry, far ex-ceed-ing all that eye has
3. Life e-ter-nal! heaven re-joic-es: Je-sus lives, who
4. Life e-ter-nal! O what won-ders crowd on faith; what

rec-tion song! Death and sor-row, earth's dark sto-ry,
yet per-ceived! Ho-liest hearts, for a-ges plead-ing,
once was dead. Join we now the death-less voic-es;
joy un-known, when, a-midst earth's clos-ing thun-ders,

to the for-mer days be-long. All a-round the
nev-er that full joy con-ceived. God has prom-ised,
child of God, lift up your head! Pa-triarchs from the
saints shall stand be-fore the throne! O to en-ter

clouds are break-ing, soon the storms of time shall cease; in
Christ pre-pares it, there on high our wel-come waits. Ev-
dis-tant a-ges, saints all long-ing for their heaven, proph-
that bright por-tal, see that glow-ing fir-ma-ment; know,

God's like-ness we, a-wak-ing, know the ev-er-last-ing peace.
ery hum-ble spir-it shares it; Christ has passed th'e-ter-nal gates.
ets, psalm-ists, seers, and sa-ges, all a-wait the glo-ry given.
with thee, O God Im-mor-tal, "Je-sus Christ whom thou has sent!"

WORDS: William J. Irons, 1873 (1 Cor. 15:20)
MUSIC: Ludwig van Beethoven, 1824; arr. by Edward Hodges, 1864

HYMN TO JOY
87.87 D

Swing Low, Sweet Chariot

703

Refrain

Swing low, sweet char-i-ot, com-ing for to car-ry me home;
swing low, sweet char-i-ot, com-ing for to car-ry me home.

1. I looked o - ver Jor - dan, and what did I see,
2. If you get there be - fore I do,
3. I'm some - times up, I'm some - times down,
4. The bright - est day that I can say,

com-ing for to car-ry me home? A band of an - gels
com-ing for to car-ry me home; tell all my friends I'm
com-ing for to car-ry me home; but still my soul feels
com-ing for to car-ry me home; when Je - sus washed my

com-ing af - ter me, com-ing for to car-ry me home.
com-ing too, com-ing for to car-ry me home.
heav-en - ly bound, com-ing for to car-ry me home.
sins a - way, com-ing for to car-ry me home.

WORDS: Afro-American spiritual (2 Kg. 2:11)
MUSIC: Afro-American spiritual; adapt. and arr. by William Farley Smith, 1987

SWING LOW
10 8.10 8 with Refrain

Adapt. and arr. © 1989 The United Methodist Publishing House

704 Steal Away to Jesus

Refrain

Steal a-way, steal a-way; steal a-way to Je-sus.

Steal a-way, steal a-way home. I ain't got long to stay here.

1. My Lord he calls me, he calls me by the thun-der; the
2. Green trees a-bend-ing, poor sin-ners stand a-trem-bling; the
3. My Lord he calls me, he calls me by the light-ning; the

trum-pet sounds with-in - a my soul. I ain't got long to stay here.

D.C.

WORDS: Afro-American spiritual (1 Cor. 15:51-52)
MUSIC: Afro-American spiritual; adapt. and arr. by William Farley Smith, 1986
Adapt. and arr. © 1989 The United Methodist Publishing House

STEAL AWAY
57.87 with Refrain

705 For Direction

Direct us, O Lord, in all our doings,
    with your most gracious favor,
and further us with your continual help,
    that in all our works,
        begun, continued, and ended in you,
        we may glorify your holy name,
        and finally, by your mercy, obtain everlasting life;
    through Jesus Christ our Lord. **Amen.**

After The Book of Common Prayer

Soon and Very Soon

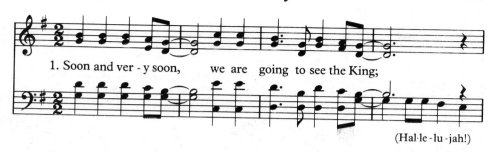

2. No more dy-ing there,
3. No more cry-ing there,

WORDS: Andraé Crouch, 1978 (Rev. 21:3-4)
MUSIC: Andraé Crouch, 1978; adapt. by William Farley Smith, 1987

VERY SOON
Irr.

707 Hymn of Promise

Unison

1. In the bulb   there is a   flow-er; in the seed,   an ap-ple tree;
2. There's a song   in ev-ery   si-lence, seek-ing word   and mel-o-dy;
3. In our end   is our be-gin-ning; in our time,   in-fin-i-ty;

in co-coons,   a hid-den prom-ise: but-ter-flies   will soon be free!
there's a dawn   in ev-ery dark-ness, bring-ing hope   to you and me.
in our doubt   there is be-liev-ing; in our life,   e-ter-ni-ty.

In the cold   and snow of win-ter there's a spring   that waits to be,
From the past   will come the fu-ture; what it holds,   a mys-ter-y,
In our death,   a res-ur-rec-tion; at the last,   a vic-to-ry,

un-re-vealed   un-til its   sea-son, some-thing God a-lone can   see.

WORDS: Natalie Sleeth, 1986
MUSIC: Natalie Sleeth, 1986

© 1986 Hope Publishing Co.

PROMISE
87.87 D

DEATH AND ETERNAL LIFE, *see further:*

Rejoice in God's Saints

1. Re - joice in God's saints, to - day and all days;
2. Some march with e - vents to turn them God's way;
3. Re - joice in those saints, un - praised and un - known,
4. Re - joice in God's saints, to - day and all days;

a world with - out saints for - gets how to praise.
some need to with - draw, the bet - ter to pray.
who bear some - one's cross or shoul - der their own.
a world with - out saints for - gets how to praise.

Their faith in ac - quir - ing the hab - it of prayer,
Some car - ry the gos - pel through fire and through flood;
They shame our com - plain - ing, our com - forts, our cares;
In lov - ing, in liv - ing, they prove it is true:

their depth of a - dor - ing, Lord, help us to share.
our world is their par - ish; their pur - pose is God.
what pa - tience in car - ing, what cour - age, is theirs!
the way of self - giv - ing, Lord, leads us to you.

WORDS: Fred Pratt Green, 1977
MUSIC: Attr. to William Croft, 1708

HANOVER
10 10.11 11

Words © 1973, 1980 Hope Publishing Co.

709 Come, Let Us Join Our Friends Above

1. Come, let us join our friends a-bove who have ob-tained the prize, and on the ea-gle wings of love to joys ce-les-tial rise. Let saints on earth u-nite to sing with those to glo-ry gone, for all the

2. One fam-i-ly we dwell in him, one church a-bove, be-neath, though now di-vid-ed by the stream, the nar-row stream of death; one ar-my of the liv-ing God, to his com-mand we bow; part of his

3. Ten thou-sand to their end-less home this sol-emn mo-ment fly, and we are to the mar-gin come, and we ex-pect to die. E'en now by faith we join our hands with those that went be-fore, and greet the

4. Our spir-its too shall quick-ly join, like theirs with glo-ry crowned, and shout to see our Cap-tain's sign, to hear his trum-pet sound. O that we now might grasp our Guide! O that the word were given! Come, Lord of

WORDS: Charles Wesley, 1759
MUSIC: Trad. English melody; arr. by Ralph Vaughan Williams, 1906

FOREST GREEN
CMD

ser - vants of our King in earth and heaven are one.
host have crossed the flood, and part are cross - ing now.
blood - be - sprin - kled bands on the e - ter - nal shore.
Hosts, the waves di - vide, and land us all in heaven.

Faith of Our Fathers 710

1. Faith of our fa - thers,* liv - ing still, in spite of dun-geon,
2. Faith of our fa - thers, we will strive to win all na-tions
3. Faith of our fa - thers, we will love both friend and foe in

fire, and sword; O how our hearts beat high with joy
un - to thee; and through the truth that comes from God,
all our strife; and preach thee, too, as love knows how

Refrain

when-e'er we hear that glo - rious word!
we all shall then be tru - ly free. Faith of our fa - thers,
by kind-ly words and vir - tuous life.

ho - ly faith! We will be true to thee till death.

"The martyrs" may be substituted for "our fathers"

WORDS: Frederick W. Faber, 1849
MUSIC: Henri F. Hemy, 1864; adapt. by James G. Walton, 1874

ST. CATHERINE
88.88.88

711 For All the Saints

Unison

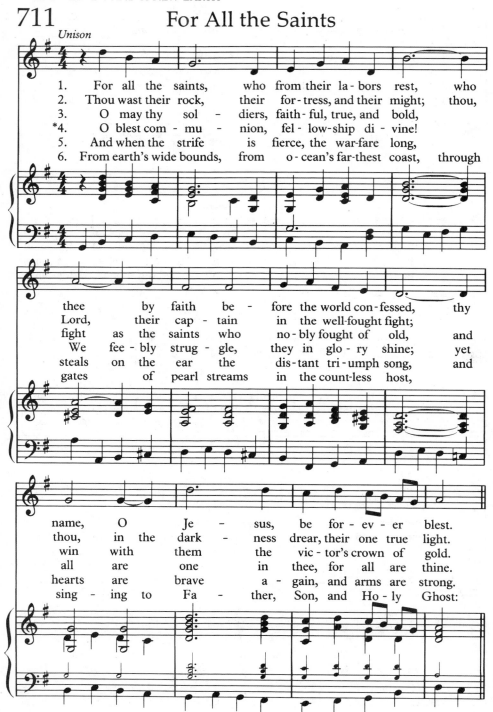

1. For all the saints, who from their la-bors rest, who
2. Thou wast their rock, their for-tress, and their might; thou,
3. O may thy sol - diers, faith-ful, true, and bold,
*4. O blest com - mu - nion, fel - low-ship di - vine!
5. And when the strife is fierce, the war-fare long,
6. From earth's wide bounds, from o - cean's far-thest coast, through

thee by faith be - fore the world con-fessed, thy
Lord, their cap - tain in the well-fought fight;
fight as the saints who no - bly fought of old, and
We fee - bly strug - gle, they in glo - ry shine; yet
steals on the ear the dis-tant tri-umph song, and
gates of pearl streams in the count-less host,

name, O Je - sus, be for - ev - er blest.
thou, in the dark - ness drear, their one true light.
win with them the vic - tor's crown of gold.
all are one in thee, for all are thine.
hearts are brave a - gain, and arms are strong.
sing - ing to Fa - ther, Son, and Ho - ly Ghost:

WORDS: William W. How, 1864 (Heb. 12:1)
MUSIC: Ralph Vaughan Williams, 1906

SINE NOMINE
10 10 10 with Alleluias

*Stanza 4 may be sung unaccompanied

712 I Sing a Song of the Saints of God

Unison

1. I sing a song of the saints of God,
2. They loved their Lord so dear, so dear, and
3. They lived not on-ly in a - ges past; there are

pa - tient and brave and true, who toiled and fought and
his love made them strong; and they fol - lowed the right for
hun - dreds of thou-sands still. The world is bright with the

lived and died for the Lord they loved and knew. And
Je - sus' sake the whole of their good lives long. And
joy - ous saints who love to do Je - sus' will. You can

one was a doc - tor, and one was a queen, and one was a
one was a sol - dier, and one was a priest, and one was
meet them in school, on the street, in the store, in church, by the

WORDS: Lesbia Scott, 1929
MUSIC: John H. Hopkins, Jr., 1940

GRAND ISLE
Irr.

shep-herd-ess on the green; they were all of them saints of
slain by a fierce wild beast; and there's not an-y rea-son,
sea, in the house next door; they are saints of God, wheth-er

God, and I mean, God help-ing, to be one too.
no, not the least, why I should-n't be one too.
rich or poor, and I mean to be one too.

All Saints 713

Almighty God,
you have knit together your elect
in one communion and fellowship,
in the mystical body of your Son Christ our Lord.
Grant us grace
so to follow your holy saints in all virtuous and godly living,
that we may come to those unspeakable joys,
which you have prepared for those who sincerely love you;
through Jesus Christ our Lord. **Amen.**

After *The Book of Common Prayer*

COMMUNION OF THE SAINTS, *see further:*

714   I Know Whom I Have Believed

1. I know not why God's won-drous grace to me he
2. I know not how this sav-ing faith to me he
3. I know not how the Spir-it moves, con-vinc-ing
4. I know not when my Lord may come, at night or

hath made known, nor why, un-wor-thy, Christ in love re-
did im-part, nor how be-liev-ing in his word wrought
us of sin, re-veal-ing Je-sus through the word, cre-
noon-day fair, nor if I walk the vale with him, or

Refrain

deemed me for his own.
peace with-in my heart.
at-ing faith in him.
meet him in the air.   But I know whom I have be-

liev-ed, and am per-suad-ed that he is a-ble to

keep that which I've com-mit-ted un-to him a-gainst that day.

WORDS: Daniel W. Whittle, 1883 (2 Tim. 1:12)
MUSIC: James McGranahan, 1883

EL NATHAN
CM with Refrain

Rejoice, the Lord Is King

715

1. Re - joice, the Lord is King! Your Lord and King a - dore;
2. Je - sus the Sav - ior reigns, the God of truth and love;
3. His king-dom can - not fail; he rules o'er earth and heaven;
4. Re - joice in glo - rious hope! Je - sus the Judge shall come,

mor - tals, give thanks and sing, and tri - umph ev - er - more.
when he had purged our stains, he took his seat a - bove.
the keys of earth and hell are to our Je - sus given.
and take his ser - vants up to their e - ter - nal home.

Lift up your heart, lift up your voice;
Lift up your heart, lift up your voice;
Lift up your heart, lift up your voice;
We soon shall hear th'arch - an - gel's voice;

re - joice; a - gain I say, re - joice.
re - joice; a - gain I say, re - joice.
re - joice; a - gain I say, re - joice.
the trump of God shall sound, re - joice!

WORDS: Charles Wesley, 1746 (1 Cor. 15:51-52)
MUSIC: John Darwall, 1770; harm. from *Hymns Ancient and Modern*, 1875, alt.

DARWALL'S 148th
66.66.88

716 Rejoice, the Lord Is King

1. Re - joice, the Lord is King! Your Lord and King a -
2. Je - sus the Sa - vior reigns, the God of truth and
3. His king - dom can - not fail; he rules o'er earth and
4. Re - joice in glo - rious hope! Je - sus the Judge shall

dore; mor - tals, give thanks and sing, and
love; when he had purged our stains, he
heaven; the keys of earth and hell are
come, and take his ser - vants up to

Refrain

1-3

tri - umph ev - er - more. Lift up your heart, lift
took his seat a - bove.
to our Je - sus given.
their e - ter - nal home.

WORDS: Charles Wesley, 1746 (1 Cor. 15:51-52)
MUSIC: G. F. Handel, ca. 1752; arr. by John Wilson, 1964

GOPSAL
66.66.88

Arr. © 1969 Hope Publishing Co.

up your voice; re-joice; a-gain I say, re-joice.

We soon shall hear the arch - an - gel's voice; the trump of

God shall sound, re - joice!

717 The Battle Hymn of the Republic

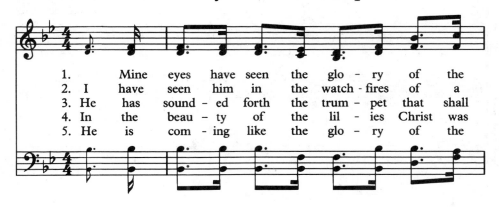

1. Mine eyes have seen the glo - ry of the
2. I have seen him in the watch - fires of a
3. He has sound - ed forth the trum - pet that shall
4. In the beau - ty of the lil - ies Christ was
5. He is com - ing like the glo - ry of the

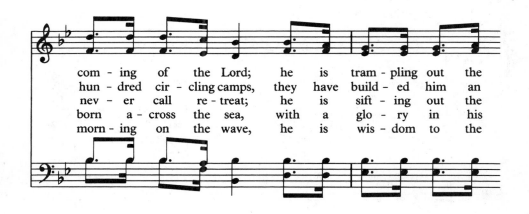

com - ing of the Lord; he is tram - pling out the
hun - dred cir - cling camps, they have build - ed him an
nev - er call re - treat; he is sift - ing out the
born a - cross the sea, with a glo - ry in his
morn - ing on the wave, he is wis - dom to the

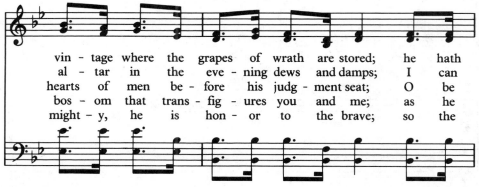

vin - tage where the grapes of wrath are stored; he hath
al - tar in the eve - ning dews and damps; I can
hearts of men be - fore his judg - ment seat; O be
bos - om that trans - fig - ures you and me; as he
might - y, he is hon - or to the brave; so the

WORDS: Sts. 1-4, Julia Ward Howe, 1861; st. 5, anon.
MUSIC: USA campmeeting tune, 19th cent.

BATTLE HYMN OF THE REPUBLIC
15 15 15.6 with Refrain

loosed the fate-ful light-ning of his ter-ri-ble swift sword;
read his righ-teous sen-tence by the dim and flar-ing lamps;
swift, my soul, to an-swer him; be ju-bi-lant, my feet!
died to make men ho-ly, let us die to make men free,
world shall be his foot-stool, and the soul of wrong his slave.

Refrain

his truth is march-ing on.
his day is march-ing on.
Our God is march-ing on. Glo-ry, glo-ry, hal-le-
while God is march-ing on.
Our God is march-ing on.

lu-jah! Glo-ry, glo-ry, hal-le-lu-jah! Glo-ry,

glo-ry, hal-le-lu-jah! His truth is march-ing on.

718 Lo, He Comes with Clouds Descending

1. Lo, he comes with clouds de-scend-ing, once for
2. Ev-ery eye shall now be-hold him, robed in
3. The dear to-kens of his pas-sion still his
4. Yea, A-men! Let all a-dore thee, high on

fa-vored sin-ners slain; thou-sand, thou-sand
dread-ful maj-es-ty; those who set at
daz-zling bod-y bears; cause of end-less
thy e-ter-nal throne; Sav-ior, take the

saints at-tend-ing swell the tri-umph of his
naught and sold him, pierced and nailed him to the
ex-ul-ta-tion to his ran-somed wor-ship-
power and glo-ry, claim the king-dom for thine

train. Hal-le-lu-jah! Hal-le-lu-jah!
tree, deep-ly wail-ing, deep-ly wail-ing,
ers; with what rap-ture, with what rap-ture,
own. Hal-le-lu-jah! Hal-le-lu-jah!

WORDS: Charles Wesley, 1758 (Rev. 1:7)
MUSIC: Trad. English melody, 18th cent.; harm. from *The English Hymnal*, 1906

HELMSLEY
87.87.47

My Lord, What a Morning 719

WORDS: Afro-American spiritual (1 Cor. 15:51-52; Rev. 6:12-17)
MUSIC: Afro-American spiritual; adapt. and arr. by William Farley Smith, 1987

BURLEIGH
Irr.

720 Wake, Awake, for Night Is Flying

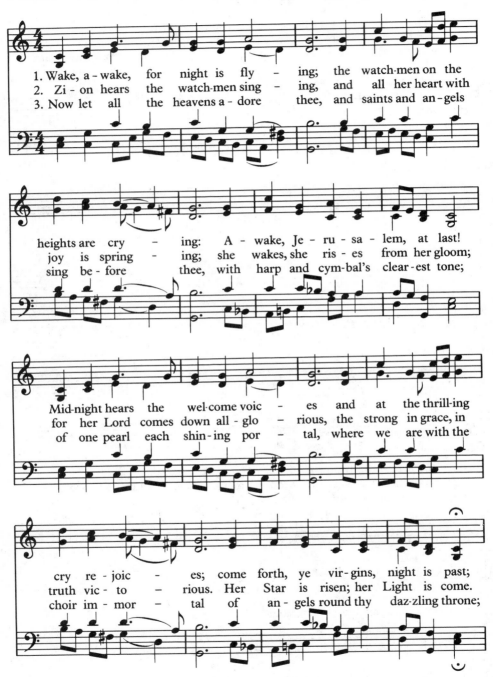

1. Wake, a-wake, for night is fly - ing; the watch-men on the
2. Zi - on hears the watch-men sing - ing, and all her heart with
3. Now let all the heavens a - dore thee, and saints and an-gels

heights are cry - ing: A - wake, Je - ru - sa - lem, at last!
joy is spring - ing; she wakes, she ris - es from her gloom;
sing be - fore thee, with harp and cym-bal's clear-est tone;

Mid-night hears the wel-come voic - es and at the thrill-ing
for her Lord comes down all - glo - rious, the strong in grace, in
of one pearl each shin-ing por - tal, where we are with the

cry re - joic - es; come forth, ye vir-gins, night is past;
truth vic - to - rious. Her Star is risen; her Light is come.
choir im - mor - tal of an - gels round thy daz-zling throne;

WORDS: Philipp Nicolai, 1599; trans. by Catherine Winkworth, 1858
(Rom. 13:11-12; Mt. 25:1-13)
MUSIC: Philipp Nicolai, 1599; harm. by J. S. Bach, 1731

WACHET AUF
Irr.

the Bride-groom comes, a - wake; your lamps with glad - ness take:
Ah come, thou bless - ed One, God's own be - lov - ed Son:
nor eye hath seen, nor ear hath yet at - tained to hear

Al - le - lu - ia! And for his mar - riage
Al - le - lu - ia! We fol - low till the
what there is ours; but we re - joice and

feast pre - pare, for ye must go and meet him there.
halls we see where thou hast bid us sup with thee.
sing to thee our hymn of joy e - ter - nal - ly.

Christ the King 721

Almighty and everlasting God,
it is your will to restore all things to Christ,
   whom you have anointed priest for ever and ruler of creation.
Grant that all the people of the earth,
   now divided by the power of sin,
   may be united under the glorious and gentle rule of Jesus Christ,
who lives and reigns for ever and ever. **Amen.**

After *The Book of Common Prayer*

RETURN AND REIGN OF THE LORD, *see further:*

722   I Want to Be Ready

Refrain

I want to be read-y, I want to be read-y,

I want to be read-y to walk in Je-ru-sa-lem just like John.

Leader

1. O John, O John, what did you say?
2. John said the cit-y was just four-square.
3. Now sin-ners, mind how you step on the cross.

All   *Leader*

Walk in Je-ru-sa-lem just like John! And he de-clared he'd
That you'd be there on
Your foot might slip and your

All

judg-ment day.
meet me there.   Walk in Je-ru-sa-lem just like John!
soul get lost.

WORDS: Afro-American spiritual (Rev. 21:2, 16)
MUSIC: Afro-American spiritual; adapt. and arr. by William Farley Smith, 1986

I WANT TO BE READY
Irr. with Refrain

Adapt. and arr. © 1989 The United Methodist Publishing House

Shall We Gather at the River   723

1. Shall we gath-er at the riv - er, where bright an-gel feet have trod,
2. On the mar-gin of the riv - er, wash-ing up its sil - ver spray,
3. Ere we reach the shin-ing riv - er, lay we ev - ery bur-den down;
4. Soon we'll reach the shin-ing riv - er, soon our pil-grim-age will cease;

with its crys-tal tide for - ev - er flow-ing by the throne of God?
we will walk and wor-ship ev - er, all the hap - py gold - en day.
grace our spir - its will de - liv - er, and pro - vide a robe and crown.
soon our hap - py hearts will quiv - er with the mel - o - dy of peace.

Refrain

Yes, we'll gath - er at the riv - er, the beau - ti - ful, the beau - ti - ful riv - er; gath - er with the saints at the riv - er that flows by the throne of God.

WORDS: Robert Lowry, 1864 (Rev. 22:1-5)
MUSIC: Robert Lowry, 1864

HANSON PLACE
87.87 with Refrain

724 On Jordan's Stormy Banks I Stand

1. On Jor-dan's* storm-y banks I stand, and cast a
2. O'er all those wide ex-tend-ed plains shines one e-
3. No chill-ing winds or poi-sonous breath can reach that
4. When I shall reach that hap-py place, I'll be for-

wish-ful eye to Ca-naan's fair and hap-py land, where
ter-nal day; there God the Son for-ev-er reigns, and
health-ful shore; sick-ness and sor-row, pain and death, are
ev-er blest, for I shall see my Fa-ther's face, and

Refrain

my pos-ses-sions lie.
scat-ters night a-way.
felt and feared no more.
in his bo-som rest. I am bound for the prom-ised land,

I am bound for the prom-ised land; oh, who will come and

Pronounced "Jerdan's"

WORDS: Samuel Stennett, 1787
MUSIC: *The Southern Harmony*, 1835; arr. by Rigdon M. McIntosh, 1895

PROMISED LAND
CM with Refrain

go with me? I am bound for the prom-ised land.

Arise, Shine Out, Your Light Has Come 725

Unison

1. A - rise, shine out, your light has come, un - fold - ing
2. A - bove earth's val - leys, thick with night, high on your
3. From walls sur - pass - ing time and space un - num - bered
4. The sounds of vi - o - lence shall cease as dwell - ings
5. The danc - ing air shall glow with light, and sun and

cit - y of our dreams. On dis - tant hills a glo - ry
walls the dawn ap - pears, and his - to - ry shall dry its
gates, like o - pen hands, shall gath - er gifts from all the
of sal - va - tion rise to spar - kle in e - ter - nal
moon give up their place, when love shines out of ev - ery

gleams: the new cre - a - tion has be - gun.
tears, as na - tions march to - ward your light.
lands and wel - come all the hu - man race.
skies from av - e - nues of praise and peace.
face, our good, our glo - ry, and de - light.

WORDS: Brian Wren, 1986 (Is. 60:1-3)
MUSIC: Vernon Griffiths, 1971

DUNEDIN
LM

726   O Holy City, Seen of John

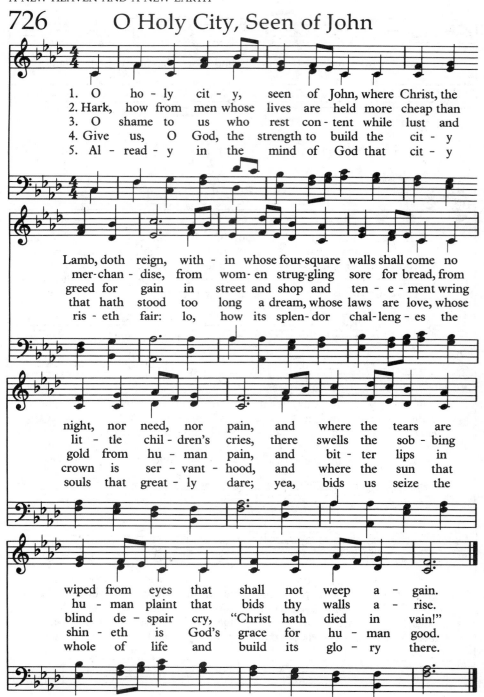

1. O ho-ly cit-y, seen of John, where Christ, the
2. Hark, how from men whose lives are held more cheap than
3. O shame to us who rest con-tent while lust and
4. Give us, O God, the strength to build the cit-y
5. Al-read-y in the mind of God that cit-y

Lamb, doth reign, with-in whose four-square walls shall come no
mer-chan-dise, from wom-en strug-gling sore for bread, from
greed for gain in street and shop and ten-e-ment wring
that hath stood too long a dream, whose laws are love, whose
ris-eth fair: lo, how its splen-dor chal-leng-es the

night, nor need, nor pain, and where the tears are
lit-tle chil-dren's cries, there swells the sob-bing
gold from hu-man pain, and bit-ter lips in
crown is ser-vant-hood, and where the sun that
souls that great-ly dare; yea, bids us seize the

wiped from eyes that shall not weep a-gain.
hu-man plaint that bids thy walls a-rise.
blind de-spair cry, "Christ hath died in vain!"
shin-eth is God's grace for hu-man good.
whole of life and build its glo-ry there.

WORDS: Walter Russell Bowie, 1909 (Rev. 21:1-22:5)
MUSIC: Wyeth's *Repository of Sacred Music, Part Second*, 1813;
  harm. by Charles H. Webb, 1987

MORNING SONG
86.86.86

O What Their Joy and Their Glory Must Be 727

1. O what their joy and their glo - ry must be,
2. Tru - ly, "Je - ru - sa - lem" name we that shore,
3. There, where no trou - bles dis - trac - tion can bring,
4. Now, in the mean - while, with hearts raised on high,
5. Low be - fore him with our prais - es we fall,

those end - less sab - baths the bless - ed ones see;
cit - y of peace that brings joy ev - er - more;
we the sweet an - thems of Zi - on shall sing;
we for that coun - try must yearn and must sigh;
of whom, and in whom, and through whom are all;

crown for the val - iant, to wea - ry ones rest;
wish and ful - fill - ment are not sev - ered there,
while for thy grace, Lord, their voic - es of praise
seek - ing Je - ru - sa - lem, dear na - tive land,
of whom, the Fa - ther; and in whom, the Son,

God shall be all, and in all ev - er blest.
nor do things prayed for come short of the prayer.
thy bless - ed peo - ple e - ter - nal - ly raise.
through our long ex - ile on Bab - y - lon's strand.
through whom, the Spir - it, with them ev - er One.

WORDS: Peter Abelard, 12th cent.; trans. by John Mason Neale, 1851
MUSIC: *Paris Antiphoner*, 1681; harm. by John B. Dykes, 1868

O QUANTA QUALIA
10 10.10 10

728 Come Sunday

*Sing cue notes last time only.

WORDS: Duke Ellington, 1966
MUSIC: Duke Ellington, 1966

© 1966, renewed G. Schirmer, Inc.

ELLINGTON
Irr.

729 O Day of Peace That Dimly Shines

1. O day of peace that dim-ly shines through all our hopes and prayers and dreams, guide us to jus-tice, truth, and love, de-liv-ered from our self-ish schemes. May swords of hate fall from our hands, our hearts from en-vy find re-lease, till by God's

2. Then shall the wolf dwell with the lamb, nor shall the fierce de-vour the small; as beasts and cat-tle calm-ly graze, a lit-tle child shall lead them all. Then en-e-mies shall learn to love, all crea-tures find their true ac-cord; the hope of

WORDS: Carl P. Daw, Jr., 1982 (Is. 11:6-7)
MUSIC: Charles Hubert Hastings Parry, 1916; harm. by Charles H. Webb, 1987

JERUSALEM
LMD

grace   our war-ring world shall see Christ's prom-ised reign of   peace.
peace shall be ful-filled,   for all the earth shall know the   Lord.

O Day of God, Draw Nigh   730

1. O   day   of   God,   draw   nigh   in   beau – ty
2. Bring   to   our   trou – bled   minds,   un –   cer – tain
3. Bring   jus – tice   to   our   land,   that   all   may
4. Bring   to   our   world   of   strife   thy   sov – ereign
5. O   day   of   God,   draw   nigh   as   at   cre –

and   in   power;   come   with   thy   time – less
and   a –   fraid,   the   qui –   et   of   a
dwell   se –   cure,   and   fine –   ly   build   for
word   of   peace,   that   war   may   haunt   the
a –   tion's   birth;   let   there   be   light   a –

judg – ment   now   to   match   our   pres – ent   hour.
stead – fast   faith,   calm   of   a   call   o – beyed.
days   to   come   foun –   da – tions   that   en – dure.
earth   no   more,   and   des – o – la – tion   cease.
gain,   and   set   thy   judg – ments   on   the   earth.

WORDS: R. B. Y. Scott, 1937
MUSIC: *Genevan Psalter*, 1551; arr. by William Crotch, 1836

ST. MICHAEL
SM

731 Glorious Things of Thee Are Spoken

1. Glo-rious things of thee are spo-ken, Zi-on, cit-y
2. See, the streams of liv-ing wa-ters, spring-ing from e-
3. Round each hab-i-ta-tion hov-ering, see the cloud and
4. Blest in-hab-i-tants of Zi-on, washed in our Re-

of our God; God, whose word can-not be bro-ken,
ter-nal love, well sup-ply thy sons and daugh-ters,
fire ap-pear for a glo-ry and a cov-ering,
deem-er's blood; Je-sus, whom our souls re-ly on,

formed thee for his own a-bode. On the Rock of A-ges
and all fear of want re-move. Who can faint while such a
show-ing that the Lord is near! Thus de-riv-ing from our
makes us mon-archs, priests to God. Us, by his great love, he

found-ed, what can shake thy sure re-pose? With sal-va-tion's
riv-er ev-er will their thirst as-suage? Grace which like the
ban-ner light by night and shade by day, safe we feed up-
rais-es, rul-ers o-ver self to reign, and as priests his

WORDS: John Newton, 1779 (Ps. 87:3; Is. 33:20-21; Ex. 13:22)
MUSIC: Croatian folk song; arr. by Franz Joseph Haydn, 1797

AUSTRIA
87.87 D

walls   sur-round-ed,   thou mayst smile   at   all   thy   foes.
Lord,   the   giv-er,   nev-er   fails from   age   to   age.
on   the   man-na   which God gives   us   when   we   pray.
sol-emn prais-es   we   for   thank-ful   of-fering bring.

Come, We That Love the Lord 732

1. Come,   we   that   love   the   Lord,   and   let   our
2. Let   those   re-fuse   to   sing   who   nev-er
3. The   hill   of   Zi-on   yields   a   thou-sand
4. Then   let   our   songs   a-bound,   and   ev-ery

joys   be   known;   join   in   a   song   with
knew   our   God;   but   chil-dren   of   the
sa-cred   sweets   be-fore   we   reach   the
tear   be   dry;   we're   march-ing   through   Em-

sweet   ac-cord,   and   thus   sur-round   the   throne.
heaven-ly   King   may   speak   their   joys   a-broad.
heaven-ly   fields,   or   walk   the   gold-en   streets.
man-uel's   ground,   to   fair-er   worlds   on   high.

WORDS: Isaac Watts, 1707
MUSIC: Aaron Williams, *The New Universal Psalmodist*, 1770

ST. THOMAS
SM

733   Marching to Zion

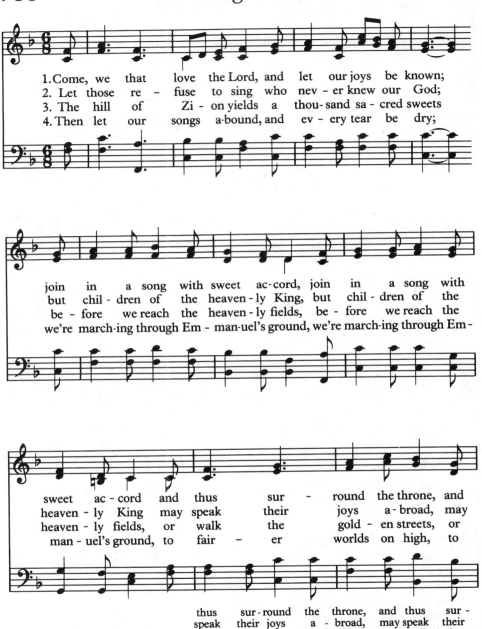

1. Come, we that love the Lord, and let our joys be known;
2. Let those re - fuse to sing who nev - er knew our God;
3. The hill of Zi - on yields a thou - sand sa - cred sweets
4. Then let our songs a-bound, and ev - ery tear be dry;

join in a song with sweet ac-cord, join in a song with
but chil - dren of the heaven - ly King, but chil - dren of the
be - fore we reach the heaven - ly fields, be - fore we reach the
we're march-ing through Em - man-uel's ground, we're march-ing through Em -

sweet ac - cord and thus sur - round the throne, and
heaven - ly King may speak their joys a - broad, may
heaven - ly fields, or walk the gold - en streets, or
man - uel's ground, to fair - er worlds on high, to

thus sur - round the throne, and thus sur -
speak their joys a - broad, may speak their
walk the gold - en streets, to walk the
fair - er worlds on high, to fair - er

WORDS: Isaac Watts, 1707; refrain by Robert Lowry, 1867
MUSIC: Robert Lowry, 1867

MARCHING TO ZION
SM with Refrain

Refrain

thus sur-round the throne. We're march - ing to Zi - on,
speak their joys a - broad. We're march - ing on to Zi - on,
walk the gold - en streets.
fair - er worlds on high.

round the throne.
joys a - broad.
gold - en streets.
worlds on high.

beau - ti - ful, beau - ti - ful Zi - on; we're march - ing up - ward to

Zi - on, the beau - ti - ful cit - y of God.
Zi - on, Zi - on, the

734 Canticle of Hope

RESPONSE *(General)*

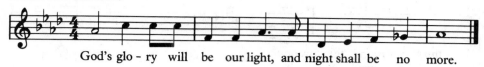

God's glo - ry will be our light, and night shall be no more.

R

We shall see a new heaven and earth,
for the old will pass away.
We shall see a new Jerusalem,
the holy city descending from heaven.

The city shall need no sun or moon,
for God's glory will be its light,
for God's Lamb will be its lamp,
and by its light the nations shall walk.   R

We shall hear a loud voice from the throne:
"Behold, God's dwelling is with mortals.
Indeed, God will dwell with them
and they will be God's people."

God shall wipe away all our tears,
and there shall be no more death.
Mourning, crying, and pain shall cease,
for all former things will pass away.   R

We shall hear One speak from the throne:
"Behold, I make all things new.
I am Alpha and Omega,
the beginning and the end."

Our Lord testifies to these things:
"Behold, I am coming soon."
The grace of the Lord is with us.
Amen. Come, Lord Jesus! Come!   R

WORDS: Revelation 22:1-6; 23-24; 22:5,12,20, adapt. by S T Kimbrough, Jr.; Response
Revelation 21:23; 22:5, adapt.
MUSIC: Carlton R. Young

Adapt. © 1988 S T Kimbrough, Jr.; Response © 1989 The United Methodist Publishing House

THE COMPLETION OF CREATION (THE CITY OF GOD), *see further:*

384 Love Divine, All Loves Excelling

PSALTER

Let everything that breathes praise the Lord!

PSALM 150

PREFACE

The book of Psalms is the hymn book of the Bible. At the heart of Judeo-Christian worship and prayer, the psalms express the rich spectrum of human emotions, attitudes, and needs in relation to God, God's family, and the world. Some of the most ancient expressions of Hebrew worship are found in psalms, (see Psalm 18 or Psalm 29). The New Testament writers often found in the psalms a confirmation of their experience of Christ (Mark 15:34). Psalms, spoken and sung, were early on a foundation of Christian worship. The church in reform and renewal has turned to the psalms. John and Charles Wesley encouraged Methodists to pray and sing the psalms. The United Methodist Liturgical Psalter links Methodism to this rich heritage and to our own renewal of interest in the psalms as central to prayer, celebration, singing, and vital worship.

This liturgical psalter, prepared for use in public worship, is based upon the New Revised Standard Version of the book of Psalms. It is faithful to the biblical text and its message and is more readable, singable than any of our previous psalters. Metaphors and forms of address for people and deity are, with few exceptions, inclusive. These 100 psalms are recommended for use with the appointed readings of the Common Lectionary, 1983 (see the Index of Scripture).

Following traditional practice, the psalms and canticles in this hymnal are arranged in a "call and response" pattern for reading and singing, using responses from Scripture and hymns of faith for emphasis and illumination.

I. *How to use the responses (R)*

The red R at the beginning of the psalm indicates that a
  solo voice or voices first sing or say the response.
The congregation then sings or says the response.
At all other places designated by R everyone sings or says the
  response together.

II. *How to read the psalms*

A leader reads the lightface type;
  then the congregation responds, reading the boldface type;
or psalms may be read by two groups, such as the right and left sections
  of a congregation;
or the psalm may be read in unison.

Both psalms and their responses may be chanted by using psalm tones (see below) and the pointing indicated by red dots above syllables or words.

The first note (♩) in each part of the tone is a reciting note, to which one or more syllables or words are sung. The point (·) above a syllable (or word) indicates the syllable (or word) where the singers move, at half cadence or ending, from the reciting note to the black notes (see example below).

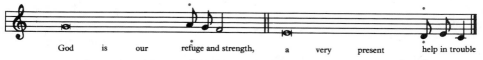

God   is   our   refuge and strength,   a   very   present   help in trouble

Therefore we will not fear though the earth should change,   though the mountains shake in the heart of the sea;

From the point (·) to the middle or end of recited text there are usually three syllables—one for each of the three remaining notes. When there are more than three syllables, the additional syllables are sung to the last half note (see example above). Occasionally a three-syllable word is sung to the two black notes by eliding the middle syllable; for example, ev-e-ry becomes ev'ry, of-fer-ing becomes off'ring, mar-ve-lous becomes marv'lous. Blessed is sung blest.

Full instructions for chanting these psalms are found in the keyboard edition.

Psalm 1

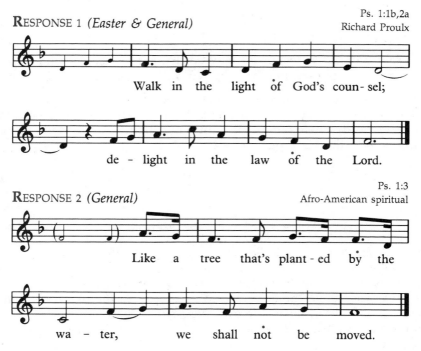

Ps. 1:1b,2a
Richard Proulx

RESPONSE 1 *(Easter & General)*

Walk in the light of God's coun-sel;

de - light in the law of the Lord.

Ps. 1:3
Afro-American spiritual

RESPONSE 2 *(General)*

Like a tree that's plant-ed by the

wa – ter, we shall not be moved.

R

1 Blessed are those
     who do not walk in the counsel of the wicked;
   **or stand in the way of sinners,
      or sit in the seat of scoffers;**
2 but their delight is in the law of the Lord,
      and on God's law they meditate day and night.
3 They are like trees
      planted by streams of water
      that yield their fruit in season,
      and their leaves do not wither.
   In all that they do, they prosper.   R

4 The wicked are not so,
      but are like chaff which the wind drives away.
5 **Therefore the wicked will not stand in the judgment;
      nor sinners in the congregation of the righteous;**
6 for the Lord knows the way of the righteous,
      but the way of the wicked will perish.   R

Psalm 2

Ps. 2:11,12a
Jane Marshall

RESPONSE 1 *(Transfiguration & General)*

Serve the Lord with fear; be hum-ble be-fore the Lord.

Job 19:25a
Psalmodia Evangelica

RESPONSE 2 *(Easter)*

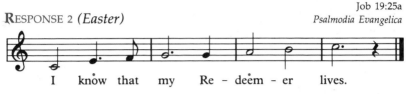

I know that my Re - deem - er lives.

R

1 Why do the nations conspire,
   and the people plot in vain?
2 The kings of the earth rise up,
   and the rulers take counsel together
   against God and God's anointed, saying,
3 **"Let us burst their bonds,**
   and cast their cords from us."
4 The One who sits in the heavens laughs,
   and holds them in derision.
5 Then God will speak to them in anger,
   and terrify them in fury, saying,
6 **"I have set my king on Zion, my holy hill."** R

7 I will tell of the decree of the Lord
   who said to me: "You are my son,
   today I have begotten you.
8 **Ask of me, and I will make the nations your heritage,**
   and the ends of the earth your possession.
9 **You shall break them with a rod of iron,**
   and dash them in pieces like a potter's vessel." R

10 Now therefore, O kings, be wise;
   be warned, O rulers of the earth.
11 **Serve the Lord with fear and trembling;**
12 humble yourselves before the Lord
   lest God be angry, and you perish in the way;
   for God's wrath is quickly kindled.
   Blessed are all who take refuge in the Lord. R

Psalm 3

Ps. 3:8a,7
Don E. Saliers

De - liv - er - ance be - longs to the Lord:

A - rise, O Lord, de - liv - er me.

R

1 O Lord, how many are my foes!
   Many are rising against me;
2 **many are saying of me,**
   "There is no help for him in God."
3 But you, O Lord, are a shield about me,
   my glory, and the lifter of my head.
4 **I cry aloud to the Lord**
   who answers me from his holy hill. R

5 I lie down and sleep;
   I wake again, for the Lord sustains me.
6 **I am not afraid of ten thousand people**
   who have set themselves against me on every side.
7 Arise, O Lord!
   Deliver me, O my God!
   For you strike all my enemies on the cheek,
   you break the teeth of the wicked.
8 **Deliverance belongs to the Lord;**
   your blessing be upon your people! R

Psalm 4

RESPONSE *(Easter & General)*   Afro-American spiritual

There is a balm in Gil-e-ad, to make the wound-ed whole.

R

1 Answer me when I call, O God of my right!
You have given me room when I was in distress.
Be gracious to me, and hear my prayer.
2 How long, O people, shall my honor suffer shame?
How long will you love vain words, and seek after lies?
3 But know that the Lord has set apart the righteous as God's own;
the Lord hears when I call. R

4 Be angry, but do not sin;
commune with your own hearts in your beds, and be silent.
5 Offer right sacrifices,
and put your trust in the Lord.
6 There are many who say, "O that we might see some good!
Lift up the light of your countenance upon us, O Lord!"
7 You have put more joy in my heart
than they have when their grain and wine abound.
8 **In peace I will both lie down and sleep;**
for you alone, O Lord, make me lie down in safety. R

Psalm 5

Ps. 5:11
Carlton R. Young

RESPONSE *(General)*

Let all who take ref-uge in you re - joice,
let them ev - er sing for joy.

R

1 Give ear to my words, O Lord;
    give heed to my groaning.
2 **Harken to the sound of my cry,**
    my Ruler and my God,
    for to you I pray.
3 O Lord, in the morning you hear my voice;
    in the morning I prepare a sacrifice for you, and watch.
4 **For you are not a God who delights in wickedness;**
    evil may not dwell with you.
5 The boastful may not stand before your eyes;
    you hate all evildoers.
6 **You destroy those who speak lies;**
    the Lord abhors the bloodthirsty and deceitful.
7 But, through the abundance of your steadfast love,
    I will enter your house.
  Toward your holy temple
    I will worship you in awe.   R

8 Lead me, O Lord, in your righteousness
    because of my enemies;
    make your way straight before me.
9 For there is no truth in their mouth;
    their heart is destruction,
  their throat is an open grave,
    they flatter with their tongue.
10 Make them bear their guilt, O God;
    let them fall by their own counsels;
  because of their many transgressions cast them out,
    for they have rebelled against you.

11 Let all who take refuge in you rejoice,
    let them ever sing for joy;
    defend them, that those who love your name may exult
       in you.
12 **For you bless the righteous, O Lord;**
    you cover them with favor as with a shield.   R

Psalm 8

Johann J. Schütz
trans. by Frances E. Cox
Bohemian
Brethren's *Kirchengesänge*

RESPONSE 1 *(New Year, Trinity & General)*

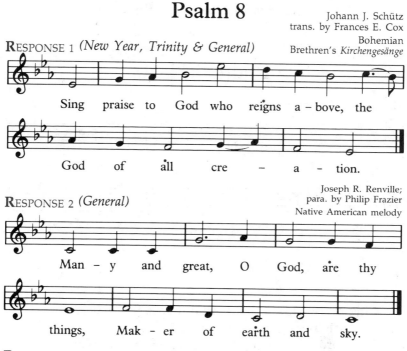

Sing praise to God who reigns a-bove, the
God of all cre - a - tion.

Joseph R. Renville;
para. by Philip Frazier
Native American melody

RESPONSE 2 *(General)*

Man - y and great, O God, are thy
things, Mak - er of earth and sky.

R

1 O Lord, our Lord,
    how majestic is your name in all the earth!
2 Your glory is chanted above the heavens
    by the mouth of babes and infants:
    you have set up a defense against your foes,
    to still the enemy and the avenger.   R

3 When I look at your heavens, the work of your fingers,
    the moon and the stars which you have established;
4 what are human beings that you are mindful of them,
    and mortals that you care for them?
5 Yet you have made them little less than God,
    and crowned them with glory and honor.

⁶ You have given them dominion over the works of your hands;
   you have put all things under their feet,
⁷ all sheep and oxen,
   and also the beasts of the field,
⁸ the birds of the air, and the fish of the sea,
   whatever passes along the paths of the seas.
⁹ O Lord, our Lord,
   how majestic is your name in all the earth!   R

Psalm 9:11-20

RESPONSE (*General*)

Ps. 9:11
Richard Proulx

We shall tell a-mong the peo - ples the glo - rious deeds of the Lord.

Alternate response at Ps. 10.

R

¹¹ Sing praises to the Lord, who dwells in Zion!
   Tell among the peoples God's deeds!
¹² The Lord who avenges blood is mindful of them,
   and does not forget the cry of the afflicted.
¹³ Be gracious to me, O Lord!
   See what I suffer from those who hate me;
   You are the One who lifts me up from the gates of death,
¹⁴   **that I may recount all your praises,**
   and, in the gates of the daughter of Zion,
   rejoice in your deliverance.   R

¹⁵ The nations have sunk in the pit which they made;
   their own foot has been caught in the net which they hid.
¹⁶ The Lord is made known! The Lord has executed judgment!
   The wicked are snared in the work of their own hands.
¹⁷ The wicked shall depart to Sheol,
   all the nations that forget God.

18 **For the needy shall not always be forgotten,**
   and the hope of the poor shall not perish for ever.
19 Arise, O Lord! Let not mortals prevail;
   let the nations be judged before you!
20 Put them in fear, O Lord;
   let the nations know that they are mortal! R

Psalm 10:12-18

RESPONSE (*General*)

S T Kimbrough, Jr. (Ps. 72:1,4,7)
Trad. English melody

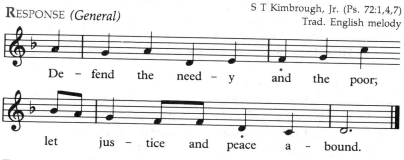

De - fend the need - y and the poor;
let jus - tice and peace a - bound.

R

12 Arise, O Lord; O God, lift up your hand;
   forget not the afflicted.
13 **Why do the wicked renounce God,**
   and say in their hearts, "You will not call to account?"
14 You indeed see, you note trouble and vexation,
   that you may take it into your hands;
   the unfortunate commit themselves to you;
   you have been the helper of the orphan. R

15 Break the arm of the wicked and evildoers;
   seek out their wickedness till you find none.
16 The Lord is Ruler for ever and ever;
   the nations shall perish from God's land. R

17 O Lord, you will hear the desire of the meek,
   you will strengthen their hearts;
   you will incline your ear
18   **to do justice to the orphan and the oppressed,**
   so that people on earth may strike terror no more. R

Psalm 13

Katharina von Schlegel
trans. by Jane Borthwick
Jean Sibelius

RESPONSE *(General)*

Be still, my soul: the Lord is on thy side.

R

1 How long, O Lord? Will you forget me for ever?
How long will you hide your face from me?
2 How long must I bear pain in my soul,
and have sorrow in my heart all the day?
How long shall my enemy be exalted over me?   R

3 Consider and answer me, O Lord my God;
lighten my eyes, lest I sleep the sleep of death;
4 lest my enemy say, "I have prevailed over him";
lest my foes rejoice because I am shaken.
5 But I trusted in your steadfast love;
my heart shall rejoice in your salvation.
6 I will sing to the Lord,
for the Lord has dealt bountifully with me.   R

Psalm 14

Alan Luff (Ezek. 37:1-14)
Richard Proulx

RESPONSE *(General)*

My hope is lost; breathe life up - on me.

R

1 Fools say in their hearts, "There is no God."
They are corrupt, they do abominable deeds,
there is none that does good.
2 The Lord looks down from heaven on all people,
to see if there are any that are wise,
who seek after God.
3 **They have all gone astray, they are all alike perverse;**
there is none that does good,
no, not one.   R

4 Have they no knowledge, the evildoers
   who eat up my people as they eat bread,
   and do not call upon the Lord?
5 **There they shall be in great terror,**
   for God is with the generation of the righteous.
6 You would confound the plans of the poor,
   but the Lord is their refuge.
7 **O that deliverance for Israel would come from Zion!**
   When the Lord restores their fortunes,
   Jacob shall rejoice and Israel shall be glad! R

Psalm 15

RESPONSE *(General)*

S T Kimbrough, Jr.
Carlton R. Young

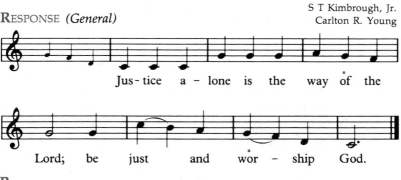

Jus-tice a - lone is the way of the Lord; be just and wor - ship God.

R

1 O Lord, who shall abide in your tent?
   Who shall dwell in your holy hill?
2 **The one who walks blamelessly, and does what is right,**
   and speaks truth from the heart;
3 who does not slander with the tongue,
   and does no evil to a friend,
   nor takes up a reproach against a neighbor;
4 **in whose eyes a reproach is despised,**
   but who honors those who fear the Lord;
5 who does not put out money at interest,
   and does not take a bribe against the innocent.
The one who does these things shall never be moved. R

Psalm 16:5-11

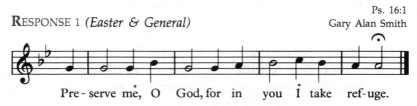

RESPONSE 1 *(Easter & General)*

Ps. 16:1
Gary Alan Smith

Pre-serve me, O God, for in you I take ref-uge.

RESPONSE 2 *(General)*

Ps. 16:8a,9a
Richard Proulx

With God al-ways be-fore me, my

heart is glad, my soul re-joic-es.

R

⁵ The Lord is my chosen portion and my cup;
you hold my lot.
⁶ **The lines have fallen for me in pleasant places;**
I have a glorious heritage.
⁷ I bless the Lord who gives me counsel;
even at night my heart instructs me.
⁸ **I have set the Lord always before me;**
the Lord is at my right hand;
I shall not be moved. R

⁹ Therefore my heart is glad, and my soul rejoices;
my body also dwells secure.
¹⁰ **For you do not give me up to Sheol,**
or let your godly one see the pit.
¹¹ You show me the path of life;
in your presence there is fullness of joy,
in your right hand are pleasures for evermore. R

Psalm 17:1-7,15

Ps. 17:8
Jane Marshall

RESPONSE *(General)*

Keep me, keep me as the ap-ple of your eye; hide me, hide me in the shad-ow of your wings.

Alternate response at Ps. 63.

R

1 Hear a just cause, O Lord; attend to my cry!
   Give ear to my prayer from lips free of deceit!
2 From you let my vindication come!
   Let your eyes see the right!
3 If you try my heart, if you visit me by night,
   if you test me, you will find no wickedness in me;
   my mouth does not transgress.
4 Concerning what others do:
   I have avoided the ways of the violent
   by following your word.
5 **My steps have held fast to your paths,**
   my feet have not slipped. R

6 I call upon you, for you will answer me, O God;
   incline your ear to me, hear my words.
7 Wondrously show your steadfast love,
   O savior of those who seek refuge
   from their adversaries at your right hand.
15 **As for me, I shall behold your face in righteousness;**
   when I awake I shall be satisfied with beholding your
   presence. R

Psalm 19

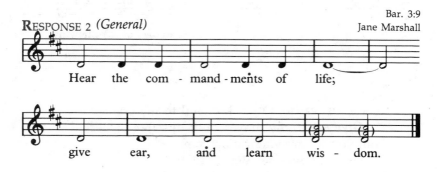

Ps. 19:7

RESPONSE 1 *(Lent, Easter & General)* Hebrew melody, from *Sacred Harmony*

The law of God is just, re - viv - ing the soul.

Bar. 3:9
Jane Marshall

RESPONSE 2 *(General)*

Hear the com - mand - ments of life;

give ear, and learn wis - dom.

R

1 The heavens are telling the glory of God;
    and the firmament proclaims God's handiwork.
2 **Day to day pours forth speech,**
    and night to night declares knowledge.
3 There is no speech, nor are there words;
    their voice is not heard;
4 **yet their voice goes out through all the earth,**
    and their words to the end of the world.
   In them God has set a tent for the sun,
5   which comes forth like a bridegroom leaving his chamber,
       and runs its course with joy like a strong man.
6 **Its rising is from the end of the heavens,**
    and its circuit to the end of them;
    and there is nothing hid from its heat.   R

7 The law of the Lord is perfect,
   reviving the soul;
   the testimony of the Lord is sure,
   making wise the simple;
8 the precepts of the Lord are right,
   rejoicing the heart;
   the commandment of the Lord is pure,
   enlightening the eyes;
9 the fear of the Lord is clean,
   enduring for ever;
   the ordinances of the Lord are true,
   and righteous altogether.
10 More to be desired are they than gold,
   even much fine gold;
   sweeter also than honey
   and drippings of the honeycomb. R

11 Moreover by them is your servant warned;
   in keeping them there is great reward.
12 **But who can understand one's own errors?**
   Clear me from hidden faults.
13 Also keep your servant from the insolent;
   let them not have dominion over me!
   Then I shall be blameless,
   and innocent of great transgression.
14 **Let the words of my mouth and the meditation of my heart**
   be acceptable in your sight,
   O Lord, my rock and my redeemer. R

Psalm 22:1-18, 25-31

Anon. Latin
trans. by Paul Gerhardt
trans. by James W. Alexander

RESPONSE 1 *(Good Friday)*

Hans L. Hassler

O sa-cred Head, now wound-ed,

with grief and shame weighed down.

Ps. 22:27

RESPONSE 2 *(Easter & General)*

Gary Alan Smith

All the ends of the earth shall re-

mem-ber and turn to the Lord.

R

1 My God, my God, why have you forsaken me?
   Why are you so far from helping me, from the words
      of my groaning?
2 O my God, I cry by day, but you do not answer;
   and by night, but find no rest.
3 Yet you, the praise of Israel,
   are enthroned in holiness.
4 **In you our forebears trusted;**
   they trusted and you delivered them.
5 To you they cried, and were saved;
   in you they trusted, and were not disappointed. R

6 But I am a worm, and not human;
   scorned by others, and despised by the people.
7 All who see me mock at me,
   they make mouths at me, they wag their heads;
8 "He committed his cause to the Lord;
   let the Lord deliver him.
   Let the Lord rescue him,
   for the Lord delights in him!"
9 **Yet it was you who took me from the womb;**
   you kept me safe upon my mother's breast.

10 Upon you I was cast from my birth,
  and since my mother bore me, you have been my God.
11 **Do not be far from me,**
    for trouble is near
      and there is none to help.   R

12 Many bulls encompass me,
    strong bulls of Bashan surround me;
13 **they open wide their mouths at me,**
    like a ravening and roaring lion.
14 I am poured out like water
    and all my bones are out of joint;
  my heart is like wax,
    it is melted within my breast;
15 my mouth is dried up like a potsherd,
    and my tongue cleaves to my jaws;
    you lay me in the dust of death.
16 Indeed, dogs surround me;
    a company of evildoers encircles me;
    they have pierced my hands and feet—
17 I can count all my bones—
    they stare and gloat over me;
18 they divide my garments among them,
    and for my raiment, they cast lots.   R

25 From you comes my praise in the great congregation;
    my vows I will pay before those who worship the Lord.
26 The poor shall eat and be satisfied;
    those who seek the Lord shall praise the Lord!
    May your hearts live for ever!
27 All the ends of the earth shall remember
    and turn to the Lord;
  and all the families of the nations
    shall worship before the Lord.
28 For dominion belongs to the Lord
    who rules over the nations.
29 **All who sleep in the earth**
    shall bow down to the Lord.
  All who go down to the dust shall bow before the Lord,
    and I shall live for God.
30 **Posterity shall serve the Lord;**
    each generation shall tell of the Lord,
31 and proclaim his deliverance to a people yet unborn.
    Surely the Lord has done it.   R

Psalm 23

Ps. 23:1

RESPONSE 1 *(Lent, Christ the King & General)*   Joseph Gelineau

My shep·herd is the Lord, noth·ing in·deed shall I want.

Jn. 10:10

RESPONSE 2 *(Easter & Funerals and Memorial Services)*   Richard Proulx

The Good Shep·herd comes that we

may have life and have it a - bun - dant - ly.

Alternate response at Ps. 25, response 2.

R

1 The Lord is my shepherd; I shall not want.
2 **The Lord makes me lie down in green pastures,**
leads me beside still waters,
3 restores my life,
leads me in right paths
for the sake of the Lord's name.
4 Even though I walk through the darkest valley,
I fear no evil;
for you are with me;
your rod and your staff,
they comfort me.   R

5 You prepare a table before me
in the presence of my enemies;
you anoint my head with oil,
my cup overflows.
6 Surely goodness and mercy shall follow me
all the days of my life;
and I shall dwell in the house of the Lord
as long as I live.   R

For King James Version (1611) see No. 137

Psalm 24

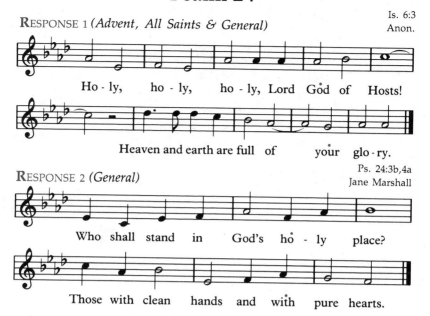

Is. 6:3
Anon.

RESPONSE 1 *(Advent, All Saints & General)*

Ho - ly,   ho - ly,   ho - ly, Lord God of Hosts!

Heaven and earth are full of   your   glo - ry.

Ps. 24:3b,4a
Jane Marshall

RESPONSE 2 *(General)*

Who shall stand in   God's ho - ly   place?

Those with clean hands and with pure hearts.

R

1 The earth is the Lord's and the fullness thereof,
   the world and those who dwell therein;
2 for God has founded it upon the seas,
   and established it upon the rivers.
3 Who shall ascend the hill of the Lord?
   And who shall stand in God's holy place?
4 Those who have clean hands and pure hearts,
   who do not lift up their souls to what is false,
   and do not swear deceitfully.
5 They will receive blessing from the Lord,
   and vindication from the God of their salvation.
6 Such is the generation of those who seek the Lord,
   who seek the face of the God of Jacob.   **R**

For King James Version (1611) see No. 212

⁷ Lift up your heads, O gates!
  and be lifted up, O ancient doors!
  that the Ruler of glory may come in.
⁸ **Who is the Ruler of glory?**
  The Lord, strong and mighty,
  the Lord, mighty in battle!
⁹ **Lift up your heads, O gates!**
  and be lifted up, O ancient doors!
  that the Ruler of glory may come in.
¹⁰ Who is this Ruler of glory?
  The Lord of hosts,
  the Lord is the Ruler of glory! R

Psalm 25:1-10

RESPONSE 1 *(Advent & General)*

Ps. 25:4a,5a
Don E. Saliers

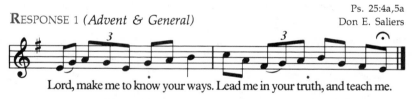

Lord, make me to know your ways. Lead me in your truth, and teach me.

RESPONSE 2 *(Lent)*

Ps. 5:8
Samuel Sebastian Wesley

Lead me, Lord, lead me in thy righ-teous-ness;

make thy way plain be - fore my face.

R

1 To you, O Lord, I lift up my soul.
2 **O my God, in you I trust,**
 let me not be put to shame;
 let not my enemies exult over me.
3 Let none that wait for you be put to shame;
 let them be ashamed who are clothed with treachery.
4 Make me to know your ways, O Lord;
 teach me your paths.
5 Lead me in your truth, and teach me,
 for you are the God of my salvation;
 for you I wait all the day long. R

6 Be mindful of your mercy, O Lord, and of your steadfast love,
 for they have been from of old.
7 **Remember not the sins of my youth, or my transgressions;**
 according to your steadfast love remember me,
 for the sake of your goodness, O Lord.
8 Good and upright is the Lord;
 therefore the Lord instructs sinners in the way,
9 and leads the humble in what is right,
 and teaches them their way.
10 **All the paths of the Lord are steadfast love and faithfulness,**
 for those who keep the Lord's covenant and
 testimonies. R

Psalm 27

Ps. 36:9
Jane Marshall

RESPONSE (*General*)

For with you is the foun-tain of life;

in your light do we see light.

R

¹ The Lord is my light and my salvation;
   whom shall I fear?
The Lord is the stronghold of my life;
   of whom shall I be afraid?
² When evildoers assail me,
   to devour my flesh,
my adversaries and foes
   shall stumble and fall.
³ **Though a host encamp against me,**
   my heart shall not fear;
though war arise against me,
   yet I will be confident.
⁴ One thing I asked of the Lord,
   that will I seek after:
that I may dwell in the house of the Lord
   all the days of my life,
to behold the beauty of the Lord,
   and to inquire in the Lord's temple. R

5 The Lord will hide me in his shelter
 in the day of trouble,
 will conceal me under the cover of his tent,
 and will set me high upon a rock.
6 **And now my head shall be lifted up**
 above my enemies round about me;
 and I will offer sacrifices in the Lord's tent
 with shouts of joy;
 I will sing and make melody to the Lord. R

7 Hear, O Lord, when I cry aloud,
 be gracious to me and answer me!
8 "Come," my heart said, "seek the Lord's face."
 Your face, O Lord, I seek.
9 Hide not your face from me.
 Turn not your servant away in anger,
 for you have been my help.
10 **Cast me not off, forsake me not,**
 O God of my salvation!
 If my father and mother should forsake me,
 the Lord would take me up. R

11 Teach me your way, O Lord;
 and lead me on a level path
 because of my enemies.
12 **Give me not up to the will of my adversaries;**
 for false witnesses have risen against me,
 and they breathe out violence.
13 I believe that I shall see the goodness of the Lord
 in the land of the living!
14 **Wait for the Lord;**
 be strong, and let your heart take courage.
 Wait for the Lord! R

Psalm 28

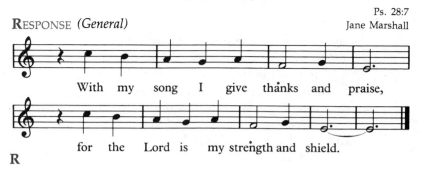

Ps. 28:7
Jane Marshall

RESPONSE (*General*)

With my song I give thanks and praise,

for the Lord is my strength and shield.

R

1 To you, O Lord, I call;
    my rock, be not deaf to me,
  lest, if you are silent to me,
    I become like those who go down to the pit.
2 **Hear the voice of my supplication,**
    as I cry to you for help,
  as I lift up my hands
    toward your most holy sanctuary.   R

3 Take me not away with the wicked,
    with those who are workers of evil,
  who speak peace with their neighbors,
    while mischief is in their hearts.
4 **Repay them according to their work,**
    and according to the evil of their deeds;
  repay them according to the work of their hands;
    render them their due reward.
5 **The Lord will break them down and build them up no more,**
    because they do not regard the deeds of the Lord,
    or the work of the Lord's hands.   R

6 Blessed be the Lord,
    who has heard the voice of my supplications!
7 **The Lord is my strength and shield**
    in whom my heart trusts;
  so I am helped, and my heart exults,
    and with my song I give thanks to the Lord.
8 The Lord is the strength of the people,
    the saving refuge of his anointed.
9 **O save your people, and bless your heritage;**
    be their shepherd, and carry them for ever.   R

Psalm 29

Charles Wesley
RESPONSE *(Baptism of the Lord, Trinity & General)*   John Hatton

With joy the Lord of Hosts pro - claim;
ex - tol the great al - might - y name.

R

1 Ascribe to the Lord, O heavenly beings,
   ascribe to the Lord glory and strength.
2 **Ascribe to the Lord the glory of his name;**
   worship the Lord in holy splendor.
3 The voice of the Lord is upon the waters;
   the God of glory thunders,
   the Lord, upon many waters.
4 **The voice of the Lord is powerful,**
   the voice of the Lord is full of majesty.   R

5 The voice of the Lord breaks the cedars,
   the Lord breaks the cedars of Lebanon.
6 The Lord makes Lebanon to skip like a calf,
   and Sirion like a young wild ox.
7 **The voice of the Lord flashes forth flames of fire.**
8 The voice of the Lord shakes the wilderness,
   the Lord shakes the wilderness of Kadesh.
9 The voice of the Lord makes the oaks to whirl,
   and strips the forests bare;
   and in his temple all cry, "Glory!"
10 The Lord sits enthroned over the flood;
   the Lord sits enthroned as Ruler for ever.
11 **May the Lord give strength to his people!**
   May the Lord bless his people with peace!   R

Psalm 30

Ps. 30:5cd
French carol melody

RESPONSE *(Easter & General)*

For the night weep - ing may tar - ry;
with the morn - ing light comes joy.

Alternate response at Ps. 135.

R

1 I will extol you, O Lord, for you have lifted me up,
   and did not let my foes rejoice over me.
2 **O Lord my God, I cried to you for help,**
   and you healed me.
3 O Lord, you brought up my soul from Sheol,
   restored me to life from among those gone down to the
   pit.   R

4 Sing praises to the Lord, O his faithful ones,
   and give thanks to his holy name.
5 **Surely the Lord's anger is but for a moment;**
   the Lord's favor is for a lifetime.
   Weeping may tarry for the night,
   but joy comes with the morning.
6 **As for me, I said in my prosperity,**
   "I shall never be moved."

7   By your favor, O Lord,
        you had established me as a strong mountain;
    you hid your face,
        I was dismayed.   R

8   To you, O Lord, I cried,
        and to the Lord I made supplication:
9   **"What profit is there in my death,**
        if I go down to the pit?
    Will the dust praise you?
        Will it tell of your faithfulness?
10 **Hear, O Lord, and be gracious to me!**
        O Lord, be my helper!"
11 You have turned my mourning into dancing;
        you have loosed my sackcloth
        and girded me with gladness,
12 that my soul may praise you and not be silent.
        O Lord, my God, I will give thanks to you forever.   R

Psalm 31:1-16

Martin Luther
trans. by Frederick H. Hedge

RESPONSE 1 *(Passion/Palm Sunday & General)*   Martin Luther

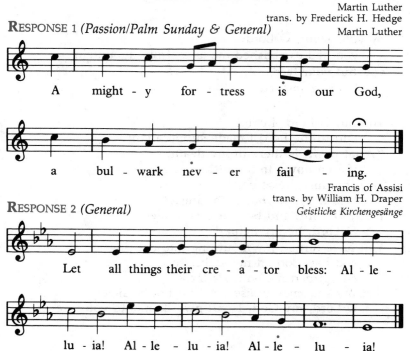

A might - y for - tress is our God,

a bul - wark nev - er fail - ing.

Francis of Assisi
trans. by William H. Draper

RESPONSE 2 *(General)*   *Geistliche Kirchengesänge*

Let all things their cre - a - tor bless: Al - le -

lu - ia! Al - le - lu - ia! Al - le - lu - ia!

R

1 In you, O Lord, I seek refuge;
      let me never be put to shame;
      in your righteousness, deliver me!
2 **Incline your ear to me,**
      rescue me speedily!
   Be a rock of refuge for me,
      a strong fortress to save me!
3 You are indeed my rock and my fortress;
      for your name's sake lead me and guide me;
4 **take me out of the net which is hidden for me,**
      for you are my refuge.

5 Into your hand I commit my spirit;
      you have redeemed me, O Lord, faithful God.
6 **I hate those who pay regard to vain idols;**
      but I trust in the Lord.
7 I will rejoice and be glad in your steadfast love,
      because you have seen my affliction,
      and have taken heed of my adversities.
8 **You have not delivered me into the hand of the enemy;**
      you have set my feet in a broad place. R

9 Be gracious to me, O Lord, for I am in distress;
      my eye is wasted from grief,
      my soul and body also.
10 **For my life is spent with sorrow,**
      and my years with sighing;
my strength fails because of my misery,
      and my bones waste away.
11 I am the scorn of all my adversaries,
      a horror to my neighbors,
an object of dread to my acquaintances;
      those who see me in the street flee from me.
12 **I have passed out of mind like one who is dead;**
      I have become like a broken vessel.
13 For I hear the whispering of many—
      terror all around!—
as they scheme together against me,
      as they plot to take my life.
14 **But I trust in you, O Lord,**
      I say, "You are my God."
15 My times are in your hand;
      deliver me from the hand of my enemies and persecutors.
16 **Let your face shine on your servant;**
      save me through your steadfast love! R

Psalm 32

Ps. 32:11
Gary Alan Smith

RESPONSE (*General*)

Be glad in the Lord and re - joice;

shout for joy, you up - right in heart.

R

1 Blessed are those whose transgression is forgiven,
   whose sin is covered.
2 **Blessed are those whom the Lord does not hold guilty,**
   and in whose spirit there is no deceit.
3 When I did not declare my sin, my body wasted away
   through my groaning all day long.
4 **For day and night your hand was heavy upon me;**
   my strength was dried up as by the heat of summer.
5 I acknowledged my sin to you,
   and I did not hide my iniquity;
   I said, "I will confess my transgressions to the Lord";
   then you forgave the guilt of my sin. R

6 Therefore let those who are godly
   offer prayer to you;
   at a time of distress, the rush of great waters
   shall not reach them.
7 You are a hiding place for me,
   you preserve me from trouble;
   you encompass me with deliverance.
8 **I will instruct you and teach you**
   the way you should go;
   I will counsel you with my eye upon you.
9 Do not be like an unruly horse or a mule, without
   understanding,
   whose temper must be curbed with bit and bridle.
10 **Many are the pangs of the wicked;**
   but steadfast love surrounds those who trust in the Lord.
11 Be glad in the Lord, and rejoice, O righteous;
   shout for joy, all you upright in heart! R

Psalm 33

RESPONSE 1 *(Lent, Easter & Trinity)*

Ps. 33:20
Richard Proulx

Our soul waits for the Lord,
who is our help and shield.

RESPONSE 2 *(General)*

Charles Wesley
Robert Williams

Praise the Lord, ye saints, and sing;
all the powers of mu - sic bring.

R

1 Rejoice in the Lord, O you righteous!
      Delight in praise, O you upright!
2 **Praise the Lord with the lyre,**
      make melody to the Lord with the harp of ten strings!
3 Sing to the Lord a new song,
      play skillfully on the strings, with loud shouts.
4 **Upright is the word of the Lord,**
      whose work is done in faithfulness.   R

5 The Lord loves righteousness and justice;
      the earth is full of the steadfast love of the Lord.
6 **By the word of the Lord the heavens were made,**
      and all their host by the breath of God's mouth.
7 The Lord gathered the waters of the sea as in a bottle
      and put the deeps in storehouses.
8 **Let all the earth fear the Lord,**
      let all the inhabitants of the world stand in awe!   R

9 For the Lord spoke, and it came to be;
    the Lord commanded, and it stood forth.
10 **The Lord brings the counsel of the nations to nothing**
    and frustrates the plans of the peoples.
11 The counsel of the Lord stands for ever,
    the thoughts of God's heart to all generations.
12 **Blessed is the nation whose God is the Lord,**
    the people whom the Lord has chosen as a heritage!   R

13 The Lord looks down from heaven,
    and sees all peoples;
14 **the Lord sits enthroned and looks forth**
    on all the inhabitants of the earth,
15 **fashioning the hearts of them all,**
    and observing all their deeds.
16 A king is not saved by his great army;
    a warrior is not delivered by his great strength.
17 **The war horse is a vain hope for victory,**
    and despite its great might it cannot save.   R

18 Behold, the eye of the Lord is on those who are faithful
    and hope for God's steadfast love
19 to deliver their soul from death,
    and to keep them alive in famine.
20 **Our soul waits for the Lord,**
    who is our help and shield.
21 Our heart is glad in the Lord,
    because we trust in God's holy name.
22 **Let your steadfast love, O Lord, be upon us,**
    even as we hope in you.   R

Psalm 34

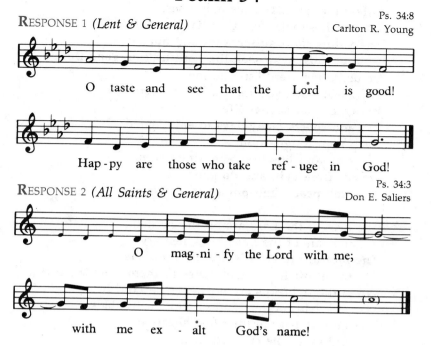

RESPONSE 1 *(Lent & General)*

Ps. 34:8
Carlton R. Young

O taste and see that the Lord is good!

Hap-py are those who take ref-uge in God!

RESPONSE 2 *(All Saints & General)*

Ps. 34:3
Don E. Saliers

O mag-ni-fy the Lord with me;

with me ex-alt God's name!

R

1 I will bless the Lord at all times;
   God's praise shall continually be in my mouth.
2 **My soul makes its boast in the Lord;**
   let the afflicted hear and be glad.
3 O magnify the Lord with me,
   and let us exalt God's name together!
4 **I sought the Lord, who answered me,**
   and delivered me from all my fears.
5 Look to God and be radiant,
   so your faces shall never be ashamed.
6 **The poor cried out, and the Lord heard,**
   and saved them out of all their troubles.
7 The angel of the Lord encamps
   around those who fear God, and delivers them.
8 **O taste and see that the Lord is good!**
   Happy are those who take refuge in God!   R

9 O fear the Lord, you his holy ones,
      for those who fear God have no want!
10 **The young lions suffer want and hunger,**
      but those who seek the Lord lack no good thing.
11 Come, O children, listen to me,
      I will teach you the fear of the Lord.
12 **Which of you desires life**
      and covets many days to enjoy good?
13 Keep your tongue from evil,
      and your lips from speaking deceit.
14 **Depart from evil, and do good;**
      seek peace, and pursue it.   R

15 The eyes of the Lord are on the righteous;
      the ears of the Lord hear their cry.
16 **The face of the Lord is against evildoers,**
      to cut off the remembrance of them from the earth.
17 When the righteous cry for help, the Lord hears,
      and delivers them out of all their troubles.
18 **The Lord is near to the brokenhearted,**
      and saves the crushed in spirit.
19 Many are the afflictions of the righteous;
      but the Lord delivers them.
20 **The Lord keeps all their bones;**
      not one of them is broken.
21 Evil shall slay the wicked;
      and those who hate the righteous will be condemned.
22 **The Lord redeems the life of his servants;**
      none of those who take refuge in God will be
      condemned.   R

Psalm 36:5-10

Ps. 36:10
Adapt. from J. S. Bach
by Gary Alan Smith

RESPONSE *(Epiphany, Holy Week & General)*

I de - sire to fol - low your way, O Lord, my

God; con - tin - ue your stead - fast love to me.

Alternate HOLY WEEK and GENERAL response at Ps. 27.

R

⁵ Your steadfast love, O Lord, extends to the heavens,
  your faithfulness to the clouds.
⁶ **Your righteousness is like the mighty mountains,**
  your judgments are like the great deep;
  O Lord, humans and animals you save!
⁷ O God, how precious is your steadfast love!
  All people may take refuge in the shadow of your wings.
⁸ **They feast on the abundance of your house,**
  and you give them drink from the river of your delights.
⁹ For with you is the fountain of life;
  in your light do we see light.
¹⁰ **O continue your steadfast love to those who know you,**
  and your salvation to the upright of heart!   R

Psalm 37:1-11

RESPONSE *(General)*

Albert F. Bayly (Mic. 6:8)
Erik Routley

Do just-ly, love mer-cy, walk hum-bly with your God.

R

1 Do not be angry because of the wicked,
    do not be envious of wrongdoers!
2 **For they will soon fade like the grass,**
    and wither like the green herb.
3 Trust in the Lord, and do good;
    so you will dwell in the land, and enjoy security.
4 **Take delight in the Lord,**
    who will give you the desires of your heart. R

5 Commit your way to the Lord;
    trust in God, who will act,
6 bringing forth your vindication as the light,
    and your right as the noonday.
7 **Be still and wait patiently before the Lord;**
    do not be angry because of those who prosper in their
    way,
    because of those who carry out evil devices! R

8 Refrain from anger, and forsake wrath!
    Do not be angry; it leads only to evil.
9 **For the wicked shall be cut off;**
    but those who wait for the Lord shall possess the land.
10 Yet a little while, and the wicked will be no more;
    though you look at their place, they will not be there.
11 **But the meek shall possess the land,**
    and delight in abundant prosperity. R

Psalm 39

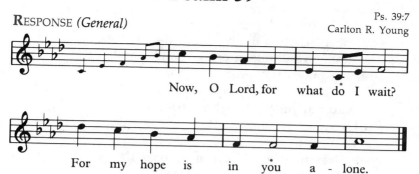

RESPONSE (*General*)

Ps. 39:7
Carlton R. Young

Now, O Lord, for what do I wait?

For my hope is in you a - lone.

R

1 I said, "I will guard my ways,
  that I may not sin with my tongue;
I will keep a muzzle on my mouth,
  so long as the wicked are in my presence."
2 I was mute and silent,
  I held my peace to no avail;
  my distress grew worse,
  my heart became hot within me.
3 As I mused the fire burned;
  then I spoke with my tongue:
4 **"Lord, let me know my end,**
  and what is the measure of my days;
  let me know how fleeting my life is!
5 **You have made my days a few handbreadths,**
  and my lifetime is as nothing in your sight.
  Surely every human being is an empty breath!
6 **Surely everyone goes about as a shadow!**
  Surely they are in turmoil for nothing;
  they heap up, and do not know who will gather! **R**

7 "And now, Lord, for what do I wait?
  My hope is in you.
8 **Deliver me from all my transgressions.**
  Make me not the scorn of the fool!
9 I am mute, I do not open my mouth;
  for it is you who have done it.
10 **Remove your stroke from me;**
  I am spent by the blows of your hand.

¹¹ When you chasten people
     with rebukes for sin,
   you consume like a moth what is dear to them;
     surely every human being is an empty breath!
¹² Hear my prayer, O Lord,
    and give ear to my cry;
    hold not your peace at my tears!
For I am your passing guest,
   a sojourner, like all my forebears.
¹³ Look away from me, that I may know gladness,
    before I depart and am no more!" R

Psalm 40:1-11

Ps. 40:11
Don E. Saliers

RESPONSE (*General*)

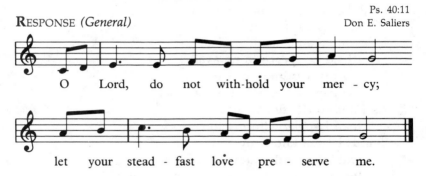

O Lord, do not with-hold your mer - cy;

let your stead - fast love pre - serve me.

R

¹ I waited patiently for the Lord,
   who inclined to me and heard my cry.
² The Lord drew me up from the desolate pit,
    out of the miry bog,
set my feet upon a rock,
    making my steps secure.
³ The Lord put a new song in my mouth,
   a song of praise to our God.
Many will see and be in awe,
    and put their trust in the Lord. R

4 Blessed are those who make
the Lord their trust,
who do not turn to the proud,
to those who go astray after false gods!
5 **O Lord my God, you have multiplied your wondrous deeds**
and your thoughts toward us;
none can compare with you!
Were I to proclaim and tell of them,
they would be more than can be numbered.
6 **Sacrifice and offering you do not desire;**
but you have given me an open ear.
Burnt offering and sin offering
you have not required.
7 **Then I said, "Lo, I come;**
in the roll of the book it is written of me;
8 **I delight to do your will, O my God;**
your law is within my heart." R

9 I have told the glad news of deliverance
in the great congregation;
lo, I have not restrained my lips,
as you know, O Lord.
10 I have not hid your saving help within my heart,
I have spoken of your faithfulness
and your salvation;
I have not concealed your steadfast love and faithfulness
from the great congregation.
11 O Lord, do not withhold
your mercy from me,
let your steadfast love and faithfulness
ever preserve me! R

Psalm 41

Ps. 139:23
Adapt. from Martin Luther
by Carlton R. Young

RESPONSE (*General*)

Search me, O God, and know my heart;
try me and know my thoughts.

R

1 Blessed are those who consider the poor!
    The Lord delivers them in the day of trouble;
2 **the Lord protects them and keeps them alive;**
    they are called blessed in the land;
    you do not give them up to the will of their enemies.
3 **The Lord sustains them on their sickbed;**
    in their illness you heal all their infirmities.   R

4 As for me, I said, "O Lord, be gracious to me;
    heal me, for I have sinned against you!"
5 **My enemies say of me in malice:**
    "When will he die, and his name perish?"
6 Those who come to see me utter empty words,
    while their hearts gather mischief;
    when they go out, they tell it abroad.
7 **All who hate me whisper together about me;**
    they imagine the worst for me.
8 They say, "A deadly thing has fastened upon him;
    he will not rise again from where he lies."
9 **Even my bosom friend in whom I trusted,**
    who ate of my bread, has lifted a heel against me.   R

But you, O Lord, be gracious to me,
    and raise me up, that I may repay them!
11 **By this I know that you are pleased with me,**
    in that my enemy has not triumphed over me.
12 But you have upheld me because of my integrity,
    and set me in your presence for ever.
13 **Blessed be the Lord, the God of Israel,**
    from everlasting to everlasting!
    Amen and Amen.   R

Psalm 42

Ezek. 36:26
Gesangbuch, Meiningen

RESPONSE *(General)*

God will give you a new heart, a new spir-it put with- in.

R

1 As a deer longs for flowing streams,
    so longs my soul for you, O God.
2 **My soul thirsts for God,**
    for the living God.
When shall I come and behold
    the face of God?
3 My tears have been my food
    day and night,
while people say to me continually,
    "Where is your God?"
4 **These things I remember**
    as I pour out my soul:
how I went with the throng,
    and led them in procession to the house of God,
with glad shouts and songs of thanksgiving,
    a multitude keeping festival.
5 Why are you cast down, O my soul,
    and why are you disquieted within me?
Hope in God whom again I shall praise,
6   **my help and my God.** R

My soul is cast down within me,
    therefore I remember you
from the land of Jordan and of Hermon,
    from Mount Mizar.
7 **Deep calls to deep**
    at the thunder of your cataracts;
all your waves and your billows
    have gone over me.
8 By day the Lord commands his steadfast love;
    and at night God's song is with me,
    a prayer to the God of my life.

9 **I say to God, my rock:**
   "Why have you forgotten me?"
Why do I mourn
   because of the oppression of the enemy?"
10 Like a deadly wound in my body,
   my adversaries taunt me;
they say to me continually,
   "Where is your God?"
11 Why are you cast down, O my soul,
   and why are you disquieted within me?
Hope in God whom again I shall praise,
   my help and my God.   R

Psalm 43

Ps. 43:3
Charles Gounod

RESPONSE (*General*)

Send out your light and your truth; let them lead me.

R

1 Vindicate me, O God, and defend my cause
   against an ungodly people;
   from the deceitful and unjust deliver me!
2 **For you are the God in whom I take refuge;**
   Why have you cast me off?
Why must I mourn
   because of the oppression of the enemy?
3 O send out your light and your truth;
   let them lead me,
   let them bring me to your holy hill
   and to your dwelling!
4 **Then I will go to the altar of God,**
   to God my exceeding joy;
   and I will praise you with the lyre,
   O God, my God.
5 Why are you cast down, O my soul,
   and why are you disquieted within me?
Hope in God whom again I shall praise,
   my help and my God.   R

Psalm 44:1-8

Ps. 44:26
Gary Alan Smith

RESPONSE (General)

Rise up, come to our help! De-
liv - er us for the sake of your love.

R

1 We have heard with our ears, O God,
    our forebears have told us,
  what deeds you performed in their days,
    in the days of old:
2 **you with your own hand drove out the nations,**
    but our forebears you planted;
  you afflicted the peoples,
    but our forebears you set free;
3 for not by their own sword did they win the land,
    nor did their own arm give them victory;
  but your right hand, and your arm,
    and the light of your countenance;
    for you delighted in them.   R

4 You are my Ruler and my God,
    who ordains victories for Jacob.
5 **Through you, we push down our foes;**
    through your name, we tread down our assailants.
6 For not in my bow do I trust,
    nor can my sword save me.
7 **But you have saved us from our foes,**
    and have put to confusion those who hate us.
8 **In God we have boasted continually,**
    and we will give thanks to your name for ever.   R

Psalm 46

Martin Luther
trans. by Frederick H. Hedge

RESPONSE 1 *(Easter & General)* — Martin Luther

A might-y for-tress is our God,
a bul-wark nev-er fail-ing.

Ps. 46:10a,11a
Carlton R. Young

RESPONSE 2 *(General)*

"Be still, and know that I am God."
The Lord of Hosts is with us.

R

1 God is our refuge and strength,
    a very present help in trouble.
2 **Therefore we will not fear though the earth should change,**
    though the mountains shake in the heart of the sea;
3 though its waters roar and foam,
    though the mountains tremble with its tumult.
4 **There is a river whose streams make glad the city of God,**
    the holy habitation of the Most High.
5 God is in the midst of the city which shall not be moved;
    God will help it at the dawn of the day.
6 **The nations rage, the kingdoms totter;**
    God's voice resounds, the earth melts.
7 The Lord of hosts is with us;
    the God of Jacob is our refuge. R

8 Come, behold the works of the Lord,
    who has wrought desolations in the earth;
9 **who makes wars cease to the end of the earth,**
    breaks the bow, shatters the spear,
    and burns the shields with fire!

10 "Be still, and know that I am God.
I am exalted among the nations,
I am exalted in the earth!"
11 **The Lord of hosts is with us;**
the God of Jacob is our refuge. R

Psalm 47

Charles Wesley
Robert Williams

RESPONSE *(Ascension & General)*

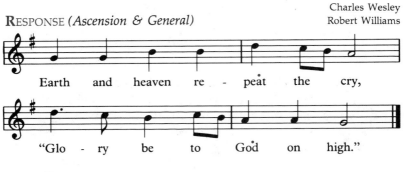

Earth and heaven re - peat the cry,

"Glo - ry be to God on high."

R

1 Clap your hands, all peoples!
Shout to God with loud songs of joy!
2 For the Lord, the Most High, is to be feared,
a great Ruler over all the earth,
3 who subdued peoples under us,
and nations under our feet,
4 **who chose our heritage for us,**
the pride of Jacob whom God loves. R

5 God has gone up with a shout,
the Lord with the sound of a trumpet.
6. Sing praises to God, sing praises!
Sing praises to our Ruler, sing praises!
7 For God is the Ruler of all the earth;
sing praises with a psalm!
8 God reigns over the nations;
God sits on his holy throne.
9 The princes of the people gather
as the people of the God of Abraham.
For the shields of the earth belong to God,
who is highly exalted! R

Psalm 48

Ps. 48:13c,14c
Thomas J. Williams

RESPONSE (General)

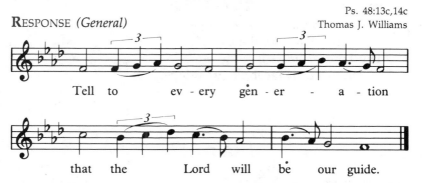

Tell to ev-ery gen-er-a-tion
that the Lord will be our guide.

R

1 Great is the Lord and greatly to be praised
   in the city of our God;
2 **whose holy mountain, beautiful in elevation,**
   is the joy of all the earth,
   Mount Zion, in the far north,
   the city of the great Ruler.
3 **Within its citadels God**
   has proven a sure defense.   R

4 For lo, the kings assembled,
   they marched together.
5 **As soon as they saw it, they were astounded,**
   they were in panic, they took to flight;
6 trembling took hold of them there,
   anguish as of a woman in travail,
7 **as when an east wind shatters**
   the ships of Tarshish.
8 As we have heard, so have we seen
   in the city of the Lord of hosts,
   in the city of our God,
   which God establishes for ever.
9 **We have thought on your steadfast love, O God,**
   in the midst of your temple.   R

10 As your name, O God,
     so your praise reaches to the ends of the earth.
Your right hand is filled with victory;
11 **let Mount Zion be glad!**
Let the daughters of Judah rejoice
     because of your judgments!
12 **Walk about Zion, go round about it,**
     number its towers,
13 consider well its ramparts,
     go through its citadels,
     that you may tell the next generation,
14 **"This is God, our God for ever and ever.**
     God will be our guide for ever." R

Psalm 50

Ps. 57:5

RESPONSE *(Transfiguration & General)*   Jane Marshall

Be ex - alt - ed, O God, a - bove the heavens!

Let your glo - ry o - ver all the earth be found.

Alternate GENERAL response at Ps. 76.

R

1 The Mighty One, God the Lord,
     speaks and summons the earth
     from the rising of the sun to its setting.
2 **Out of Zion, the perfection of beauty,**
     God shines forth.
3 Our God comes, and does not keep silence,
     before whom is a devouring fire,
     round about whom is a mighty storm.
4 **God calls to the heavens above**
     and to the earth, that the people may be judged:

5 "Gather to me my faithful ones,
 who made a covenant with me by sacrifice!"
6 **The heavens declare God's righteousness,**
 for God alone is judge!   R

7 "Hear, O my people, and I will speak,
 O Israel, I will testify against you.
 I am God, your God.
8 **I do not reprove you for your sacrifices;**
 your burnt offerings are continually before me.
9 But I will not accept a bull from your house,
 nor a he-goat from your folds.
10 **For every beast of the forest is mine,**
 the cattle on a thousand hills.
11 I know all the birds of the air,
 and all that moves in the field is mine.
12 **If I were hungry, I would not tell you;**
 for the world and all that is in it is mine.
13 Do I eat the flesh of bulls,
 or drink the blood of goats?
14 **Offer to God a sacrifice of thanksgiving,**
 and pay your vows to the Most High;
15 **and call upon me in the day of trouble;**
 I will deliver you, and you shall glorify me."   R

16 But to the wicked God says:
 "What right have you to recite my statutes,
 or take my covenant on your lips?
17 **For you hate discipline,**
 and you cast my words behind you.
18 If you see thieves, you are their friends;
 and you keep company with adulterers.
19 **You give your mouth free rein for evil,**
 and your tongue frames deceit.
20 You sit and speak against your brother;
 you slander your mother's son.
21 **These things you have done and I have been silent;**
 you thought that I was one like yourself.
 But now I rebuke you, and lay the charge before you.
22 Mark this, then, you who forget God,
 lest I rend, and there be none to deliver!
23 **Those who bring thanksgiving as their sacrifice honor me;**
 to those who order their way aright
 I will show the salvation of God!"   R

Psalm 51:1-17

RESPONSE 1 *(Ash Wednesday)*
Ps. 51:11
Carlton R. Young

Cast me not a - way from your pres - ence,

and take not your Ho - ly Spir - it from me.

RESPONSE 2 *(Lent & General)*
Ps. 51:10
Alan Luff

Cre - ate in me a clean heart, O

God, and re - new a right spir - it with - in me.

R

1 Have mercy on me, O God,
        according to your steadfast love;
    according to your abundant mercy
        blot out my transgressions.
2 Wash me thoroughly from my iniquity,
        and cleanse me from my sin!
3 **For I know my transgressions,**
        and my sin is ever before me.
4 Against you, you only, have I sinned,
        and done that which is evil in your sight,
    so that you are justified in your sentence
        and blameless in your judgment.
5 **Behold, I was born into iniquity,**
        and I have been sinful since my mother conceived
        me. R

6 Behold, you desire truth in the inward being;
   therefore teach me wisdom in my secret heart.
7 **Purge me with hyssop, and I shall be clean;**
   wash me, and I shall be whiter than snow;
8 Make me hear with joy and gladness;
   let the bones which you have broken rejoice.
9 **Hide your face from my sins,**
   and blot out all my iniquities.   R

10 Create in me a clean heart, O God,
   and put a new and right spirit within me.
11 **Cast me not away from your presence,**
   and take not your holy Spirit from me.
12 Restore to me the joy of your salvation,
   and sustain in me a willing spirit.
13 **Then I will teach transgressors your ways,**
   and sinners will return to you.
14 Deliver me from death, O God, God of my salvation,
   and my tongue will sing aloud of your deliverance.
15 **O Lord, open my lips,**
   and my mouth shall show forth your praise.
16 For you have no delight in sacrifice;
   were I to give a burnt offering, you would not be pleased.
17 **The sacrifice acceptable to God is a broken spirit;**
   a broken and contrite heart, O God, you will not
   despise.   R

Psalm 62:5-12

Ps. 138:1,8a
Gary Alan Smith

RESPONSE *(General)*

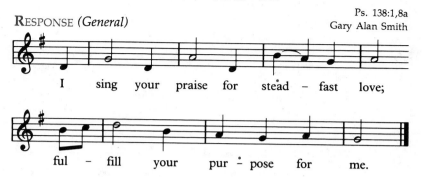

I sing your praise for stead - fast love;
ful - fill your pur - pose for me.

R

5 For God alone my soul waits in silence,
  for my hope is from God,
6 **who alone is my rock and my salvation,**
  my fortress; I shall not be shaken.
7 On God rests my deliverance and my honor;
  my mighty rock, my refuge is God.
8 **Trust in God at all times, O people;**
  pour out your heart before God who is a refuge for us. R

9 Those of low estate are but a breath,
  those of high estate are a delusion;
  in the balances they go up;
  they are together lighter than a breath.
10 **Put no confidence in extortion,**
   set no vain hopes on robbery;
   if riches increase, set not your heart on them.
11 Once God has spoken,
   twice have I heard this:
   power belongs to God;
12 **and to you, O Lord, belongs steadfast love,**
   for you repay all according to their work. R

Psalm 63

Ps. 63:1a
Richard Proulx

RESPONSE (*General*)

My soul is thirst-ing for you, O Lord, thirst-ing for you my God.

R

1 O God, you are my God, I seek you,
    my soul thirsts for you;
  my flesh faints for you,
      as in a dry and weary land where no water is.
2 **So I have looked upon you in the sanctuary,**
    beholding your power and glory.
3 Because your steadfast love is better than life,
    my lips will praise you.
4 **So I will bless you as long as I live;**
    I will lift up my hands and call on your name. R

5 My soul is feasted as with marrow and fat,
    and my mouth praises you with joyful lips,
6 when I think of you upon my bed,
    and meditate on you in the watches of the night;
7 **for you have been my help,**
    and in the shadow of your wings I sing for joy.
8 **My soul clings to you;**
    your right hand upholds me. R

9 But those who seek to destroy my life
    shall go down into the depths of the earth;
10 **they shall be given over to the power of the sword,**
    they shall be prey for jackals.
11 But the king shall rejoice in God;
      all who swear in God's name shall glory;
      but the mouths of liars will be stopped. R

Psalm 65

Martin Rinkart
trans. by Catherine Winkworth

RESPONSE *(Thanksgiving & General)*

Johann Crüger

Now thank we all our God with heart and hands and voic-es.

R

1 Praise is due to you,
       O God, in Zion;
   and to you shall vows be performed.
2 To you who hear prayer
       all flesh shall come because of their sins.
3 **When our transgressions prevail over us,**
       you forgive them.
4 Blessed are those whom you choose and bring near,
       to dwell in your courts!
   We shall be satisfied with the goodness of your house,
       your holy temple!   R

5 By dread deeds you answer us with deliverance,
       O God of our salvation,
   who is the hope of all the ends of the earth,
       and of the farthest seas;
6 **who by your strength established the mountains,**
       being girded with might;
7 who stills the roaring of the seas,
       the roaring of their waves,
       the tumult of the peoples;
8 so that those who dwell at earth's farthest bounds
       are afraid at your signs;
   you make the morning and the
       evening resound with joy.   R

9 You visit the earth and water it,
       you greatly enrich it;
   the river of God is full of water;
       you provide its grain,
       for so you have prepared it.

10 You water its furrows abundantly,
   settling its ridges,
softening it with showers,
   and blessing its growth.
11 **You crown the year with your bounty;**
   the tracks of your chariot drip with fatness.
12 The pastures of the wilderness drip,
   the hills gird themselves with joy,
13 **the meadows clothe themselves with flocks,**
   the valleys deck themselves with grain,
   they shout and sing together for joy. R

Psalm 66:8-20

RESPONSE *(Easter & General)*

Ps. 67:4a,7
Carlton R. Young

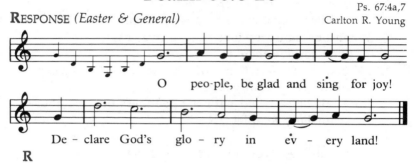

O people, be glad and sing for joy!
De - clare God's glo - ry in ev - ery land!

R

8 Bless our God, O peoples,
   let the sound of God's praise be heard,
9 who has kept us among the living,
   and has not let our feet slip.
10 **For you, O God, have tested us;**
   you have tried us as silver is tried.
11 You brought us into the net;
   you laid affliction on our loins;
12 **you let people ride over our heads;**
   we went through fire and through water;
   yet you have brought us forth to a spacious place. R

13 I will come into your house with burnt offerings;
   I will pay you my vows,
14 that which my lips uttered
   and my mouth promised when I was in trouble.
15 **I will offer to you burnt offerings of fatlings,**
   ' with the smoke of the sacrifice of rams;
   I will make an offering of bulls and goats. R

16 Come and hear, all you who worship God,
   and I will tell what God has done for me.
17 **I cried aloud to God,**
   who was highly praised with my tongue.
18 If I had cherished iniquity in my heart,
   the Lord would not have listened.
19 **But truly God has listened,**
   and has given heed to the voice of my prayer.
20 **Blessèd be God,**
   who has not rejected my prayer
   or removed his steadfast love from me.   R

Psalm 67

RESPONSE (*Easter & General*)

Ps. 67:4a,7
Carlton R. Young

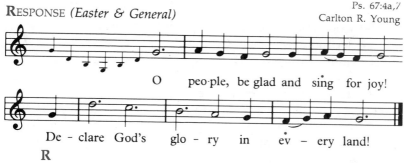

O people, be glad and sing for joy!
De - clare God's glo - ry in ev - ery land!
R

1 O God, be gracious to us and bless us
   and make your face to shine upon us,
2 **that your way may be known upon earth,**
   your saving power among all nations.
3 Let the peoples praise you, O God;
   let all the peoples praise you!
4 **Let the nations be glad and sing for joy,**
   for you judge the peoples with equity
   and guide the nations upon earth.   R

5 Let the peoples praise you, O God;
   let all the peoples praise you!
6 **The earth has yielded its increase;**
   God, our God, has blessed us.
7 God has blessed us;
   let all the ends of the earth fear God!   R

Psalm 68:1-10, 32-35

Ps. 8:2,9

Chinese melody
adapt. by Bliss Wiant

RESPONSE (*Easter & General*)

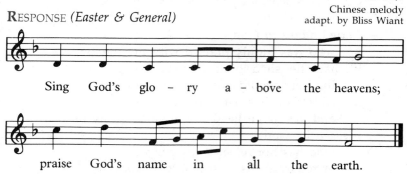

Sing God's glo - ry a - bove the heavens;
praise God's name in all the earth.

Alternate response at Ps. 67.

R

¹ Let God arise, let God's enemies be scattered;
   let those who hate God flee!
² **As smoke is driven away, so drive them away;**
   as wax melts before fire,
   let the wicked perish before God!
³ But let the righteous be joyful;
   let them exult before God;
   let them be jubilant with joy!
⁴ **Sing to God, sing praises to God's name;**
   lift up a song to the One who rides upon the clouds;
   exult before the One whose name is Lord!   R

⁵ In the holy habitation, God is father of orphans
   and protector of widows.
⁶ **God gives the desolate a home to dwell in,**
   and leads out the prisoners to prosperity;
   but the rebellious dwell in a parched land.
⁷ O God, when you went forth before your people,
   when you marched through the wilderness,
⁸ **the earth quaked, the heavens poured down water,**
   at the presence of God, the God of Sinai,
   at the presence of God, the God of Israel.
⁹ Rain in abundance, O God, you shed abroad;
   you restored your heritage as it languished;
¹⁰ **your flock found a dwelling in it;**
   in your goodness, O God, you provided for the needy.   R

32   Sing to God, O kingdoms of the earth;
      sing praises to the Lord.
33   **O Rider in the heavens, the ancient heavens;**
      God's voice goes forth, a mighty voice.
34   Ascribe power to God,
      whose majesty is over Israel,
      and whose power is in the skies.
35   **Wondrous is God in the sanctuary,**
      the God of Israel,
      who gives power and strength to the people.   R

Psalm 70

Martin Luther (Ps. 130:1,2)
trans. by Catherine Winkworth
Attr. to Martin Luther

RESPONSE (*Holy Week & General*)

Out of the depths I cry to thee;
Lord, hear me, I im - plore thee!

R

1   Be pleased, O God, to deliver me!
      O Lord, make haste to help me!
2   Let them be put to shame and confusion
      who seek my life!
      Let them be turned back and brought to dishonor
      who desire my pain!
3   Let them turn back because of their shame
      who say, "Aha, Aha!"
4   **May all who seek you**
      rejoice and be glad in you!
      May those who love your salvation
      say evermore, "God is great!"
5   **But I am poor and needy;**
      hasten to me, O God!
      You are my help and my deliverer;
      O Lord, do not tarry!   R

Psalm 71:1-12

RESPONSE (*Holy Week & General*)

Ps. 71:5
Lewis Edson

O Lord, you are my hope, my trust, Lord, from my youth.

R

1 In you, O Lord, do I take refuge;
   let me never be put to shame!
2 **In your righteousness deliver me and rescue me;**
   incline your ear to me, and save me!
3 Be to me a rock of refuge,
   a strong fortress, to save me,
   for you are my rock and my fortress.
4 **Rescue me, O my God, from the hand of the wicked,**
   from the grasp of the unjust and cruel.
5 For you, O Lord, are my hope,
   my trust, O Lord, from my youth.
6 **Upon you I have leaned from my birth;**
   it was you who took me from my mother's womb.
   My praise is continually of you.   R

7 I have been an example to many,
   for you are my strong refuge.
8 **My mouth is filled with your praise**
   and with your glory all the day.
9 Do not cast me off in the time of old age;
   forsake me not when my strength is spent.
10 **For my enemies speak concerning me,**
    those who watch for my life consult together, saying,
11 **"God has forsaken him;**
    pursue and seize him,
    for there is no deliverer."
12 O God, be not far from me;
    O my God, make haste to help me!   R

Psalm 72:1-17

Is. 49:6

RESPONSE 1 *(Advent, Epiphany & General)*

Gary Alan Smith

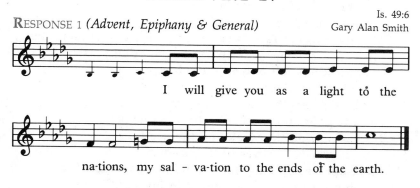

I will give you as a light to the nations, my sal - va-tion to the ends of the earth.

S T Kimbrough, Jr. (Ps. 72:1,4,7)

RESPONSE 2 *(General)*

Trad. English melody

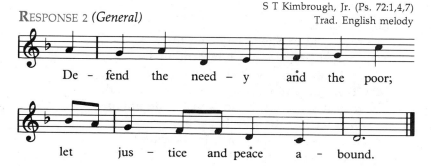

De - fend the need - y and the poor; let jus - tice and peace a - bound.

R

1 Give the king your justice, O God,
   and your righteousness to the royal son!
2 May he judge your people with righteousness,
   and your poor with justice!
3 Let the mountains bear prosperity for the people,
   and the hills, in righteousness!
4 **May he defend the cause of the poor of the people,**
   give deliverance to the needy,
   and crush the oppressor!
5 May he live while the sun endures,
   and as long as the moon, throughout all generations!
6 **May he be like rain that falls on the mown grass,**
   like showers that water the earth!
7 In his days may righteousness flourish,
   and peace abound, till the moon be no more!
8 **May he have dominion from sea to sea,**
   and from the river to the ends of the earth!   R

⁹ May his foes bow down before him,
    and his enemies lick the dust!
¹⁰ May the kings of Tarshish and of the isles render him tribute,
    may the kings of Sheba and Seba bring gifts!
¹¹ **May all kings fall down before him,**
    all nations serve him!
¹² For he delivers the needy when they call,
    the poor and those who have no helper.
¹³ **He has pity on the weak and the needy,**
    and saves the lives of the needy.
¹⁴ **From oppression and violence he redeems their life;**
    and precious is their blood in his sight.   R

¹⁵ Long may he live,
    may gold of Sheba be given to him!
May prayer be made for him continually,
    and blessings invoked for him all the day!
¹⁶ **May there be abundance of grain in the land;**
    may it wave on the tops of the mountains;
    may its fruit be like Lebanon;
and may they blossom forth in the cities
    like the grass of the field!
¹⁷ **May his name endure for ever,**
    his fame continue as long as the sun!
May people bless themselves by him,
    all nations call him blessed!   R

Psalm 76

Amos 5:24
Carlton R. Young

RESPONSE (*General*)

Let jus-tice roll down like wa-ters, and righ-teous-ness like flow-ing streams.

R

1 In Judah God is known,
    whose name is great in Israel,
2 whose abode has been established in Salem,
    whose dwelling place is in Zion.
3 **There God broke the flashing arrows,**
    the shield, the sword, and the weapons of war.
4 You are glorious, more majestic
    than the everlasting mountains.
5 **The stouthearted were stripped of their spoil;**
    they sank into sleep;
    all the soldiers
    were unable to use their hands.
6 **At your rebuke, O God of Jacob,**
    both rider and horse lay stunned.   R

7 You indeed are to be feared!
    Who can stand before you when once your anger is
    roused?
8 From the heavens you uttered judgment;
    the earth feared and was still,
9 when God arose to establish judgment
    to save all the oppressed of the earth.
10 **Surely human wrath shall praise you;**
    the residue of wrath you will gird upon you.
11 Make vows to the Lord your God, and keep them;
    let those who surround God bring gifts
    to the One to be feared,
12 **who cuts off the spirit of monarchs,**
    and makes the rulers of the earth afraid.   R

Psalm 77:1-2, 11-20

Ps. 105:5a,2a
Carlton R. Young

RESPONSE (General)

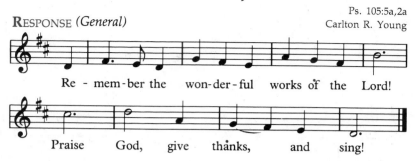

Re - mem-ber the won-der-ful works of the Lord!
Praise God, give thanks, and sing!

R

¹ I cry aloud to God,
aloud that God may hear me.
² In the day of my trouble I seek the Lord,
in the night my hand is stretched out continually;
my soul refuses to be comforted.
¹¹ I will call to mind the deeds of the Lord;
I will remember your wonders of old.
¹² I will meditate on all your work,
and muse on your mighty deeds.
¹³ Your way, O God, is holy.
What god is great like our God?
¹⁴ You are the God who works wonders,
you manifested your might among the peoples.
¹⁵ You redeemed with your arm your people,
the descendants of Jacob and Joseph. R

¹⁶ When the waters saw you, O God,
when the waters saw you, they were afraid,
the very deeps trembled.
¹⁷ The clouds poured out water;
the skies gave forth thunder;
your arrows flashed on every side.
¹⁸ The crash of your thunder was in the whirlwind;
your lightnings illumined the world;
the earth trembled and shook.
¹⁹ Your way was through the sea,
your path through the great waters;
yet your footprints were unseen.
²⁰ You led your people like a flock
by the hand of Moses and Aaron. R

Psalm 78:1-4, 9-20, 32b-38a

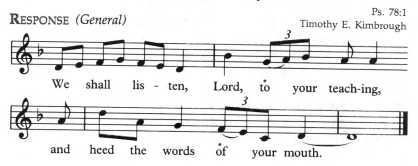

RESPONSE *(General)*

Ps. 78:1
Timothy E. Kimbrough

We shall lis-ten, Lord, to your teach-ing,

and heed the words of your mouth.

Alternate response at Ps. 25, response 2.

R

1   Give ear, O my people, to my teaching:
        incline your ears to the words of my mouth!
2   **I will open my mouth in a parable;**
        I will utter dark sayings from of old,
3   things that we have heard and known,
        that our forebears have told us.
4   **We will not hide them from their children,**
        but tell to the coming generation
    the glorious deeds of the Lord, the might,
        and wonders God has wrought.   R

9   The Ephraimites, armed with the bow,
        turned back on the day of battle.
10 **They did not keep God's covenant,**
        but refused to walk according to God's law.
11 They forgot the deeds of the Lord,
        the miracles that God had shown them.
12 **The Lord wrought marvels in the sight of their forebears**
        in the land of Egypt, in the fields of Zoan,
13 the Lord divided the sea and let them pass through it,
        and made the waters stand like a heap,
14 **led them with a cloud in the daytime,**
        and all the night with a fiery light,
15 cleft rocks in the wilderness,
        and gave them drink abundantly as from the deep,
16 **made streams come out of the rock,**
        and caused waters to flow down like rivers.   R

17 Yet they sinned still more against God,
     rebelling against the Most High in the desert.
18 They tested God in their heart
     by demanding the food they craved.
19 They spoke against God, saying,
   "Can God spread a table in the wilderness?
20   **Indeed! God struck the rock so that water**
        gushed out and streams overflowed!
   Can God also give bread,
        or provide meat for the people?"   R

32 They did not believe in his wonders,
33   so God made their days like a breath,
        turned their years into terror.
34 **Whenever God slew them, they would inquire after God,**
     repent, and seek God earnestly.
35 They remembered that God was their rock,
     the Most High God their redeemer,
36 **whom they flattered with their mouths,**
     to whom they lied with their tongues.
37 Their heart was not steadfast toward God;
     they were not true to God's covenant.
38 **Yet God, being compassionate,**
     forgave their iniquity,
     and did not destroy them.   R

Psalm 80

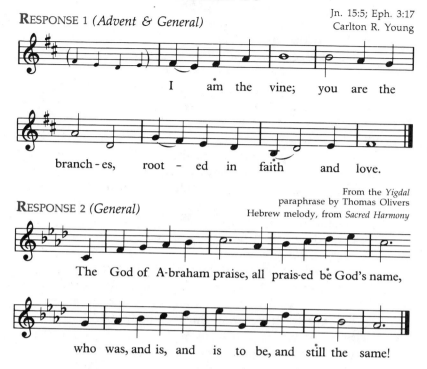

RESPONSE 1 (*Advent & General*)

Jn. 15:5; Eph. 3:17
Carlton R. Young

I am the vine; you are the branch-es, root - ed in faith and love.

RESPONSE 2 (*General*)

From the *Yigdal*
paraphrase by Thomas Olivers
Hebrew melody, from *Sacred Harmony*

The God of A-braham praise, all prais-ed be God's name, who was, and is, and is to be, and still the same!

R

1 Give ear, O Shepherd of Israel,
   you who lead Joseph like a flock!
   You who are enthroned upon the cherubim, shine forth!
2 In the presence of Ephraim and Benjamin and Manasseh,
   stir up your might, and come to save us!
3 **Restore us, O God;**
   let your face shine, that we may be saved!
4 O Lord God of hosts,
   how long will you be angry with your people's prayers?
5 **You have fed them with the bread of tears,**
   and given them tears to drink in full measure.
6 You make us the scorn of our neighbors;
   and our enemies laugh among themselves.
7 **Restore us, O God of hosts;**
   let your face shine, that we may be saved! R

8   You brought a vine out of Egypt;
      you drove out the nations and planted it.

9   **You cleared the ground for it;**
      it took deep root and filled the land.

10   The mountains were covered with its shade,
      the mighty cedars with its branches;

11   **it sent out its branches to the sea,**
      and its shoots to the river.

12   Why then have you broken down its walls,
      so that all who pass along the way pluck its fruit?

13   **The boar from the forest ravages it,**
      and all that move in the field feed on it.   R

14   Turn again, O God of hosts!
      Look down from heaven, and see:
  have regard for this vine,

15   **the stock which your right hand planted.**

16   They have burned it with fire, they have cut it down;
      may they perish at the rebuke of your countenance!

17   **But let your hand be upon those of your right hand,**
      the ones whom you have made strong for yourself!

18   Then we will never turn back from you;
      give us life, and we will call on your name!

19   **Restore us, O Lord God of hosts!**
      let your face shine, that we may be saved!   R

Psalm 81:1-10

Ps. 81:1
Randolph Currie

RESPONSE (General)

Repeat ad lib.

Sing with joy to God! Sing to God our help!

R

1 Sing aloud to God our strength;
      shout for joy to the God of Jacob!
2 **Raise a song, sound the tambourine,**
      the sweet lyre with the harp.
3 Blow the trumpet at the new moon,
      at the full moon, on our feast day.
4 **For it is a statute for Israel,**
      an ordinance of the God of Jacob,
5 **who made it a decree in Joseph,**
      when God went out over the land of Egypt.   R

I hear a voice I do not know:
6 **"I relieved your shoulder of the burden;**
      your hands were freed from the basket.
7 In distress you called, and I delivered you;
      I answered you in the secret place of thunder;
      I tested you at the waters of Meribah.
8 **Hear, O my people, while I admonish you!**
      O Israel, if you would but listen to me!
9 There shall be no strange god among you;
      you shall not bow down to a foreign god.
10 **I am the Lord your God,**
      who brought you up out of the land of Egypt.
      Open wide your mouth, and I will fill it."   R

Psalm 82

Ps. 3:8a,7a
Richard Proulx

RESPONSE (General)

De-liv-er-ance   be-longs to the Lord. A - rise, O Lord, de - liv - er us.

R

1 God is seated in the divine council;
   and in the midst of the gods holds judgment:
2 **"How long will you judge unjustly**
   and show partiality to the wicked?
3 Give justice to the weak and the orphan;
   maintain the right of the afflicted and the destitute.
4 **Rescue the weak and the needy;**
   deliver them from the hand of the wicked."
5 They have neither knowledge nor understanding,
   they walk about in darkness;
   all the foundations of the earth are shaken.
6 **I said, "You are gods,**
   godlike offspring, all of you;
7 nevertheless you shall die like mortals,
   and fall like any prince."
8 **Arise, O God, judge the earth,**
   for to you belong all the nations!   R

Psalm 84

Ps. 84:2a;16:11b
Gary Alan Smith

RESPONSE (General)

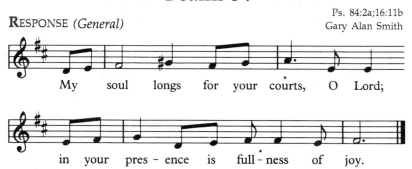

My   soul   longs   for   your   courts,   O   Lord;
in   your   pres - ence   is   full - ness   of   joy.

R

1 How lovely is your dwelling place,
    O Lord of hosts!
2 **My soul longs, indeed it faints**
    for the courts of the Lord;
  my heart and flesh sing for joy
    to the living God.
3 O Lord of hosts, my Ruler and my God,
    at your altars even the sparrow finds a home,
    and the swallow a nest for herself,
    where she may lay her young.
4 **Blessed are those who dwell in your house,**
    ever singing your praise!   R

5 Blessed are those whose strength is in you,
    in whose heart are the highways to Zion.
6 **As they go through the valley of tears,**
    they make it a place of springs;
    the early rain also covers it with pools.
7 They go from strength to strength;
    the God of gods will be seen in Zion.
8 **O Lord God of hosts, hear my prayer;**
    give ear, O God of Jacob!
9 **Behold our shield, O God;**
    look upon the face of your anointed!   R

10 For a day in your courts is better
    than a thousand elsewhere.
  I would rather be a doorkeeper in the house of my God
    than dwell in the tents of wickedness.
11 For the Lord God is a sun and shield,
    and bestows favor and honor.
  No good thing does the Lord withhold
    from those who walk uprightly.
12 **O Lord of hosts,**
    blessed are those who trust in you!   R

Psalm 85

Is. 40:5
Jane Marshall

RESPONSE *(Advent & General)*

The glo-ry of the Lord shall be re-vealed,

and all flesh shall see it to-geth-er.

Alternate response at Ps. 91.

R

1 Lord, you showed favor to your land;
   you restored the fortunes of Jacob.
2 **You forgave the iniquity of your people;**
   you pardoned all their sin.
3 You withdrew all your wrath;
   you turned from your hot anger.
4 **Restore us again, O God of our salvation,**
   and put away your indignation toward us!
5 Will you be angry with us forever?
   Will you prolong your anger to all generations?
6 Will you not revive us again,
   that your people may rejoice in you?
7 **Show us your steadfast love, O Lord,**
   and grant us your salvation. R

8 Let me hear what God will speak,
   for the Lord will speak peace to his people,
   to his faithful, to those who turn to the Lord in their hearts.
9 **Surely salvation is at hand for those who fear the Lord,**
   that glory may dwell in our land.
10 Steadfast love and faithfulness will meet;
   righteousness and peace will kiss each other.
11 **Faithfulness will spring up from the ground,**
   and righteousness will look down from the sky.
12 The Lord will give what is good,
   and our land will yield its increase.
13 **Righteousness will go before the Lord,**
   and make God's footsteps a way. R

Psalm 89:1-4, 19-37

R

¹ I will sing of your steadfast love, O Lord, for ever;
  with my mouth I will proclaim your faithfulness to all
  generations.
² **Your steadfast love is established for ever,**
  your faithfulness is firm as the heavens.
³ You have said, "I have made a covenant with my chosen one,
  I have sworn to David my servant:
⁴ **'I will establish your descendants for ever,**
  and build your throne for all generations.'" R

19 Then you spoke in a vision to your faithful one, and said:
    "I have set the crown upon one who is mighty,
    I have exalted one chosen from the people.
20 I have found David, my servant;
    with my holy oil I have anointed him;
21 **so that my hand shall ever abide with him,**
    my arm also shall strengthen him.
22 The enemy shall not outwit him,
    the wicked shall not humble him.
23 **I will crush his foes before him**
    and strike down those who hate him.
24 My faithfulness and my steadfast love shall be with him,
    and in my name shall his horn be exalted.
25 **I will set his hand on the sea**
    and his right hand on the rivers.   R

26 "He shall cry to me, 'You are my Father,
    my God, and the Rock of my salvation.'
27 **And I will make him the first-born,**
    the highest of the kings of the earth.
28 My steadfast love I will keep for him for ever,
    and my covenant will stand firm for him.
29 **I will establish his line for ever**
    and his throne as the days of the heavens.
30 If his children forsake my law
    and do not walk according to my ordinances,
31 **if they violate my statutes**
    and do not keep my commandments,
32 then I will punish their transgression with the rod
    and their iniquity with scourges;
33 **but I will not remove from him my steadfast love,**
    or be false to my faithfulness.
34 I will not violate my covenant,
    or alter the word that went forth from my lips.
35 **Once for all I have sworn by my holiness;**
    I will not lie to David.
36 His line shall endure for ever,
    his throne as long as the sun before me.
37 **Like the moon it shall be established for ever;**
    it shall stand firm while the skies endure."   R

Psalm 90

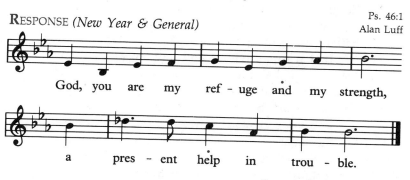

R<small>ESPONSE</small> *(New Year & General)*

Ps. 46:1
Alan Luff

God, you are my ref - uge and my strength,

a pres - ent help in trou - ble.

R

Alternate response at Ps. 46, response 1.

¹ Lord, you have been our dwelling place
   in all generations.
² Before the mountains were brought forth,
   or ever you had formed the earth and the world,
   from everlasting to everlasting you are God.
³ You turn us back to the dust,
   and say, "Turn back, O mortal ones!"
⁴ For a thousand years in your sight
   are but as yesterday when it is past,
   or as a watch in the night.
⁵ You sweep them away; they are like a dream,
   like grass which is renewed in the morning:
⁶ in the morning it flourishes and is renewed;
   in the evening it fades and withers.   R

⁷ For we are consumed by your anger;
   by your wrath we are overwhelmed.
⁸ You have set our iniquities before you,
   our secret sins in the light of your countenance.
⁹ For all our days pass away under your wrath,
   our years come to an end like a sigh.
¹⁰ The years of our life are threescore and ten,
   or even by reason of strength fourscore;
   yet their span is but toil and trouble;
   they are soon gone, and we fly away.
¹¹ Who considers the power of your anger,
   the awesomeness of your wrath?
¹² So teach us to number our days
   that we may receive a heart of wisdom.   R

13   Return, O Lord! How long?
    Have pity on your servants!
14   **Satisfy us in the morning with your steadfast love,**
    that we may rejoice and be glad all our days.
15   Make us glad as many days as you have afflicted us,
    and as many years as we have seen evil.
16   **Let your work be manifest to your servants,**
    and your glorious power to their children.
17   Let the favor of the Lord our God be upon us,
    and establish the work of our hands;
    yes, establish the work of our hands.   R

Psalm 91

Ps. 91:16,15,2
Carlton R. Young

Response *(Lent & General)*

Grant us sal - va-tion, Lord; in trou-ble be our ref-uge.

Alternate responses at Ps. 121, response 2, and Ps. 124.

R

1   Those who dwell in the shelter of the Most High,
    who abide in the shadow of the Almighty,
2   will say to the Lord,
    "My refuge and my fortress;
    my God, in whom I trust."
3   For the Lord will deliver you from the snare of the fowler
    and from the deadly pestilence
4   and will cover you with his pinions;
    under the Lord's wings you will find refuge.
    God's faithfulness is a shield and buckler.   R

5   You will not fear the terror of the night,
    nor the arrow that flies by day,
6   **nor the pestilence that stalks in darkness,**
    nor the destruction that wastes at noonday.
7   A thousand may fall at your side,
    ten thousand at your right hand,
    but it will not come near you.
8   **You will only look with your eyes**
    and see the recompense of the wicked.

⁹ Because you have made the Lord your refuge,
    the Most High your habitation,
¹⁰ **no evil shall befall you,**
    no scourge come near your tent. R

¹¹ For God will give his angels charge over you
    to guard you in all your ways.
¹² **They will bear you up on their hands**
    lest you dash your foot against a stone.
¹³ **You will tread on the lion and the adder,**
    the young lion and the serpent you will trample under
    foot.
¹⁴ Because they cleave to me in love, I will deliver them;
    I will protect them, because they know my name.
¹⁵ When they call to me, I will answer them;
    I will be with them in trouble,
    I will rescue them and honor them.
¹⁶ **I will satisfy them with long life**
    and show them my salvation. R

Psalm 92

RESPONSE *(General)*

Ps. 92:15,18:2
Johann Crüger

Sing praise to God our rock, in whom we take our ref-uge.

R

¹ It is good to give thanks to the Lord,
    to sing praises to your name, O Most High;
² **to declare your steadfast love in the morning,**
    and your faithfulness by night,
³ to the music of the lute and the harp,
    to the melody of the lyre.
⁴ **For you, O Lord, have made me glad by your work;**
    at the works of your hands I sing for joy. R

5 How great are your works, O Lord!
  Your thoughts are very deep!
6 **The dull ones cannot know,**
  the foolish cannot understand this:
7 though the wicked sprout like grass
    and all evildoers flourish,
    they are doomed to destruction for ever,
8   but you, O Lord, are on high for ever.
9 **For your enemies, O Lord,**
  for your enemies shall perish;
  all evildoers shall be scattered.
10 But you have exalted my horn like that of the wild ox;
    you have poured over me fresh oil.
11 **My eyes have seen the downfall of my enemies,**
  my ears have heard the doom of my evil assailants.   R

12 The righteous flourish like the palm tree,
    and grow like a cedar in Lebanon.
13 **They are planted in the house of the Lord,**
  they flourish in the courts of our God.
14 They still bring forth fruit in old age,
    they are ever full of sap and green
15   to show that the Lord is upright.
  The Lord is my rock, in whom there is no
  unrighteousness.   R

Psalm 93

Ps. 57:5
Jane Marshall

RESPONSE (*Christ the King & General*)

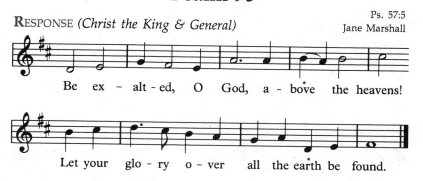

Be ex - alt - ed, O God, a - bove the heavens!

Let your glo - ry o - ver all the earth be found.

R

1 The Lord reigns and is robed in majesty;
    the Lord is robed and is girded with strength.
  The Lord has established the world;
    it shall never be moved.

2 Your throne has been established from of old;
    you are from everlasting!

3 **The floods have lifted up, O Lord,**
    the floods have lifted up their voice,
    the floods lift up their roaring.

4 Mightier than the thunders of many waters,
    mightier than the waves of the sea,
    the Lord on high is mighty!

5 **Your decrees are very sure;**
    holiness befits your house,
    O Lord, for evermore.   R

Psalm 95

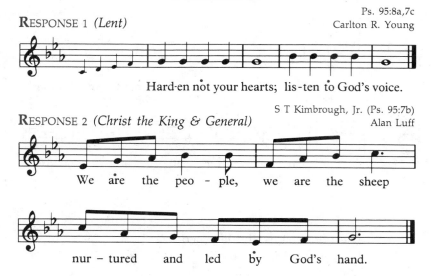

Ps. 95:8a,7c

RESPONSE 1 *(Lent)*

Carlton R. Young

Hard-en not your hearts; lis-ten to God's voice.

S T Kimbrough, Jr. (Ps. 95:7b)

RESPONSE 2 *(Christ the King & General)*

Alan Luff

We are the peo - ple, we are the sheep

nur - tured and led by God's hand.

R

1   O come, let us sing to the Lord;
    let us make a joyful noise to the rock of our salvation!
2   Let us come into God's presence with thanksgiving;
    let us make a joyful noise with songs of praise!
3   For the Lord is a great God,
    and a great Ruler above all gods,
4   in whose hands are the depths of the earth
    and also the heights of the mountains.
5   **The sea belongs to God who made it,**
    and the dry land, because God formed it.   R

6   O come, let us worship and bow down,
    let us kneel before the Lord, our Maker!
7   For the Lord is our God,
    we are the people of God's pasture,
    the sheep of God's hand.

For Coverdale Version (1535) see No. 91

Hear the voice of the Lord today!
8   Harden not your hearts, as at Meribah,
          as on the day at Massah in the wilderness,
9   when your forebears tested me,
          and put me to the proof, though they had seen my work.
10 **For forty years I loathed that generation**
          and said, "They are a people who err in heart,
          and they do not regard my ways."
11 **Therefore I swore in my anger**
          that they should not enter my rest.   R

Psalm 96

RESPONSE (*Christmas, Epiphany & General*)

Ps. 96:13,11-12
Gary Alan Smith

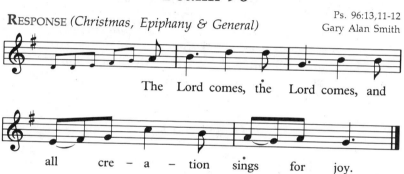

The Lord comes, the Lord comes, and all cre-a-tion sings for joy.

R

1   O sing to the Lord a new song;
          sing to the Lord, all the earth!
2   **Sing to the Lord, bless God's name;**
          proclaim God's salvation from day to day.
3   Declare the Lord's glory among the nations,
          the Lord's marvelous works among all the peoples!
4   **For great is the Lord and greatly to be praised,**
          to be feared above all gods.
5   For all the gods of the peoples are idols;
          but the Lord made the heavens.
6   **Honor and majesty are before the Lord**
          in whose sanctuary are strength and beauty.   R

7 Ascribe to the Lord, O families of the peoples,
  ascribe to the Lord glory and strength!
8 **Ascribe to the Lord the glory of his name!**
  Bring an offering, and come into the courts
  of the Lord!
9 Worship the Lord in holy splendor;
  tremble before the Lord, all the earth! R

10 Say among the nations, "The Lord reigns!
   The Lord has established the world, it shall
   never be moved.
   The Lord will judge the peoples with equity."
11 Let the heavens be glad, and let the earth rejoice;
   let the sea roar, and all that fills it;
12   let the field exult, and everything in it!
   Then shall all the trees of the wood sing for joy
13   **before the Lord, who comes to judge the earth.**
   The Lord will judge the world with righteousness,
   and the peoples with his truth. R

Psalm 97

Ps. 97:1a

RESPONSE 1 *(Christmas, Epiphany, Easter & General)*   Jane Marshall

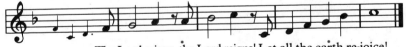

The Lord reigns, the Lord reigns! Let all the earth rejoice!

James Weldon Johnson
J. Rosamond Johnson

RESPONSE 2 *(General)*

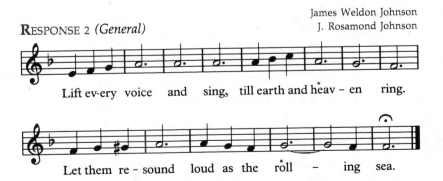

Lift ev-ery voice and sing, till earth and heav-en ring.

Let them re-sound loud as the roll - ing sea.

R

1 The Lord reigns; let the earth rejoice;
  let the many coastlands be glad!
2 **Clouds and thick darkness surround the Lord;**
  righteousness and justice are the foundation of
  God's throne.
3 Fire goes before the Lord,
  and burns up his adversaries round about.
4 **The Lord's lightnings illumine the world;**
  the earth sees and trembles.
5 The mountains melt like wax before the Lord,
  before the Lord of all the earth.
6 **The heavens proclaim God's righteousness**
  and all the peoples behold God's glory. R

7 All worshipers of images are put to shame,
  who make their boast in worthless idols;
  all gods bow down before the Lord.
8 **Zion hears and is glad,**
  and the daughters of Judah rejoice,
  because of your judgments, O God.
9 For you, O Lord, are most high over all the earth;
  you are exalted far above all gods.
10 **The Lord loves those who hate evil,**
   preserves the lives of his faithful,
   and delivers them from the hand of the wicked.
11 Light dawns for the righteous,
   and joy for the upright in heart.
12 **Rejoice in the Lord, O you righteous,**
   and give thanks to God's holy name! R

Psalm 98

Ps. 98:1a,3c

RESPONSE 1 *(Easter, Epiphany, Christmas & General)* Carlton R. Young

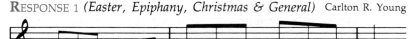

Sing a new song to the Lord,

who re - stores the ends of the earth.

Isaac Watts
Arr. from G. F. Handel
by Lowell Mason

RESPONSE 2 *(Epiphany & Christmas)*

Joy to the world! the Lord is come.

R

¹ O sing to the Lord a new song,
for the Lord has done marvelous things!
God's right hand and holy arm
have gotten the victory.
² **The Lord has declared victory,**
and has revealed his vindication in the sight of
the nations.
³ The Lord has remembered his steadfast love and faithfulness
to the house of Israel.
All the ends of the earth have seen
the victory of our God.   R

⁴ Make a joyful noise to the Lord, all the earth;
break forth into joyous song and sing praises!
⁵ Sing praises to the Lord with the lyre,
with the lyre and the sound of melody!
⁶ **With trumpets and the sound of the horn**
make a joyful noise before the Ruler, the Lord!   R

7 Let the sea roar, and all that fills it,
    the world and those who dwell in it!
8 **Let the floods clap their hands;**
    let the hills sing for joy together before the Lord,
9   **who comes to judge the earth.**
  The Lord will judge the world with righteousness,
    and the peoples with equity.   R

Psalm 99

Ps. 57:5
Jane Marshall

RESPONSE *(Transfiguration & General)*

Be ex - alt - ed, O God, a - bove the heavens!

Let your glo - ry o - ver all the earth be found.

R

1 The Lord reigns; let the peoples tremble!
    The Lord sits enthroned upon the cherubim;
      let the earth quake!
2 **The Lord is great in Zion,**
    and is exalted over all the peoples.
3 Let them praise your great and wondrous name!
    Holy is the Lord!
4 Mighty Ruler, lover of justice,
    you have established equity;
  you have executed justice
    and righteousness in Jacob.
5 Extol the Lord our God.
    Worship at the Lord's footstool!
    Holy is the Lord!   R

6 Moses and Aaron were among God's priests,
> Samuel also was among those who called on God's
> name.
They cried to the Lord, who answered them,
7 > **who spoke to them in the pillar of cloud.**
They kept God's testimonies,
> and the statutes God gave them.
8 **O Lord, our God, you answered them;**
> **you were a forgiving God to them,**
> **but an avenger of their wrongdoings.**
9 Extol the Lord our God,
> and worship at his holy mountain.
> **Surely the Lord our God is holy!   R**

Psalm 100

Edward H. Plumptre
Arthur H. Messiter

RESPONSE 1 *(Thanksgiving, Morning Prayer & General)*

Re - joice, re - joice, re - joice, give thanks, and sing.

Charles Wesley
Timothy E. Kimbrough

RESPONSE 2 *(General)*

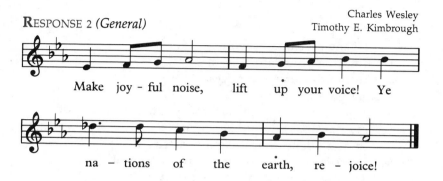

Make joy - ful noise, lift up your voice! Ye

na - tions of the earth, re - joice!

R

1 Make a joyful noise to the Lord, all the lands!
2 **Serve the Lord with gladness!**
     Come into God's presence with singing!
3 Know that the Lord, who made us, is God.
     We are the Lord's;
     we are the people of God,
     the sheep of God's pasture.
4 Enter God's gates with thanksgiving,
     and God's courts with praise!
     Give thanks and bless God's name!
5 For the Lord is good;
     God's steadfast love endures for ever;
     God's faithfulness to all generations.   R

Psalm 102

John Holbert (Ps. 102:2,20)
Gary Alan Smith

RESPONSE (General)

In our dis-tress we cry to you; come, Lord, and set us free!

R

1 Hear my prayer, O Lord;
    let my cry come to you!
2 **Do not hide your face from me**
    in the day of my distress!
Incline your ear to me;
    answer me speedily in the day when I call!
3 For my days pass away like smoke,
    and my bones burn like a furnace.
4 **My heart is smitten like grass, and withered;**
    I am too wasted to eat my bread.
5 Because of my loud groaning,
    my bones cleave to my flesh.
6 **I am like an owl of the wilderness,**
    like a little owl of the waste places;
7 I lie awake,
    I am like a lonely bird on the housetop.
8 **All the day my enemies taunt me,**
    those who deride me use my name for a curse.
9 For I eat ashes like bread,
    and mingle tears with my drink,
10 because of your indignation and anger.
    You have taken me up and thrown me away.
11 **My days are like an evening shadow;**
    I wither away like grass.   R

12 But you, O Lord, are enthroned for ever;
    your name endures to all generations.
13 **You will arise and have pity on Zion;**
    it is the time to favor it;
    the appointed time has come.

14 For your servants hold its stones dear,
     and have pity on its dust.
15 **The nations will fear the name of the Lord,**
     and all the kings of the earth your glory.
16 For the Lord will build up Zion,
     and will appear in his glory;
17 **the Lord will regard the prayer of the destitute,**
     and will not despise their prayer.   R

18 Let this be recorded for a generation to come,
     so that a people yet unborn may praise the Lord:
19 **that the Lord looked down from his holy height,**
     from heaven the Lord looked at the earth,
20 **to hear the groans of the prisoners,**
     to set free those who were doomed to die;
21 **that the name of the Lord may be declared in Zion,**
     and God's praise in Jerusalem,
22 **when peoples and kingdoms gather together to worship the**
     Lord.   R

23 The Lord has broken my strength in mid-course,
     and has shortened my days.
24 **"O my God," I say, "Do not take me away**
     in the midst of my days,
     you whose years endure
     throughout all the generations!"
25 Of old you laid the foundation of the earth,
     and the heavens are the work of your hands.
26 **They will perish, but you endure;**
     they will all wear out like a garment.
   You change them like raiment, and they pass away;
27   but you are the same, and your years have no end.
28 **The children of your servants shall dwell secure;**
     their posterity shall be established before you.   R

Psalm 103:1-18

Ps. 103:12
Richard Proulx

RESPONSE *(Lent & General)*

As far as the east is from the west, so far the Lord re-moves our sins from us.

R

¹ Bless the Lord, O my soul!
    and all that is within me,
    bless God's holy name!
² **Bless the Lord, O my soul,**
    and forget not all God's benefits,
³ who forgives all your iniquity,
    who heals all your diseases,
⁴ **who redeems your life from the pit,**
    who crowns you with steadfast love and mercy,
⁵ **who satisfies you with good as long as you live**
    so that your youth is renewed like the eagle's. **R**

⁶ The Lord, who works vindication
    and justice for all who are oppressed,
⁷ has made known God's ways to Moses,
    God's acts to the people of Israel.
⁸ **The Lord is merciful and gracious,**
    slow to anger and abounding in steadfast love.
⁹ The Lord will not always chide,
    nor harbor anger for ever.
¹⁰ **The Lord does not deal with us according to our sins,**
    nor repay us according to our iniquities.

11 For as the heavens are high above the earth,
   so great is the Lord's steadfast love toward the faithful;
12 **as far as the east is from the west,**
   so far does the Lord remove our transgressions from us.
13 As a father shows compassion to his children,
   so the Lord shows compassion to the faithful.
14 **For the Lord knows our frame,**
   and remembers that we are dust.   R

15 As for mortals, their days are like grass;
   they flourish like a flower of the field;
16 for the wind passes over it, and it is gone,
   and its place knows it no more.
17 **But the steadfast love of the Lord**
   is from everlasting to everlasting upon the faithful,
and the righteousness of the Lord to children's children,
18 **to those who keep his covenant**
   and remember to do his commandments.   R

Psalm 104:1-13, 24-35

Joachim Neander
trans. by Catherine Winkworth, alt.

RESPONSE *(Pentecost & General)*   *Erneuerten Gesangbuch*

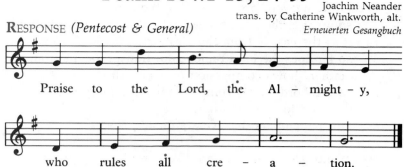

Praise to the Lord, the Al - might - y,

who rules all cre - a - tion.

R

1   Bless the Lord, O my soul!
    O Lord my God, you are very great!
    You are clothed with honor and majesty,
2   and cover yourself with light as with a garment;
    you have stretched out the heavens like a tent,
3   **and have laid the beams of your chambers on the**
           waters;
    you make the clouds your chariot,
       and ride on the wings of the wind;
4   **you make the winds your messengers,**
    fire and flame your ministers.
5   You set the earth on its foundations,
       so that it should never be shaken.
6   **You covered it with the deep as with a garment;**
    the waters stood above the mountains.
7   At your rebuke they fled;
    at the sound of your thunder they took to flight.
8   They rose up to the mountains, ran down to the valleys,
       to the place which you appointed for them.
9   **You set a bound which they should not pass,**
    so that they might not again cover the earth.   R

10 You make springs gush forth in the valleys;
    they flow between the hills;
11 **they give drink to every beast of the field;**
    the wild asses quench their thirst.
12 Above the springs the birds of the air have their nests;
    they sing among the branches.
13 **From your lofty place you water the mountains;**
    with the fruit of your work the earth is satisfied. R

24 O Lord, how manifold are your works!
    In wisdom you have made them all;
    the earth is full of your creatures.
25 Yonder is the sea, great and wide,
    creeping things innumerable are there,
    living things both small and great.
26 There go the ships,
    and Leviathan whom you formed to play in it.
27 **These all look to you,**
    to give them their food in due season.
28 When you give to them, they gather it;
    when you open your hand, they are filled with good
      things.
29 When you hide your face, they are dismayed;
    when you take away their breath, they die
    and return to their dust.
30 When you send forth your spirit, they are created;
    and you renew the face of the ground.
31 May the glory of the Lord endure for ever,
    may the Lord rejoice in his works,
32 **who looks on the earth and it trembles,**
    who touches the mountains and they smoke!
33 I will sing to the Lord as long as I live;
    I will sing praise to my God while I have being.
34 May my meditation be pleasing to the Lord
    in whom I rejoice.
35 **Let sinners be consumed from the earth,**
    and let the wicked be no more!
Bless the Lord, O my soul!
    Praise the Lord! R

Psalm 105:1-11

RESPONSE *(Lent & General)*

Is. 40:31a
Don E. Saliers

They who wait for the Lord shall re-new their strength.

Alternate GENERAL response at Ps. 77.

R

1 O give thanks to the Lord, call on God's name,
   make known God's deeds among the peoples!
2 **Sing to the Lord, sing praises!**
   Tell of all God's wonderful works!
3 Glory in God's holy name;
   let the hearts of those who seek the Lord rejoice!
4 **Seek the Lord and his strength;**
   seek the Lord's presence continually!
5 Remember the wonderful works God has done,
   the miracles and judgments God has uttered,
6 **O offspring of Abraham, God's servant,**
   children of Jacob, God's chosen ones.   R

7 The Lord is our God,
   whose judgments are in all the earth.
8 **The Lord is mindful of his everlasting covenant,**
   of the word commanded for a thousand generations,
9 the covenant made with Abraham,
   his promise sworn to Isaac,
10 and confirmed to Jacob as a statute,
   to Israel as an everlasting covenant, saying,
11 **"To you I will give the land of Canaan**
   as your portion for an inheritance."   R

Psalm 106:1-12, 19-23, 47-48

Folliot S. Pierpoint
Conrad Kocher

RESPONSE *(General)*

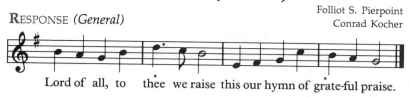

Lord of all, to thee we raise this our hymn of grateful praise.

R

1 Praise the Lord!
   O give thanks to the Lord who is good;
      whose steadfast love endures for ever!
2 Who can utter the mighty doings of the Lord,
      or show forth all God's praise?
3 **Blessed are they who observe justice,**
      who do righteousness at all times!
4 Remember me, O Lord, when you show favor to your people;
      help me when you deliver them,
5 **that I may see the prosperity of your chosen ones,**
      that I may rejoice in the gladness of your nation,
      that I may glory with your heritage.   R

6 Both we and our forebears have sinned;
      we have committed iniquity, we have done wickedly.
7 **Our forebears, when they were in Egypt,**
      did not consider your wonderful works;
   they did not remember the abundance of your steadfast love,
      but rebelled against the Most High at the Red Sea.
8 **God saved them for the sake of his holy name,**
      to make known the mighty power of God.
9 God rebuked the Red Sea, and it became dry;
      and led them through the deep as through a desert.
10 **So God saved them from the hand of the foe,**
      and delivered them from the hand of the enemy.
11 And the waters covered their adversaries;
      not one of them was left.
12 **Then they believed God's words:**
      they sang God's praise.   R

¹⁹ They made a calf in Horeb
    and worshiped a molten image.
²⁰ They exchanged the glory of God
    for the image of an ox that eats grass.
²¹ They forgot God, their Savior,
    who had done great things in Egypt,
²² wondrous works in the land of Ham,
    and terrible things by the Red Sea.
²³ Therefore the Lord intended to destroy them
    had not Moses, his chosen one,
    stood in the breach,
    to turn away God's wrath from destroying them.
⁴⁷ Save us, O Lord our God,
    and gather us from among the nations,
    that we may give thanks to your holy name
    and glory in your praise.
⁴⁸ Blessed be the Lord, the God of Israel,
    from everlasting to everlasting!
And let all the people say, "Amen!"
    Praise the Lord!   R

Psalm 107:1-9, 33-43

RESPONSE (*General*)

Ps. 107:8
Richard Proulx

Give thanks to the Lord for stead-fast love,

for all God's won-der-ful works.

R

¹ O give thanks to the Lord, who is good,
    whose steadfast love endures for ever!
² Let the redeemed of the Lord say so,
    whom the Lord has redeemed from trouble
³ **and gathered in from the lands,**
    from the east and from the west,
    from the north and from the south.

4 Some wandered in the desert wastes,
  finding no way to a city in which to dwell;
5 **hungry and thirsty,**
  their soul fainted within them.
6 Then in their trouble, they cried to the Lord,
  who delivered them from their distress,
7 **and led them by a straight way,**
  till they reached a city in which to dwell.
8 Let them thank the Lord for his steadfast love,
  for his wonderful works to humankind.
9 **For the Lord satisfies those who are thirsty,**
  and fills the hungry with good things.   R

33 The Lord turns rivers into a desert,
   springs of water into thirsty ground,
34 **a fruitful land into a salty waste,**
   because of the wickedness of its inhabitants.
35 The Lord turns a desert into pools of water,
   a parched land into springs of water.
36 **The Lord lets the hungry dwell there,**
   and they establish a city in which to live;
37 they sow fields, and plant vineyards,
   and get a fruitful yield.
38 **They multiply greatly by the blessing of the Lord**
   who does not let their cattle decrease.   R

39 When they are diminished and brought low
   through oppression, trouble, and sorrow,
40 the Lord pours contempt upon princes
   and makes them wander in trackless wastes;
41 **but the Lord raises up the needy out of affliction,**
   and makes their families like flocks.
42 The upright see it and are glad;
   and all wickedness stops its mouth.
43 **Whoever is wise, give heed to these things;**
   consider the steadfast love of the Lord.   R

Psalm 111

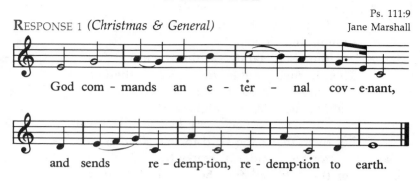

Ps. 111:9
Jane Marshall

RESPONSE 1 (*Christmas & General*)

God com - mands an e - ter - nal cov - e-nant, and sends re - demp-tion, re - demp-tion to earth.

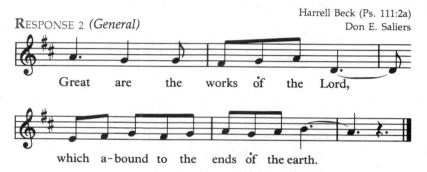

Harrell Beck (Ps. 111:2a)
Don E. Saliers

RESPONSE 2 (*General*)

Great are the works of the Lord, which a-bound to the ends of the earth.

R

1   Praise the Lord.
    I will give thanks to the Lord with my whole heart,
        in the company of the upright, in the congregation.
2   Great are the works of the Lord,
        studied by all who have pleasure in them.
3   **Full of honor and majesty are the works of the Lord**
        whose righteousness endures for ever,
4   who has caused his wonderful works to be remembered;
        the Lord is gracious and merciful.
5   **The Lord provides food for the faithful**
        and is ever mindful of his covenant.   R

6   The Lord has shown his people the power of his works
        by giving them the heritage of the nations.
7   **The works of the Lord's hands are faithful and just;**
        the precepts of the Lord are trustworthy;
8   they are established for ever and ever,
        to be performed with faithfulness and uprightness.

9 The Lord sent redemption to his people
      and has commanded his covenant for ever.
      Holy and wondrous is God's name!
10 **The fear of the Lord is the beginning of wisdom;**
      all those who practice it have a good understanding.
      The praise of the Lord endures for ever.   R

Psalm 112

RESPONSE *(General)*

S T Kimbrough, Jr. (Ps. 112:4,5)
Carlton R. Young

Light ris - es in dark-ness when jus - tice rules our lives.

Alternate response at Ps. 10.

R

1 Praise the Lord.
      Blessed are those who fear the Lord,
      who greatly delight in God's commandments!
2 **Their descendants will be mighty in the land;**
      the generation of the upright will be blessed.
3 Wealth and riches are in their house,
      and their righteousness endures for ever.
4 **They rise in the darkness as a light for the upright;**
      they are gracious, merciful and righteous.
5 It is well with those who deal generously and lend,
      who conduct their affairs with justice.
6 **For the righteous shall never be moved;**
      they will be remembered for ever.   R

7 They are not afraid of evil tidings;
      their hearts are firm, trusting in the Lord.
8 **When they see their adversaries,**
      their hearts are steady, they will not be afraid.
9 They have distributed freely, they have given to the poor;
      their righteousness endures for ever;
      their horn is exalted in honor.
10 **The wicked see it and are angry;**
      they gnash their teeth and melt away;
      the desire of the wicked comes to nothing.   R

Psalm 113

Lk. 7:16
Gary Alan Smith

RESPONSE *(General)*

Praise the Lord, praise the Lord, for God has vis-it-ed and re-deemed us.

R

¹ Praise the Lord!
Praise, O servants of the Lord,
    praise the name of the Lord!
² Blessed be the name of the Lord
    from this time forth and for evermore!
³ **From the rising of the sun to its setting**
    the name of the Lord is to be praised!
⁴ The Lord is high above all nations,
    God's glory above the heavens!
⁵ **Who is like the Lord our God,**
    who is seated on high,
⁶ **who looks far down**
    upon the heavens and the earth?
⁷ God raises the poor from the dust,
    and lifts the needy from the ash heap,
⁸ to make them sit with princes,
    with the princes of God's people.
⁹ **God gives the barren woman a home,**
    making her the joyous mother of children.
Praise the Lord! R

Psalm 114

Ps. 114:7
Richard Proulx

RESPONSE *(Easter & General)*

Trem-ble, O earth, at the pres-ence of the Lord.

R

1 When Israel went forth from Egypt,
    the house of Jacob from a people of strange language,
2 **Judah became God's sanctuary,**
    Israel God's dominion.
3 The sea looked and fled,
    Jordan turned back.
4 **The mountains skipped like rams,**
    the hills like lambs.
5 What ails you, O sea, that you flee?
    O Jordan, that you turn back?
6 **O mountains, that you skip like rams?**
    O hills, like lambs?
7 Tremble, O earth, at the presence of the Lord,
    at the presence of the God of Jacob,
8 **who turns the rock into a pool of water,**
    the flint into a spring of water. R

Psalm 115:1-11

Ps. 115:9a,18b
Don E. Saliers

RESPONSE *(General)*

We will trust in the Lord from this time forth and for ev - er.

R

1 Not to us, O Lord,
  not to us, but to your name give glory,
  for the sake of your steadfast love and faithfulness!
2 Why should the nations say,
  "Where is their God?"
3 **Our God is in the heavens;**
  whatever God pleases, God does. R

4 Their idols are silver and gold,
  the work of human hands.
5 **They have mouths, but do not speak;**
  eyes, but do not see.
6 They have ears, but do not hear;
  noses, but do not smell.
7 **They have hands, but do not feel;**
  feet, but do not walk;
  throats, but make no sound.
8 Those who make idols are like them;
  so are all who trust in them. R

9 O, Israel, trust in the Lord!
  The Lord is their help and their shield.
10 O house of Aaron, trust in the Lord!
  The Lord is their help and their shield.
11 You who fear the Lord, trust in the Lord!
  The Lord is their help and their shield. R

Psalm 116

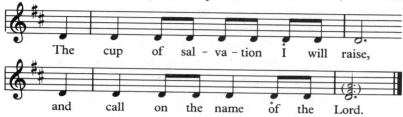

RESPONSE 1 *(Easter & General)*

Ps. 116:19b,8
Carlton R. Young

O praise the Lord, who de-liv-ers your soul from death.

RESPONSE 2 *(Lent & Holy Thursday)*

Ps. 116:13
Jane Marshall

The cup of sal - va - tion I will raise,

and call on the name of the Lord.

R

1   I love the Lord, who has heard
        my voice and my supplications,
2 and has inclined his ear to me
        whenever I called.
3 **The snares of death encompassed me;**
        the pangs of Sheol laid hold on me;
        I suffered distress and anguish.
4 Then I called on the name of the Lord:
        "O Lord, I beseech you, save my life!"   R

5 Gracious is the Lord, and righteous;
        our God is merciful.
6 **The Lord preserves the simple;**
        when I was brought low, the Lord saved me.
7 Return, O my soul, to your rest;
        for the Lord has dealt bountifully with you.
8 For you have delivered my soul from death,
        my eyes from tears,
        my feet from stumbling;
9 **I walk before the Lord**
        in the land of the living.
10 I kept my faith, even when I said,
        "I am greatly afflicted."
11 **I said in my consternation,**
        "All humans are a vain hope."   R

12 What shall I return to the Lord
        for all my benefits?
13 I will lift up the cup of salvation
        and call on the name of the Lord,
14 I will pay my vows to the Lord
        in the presence of all his people.
15 Precious in the sight of the Lord
        is the death of his faithful ones.
16 O Lord, I am your servant;
        I am your servant, the child of your handmaid.
        You have loosed my bonds.
17 I will offer to you the sacrifice of thanksgiving
        and call on the name of the Lord.
18 I will pay my vows to the Lord,
        in the presence of all his people,
19 in the courts of the house of the Lord,
        in your midst, O Jerusalem.
Praise the Lord!   R

Psalm 117

RESPONSE *(New Year & General)*

Alan Luff (Rev. 21:1-6)
Gary Alan Smith

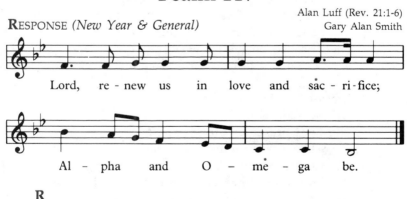

Lord, re-new us in love and sac-ri-fice;
Al-pha and O-me-ga be.

R

1 Praise the Lord, all nations!
        Extol the Lord, all peoples!
2 The Lord's steadfast love toward us is great!
        The faithfulness of the Lord endures for ever!
Praise the Lord!   R

Psalm 118:14-29

Ps. 118:26
William Mathias

RESPONSE 1 *(Passion/Palm Sunday)*

Bless-ed is the one who comes in the

name of the Lord! Ho-san-na in the high-est!

RESPONSE 2 *(Easter & General)*

Ps. 118:24
Richard Proulx

This is the day the Lord has made;

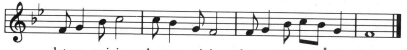

let us re-joice, let us re-joice, let us re-joice and be glad.

*May be sung as a canon.

R

14 The Lord is my strength and my power;
    the Lord has become my salvation.
15 **There are joyous songs of victory**
    in the tents of the righteous:
    "The right hand of the Lord does valiantly,
16   the right hand of the Lord is exalted,
    the right hand of the Lord does valiantly!"
17 I shall not die, but I shall live,
    and recount the deeds of the Lord.
18 **The Lord has chastened me sorely,**
    but has not given me over to death.
19 Open to me the gates of righteousness,
    that I may enter through them
    and give thanks to the Lord.
20 **This is the gate of the Lord;**
    the righteous shall enter through it.   **R**

21   I thank you that you have answered me
      and have become my salvation.
22   **The stone which the builders rejected**
      has become the cornerstone.
23   This is the Lord's doing;
      it is marvelous in our eyes.
24   **This is the day which the Lord has made;**
      let us rejoice and be glad in it.   R

25   Save us, we beseech you, O Lord!
      O Lord, we beseech you, give us success!
26   Blessed is the one who comes in the name of the Lord!
      We bless you from the house of the Lord.
27   The Lord is God,
      who has given us light.
      Lead the festal procession with branches,
      up to the horns of the altar!
28   You are my God, and I will give thanks to you;
      you are my God, I will extol you.
29   **O give thanks to the Lord, who is good;**
      for God's steadfast love endures for ever!   R

Psalm 119:1-8, 33-48, 129-144

RESPONSE 1 *(General)*

Ps. 119:105
Jane Marshall

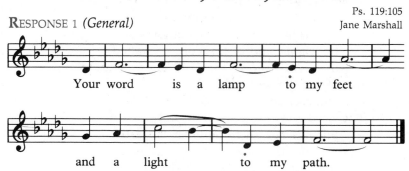

Your word is a lamp to my feet
and a light to my path.

RESPONSE 2 *(General)*

Ps. 119:45
Don E. Saliers

I shall walk at lib - er - ty,

for I have sought your pre - cepts.

RESPONSE 3 *(General)*

Ps. 119:105
Amy Grant and Michael W. Smith

Thy word is a lamp un - to my feet

and a light un - to my path.

R

1 Blessed are those whose way is blameless,
  who walk in the law of the Lord!
2 **Blessed are those who keep God's testimonies,**
  who seek God with their whole heart,
3 who also do no wrong,
  but walk in God's ways!
4 **You have commanded your precepts**
  to be kept diligently.
5 O that my ways may be steadfast
  in keeping your statutes!
6 **Then I shall not be put to shame,**
  having my eyes fixed on all your
  commandments.
7 I will praise you with an upright heart,
  when I learn your righteous ordinances.
8 **I will observe your statutes;**
  O forsake me not utterly! R

33 Teach me, O Lord, the way of your statutes;
   and I will keep it to the end.
34 **Give me understanding, that I may keep your law**
   and observe it with my whole heart.
35 Lead me in the path of your commandments,
   for I delight in it.
36 **Incline my heart to your testimonies,**
   and not to gain!
37 Turn my eyes from looking at vanities;
   and give me life in your ways.
38 **Confirm to your servant your promise,**
   which is for those who fear you.
39 Turn away the reproach which I dread;
   for your ordinances are good.
40 **Behold, I long for your precepts;**
   in your righteousness give me life! R

41 Let your steadfast love come to me, O Lord,
   your salvation according to your promise;
42 **then shall I have an answer for those who taunt me,**
   for I trust in your word.
43 And take not the word of truth utterly out of my mouth,
   for my hope is in your ordinances.
44 **I will keep your law continually,**
   for ever and ever;
45 and I shall walk at liberty,
   for I have sought your precepts.
46 **I will also speak of your testimonies before rulers,**
   and shall not be put to shame;
47 for I find my delight in your commandments,
   which I love.
48 **I revere your commandments, which I love,**
   and I will meditate on your statutes. R

129 Your testimonies are wonderful;
    therefore my soul keeps them.
130 **The unfolding of your words gives light;**
    it imparts understanding to the simple.
131 With open mouth I pant,
    because I long for your commandments.
132 **Turn to me and be gracious to me,**
    for you are just to those who love your name.
133 Keep steady my steps according to your promise,
    and let no iniquity get dominion over me.
134 **Redeem me from human oppression,**
    that I may keep your precepts.
135 Make your face shine upon your servant,
    and teach me your statutes.
136 **My eyes shed streams of tears,**
    because your law is not kept. **R**

137 Righteous are you, O Lord,
    and right are your judgments.
138 **You have appointed your testimonies in righteousness**
    and in all faithfulness.
139 My zeal consumes me,
    because my foes forget your words.
140 **Your promise is well tried,**
    and your servant loves it.
141 I am small and despised,
    yet I do not forget your precepts.
142 **Your righteousness is righteous for ever,**
    and your law is true.
143 Trouble and anguish have come upon me,
    but your commandments are my delight.
144 **Your testimonies are righteous for ever;**
    give me understanding that I may live. **R**

Psalm 121

RESPONSE 1 *(Evening Prayer & General)*

Eph. 6:10
Carlton R. Young

Be strong in the Lord and in the strength of God's might.

RESPONSE 2 *(General)*

Ps. 63:7
Michael Joncas

In the shad-ow of your wings I sing for joy.

Wis. of Sol. 5:15
Arr. from *Gesangbuch,* Meiningen
RESPONSE 3 *(Funerals and Memorial Services)* by Timothy E. Kimbrough

The righ-teous live for ev - er,

their re - ward is with the Lord.

R

1 I lift up my eyes to the hills.
   From whence does my help come?
2 **My help comes from the Lord,**
   who made heaven and earth.
3 The Lord will not let your foot be moved,
   the Lord who keeps you will not slumber.
4 **Behold, the One who keeps Israel**
   will neither slumber nor sleep.
5 The Lord is your keeper;
   the Lord is your shade
   on your right hand.
6 The sun shall not smite you by day,
   nor the moon by night.
7 The Lord will keep you from all evil,
   and will keep your life.
8 **The Lord will keep**
   your going out and your coming in
   from this time forth and for evermore. R

Psalm 122

RESPONSE 1 *(Advent & General)*

James Montgomery
Gesangbuch der H. W. k. Hofkapelle

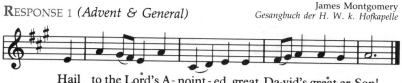

Hail   to the Lord's A-noint-ed, great Da-vid's great-er Son!

RESPONSE 2 *(General)*

Ps. 122:6a,7a
Jane Marshall

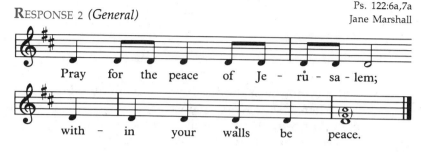

Pray   for   the   peace   of   Je - ru - sa - lem;

with - in   your   walls   be   peace.

R

1 I was glad when they said to me,
     "Let us go to the house of the Lord!"
2 **Our feet were standing**
     within your gates, O Jerusalem!
3 Jerusalem is built as a city
     and is bound firmly together,
4 to which the tribes go up,
     the tribes of the Lord,
   to give thanks to the name of the Lord,
     as was decreed for Israel.
5 **Thrones for judgment were set there,**
     the thrones of the house of David.   R

6 Pray for the peace of Jerusalem!
   "May they prosper who love you!
7   **Peace be within your walls,**
     and security within your towers!"
8 For the sake of my relatives and friends
     I will say, "Peace be within you!"
9 **For the sake of the house of the Lord our God,**
     I will seek your good.   R

Psalm 124

RESPONSE *(General)*   Charles Albert Tindley

When the storms of life are rag-ing, stand by me.

R

1 If it had not been the Lord who was on our side—
   let Israel now say—
2 **if it had not been the Lord who was on our side,**
   when foes rose up against us,
3 **then they would have swallowed us up alive,**
   when their anger was kindled against us;
4 then the flood would have swept us away,
   the torrent would have gone over us;
5 **then the raging waters**
   would have gone over us.
6 Blessed be the Lord,
   who has not given us
   as prey to their teeth!
7 **We have escaped as a bird**
   from the snare of the fowlers;
   the snare is broken,
   and we have escaped!
8 **Our help is in the name of the Lord**
   who made heaven and earth. R

Psalm 126

RESPONSE 1 (*Thanksgiving & General*)

Ps. 126:3
Trad. English melody

The Lord has done great things for us, and we are filled with joy.

RESPONSE 2 (*Advent & Lent*)

Ps. 30:5cd
French carol melody

For the night weep - ing may tar - ry;

with the morn - ing light comes joy.

R

1 When the Lord restored the fortunes of Zion,
    we were like those who dream.
2 **Then our mouth was filled with laughter,**
    and our tongue with shouts of joy;
  then they said among the nations,
    "The Lord has done great things for them."
3 **The Lord has done great things for us;**
    we are glad.   R

4 Restore our fortunes, O Lord,
    like the watercourses in the Negeb!
5 **May those who sow in tears**
    reap with shouts of joy!
6 Those who go forth weeping,
    bearing the seed for sowing,
  shall come home with shouts of joy,
    carrying their sheaves.   R

Psalm 130

Ps. 120:1-2a
Jane Marshall

RESPONSE (*Lent, Funerals and Memorial Services & General*)

In my dis - tress I cry to the Lord:

"De - liv - er me, O Lord."

R

1 Out of the depths I cry to you, O Lord!
2   Lord, hear my voice!
  Let your ears be attentive
      to the voice of my supplications!
3 If you, O Lord, should mark iniquities,
      Lord, who could stand?
4 **But there is forgiveness with you,**
      that you may be worshiped.
5 I wait for the Lord, my soul waits,
      in the Lord's word I hope;
6 **my soul waits for the Lord**
      more than those who watch for the morning,
      more than those who watch for the morning.
7 O Israel, hope in the Lord!
      For with the Lord there is steadfast love,
      with the Lord is plenteous redemption.
8 **And the Lord will redeem Israel**
      from all iniquities. R

For Coverdale Version (1535) see No. 516.

Psalm 132:1-5, 11-18

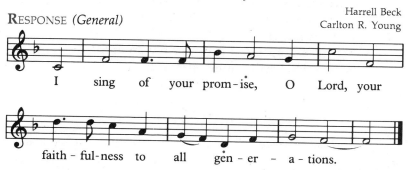

RESPONSE *(General)*

Harrell Beck
Carlton R. Young

I sing of your prom-ise, O Lord, your faith – ful-ness to all gen – er – a – tions.

Alternate response at Ps. 122, response 2.

R

1 O Lord, in David's favor
    remember all the hardships he endured;
2 how he swore to the Lord
    and vowed to the Mighty One of Jacob,
3 **"I will not enter my house**
    or get into my bed;
4 I will not give sleep to my eyes
    or slumber to my eyelids,
5 **until I find a place for the Lord,**
    a dwelling place for the Mighty One of Jacob." **R**

11 The Lord swore to David a sure oath
    and from it will not turn back:
"One of the sons of your body
    I will set on your throne.
12 If your sons keep my covenant
    and my testimonies which I shall teach them,
their sons also for ever
    shall sit upon your throne." **R**

13 For the Lord has chosen Zion,
    and has desired it for God's habitation:
14 **"This is my resting place for ever;**
    here I will dwell, for I have desired it.
15 I will abundantly bless its provisions;
    I will satisfy its poor with bread.

16 **Its priests I will clothe with salvation,**
   and its faithful will shout for joy.
17 There I will make a horn to sprout for David;
   I have prepared a lamp for my anointed.
18 **His enemies I will clothe with shame,**
   but his crown will shine upon him." R

Psalm 133

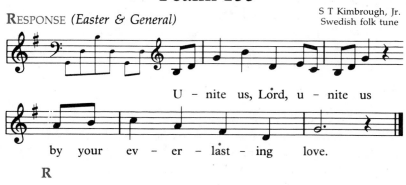

RESPONSE (*Easter & General*)

S T Kimbrough, Jr.
Swedish folk tune

U – nite us, Lord, u – nite us
by your ev – er – last – ing love.

R

1 Behold, how good and pleasant it is
   when we live together in unity!
2 **It is like the precious oil upon the head,**
   running down upon the beard,
   upon the beard of Aaron,
   running down on the collar of his robes!
3 It is like the dew of Hermon
   which falls on the mountains of Zion!
   For there the Lord has commanded the blessing,
   life for evermore. R

Words Response © 1989 The United Methodist Publishing House

Psalm 134

RESPONSE (*Evening Prayer & General*)

Ps. 141:2
Arlo D. Duba

My prayers rise like in – cense, my
hands like the eve – ning sac – ri – fice.

Music © 1980 Arlo D. Duba

R

1 Come, bless the Lord, all you servants of the Lord,
who stand by night in the house of the Lord!
2 Lift up your hands in the holy place,
and bless the Lord!
3 **May the Lord who made heaven and earth
bless you from Zion.   R**

Psalm 135:1-14

Johann J. Schütz
trans. by Frances E. Cox
Bohemian Brethren's *Kirchengesänge*

RESPONSE *(General)*

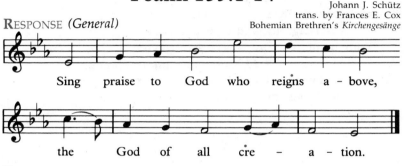

Sing praise to God who reigns a - bove, the God of all cre - a - tion.

R

1 Praise the Lord!
Praise the name of the Lord!
Give praise, O servants of the Lord,
2 **you that stand in the house of the Lord,
in the courts of the house of our God!**
3 Praise the Lord, for the Lord is good;
sing to the Lord's name, for the Lord is gracious!
4 **For the Lord has chosen Jacob as God's own,
Israel as God's own possession.   R**

5 For I know that the Lord is great,
and that our Lord is above all gods.
6 Whatever the Lord pleases, the Lord does,
in heaven and on earth,
in the seas and all deeps.
7 **It is the Lord who makes the clouds rise at the end of the earth,
makes lightnings for the rain
and brings wind from the storehouse of God.   R**

8 It was the Lord who struck the first-born of Egypt,
    both of human beings and animals;
9 **who in your midst, O Egypt,**
    sent signs and wonders
    against Pharaoh and all his servants;
10 who struck many nations
    and slew mighty kings,
11 Sihon, king of the Amorites,
    and Og, king of Bashan,
    and all the kingdoms of Canaan,
12 **and gave their land as a heritage,**
    a heritage to God's people Israel.
13 Your name, O Lord, endures for ever,
    your renown, O Lord, throughout all ages.
14 **For the Lord will vindicate his people,**
    and have compassion on his servants.   R

Psalm 137

RESPONSE *(Lent & General)*

Ps. 39:7
Jane Marshall

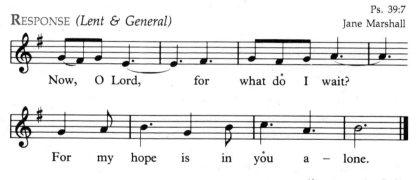

Now, O Lord, for what do I wait?

For my hope is in you a - lone.

Alternate response at Ps. 76.

R

1 By the rivers of Babylon,
    there we sat down and wept,
    when we remembered Zion.
2 **On the willows there**
    we hung up our lyres.
3 For there our captors
    required of us songs,
    and our tormentors, mirth, saying,
    "Sing us one of the songs of Zion!"

4 **How shall we sing the Lord's song**
   in a foreign land?
5 If I forget you, O Jerusalem,
   let my right hand wither!
6 **Let my tongue cleave to the roof of my mouth,**
   if I do not remember you,
   if I do not set Jerusalem
   above my highest joy!
7 O Lord, remember against the Edomites
   the day of Jerusalem,
   how they said, "Raze it, raze it!
   Down to its foundations!"
8 O daughter of Babylon, you devastator!
   Happy shall they be who repay you
   with what you have done to us!
9 **Happy shall they be who take your little ones**
   and dash them against the rock! R

Psalm 138

RESPONSE *(General)*

Ps. 138:1,2,6
Gary Alan Smith

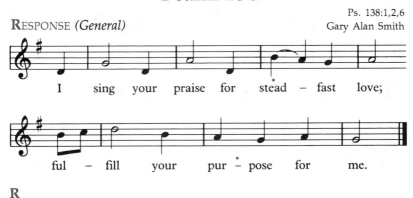

I sing your praise for stead - fast love;

ful - fill your pur - pose for me.

R

1 I give you thanks, O Lord, with my whole heart;
   before the gods I sing your praise;
2 **I bow down toward your holy temple**
   and give thanks to your name for your steadfast
   love and faithfulness;
   for you have exalted your name
   and your word above everything.
3 **On the day I called, you answered me,**
   you strengthened my life. R

4 All the rulers of the earth shall praise you, O Lord,
   for they have heard the words of your mouth;
5 and they shall sing of the ways of the Lord,
   for great is the glory of the Lord.
6 For the Lord is high, but regards the lowly;
   yet knows the haughty from afar.   R

7 Though I walk in the midst of trouble,
     you preserve my life;
   you stretch out your hand against the wrath of my enemies
   and your right hand delivers me.
8 O Lord, fulfill your purpose for me;
   O Lord, may your steadfast love endure for ever.
   Do not forsake the work of your hands.   R

Psalm 139

Ps. 139:23
Adapt. from Martin Luther
by Carlton R. Young

RESPONSE(*General*)

Search   me,   O   God,   and   know   my   heart;

try   me   and   know   my   thoughts.

R

1 O Lord, you have searched me and known me!
2 **You know when I sit down and when I rise up;**
   you discern my thoughts from afar.
3 You search out my path and my lying down,
     and are acquainted with all my ways.
4 **Even before a word is on my tongue, O Lord,**
   you know it altogether.
5 You pursue me behind and before,
     and lay your hand upon me.
6 **Such knowledge is too wonderful for me;**
   it is high, I cannot attain it.   R

7 Whither shall I go from your spirit?
Or whither shall I flee from your presence?
8 If I ascend to heaven, you are there!
If I make my bed in Sheol, you are there!
9 **If I take the wings of the morning**
and dwell in the uttermost parts of the sea,
10 **even there your hand shall lead me,**
and your right hand shall hold me.
11 If I say, "Let only darkness cover me,
and the light about me be night,"
12 **even the darkness is not dark to you,**
the night is bright as the day;
for darkness is as light with you.   R

13 For it was you who formed my inward parts,
you knit me together in my mother's womb.
14 I praise you, for you are fearful and wonderful.
Wonderful are your works!
You know me very well;
15 **my frame was not hidden from you,**
when I was being made in secret,
intricately wrought in the depths of the earth.
16 Your eyes beheld my unformed substance;
in your book were written
the days that were formed for me,
every day, before they came into being.
17 How profound to me are your thoughts, O God!
How vast is the sum of them!
18 **If I would count them, they are more than the sand.**
When I awake, I am still with you.   R

19 O that you would slay the wicked, O God,
and that the bloodthirsty would depart from me,
20 **those who maliciously defy you,**
who lift themselves up against you for evil.
21 Do I not hate them that hate you, O Lord?
And do I not loathe them that rise up against you?
22 **I hate them with perfect hatred;**
I count them my enemies.
23 Search me, O God, and know my heart!
Try me and know my thoughts;
24 **and see if there be any wicked way in me,**
and lead me in the way everlasting!   R

Psalm 143:1-10

RESPONSE 1 *(Lent & General)*

Alan Luff (Ezek. 37:1-14)
Richard Proulx

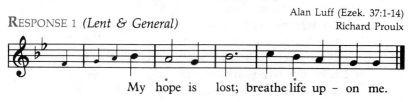

My hope is lost; breathe life up - on me.

RESPONSE 2 *(General)*

Ps. 46:1
Juan Antonio Espinosa

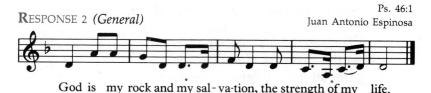

God is my rock and my sal-va-tion, the strength of my life.

R

1 Hear my prayer, O Lord;
    in your faithfulness give ear to my supplications;
    in your righteousness answer me!

2 **Enter not into judgment with your servant;**
    for no one living is righteous before you.

3 For enemies have pursued me;
    they have crushed my life to the ground;
    they have made me sit in darkness like those long dead.

4 **Therefore my spirit faints within me;**
    my heart within me is appalled. R

5 I remember the days of old,
    I meditate on all that you have done;
    I muse on what your hands have wrought.

6 **I stretch out my hands to you;**
    my soul thirsts for you like a parched land.

7 Make haste to answer me, O Lord!
    My spirit fails!
Hide not your face from me,
    lest I be like those who go down to the pit.

8 In the morning let me hear of your steadfast love,
    for in you I put my trust.
Teach me the way I should go,
    for to you I lift up my soul. R

9 Deliver me, O Lord, from my enemies!
   I have fled to you for refuge!
10 Teach me to do your will,
   for you are my God!
   Let your good Spirit lead me
   on a level path! R

Psalm 145:8-21

RESPONSE (*Easter & General*)   Ps. 85:7
Adapt. from Leisentritt's *Gesangbuch*

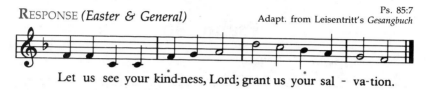

Let us see your kind-ness, Lord; grant us your sal - va-tion.

R

8 The Lord is gracious and merciful,
   slow to anger and abounding in steadfast love.
9 **The Lord is good to all,**
   his compassion is over all his creation.
10 All your works shall give thanks to you, O Lord,
   and your faithful ones shall bless you!
11 They shall speak of the glory of your kingdom,
   and tell of your power,
12 to make known to all people your mighty deeds,
   and the glorious splendor of your kingdom.
13 Your kingdom is an everlasting kingdom,
   and your dominion endures throughout all
   generations. R

14 The Lord upholds all who are falling,
   and raises up all who are bowed down.
15 The eyes of all look to you,
   and you give them their food in due season.
16 You open your hand,
   you satisfy the desire of every living thing.
17 All the Lord's ways are just,
   all the Lord's doings are kind.

¹⁸ The Lord is near to all who call,
   to all who call upon the Lord in truth.
¹⁹ The Lord fulfills the desire of all the faithful,
   and hears their cry and saves them.
²⁰ All who love the Lord, the Lord preserves.
   All the wicked the Lord destroys.
²¹ My mouth will speak the praise of the Lord;
   let all flesh bless God's holy name for ever and ever.   R

Psalm 146

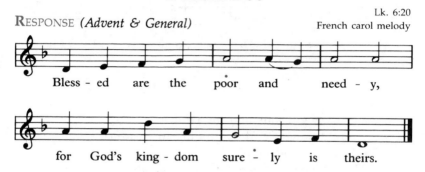

R

¹ Praise the Lord!
   Praise the Lord, O my soul!
² **I will praise the Lord as long as I live;**
   I will sing praises to my God while I have being.
³ Put not your trust in princes,
   in mortals, in whom there is no help.
⁴ **Their breath departs, they return to the earth;**
   on that very day their plans perish.
⁵ Happy are those whose help is in the God of Jacob,
   whose hope is in the Lord, their God,
⁶ who made heaven and earth,
   the sea, and all that is in them;
   who keeps faith for ever;
⁷   **who executes justice for the oppressed;**
   who gives food to the hungry.   R

The Lord sets the prisoners free;
8   **the Lord opens the eyes of the blind.**
The Lord lifts up those who are bowed down;
        the Lord loves the righteous.
9   The Lord watches over the sojourners,
        and upholds the widow and the orphan;
        but the Lord brings the way of the wicked to ruin.
10   The Lord will reign for ever,
        your God, O Zion, from generation to generation.
Praise the Lord!   R

Psalm 147

RESPONSE *(Christmas, Epiphany & General)*

Charles Wesley
Robert Williams

Praise the Lord who reigns a-bove: Al - le - lu - ia!

R

1   Praise the Lord!
        For it is good to sing praises to our God;
        a song of praise is fitting.
2   **The Lord builds up Jerusalem;**
    and gathers the outcasts of Israel.
3   The Lord heals the brokenhearted,
        and binds up their wounds.
4   **The Lord determines the number of the stars,**
    and gives to all of them their names.
5   Great is our Lord, and abundant in power,
        whose understanding is beyond measure.
6   **The Lord lifts up the downtrodden,**
    but casts the wicked to the ground.   R

7　Sing to the Lord with thanksgiving;
　　make melody upon the lyre to our God
8　who covers the heavens with clouds,
　　prepares rain for the earth,
　　makes grass grow upon the hills.
9　**The Lord gives to the beasts their food,**
　　and to the young ravens that cry.
10　The Lord takes no delight in the might of a horse
　　nor pleasure in the strength of a runner,
11　**but the Lord takes pleasure in the faithful,**
　　in those who hope in the Lord's steadfast love.　R

12　Praise the Lord, O Jerusalem!
　　Praise your God, O Zion!
13　**The Lord strengthens the bars of your gates,**
　　blesses your children in your midst,
14　makes peace in your borders,
　　fills you with the finest wheat.
15　**The Lord sends forth commands to the earth;**
　　the word runs swiftly.
16　The Lord gives snow like wool,
　　scatters hoarfrost like ashes,
17　**casts forth ice like morsels;**
　　who can withstand its cold?
18　The Lord sends forth the word and melts them;
　　makes the wind blow, and the waters flow.
19　**The Lord declares the word to Jacob,**
　　the statutes and ordinances to Israel.
20　The Lord has not dealt thus with any other nation;
　　they do not know God's ordinances.
Praise the Lord!　R

Psalm 148

Francis of Assisi
trans. by William H. Draper
Geistliche Kirchengesänge

Response *(Morning Prayer & General)*

Let all things their cre - a - tor bless: Al - le -
lu - ia! Al - le - lu - ia! Al - le - lu - ia!

R

1 Praise the Lord!
  Praise the Lord from the heavens,
  praise the Lord, in the heights!
2 **Praise the Lord, all his angels,**
  praise the Lord, all his hosts!
3 Praise the Lord, sun and moon,
  praise the Lord, all shining stars!
4 **Praise the Lord, highest heavens,**
  and all waters above the heavens! R

5 Let them praise the name of the Lord,
  who commanded and they were created,
6 **who established them for ever and ever,**
  and fixed their bounds which cannot be passed.
7 Praise the Lord from the earth,
  sea monsters and all deeps,
8 **fire and hail, snow and smoke,**
  stormy wind fulfilling God's command! R

9 Mountains and all hills,
  fruit trees and all cedars!
10 **Beasts and all cattle,**
   creeping things and flying birds!
11 Kings of the earth and all peoples,
   princes and all rulers of the earth!
12 **Young men and maidens together,**
   old men and children!

¹³ Let them praise the name of the Lord,
    whose name alone is exalted,
    whose glory is above earth and heaven.
¹⁴ **God has raised up a horn for his people,**
    praise for all his faithful ones,
    for the people of Israel who are near their God.
    Praise the Lord! R

Psalm 150

RESPONSE 1 *(Easter)*

Lk. 24:34
Giovanni P. da Palestrina

Al- le - lu - ia! Al- le - lu - ia! Christ is ris - en!

RESPONSE 2 *(Morning Prayer & General)*

Ps. 95:1
Carlos Rosas

Al - le - lu- ia! Al - le - lu- ia! Let's

sing un - to the Lord: Al - le - lu - ia!

R

¹ Praise the Lord!
    Praise God in his sanctuary;
    praise God in his mighty firmament!
² Praise God for his mighty deeds;
    praise God for his exceeding greatness!
³ Praise God with trumpet sound;
    praise God with lute and harp!
⁴ Praise God with tambourine and dance;
    praise God with strings and pipe!
⁵ Praise God with sounding cymbals;
    praise God with loud clashing cymbals!
⁶ Let everything that breathes praise the Lord!
    Praise the Lord! R

OTHER GENERAL SERVICES
& ACTS OF WORSHIP

There is one God
  and there is one mediator, Jesus Christ,
who came as a ransom for all,
  to whom we testify.

I TIMOTHY 2:5-6

A SERVICE OF CHRISTIAN MARRIAGE

This service of Christian marriage is provided for couples who wish to solemnize their marriage in a service of Christian worship, parallel in its structure to the Sunday service, which includes the proclamation of the Word with prayer and praise. Christian marriage is proclaimed as a sacred covenant reflecting Christ's covenant with the church. Everything about the service is designed to witness that this is a Christian marriage.

Both words and actions consistently reflect the belief that husband and wife are equal partners in Christian marriage and that they are entering into the marriage of their own volition.

Those present are understood to be an active congregation rather than simply passive witnesses. They give their blessing to the couple and to the marriage, and they join in prayer and praise.

Holy Communion may or may not be celebrated. If it is, it is most important that its significance be made clear. Specifically: (1) The marriage rite is included in a Service of Word and Table. (2) Not only the husband and wife but the whole congregation are to be invited to receive Communion. It is our tradition to invite all Christians to the Lord's table. (3) There should be no pressure that would embarrass those who for whatever reason do not choose to receive Communion.

Other approved services are found in The Book of Ritual *of the former Evangelical United Brethren Church (1959), pages 34-38, and* The Book of Worship for Church and Home *of the former Methodist Church (1965), pages 28-31.*

ENTRANCE

GATHERING

While the people gather, instrumental or vocal music may be offered.

During the entrance of the wedding party, there may be instrumental music, or a hymn, a psalm, a canticle, or an anthem.

GREETING

Pastor to people:

Friends, we are gathered together in the sight of God
to witness and bless the joining together of *Name* and *Name*
   in Christian marriage.
The covenant of marriage was established by God,
   who created us male and female for each other.
With his presence and power
   Jesus graced a wedding at Cana of Galilee,
and in his sacrificial love
   gave us the example for the love of husband and wife.
Name and *Name* come to give themselves to one another
   in this holy covenant.

DECLARATION OF INTENTION

DECLARATION BY THE MAN AND THE WOMAN

Pastor to the persons who are to marry:

I ask you now, in the presence of God and these people,
to declare your intention
to enter into union with one another
through the grace of Jesus Christ,
　　who calls you into union with himself
　　as acknowledged in your baptism.

Pastor to the woman:

Name, will you have *Name* to be your husband,
　　to live together in holy marriage?
Will you love him, comfort him, honor and keep him,
　　in sickness and in health,
and forsaking all others, be faithful to him
　　as long as you both shall live?

Woman: **I will.**

Pastor to the man:

Name, will you have *Name* to be your wife,
　　to live together in holy marriage?
Will you love her, comfort her, honor and keep her,
　　in sickness and in health,
and forsaking all others, be faithful to her
　　as long as you both shall live?

Man: **I will.**

RESPONSE OF THE FAMILIES AND PEOPLE

Pastor to people:

The marriage of *Name* and *Name* unites their families
　　and creates a new one.
They ask for your blessing.

Parents or other representatives of the families may respond:

**We rejoice in your union,
and pray God's blessing upon you.**

Pastor to people:

Will all of you, by God's grace,
do everything in your power
to uphold and care for these two persons
　　in their marriage?

People: **We will.**

PRAYER

The Lord be with you.

And also with you.

Let us pray.

God of all peoples,
you are the true light illumining everyone.
You show us the way, the truth, and the life.
You love us even when we are disobedient.
You sustain us with your Holy Spirit.
We rejoice in your life in the midst of our lives.
We praise you for your presence with us,
    and especially in this act of solemn covenant;
through Jesus Christ our Lord.

Amen.

PROCLAMATION AND RESPONSE

SCRIPTURE LESSON(S)

A hymn, psalm, canticle, anthem, or other music may be offered before or after the readings.

SERMON OR OTHER WITNESS TO CHRISTIAN MARRIAGE

INTERCESSORY PRAYER

An extemporaneous prayer may be offered, or the following may be prayed by the pastor or by all:

Let us pray.

Eternal God, creator and preserver of all life,
    author of salvation, giver of all grace:
Bless and sanctify with your Holy Spirit
    Name and *Name*, who come now to join in marriage.
Grant that they may give their vows to each other
    in the strength of your steadfast love.
Enable them to grow in love and peace
    with you and with one another all their days,
    that they may reach out
    in concern and service to the world;
    through Jesus Christ our Lord.

Amen.

THE MARRIAGE

EXCHANGE OF VOWS

The woman and man face each other, joining hands.

Man to woman:

In the name of God,
I, *Name,* take you, *Name,* to be my wife,
   to have and to hold
   from this day forward,
   for better, for worse,
   for richer, for poorer,
   in sickness and in health,
   to love and to cherish,
   until we are parted by death.
This is my solemn vow.

Woman to man:

In the name of God,
I, *Name,* take you, *Name,* to be my husband,
   to have and to hold
   from this day forward,
   for better, for worse,
   for richer, for poorer,
   in sickness and in health,
   to love and to cherish,
   until we are parted by death.
This is my solemn vow.

BLESSING AND EXCHANGE OF RINGS

The pastor may say:

These rings (symbols)
are the outward and visible sign
   of an inward and spiritual grace,
signifying to us the union
   between Jesus Christ and his church.

The pastor may bless the giving of rings or other symbols of the marriage:

Bless, O Lord, the giving of these rings (symbols),
that they who wear them may live in your peace
   and continue in your favor
   all the days of their life;
through Jesus Christ our Lord.

Amen.

The giver(s) may say to the recipient(s):

Name, I give you this *ring*
    as a sign of my vow,
and with all that I am,
    and all that I have,
    I honor you;
in the name of the Father,
    and of the Son,
    and of the Holy Spirit.

DECLARATION OF MARRIAGE

*The wife and husband join hands. The pastor may place a hand on,
or wrap a stole around, their joined hands.*

Pastor to husband and wife:

You have declared your consent and vows
    before God and this congregation.
May God confirm your covenant
    and fill you both with grace.

Pastor to people:

Now that *Name* and *Name*
    have given themselves to each other by solemn vows,
    with the joining of hands,
    [and the giving and receiving of *rings*,]
I announce to you that they are husband and wife;
    in the name of the Father,
    and of the Son,
    and of the Holy Spirit.
Those whom God has joined together,
    let no one put asunder.

Amen.

A doxology or other hymn may be sung.

Intercessions may be offered for the church and for the world.

BLESSING OF THE MARRIAGE

The husband and wife may kneel, as the pastor prays:

O God,
you have so consecrated
    the covenant of Christian marriage
    that in it is represented
    the covenant between Christ and his church.
Send therefore your blessing upon *Name* and *Name*,
    that they may surely keep their marriage covenant,
    and so grow in love and godliness together
    that their home may be a haven of blessing and peace;
through Jesus Christ our Lord.

Amen.

If Holy Communion is to be celebrated, the service continues with A Service of Word and Table III (page 15).

If Holy Communion is not to be celebrated, the service continues with the Lord's Prayer (Nos. 894-896).

In either event, the service concludes with the sending forth.

SENDING FORTH

Here may be sung a hymn or psalm.

DISMISSAL WITH BLESSING

Pastor to wife and husband:

God the Eternal keep you in love with each other,
   so that the peace of Christ may abide in your home.
Go to serve God and your neighbor in all that you do.

Pastor to people:

Bear witness to the love of God in this world,
   so that those to whom love is a stranger
      will find in you generous friends.
The grace of the Lord Jesus Christ,
   and the love of God,
   and the communion of the Holy Spirit
   be with you all.

Amen.

THE PEACE

The peace of the Lord be with you always.

And also with you.

The couple and pastor(s) may greet each other, after which greetings may be exchanged through the congregation.

GOING FORTH

A hymn may be sung or instrumental music played as the couple, the wedding party, and the people leave.

A SERVICE OF DEATH AND RESURRECTION

This is a service of Christian worship suitable for funerals and memorial services. It should be held in the church if at all possible, and at a time when members of the congregation can be present.

The pastor should be notified immediately of the death of a member or constituent of the congregation. All arrangements should be made and approved in consultation with the pastor.

This order is intended for use with the body of the deceased present, but it can be adapted for use at memorial services or other occasions. The coffin remains closed throughout the service and thereafter. It may be covered with a pall.

Use of the term "Service of Death and Resurrection" is not intended to discourage use of the more familiar terms "funeral," "burial of the dead," or "memorial service." "Funeral" is appropriate for a service with the body of the deceased present. "Burial of the dead" is appropriate for a service where the remains of the deceased are buried. "Memorial service" is appropriate where the body of the deceased is not present. "Service of Death and Resurrection" was selected as being appropriate to any of the wide variety of situations in which this service might be used. It expresses clearly the twofold nature of what is done: the facts of death and bereavement are honestly faced, and the gospel of resurrection is celebrated in the context of God's baptismal covenant with us in Christ.

ENTRANCE

GATHERING

The pastor may greet the family.

Music for worship may be offered while the people gather.

Hymns and songs of faith may be sung during the gathering.

The pall may be placed on the coffin or urn with these words:

Dying, Christ destroyed our death.
Rising, Christ restored our life.
Christ will come again in glory.
As in baptism *Name* put on Christ,
  so in Christ may *Name* be clothed with glory.
Here and now, dear friends, we are God's children.
What we shall be has not yet been revealed;
but we know that when he appears, we shall be like him,
  for we shall see him as he is.
Those who have this hope purify themselves
  as Christ is pure.

The coffin or urn may be carried into the place of worship in procession, the pastor going before it and saying the word of grace, the congregation standing. Or, if the coffin or urn is already in place, the pastor says the following from in front of the congregation.

THE WORD OF GRACE

Jesus said, I am the resurrection and I am life.
Those who believe in me, even though they die, yet shall they live,
   and whoever lives and believes in me shall never die.
I am Alpha and Omega, the beginning and the end, the first and the last.
I died, and behold I am alive for evermore,
   and I hold the keys of hell and death.
Because I live, you shall live also.

GREETING

Friends, we have gathered here to praise God
   and to witness to our faith as we celebrate the life of *Name*.
We come together in grief, acknowledging our human loss.
May God grant us grace, that in pain we may find comfort,
   in sorrow hope, in death resurrection.

If the pall was not placed on the coffin or urn earlier, the sentences used above for that act may be used here instead.

HYMN OR SONG

PRAYER

The following or other prayers may be offered, in unison if desired. Petition for God's help, thanksgiving for the communion of saints, confession of sin, and assurance of pardon are appropriate here.

The Lord be with you.

And also with you.

Let us pray.

O God, who gave us birth,
you are ever more ready to hear
   than we are to pray.
You know our needs before we ask,
   and our ignorance in asking.
Give to us now your grace,
   that as we shrink before the mystery of death,
   we may see the light of eternity.
Speak to us once more
   your solemn message of life and of death.
Help us to live as those who are prepared to die.
And when our days here are accomplished,
   enable us to die as those who go forth to live,
   so that living or dying, our life may be in you,
   and that nothing in life or in death will be able to separate us
   from your great love in Christ Jesus our Lord.
Amen.

and/or

Eternal God,
we praise you for the great company of all those
   who have finished their course in faith
   and now rest from their labor.
We praise you for those dear to us
   whom we name in our hearts before you.
Especially we praise you for *Name,*
   whom you have graciously received into your presence.
To all of these, grant your peace.
Let perpetual light shine upon them;
and help us so to believe where we have not seen,
   that your presence may lead us through our years,
   and bring us at last with them
     into the joy of your home
     not made with hands but eternal in the heavens;
through Jesus Christ our Lord.
Amen.

The following prayer of confession and pardon may also be used:

Holy God, before you our hearts are open,
   and from you no secrets are hidden.
We bring to you now
   our shame and sorrow for our sins.
We have forgotten
   that our life is from you and unto you.
We have neither sought nor done your will.
We have not been truthful in our hearts,
   in our speech, in our lives.
We have not loved as we ought to love.
Help us and heal us,
   raising us from our sins into a better life,
   that we may end our days in peace,
   trusting in your kindness unto the end;
through Jesus Christ our Lord,
   who lives and reigns with you
   in the unity of the Holy Spirit,
   one God, now and for ever.
Amen.

Who is in a position to condemn?
Only Christ, Christ who died for us, who rose for us,
   who reigns at God's right hand and prays for us.
Thanks be to God who gives us the victory
   through our Lord Jesus Christ.

PSALM 130*

Out of the depths I cry unto thee, O Lord!
Lord, hear my cry.
Let thine ears be attentive
   to the voice of my supplication.
If thou, Lord, should mark iniquities,
   Lord, who could stand?
But there is forgiveness with thee,
   that thou may be feared.
I wait for the Lord, my soul waits,
   and in his word do I hope.
My soul waits for the Lord
   more than those who watch for the morning.
O Israel, hope in the Lord!
   For with the Lord is great mercy.
With him is plenteous redemption,
   and he will redeem Israel from all their sins.

PROCLAMATION AND RESPONSE

OLD TESTAMENT LESSON

PSALM 23**

Sung or said by the people standing.

The Lord is my shepherd; I shall not want.
He maketh me to lie down in green pastures:
   he leadeth me beside the still waters.
He restoreth my soul:
   he leadeth me in the paths of righteousness
     for his name's sake.
Yea, though I walk
   through the valley of the shadow of death,
   I will fear no evil:
for thou art with me;
   thy rod and thy staff they comfort me.
Thou preparest a table before me
   in the presence of mine enemies;
thou anointest my head with oil;
   my cup runneth over.
Surely goodness and mercy shall follow me
   all the days of my life:
   and I will dwell in the house of the Lord for ever.

*For other versions, see Nos. 515, 516, and page 848
**For other versions, see Nos. 136-138, and page 754

NEW TESTAMENT LESSON

PSALM, CANTICLE OR HYMN

GOSPEL LESSON

SERMON

A sermon may be preached, proclaiming the gospel in the face of death. It may lead into, or include, the following acts of naming and witness.

NAMING

The life and death of the deceased may be gathered up by the reading of a memorial or appropriate statement, or in other ways, by the pastor or others.

WITNESS

Family, friends, and members of the congregation may briefly voice their thankfulness to God for the grace they have received in the life of the deceased and their Christian faith and joy. Signs of faith, hope, and love may be exchanged.

HYMN OR SONG

CREED or AFFIRMATION OF FAITH (Nos. 880-889)

If the creed has not been preceded by, it may be followed by, a hymn or musical response.

COMMENDATION

PRAYERS

One or more of the following prayers may be offered, or other prayers may be used. They may take the form of a pastoral prayer, a series of shorter prayers, or a litany. Intercession, commendation of life, and thanksgiving are appropriate here.

God of us all, your love never ends.
When all else fails, you still are God.
We pray to you for one another in our need,
   and for all, anywhere, who mourn with us this day.
To those who doubt, give light;
   to those who are weak, strength;
   to all who have sinned, mercy;
   to all who sorrow, your peace.
Keep true in us
   the love with which we hold one another.
In all our ways we trust you.
And to you,
   with your church on earth and in heaven,
   we offer honor and glory, now and for ever.
Amen.

O God, all that you have given us is yours.
As first you gave *Name* to us,
   so now we give *Name* back to you.

Here the pastor, with others, standing near the coffin or urn, may lay hands on it, continuing:

Receive *Name* into the arms of your mercy.
Raise *Name* up with all your people.
Receive us also, and raise us into a new life.
Help us so to love and serve you in this world
    that we may enter into your joy in the world to come.

Amen.

Into your hands, O merciful Savior,
    we commend your servant *Name.*
Acknowledge, we humbly beseech you,
    a sheep of your own fold,
    a lamb of your own flock,
    a sinner of your own redeeming.
Receive *Name* into the arms of your mercy,
    into the blessed rest of everlasting peace,
    and into the glorious company of the saints of light.

Amen.

The pastor may administer Holy Communion to all present who wish to share at the Lord's table, using A Service of Word and Table III (page 15). Otherwise, the service continues as follows:

PRAYER OF THANKSGIVING

God of love, we thank you
    for all with which you have blessed us
        even to this day:
for the gift of joy in days of health and strength,
    and for the gifts of your abiding presence and promise
        in days of pain and grief.
We praise you for home and friends,
    and for our baptism and place in your church
    with all who have faithfully lived and died.
Above all else we thank you for Jesus,
    who knew our griefs,
    who died our death and rose for our sake,
    and who lives and prays for us.
And as he taught us, so now we pray.

THE LORD'S PRAYER (Nos. 894-896)

HYMN

DISMISSAL WITH BLESSING

A service of committal follows at the final resting place.

ORDERS OF DAILY PRAISE AND PRAYER

From the earliest days of the church, Christian worshipers saw the rising of the sun and the lighting of the evening lamps as symbolic of Christ's victory over death. "An Order for Morning Praise and Prayer" and "An Order for Evening Praise and Prayer" enable United Methodists to celebrate daily the life, death, and resurrection of Jesus Christ.

These services focus upon the praise of God and prayer for God's creation rather than the proclaiming of the Word. Therefore, preaching or other devotional talks are inappropriate in these services. When Scripture is used, passages should be chosen that will encourage the community in its praise and prayer.

Each order reflects a simple yet flexible pattern. The openings, hymns, songs of praise, responses to prayers, and Lord's Prayer may all be sung, with or without accompaniment. Scripture, silence, and prayer are optional, as indicated by brackets.

Each order is to be celebrated in a community of Christians at various occasions in their life together. These orders may be used on any occasion when Christians gather, but they are not adequate substitutes for the full Sunday Service of Word and Table.

Laity are encouraged to lead these services. Different parts of the service may be led by different people.

The communal quality of prayer is emphasized when the people stand or sit in a circle or other arrangement facing one another. There may be a simple setting with a focus such as a cross or candle.

AN ORDER FOR MORNING PRAISE AND PRAYER

This service is for groups as they begin their day in prayer.

CALL TO PRAISE AND PRAYER *Sung or spoken:*

O Lord, open our lips.

And we shall declare your praise.

MORNING HYMN

A hymn appropriate to the morning may be sung.

PRAYER OF THANKSGIVING

The following or other prayer of thanksgiving may be said:

New every morning is your love, great God of light,
  and all day long you are working for good in the world.
Stir up in us desire to serve you,
    to live peacefully with our neighbors,
    and to devote each day to your Son,
    our Savior, Jesus Christ the Lord.

Amen.

SCRIPTURE

Psalm 51 (page 785), 63 (page 788), or 95 (page 814); Deuteronomy 6:4-9; Isaiah 55:1-3; John 1:1-5, 9-14; Romans 12:1-2; or other readings appropriate to the morning, or to the day or season of the Christian year, or to the nature of the occasion, may be used.

SILENCE

Silent meditation on the Scripture that has been read. This may be concluded with a short prayer.

SONG OF PRAISE

Psalm 100 (page 821), 148 (page 861), or 150 (page 862); Canticle of God's Glory (Nos. 82, 83); Canticle of the Holy Trinity (No. 80); Canticle of Light and Darkness (No. 205); Canticle of Moses and Miriam (No. 135); Canticle of Praise to God (No. 91); Canticle of Thanksgiving (No. 74); Canticle of Zechariah (No. 208); or other Scripture song or hymn may be sung.

PRAYERS OF THE PEOPLE

The following or other litany of intercession may be prayed, during which any person may offer a brief prayer of intercession or petition.
After each prayer, the leader may conclude: Lord, in your mercy,
and all may respond: **Hear our prayer.**

Together, let us pray for

   the people of this congregation . . .

   those who suffer and those in trouble . . .

   the concerns of this local community . . .

   the world, its people, and its leaders . . .

   the church universal—its leaders, its members, and
     its mission . . .

   the communion of saints . . .

Following these prayers, all may sing: "Hear Us, O God" (No. 490), "Jesus, Remember Me" (No. 488), "Let Us Pray to the Lord" (No. 485), "Remember Me" (No. 491), or "This Is Our Prayer" (No. 487).

THE LORD'S PRAYER *Sung or spoken. See Nos. 270, 271, 894-896.*

BLESSING

> The grace of the Lord Jesus Christ,
> and the love of God,
> and the communion of the Holy Spirit
> be with you all.

> **Amen.**

THE PEACE

Signs of peace may be exchanged.

AN ORDER FOR EVENING PRAISE AND PRAYER

This service is for groups as they end their day in prayer.

PROCLAMATION OF THE LIGHT

A candle may be lit and lifted in the midst of the community. The following may be sung or spoken:

Light and peace in Jesus Christ.

Thanks be to God.

EVENING HYMN

"O Gladsome Light" (No. 686) or other hymn appropriate to the evening may be sung.

PRAYER OF THANKSGIVING

The following or other prayer of thanksgiving may be said:

> We praise and thank you, O God,
>   for you are without beginning and without end.
> Through Christ, you created the whole world;
>   through Christ, you preserve it.
> You made the day for the works of light
>   and the night for the refreshment of our minds and our bodies.
> Keep us now in Christ; grant us a peaceful evening,
>   a night free from sin; and bring us at last to eternal life.
> Through Christ and in the Holy Spirit,
>   we offer you all glory, honor, and worship,
>   now and for ever.

> **Amen.**

SCRIPTURE

Psalm 23 (No. 137 and page 754), 90 (page 809), 121 (page 844), 141; Genesis 1:1-5, 14-19; Exodus 13:21-22; Matthew 25:1-13; Romans 5:6-11; 1 Thessalonians 5:1-10;

Revelation 22:1-5; or other readings appropriate to the evening, or to the day or season of the Christian year, or to the nature of the occasion, may be used.

SILENCE

Silent meditation on the Scripture that has been read. This may be concluded with a short prayer.

SONG OF PRAISE

Psalm 134 (page 850), Canticle of Covenant Faithfulness (No. 125), Canticle of Hope (No. 734), Canticle of Light and Darkness (No. 205), Canticle of Mary (No. 199), Canticle of Simeon (No. 225), or other Scripture song or hymn may be sung.

PRAYERS OF THE PEOPLE

The following or other litany of intercession may be prayed, during which any person may offer a brief prayer of intercession or petition.

After each prayer, the leader may conclude: Lord, in your mercy, *and all may respond:* **Hear our prayer.**

Together, let us pray for

the people of this congregation . . .

those who suffer and those in trouble . . .

the concerns of this local community . . .

the world, its peoples, and its leaders . . .

the church universal—its leaders, its members, and its mission . . .

the communion of saints . . .

Or, prayers of confession and words of pardon may be offered. See Nos. 890-893.

Following these prayers, all may sing: "Hear Us, O God" (No. 490), "Kyrie Eleison" (Nos. 483, 484), "Lord, Have Mercy" (No. 482), or "Remember Me" (No. 491).

THE LORD'S PRAYER *Sung or spoken. See Nos. 270, 271, 894-896.*

BLESSING

The grace of Jesus Christ enfold you this night.
Go in peace.

Thanks be to God.

THE PEACE

Signs of peace may be exchanged, or all may depart in silence.

AFFIRMATIONS OF FAITH

880   THE NICENE CREED

We believe in one God,
  the Father, the Almighty,
  maker of heaven and earth,
  of all that is, seen and unseen.

We believe in one Lord, Jesus Christ,
  the only Son of God,
  eternally begotten of the Father,
  God from God, Light from Light,
  true God from true God,
  begotten, not made,
  of one Being with the Father;
  through him all things were made.
  For us and for our salvation
    he came down from heaven,
    was incarnate of the Holy Spirit and the Virgin Mary
    and became truly human.
    For our sake he was crucified under Pontius Pilate;
    he suffered death and was buried.
    On the third day he rose again
    in accordance with the Scriptures;
    he ascended into heaven
    and is seated at the right hand of the Father.
    He will come again in glory
    to judge the living and the dead,
    and his kingdom will have no end.

We believe in the Holy Spirit, the Lord, the giver of life,
  who proceeds from the Father and the Son,
  who with the Father and the Son
    is worshiped and glorified,
  who has spoken through the prophets.
  We believe in the one holy catholic* and apostolic church.
  We acknowledge one baptism
    for the forgiveness of sins.
  We look for the resurrection of the dead,
    and the life of the world to come. Amen.

*universal

THE APOSTLES' CREED, TRADITIONAL VERSION   881

I believe in God the Father Almighty,
  maker of heaven and earth;

And in Jesus Christ his only Son our Lord:
  who was conceived by the Holy Spirit,
    born of the Virgin Mary,
    suffered under Pontius Pilate,
    was crucified, dead, and buried;*
  the third day he rose from the dead;
  he ascended into heaven,
    and sitteth at the right hand of God the Father Almighty;
  from thence he shall come to judge the quick and the dead.

I believe in the Holy Spirit,
  the holy catholic** church,
  the communion of saints,
  the forgiveness of sins,
  the resurrection of the body,
  and the life everlasting. Amen.

THE APOSTLES' CREED, ECUMENICAL VERSION   882

I believe in God, the Father Almighty,
  creator of heaven and earth.

I believe in Jesus Christ, his only Son, our Lord,
  who was conceived by the Holy Spirit,
  born of the Virgin Mary,
  suffered under Pontius Pilate,
  was crucified, died, and was buried;
  he descended to the dead.
  On the third day he rose again;
  he ascended into heaven,
  is seated at the right hand of the Father,
  and will come again to judge the living and the dead.

I believe in the Holy Spirit,
  the holy catholic** church,
  the communion of saints,
  the forgiveness of sins,
  the resurrection of the body
  and the life everlasting. Amen.

*Traditional use of this creed includes these words: "He descended into hell."
**universal

883 A STATEMENT OF FAITH OF THE UNITED CHURCH OF CANADA

We are not alone, we live in God's world.
We believe in God:
  who has created and is creating,
  who has come in Jesus, the Word made flesh,
    to reconcile and make new,
  who works in us and others by the Spirit.
We trust in God.
We are called to be the church:
  to celebrate God's presence,
  to love and serve others,
  to seek justice and resist evil,
  to proclaim Jesus, crucified and risen,
    our judge and our hope.
In life, in death, in life beyond death,
  God is with us.
We are not alone.
Thanks be to God. Amen.

By permission of The United Church of Canada

884 A STATEMENT OF FAITH OF THE KOREAN METHODIST CHURCH

We believe in the one God,
  creator and sustainer of all things, Father of all nations,
  the source of all goodness and beauty, all truth and love.
We believe in Jesus Christ,
  God manifest in the flesh,
  our teacher, example, and Redeemer, the Savior of the world.
We believe in the Holy Spirit,
  God present with us for guidance, for comfort, and for strength.
We believe in the forgiveness of sins,
  in the life of love and prayer,
  and in grace equal to every need.
We believe in the Word of God
  contained in the Old and New Testaments
  as the sufficient rule both of faith and of practice.
We believe in the church,
  those who are united in the living Lord
  for the purpose of worship and service.
We believe in the reign of God
  as the divine will realized in human society,
  and in the family of God,
  where we are all brothers and sisters.
We believe in the final triumph of righteousness
  and in the life everlasting. Amen.

Adapt. © 1989 The United Methodist Publishing House

A MODERN AFFIRMATION

885

Pastor:

Where the Spirit of the Lord is,
there is the one true church, apostolic and universal,
whose holy faith let us now declare:

Pastor and People:

We believe in God the Father,
  infinite in wisdom, power, and love,
  whose mercy is over all his works,
  and whose will is ever directed to his children's good.
We believe in Jesus Christ,
  Son of God and Son of man,
  the gift of the Father's unfailing grace,
  the ground of our hope,
  and the promise of our deliverance from sin and death.
We believe in the Holy Spirit
  as the divine presence in our lives,
  whereby we are kept in perpetual remembrance
  of the truth of Christ,
  and find strength and help in time of need.
We believe that this faith should manifest itself
  in the service of love
  as set forth in the example of our blessed Lord,
  to the end
  that the kingdom of God may come upon the earth. Amen.

THE WORLD METHODIST SOCIAL AFFIRMATION 886

We believe in God, creator of the world and of all people;
  and in Jesus Christ, incarnate among us,
    who died and rose again;
  and in the Holy Spirit,
    present with us to guide, strengthen, and comfort.

We believe;
God, help our unbelief.

We rejoice in every sign of God's kingdom:
    in the upholding of human dignity and community;
    in every expression of love, justice, and reconciliation;
    in each act of self-giving on behalf of others;
    in the abundance of God's gifts
      entrusted to us that all may have enough;
    in all responsible use of the earth's resources.

Glory be to God on high;
and on earth, peace.

We confess our sin, individual and collective,
> by silence or action:
>> through the violation of human dignity
>>> based on race, class, age, sex, nation, or faith;
>> through the exploitation of people
>>> because of greed and indifference;
>> through the misuse of power
>>> in personal, communal, national, and international life;
>> through the search for security
>>> by those military and economic forces
>>> that threaten human existence;
>> through the abuse of technology
>>> which endangers the earth and all life upon it.

Lord, have mercy;
Christ, have mercy;
Lord, have mercy.

We commit ourselves individually and as a community
> to the way of Christ:
>> to take up the cross;
>> to seek abundant life for all humanity;
>> to struggle for peace with justice and freedom;
>> to risk ourselves in faith, hope, and love,
>>> praying that God's kingdom may come.

Thy kingdom come on earth as it is in heaven. Amen.

887 AFFIRMATION FROM ROMANS 8:35, 37-39

Leader:

Who shall separate us from the love of Christ?
Shall tribulation or distress,
> or persecution or famine,
> or nakedness or peril or sword?

People:

No!
In all things we are more than conquerors
> through the One who loved us.
We are sure that neither
> death nor life,
> nor angels, nor principalities,
> nor things present, nor things to come,
> nor powers, nor height, nor depth,
> nor anything else in all creation,
will be able to separate us from the love of God
> in Christ Jesus our Lord.
Thanks be to God! Amen.

AFFIRMATION FROM I CORINTHIANS 15:1-6 AND COLOSSIANS 1:15-20   888

Leader:

This is the good news
  which we have received,
  in which we stand,
  and by which we are saved:

People:

Christ died for our sins,
  was buried,
  was raised on the third day,
  and appeared first to the women,
    then to Peter and the Twelve,
    and then to many faithful witnesses.

We believe Jesus is the Christ,
  the Anointed One of God,
  the firstborn of all creation,
    the firstborn from the dead,
    in whom all things hold together,
    in whom the fullness of God
      was pleased to dwell
      by the power of the Spirit.

Christ is the head of the body, the church,
  and by the blood of the cross
  reconciles all things to God. Amen.

Adapt. © 1989 The United Methodist Publishing House

AFFIRMATION FROM I TIMOTHY 2:5-6; 1:15; 3:16   889

Leader:

There is one God
and there is one mediator, Christ Jesus,
  who came as a ransom for all,
  to whom we testify.

People:

This saying is sure
  and worthy of full acceptance:
That Jesus Christ came into the world to save sinners,
  and was manifested in the flesh,
  vindicated in the Spirit,
  seen by angels,
  proclaimed among the nations,
  believed in throughout the world,
  taken up in glory.
Great indeed is the mystery of the gospel. Amen.

Adapt. © 1989 The United Methodist Publishing House

PRAYERS OF CONFESSION, ASSURANCE, AND PARDON

890   Most merciful God,
     we confess that we have sinned against you
     in thought, word, and deed,
     by what we have done,
     and by what we have left undone.
     We have not loved you with our whole heart;
     we have not loved our neighbors as ourselves.
     We are truly sorry and we humbly repent.
     For the sake of your Son Jesus Christ,
     have mercy on us and forgive us;
     that we may delight in your will,
     and walk in your ways,
     to the glory of your name. Amen.

     All pray in silence.

     Almighty God have mercy on you,
     forgive all your sins through our Lord Jesus Christ,
     strengthen you in all goodness,
     and by the power of the Holy Spirit
     keep you in eternal life. **Amen.**

891   Almighty and most merciful God,
     we have erred and strayed from thy ways like lost sheep.
     We have followed too much
     the devices and desires of our own hearts.
     We have offended against thy holy laws.
     We have left undone
     those things which we ought to have done,
     and we have done
     those things which we ought not to have done.
     But thou, O Lord, have mercy upon us.
     Spare thou those, O God, who confess their faults.
     Restore thou those who are penitent,
     according to thy promises declared in Christ Jesus our Lord.
     And grant, O most merciful God, for his sake,
     that we may hereafter live a godly, righteous, and sober life;
     to the glory of thy holy name. Amen.

     All pray in silence.

     If we confess our sins,
     God is faithful and just,
     and will forgive our sins
     and cleanse us from all unrighteousness.
     Thanks be to God.

Our heavenly Father,
who by thy love hast made us,
and through thy love hast kept us,
and in thy love wouldst make us perfect:
We humbly confess that we have not loved thee
with all our heart and soul and mind and strength,
and that we have not loved one another
as Christ hath loved us.
Thy life is within our souls,
but our selfishness hath hindered thee.
We have not lived by faith.
We have resisted thy Spirit.
We have neglected thine inspirations.
Forgive what we have been;
help us to amend what we are;
and in thy Spirit direct what we shall be;
that thou mayest come into the full glory of thy creation,
in us and in all the people;
through Jesus Christ our Lord. Amen.

All pray in silence.

The saying is sure and worthy of full acceptance,
that Christ Jesus came into the world to save sinners.
If any one sins, we have an advocate with the Father,
Jesus Christ the righteous;
and he is the expiation for our sins,
and not for ours only
but also for the sins of the whole world.
Thanks be to God.

Lord, we confess our day to day failure to be truly human.
    Lord, we confess to you.
Lord, we confess that we often fail to love with all we have and are,
often because we do not fully understand what loving means,
often because we are afraid of risking ourselves.
    Lord, we confess to you.
Lord, we cut ourselves off from each other and we erect barriers of division.
    Lord, we confess to you.
Lord, we confess that by silence and ill-considered word
    we have built up walls of prejudice.
Lord, we confess that by selfishness and lack of sympathy
    we have stifled generosity and left little time for others.
Holy Spirit, speak to us. Help us listen to your word of forgiveness, for we are
very deaf. Come, fill this moment and free us from sin.

892

893

THE LORD'S PRAYER

894 ECUMENICAL TEXT

Our Father in heaven,
  hallowed be your name,
  your kingdom come,
  your will be done, on earth as in heaven.
Give us today our daily bread.
Forgive us our sins
  as we forgive those who sin against us.
Save us from the time of trial
  and deliver us from evil.
For the kingdom, the power, and the glory are yours
  now and for ever. Amen.

895 FROM THE RITUAL OF THE FORMER METHODIST CHURCH

Our Father, who art in heaven,
  hallowed be thy name.
  Thy kingdom come,
  thy will be done on earth as it is in heaven.
Give us this day our daily bread.
And forgive us our trespasses,
  as we forgive those who trespass against us.
And lead us not into temptation,
  but deliver us from evil.
For thine is the kingdom, and the power, and the glory,
  forever. Amen.

896 FROM THE RITUAL OF THE FORMER EVANGELICAL UNITED BRETHREN CHURCH

Our Father, who art in heaven,
  hallowed be thy name;
  thy kingdom come,
  thy will be done, on earth as it is in heaven.
Give us this day our daily bread;
and forgive us our debts,
  as we forgive our debtors;
and lead us not into temptation,
  but deliver us from evil.
For thine is the kingdom and the power and the glory,
  forever. Amen.

AMENS

897

898

A-men, a - men.

A-men, a-men, a - men.

MUSIC: Dresden

MUSIC: Danish

899

A - men, A - men.

MUSIC: Vincent Persichetti, 1956

© 1956, Elkan-Vogel, Inc.

900

A - men, a - men, a - men.

MUSIC: Vincent Persichetti, 1956

© 1956, Elkan-Vogel, Inc.

901

Al - le-lu - ia, a - men, a - men.

MUSIC: Carl Wiltse, 1982

© 1989 The United Methodist Publishing House

902

MUSIC: John Rutter, 1981 adapt. by the composer from the anthem *The Lord Bless You and Keep You*

903

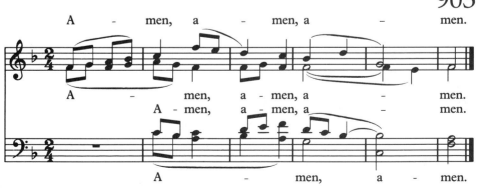

MUSIC: Philip E. Baker, 1972

904

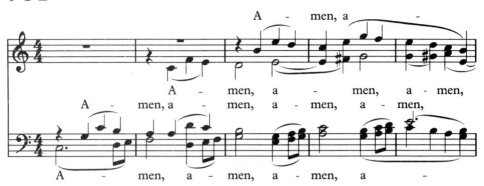

MUSIC: Peter Christian Lutkin, 1900

INDEXES

ACKNOWLEDGMENTS

United Methodist congregations may reproduce for worship and educational purposes any single item from *The United Methodist Hymnal* for one-time use, as in a bulletin, special program, or lesson resource, provided the item bears a United Methodist Publishing House or Abingdon Press copyright notice; that the copyright notice as shown on the page is included on the reproduction; and that *The United Methodist Hymnal* is acknowledged as the source. Permission requests for use of more than one United Methodist Publishing House or Abingdon Press item should be addressed to Permission Office, Abingdon Press; 201 8th Avenue, South; Nashville, Tennessee 37202.

Permissions have been obtained for *The United Methodist Hymnal* with the restriction that its distribution is limited to the United States of America, its possession and territories. Some items showing no copyright information may have copyright protection in other countries. Every effort has been made to trace the owner(s) and/or administrator(s) of each copyright. The Publisher regrets any omission and will, upon written notice, make the necessary correction(s) in subsequent printings.

Scripture, unless otherwise indicated, is adapted from the Revised Standard Version of the Bible, © 1946, 1952, 1957, 1971 by Division of Christian Education of the National Council of Churches of Christ in the USA and is used by permission.

Pages 2-54, 864-79, containing the General Services, and Nos. 880-96, containing the Other Acts of Worship of The United Methodist Church are copyrighted as follows:

  2   *The Basic Pattern of Worship*, © 1976 Abingdon Press; © 1980, 1984, 1989 The United Methodist Publishing House.

3-5   *An Order of Sunday Worship*, © 1985, 1989 The United Methodist Publishing House.

6-11   *A Service of Word and Table I*, © 1972, 1980, 1985, 1989 The United Methodist Publishing House.

12-15   *A Service of Word and Table II*, © 1972, 1980, 1985, 1989 The United Methodist Publishing House.

15-16   *A Service of Word and Table III*, © 1980, 1985, 1989 The United Methodist Publishing House.

17-20, 22-24   Musical Settings, © 1989 The United Methodist Publishing House.

26-31   *A Service of Word and Table IV*, © 1957 Board of Publication, Evangelical United Brethren Church; © 1964, 1965, 1989 The United Methodist Publishing House.

  32   Concerning the Services, © 1989 The United Methodist Publishing House.

33-43   Baptismal Covenants I, II, © 1976, 1980, 1985, 1989 The United Methodist Publishing House.

  44   Congregational Pledge 1, © 1959 Board of Publication, Evangelical United Brethren Church; Congregational Pledge 2, © 1964 The United Methodist Publishing House.

45-49   The Baptismal Covenant III, © 1964, 1965, 1966 The United Methodist Publishing House.

50-53   The Baptismal Covenant IV, © 1976, 1980, 1985, 1989 The United Methodist Publishing House.

738-862   The United Methodist Liturgical Psalter, edited by Harrell Beck, John Holbert, S T Kimbrough, Jr., and Alan Luff, © 1989 The United Methodist Publishing House, based on the New Revised Standard Version Bible, 1989, and adapted by permission of the Division of Christian Education of the National Council Churches of Christ in the USA, all rights reserved.

864-69   A Service of Christian Marriage, © Abingdon Press; © 1979, 1980, 1985, 1989 The United Methodist Publishing House.

870-75   A Service of Death and Resurrection, © Abingdon Press; © 1979, 1980, 1985, 1989 The United Methodist Publishing House.

876-79   Orders of Daily Praise and Prayer, © 1989 The United Methodist Publishing House.

877   Prayer of Thanksgiving, *The Worshipbook—Services*, Philadelphia, PA, The Westminster Press, 1972.

885   A Modern Affirmation © 1932, 1935, 1989, adapt. The United Methodist Publishing House.

892   Prayer of Confession, © 1932, 1935, 1989, adapt. The United Methodist Publishing House.

Permission for use of items controlled by other copyright owners must be obtained from the respective owners listed below.

Book of Common Prayer, 1928:.
    Prayer of confession 2, No. 891.

English Language Liturgical Consultation; 1275 "K" St, NW, #1202; Washington, D.C. 20005-4097, revision of ICET translations:.
    Apostles' Creed, Ecumenical version, lines 3, 11, 12 alt. pp. 7, 35, 41, 46, 51, No. 882.
    Nicene Creed, No. 880.
    Sursum Corda, pp. 9, 13, 15, 17, 18, 20, 23, 24.

International Commission on English in the Liturgy; 1275 "K" St, NW, #1202; Washington, D.C. 20005-4097:.
    Memorial Acclamation, pp. 10, 14, 16, 18, 20, 22, 24, 25, from *The Roman Missal* © 1973 ICEL.

International Consultation on English Texts; 1275 "K" St, NW, #1202; Washington, D.C. 20005-4097, translations 1975:.
    The Lord's Prayer, Ecumenical Text, pp. 10-11, No. 894.
    Sanctus and Benedictus, pp. 9, 13, 16, 17, 19, 21, 23, 25.

Orbis Books; Maryknoll, NY 10545.
    Confession, Assurance and Pardon 4. *Vigil of Prayer for Detainees*, © 1986 John de Grucy, p. 893.

The Book of Common Prayer, 1979:.
    Opening Prayer, p. 6;.
    Prayer of Confession 1, p. 890;.
    Declaration of Intention, pp. 865;.
    Marriage Vows, Exchange of Rings, Declaration of Marriage, Blessing, pp. 867-869;.
    Commendation 3, p. 875.

The Upper Room Worshipbook, © 1985 The Upper Room; PO Box 189; Nashville, Tn 37202-0189. Prayer of Thanksgiving, p. 878.

The Worshipbook—Services, The Westminster Press; 100 Witherspoon St; Louisville, KY 40202-1396. Prayer of Thanksgiving, p. 877.

21   Adapt: G.I.A. Publications, Inc., 7404 S Mason Ave., Chicago, IL 60638

25   Music: Oxford University Press; 200 Madison Ave; New York, NY 10016.

53   Musical Settings: The United Methodist Publishing House.

54   Musical Settings: The United Methodist Publishing House.

59   Trans: The United Methodist Publishing House.

60   Harm: The United Methodist Publishing House.

62   Adapt: The United Methodist Publishing House.

67   Arr: Abingdon Press; 201 8th Ave, S; Nashville, TN 37202. From *The Book of Hymns*.

68   Words: Hope Publishing Co.; 380 S. Main Pl; Carol Stream, IL 60188.

69   Alt: The United Methodist Publishing House.

72 Music: Les Presses de Taizé c/o G.I.A. Publications, Inc.; 7404 South Mason Ave; Chicago, IL 60638. Used by permission.

74 Resp. 1: The United Methodist Publishing House.

77 Words, Music: Manna Music, Inc.; 2111 Kenmore Ave; Burbank, CA 91504.

78 Transcription: The United Methodist Publishing House.

79 Words (5-7): The Church Hymnal Corporation; 800 Second Ave; New York, NY 10017.

80 Words: International Consultation on English Texts, revised by English Language Liturgical Consultation; 1275 "K" St, NW, #1202; Washington, DC 20005-4097.

81 Words, Music, Trans: The United Methodist Publishing House. ·

83 Words: International Consultation on English Texts, revised by English Language Liturgical Consultation; 1275 "K" St, NW, #1202; Washington, DC 20005-4097. Music: G.I.A. Publications, Inc.; 7404 S Mason; Chicago, IL 60638.

84 Adapt, Arr: The United Methodist Publishing House.

86 Words, Music, Trans: The United Methodist Publishing House.

87 Words, Music: Hope Publishing Co.; 380 S Main Pl; Carol Stream, IL 60188.

93 Music: Hinshaw Music, Inc.; PO Bx 470; Chapel Hill, NC 27514. Reprinted by permission.

94 Adapt: The United Methodist Publishing House.

97 Words: Hope Publishing Co.; 380 S Main Pl; Carol Stream, IL 60188. Music: Francis Jackson; Nether Garth; Acklam, Malton Y07 9RG Burythorpe 395 England.

99 Words, Music: Communiqué Music, Inc./ASCAP, used by permission of Spectra Copyright Management Corp; 23 Music Sq, E; Nashville, TN 37203.

100 Words: William Boyd Grove; 900 Washington St, E; Charleston, WV 25301. Used by permission.

105 Words, Music: Hope Publishing Co.; 380 S Main Pl; Carol Stream, IL 60188.

106 Words: Joan Daves; 21 W 26th St; New York, NY 10010-1083. Adapt. from Martin Luther King, Jr., "Our God Is Able", in *Strength to Love* (New York: Pocket Books, 1968). © 1968 Coretta Scott King.

107 Words, Music: Juan Luis García; 423 SW Beacon Blvd; Miami, FL 33135. Trans: The United Methodist Publishing House.

108 Words: The Hymn Society of America c/o Hope Publishing Co.; 380 S Main Pl; Carol Stream, IL 60188.

109 Words: The Hymn Society of America c/o Hope Publishing Co.; 380 S Main Pl; Carol Stream, IL 60188.

111 Words: Hope Publishing Co.; 380 S Main Pl; Carol Stream, IL 60188.

112 Adapt, Resp 1: The United Methodist Publishing House.

113 Words, Music: Oxford University Press; 200 Madison Ave; New York, NY 10016.

114 Words, Music: Al Carmines; 400 W 43rd St, #24N; New York, NY 10036. Hymn composed for the Quadrennial 1973 Convocation of United Methodist Women.

115 Words: The United Methodist Publishing House.

118 Harm: Oxford University Press; Ely House; 37 Dover St; London, England W1X 4AH.

119 Trans: Christian Conference of Asia; Attn: Tosh Aria; 57 Peking Rd, 5/F; Kowloon, Hong Kong. Music: Elena Maquiso; Silliman Univ.; Ulahingan Research Proj; Dumaguete City, 6200, Philippines. Harm: The United Methodist Publishing House.

120 Trans: Hope Publishing Co.; 380 S Main Pl; Carol Stream, IL 60188. Music: Lars Lundberg; Parmmatarg.1 S11224 Stockholm, Sweden. Harm: The United Methodist Publishing House.

121 Harm: The United Methodist Publishing House.

122 Words: Jaroslav J. Vajda; 3303 Meramec; St. Louis, MO 63118. Music: G.I.A. Publications, Inc.; 7404 S Mason Ave., Chicago, IL 60638

123 Words, Music: LITA Music; Attn: Justin Peters; 3609 Donna Kay Dr; Nashville, TN 37211.

124 Words: Hope Publishing Co.; 380 S Main Pl; Carol Stream, IL 60188. Music: The Church Hymnal Corporation; 800 Second Ave; New York, NY 10017.

125 Adapt, Words Response: The United Methodist Publishing House.

132 Trans: Hope Publishing Co.; 380 S Main Pl; Carol Stream, IL 60188. Music: Novello and Co. Ltd.; Fairfield Rd; Borough Green; Sevenoaks; Kent, England TN15 8DT.

134 Adapt, Arr: The United Methodist Publishing House.

135 Text, Words, Music: The United Methodist Publishing House.

136 Harm: Oxford University Press; Ely House; 37 Dover St; London, England W1X 4AH. Used by permission.

137 Resp 1: The Grail c/o G.I.A. Publications, Inc.; 7404 S Mason Ave; Chicago, IL 60638. Used by permission. Resp. 2: The United Methodist Publishing House.

139 Trans (2-4): The United Methodist Publishing House.

140 Words, Music: Hope Publishing Co.; 380 S Main Pl; Carol Stream, IL 60188.

141 Trans: Augsburg/Fortress; 426 S Fifth St; Minneapolis, MN 55440.

143 Words, Music: North American Liturgy Resources; 10802 N 23rd Ave; Phoenix, AZ 85029. 602/864-1980. This and other titles are available from NALR.

145 Words: David Higham Associates, Ltd.; 5-8 Lower John St; Golden Square; London, England W1R 4HA. Used by permission. Harm: The United Methodist Publishing House.

146 (1) Morrow Junior Books (a Division of William Morrow and Company, Inc.); 105 Madison Ave; New York, NY 10016. (2) The Society for Promoting Christian Knowledge; Holy Trinity Church; Marylebone Rd; London, England NW1 4DU.

148 Harm: G.I.A. Publications, Inc.; 7404 S Mason Ave; Chicago, IL 60638.

149 Words, Music: Resource Publications, Inc.; 160 E Virginia St, #290; San Jose, CA 95112. Trans, Arr: The United Methodist Publishing House.

150 Words: Hope Publishing Co.; 380 S Main Pl; Carol Stream, IL 60188.

151 Trans: Boris and Clare Anderson. Harm: The United Methodist Publishing House.

158 Harm: Abingdon Press; 201 8th Ave, S; Nashville, Tn 37202. From *The Book of Hymns*.

159 Words, Music: Hope Publishing Co.; 380 S Main Pl; Carol Stream, IL 60188.

161 Music: Harold Flammer, Inc.; Delaware Water Gap, PA 18327-1099.

162 Words, Music: The Word of God; PO Bx 8617; Ann Arbor, MI 48107, USA. All rights reserved.

166 Words: The Church Hymnal Corp; 800 Second Ave; New York, NY 10017.

167 Adapt, Resp 1: The United Methodist Publishing House. Music, Resp 2: Oxford University Press; Ely House; 37 Dover St; London, England W1X 4AH.

168 Music: Oxford University Press; Ely House; 37 Dover St; London, England W1X 4AH.

171 Words, Music: William J. Gaither c/o Gaither Music Co.; PO Bx 737; Alexandria, IN 46001. Used by permission.

174 Words, Music: Manna Music, Inc.; 2111 Kenmore Ave; Burbank, CA 91504.

176 Words, music: Rocksmith Music c/o Trust Music Management; PO Bx 9256; Calabasas, CA 91302.

177 Arr: Word, Inc.; 5221 N O'Connor Blvd, #1000; Irving, TX 75039. All rights reserved. International copyright secured. Used by permission.

178 Words: The Hymn Society of America c/o Hope Publishing Co.; 380 S Main Pl; Carol Stream, IL 60188. Music: Abingdon Press; 201 8th Ave, S; Nashville, TN 37202. From *The Book of Hymns*.

180 Trans: The United Methodist Publishing House.

182 Words: Geoffrey Chapman Publishers (a Division of Cassell Publishers, Ltd); Artillery House/Artillery Row; London, England SW 1P 1RT. Reprinted by permission.

184 Arr: The Church Hymnal Corp; 800 Second Ave; New York, NY 10017.

186 Words, Music: Manna Music, Inc.; 25510 Ave. Stanford, #101; Valencia, CA 91355.

187 Words, Music: Augsburg Fortress; 426 S Fifth St; Minneapolis, MN 55440.

188 Words: Hope Publishing Co.; 380 S Main Pl; Carol Stream, IL 60188. Harm: Oxford University Press; Ely House; 37 Dover St; London, England W1X 4AH.

191 Cherokee trans, Japanese phonetic transcription: The United Methodist Publishing House.

192 Words: Hope Publishing Co.; 380 S Main Pl; Carol Stream, IL 60188.

194 Words: J. W Shore; 158 Hill Top Dr; Kirk Holt, Rochdale; Lancashire, England OL112RZ.

195 Words, Music: The Hymnal Committee of the United Church of Christ in Japan; 2-3-18 Nishiwaseda; Shinjuku, Tokyo, Japan 169. Trans: The United Methodist Publishing House.

197 Words (4): The Church Hymnal Corp; 800 Second Ave; New York, NY 10017. Music: G.I.A. Publications, Inc.; 7404 S Mason Ave; Chicago, IL 60638.

198 Words: Medical Mission Sisters; Permissions Dept; 92 Sherman St; Hartford, CT 06105. Harm: The United Methodist Publishing House.

199 Words: International Consultation on English Texts, revised by English Language Liturgical Consultation; 1275 "K" St, NW, #1202; Washington, DC 20005-4097. Resp: The United Methodist Publishing House.

200 Words: Hope Publishing Co.; 380 S Main Pl; Carol Stream, IL 60188. Music: Oxford University Press; Ely House; 37 Dover St; London, England W1X 4AH.

201 Alt: The United Methodist Publishing House.

202 Words: David Higham Associates, Ltd; 5-08 Lower John St; Golden Square; London, England W1R 4HA. Harm: Oxford University Press; Walton St; Oxford, England OX2 6DP. From the *Oxford Book of Carols.*

204 Words, Music: C. A. Music c/o Music Services; 2021 N Brower Ave; Simi Valley, CA 93065. License #120125. Used by permission.

205 Adapt, Resp 1, 2: The United Methodist Publishing House.

206 Words, Music: Celebration, administered by Maranatha! Music; PO Bx 31050; Laguna Hills, CA 92654-1050. All rights reserved. International copyright secured. Used by permission.

207 Music: Les Presses de Taizé c/o G.I.A. Publications, Inc; 7404 S Mason; Chicago, IL 60638

208 Words: International Consultation on English Texts, revised by English Language Liturgical Consultation; 1275 "K" St, NW, #1202; Washington, DC 20005-4097.

209 Words, Music: Hope Publishing Co.; 380 S Main Pl; Carol Stream, IL 60188.

210 Words, Music: Alberto Taulé c/o Virgil Funk; Pastoral Musicians; 225 Sheridan St, NW; Washington DC 20001. Trans: The United Methodist Publishing House. Harm: Skinner Chávez-Melo; 200 W 79th St; #12-F; New York, NY 10024.

211 Words (st. 1,3,5ab,6cd,7ab): The Church Hymnal Corp; 800 Second Ave; New York, NY 10017. Trans (st 4,5cd,6ab,7cd): The United Methodist Publishing House; O Antiphons Text: The Sisters of St. Benedict; The Liturgical Press; Collegeville, MN 56301, from *Meditations on the O Antiphons.*

212 Resp 2: The United Methodist Publishing House.

214 Words (3-5): Concordia Publishing House; 3558 Jefferson Ave; St. Louis, MO 62118.

215 Words, Music: Hope Publishing Co.; 380 S Main Pl; Carol Stream, IL 60188.

216 Words (st. 3): The Church Hymnal Corp; 800 Second Ave; New York, NY 10017.

222 Trans: The United Methodist Publishing House.

223 Trans (2-3): Hope Publishing Co.; 380 S Main Pl; Carol Stream, IL 60188.

224 Harm: The United Methodist Publishing House.

225 Words: International Consultation on English Texts, revised by English Language Liturgical Consultation; 1275 "K" St, NW, #1202; Washington, DC 20005-4097. Music: G.I.A. Publications, Inc.; 7404 S Mason Ave; Chicago, IL 60638.

226 Words: A P Watt, Ltd; 20 John St; London, England WC1N 2DR. Used by permission on behalf of The Grail, England. Harm: The United Methodist Publishing House.

227 Harm: The United Methodist Publishing House.

228 Harm: The United Methodist Publishing House.

229 Harm: Abingdon Press; 201 8th Ave, S; Nashville, TN 37202. From The *Book of Hymns.*

231 Alt: The United Methodist Publishing House.

232 Trans: Augsburg Fortress; 426 S Fifth St; Minneapolis, MN 55440.

233 Trans: Augsburg Fortress; 426 S Fifth St; Minneapolis, MN 55440. Span. trans, harm: Skinner Chávez-Melo; 200 W 79th; #12-F; New York, NY 10024.

235 Trans: Jaroslav J. Vajda; 3303 Meramec; St. Louis, MO 63118. Music: Oxford University Press; Walton St; Oxford, England OX2 6DP. From the *Oxford Book of Carols.*

237 Harm: Oxford University Press; Walton St; Oxford, England OX2 6DP. From the *Oxford Book of Carols.*

238 Harm: Abingdon Press; 201 8th Ave, S; Nashville, TN 37202. From The *Book of Hymns.*

241 Words, Music: Hope Publishing Co.; 380 S Main Pl; Carol Stream, IL 60188.

242 Harm: Oxford University Press; Ely House; 37 Dover St; London, England W1X 4AH.

243 Trans: Walton Music Corp; 170 NE 33rd St; Ft. Lauderdale, FL 33334. Used by permission.

244 Trans. Frederick Harris Music Co., Ltd; 529 Speers Rd; Oakville, Ontario, Canada L6K 2G4.

247 Trans (3): Augsburg Fortress; 426 S Fifth St; Minneapolis, MN 55440.

251 Adapt, Arr: The United Methodist Publishing House.

252 Words: Hope Publishing Co.; 380 S Main Pl; Carol Stream, IL 60188. Harm: The United Methodist Publishing House.

255 Words: The United Methodist Publishing House.

257 Words: Hope Publishing Co.; 380 S Main Pl; Carol Stream, IL 60188. Music: The United Methodist Publishing House.

259 Words: The United Methodist Publishing House.

260 Words, Music: Hope Publishing Co.; 380 S Main Pl; Carol Stream, IL 60188.

261 Words, Music: Galliard, Ltd. c/o Galaxy Music Corp; 131 W 86th St; New York, NY 10024.

262 Words, Music: Hope Publishing Co.; 380 S Main Pl; Carol Stream, IL 60188.

263 Words, Music: Stainer & Bell, Ltd. c/o Galaxy Music Corp; 131 W 86th St; New York, NY 10024.

264 Words: Oxford University Press; 200 Madison Ave; New York, NY 10016.

265 Words: Hope Publishing Co.; 380 S Main Pl; Carol Stream, IL 60188.

268 Words: Augsburg Fortress; 426 S Fifth St; Minneapolis, MN 55440.

269 Harm: The United Methodist Publishing House

271 Adapt: Abingdon Press; 201 8th Ave, S; Nashville, TN 37202. Arr: The United Methodist Publishing House. From *Songs of Zion.*

272 Music: Skinner Chávez-Melo; 200 W 79th, #12-F; New York, NY 10024.

273 Words: A. S. Hopkinson; Down PL.; South Harting; Petersfield, GL315PN. Harm: The United Methodist Publishing House.

274 Words: Hope Publishing Co.; 380 S Main Pl; Carol Stream, IL 60188. Music: The United Methodist Publishing House.

275 Words, Music: Hope Publishing Co.; 380 S Main Pl; Carol Stream, IL 60188.

276 Words, Music: Linda Wilberger Egan; 302 Woodward Rd; Moylan, PA 19065. Used by permission.

279 Words, Music: The United Methodist Publishing House.

281 Words: Augsburg Fortress; 426 S Fifth St; Minneapolis, MN 55440.

285 Words: Hope Publishing Co.; 380 S Main Pl; Carol Stream, IL 60188.

288 Adapt, Arr: The United Methodist Publishing House.

291 Adapt, Arr: The United Methodist Publishing House.

292 Harm: Augsburg Fortress; 426 S Fifth St; Minneapolis, MN 55440.

300 Words, Music: The United Methodist Publishing House.

304 Words: The United Methodist Publishing House.

305 Words, Music: Ediciones Paulinas, sole U.S. Agent: OCP Publications; 5536 NE Hassalo; Portland OR 97213. All rights reserved. Used by permission. Trans: The United Methodist Publishing House. Harm: Juan Luis García; 423 Beacom Blvd; Miami, FL 33135.

307 Words: Hope Publishing Co.; 380 S Main Pl; Carol Stream, IL 60188. Harm: Abingdon Press, 201 8th Ave, S; Nashville, TN 37202.

308 Trans: World Student Christian Federation; 5, Route des Morillons; 1218 Grand Sacannes; Geneva, Switzerland. Used by permission.

309 Words: The United Methodist Publishing House. Music: Hope Publishing Co.; 380 S Main Pl; Carol Stream, IL 60188.

310 Words, Music: The Rodeheaver Co. c/o Word, Inc.; 5221 N O'Connor Blvd, #1000; Irving, TX 75039. All rights reserved. International copyright secured. Used by permission.

311 Harm: Oxford University Press; Walton St; Oxford, England OX2 6DP.

312 Harm: Oxford University Press; Ely House; 37 Dover St; London, England W1X 4AH.

313 Words, Music: Metho Press, Ltd. c/o Ediciones La Aurora; Dean Funes 1823; 1244 Buenos Aires, Argentina. Trans: Hope Publishing Co; 380 S Main Pl; Carol Stream, IL 60188

314 Adapt: The United Methodist Publishing House.

316 Adapt, Arr: The United Methodist Publishing House.

317 Harm: The United Methodist Publishing House.

318 Words: Hope Publishing Co.; 380 S Main Pl; Carol Stream, IL 60188.

321 Words, Music: Augsburg Fortress; 426 S Fifth St; Minneapolis, MN 55440.

323 Words: The United Methodist Publishing House.

328 Words, Music: Lanny Wolfe Music/ASCAP, a division of Pathway Press; PO Bx 2250; Cleveland, TN 37320.

330 Words, Music: The United Methodist Publishing House.

331 Words: Faber Music Ltd.; 3 Queens Sq; London, England WC1N 3AU. Reprinted from *The New Catholic Hymnal* by permission. Music: Hope Publishing Co; 380 S Main Pl; Carol Stream, IL 60188.

333 Adapt: The United Methodist Publishing House.

334 Words, Music: Manna Music, Inc.; 25510 Ave Stanford, #101; Valencia, CA 91355.

335 Words: The Society for Promoting Christian Knowledge; Holy Trinity Church; London, England WN1 4DU. Used by permission.

336 Words: Hope Publishing Co.; 380 S Main Pl; Carol Stream, IL 60188.

340 Harm: The United Methodist Publishing House.

343 Words, Music: The United Methodist Publishing House.

344 Words, Music: Ediciones Paulinas, sole US agent: OCP Publications; 5536 NE Hassalo; Portland, OR 97213. All rights reserved. Used with permission. Trans: The United Methodist Publishing House. Harm: Skinner Chávez-Melo; 200 W 79th, #12-F; New York, NY 10024.

345 Adapt, Arr: The United Methodist Publishing House.

347 Words, Music: Mercy Publishing c/o Maranatha! Music; PO Bx 31050; Laguna Hills, CA 92654-1050. All rights reserved. International copyright secured. Used by permission.

349 Words, Music: Singspiration Music c/o The Benson Company; 365 Great Circle Rd; Nashville, TN 37209.

350 Trans: The United Methodist Publishing House.

352 Arr: The United Methodist Publishing House.

353 Words: The United Methodist Publishing House.

356 Trans: The United Methodist Publishing House.

360 Trans: Fortress Press; 2900 Queen Ln; Philadelphia, PA 19129. Permission granted by the publisher.

364 Words, Music: William J. Gaither c/o Gaither Music Co; PO Bx 737; Alexandria, IN 46001. Used by permission.

366 Words: Harper & Row Publishers, Inc. 10 E 53rd St; New York, NY 10022. From *The World At One in Prayer*, Daniel Fleming. Reprinted by permission.

367 Words, Music: William J. Gaither c/o Gaither Music Co; PO Bx 737; Alexandria, IN 46001. Used by permission.

370 Words, Music: Assigned to Albert E. Brumley & Sons; Down in Memory Valley; Powell, MO 65730. All rights reserved. Used by permission.

375 Adapt, Arr: The United Methodist Publishing House.

383 Words, Music: Hope Publishing Co.; 380 S Main Pl; Carol Stream, IL 60188.

386 Harm: Abingdon Press; 201 8th Ave, S; Nashville, TN 37202. From *The Book of Hymns*.

389 Words, Music: Communiqué Music, Inc. c/o Spectra Copyright Management, Inc., 23 Music Square, E; Nashville, TN 37203. Used by permission.

390 Words: Oxford University Press; Ely House; 37 Dover St; London, England W1X 4AH.

392 Words: Alfred A. Knopf, Inc. and Faber and Faber, Ltd.; 201 50th St; New York, NY 10022. From *Markings* by Dag Hammarskjold, trans. by Leif Sjoberg and W. H. Auden, trans. © 1964. Reprinted by permission.

393 Words, Music: Moody Press; 820 N Lasalle Dr; Chicago, IL 60610.

394 Words, Music: William J. Gaither c/o Gaither Music Co; PO Bx 737; Alexandria, IN 46001. Used by permission.

401 Words: Howard Thurman Educational Trust; 2020 Stockton St; San Francisco, CA 94133. From *Meditations of the Heart*, Harper & Row Publishers, Inc. (1953). Reprinted by Friends United Press; Richmond, IN (1976).

402 Adapt, Arr: The United Methodist Publishing House.

404 Adapt, Arr: The United Methodist Publishing House.

405 Words, Music: Maranatha! Music; PO Bx 31050; Laguna Hills, CA 92654-1050. All rights reserved. International copyright secured. Used by permission.

406 Adapt: Division of Christian Education of the National Council of Churches in the USA. From the Revised Standard Version of the Bible. Music: Galliard, Ltd. c/o Galaxy Music Corp; 131 W 86th St; New York, NY 10024.

408 Words, Music: Hope Publishing Co; 380 S Main Pl; Carol Stream, IL 60188.

411 Words, Music: The United Methodist Publishing House.

416 Adapt, Arr: The United Methodist Publishing House.

418 Adapt, Arr: The United Methodist Publishing House.

425 Words: The Community of the Resurrection; Mirfield; West Yorkshire, England WF14OBN. Used by permission. Harm: Oxford University Press; Ely House; 37 Dover St; London, England; WlX4AH. Used by permission.

426 Words: Hope Publishing Co; 380 S Main Pl; Carol Stream, IL 60188. Music: Max Miller; 45 Hunnewell Ave; Newton, MA 02158.

428 Words: Hope Publishing Co.; 380 S Main Pl; Carol Stream, IL 60188.

429 Words: Harper & Row, Publishers, Inc.; 10 E 53rd St; New York, NY 10022. "Our Lord of Light", from *Meditations*, Toyohiko Kagawa. Reprinted by permission.

431 Words, Music: Jan-Lee Music; 260 El Camino; Beverly Hills, CA 90212.

432 Words, Music: Hope Publishing Co; 380 S Main Pl; Carol Stream, IL 60188.

433 Words: Galliard, Ltd. c/o Galaxy Music Corp; 131 W 86th St; New York, NY 10024. Harm: Abingdon Press; 201 8th Ave, S; Nashville, TN 37202. From *The Book of Hymns*.

434 Words, Music: Ediciones Paulinas, sole U.S. Agent: c/o OCP Publications; 5536 NE Hassalo; Portland, OR 95745. All rights reserved. Used with permission; Trans: The United Methodist Publishing House.

435 Words: The Hymn Society of America c/o Hope Publishing Co.; 380 S Main Pl; Carol Stream, IL 60188. Harm: Oxford University Press; Ely House; 37 Dover St; London, England W1X 4AH.

437 Words (1-3): Lorenz Publishing Co; 501 E Third St; Dayton, OH 45401-0802. Arr: The Westminster/John Knox Press; 100 Witherspoon St; Louisville, KY 40202-1396.

439 Words: Hope Publishing Co.; 380 S Main Pl; Carol Stream, IL 60188.

440 Music: Mrs. Robert J. B. Fleming; 6015 Tisdall St, #222; Vancouver, BC Canada V5Z3N1.

441 Words: Oxford University Press; Ely House; 37 Dover St; London, England W1X 4AH. Music: Hope Publishing Co.; 380 S Main Pl; Carol Stream, IL 60188.

442 Words: Inter-Lutheran Commission on Worship c/o Chantry Music Press, Inc.; Bx 1101; Springfield, OH 45501. Music: Chantry Music Press, Inc.; Bx 1101; Springfield, OH 45501. Harm: G.I.A. Publications, Inc; 7404 S Mason; Chicago, IL 60638.

443 Words: The United Methodist Publishing House. Music: Augsburg Fortress; 426 S Fifth St; Minneapolis, MN 55440.

447 Words: The Church Hymnal Corp; 800 Second Ave; New York, NY 10019.

448 Adapt, Arr: The United Methodist Publishing House.

450 Words: The Methodist Publishing House; 20, Ivatt Way; Peterborough, England PE3 7PG.

451 Alt: The United Methodist Publishing House. Harm: Abingdon Press; 201 8th Ave, S; Nashville, TN 37202. From *The Book of Hymns*.

456 Words: Seabury Press, Inc. c/o Harper & Row Publishers, Inc.; 10 E 53rd St; New York, NY 10022. From *Instrument of Thy Peace* by Alan Paton. Reprinted by permission.

457 Alt: The United Methodist Publishing House.

458 Words: Dohnavur Fellowship c/o Christian Literature Crusade; Ft. Washington, PA; London: Society for Promoting Christian Knowledge. Used by permission. Music: Oxford University Press; Ely House; 37 Dover St; London, England W1X 4AH. Used by permission.

460 Words: Abingdon Press; 201 8th Ave, S; Nashville, TN 37202. From *The Glory of God* by Georgia Harkness.

461 Words: The United Methodist Publishing House.

464 Adapt, Arr: The United Methodist Publishing House.

466 Words: A. R. Mowbray & Co., Ltd; a division of Cassell Publishers Ltd.; Villiers House; 41/47 Strand; London WC2N5JE England. From *The Orthodox Way*, Kallistos Ware, 1979. Reproduced by permission.

471 Words, Music: Richard Alan Henderson; PO Bx 45; Anderson, IN 46015. Partial arrangement. Used by permission.

474 Words, Music: Unichappell Music, Inc. c/o Hal Leonard Publishing Corp; PO Bx 13819; Milwaukee, WI 53213. International copyright secured. Made in USA. All rights secured.

476 Words, Music: The United Methodist Publishing House.

478 Phonetic transcription: The United Methodist Publishing House.

482 Music: The United Methodist Publishing House.

484 Music: Les Presses de Taizé c/o G.I.A. Publications, Inc.; 7404 S Mason Ave; Chicago, IL 60638.

485 Harm: G.I.A. Publications, Inc; 7404 S Mason Ave; Chicago, IL 60638.

486 Music: G.I.A. Publications, Inc; 7404 S Mason Ave; Chicago, IL 60638.

487 Words, Music: The United Methodist Publishing House.

488 Music: Les Presses de Taizé c/o G.I.A. Publications, Inc.; 7404 S Mason Ave; Chicago, IL 60638.

489 Words: Howard Thurman Educational Trust; 2020 Stockton St; San Francisco, CA 94133. From *Meditations of the Heart*, Harper & Row Publishers, Inc.(1953). Reprinted by Friends United Press; Richmond, IN (1976).

490 Words, Music: The United Methodist Publishing House.

491 Harm: Abingdon Press; 201 8th Ave, S; Nashville, TN 37202. From *Songs of Zion*.

494 Harm: The United Methodist Publishing House.

497 Words, Music: Utryck c/o Walton Music Corp; 170 NE 33rd St; Ft. Lauderdale, FL 33334.

498 Words, Music: Nguyen D. Viet-Chau, Publisher-Editor; Dan Chua Catholic Magazine & Publications; PO Bx 1419; Gretna, LA 70053. Used by permission.

499 Music: Associated Music Publishers, Inc. c/o G. Schirmer, Inc.; 24 E 22nd St; New York, NY 10010. Used by permission.

502 Words, Music: Gracia Grindal; Lutheran Theological Seminary; 2481 Como Ave; St. Paul, MN 55108.

503 Words, Music: Martin & Morris Music, Inc.; 4312 Indiana, Chicago, IL 60653.

505 Words: Hope Publishing Co.; 380 S Main Pl; Carol Stream, IL 60188.

506 Words, Music: Medical Mission Sisters; Permissions Dept; 92 Sherman St; Hartford, CT 06105.

507 Words, Music: Manna Music, Inc.; 25510 Ave Stanford, #101; Valencia, CA 01355.

508 Words, Trans, Music: Hope Publishing Co.; 380 S Main Pl; Carol Stream, IL 60188.

512 Arr: The United Methodist Publishing House.

515 Trans: Augsburg Fortress; 426 S 5th St; Minneapolis, MN 55440. Harm: Abingdon Press; 201 8th Ave, S; Nashville, TN 37202. From *The Book of Hymns*.

516 Resp: The United Methodist Publishing House.

517 Trans: Hope Publishing Co; 380 S Main Pl; Carol Stream, IL 60188.

518 Harm: Abingdon Press; 201 8th Ave, S; Nashville, TN 37202. From *The Book of Hymns*.

519 Words, Music: Edward B. Marks Music Co. c/o Hal Leonard Publishing Corp; PO Bx 13819; Milwaukee, WI 53213. Used by permission. International copyright secured. Made in USA. All rights reserved.

520 Adapt, Arr: The United Methodist Publishing House.

521 Adapt: The United Methodist Publishing House.

522 Words, Music: Hope Publishing Co.; 380 S Main Pl; Carol Stream, IL 60188.

523 Trans, Arr: Christian Conference of Asia; Communications; 4/F 57 Peking Rd; Kowloon, Hong Kong. Used by permission.

524 Arr: J. Edward Hoy; 762-S Broad St; Philadelphia, PA 19146.

527 Adapt, Arr: The United Methodist Publishing House.

533 Adapt: The United Methodist Publishing House.

534 Arr: The Westminster Press/John Knox Press; 100 Witherspoon St; Louisville, KY 40202-1396.

537 Words: Mrs. J. R. Peacey; 10 Park Cottages; Manor Rd; Hurstpierpoint, West Sussex, England BN6 9UW. Used by permission. Music: Hope Publishing Co.; 380 S Main Pl; Carol Stream, IL 60188.

538 Words, Music: Oxford University Press; 200 Madison Ave; New York, NY 10016. Used by permission.

541   Harm: Abingdon Press; 201 8th Ave, S; Nashville, TN 37202. From *The Book of Hymns*.

542   Words: The United Methodist Publishing House.

543   Music: The United Methodist Publishing House.

544   Words, Music: Hope Publishing Co.; 380 S Main Pl; Carol Stream, IL 60188.

546   Adapt: The United Methodist Publishing House.

547   Words: The Hymn Society of America c/o Hope Publishing Co.; 380 S Main Pl; Carol Stream, IL 60188.

548   Words (3): The United Methodist Publishing House.

549   Trans: World Library Publications, Inc.; 3815 N Willow Rd; Schiller Park, IL 60176. All rights reserved. Used by permission.

551   Words: Augsburg Fortress; 426 S Fifth St; Minneapolis, MN 55440. Music: Max Miller; 45 Hunnewell Ave; Newton, MA 02158.

552   Words, Phonetic transcription: The United Methodist Publishing House. Music: JASRAC; 1-7-13 Nishishimbashi, Minato-ku, Tokyo 105, Japan.

554   Harm: Abingdon Press; 201 8th Ave, S; Nashville, TN 37202. From *The Book of Hymns*.

556   Words: Crossroad Publishing Co.; 370 Lexington Ave; New York, NY 10017. Reprinted by permission.

558   Words, Music: Hope Publishing Co.; 380 S Main Pl; Carol Stream, IL 60188.

560   Words, Music: Hope Publishing Co.; 380 S Main Pl; Carol Stream, IL 60188.

563   Trans: The Church Hymnal Corp; 800 Second Ave; New York, NY 10017. Music: Elkan-Vogel, Inc. c/o Theodore Presser Co.; Presser Pl; Bryn Mawr, PA 19010. Used by permission.

565   Trans: The Church Hymnal Corp; 800 Second Ave; New York, NY 10017. Harm: Hope Publishing; 380 S Main Pl; Carol Stream, IL 60188.

571   Words: Abingdon Press; 201 8th Ave, S; Nashville, TN 37202. From *The Book of Hymns*.

572   Words, Music: Communiqué Music, Inc. c/o Spectra Copyright Management, Inc.; 23 Music Square, E, #101; Nashville, TN 37203. Used by permission.

574   Words: Orbis Books, Inc.; Maryknoll, NY 10545. From *Cry Justice*.

577   Words: Elinor Fosdick Downs; 63 Atlantic Ave; Boston, MA 02110. Used by permission.

579   Words: Hope Publishing Co.; 380 S Main Pl; Carol Stream, IL 60188.

581   Words: Oxford University Press; Ely House; 37 Dover St; London, England W1X 4AH. Used by permission. Harm: Augsburg Fortress; 426 S Fifth St; Minneapolis, MN 55440

582   Words: Hope Publishing Co.; 380 S Main Pl; Carol Stream, IL 60188.

583   Words, Music: Ediciones Paulinas, sole US agent: OCP Publications; 5536 NE Hassalo; Portland, OR. All rights reserved. Used with permission. Trans: The United Methodist Publishing House. Harm: Skinner Chávez-Melo; 200 W 79th; 12-F; New York, NY 10024.

584   Words, Music: Hope Publishing Co.; 380 S Main Pl; Carol Stream, IL 60188.

585   Adapt: The United Methodist Publishing House.

586   Words: The United Methodist Publishing House.

589   Words: Hope Publishing Co.; 380 S Main Pl; Carol Stream, IL 60188. Music: Theodore Presser Co.; Presser Pl; Bryn Mawr, PA 19010. Used by permission.

590   Words, Music: Hope Publishing Co.; 380 S Main Pl; Carol Stream, IL 60188.

592   Words: Hope Publishing Co.; 380 S Main Pl; Carol Stream, IL 60188. Music: Oxford University Press; Ely House; 37 Dover St; London, England W1X 4AH. Used by permission.

593   Words, Music: North American Liturgy Resources; 10802 N 23rd Ave; Phoenix, AZ 85029. Recordings of this and other titles are available from NALR.

601   Words, Music: Meadowgreen Music Co./ Bug and Bear Music. Meadowgreen Music Co. adm. by Tree Publishing Co., Inc.; 8 Music Sq, W, Nashville, TN 37203. Bug and Bear Music adm. by LCS Music Group, Inc.; PO Bx 7409; Dallas TX

604   Words: H. Francis Yardley; 116 Silver Crest Dr, NW, #41; Calgary, Alberta, Canada T3B 4N9. Harm: Oxford University Press; Ely House; 37 Dover St; London, England W1X 4AH.

605   Words: The United Methodist Publishing House. Harm: Augsburg Fortress; 426 S Fifth St; Minneapolis, MN 55440.

608   Words: The Rev. Thomas E. Herbranson; 978 SW 5th St; New Brighton, MN 55112.

609   Words, Music: International Commission on English in the Liturgy; 1275 "K" St, NW; Washington, DC 20005-4097. From Rite of Baptism for Children and Music for the Rite of Funerals and Rite of Baptism for Children. All rights reserved.

610   Words: John B. Geyer; 5 Wealey Hill; Birmingham, England B29 4AA.

611   Words: Ronald S. Cole-Turner; Memphis Theological Seminary; 168 E Parkway S; Memphis, TN 38104. Used by permission.

613   Harm: The United Methodist Publishing House

614   Music: Hope Publishing Co.; 380 S Main Pl; Carol Stream, IL 60188.

615   Phonetic Transcription, Music: The United Methodist Publishing House.

617   Words: Hope Publishing Co.; 380 S Main Pl; Carol Stream, IL 60188. Harm: The United Methodist Publishing House.

618   Adapt, Arr: The United Methodist Publishing House.

619   Words, Music: Hope Publishing Co.; 380 S Main Pl; Carol Stream, IL 60188.

620   Words, Music: North American Liturgy Resources; 10802 N 23rd Ave; Phoenix, AZ 85029. Recordings of this and other titles are available from NALR.

625   Words (4), Harm: Augsburg Fortress; 426 S Fifth St; Minneapolis, MN 55440. Trans (1-3), Music: Lutheran World Federation; Route de Ferney 150; 1211 Geneva, Switzerland 20. Used by permission.

627   Music: Hope Publishing Co.; 380 S Main Pl; Carol Stream, IL 60188.

628   Words, Music: Les Presses de Taizé France c/o G.I.A. Publications, Inc.; 7404 S Mason Ave; Chicago, IL 60638.

629   Words, Music: Archdiocese of Philadelphia; Archdiocesan Music Ofc; 222 N Seventeenth St; Philadelphia, PA 19103.

630   Words: The Westminster/John Knox Press; 100 Witherspoon St; Louisville, KY 40202-1396. From *The Worshipbook—Services and Hymns*. Used by permission.

632   Words: Oxford University Press; Ely House; 37 Dover St; London, England W1X 4AH. Used by permission. Music: The H. W. Gray Co., a division of CCP/Belwin, Inc.; PO Bx 4340; Miami, FL 33014. All rights reserved. Used by permission.

633   Phonetic Transcription, Harm: The United Methodist Publishing House.

634   Words: Hope Publishing Co.; 380 S Main Pl; Carol Stream, IL 60188.

636   Words: The Saint Andrew Press; Church of Scotland; 121 George St; Edinburgh, Scotland, EH2 4YN. Used by permission.

637   Words, Music: Ediciones Musical PAX, sole US agent: OCP Publications; 5536 NE Hassalo; Portland, OR 97213; All rights reserved; Used with permission. Trans: The United Methodist Publishing House. Harm: Skinner Chávez-Melo; 200 W 79th, #12-F; New York, NY 10024

638   Words: Augsburg Fortress; 426 S Fifth St; Minneapolis, MN 55440. Music: Richard Hillert; 1620 Clay Ct; Melrose Park, IL 60160.

639 Trans: Fortress Press; 2900 Queen Ln; Philadelphia, PA 19129.

640 Words, Music: G.I.A. Publications, Inc.; 7404 S Mason Ave; Chicago, IL 60638.

641 Words, Music: Assigned to Sacred Songs, a division of Word, Inc.; 5221 N O'Connor Blvd, #1000; Irving, TX 75039. All rights reserved. International copyright secured. Used by permission.

642 Words: Hope Publishing Co.; 380 S Main Pl; Carol Stream, IL 60188.

643 Words, Music: Hope Publishing Co.; 380 S Main Pl; Carol Stream, IL 60188.

646 Adapt: S T Kimbrough, Jr.; Center of Theological Inquiry; 50 Stockton St; Princeton, NJ 08540. Resp 1 and 2: The United Methodist Publishing House.

647 Words: Russell Schulz-Widmar; PO Bx 2247; Austin, TX 78768. Used by permission. Music: M. Lee Suitor; 284 "M" St; Salt Lake City, UT 84103.

648 Words: Hope Publishing Co.; 380 S Main Pl; Carol Stream, IL 60188.

649 Words: Hope Publishing Co.; 380 S Main Pl; Carol Stream, IL 60188.

652 Text, Response Words, Music: The United Methodist Publishing House.

653 Words: Hope Publishing Co.; 380 S Main Pl; Carol Stream, IL 60188.

654 Words: The Hymn Society of America c/o Hope Publishing Co.; 380 S Main Pl; Carol Stream, IL 60188.

655 Adapt, Arr: The United Methodist Publishing House.

657 Words, music: Scripture in Song c/o Maranatha! Music; PO Bx 31050; Laguna Hills, CA 92654-1050. All rights reserved. International copyrights secured. Used by permission.

659 Trans, Music Transcription: Mennonite Indian Leaders' Council; Box 37; Busby, MT 59016.

660 Words, Music: Hope Publishing Co.; 380 S Main Pl; Carol Stream, IL 60188.

661 Trans, Versification: Abingdon Press; 201 8th Ave, S; Nashville, TN 37202. From *The Book of Hymns.*

664 Words: World Library Publications, Inc.; 3815 N Willow Rd; Schiller Park, IL 60176. Harm: Augsburg Fortress; 426 S Fifth St; Minneapolis, MN 55440.

665 Words, Music: Hinshaw Music, Inc.; PO Bx 470; Chapel Hill, NC 27514. Reprinted by permission.

666 Words, Harm: The United Methodist Publishing House.

667 Trans: The United Methodist Publishing House.

668 Adapt: Concordia Publishing House; 3558 Jefferson Ave; St. Louis, MO 63118. Used by permission.

670 Words: Mrs. J. R. Peacey; 10 Park Cottages; Manor Rd; Hurstpierspoint, England BN6 9VW.

677 Words: Viking Penguin, Inc.; 40 W 23rd St; New York, NY 10022. From *God's Trombones* by James Weldon Johnson. All rights reserved. Reprinted by permission.

678 Trans: Allen A. Wiant, Executor; 325 Gudrun Rd; Columbus, OH 43202. Used by permission of Mildred A. and Allen A. Wiant.

680 Harm: Oxford University Press; Ely House; 37 Dover St; London, England W1X 4AH. Used by permission.

681 Alt: The United Methodist Publishing House.

684 Words: The United Methodist Publishing House. Music: G.I.A. Publications; 7404 S Mason Ave; Chicago, IL 60638.

689 Words: Macmillan Publishing Co., Inc.; 866 Third Ave; New York, NY 10022. Used by permission.

692 Trans, Harm: The Church Hymnal Corp; 800 Second Ave; New York, NY 10017.

695 Words: The Hymn Society of America c/o Hope Publishing Co.; 380 S Main Pl; Carol Stream, IL 60188. Harm: The United Methodist Publishing House

703 Adapt, Arr: The United Methodist Publishing House.

704 Adapt, Arr: The United Methodist Publishing House.

706 Words, Music: Communiqué Music, Inc. and Crouch Music Corp./ASCAP c/o Spectra Copyright Management, Inc.; 23 Music Square, E; Nashville, TN 37205. Used by permission.

707 Words, music: Hope Publishing Co.; 380 S Main Pl; Carol Stream, IL 60188.

708 Words: Hope Publishing Co.; 380 S Main Pl; Carol Stream, IL 60188.

716 Arr: Hope Publishing Co.; 380 S Main Pl; Carol Stream, IL 60188.

719 Adapt, Arr: The United Methodist Publishing House.

722 Adapt, Arr: The United Methodist Publishing House.

725 Words: Hope Publishing Co.; 380 S Main Pl; Carol Stream, IL 60188. Music: Faber Music Limited; 3 Queens Square; London, England WC1N 3AU. Reprinted from *The New Catholic Hymnal* by permission.

726 Harm: The United Methodist Publishing House.

728 Words, Music: G. Schirmer, Inc.; 24 E 22nd St; New York, NY 10010. Used by permission.

729 Words: Hope Publishing Co.; 380 S Main Pl; Carol Stream, IL 60188. Harm: The United Methodist Publishing House.

734 Adapt: S T Kimbrough, Jr.; Center of Theological Inquiry; 50 Stockton St; Princeton, NJ 08540. Resp: The United Methodist Publishing House.

738 Music Resp 1: The United Methodist Publishing House.

739 Music Resp 1: The United Methodist Publishing House.

740 Music: The United Methodist Publishing House.

742 Music: The United Methodist Publishing House.

744 Music: The United Methodist Publishing House.

745 Words Response: The United Methodist Publishing House.

746 Adapt, Words, Music: The United Methodist Publishing House.

747 Adapt, Words, Music: The United Methodist Publishing House.

748 Music: The United Methodist Publishing House.

749 Music: The Choristers Guild; 2834 W Kingsley Rd; Garland, TX 75041.

750 Music Resp. 2: The United Methodist Publishing House.

752 Music Resp 2: The United Methodist Publishing House.

754 Music Resp 1: The Grail c/o G.I.A. Publications, Inc.; 7404 S Mason Ave; Chicago, IL 60638. Used by permission. Music Resp. 2: The United Methodist Publishing House.

755 Music Resp 2: The United Methodist Publishing House.

756 Music Resp 1: The United Methodist Publishing House.

758 Music: The United Methodist Publishing House.

760 Music: The United Methodist Publishing House.

766 Music: The United Methodist Publishing House.

767 Music Resp 1: The United Methodist Publishing House.

769 Music: The United Methodist Publishing House.

771 Adapt: The United Methodist Publishing House.

772 Words: Oxford University Press; Ely House; 37 Dover St; London, England W1X 4AH. Music: Hope Publishing Co.; 380 S Main Pl; Carol Stream, IL 60188.

773 Music: The United Methodist Publishing House.

774 Music: The United Methodist Publishing House.

776 Adapt: The United Methodist Publishing House.

779 Music: The United Methodist Publishing House.

780 Music Resp 2: The United Methodist Publishing House.

783 Music: The United Methodist Publishing House.

785 Music: The United Methodist Publishing House.

787 Music: The United Methodist Publishing House.

788 Music: G.I.A. Publications, Inc.; 7404 S Mason Ave; Chicago, IL 60638.

790 Music: The United Methodist Publishing House.

791 Music: The United Methodist Publishing House.

795 Music Resp 1: The United Methodist Publishing House. Adapt Resp 2: The United Methodist Publishing House.

797 Music: The United Methodist Publishing House.

798 Music: The United Methodist Publishing House.

799 Music: The United Methodist Publishing House.

801 Music Resp 1: The United Methodist Publishing House.

803 Music: G.I.A. Publications, Inc.; 7404 S Mason; Chicago, IL 60638.

804 Music: The United Methodist Publishing House.

804 Music: The United Methodist Publishing House.

806 Music: The United Methodist Publishing House.

807 Music: The United Methodist Publishing House.

809 Music: The United Methodist Publishing House.

810 Music: The United Methodist Publishing House.

813 Music: The United Methodist Publishing House.

814 Music: The United Methodist Publishing House.

815 Music: The United Methodist Publishing House.

816 Music Resp 1: The United Methodist Publishing House. Words, Music Resp 2: Edward B. Marks Music Co. c/o Hal Leonard Publishing Company; PO Bx 13819; Milwaukee, WI 53213.

818 Music: The United Methodist Publishing House.

819 Music: The United Methodist Publishing House.

821 Music Resp 2: The United Methodist Publishing House.

822 Adapt, Music: The United Methodist Publishing House.

824 Music: The United Methodist Publishing House.

828 Music: The United Methodist Publishing House.

830 Music: The United Methodist Publishing House.

832 Music: The United Methodist Publishing House.

833 Adapt, Words, Music: The United Methodist Publishing House.

834 Music: The United Methodist Publishing House.

835 Music: The United Methodist Publishing House.

836 Music: The United Methodist Publishing House.

837 Music: The United Methodist Publishing House.

838 Music: The United Methodist Publishing House.

839 Music Resp 1: Oxford University Press; 200 Madison Ave; New York, NY 10016. Music Resp 2: G.I.A. Publications, Inc.; 7404 S Mason; Chicago, IL 60638.

840 Music Resp 1: The United Methodist Publishing House.

841 Music Resp 2: The United Methodist Publishing House.

841 Music Resp 3: Meadowgreen/Bug & Bear Music, administered by Tree Pub. Co., Inc.; 8 Music Square, W; Nashville, TN 37203. International copyright secured. All rights reserved. Used by permission.

844 Music Resp 1: The United Methodist Publishing House. Music Resp 2: G.I.A. Publications, Inc.; 7404 S Mason; Chicago, IL 60638. Arr Resp 3: The United Methodist Publishing House.

845 Music Resp 2: The United Methodist Publishing House.

848 Music: The United Methodist Publishing House.

849 Words, Music: The United Methodist Publishing House.

850 Words: The United Methodist Publishing House.

850 Music: Arlo D. Duba; Univ. of Dubuque Theological Seminary; 2000 University Ave; Dubuque, IA 52001.

852 Music: The United Methodist Publishing House.

853 Music: The United Methodist Publishing House.

854 Adapt: The United Methodist Publishing House.

856 Resp 1: The United Methodist Publishing House. Music Resp 2: Ediciones Apostalade de la Prensa, sole US agent: OCP Publications; 5536 NE Hassalo; Portland, OR 97213. All rights reserved. Used with permission.

862 Music Response 2: Resource Publications, Inc.; 160 E Virginia St, #290; San Jose, CA 95112.

883 Text: The United Church of Canada; 85 St. Clair Ave, E; Toronto, Canada M4T1M8

884 Adapt: The United Methodist Publishing House.

886 Text: World Methodist Council; Lake Junaluska, NC

887 Adapt: The United Methodist Publishing House.

888 Adapt: The United Methodist Publishing House.

889 Adapt: The United Methodist Publishing House.

893 Adapt: The United Methodist Publishing House.

899 Musical Setting: Elkan-Vogel, Inc. c/o Theodore Presser Co.; Presser Pl. Bryn Mawr, PA 19010. From *Hymns and Responses for the Church Year* by Vincent Persichetti. Used by permission.

900 Musical Setting: Elkan-Vogel, Inc. c/o Theodore Presser Co.; Presser Pl. Bryn Mawr, PA 19010. From *Hymns and Responses for the Church Year* by Vincent Persichetti. Used by permission.

901 Musical Setting: The United Methodist Publishing House.

902 Musical Setting: Oxford University Press; Walton St; Oxford, England 0x2 6DP. Extracted and adapted by the composer from the anthem *The Lord Bless you and Keep you.* Used by permission.

903 Musical Setting: The United Methodist Publishing House.

INDEX OF COMPOSERS, ARRANGERS, AUTHORS, TRANSLATORS, AND SOURCES

INDEX OF SCRIPTURE:
Services, Psalter, Acts of Worship

INDEX OF SCRIPTURE:
Hymns, Canticles, Prayers & Poems

METRICAL INDEX

INDEX OF TUNE NAMES

INDEX OF TOPICS AND CATEGORIES

Italic type indicates poetry and prayers
Psalms without reference numbers are found in the Psalter, pages 738-862

ADORATION AND PRAISE 57-152. *Also:*

280 All glory, laud, and honor
554 All praise to our redeeming Lord
553 And are we yet alive
675 As the sun doth daily rise
199 Canticle of Mary
684 Christ, mighty Savior
260 Christ, upon the mountain peak
411 Dear Lord, lead me day by day
612 Deck thyself, my soul, with gladness
711 For all the saints
705 *For Direction*
477 *For Illumination*
731 Glorious things of thee are spoken
660 God is here
325 Hail, thou once despised Jesus
478 Jaya ho jaya ho
718 Lo, he comes with clouds descending
498 My prayer rises to heaven
198 My soul gives glory to my God
686 O gladsome light
267 O love, how deep, how broad
727 O what their joy and their glory must be
258 O wondrous sight! O vision fair
248 On this day earth shall ring
604 Praise and thanksgiving be to God
715 Rejoice, the Lord is King
716 Rejoice, the Lord is King
296 Sing, my tongue, the glorious battle
702 Sing with all the saints in glory
662 Stand up and bless the Lord
200 Tell out, my soul
303 The day of resurrection
690 The day thou gavest, Lord, is ended
657 This is the day
658 This is the day the Lord hath made
720 Wake, awake, for night is flying (st. 3)
292 What wondrous love is this (sts. 3, 4)
701 When We All Get to Heaven

ADVENT. *See* **Christian Year**

AFFIRMATION OF FAITH
Musical. *See* **Service Music**
Texts 880-889

AFFLICTION AND TRIBULATION

517 By gracious powers
340 Come, ye sinners, poor and needy
330 Daw-Kee, Aim Daw-Tsi-Taw
448 Go Down, Moses
522 Leave It There
474 Precious Lord, take my hand
491 Remember me
348 Softly and tenderly Jesus is calling

347 Spirit Song
374 Standing on the promises
375 There is a balm in Gilead
380 There's within my heart a melody
525 We'll Understand It Better By and By
526 What a friend we have in Jesus

ALDERSGATE

363 And can it be that I should gain
550 Christ, from whom all blessings flow
603 Come, Holy Ghost, our hearts inspire
651 Come, Holy Ghost, our souls inspire
386 Come, O thou Traveler unknown
387 *Come, O thou Traveler unknown*
58 *Glory to God, and praise and love*
59 *Mil voces*
57 O for a thousand tongues to sing
515 Out of the depths I cry to you
342 *Where shall my wondering soul begin*

ALL SAINTS DAY. *See* **Christian Year**

AMENS 897-904

ANNIVERSARIES. *See* **Church Anniversaries; Heritage**

ASCENSION. *See* **Christian Year**

ASH WEDNESDAY. *See* **Christian Year**

ASPIRATION AND RESOLVE

451 Be thou my vision
80 Canticle of the Holy Trinity
173 Christ, whose glory fills the skies
594 *Come, divine Interpreter*
475 Come down, O Love divine
508 Faith, while trees are still in blossom
409 *For Grace to Labor*
397 I need thee every hour
410 I want a principle within
402 Lord, I want to be a Christian
421 Make me a captive, Lord
373 Nothing between my soul and my Savior
388 O come, and dwell in me
480 O Love that wilt not let me go
329 *Prayer to the Holy Spirit*
500 Spirit of God, descend
493 *Three Things We Pray*
76 *Trinity Sunday*

ASSURANCE 368-381. *Also:*

700 Abide with me
163 Ask ye what great thing I know
517 By gracious powers
127 Guide me, O thou great Jehovah

213 Lift up your heads
427 Where cross the crowded ways

CLOSING HYMNS 663-673. *Also:*

530 Are ye able
566 Blest be the dear uniting love
305 Camina, pueblo de Dios
590 Christ loves the church
537 Filled with the Spirit's power
438 Forth in thy name
571 Go, make of all disciples
251 Go, tell it on the mountain
578 God of love and God of power
623 Here, O my Lord, I see thee (sts. 4, 5)
580 Lead on, O King eternal
581 Lord, whose love through humble service
634 Now let us from this table rise
336 Of all the Spirit's gifts to me
309 On the day of resurrection
356 Pues si vivimos
708 Rejoice in God's saints
664 Sent forth by God's blessing
583 Sois la semilla
513 Soldiers of Christ, arise
303 The day of resurrection
436 The voice of God is calling
582 Whom shall I send
181 Ye servants of God
   See also **Commitment; Discipleship and Service**

COMFORT

700 Abide with me
534 Be still, my soul
141 Children of the heavenly Father
510 Come, ye disconsolate
461 *For Those Who Mourn*
130 God Will Take Care of You
128 He leadeth me
529 How firm a foundation
464 I will trust in the Lord
142 If thou but suffer God to guide thee
60 I'll praise my Maker (st. 2, 3)
377 It Is Well with My Soul
469 Jesus is all the world to me
479 Jesus, lover of my soul
133 Leaning on the Everlasting Arms
472 Near to the Heart of God
528 Nearer, my God, to thee
520 Nobody knows the trouble I see
373 Nothing between my soul and my Savior
518 O Thou, in whose presence
474 Precious Lord, take my hand
536 Precious Name
137 Psalm 23 (King James Version)
754 Psalm 23
523 Saranam, Saranam
512 Stand By Me
496 Sweet hour of prayer
138 The King of love my shepherd is
136 The Lord's my shepherd
153 Thou hidden source of calm repose
502 Thy holy wings, O Savior
85 We believe in one true God
506 Wellspring of wisdom

COMMITMENT

413 A charge to keep I have

289 Ah, holy Jesus
294 Alas! and did my Savior bleed
359 Alas! and did my Savior bleed
186 Alleluia
168 At the name of Jesus
566 Blest be the dear uniting love
517 By gracious powers
728 Come Sunday
676 *For a New Day*
100 God, whose love is reigning o'er us
382 Have thine own way, Lord
593 Here I am, Lord
465 Holy Spirit, Truth divine
397 I need thee every hour
354 I Surrender All
206 I want to walk as a child of the light
221 In the bleak midwinter
377 It Is Well with My Soul
183 *Jesus, thy boundless love to me*
398 Jesus calls us o'er the tumult
157 Jesus shall reign
661 Jesus, we want to meet
273 Jesus' hands were kind hands
357 Just as I am, without one plea
431 Let there be peace on earth
463 Lord, speak to me
242 Love came down at Christmas
421 Make me a captive, Lord
471 Move me
424 Must Jesus bear the cross alone
172 My Jesus, I love thee
222 Niño lindo
396 O Jesus, I have promised
480 O Love that wilt not let me go
430 O Master, let me walk with thee
247 O Morning Star, how fair and bright
501 O Thou who camest from above
454 Open my eyes, that I may see
392 *Prayer for a New Heart*
497 Send me, Lord
399 Take my life, and let it be consecrated
640 Take our bread
415 Take up thy cross
241 That boy-child of Mary
192 There's a Spirit in the air
585 This little light of mine
467 Trust and Obey
298 When I survey the wondrous cross
299 When I survey the wondrous cross
252 When Jesus came to Jordan
338 Where He Leads Me

COMMUNION. *See* Holy Communion

COMMUNITY IN CHRIST. *See* Church

CONFESSION

468 Dear Jesus, in whose life I see
355 Depth of mercy
564 *For the Unity of Christ's Body*
577 God of grace and God of glory
115 How like a gentle spirit
478 Jaya ho jaya ho
479 Jesus, lover of my soul
357 Just as I am, without one plea
586 Let my people seek their freedom
579 Lord God, your love has called us here
726 O holy city, seen of John

ORDINATION 648-651. *Also:*

413 A charge to keep I have
566 Blest be the dear uniting love
571 Go, make of all disciples
578 God of love and God of power
593 Here I Am, Lord
580 Lead on, O King eternal
584 Lord, you give the great commission
582 Whom shall I send
See also **Installation Services**

PARDON 361-367. *See also* **Forgiveness**

PASSION/PALM SUNDAY. *See* **Christian Year**

PEACE, INNER. *See* **Calmness and Serenity**

PEACE, PASSING OF. *See* **Service Music**

PEACE, WORLD

433 All who love and serve your city
426 Behold a broken world
188 Christ is the world's light
450 Creator of the earth and skies
327 Crown him with many crowns
376 Dona nobis pacem
428 For the healing of the nations
567 Heralds of Christ
178 Hope of the world
218 It came upon the midnight clear
580 Lead on, O King eternal
440 Let there be light
431 Let there be peace on earth
159 Lift high the cross
556 *Litany for Christian Unity*
211 O come, O come, Emmanuel
730 O day of God, draw nigh
729 O day of peace that dimly shines
435 O God of every nation
449 *Our earth we now lament to see*
437 This is my song
533 We shall overcome
439 We utter our cry
442 Weary of all trumpeting

PENITENCE

682 All praise to thee, my God, this night
624 Bread of the world
516 Canticle of Redemption
450 Creator of the earth and skies
597 *For the Spirit of Truth*
262 Heal me, hands of Jesus
266 Heal us, Emmanuel
265 O Christ, the healer
425 O crucified Redeemer
435 O God of every nation
443 O God who shaped creation
286 O sacred Head, now wounded
515 Out of the depths I cry to you
361 Rock of Ages, cleft for me
264 Silence, frenzied, unclean spirit
380 There's within my heart a melody
442 Weary of all trumpeting
298 When I survey the wondrous cross
299 When I survey the wondrous cross
See also **Confession**

PENTECOST. *See* **Christian Year**

PETITION PRAYER. *See* **Service Music**

PILGRIMAGE

407 Close to Thee
386 Come, O thou Traveler unknown
387 *Come, O thou Traveler unknown*
732 Come, we that love the Lord
733 Come, we that love the Lord
434 Cuando el pobre
127 Guide me, O thou great Jehovah
128 He leadeth me
142 If thou but suffer God to guide thee
580 Lead on, O King eternal
133 Leaning on the Everlasting Arms
631 O food to pilgrims given
724 On Jordan's stormy banks I stand
723 Shall we gather at the river

PRAYER

358 Dear Lord and Father of mankind
404 Every time I feel the Spirit
498 My prayer rises to heaven
119 O God in heaven
492 Prayer is the soul's sincere desire
113 Source and Sovereign, Rock and Cloud
500 Spirit of God, descend upon my heart
352 Standing in the Need of Prayer
496 Sweet hour of prayer
395 Take time to be holy
437 This is my song
See also **Lord's Prayer**

PRAYER RESPONSES. *See* **Service Music**

PRAYERS OF CONFESSION, ASSURANCE, AND PARDON 890-893

PRESENCE (Holy Spirit)

110 A mighty fortress is our God
420 Breathe on me, Breath of God
125 Canticle of Covenant Faithfulness
475 Come down, O Love divine
 61 Come, thou almighty King
330 Daw-Kee, Aim Daw-Tsi-Taw
461 *For Those Who Mourn*
560 Help us accept each other
331 Holy Spirit, come, confirm us
152 I sing the almighty power of God
503 Let it breathe on me
518 O Thou, in whose presence my soul
143 On Eagle's Wings
412 *Prayer of John Chrysostom*
124 Seek the Lord
126 Sing praise to God who reigns above
113 Source and Sovereign, Rock and Cloud
393 Spirit of the living God
328 Surely the presence of the Lord
334 Sweet, Sweet Spirit
138 The King of love my shepherd is
136 The Lord's my shepherd
121 There's a wideness in God's mercy
144 This is my Father's world
See also **Jesus Christ: Presence**

PROCESSIONALS

 62 All creatures of our God and King
280 All glory, laud, and honor
154 All hail the power of Jesus' name

INDEX OF FIRST LINES AND COMMON TITLES OF HYMNS, CANTICLES AND ACTS OF WORSHIP